The Complete
HUNTER'S
CATALOG

Other Books by the Editors

The Hunter's Almanac
by Norman Strung

The Fisherman's Almanac
by Norman Strung and Dan Morris

Family Fun Around the Water
by Norman Strung and Dan Morris

Camping in Comfort
by Norman Strung and Sil Strung

Spinfishing
by Norman Strung and Milt Rosko

Deer Hunting
by Norman Strung

Whitewater!
by Norman Strung, Sam Curtis, and Earl Perry

Misty Mornings and Moonless Nights
by Norman Strung

Communicating the Outdoor Experience
edited by Norman Strung

An Encyclopedia of Knives
by Norman Strung

The Complete
HUNTER'S
CATALOG

NORMAN STRUNG

J. B. LIPPINCOTT COMPANY
Philadelphia & New York

Grateful acknowledgment is made for the use of the following:

Pages 20, 21, 23, and 31: quotations reprinted from "The Short Happy Life of Francis Macomber" (copyright 1936 Ernest Hemingway) by permission of Charles Scribner's Sons from *The Short Stories of Ernest Hemingway.*

Page 33: quotation from *The Tender Carnivore and the Sacred Game* by Paul Shepard (copyright 1972 Paul Shepard) reprinted by permission of Charles Scribner's Sons.

Pages 39, 69, 75, 85, 163, 165, 259, and 417: quotations from *Round River: From the Journals of Aldo Leopold* by Aldo Leopold and Luna Leopold. Copyright 1953 by Oxford University Press, Inc. Reprinted by permission.

Pages 113 and 209: quotations from "The Bear" by William Faulkner. Copyright 1942 and renewed 1970 by Estelle Faulkner and Jill Faulkner Summers. Reprinted by permission of Random House, Inc. An expanded version of this story appears in *Go Down, Moses* by William Faulkner.

Pages 137, 203, 213, 221, 233, 245, 249, 253, 263, 273, and 317: quotations from *A Sand County Almanac: And Sketches Here and There* by Aldo Leopold. Copyright 1949 and renewed 1976 by Oxford University Press, Inc. Reprinted by permission.

Page 152: quotation reprinted by permission of Charles Scribner's Sons from *The Green Hills of Africa* by Ernest Hemingway. Copyright 1935 by Charles Scribner's Sons.

Page 193: "The Rabbit Hunter" by Robert Frost, from *The Poetry of Robert Frost*, edited by Edward Connery Lathem. Copyright 1942 by Robert Frost. Copyright © 1969 by Holt, Rinehart and Winston. Copyright © 1970 by Lesley Frost Ballantine. Reprinted by permission of Holt, Rinehart and Winston.

Page 202: "Hunting Song" by Jane Yolen, reprinted from *Cricket* magazine, November 1976. Copyright © 1976 by Jane Yolen. Used by permission of Curtis Brown, Ltd.

U.S. Library of Congress Cataloging in Publication Data

Main entry under title:

The Complete hunter's catalog.

Includes index.
1. Hunting—Implements and appliances—Catalogs.
2. Hunting.   I. Strung, Norman.
SK283.2.C65   799.2   77-23867
ISBN-0-397-01217-9
ISBN-0-397-01242-X (pbk.)

DEDICATED

TO

The Lovers of Legitimate Sport.

Staff

Editor	Norman Strung
Managing Editor	John Barsness
Field Editors	Fred Scholl
	Sil Strung
Art Director	C. W. "Wally" Hansen

Acknowledgments

Over 1,000 "thank yous" go to those manufacturers' representatives who helped put this book together with words, pictures, and deeds. It would be good and right to list them all here, though impractical, and in a way it isn't necessary. Their presence and help is evident in every catalog listing.

Special thanks go to the following folks for aid beyond the call of duty, mostly through their gracious provision of old catalog and calendar art: Bear Archery, Fred Bear; Ithaca Gun Company, Kris Driscoll and Jim Kristoff; Marlin Firearms, Bob Behn; Remington Arms, Ted McCawley and Dick Dietz; Savage Arms, E. G. Harrington; Stoeger Industries, Robert Scott; and the Personal Firearms Record Book Company of Santa Fe, New Mexico.

—The Editors

CONTENTS

Like a TV or radio commercial, a handbill, or a newspaper advertisement, a catalog is a purveyor of products. Yet there is a special magic in a catalog that transcends the appeal of these other forms of promotion. A catalog is a consumer's dream book, instant gratification for all those things we wish we had. Turn to any page and imagined possessions, large and small, new and bright, cheap and dear, seduce us, their effect heightened by our natural conviction that if we just had them, we could do so much better.

Take a can of beer and a few stolen moments in an easy chair, or the daily solitude behind the bathroom door, and look: Mr. Burpee's tomatoes bloom into basketballs in our garden; with two pages of Sears tools before us, we reconstruct the world.

It is in cognizance of this appeal that *The Complete Hunter's Catalog* is written. It is a hunter's and shooter's dream book; a parade of all those tools of the trade that are available to sportsmen: shotguns, rifles, scopes, clothing, duckboats, decoys, dogs, and the thousand other accoutrements one could conceivably employ to complement the shooting sports.

But *The Complete Hunter's Catalog* is much more than mere product exposure. Most catalogs incorporate an element of cruelty in their appeal. They whet the appetite and trigger the taste buds, without really satisfying. Then too, one questions their accuracy, for they are ultimately a company's sales pitch; everything presented is the best, the highest quality. There is no opportunity for comparison or evaluation.

While the backbone of *The Complete Hunter's Catalog* is products for the sportsman, they are presented in an uncommon light that exposes features seldom examined in company-sponsored mail-order promotions. Where several brands of the same product exist, the staff has endeavored to make comparative evaluations, balancing cost versus quality, and tempering those recommendations with serviceability, inherent flaws, and features of unusual excellence in mind. That light shines most brightly because we have no axe to grind or advertisers to please. We're not salespersons, nor have we sold ad space. Our judgments, endorsements, and criticism are based on long experience as hunters, shooters, and outdoorspeople, and nothing more.

The Complete Hunter's Catalog also goes several steps beyond material display and into the realm of reader satisfaction. Information on products available for the shooter is complemented by a treasury of outdoor tips, anecdotes, history, literature, and advice that illuminates topics from ammo to zoom optics, and antelope to zebra. Contributors cover a similar spectrum, and their writings include excerpts from years gone by. Charles Hallock, editor of *Forest & Stream*, who a hundred years ago warned of the extinction of the buffalo and moose and chronicled the best ways to hunt passenger pigeons and whooping crane; Nessmuk, judged by many to be the father of outdoor writing; Hemingway on Africa, Faulkner on bear hunting, Leopold on geese, and other observations from great writers, conservationists, and hunters of the past.

The present is well represented by contributors who include the top hunters, shooters, and outdoor writers in America today, a multiplicity of talent that begins with Stu Apte, ends with Zack Taylor, and scores over seventy hits with experts in between. In addition, hundreds of how-to hints, helpful to the hunter and shooter, have been assembled by the staff.

In a way then, there's good argument that *The Complete Hunter's Catalog* represents the ultimate in books of this genre. It is a dream book, true, yet it works in a large part to bring all the dreams of hunters and shooters up to the moment of accurate reality.

INTRODUCTION

The staff of *The Complete Hunter's Catalog* has endeavored to bring together every product that's available to today's shooting sportsmen. We've probably missed a few, but nonetheless our work represents a treasury of goods, services, and gadgets that will entertain, amuse, educate, intrigue, and generally improve your lot if you're a hunter, target shooter, or gun collector.

In order to do this in some semblance of order and logic, *The Complete Hunter's Catalog* is divided into six sections. They are: Big Game, Upland Game, Waterfowl, Varmint and Target Shooting, Black-Powder Guns and Other Collectibles, and Archery.

Each section is then further broken down into component parts. The big-game section, for example, leads off with guns for big game, followed by ammunition, sights and scopes, big-game clothing and footwear, and all the other accoutrements of comfort and aid you might need to pursue big game on this continent and abroad. In listing each item, we've endeavored to include three things:

• A description of the product, by word or picture, that reveals something about its quality or its construction or its most practical application. In some cases, we've included comments on all three things.

• The item's retail price. To some extent this is opening a can of worms, as prices are bound to fluctuate, but at least those figures give you some idea of the out-of-pocket cash it's going to take to buy a particular product. Listing the manufacturer's suggested retail price also serves as a kind of consumer's guide. Many of the goods we've featured are sold through retail outlets. When your local sporting goods store advertises a super sale, by comparing his price with those listed here, you'll at least get some idea of just how "super" it is.

• An address. In many cases, you can order these products directly through the mail from this address. In some cases, the listed manufacturer sells only to mail-order houses, sports stores, and other retail outlets. In any case, a letter to that address should get you more detailed information on the product and, if the goods are not sold mail order, the location of the nearest retail outlet where the items may be purchased.

Just because we include an item in the catalog doesn't necessarily mean we endorse it. It does, however, mean that it has struck our eye, or our fancy, or represents some class of goods we have found to be useful in our experience as hunters and shooters. In short, everything we've included we've found interesting, and it's our sincere hope that you will too.

Part I

BIG GAME

Part 1

BIG GAME

FOREIGN BIG-GAME HUNTING

Of all the hunting opportunities in the world, none packs quite the same aura of romance and high adventure as the safari. The mere mention of the word brings forth images of dashing white hunters, charging rhinos, and the spirit and substance of the man called Hemingway.

If the idea of a safari appeals to you, we suggest the following: contact a reputable booking agent who specializes in hunting safaris, and learn all you can about the social, cultural, and wildlife conditions that prevail in the country where you plan to hunt. The details associated with a safari, from political conflicts to inoculations needed to gun permits and game licenses, will likely be a tangled snarl of regulations and current events that only a trained professional can unravel.

Start planning your hunt a year in advance. You'll need at least that much time to gather together all those loose ends of equipment and bureaucratic fiat you're bound to encounter.

And start off with a fat checkbook, for you'll soon find out that safari is very, very expensive sport. But if you can afford it, do it. It is one of those experiences a serious hunter owes himself, if only once in his lifetime.

FIRST SAFARI ADVICE
by Walter Cook

Kenya is surely the most popular country for a first safari, though Botswana probably rates the highest among safari veterans. Hunting is generally available all year, though the dry season is the favored time—roughly early November through the middle of May.

All things taken into consideration (such as cost and convenience), for hunting in Rhodesia, Botswana, South Africa, or Southwest Africa, I prefer to fly South African Airways from Kennedy Airport, New York, to Rio, then to Johannesburg. In the past, this flight has been available only on certain days of the week. An alternative is to fly from Kennedy to Cape Verde Island and then to Johannesburg. Either route is much faster than going by way of Europe.

Should you choose East Africa for your safari (Sudan, Kenya), fly Pan Am or British Air Lines from New York to West Africa, and then on to Nairobi, Kenya.

While I favor Botswana, if you're looking for the biggest of big game, elephant, there have been some heavy tusks taken in Kenya in the recent past. There is also big ivory in the Central African Republic, and in Southern Sudan.

One of the hassles you'll face hunting in Africa is the long wait for raw skins to be tanned. I strongly recommend that you spend the extra money to have them transported by air freight. If you ship by ocean carrier, you might have to wait up to a year for your skins.

While safari costs are high, you do get your money's worth in accommodations and services, not to mention excellent hunting that often turns up the unusual. On my first hunt in Kenya, we were in concession block 58, an area that's roughly a four-hour drive from Nairobi. My party consisted of two trackers, a guide, and myself, and we were looking for a good buff. Buffalo are notoriously difficult to bring down, so I was carrying a heavy gun—a .375 Holland & Holland with steel-jacketed bullets. I had a license for one buffalo, though two are allowed if you buy a second permit.

We saw nothing for the first day, and started out at sunup the second day. We followed tracks until 10 A.M., at which time the trackers spotted a herd of twelve buffs. There was one good bull 40 yards away, and I took a shot from a kneeling position, hitting the animal in the shoulder. He went down as if pole-axed . . . and so did a second bull standing a few yards away!

When we checked the second buffalo, we found the bullet had been deflected, perhaps by bone, and had connected with the boss of the second bull's horn. Neither guide nor trackers had ever seen two buffalo go down with one shot, and though I plan to hunt Africa several times a year, I doubt that I'll ever see it again either.

Walter Cook is a New York businessman who has hunted around the world.

As we go to press, Kenya's borders are closed to hunters, but—African politics being what they are—they might well reopen in the near future.

G7064C

WINCHESTER MODEL 70 AFRICAN

Since the first English big-game hunters ventured into Africa back in the muzzle-loading days, guns and loads for the big game of that continent—especially the elephant, rhino, and Cape buffalo—were almost exclusively British in origin and design. The list of cartridges sufficient in power to kill the big African beasts at one time was almost as long as the great Rift Valley itself. Holland & Holland and Westley-Richards were as much a part of Africa as Kenya and the Nile. The big double rifles that handled these cartridges were always branded as "English" rifles, even if they happened to have been built in Spain. The only American guns that might qualify for African hunting were the few bolt guns chambered for the .375, a Holland & Holland development, and a cartridge which many considered on the light side for the really big game.

In 1956, Winchester decided to change all that. They designed a case short enough to work through the standard .30-06 length magazine but loaded to higher pressures than the sometimes gigantic British rounds, for the same performance in a smaller package. The .458 Winchester Magnum turns a 500-grain bullet loose at 2,130 fps with over 5,000 pounds of muzzle energy—what most elephant and buffalo hunters had decided was about the optimum. If bullets are much smaller they lack the bullet weight in certain situations to break heavy bone. If they are much larger, recoil goes sky high, without really increasing efficiency. After all,

if a .458 will break both shoulders on a buffalo or shoot through an elephant's head, why put up with a round such as the 600 Nitro Express which is just as apt to mash the shooter as the game?

There were already rounds on the market such as the .470 and .425 Westley-Richards that approximated this performance, but the Winchester round was available in a rifle that cost only about 20 percent of what many of the double rifles cost. It also was loaded with an excellent steel-jacketed solid that quickly acquired a reputation for reliable penetration that some of the British products lacked. True, the Winchester bolt gun wasn't as fast as a double that could be fired twice in as much time as it took the shooter to recover from recoil, but professional hunters—men who *use* their guns—found that the bolt could be worked pretty fast, after a bit of practice, and offered three shots to the double's two.

The .458 is now probably the most popular cartridge for big game in Africa. A great many of the African game departments stock the Winchester African Model 70 as their "official" rifle, to be used on control hunts or on safari. It hasn't replaced the double rifle totally—the two-barrel gun is still preferred by most hunters in following up wounded dangerous game—but it is truly the number-one dangerous-game rifle on the market today. Price: $440. Winchester-Western, 275 Winchester Avenue, New Haven, CT 06504.

—J.B.

WINCHESTER
TRADE MARK

BOTSWANA SAFARI

The Republic of Botswana is a country of 275,000 square miles in the central highlands of southern Africa. The country's population is clustered in the southeastern part of the nation, leaving the game-rich northern sections virtually uninhabited. In recent years, a team of visiting scientists from the United Nations found Botswana to contain the largest herds of game in Africa today.
Large Game: buffalo, eland, elephant, gemsbok, impala, kudu, lion, sable, sitatunga, sassaby; *Small Game:* guinea fowl, francolin, sandgrouse, doves, ducks, and geese.
Costs (21-day safari):
Client and one professional
hunter . . . . $375 per day
Concession tax $1,100

Representative supplementary license fees (each animal is bought separately)
    Buffalo $85
    Elephant $213
             (plus export duty)
    Eland $198
    Lion $738
    Sable $383
Services: Professional hunter and staff (including tracker, gun bearers), camp shelter, camp equipment, food, field preparation of trophies, transportation within the concession area, two-way radio contact with Kasane, tips for the safari crew, and a sitatunga boat.
Bookings: Reservations are confirmed upon 25 percent deposit against the safari quotation. Contact Hunters Africa Ltd., Box 11, Kasane, Botswana (cable "Wytehunter," Kasane, Botswana).

THE WORLD'S GREATEST GAME ANIMAL

by F. Wallace "Wally" Taber

Perhaps I rate the leopard uncommonly high as the hunters' number-one adversary, but it defied me inordinately long. It was my third safari in British East Africa before I lucked by chance into a cat in Tanganyika. In intervening years, many things have changed. Tanganyika is now Tanzania and Africa is scarcely the Africa I once knew. Yet the leopard reigns on, indomitable, more so even than lion or tiger the king of the cats!

I admire the fact that the leopard fights back, that it appears to reason more than the lion or tiger, that it doesn't hesitate to press the attack, to make hunted of the hunter, to lie in ambush, to exhibit infinite patience; even to stalk man, to kill his dogs, and, in the final analysis, to kill, and even devour, man himself.

Leopards are well known dog-eaters and lesser known man-eaters throughout Africa and Asia. From the snows of Kilimanjaro to the seared sands of the Sahara and from the oil-producing deserts of Arabian nights to the mighty Parmirs—roof of the world—separating Russia from China, leopards daily prove their superiority merely by continuing to coexist with a mankind that has waged unrelenting war since first the mold for both was cast, long eons ago.

Whoever put the leopard on the endangered-species list knew not the ways of this incredible cat. For the hunter never lived that can regularly outsmart a leopard. Even as the spots of the leopard are as individualistic as the fingerprints of man, so the character of each cat seems just as individual.

In happier days in Uganda I safaried with a stalwart Britisher, a second-generation African-born subject of Her Majesty's then far-flung empire. Ian had been born and reared on a Mount Kenya ranch where leopards were as common as raccoons on an Ohio farm. Nightly forays were conducted against the domestic animals, and constant warfare with the spotted feline was a way of life for young Ian as he struggled into manhood.

"I never kept tally," Ian answered my query, "but I am sure it reaches over a hundred." Then he added, "And I respected every regal hide of the bloody lot I dispatched."

Nor will I forget the night I drove to Entebbe. Because of the dense elephant grass around town, my hired men pitched our tents on the very airstrip where more recently the Israeli Commandos defied both Palestinian guerrillas and Idi Amin's finest to rescue a hundred hostages. I remained in Entebbe the better part of a week, camped on the mowed airstrip before rejoining Ian on safari.

The night I had driven out of camp headed for Entebbe, Ian tied Tiger, his beloved Dalmatian, to the leg of his cot, a nightly precaution against marauding leopards. Well before daylight, Ian was conscious of the drip, drip, drip on his tent and awakened at dawn expecting to see the desolate, dry Karamojan countryside transformed overnight with life-giving rain. When no rain-refreshed bush loomed beyond the tent flaps, he slipped into his slippers and stepped outside, unconscious of Tiger's absence from the tent floor.

Observing no evidence of even a shower, Ian looked at his tent to observe, not rain, but blood dripping onto the corner of his tent. From Tiger's limp carcass, firmly wedged in the crotch of the overhanging fever tree branches, blood still dripped spasmodically. Half of the carcass had been devoured and, in typical fashion, the remainder wedged for later leopard attention, comfortably safe from both hyena and lion.

With tears in his voice, Ian explained how soundly he must have slept not to have heard the leopard kill Tiger in the tent, chew the leather leash in two, and carry his beloved pet outside. That he ultimately achieved revenge with a single blast of buckshot after three nights of vigilance while awaiting the leopard's return, was, as Ian put it, "beastly poor consolation."

Although the leopard exists in every life zone on both African and Asian continents, success to the questing gunner comes once in three safaris and is even less frequent on shikar. Rarely is the leopard taken in fair chase; more frequently it is by accidental encounter from questing safari cars. Successful safarists get that way over bait in Africa and in front of beaters or on bait in Asia. Seldom is the challenging critter taken in fair chase, even less frequently through accidental encounter afoot.

Come to think of it, I have never heard or read of anyone, not even tiger-stalking Jim Corbett, taking to the spoor of a leopard and stalking it to a kill. And, while my wife boasts of a pair of do-it-yourself leopard coats, one from India and one from Africa, in honesty I must admit that the leopards were encountered accidentally from our vehicle or taken over bait, which seems at least a cut above the usual method for taking the beautifully spotted furs for milady's coats, by the wholly unsporting and illegal means of set-guns, snares, and traps.

F. Wallace (Wally) Taber has hunted, fished, and filmed in most "corners" of the world. His Safari Shows, revealing in living color and personal narration the hunting, fishing, wildlife, and native life of the world, annually entertain upwards of 100,000 persons in live audiences and untold millions on television.

STROBE STRIPES

Most striped, spotted, or dapple-furred animals evolved their exterior coloration as a means to hide in the shade- and sunlight-splashed environment of a forest floor. Zebras, however, are creatures of the open plain, where overhead shadows are virtually nonexistent. Their coloration provides protection by way of a stroboscopic effect.

Predators like the big cats and hyenas are keyed by nature to pick out and concentrate upon one animal for the kill. When zebras are threatened, they immediately gather together and mill before breaking and running. This creates a confusing pattern of converging lines, not unlike the effect of a modern strobe-lit show, giving the animals at least a chance to outdistance their bleary-eyed pursuer.

Protecto ABS Plastic Cases for Just About Everything

THE MOST DANGEROUS GAME

I don't know what there is about buffalo that frightens me so. Lions and leopards and rhinos excite me but don't frighten me. But that buff is so big and mean and ugly and hard to stop, and vindictive and cruel and surly and ornery. He looks like he hates you personally. He looks like you owe him money. He looks like he is hunting you.

—Robert Ruark, *Horn of the Hunter*

SAFARI OUTFITTERS

This Chicago-based firm books hunts worldwide. It is worthy of note on several counts. First, it publishes an excellent newsletter with up-to-date information on hunting opportunities around the world, including whatever effect political upheavals, revolutions, and current events might have on the hunting scene in each country.

Second, it also publishes an easy-to-read brochure entitled "Safaris With Gun and Camera" that plainly sets down costs (including air fare via Pan Am), conditions, and the types of game available on every safari-shikar tour they book.

Third, the firm is lightning-quick to reply to your inquiries, and thorough in its answer. Contact Mr. Roman H. Hupalowski, President, Safari Outfitters, Inc., 8 South Michigan Avenue, Chicago, IL 60603.

Whether you're flying to Africa or Arkansas, air travel dictates solid, sturdy protection for firearms, and Protecto Plastics makes a case for every conceivable gun and then some.

Their cases meet FAA requirements for commercial aircraft transportation and consist of a tough outer shell with a foam interior, clasp-type latches, and a keyed lock. There are thirty-four case models in this product line, and their variety of dimensions will accommodate rifles, shotguns, handguns, Kentucky long rifles, recurve bows, compound bows (with arrows), spotting scopes, cameras, lenses, you name it. If you want to case it, they've got it.

The Wally Taber Safari Case (13½ by 52½ by 3½ inches), $55.95. Protecto Plastics, Inc., 201 Alpha Road, Wind Gap, PA 18091.

THE .510 WELLS EXPRESS

The .510 Wells Express is the newest entry into the African sporting arms field. Custom built on a special Magnum Mauser action, the .510 shoots a range of bullets from 400 to 700 grains, in soft nose or solids. Muzzle velocity is approximately 2,700 fps, with a 700-grain bullet, that develops 12,000 pounds of muzzle energy. Clearly, if you hit an elephant in the butt with this one, his eyes would bulge out.

The rifle can be built from 11 pounds on up, and you have a choice of a four- or five-shell magazine.

The Wells Express is built only to order by custom gunmaker Fred F. Wells of Prescott, Arizona. Cost of the basic arm is $5,500. You can also get a specifically fitted leather case for $1,800. Custom ammunition is available through the Colorado Custom Bullet Company.

KENYA COAT

This all-cotton safari-style jacket comes in both long- and short-sleeved models. Features include leather butt pads, four pleated pockets, a deep pleated-action back, and a center-vented coattail. The short-sleeved jacket may be worn as a shirt when the weather gets beastly hot. Kenya shirt, $37.50; Kenya jacket, $39.50, from 10-X Manufacturing Company, P.O. Box 3408, Boulder, CO 80303.

Hemingway on Where to Hit a Buff

When a buff comes, he comes with his head high and thrust straight out. The boss of the horns covers any sort of brain shot. The only shot is straight into the nose. The only other shot is into his chest or, if you're to one side, into the neck or the shoulders.

—From *The Short Happy Life of Francis Macomber*

"In Africa, no woman ever misses her lion and no white man ever bolts."
—Ernest Hemingway, "The Short Happy Life of Francis Macomber"

21

SOLID BULLETS

Technically speaking, there isn't a solid bullet to be found on the market, as these are really nonexpanding bullets made from a combination of lead, gilding metal, steel, or what-have-you. They are used when hunting dangerous, thick-skinned game, such as elephant, rhino, and Cape buffalo, where extreme penetration and bone-breaking ability are needed. Both the .458 and the .375 Holland & Holland are available in good factory loads with solid bullets, as are the Weatherby counterparts, the .460 and the .378. If you wish to use calibers other than these or prefer to load your own, there are two good sources of solids in the United States today. Hornady Manufacturing Company, P.O. Box 1848, Grand Island, NE 68801, makes an excellent steel-jacketed solid in .30, .338, .375, and .458 calibers in 220-, 250-, 300-, and 500-grain weights respectively. The steel is coated with gilding metal so the bore won't be harmed. Reloading information for these is available in the *Hornady Handbook of Cartridge Reloading*, Vol. 2. One reason the .338 has never really dented the .375's popularity is the lack of a solid bullet load for it—the 250-grain Hornady is a good bullet but doesn't quite match the 300-grain .375 in performance. If you'd like heavier bullets, Colorado Custom bullets, Box 215, American Fork, UT 84003, makes a whole line of solid bullets in just about any caliber from .270 on up. The solid bullets in each caliber (they also manufacture

a very good line of expanding bullets) are of heavier-than-standard weight. The .270, for instance, is a 180 grain, the .338 a 300, the .375 a 350, and the .458 comes in both 500- and 600-grain weights. They go on up to 900-grain .620 diameter for loading the 600 Nitro Express. The construction of the Colorado bullets is the opposite of the Hornadys, in a way. Whereas the Hornady is built as strong as possible to withstand the impact of heavy bone, the Colorado bullets are made of pure copper and lead, on the theory that they will give a little and bend instead of breaking. It seems to work—I inspected a .375 solid that had been shot through 54 inches of a live cottonwood tree, two 2 by 6 planks, and a 55-gallon oil drum filled with water. The only visible evidence of its journey other than the rifling marks was a slight flattening where it hit the oil drum. I've been testing the .270 180-grain solid on various hard objects and it's held up well.

Solid bullets aren't cheap, but if you're going to Africa you'll most likely be able to afford them. The 500-grain Hornady .458 is priced at $34.50 for 100, the Colorado of the same dimensions at $32.40 (prices subject to change). The 600 Nitro bullets from Colorado, in case you're interested, run $32.00 for *20*, or you can buy them individually at $1.75.

—J.B.

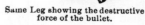

Already I was beginning to fall into the African way of thinking: that if you properly respect what you are after, and shoot it cleanly and on the animal's terrain, if you imprison in your mind all the wonder of the day from sky to smell to breeze to flowers—then you have not merely killed an animal. You have lent immortality to a beast you have killed because you loved him and wanted him forever so you could always recapture that day. You could always remember how blue the sky was and how you sat on the high hill with the binoculars under the great umbrella of the mimosa, waiting for the first buzzard to slide down out of the sky, waiting for the first lioness to sneak out of the bush, waiting for the old man to take his heavy head and brilliant mane and burly chest out of the bush and into the clear golden field where the dead topi lay. This is better than letting him grow a few years older, to be killed or crippled by a son and eaten, still alive, by hyenas. Death is not a dreadful thing in Africa—not if you respect the thing you kill, not if you kill to feed your people or your memory.

—Robert Ruark, *Horn of the Hunter*

CHUKKA BOOTS

There are a thousand pleasures associated with any hunt, and one of them is when the day is over and you peel off a pair of damp, heavy boots. Your feet feel like new: light, cool, and suddenly free. They smile.

Keep the little fellers happy by donning a pair of Chukka boots, which, in fact, are the traditional camp shoe on safari. They are light, roomy, and so comfortable that you'll want to wear them everywhere, and they're dressy enough so you can.

This particular Chukka is one of the best (Chukka styles can be found in most shoe stores from around $16.00 and up). It includes a cushioned ankle top, a glove-leather lining, cushioned leather insoles, and an English moccasin toe. The soles are crepe—long on both comfort and wear—and they're bonded, not nailed, to the uppers. Price: $37.95. Browning, Route 1, Morgan, UT 84050.

THE TREE WHERE MAN WAS BORN/ THE AFRICAN EXPERIENCE

by Peter Mathiessen, photos by Eliot Porter

New York: E. P. Dutton & Company, $35.00.

Here is a book that deserves more than complimentary adjectives or hollow superlatives. It is a graphic portrayal of the guts of Africa: its people, its lands, its wildlife.

Mathiessen's text is at once poetic and reportorial, transcending the limitations of both to present a blend that is solid, substantial, and lifelike. Porter's photography brings the written word to visual life: the tranquillity of moss and ferns in a Mount Kenya forest, the gentle, filial humanity of Llo-molo tribesmen touching as they dance, and the grace of nature's perfect injustice as a cheetah brings down a gazelle in Amboseli.

The genre to which this work belongs is "coffee table books," but to relegate it to such vanity does it a disservice. It is work of word and picture art about Africa that comes very close to putting you there.

WEATHERBY MARK IV

The .460 Weatherby Magnum, according to the Weatherby people, is the most powerful factory cartridge in the world. I doubt that there's anyone who would dispute the point. In keeping with the Weatherby tradition that puts more powder than anyone else behind a given bullet, the big .460 case (basically the same as the British .416 Rigby round, except that it has a belt and is loaded to higher pressure than the Rigby) pushes a 500-grain bullet at 2,700 fps with just over 8,000 pounds of energy. That's more than 2½ times as powerful as your faithful '06, friends. There are some experienced African hunters who hold, however, that the most effective velocity for penetration (the major factor in elephant, Cape buffalo, and rhino rifles) is around 2,300 to 2,400 fps—below that, they say, penetration isn't all it could be, and above that, performance can become erratic. However that may be, the .460 makes a big impression on anything it hits. The same case necked down to .375 is Weatherby's .378 Magnum, which is sort of a super .270 or 7mm Magnum in that it shoots a 270-grain bullet at 3,180 fps, or a 300 grain at 2,925. It also, with the proper bullets, is fine for whales and/or brontosaurus. The smaller Weatherby rounds, from .240 to .340, are all useful on various sizes of African game—or game all over the world—with the most popular being the .300. Some people feel that it's the ultimate all-around rifle, good on everything from antelope to elephant, and indeed some have used it for those species and everything between. The average hunter, though, would be well advised to stick to game under a ton. Prices: .300, $449.50; .460, $649.50. Weatherby, Inc., 2781 Firestone Boulevard, South Gate, CA 90280.

—J.B.

"A brave man is always frightened three times by a lion; when he first sees his track, when he first hears him roar, and when he first confronts him."
—Hemingway, "The Short Happy Life of Francis Macomber"

23

BOB LEE'S HUNTING WORLD CATALOG

Here's a source for quality, conversation pieces, and an attitude. Featured within these slick pages are things like elephant-skin shoes and belts, Guy Coheleach oils (originals), and tweed deerstalker hats.

Aside from the kinds of products featured, this catalog is remarkable in that it captures the ambience of the hunting sport as it is pursued by the very rich. You get a sense of what one should wear on the Scottish moors or the African veldt, the kind of crystal to grace a bar in a proper trophy room, and the elegant understatement inherent in an elephant-leather car-key fob with your Rolls-Royce emblem emblazoned upon it.

This isn't just a catalog for the wealthy, though. There are some useful items that are well within the reach of the average sportsman: Bob Lee's Safari Table that seats four and folds into its own compact carrying case ($57.00), and an innovative combination mitt and glove for cold-weather shooting ($25.00), for example. Still, its real appeal lies in the display of all those things we wish we could afford, but obviously can't.

Hunting World's credo is, "We do not build a product to a price . . . we'll always pay more to improve our quality." O.K., Bob, you got me; I'm sending in an order for an elephant-leather watch fob for my Ford pickup.

Free catalog from Hunting World, 16 East 53rd Street, New York, NY 10022.
—N.S.

MARLIN REPEATING RIFLES.

The above cut shows pistol grip, selected stock and engraved.

32-40 and 38-55 calibre have rifle butts.

PRICE LIST
OF

MARLIN REPEATING RIFLE.

32 Calibre, 40 Grains Powder, 165 Grains Lead.

				Single Trigger.	Double Set Triggers.
24 inch Octagon Barrel,	8 shots, 7¼ lbs., Rifle Butt.			$15 00	$18 00
28 " "	"	10 "	7½ " "	16 15	19 15
30 " "	"	10 "	8½ " "	18 75	21 75

24 and 28 inch can be furnished with extra heavy barrel, 1 lb. more than above weights, for $1.00 extra.

38 Calibre, 55 Grains Powder, 255 Grains Lead.

24 inch Octagon Barrel,	8 shots, 7¼ lbs., Rifle Butt..			$15 00	$18 00
28 " "	"	10 "	7½ " "	16 15	19 15
30 " "	"	10 "	8½ " "	18 75	21 75

24 and 28 inch can be furnished with extra heavy barrel, 1 lb. more than above weights, for $1.00 extra.

40 Calibre, 60 Grains Powder, 260 Grains Lead.

24 inch Octagon Barrel,	8 shots, 9 lbs., Shot Gun Butt......			$15 75	$18 75
28 " "	"	10 "	9½ " "	16 90	20 00
30 " "	"	10 "	11 " "	18 75	21 75

45 Calibre, 70 or 85 Grains Powder, 405 or 285 Grains Lead.

24 inch Octagon Barrel,	8 shots, 9 lbs., Shot Gun Butt......			$15 75	$18 75
28 " "	"	10 "	9½ " "	16 90	20 00
30 " "	"	10 "	11 " "	18 75	21 75

If preferred, the 32 and 38 calibre rifles can be furnished with shot gun butt, and the 40 and 45 calibre rifles with rifle butt, at an extra charge of $1.00.

Any of the above styles can also be supplied with a half length magazine holding four cartridges, at same prices.

The receivers are blued, and butt plates, levers and fore-arm tips case-hardened.

The regular sights on these rifles are Rocky Mountain rear, and Knife-edge German silver front. Any of the other sights shown in the back of this catalogue can also be readily attached.

Each rifle is accompanied by a four-jointed wooden cleaning rod.

EXTRAS.

Full Nickel Plating.............	$4 00	Case Hardened Receiver............	$1 00
Nickel Plated Trimmings........	2 50	Swivel and Sling Strap..........	1 50
Gold Plated Trimmings..........	8 00	Pistol Grip Stock, selected and finely Checked........	12 00
Selected Walnut Stock and Forearm finely checked.............	8 00	Engraving from $5.00 up.	

Shortening or lengthening butt stock..........................	$3 00
Leaving off rear sight slot or changing its position..................	2 00
Blank piece to fill the rear sight slot......................	25

Pistol Grip with Checking, on any size, $4.00 extra.

An old Marlin price list.

STATION WAGON BAGS

In the back of your station wagon, or on a plane heading for the Sudan and a safari, these sturdy bags make a lot of sense. They always seem to have enough room left to take that overlooked pair of shoes, and even fully loaded they fit into place anywhere.

Virtually every outdoor writer I know, and most of the better outdoorsmen, are quick to spot at an airport because they'll be carrying these bags. My one complaint: I have never yet been able to carry a bottle of gin inside one, no matter how carefully I pack it, without the bottle breaking. I once crammed a bottle of Beefeaters into an insulated leather hunting boot, in the middle of all my duffle, and still the baggage handlers figured out how to smash it. I can abide champagne from a glass slipper, but martinis from an old hunting boot are another matter.

My solution: I now carry my booze in an aluminum backpacker's quart fuel container and always arrive prepared for cocktail hour.

Station wagon bags: 24" by 10" by 20", $29.50; 26" by 12" by 13", $32.50; 30" by 13" by 14", $37.50. Orvis, Manchester, VT 05254.

Fuel Container: $4.95. Recreational Equipment, Inc., 1525 11th Avenue, Seattle, WA 98122.
—N.S.

BIG CATS

The cheetah, leopard, tiger, jaguar, ocelot, snow leopard, margay, and tiger cat are on the U.S. endangered species list, which for all practical purposes makes them illegal to import. Of the "big cats" only the African and American lion are not endangered.

FERLACH DOUBLE RIFLES

If you really want to do things right on your safari, you need a double rifle. You can rent one in Nairobi or borrow one from your local white hunter, but if you want to go first class, buy one. If you get about $1,000 worth of engraving on it it will look nice next to the buffalo head in your trophy room back home in Toledo. It will also increase the cost of your safari from 20 percent to 50 percent.

The traditional double is a side-by-side. Ferlach imports the Holland & Holland side-by-side in standard monster calibers such as .458 Winchester and .470 Nitro Express, built to your specifications with the engraving you desire, barrel length you want, and so on. Base price is $6,670 for the big calibers (smaller calibers are available for $4,900 base; there is a $1,770 charge for pachyderm stoppers). There is also a standard delivery time of several months (this is all part of the mystique of the double rifle).

Also available is the Ferlach over-under double rifle built by Franz Sodia Jagdgewehrfabrik of Austria. It is available in big calibers at a base price of $2,900, with $281 extra for the bigger chamberings. It does not bear the hallowed Holland & Holland name but is an excellent gun nonetheless.

Ferlach also imports H&H shotguns, along with Franz Sodia's three-barrel guns (drillings) in an array of caliber/gauge combinations. Standard chamberings in the Model 50 (two shotgun barrels over one rifle barrel) include 12, 16, and 20 gauge over the rimmed versions of the 6.5-, 7-, and 8-millimeter Mauser rounds, along with the .270 Winchester. For the man who feels there might be a Scottish stag hunt or a traipse through Germany's Black Forest in his future, this is the arm. Base price: $2,100.

H&H double with automatic ejectors.

The Ferlach [Austria] catalog (Write: Ferlach of North America, P.O. Box 143435, South Miami, FL 33143) is in both German and English and is highly entertaining, especially as some of the German syntax finds its way into English.

—J.B.

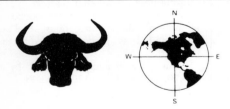

Jack Atcheson & Sons
INTERNATIONAL HUNTING CONSULTANTS & TAXIDERMISTS

Butte, Mont.: Jack Atcheson & Sons (3210 Ottawa Street), $2.00.

This 100-page outsized paperback contains extensive information on a wide variety of safari-style expeditions, all of which may be booked through Jack Atcheson.

Although the book is promotional, there is more than enough solid information to justify its cost, and the pictures aren't bad either. A typical entry includes the types of game available in a given area (for example, Northern Kenya), the precise locations of game concessions, the time you'll

THE INTERNATIONAL HUNTER
by Jack Atcheson

probably need to down each trophy available, the personal equipment you'll have to bring, customs information, camp facilities, and the cost of the safari, which is bound to turn a head or two.

Of particular note is the depth of detail contained in the publication. Atcheson goes so far as to list things like rubber mattresses and steel divans in his descriptions

of what you can expect at camp, and the temperatures and weather conditions that are probable in every month. The collective weight of this kind of detail begins to read like a novel; you develop a sense of what it's like to be there, and for that reason, even if you can't afford a safari, *The International Hunter* makes for good armchair reading.

Countries covered include all of Africa, Mongolia, Australia, New Zealand, parts of South America, Iran, Alaska, Canada, and certain portions of the United States.

LOOKING AT ANIMALS: A ZOOLOGIST IN AFRICA
by Hugh B. Cott

New York: Charles Scribner's Sons, $14.95.

This isn't about hunting but should interest anyone wanting to know more about African wildlife. It has numerous black-and-white photos and the author's excellent illustrations, along with both scientific and more mundane information on the birds, land animals, and water animals of Africa (no fish). There are a few color photos. A comprehensive book written by someone who obviously knows his stuff (Cott is an Englishman who was educated at Cambridge) and cares about it.

ZAMBIA NATIONAL TOURIST BUREAU

SAFARI HAT

Going on safari without a proper hat would be like attending a tuxedo ball in tennis runners. The White Hunter has all those qualities that will enhance your Stewart Granger image: 100 percent pure felt for rugged wear, 3¼-inch raw-edge brim styled to be worn "all around down," and a genuine zebra band that contrasts dramatically with the hat's impala brown. Price: $75.00 from Hunting World, 16 East 53rd Street, New York, NY 10022.

Savannah Safari Shirt

This is about as comfortable a shirt as you'll find for warm-weather wear which is still suitable for places that refuse service to people with bare feet and chests. There is a cool crispness about the material and the cut that subdues oppressive sun and allows lots of air circulation.

The unquestionably good-looking shirt design includes large button-down pockets and epaulets, and it's available with long sleeves for when the hunting gets buggy.

Short-sleeve: $16.00; long-sleeve: $17.50, from 10-X Manufacturing Company, P.O. Box 3408, Boulder, CO 80303.

KIT BAG

Pack up your troubles, and the small stuff that always seems to sift down out of reach in conventional luggage, in one of these kit bags. Their many pockets are ideal for different calibers and weights of shells, binoculars, cameras, lenses, film—just about any kind of support material a hunter could want to tote with him. The bags include a shoulder strap, and they'll fit under an airplane seat. Small, $22.50; medium, $28.50; large, $38.00. From Orvis, Manchester, VT 05254.

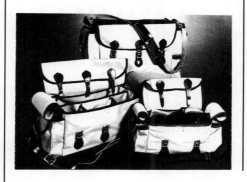

Game Conservation International, or "Game Coin," as it is more commonly known, is an international nonprofit organization dedicated to conserving the wildlife of the world, their habitats and ecosystems.

While their concern and conservation work are, in truth, international, their most outstanding achievements have been in the area of African big game. They have

Game Conservation International

also established and administer a legal defense fund whose purpose is to defend hunters and their sport from suits and harassment brought about by antihunting organizations.

They publish a newsletter, *Hook 'n' Bullet News*, four times a year. It is a well-edited and -conceived blend of organizational news, conservation trends and achievements, and hunting and fishing information on an international scale. For membership information write: Game Conservation International, Petroleum Center, Suite D-211, San Antonio, TX 78209.

POACHING ON A GRAND SCALE

Elephant poachers are doing a huge business in ivory. In past years, the price of ivory has risen from $2.80 to $22.00 a pound, creating a market for tusks that has made many an illegal hunter wealthy.

Getting the ivory is no problem. In a day, a man can drop a big bull in one of Africa's many preserves or parks and be back in his truck with 50 pounds of ivory by nightfall. The National Audubon Society estimates this hunger for ivory is responsible for the killing of 1,000 elephants annually in Kenya alone!

Outdoors Adventures with Flying Colors

This free catalog is published by Braniff International and details the many hunting and fishing opportunities in Latin, Central, and South America. What are the hunting opportunities? Well, except for ducks, geese, and quail, they're largely undeveloped and unexplored, which in turn reflects itself in much lower prices than you encounter in "traditional" safari country like Africa or India. If you have limited funds and a sense of adventure and like to go it on your own, hunting in South America might well be for you. Contact: Braniff Outdoor Council, Suite 201, Outdoors Building, Columbia, MO 65201.

BRANIFF INTERNATIONAL
U.S. MAINLAND HAWAII MEXICO SOUTH AMERICA
BRANIFF INTERNATIONAL
TERRITORIO CONTINENTAL DE LOS EE. UU. HAWAI MEXICO SUR AMERICA

Russian tur may be hunted on the Kubinsky Hunting Reserve or the North Ossetian Hunting Reserve.

Should you choose the Kubinsky Reserve, you fly from Moscow to Buku, take a car from Sumgait to Derk, then ride 25 kilometers on horseback into camp. Season: July 1 to September 15; probable length of hunt, 4 to 6 days; hunting method: stalking.

The North Ossetian Hunting Reserve may be reached via a 3-hour flight from

Hunt Tur in Russia

Moscow to Mineralnyje Vody, then a 4-hour drive to Ordjonikidze. Season: August 15 to November 5; probable duration of hunt, 6 to 8 days; hunting method: "surrounding."

Costs: Round-trip air, Moscow/drop-off point .... 70 rubles
Daily fee .... 70 rubles
(includes accommodations, guide, and so on)
Tur license .... 500 rubles
"Processing" of tur ..... 10 rubles
Air fare, New York/Moscow, first class $1,610
Contact: Safari Outfitters, Inc., 8 South Michigan Avenue, Chicago, IL 60603.
—P.S.

TIGERS OFF THE GAME LIST

The World Wildlife Fund estimates wild tiger populations at less than 5,000. Hunting tigers has been banned worldwide, but a combination of an illegal skin trade and declining habitat continues to reduce populations. The fund is currently involved in a million-dollar campaign to expand and improve key wildlife preserves in an effort to save threatened species from extinction.

BIG-GAME HUNTING IN MEXICO

Mexico offers hunting for mule deer and javelina in the northern states and for whitetail deer and several species of cats in the southern states. Driven hunts are the rule; you are posted at a game pass, and beaters push the game by you.

Rates are reasonable: around $100 a day, which includes guides, beaters, gun rental, and a license, though usually an additional fee is charged for the animals bagged. If you prefer the economy route, you can go alone, buying the necessary gun permits for two rifles and fifty rounds of ammo and a license for the state where you wish to hunt for around $100.

However, there are a few problems associated with freelance hunting in Mexico. Laws change yearly, so inquire as to recent regulations and restrictions at a Mexican consulate well in advance of your trip. Be very careful to learn the gun importation procedure by chapter and verse, as it can be awfully confusing, especially if you don't speak Spanish.

Finding game can be tough too, as most "public" areas are subject to illegal night hunting with lights by natives, and game is more than skittish at all times. If you take the time to ask around, however, it's often possible to find a friendly landowner who protects his wildlife and who will let you hunt either for free or for a small fee.

Guides aren't faultless, either. For example, you'll have no problem booking an expensive jaguar hunt, and you'll likely get your *tigre*, as they are known in Mexico. But it's doubtful if anyone will have told you that they are on the

endangered species list and therefore their hides and heads cannot be brought back into the United States.

So look carefully before you leap into Mexico, especially if you intend to go it alone. If you wish a guided hunt, Hermanos Avilles, Mazatlán, Sinaloa, Mexico, have a good reputation, and both brothers speak perfect English. —N.S.

"In Africa, all you need is a down jacket, good boots, and a British guide."
—Anon.

27

HUNTING IN SOUTH AMERICA
by E. L. (Buck) Rogers

The last jaguar I bagged was hit in the chest at a distance of fifteen feet and landed in a squirming, claw-raking ball in the underbrush at my feet. My companions were up trees or dangling from vines by this time, and I was left alone in the dark with a head lamp knocked askew and a second cartridge in the chamber, too damn scared to know what to do next. Fortunately, nothing else was required. By the time we got organized, the cat was dead and my little brown-skinned compadres were whooping around in a circle congratulating each other.

Like I said, that was my last jaguar hunt. Now I'm concentrating on peacock bass and fast-flying doves.

South America does not have the many species of big game that Africa does, nor even the varieties of hoofed game that abound in our own country. But it still is the last wilderness frontier left on earth, and for the man as interested in exploring wild places as he is in pulling the trigger, this continent is the place to go.

Two big cats, the jaguar and the puma (mountain lion), are common throughout South America. Recently I saw fresh tracks of a big jaguar on the north coast of Colombia, a scant hundred meters from a beach bombarded by a Caribbean surf, and the species extends southward to the temperate grasslands of central Argentina. The puma is also common through this region and is known to range even farther southward, to Tierra del Fuego.

These big cats, particularly *el tigre*, are difficult to bag in tropical South America because of dense jungle growth. Hunts here are usually nocturnal vigils spent perched over a bleating goat or a fresh kill or hunkered beside a grizzled guide making sex-talk with a gourd. Shots are rare, but when they occur they are usually at short range with an irate cat coming head on.

A few exceptions are the open areas of this continent. One is the vast Llanos region of Colombia and Venezuela, prairies which stretch eastward from the slopes of the northern Andes to the Atlantic. Another is the open, scrub-studded Gran Chaco region of Paraguay and Bolivia. The Mato Grosso region of Brazil is a good bet, as are the open Brazilian highlands and the Argentine pampas. Here the big cats are hunted with dogs, and the odds of a successful hunt are relatively good.

South America has eight native species of deer, but most are too small to be considered hunting trophies. Largest is the swamp deer, about the same size as our mule deer, but it is so elusive that it is rarely bagged by sportsmen hunters.

The large European red deer, cousin to our American elk, was imported into Argentina many years ago and is now more common there than in its original habitat. Today, this species is particularly abundant in the western part of the country, and organized hunts are available which usually produce the trophies desired.

A hunter poking around in the Amazon bush will encounter two species of wild peccary. One is the collared variety, which is also common in Central America and Mexico. The other, a larger kind, is the white-tipped peccary, which ranges in large herds in the jungle and makes a formidable antagonist when a man has to take on fifty at a time. Three-hundred-pound tapirs inhabit these jungles, as do capybaras and other lesser animals of this type. Most of these game species are bagged for table fare rather than trophies, but they are wary enough to provide good sport under difficult hunting conditions.

Bird hunting in South America is something else. The goose shooting in Argentina, for instance, has to be the best in the world. Seasons are the reverse of ours, so when we're getting our tackle ready for spring fishing, the honkers are winging northward from Antarctica toward the lush Argentine grain fields. Geese are everywhere. There are no limits, and almost no hunters. This is hunting which must be experienced to be believed.

The same situation is true with dove shooting near Cali, Colombia. This Andes species is big, fast-flying, and endless in number. Hunters shoot from stands there, European style, and the only limit is the amount of pounding a man's shoulder can withstand in a day's shooting.

Most of the teal which fly over our blinds in early autumn end up wintering in the coastal marshes of Colombia. Duck hunting is superb as a result, but, again, there are no limits and very few hunters.

A variety of quail and partridge abounds in tropical valleys and on grassy Andes slopes, and in some areas big blue pigeons offer even more exciting sport. And with no hunters to thin their ranks, regulations and bag limits are unheard of.

South America—the continent is almost as large as the United States and Canada combined. A book could never cover all the opportunities—where or how to go—but the hunting is there. Competent outfitters are available through some travel agencies, but the best source is through one of the U.S. airlines serving the South American continent.

E. L. (Buck) Rogers, outdoor writer, photographer, and traveler, has been all over the world with rod and gun in hand but in past years has specialized in South America.

WHAT'S AN EXOTIC?

By definition, something that is exotic is foreign or imported, and this is precisely the case with exotic United States animals. What many folks fail to realize is that there is an awful lot of exotic wildlife in the United States that we think of as being American as apple pie: pheasant, Hungarian partridge, English sparrows, and carp, to name just a few.

Among species of big game, however, imports have not established themselves so firmly in a truly wild state. Various plantings of axis, fallow, and red deer have been attempted on public lands and forests in the South and Southwest, but except for a few token populations that afford hunting so limited as to be nonexistent, these animals have not adapted to their new environments.

One exception lies in the state of Texas. There the climate, soil, and plants make for a suitable habitat for a wide range of exotic deer, goats, and sheep, but because of this state's initial status as a sovereign nation before entry into the Union, all lands in Texas are in private hands. Importations of exotics there were essentially private ventures, and

Aoudad sheep look like a big, wooly version of the Rocky Mountain goat. They weigh up to 300 pounds and stand up to four feet at the shoulder. Their color is light brown, and they have a long chest mane that resembles a cowboy's chaps. Their horns are much larger than a mountain goat's, sweeping up and out, and curling back upon themselves. They are native to North Africa. Price: $500 to $950.

Axis deer are roughly comparable in size and appearance to whitetail deer, though they sport fawnlike spotted coats throughout their lives and carry elklike, three-tined antlers. They are native to India. Price: $600 to $950.

Blackbuck antelope have graceful, spiraling horns that shoot up and out from the tops of their heads. Their backs, heads, and extremities are covered with a dark saddle. Their undersides are light and in sharp contrast to the saddle. Their body structure, size, and temperament are roughly comparable to the American pronghorn. They are native to India. Price: $500 to $750.

Corsican rams are native to Corsica and Sardinia. They resemble a cross between a Stone sheep and a domestic goat and weigh between 100 and 150 pounds. Price: $100 to $300.

Fallow deer carry a palmated rack, a bit like a caribou, and have a body structure that looks like a cross between a moose and a deer. Individuals may exhibit brown, spotted, white, and black color phases. They weigh up to 175 pounds and are native to Southern Europe and Asia Minor. Price: $350 to $500.

consequently this "game" is legally the property of the land-owner.

The effect of this situation is that U.S. exotic hunting is largely a pay-for-your-animal venture. Ranchers regard this game as a source of revenue, like cattle, and you are generally charged by the head(s) of game you take. Exotic hunting on these private lands is usually open all year long, and the hunt is usually "guaranteed" . . . no game, no pay. A sampling of the species available, and the price for each, follows.

Ibex look like a billy goat turned prize fighter. They are thick-set animals that stand three feet at the shoulder and sport immense, scimitar-shaped horns. They are native to the high mountains of Asia and Europe. Price: $500 to $950.

Mouflon are wild sheep from the Greek islands. They average 27 inches at the shoulder, and a mature ram will weigh around 150 pounds. They closely resemble small Stone sheep. Price: $250 to $500.

Red stag look very much like our wapiti or elk. They are native to Europe. Price: $1,000 to $1,500.

Sika deer come from Eastern Asia. Their body weight and structure are comparable to the whitetail, and their antlers are elklike, usually sporting four tines on a side. Price: $350 to $700.

THE GREAT MONSOON YAK HUNT
by Chuck Durang

High in the Tibetan regions of the Himalayan Mountains, the sun beats down powerfully almost from dawn to dusk. Dry atmosphere makes the climate even less bearable, and the rapid heating of the plateaus causes howling winds to tumble from the mountaintops. Trees cannot grow here, nor can shallow-rooted grasses. Almost the only vegetation consists of two-foot-high shrubs.

The usual range of Tibetan fauna is also absent. Nowhere to be found are the *languar* (a monkey), rhinocerous, elephant, tiger, or even the goatlike serow or goral. Not even the butterfly, the anteater, or the python live here. Who does live here? Only the yak, the yeti, and Clyde Darjeeling, the White Hunter.

The yeti—the abominable snowman—is said to be mythical. The yak looks more like a mop than an animal and is hunted for sport, as it has little in the way of useful by-products. (The female yak gives yak milk, as might be expected, but it is not easy to tell a female yak from a male yak. Or even from a haystack). Clyde Darjeeling is relatively abominable, and does not give yak milk (he does *sell* it).

We approached Darjeeling's little hut, Dr. Alfred Stonewhistle and I. The sign said, "Native Bearers, Cash and Carry," and soon we had seven Sherpas to pack our gear on an upland yak hunt. We were told by our guide that hunting the yak is fairly simple. In the first place, it is difficult to miss a yak when the only other feature on the landscape is a two-foot bush or a bamboo rat. Further, if one moves before the wind, he is rather likely to come upon a yak, and perhaps even undetected, as the yak always stands with its hind quarters to the wind. Its tail thus serves as a unique windscreen; however, it is able to smell only yak.

We found our yak at 12,000 feet (we had lost our bearers at 10,000 when we heard what they supposed to be a yeti. We agreed it was best, as we had been paying them 20 cents a day . . .). Unfortunately, the temperature ranges 60 degrees a day in the Tibetan Mountains, and we spotted the yak at the moment we were changing from our morning heavy clothes to our noontime garb of Hawaiian shirts and polo shorts. We were clad in our woolen long johns when, simultaneously, there appeared the yak and the monsoon rains.

The Indian monsoon provides most of the rain for the Himalayas, though only about ten inches a year reaches Tibet. However, when it arrived, it caused our unmentionables to shrink and immobilize us. By the time the Sherpas arrived to cut us loose, our yak was gone, having eaten our summer clothing before departing.

Chuck Durang is a functional illiterate who holds a black belt in mah jongg. He is living in Port Byron, New York, until his neighbors find out.

RUGER 77

If you are going on safari in Africa or on an exotic hunt in the United States, you'll need what is known as a "light" rifle. In Africa, this is opposed to your "heavy" rifle, that .375-on-up cannon used for pachyderms and fanged beasts. Your light rifle will be the one you use to kill kudu, sable, impala, oryx, and Thompson gazelle, which are animals ranging in size from an elk down to a coyote. Here in the United States it'll be used on species ranging from the size of whitetail (black buck, axis deer) on up to elk (oryx). An excellent choice for this would be the Ruger 77 bolt rifle, and probably the three best calibers would be the .270, 7mm Remington Magnum, and the .30-06. The Ruger rifle has a theoretical advantage over most other American sporting guns in that it employs the wide Mauser extrac-

tor, which might be an aid in extraction in the warm climates where these animals are hunted. That's theory, however. What you can't get around is the innovation and quality in the rifle. The slanting recoil lug, the integral scope bases, and the clean hand-checkered stock all point up the thinking and care that go into this gun. And the most amazing thing is the price: $215, and that includes the scope mounts! It's also the first American rifle in many years to be chambered for the 7x57 (which is also a good choice as a light rifle), .257 Roberts, and .220 Swift, and the first bolt rifle available in .250 Savage for many years. One of the best rifles made. From Sturm, Ruger & Co., Inc., Lacey Place, Southport, CT 06490.

—J.B.

DANA ADAMS

Y.O. RANCH—TEXAS' BESTES'

The Y.O. Ranch encompasses 125 square miles of Texas Divide country. It is located near Kerrville and was one of the first ranches in the nation to establish viable, free-roaming herds of exotic wildlife. It is generally recognized as having the best exotic hunting in the United States, when you take accommodations and the quality of the game and of the hunt into account.

The Y.O. package includes bunkhouse or individual housing, meals, and one guide for two hunters. Transportation is via a radio-equipped four-wheel drive, and they estimate the time it will take to get your game at between one and two days.

While the accommodations are more than agreeable, the Y.O. does not go overboard in a posh, country-clubbish way. There's a telling line in their brochure that reads, "Swimming, fishing or golfing? . . . no time or facilities. This is a hunting area, not a resort"; and another about available nighttime activities suggests that "most hunters like to get a little sleep."

Prices per head of game run from $200 for a Spanish goat to $950 for an ibex, aoudad, or axis deer. First-class lodging is $40 per night, and bunkhouse beds $30. Both prices include meals.

They have a fully illustrated, informative brochure on the Y.O. operation, reservations, types of game available, and the equipment you'll need. Like everything else about this spread, it's quality. Write: Y.O. Ranch, P.O. Box 222, Mountain Home, TX 78058.

"[Hunting] cleans out your liver . . . damn funny things happen to people."
—Hemingway, *"The Short Happy Life of Francis Macomber"*

31

Mongolian Argali Safari

Hunt argali in North Altai, Mid Altai, or the South Gobi. Price of safari includes: two magnificent days in Ulan Bator, Mongolia; licenses for one argali and one ibex, plus round-trip ticket on Air Mongol Airlines from Ulan Bator to your hunting area.

Seasons: July through October in the North and Mid Altai. In the South Gobi, you can hunt all year long, and at bargain-basement rates!

Rates: 12-day safari, North Altai . . $10,000
12-day safari, Mid Altai . . . $ 5,320
12-day safari, South Gobi . . $ 3,625
Air Fare: New York to Ulan Bator, first class, $2,493.80.
Contact: Safari Outfitters Inc., 8 South Michigan Avenue, Chicago, IL 60603.

THE EXOTIC HUNT
by Hal Swiggett

Hunting exotic big game in the United States amounts to hunting inside fences, which seems to turn some folks off—basically those who haven't tried it. It just ain't that easy.

Sure, there are those places, I refuse to call them either ranches or preserves, which turn animals out in a small pasture where fences can be seen on all sides at the same time, and sure, there are those who partake of this "sport." Neither the "doee" nor the "doer" rates as a sportsman in this case in any sense of the word.

Many large ranches specialize in foreign game, particularly in Texas. Known as "exotics," these animals are free to roam over several thousand acres at will. In most cases they receive no food supplement. They are wild in every way. Every natural instinct of survival is brought into play as they fend for themselves. These same instincts help them avoid hunters.

I've probably had as much contact with hunting exotic game as any writer in the business and know for a positive fact they are as hard to reduce to a wall-hanging trophy or table fare as any native game, assuming you're on a real honest-to-goodness hunting ranch, of course.

Certainly, as mentioned earlier, there are places where you're not really hunting, but don't let "guaranteed hunting" scare you off. All that means, in the case of big ranches, is that you don't pay until you kill something. It doesn't mean getting the game is a sure cinch.

I'm not defending the sport of exotic hunting because it doesn't need such action. I'm just pointing out that it can be either good or bad, as with any other type of hunting.

Exotics are seldom shot while watching a baited blind, as are animals in Africa and sometimes in the United States. Neither are they hunted at waterholes, as is common with native game the world over. Nor are they called, as are elk, or rattled up, as with whitetails in the Southwest. To bag a fine exotic trophy, the hunter gets in where the animals live and seeks them out on their terms.

Blackbuck antelope, from India, have a tendency to run at the first hint of something wrong. These "hints" are usually picked out once the hunter is in the vicinity of 350 to 400 yards. Sometimes blackbuck find it necessary to be someplace else when hunters are twice that distance away.

Axis deer, also from India, are, in my opinion, the most handsome of all exotics. Their choice of habitat, normally, is the thickest brush in the pasture. Often a trophy buck will be only 50 or 60 yards away and all the hunter can see is a leg or an antler. An open shot is very uncommon.

The various sheep and goats are similar all over the world. They prefer open country, where they tend to bunch up, making the trophy male hard to get.

Sika deer, from Japan, and fallow deer, from the Mediterranean, behave much as our own whitetails and are hunted in the same manner.

Rifles used for medium native game in the United States, like the .270 or 25-.06, should be brought into play. Shots will vary from an exceptional 40 or so yards for some of the brush-lovers to 500 for the capable shooter.

The only difference in hunting exotics on a real hunting ranch and hunting native game is the trophy you end up with.

If the outfit you are dealing with refuses to mention the size of the hunting area, be prepared to lean on one fence and shoot your game against another. Real exotic hunting ranches are quick to point out how many thousands of acres they have, often referred to as square miles because acres means nothing to most city-bred hunters. In some instances, sections might be used as the size reference. A section is a square mile—640 acres.

Choose your exotic hunting with the same care you apply to elk or sheep hunting, and you won't be disappointed.

Hal Swiggett was born in 1921. He has been hunting since 1927 and writing about it since 1947. He has had more than 1,000 articles published and is a specialist at hunting with big-bore handguns and muzzle-loading rifles and shotguns.

ECONOMICAL EXOTICS

The Inks Ranch in Llano, Texas, offers an intriguing and frank package. These people are more interested in raising cattle than messing around with a bunch of wacky wildlife and crazy hunters, so when you book into their operation, you go it on your own.

There are no guides, no quarters, no meals, no nuthin', except for a camping area with water and electricity that you can use if you've got your own equipment. You're shown a "pasture" (which is a misleading term in Texas . . . remember, things are bigger in Texas, and a Vermont "pasture" down there converts to the proportions of an African "concession"), you're told what kind of game to expect, and you're turned loose.

This do-it-yourself approach results in substantially lower fees than are common among the more sophisticated hunting preserves; your aoudad will cost you half as much.

Aside from savings, there's the challenge of learning about your game from the ground up, which to us has always been an important part of hunting anyway. Write: Jim Inks, Inks Ranch, P.O. Box 444, Llano, TX 78643.

BOAR HUNTING

Boar hunting in the United States is a very questionable practice, questionable in that it's difficult to determine exactly what one is hunting.

At one time or another, Russian, European, or blue boar were released in the wilds across this nation, but it's doubtful if pure strains still exist. Foreign boars, not having the language or political barriers we humans have established, will very gladly mate with an American sow of the barnyard variety, producing offspring with a genealogy as varied as all outdoors.

What's more, the greatest concentration of "wild boars" in this country is in Florida, and that particular strain can be traced to the Spaniards. When the conquistadors first visited Florida's shores, they had with them "domestic" pigs of that age. These animals were a far cry from the fat hogs of today. They were lean, big-headed, mean beasts, more wild than tame, and they escaped from the crude stockades in which they were kept to forage, survive, and multiply in Florida's swamps and piney woods. When settlers from the North first pushed into Florida, they dubbed these wild boars "razorbacks" because of their sharp, bony spines and erect guard hairs and hackles. These were tough critters, make no mistake, but, as happened elsewhere, they cross-bred with domestic stock, and that strain too was largely lost.

So for all practical purposes, America's "wild boars" are closer to feral hogs. Don't let that semantic twist fool you though; at bay, a 150-pound wild boar is a lot more menacing and dangerous than a 150-pound black bear. They will retreat when given the opportunity, but when they must stand and fight, knife-sharp tusks pop and clack like small firecrackers from the gloom of thick palmetto. They can disembowel a dog in the flick of an eyelid. A good friend of mine very nearly lost his kneecap when he was hooked by such a pig, and had he not kept his footing he could have lost his life.

They are also uncanny in their intelligence. A pig is reputed to be the smartest animal in the barnyard, and there is good argument that the feral pig is the most intelligent animal in the wilds. I have never met a hunter who has been able to creep up on one; they are just too alert. Without the aid of dogs, about the only way you can hope to bag a boar is to post along a trail they've been using and hope they'll come to you. With well-trained dogs, they are not that difficult to bring to bay and can be shot with a pistol, but training a good hog dog is a labor of love itself, and many, many are lost to those flashing tusks. Plainly, I consider hunting wild hogs one of the most exciting sports in the United States today.

Where can you find good hog hunting? Well, there are lots of preserve-type shoots available in Tennessee and North and South Carolina, and a few in Pennsylvania, but most of those I've investigated have been put-and-take operations, stocked with hogs that were trapped in Florida and southern Georgia. The most exciting and sporty hunts I've experienced have been in Florida, either on large tracts of private land or in national forests and wildlife management units. Places I've hunted include Fort Pierce, the Ocala National Forest, and the Parker Management Unit near Wewahitchka up on the Panhandle. One guide I can fully recommend is John Tanner, Route 4, P.O. Box 193, Orlando, FL 32803. He is one of the most competent outdoorsman I have ever met, and a hog hunter extraordinaire.

—N.S.

"Hunters, like poets, are born, not made. The art cannot be taught on paper."
—Nessmuk

33

Exotic Hunting Outside of Texas

The Exotic Wildlife Association, P.O. Box 1365, Kerrville, TX 78028, lists members in Michigan, Tennessee, Oklahoma, Nebraska, Pennsylvania, and elsewhere. If a trip to Texas is too far for your hunting plans, you might look into their membership list for places closer to home. A word of warning, though: a lot of the northern exotic hunting I've looked into is strictly put-and-take and not always sporty.

—N.S.

Wayne Preston, Exotic Bookings

If you don't want the hassle of writing letters, making decisions, and getting airline reservations for your exotic hunt, Wayne Preston, 3444 Northaven Road, Dallas, TX 75229, is the one travel agent specializing in this field.

His motto is, "When the wilderness calls, call Wayne Preston (214-358-4477)." If you get no answer, try again in five minutes. He might be in the shower.

Hunting with Cameras

The idea of the hunt as metaphor applies to man's search for knowledge and is therefore vulnerable to being invaded by its analogies—to hunt with a microphone or camera, for example. It has been argued that by these other ways allow for the play of venatic talents-scanning, stalking, "shooting" and retrieving—without the cruelty of death. But photography as a substitute for hunting is a mockery. It is a platonic hunting . . . the maximum tradition of affected piety.

—Paul Shepard, *The Tender Carnivore and the Sacred Game*

LONG-RANGE BIG-GAME RIFLES

Every big-game hunter, at one time or another, comes in contact with long-range shooting, if perhaps only through the pages of his favorite monthly magazine. There is something intriguing to most of us in the notion of a rifleman knocking off a pronghorn buck a quarter of a mile away, even if all we ever hunt is whitetail deer at ranges that barely break out a sweat on the plodding .30-30. There is a romance involved in long-range shooting, a myth all tied up in outdoorsmen like Daniel Boone and Davy Crockett and their supposed ability to shoot all game "between the eyes" at distances far beyond those deemed possible by mere mortals. But every American hunter likes to think he has those same abilities, and a great many are under the impression that the mere possession of a rifle bestows them, no matter how infrequently the hunter handles that arm.

(continued on next page)

BARBARY SHEEP IN NEW MEXICO

Barbary sheep are one of the few big-game exotic animals that afford public hunting in the United States. A male will run between 250 and 300 pounds with horn lengths sometimes exceeding 30 inches. These imported sheep are comparable to the bighorn, and they began their residence on a private New Mexico ranch in 1941.

Their successful adaptation to a southwestern U.S. environment impressed fish and game officials, and in the 1950s small herds were released in Texas and New Mexico. Total herd estimates are currently 3,000 for Texas and 2,000 for New Mexico, and about 65 animals are taken by hunters in New Mexico annually.

For more information, write: New Mexico Department of Game and Fish, State Capitol, Villagra Building, Santa Fe, NM 87503.

People blast away at game at incredible distances, often with inferior weapons, and with no idea of where the bullets are headed. I have seen "hunters"—who would be hard put to hit a moose prone at 100 yards—stand up and let loose at antelope that were running half a mile away.

This is not to say that long-range shooting at big game is impossible or even undesirable. However, the hunter should always make every attempt to get as close as possible and to shoot from as steady a position as possible. In my experience even pronghorn antelope can usually be approached within 250 yards, which is a comparatively easy shot, though from some stories you read you might suppose that every one was shot at over 400 yards.

But there is the occasional need for a long shot, and for a well-trained marksman with a good rifle kills up to 500 yards are not uncommon. Just what are the requirements for a "good" long-range rifle? A flat trajectory is most often given as the prime prerequisite. The flatter the trajectory of the bullet the farther away a hunter can aim "right on" a game animal without having to allow for the drop of the bullet. The most common method of sighting in a gun for long-range shooting is to have it striking three inches high at 100 yards; most modern rounds will then strike at point of aim at somewhere between 225 and 290 yards, and not drop below three inches of point of aim until they are out to 250 or 325 yards. This three-inch allowance is acceptable even on the smallest of big game, such as antelope, if shots are aimed at the heart–lung area, which is accepted as the best place to shoot for a quick, reliable kill. The loads at the low end of the spectrum would be the .308 Winchester with 150-grain bullet, the .30-06 with 180-grain, and similar loads with a muzzle velocity of around 2,700 to 2,800 fps. This is about the minimum for a long-range round. The cartridges at the upper end would be the rounds that have velocities in the 3,200-plus area, such as the .264 Magnum, 150-grain 7mm Magnum, and the .300 Weatherby. With these the "hold-right-on" range would be about 75 yards farther than with the minimum rounds.

Actually, in practical terms, there is little advantage in one of the super-magnums for most shooting. Beyond a certain point, which is in a fairly narrow range of 250–325 yards, the rifleman must know the trajectory of his arm if he is to hit anything, whether he's shooting a mild 7x57 Mauser or a .300 Weatherby. What does matter more is accuracy. If a rifle is inaccurate it won't be worth beans for a cross-canyon shot even if it shoots flatter than Kansas.

Accuracy is perhaps harder to come by than any other requirement for a long-range rifle. Anybody can buy a powerful flat-shooting arm, but to say it will be accurate enough to knock off a mule deer at over 300 yards is not so certain. To consistently take game at ranges of 400 yards, the rifle must be able to place all its shots in a circle 12 inches or so across at that range; this is speaking in terms of the rifle's basic accuracy and not the limits of the shooter. To do this the rifle must place all its shots in 1½ inches at 100 yards.

The bolt action has long been held up as *the* accurate action, for a variety of reasons. It locks up more tightly and more consistently than any other repeating action, giving more consistent cartridge positioning in the chamber. The

trigger system doesn't have to be designed to put up with the slam-banging and the necessarily greater tolerances of a slide, lever, or semiauto, and hence can be made more precise. The bolt is easier to tune for accuracy than other actions because its one-piece stock, usually attached to the action with two or three screws, can be easily modified in its relationship with the metal parts of the gun, especially the barrel. The bolt action will also digest handloads more easily than any other action, as its design is essentially an interrupted-thread that has the camming power to chamber and extract oversize or high-pressure loads, and handloads have long been held essential to real accuracy.

The other actions—slide, lever, self-loading, and, to a lesser extent, the single-shot—have all been denounced as having one or more faults that disqualify them from long-range consideration. The slide, lever, and semiauto all purportedly suffer from inferior accuracy and from generally being limited to less-powerful rounds that don't have the flat trajectory required, and the single-shot is hampered by the lack of a reasonably fast repeat shot, which can come in handy even in long-range hunting.

Most of these assumptions are not as valid as they once were. Modern pump, auto, and lever guns will handle cartridges that are flat-shooting, though because these actions do not have the camming power of the bolt they can never quite match the velocities of the bolt when handloads are "worked up." While off-the-shelf bolt rifles may average better in accuracy than other types, nowadays there is less and less difference. Triggers on the fast-repeating rifles are better, and more is known about tuning two-piece stocks. The Browning BAR is usually accurate enough for long-range big-game hunting, with groups under the 1½-inch standard being not uncommon, and it is chambered for some booming rounds, such as the 7mm Remington and .300 Winchester magnums. The Remington slide and auto guns are reported to be much better than in years past, though the two or three I've fooled around with haven't impressed me. The Savage 99 lever gun, which is the most popular of the modern lever actions, even if it came to life in the last century, can be very good and is easily tuned, more so than the slides and autos with their machinery in the forearm. I once had a 99 in .308 that, after tension had been relieved in the forearm, would consistently put three shots into 1¼ inches with factory ammo. The two modern single-shots, the Ruger No. 1 and the Browning, have more efficient ejection systems than the actions they were based on—the Farquharson and the Winchester Hi-Wall, respectively—and can be fired and reloaded fairly rapidly, at least rapidly enough for most long-range hunting.

Factory ammunition, too, is much improved, and more often than not can scarcely be bettered in the accuracy department by the shooters who handload for big game, so another of the bolt action's supposed advantages is not so big as it once was.

Once we get down to the nitty-gritty it matters not what kind of action you use as long as the gun is accurate. If you like the slide, semiauto, lever, or single-shot, use them. I personally still feel the bolt has an edge on the others. It is easier to handload for, and while factory rounds have im-

"Hunting is the sport of kings, the image of war without its guilt, and only five and twenty percent of its danger."
—Robert Smith Surtees, Handley Cross (1843)

35

proved, the handloader has enormous latitude in his loads, he can afford to shoot more as hand loading is cheaper (there is nothing like lots of practice to ensure accurate long-range shooting), and he can take advantage of such excellent big-game bullet designs as the Nosler. The handloader can load shells to higher pressures and velocities than he can in any other repeating rifle. The bolt is more easily tuned and is usually lighter and cheaper than the other repeaters. The most accurate of the autoloaders, the Browning, will weigh at least a pound more than most bolt-actions and cost twice as much. The weight won't be important on a plains hunt for pronghorn, but on a sheep mountain it might.

tionship of caliber to weight is called sectional density and is expressed by ballisticians in terms of a decimal. The SD of a 150-grain .30 bullet, for instance, is .225. This is a relatively low figure, approximately equivalent to a 90-grain 6mm bullet or a 120-grain 7mm; these bullets are usually used for varmint shooting where a high velocity (to ensure breakup in preventing ricochets and an initially flat trajectory) is desirable and high retained energy isn't necessary. The better long-range bullets have sectional densities of around .250 or better. The 165-grain .30 bullet, which has an SD of .248, is a much more efficient bullet past 300 yards than the 150-grain, and is now available in a factory load from Federal with a muzzle velocity of 2,800 fps. Hand-

No matter what action you choose, to bring out the full capabilities of a long-range rifle you need a telescopic sight. There is no sense in owning a rifle capable of taking game out beyond 300 yards and then not having sights that are capable of similar ranges. Iron sights, while satisfactory for close-in hunting, are useless when you're trying to pick a gray mule deer from a gray rock 400 yards away. Nor will you be able to place your shots with any precision at ranges over 250 yards, even if you're the best of shooters.

Besides accuracy and a flat trajectory, a long-range arm needs to retain its power as much as possible out to where the game is. An efficient bullet of at least moderate weight is needed to do this. It may seem elementary to some that only pointed (spitzer) bullets should be used in long-range hunting, but I once had an acquaintance who bought a new 7mm Magnum equipped with a quality 3 to 9x scope and then used round-nosed bullets in it. Needless to say, he didn't have the long-range elk gun he wanted. Bullets light for their diameter also lose velocity quickly, and energy more quickly, as energy is a function of the square of the velocity. I had another friend who bought a .25-06 for use on antelope and mule deer at long range; he also bought several boxes of 90-grain ammunition for it, as he was impressed with its 3,400-plus muzzle velocity. He failed to note that the more pedestrian 120-grain bullet (at 3,050) caught up to the 90-grain load in terms of velocity at around 250 yards, and at 400 yards, out where he expected to be shooting game, the heavier bullet had twice the energy! The lighter bullet was also much more susceptible to wind drift. After a bad experience or two he became convinced that the .25-06 was a bum big-game rifle.

Actually, I am convinced that the popular 150-grain load in the .30-06 is not nearly as effective for long ranges as the heavier 180-grain, even in terms of deer and antelope. The reason is, again, that it is light for its caliber. The rela-

loads can get this bullet moving at over 2,900, which results in a load that compares very favorably with the 175-grain 7mm Magnum. I have used a handload like this on antelope and deer, and found it extremely effective. If the wind is blowing the 180-grain would be even better. Elmer Keith, the Salmon, Idaho, hunter and writer, has long recommended that the heaviest pointed bullet available in any caliber be used for long-range shooting. A great many people have found it easy to laugh at Elmer's ideas, as he does things that are considered slightly unnecessary, like hunting antelope with a .338 Magnum; other writers have maintained that a medium-weight bullet shoots just as flat up to 500 yards and will kill quicker in spite of less energy because the lighter bullet will expand more reliably. Both arguments have merits; when the wind is blowing I would tend to agree with Elmer. I have used both the 130- and 150-grain bullets in a .270 fairly extensively and can see no appreciable difference in killing power or trajectory when both are loaded to their maximum velocity. I can, however, detect a difference in how much the wind affects them at long range. Boattail bullets, in addition to supplying a slightly flatter trajectory, will drift less in the wind.

There is a trend now among hunters to use rifles as short and light as possible. For the mountain hunter this is a good idea, as an eight-pound .270 or .30-06 will have all the power and trajectory characteristics needed for the long shots that occasionally present themselves when you're after mule deer, goats, sheep, and elk. The plains hunter, however, might seriously consider going back to Grandpa's idea of a long-range rifle, a heavier arm with a longer barrel, not because of Grandpa's notion that a longer barrel is more accurate but because such a gun would hold steadier and give higher velocity. In 99 percent of the situations encountered, the light mountain rifle would do as well, but in the 1 percent situations the heavier gun might be worth it.

What caliber? Actually, anything with a velocity of 2,700 fps and above qualifies. The flatter rounds will give about 75 yards both in point-blank range and at the other end, out at 400 or 500 yards where trajectory starts to be so steep that a misjudgment of 50 yards one way or the other can result in a miss, or at least a misplaced hit. For deer and antelope I have found the .243/6mm good to the limits of my riflery, as much because of their accuracy as anything else. I might hesitate to bust a big mountain muley or a heavy ram with one at 450 yards, but I have taken enough deer well past 300 to know their capabilities. The .270 and 7mm Magnum might give an edge on those animals, and they are suitable for elk and moose when shots can be placed well, as they usually can be in long-range hunting. I have used the .308 and .30-06 enough to know that they are accurate and suitable, though the hunter must be more aware of his trajectory, particularly with the .308. The .25-06 is very good on game up to sheep size, and some even use it on elk, though I would hesitate to recommend it for that purpose. The .264 Winchester is the flattest shooting factory round we have that is suitable for big game, but it has a reputation for being persnickety as to what loads it will shoot accurately. For the determined handloader, though, it has possibilities. Anything bigger than the .270–.30-06–7mm Magnum rounds has more recoil than most of us can handle (and a great many of us can't even handle those), but for the hunter who feels he needs it and can tame it, a .300 Magnum or even a .338 has an edge in long-range power that can be useful on our biggest game.

What it comes down to, though, is the shooter's skill. It takes practice to become a long-range shooter. Off-season varmint hunting with your big-game rifle (and big-game loads if possible, where population is thin enough so that there is no danger of ricochets harming anything) is still one of the best ways to learn to judge wind and distance. Actually, the long-range shooter is defined not by how far away he will shoot at things but by his awareness of his limitations. When you can hit a gallon can five-out-of-five at 400 yards on a calm day from a prone position, you can begin to think of yourself as a long-range shooter. When you pull down on a trophy buck someday at that distance when the wind is howling and the best shooting position you can get into is not as steady as you'd like, when your pulse is pounding and the crosshairs are doing a lively dance all over the deer, if you then have sense enough not to shoot— no matter how many times you plugged that can back on the range—you can begin to think of yourself as a long-range *hunter*.

—J.B.

REMINGTON 788

The Remington 788 was conceived as a low-cost bolt rifle for those shooters not wanting to lay out the cash for the 700. Inflation being what it is, the 788 now costs about what the 700 did when the 788 was introduced. For those unconcerned with fancy stocks, milled trigger guards, and the like, it is an excellent choice. It has a clip magazine and is also a very accurate arm. This is partially due to its fast lock time (even faster than the 700s), and there are quite a few benchrest rifles built on this action. In .243, 6mm, and .308 calibers it can handle 90 percent of the long-range big-game hunting in North America. It is also the lowest-priced bolt-action rifle available in a left-hand version (the left-hand version is in 6mm and .308 only). Price for the right-hand version is $144.95, the left, $149.95. Remington Arms Co., Inc., 939 Barnum Avenue, Bridgeport, CT 06602.

MOSSBERG 810 AND 800 RIFLES

The Mossberg 810 and 800 rifles are simply long-action and short-action versions of the same action. The long-action is chambered for the .270, .30-06, and 7mm Magnum, and the short for the .243 and .308 in big-game calibers. Price is $184.95 for the .270 and '06, $197.50 for 7mm Magnum, though Lord knows why, as the only difference is a 2-inch increase in the length of the barrel (22 to 24 inches) in the Magnum over the standard rounds. The 800 is $174.95. Weight of the 810 is 8 pounds, that of the 800, 6½. Trigger is adjustable, and sling swivels are included. The action differs from most bolt types in that it has six locking lugs and a short throw. O. F. Mossberg and Sons, Inc., 7 Grasso Avenue, North Haven, CT 06473.

—J.B.

"At least if the species has lost its animal strength its individual members can have the fun of finding it again."
—Renny Russe

37

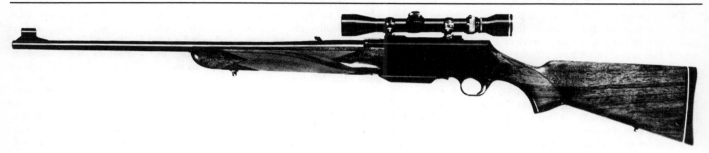

BROWNING AUTOMATIC RIFLE

This rifle is the most consistently accurate semiautomatic on the market, equal to many bolt rifles, and it comes in powerful flat-shooting rounds: .243, .270, .308, .30-06, 7mm Magnum, and .300 Winchester Magnum. It has a hand-checkered stock and a four-round box magazine that is easily removed for loading and unloading. The trigger is one of the best of any semiautomatic. Weight is about 7½ pounds in standard calibers, 8½ in magnums. It comes in two grades, the Mark I, which is

$439.50 in standard calibers and $479.50 in magnum, and the Mark IV, which features an engraved grayed steel receiver, and a fancy-grade walnut stock with fancier checkering than the Mark I. Price is $1,000 for standard calibers and, again, $40 more for magnums. It also comes without the good, open sights of the MK I.

Since ejection is to the side, the BAR is easily scoped, but because of the angle at which the ejector kicks the empties out (about 45 degrees upward) some scope mounts that feature large-headed side screws, such as the Weaver mount, can cause ejection problems if the screws are on the same side of the receiver as the ejection port. Simply reversing the rings so that the screw heads are on the other side solves this problem, however.

Browning, Route 1, Morgan, UT 84050.

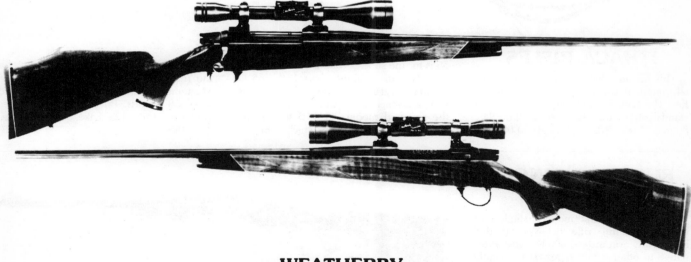

WEATHERBY VANGUARD

For those shooters who want a Weatherby rifle without the hassle of obtaining Weatherby ammo or the recoil that results when you touch it off, there is the Weatherby Vanguard. It comes in .243, .25-06, .270, and 7mm Magnum, .30-06 and .300

Winchester Magnum, with the standard Weatherby-style Monte Carlo stock with white-line spacers and angled fore-end cap. It is on a more standard-designed bolt

action than the Weatherby Mark V, having two bolt lugs instead of the projectionless 9 lugs of the Mark V. All barrels are 24-inch, weight is just under 8 pounds. Price: $269.50. Weatherby, 2781 Firestone Boulevard, South Gate, CA 90280. —J.B.

REMINGTON 700

The Remington 700 has the reputation of being one of the most consistently accurate sporting rifles to be produced in the world. It is also a very strong action, which can handle the pressures of maximum handloads. It is available in just about any caliber the big-game hunter might want, from the little .243 and 6mm to the booming .338, .375, and .458. It also has an advantage in that it is available to left-handed shooters for only an extra five bucks over the regular version, bringing the advantages of the bolt gun to the southpaw shooter who has traditionally either had to go through some amazing gymnastics to get another round in the chamber of right-handed bolt rifles or resort to lever, pump, or semiauto designs. The left-handed version is only available in the most popular rounds, the .270, .30-06, or 7mm Magnum, but if the shooter really wanted a different caliber he could easily have a 700 rebarreled to .25-06 or .338 or whatever.

The 700 is available in two grades ADL (without floorplate and sling) and BDL (which includes those things and a dressed-up stock). The ADL runs $214.95 and the BDL $244.95 for "standard" rounds like the .270 and '06, or $259.95 for magnums, with the left-hand being available in only the BDL version for the aforementioned $5 extra. The .375 and .458 cost $435 and are known as Safari Grade. Remington Arms Co., Inc., 939 Barnum Avenue, Bridgeport, CT 06602. —J.B.

Ithaca CF-2.

ITHACA RIFLES

This famous shotgun firm makes (actually imports) two bolt-action big-game rifles. The LSA 55 and 65 are chambered for standard-type rounds such as the .243, 6mm, .25-06, .270, .308, and .30-06. The 55 is for the shorter rounds and weighs 6½ pounds, with a 22-inch barrel; the 65 for the longer cartridges and weighs 7 pounds, with a 23-inch tube. Price is $299.95 for the standard model, $329.95 for the deluxe, which has a fancier stock. The Ithaca/BSA CF-2 is their magnum rifle, for the 7mm Remington and .300 Winchester Magnums; it has a 24-inch barrel and weighs 8 pounds. Price is $319.95. Ithaca Gun Co., Inc., 123 Lake Street, Ithaca, NY 14850. —J.B.

RUGER #1 SINGLE SHOT

This was the first modern single-shot centerfire hunting rifle that was intended as a quality arm instead of a low-cost alternative to other action types. It is roughly based on the old British Farquharson action but is much improved. This is an excellent gun in all respects: quality, function, and price. It comes in just about all popular long-range big-game calibers in a variety of barrel lengths and weights. The standard rifle, which comes without open

sights, has Ruger scope rings included. This may be the strongest commerical rifle action in existence. Price for the rifle (including sling swivels, rubber butt pad, and classic-style stock) is $265.00, or $140.00 for a barreled action. From Sturm, Ruger & Co., Inc., Lacey Place, Southport, CT 06490. —J.B.

"That wildlife is merely something to shoot at or look at is the grossest of fallacies. It often represents the difference between rich country and mere land."
—Aldo Leopold

39

SAKO BOLT RIFLE

The Sako M74 sporter comes in most popular big-game calibers, including the 7x57 Mauser, .338 Winchester, and .375 H&H as well as the standard .243, .25-06, .270, 7mm Magnum, .30-06, and .300 Winchester Magnum. Barrel length for all except the .243 is 24 inches; the .243 is 23 inches. Don't ask me why. It is a very handsome rifle and is available in two grades, standard and deluxe. The standard costs $329.00 and the deluxe $485.00. The 7x57 is only available in the standard grade; for some reason the .308 Winchester is substituted for it in the deluxe. The Sako action is dovetailed for Sako scope rings, making for a good, solid mounting system. Imported by the Garcia Corporation, 329 Alfred Avenue, Teaneck, NJ 07666. —J.B.

COLT SAUER HIGH-POWER RIFLE

This is the revolver people's big-game gun. It has a unique bolt that has no projecting locking lugs; the lugs lie flat on the bolt until the handle is turned down, at which time they rise out of the bolt body (by means of a cam) to lock the cartridge solidly in the chamber. This design makes the Colt rifle one of the slickest-working bolt actions yet. It is available in two action lengths, the long for the .25-06, .270, .30-06, 7mm Magnum, .300 Winchester and Weatherby magnums; the short for the .22-250, .243, and .308. It is a bit heavier than some other rifles, probably due to the Monte Carlo-type stock, which is exaggerated just a bit more than need be. Barrel length is 24 inches in all calibers, which also makes for unnecessary weight and length in some calibers. The stock has a high-gloss finish and the typical white spacers at butt, grip, and fore-end that go with the high Monte Carlo stock. Cost: $549.50, from Colt Industries, 150 Huyshope Avenue, Hartford, CT 06102.—J.B.

SHILEN SPORTER

The Shilen company, which has long been known for super-accurate target rifles, particularly benchrest types, has come out with a sporter rifle embodying most of the accurizing features of the target arms. The DGA sporter is purely a hunting arm, and somebody who is interested in showing off his gun and not in how it shoots might look askance at the $489.50 price tag on a gun that looks so plain. There isn't any checkering on the stock and the finish isn't some super-gloss plastic. The blueing on the barrel and action is dull compared to many guns, almost a military type. But what matters is what's inside the gun. The quick ignition of the Shilen action, the adjustable, clean trigger, the meticulously made barrel all point to accuracy, which means under 1-inch groups at 100 yards, from the reports I've seen, when whoever is shooting it knows what he's doing and the proper load is used. For a rifle in the 7½-pound weight range, it cannot be bettered. Right now it is only available in a short action with the standard calibers of .243, 6mm, and .308, as well as rounds not commonly chambered in factory rifles any more, such as the .250 Savage, .257 Roberts, .284 Winchester, and .358 Winchester. For the long-range big-game hunter the .284 would make an excellent choice, as it basically duplicates the .270. The dull finish on the gun is an advantage in the field as it doesn't glare to warn game of the hunter's presence. The barrel is 24 inches long, and magazine capacity is three rounds. In the future I hope there will be a long action for rounds such as the .270, .30-06, and 7mm Magnum, though the hunter is by no means handicapped by the choice provided. Shilen Rifles, Inc., 205 Metro Park Boulevard, Ennis, TX 75119. —J.B.

BROWNING SINGLE SHOT

This is essentially the old Winchester Hi-Wall action modernized; it is available in .22-250, 6mm Remington, .25-06, .30-06, 7mm Magnum, and .45-70. All these calibers except for the .22-250 and the .45-70 would make good choices for long-range shooting of some types of big game. The 78 comes with a 26-inch barrel, either round or octagonal, and the .45-70 with a 24-inch barrel, octagonal only (the .45-70 version would make an OK woods gun if you're not too worried about fast repeat shots). Trigger is adjustable and the forearm isn't attached to the barrel—instead it is mounted on a hanger that is attached to the receiver, allowing precise bedding adjustments, which helps accuracy considerably. Because the single-shot design has no magazine, overall length is about 4 inches less than in bolt-action sporters, so the 26-inch barrel is no handicap in handling quality. Extraction and ejection are positive, and there is a deflector at the rear of the receiver that can angle the ejected shells to right or left. A man with a couple of shells stuck between the fingers of his forearm hand can reload this gun fairly quickly. Price: $344.95. Browning, Route 1, Morgan, UT 84050.

—J.B.

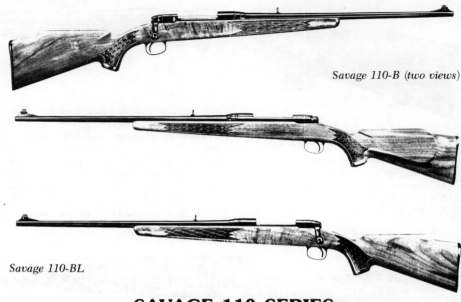

Savage 110-B (two views)

Savage 110-BL

SAVAGE 110 SERIES

The Savage 110 in its various versions is a good, relatively inexpensive bolt-action rifle for big-game hunting. It is available in left-hand as well as right-hand versions in .243, .270, 7mm Magnum, and .30-06. Prices range from $154.50 for the 110-E (right-hand only in .243 and .30-06) to $210.50 for the 110-CL (left-hand, 7mm Magnum version). The 111 Chieftain is a dolled-up 110 and is available in 7x57 as well as the other calibers; it includes a sling and fancier stock. Price: $224.50 for standard or $235.00 for magnum. Savage Arms, Springdale Road, Westfield, MA 01085.

—J.B.

BRING 'EM BACK ALIVE

. . . with a pneumatic syringe rifle. The ultimate solution to the anti-hunter debate. Shoot a grizzly or a cranky mountain lion with a tranque gun, box him up, and ship him off to Cleveland Amory or Alice Herrington COD. Let them figure out what to do next . . . after all, you've done your part, right?

CO_2 dart projector (40-yard range) with 3-syringe capacity, $249.00; 10cc syringe $11.50. Free catalog that lists syringe rifles, pistols, drugs, and such.

Wiley & Sons, P.O. Box 86, Route 1, Wills Point, TX 75169.

Through the jungle very softly flits a shadow and a sigh,
He is Fear, O Little Hunter, he is Fear!
—Rudyard Kipling, "Song of the Little Hunter"

41

SAVAGE 99

The Savage 99 lever rifle came to life in 1899, which is where it got its name, but it is a modern lever action in the sense that it will handle high-pressure rounds and pointed bullets, which qualifies it as a long-range rifle as well as a woods gun. It is available in .243, .250 Savage, .300 Savage, and .308 Winchester. The .243 and .250 are excellent flat-shooting rounds for light big game, and the .300 and .308 will handle game to elk and moose size out to 250 yards or so with proper loads. The "modern" 99 at one time was chambered for the .284 Winchester—which is a sort of lever-action .270—and the .358 Winchester, which at ranges under 200 yards will handle anything in North America. A used 99 in .284 would probably be superior to any of the available rounds for all-around big-game hunting, and the .358 for larger game.

The one fault of the 99 has always been its drooping butt stock, which made quick scope-sighting difficult (and the 99 is accurate and powerful enough to need a scope) and recoil a pain in larger calibers. Savage supposedly solved this by sticking a Monte Carlo comb on it and calling it the 99-CD. This new design, however, adds 1¼ pounds to the trim 7 pounds of the regular model, and so instead of a light woods or mountain rifle you end up with an over-9-pound clunker when scoped. A better solution would have been simply to angle the butt higher until scope sighting was feasible; this design would have been more efficient in controlling recoil also. Be that as it may, the 99-CD looks "modern" as it comes complete with white spacers under butt plate and grip cap along with the Monte Carlo and a mysterious fluted forend. The other versions, however, are straighter-combed than they used to be, though there is still room for improvement, and the straight-gripped 99-A is back, which to my conservative eye has always been the best-looking of the bunch, as well as the lightest. The 99-CD and 99-C have clip magazines as opposed to the traditional (and reliable) rotary of the old 99's, and the CD, C, and A models have tang safeties, which is a real improvement over the lever-positioned safety that still comes on the 99-E. One other fault of the 99 is a sometimes miserable trigger pull, but any competent gunsmith can greatly improve this. If your tastes run to the lever rifle, this one will do at the longer ranges as well as the traditional "woods" shooting that lever guns are known for. Prices run $178.50 for the 99-E to $235.00 for the CD. Savage Arms, Springdale Road, Westfield MA 01085.

—J.B.

Savage Rifle, Model 1899.

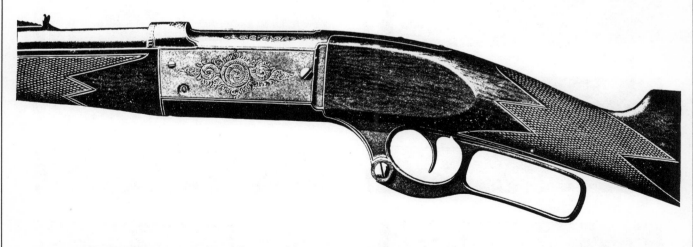

Round Barrel Rifle,	.	$20.00
Grade A Engraving,	.	5.00
Checking,	.	5.00

The engraving is carefully executed scroll work on both sides and top of the receiver, and also lines following the contour of the receiver.

Any kind of barrel and stocks can be had with this grade.

From the 1900 Savage Arms Company catalog.

BIG-GAME GUN FEATURES

In general, most rifles and shotguns are stocked with hardwood, usually walnut. Walnut, even in the cheaper, less-figured grades, has become increasingly rare and expensive and is the main reason for the increase in gun prices over the past few years, more so than inflation. The finish on most guns is now some sort of epoxy or polyurethane plastic, depending on the maker; these finishes are rugged and protect the wood well, though they are perhaps not as attractive as some of the older oil-type finishes. The better-quality guns usually have sling swivels and sometimes slings attached, and a great many feature cut checkering, as opposed to the impressed checkering that was in vogue a few years ago. (The impressed checkering was used to cut costs; now there are machines that can do cut checkering, and so expensive hand labor is not needed in most cases.) Barrel length is fairly standardized now. In the "standard" cartridges—those with .30-06 size heads (.470″)—a length of 22 inches is most common; for magnum cartridges—those with belted heads (.530″)—24 inches is the standard length. The one consistent cartridge exception to this is the .25-06; while it has a .30-06-sized head it usually is given a 24-inch barrel, as it is essentially a "magnum" without the belted head. "Brush" guns are thought of as shorter-barreled, 20 inches being the most common length, though there is less consistency with this type of arm. Barrels for single-shots are often longer, up to 26 inches, as no magazine is employed, thus reducing overall length by about 4 inches. Magnum rifles are usually factory-

equipped with recoil pads, also. Most companies still include open sights on their big-game guns, though they are easily removable in most cases.

Bolt actions can come in various lengths—a "short" type for cartridges like the .243, 6mm, and .308, and a "long" type for the .25-06, .270, .30-06, and the magnums—though some companies simply use a long type for all rounds and block the magazine if a shorter round is used. The Winchester Model 70 is an example of this. More and more companies are going to the two-action system, as it makes little sense to buy a gun in .308, for example, if it is just as long and heavy as the same model of .30-06. One of the virtues of the short cartridges is that smaller guns can be made to use them.

All factory centerfire rifles of the sporting type are drilled and tapped to take scope bases, unless they have a base machined onto the action to take special mounts, as in the Ruger and Sako bolt guns.

Bolt-action magazines are usually of the "box" type; the more expensive guns generally have floorplates under the magazine so that the shells can be removed without running them through the action. Pump and auto rifles generally have clips; lever actions have the most variance of all, with clips, tubes, and rotary magazines all used.

Shotguns especially for big-game use (usually intended for slugs) are generally equipped with recoil pads; some have sling swivels. All have open sights.

—J.B.

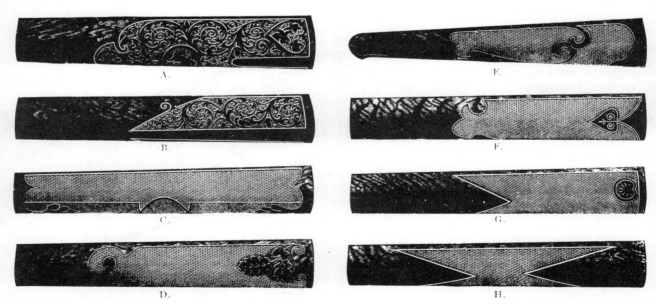

HIGHLY FINISHED WINCHESTER RIFLES.

STYLES OF CARVING AND CHECKING.

Style A, Stock and Forearm, $60.00.	Style E, Stock and Forearm, $12.50.
Style B, Stock and Forearm, 35.00.	Style F, Stock and Forearm, 7.50.
Style C, Stock and Forearm, 30.00.	Style G, Stock and Forearm, 7.50.
Style D, Stock and Forearm, 25.00.	Style H, Stock and Forearm, 5.00.

The above prices are only for carving or checking the forearm and butt stock and are in addition to the charge for fancy walnut.

From an 1890s catalog.

"A southerly wind and a cloudy sky proclaim a hunting morning;
Before the sun rises we nimbly fly, dull sleep and a downy bed scorning."
—Anon.

43

Fraternally Yours
Chas. Hallock

ONE HUNDRED YEARS AGO:
HUNTING WITH CHARLES HALLOCK

When my editor, Ed Burlingame, and I first sat down to discuss *The Complete Hunter's Catalog*, I was overcome with the enormity of such a project. Obviously, I accepted, but I felt a heavy weight in the task that lay ahead . . . until I met Charles Hallock.

Well, "met" is a poor term. Charles has long since found his happy hunting grounds. I was "introduced" to Mr. Hallock through an old friend, who found his book in a neighbor's attic.

The Sportsman's Gazetteer and General Guide was its title. There were all kinds of funky things inside, engravings and maps and archaic syntax, and it was published by Forest and Stream Publishing Company in 1877 . . . exactly 100 years ago.

The book numbers 894 pages, and the print is fine. Out of mild curiosity, I glanced through a few passages, and then more, and more, and as I read, I began to perceive what an enormous task *he* had accomplished.

It is an attempt to record everything pertinent to outdoor sport extant at that time: profiles of game, hunting techniques, conservation ethic, dogs and dog handling, taxidermy, woodcraft, and even an exhaustive "where-to-go" chapter that details the hunting and fishing meccas, as they were known, on the entire North American continent. Judging just by what little sporting history I'm familiar with, his information was as accurate as an Olympic match .22.

After reading Hallock, I began to feel as though I had been in the company of a sportsman's Leonardo Da Vinci. Perhaps this was the last man to know all there was to know about hunting and the wild, untamed world we hunters seek out for sustenance.

And yet there were other dimensions to surface in his book. At a time when passenger pigeons were being killed by the billions and buffalo wantonly slaughtered, he spoke of care, and limits to killing, and preserves for wildlife, and conservation. He wasn't always right. For example, he discusses the whooping crane and passenger pigeon as game birds, and warns about the imminent extinction of moose (but then, who knows if his words didn't save the moose?). But he also proposes preserves for buffalo, and he views wolves in a light that is wholly compatible with what we have decided in our enlightened wisdom of the last ten years: that they are a natural part of the wild world and should not be exterminated.

Hallock wrote less than a hundred years after Lewis and Clark first explored the West. At that time the Civil War was too fresh to be called history, a brace of canvasback were selling for 47 cents in New York and Custer had just gone to his questionable glory in Montana Territory. Yet he saw fit to write, in his preface regarding his "where-to-go" section, "Although I may whisper it privately . . . I have purposely refrained from indicating many places where the woodcock, the snipe, the trout, and the salmon, have their sequestered haunts. These shall be held as sacred from intrusion as the penetralia of the Vestals . . . if you wish to seek them out on your own, Godspeed. That is the essence of our sport."

His words are still timely today, and endurance is one test of greatness. For that reason, and a lot of others, we dedicated this book to him and to the "lovers of legitimate sport," as his dedication read, in his book, published 100 years ago.

—N.S.

WHERE TO FIND MULIES
by Ken Heuser

Better-than-average mule deer bucks are like gold nuggets, they're where you find them. Of course, there were some prospectors who never did find a gold nugget. The biggest reason—they never looked in the right places, and if they did, they walked right by the gold. Well, there are hunters like that too—they just never look in the right places for that big buck. But if a hunter gets in the right places enough of the time, he's going to see one sooner or later.

Big bucks get that way by being more careful than others. They either select places that have excellent vantage points for them to relax and watch from, timber pockets that are often passed up by hunters as being too small or not right, or areas that are so far off the beaten track it would take a prospector to find them. On nice days, look for the bucks on the points of ridges or in drainages just under the tops. This gives them an excellent view in all directions but the top of the ridge (keep that in mind). The thermal wind currents also rise until the warmest part of the day, which gives the buck the "smell" of anything that's moving below him (keep that in mind). Glass the points from at least half a mile away, looking carefully in shady spots. When you spot a buck, plan your stalk. On miserable days the deer will pick the southern exposures about two thirds of the way up the slope. Bucks will be off to one side or above the does. If a doe gets up in alarm, the bucks will evaporate into thin air, so be careful.

The mulies' favorite hangout—bar none—is a quakie patch. It not only offers almost instant escape routes in many directions but usually is so noisy underfoot that the only way to approach the deer silently would be to fly in on owls' wings (which, at this writing, are not yet on the market). Mule deer are not overly fond of sheep, so when you are scouting, keep that in mind. The next trick is to pick those timber pockets that are not too large (5 to 25 acres). Some of the most overlooked and bypassed hot spots for mule deer are these timber pockets in the rolling foothills and sage flats. Not only are they readily accessible, they are easily hunted and, after you catch on to how to do it, very productive. Mule deer seek good cover, plenty of food, a reliable watering spot, and hassle-free living. These timber pockets are made to order. Hikers, backpackers, and fishermen usually seek the higher places to do their thing, so the deer remain undisturbed all summer.

The mulie no longer feels that he has to migrate to the high country anymore than you feel that you have to go to Auntie Margaret's every summer. Lots, and I really mean lots, of mulies spend the whole year in the lower country. For some other strange reason, good bucks will sometimes develop a habit of spending a lot of time around small ranches, fairly close to the buildings if there is any cover, like a timber patch or a deep gully. Surprise your buddies by telling them you've got a sore leg and can't walk too far, then hunt carefully and thoroughly around the ranch for a day. I'm sure these bucks welcome the good feed, cover, and water that are always handy.

If you've got the get-up-and-go, you'll always find mulies in the remote canyons at least a mile away from any road. The deer don't get disturbed at all in these areas, and that's the point. Mulies are basically lazy deer and hate to be bothered by humans, so when they find such a place they'll camp there until something happens. Mulie bucks in these areas are generally less wary, at least until they're shot at. Look for them near the heads of these canyons, under the rimrocks, or in among the big rocks and rocky ledges. Go slowly and look ahead a couple of hundred yards, glass four steps, then move forward one—or, better yet, take a compatible partner, and each of you take a side of the canyon, but go slow and look much.

Mule deer, being free spirits like most Americans, are everywhere, but they do like certain accommodations best. I remember the first rancher I ever asked, "Where are the mulies?" His answer: "West of the Mississippi usually, but don't bank on it." Look for this newly educated deer in the out-of-the-way places; high or low, it doesn't make a lot of difference.

A Mexican sheepherder my wife, Marg, and I met last year said it well. We were looking for an elklike buck that we knew spent his time in one of two rough canyons. Figuring to save some time and energy, we thought we'd ask the herder if he might have seen the old boy lately. We pulled up our horses to talk. After a proper length of conversation and admiring the sheepherder's new store-boughten teeth which he very prominently displayed, I asked the old man if he knew where the big buck was. He had a twinkle in his eye and a sparkle on his teeth when he said, "You could try that canyon over there"—pointing to the first one—"and eef you do not find heem there, you could try the other!"

Ken Heuser is a free-lance writer who specializes in deer hunting, with over a hundred articles and books published dealing with this subject. He lives near Rifle, Colorado.

The does of the mule deer are found throughout the foothills the whole year, but the bucks retire in the spring to the highest mountains, to "grow their horns," where they remain until about the first of October. While on the mountaintops they collect generally in small bands of four or five. They are generally found near timber line, in the heat of the day, but in the

MULE DEER

morning and evening they leave the shade of the forest and go further up the mountains to the grassy tops, to feed on the young rich growth which is nourished and fed by the water from the snow banks on the mountain peaks. When thus feeding, it requires the utmost skill of the hunter to approach them within shooting distance.
—Charles Hallock, 1877

"Come, Watson come! The game is afoot."
—Sir Arthur Conan Doyle

45

WHAT DID IT WEIGH ON THE HOOF?

Add one pound for every three pounds of field-dressed weight to determine the live weight of your deer.

HUNTING BIG-GAME TROPHIES
by Tom Brakefield

New York: E. P. Dutton & Company, (an Outdoor Life Book), $10.95.

This is a complete guide to trophy hunting—where to go, when to go, whom to contact, economies vs. amenities, camp savvy, animal lore, conservation principles. And there are individual chapters on each of the major trophy animals: whitetail, mule deer, pronghorn, moose, caribou, elk, sheep, goat, and bear. Anecdotes make the book interesting to read. It teaches you about equipment, camp and field life, using a camera, using a taxidermist, and Boone & Crockett's role in establishing standards for hunt conduct and trophy recognition. Also included is an appendix describing the Pope and Young Club's trophy award program for bow hunters, and an extensive list of sources of hunting equipment, maps, and other information.

SHOOTER'S BIBLE

South Hackensack, N.J.: Stoeger Publishing Company, $7.95.

This book is published by the Stoeger Publishing Company and is a catalog of common shooting equipment—guns, sights, ammo, and reloading products—plus several articles concerning the shooting sports on both historical and modern topics. The 1977 *Shooter's Bible* costs $7.95; an edition is published every year with updated information and new articles.

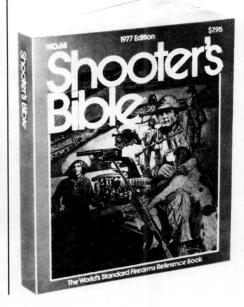

MULE DEER TROPHY

If you're after a record mule deer, Colorado is the place to go. Boone and Crockett records reveal that 97 of the 229 typical mule deer that made the books were taken in Colorado. This impressive tally represents three times as many animals as are listed by any other state.

Most mule deer bucks have ears that measure between 7½ and 8 inches. When the ears are extended from the head, they cover approximately 20 inches. Using this as a scale, you can guesstimate whether you have a trophy in your sights or not. A 24-inch spread is more than worthy of a mount.

BUYING GUNS AND AMMO THROUGH THE MAIL

The Gun Control Act of 1964 has made it impossible to buy firearms or ammunition through the mail from a state other than your own. It is possible, however, to purchase any gun or ammunition listed in this catalog, but it has to be done through a licensed federal firearms dealer.

You must purchase the gun in the state of your residence. Every sporting goods store that sells guns has one of these licenses, and most gunsmiths also have dealer licenses. Either should be willing to order, receive, and transfer your gun, though they will probably and properly expect to be paid for their time and trouble.

THE MODERN RIFLE
by Jim Carmichael

New York: Winchester Press, $12.95.

Here is a book that traces and explains the evolution of the modern rifle and analyzes the impact of important designs on today's hunting and related shooting sports. The author is shooting and hunting editor for *Outdoor Life* and has been a competitive shooter, gunsmith, and builder of custom rifles, as well as having hunted all over the world.

Why one rifle is more accurate than another of the same general type, what features contribute to accuracy, to smooth functioning and reliability, and what a buyer should look for in a high-performance rifle are all topics covered in the book, along with a discussion of how consumer demands shape the course of rifle development and why certain designs succeed and others fail.

THE HUNTING RIFLE
by Jack O'Connor

New York: Winchester Press, $8.95 (hardcover); South Hackensack, N.J.: Stoeger Publishing Company, $5.95 (soft-cover).

Jack O'Connor, for many years shooting editor of *Outdoor Life* and now associated with *Petersen's Hunting*, is perhaps the most widely read shooting and hunting writer we've ever had. Not only has he had vast experience in guns and game, he is one of the best writers in the business, and he reports everything as he sees it. This book is a full rundown on guns and scopes for all types of hunting, though mostly big game, interspersed with his anecdotes and comments on hunting and life in general.

Sock It to Your Gun

The simplest way to protect your guns in transit is to sock 'em. These gun socks fit any gun, scoped or unscoped, and they're available in a choice of gold, blue, or red, so you can color-code the sporting arms inside. Price: $2.20. Orvis, Manchester, VT 05254.

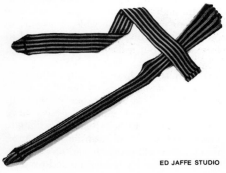

ED JAFFE STUDIO

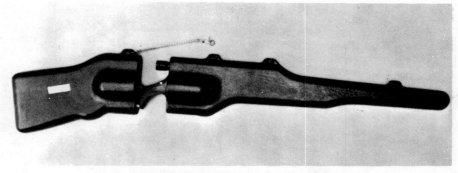

GUN BOOT, A CASE OF MANY USES

The Gun Boot is a seamless hard-shell polyethylene gun case that slides apart in the middle, a little like a plastic cigarette pack protector. It's dustproof, waterproof, and shock proof and will accept rifles or shotguns, with or without scopes.

The gun boot can be padlocked closed, and it can be padlocked to a stationary object should you want to leave the gun in a car or in camp. In addition, it works like a scabbard, and you can use it to hold your gun while riding a horse, trail bike, or snowmobile.

It's also suitable for shipping firearms via the airlines . . . truly a case of many uses. Price: $52.00. Kolpin Manufacturing, Inc., P.O. Box 231, Berlin, WI 54923.

NEW EASY WAY DEER DRAG

To Drag a Deer

When you down a deer alone, one easy way to get the critter out is via an 8-foot rope and a wide belt like the old marine-style garrison belt. Tie it on around the deer's neck and throw a half-hitch around the deer's muzzle. This keeps the head pointed forward and discourages it from snagging on underbrush.

Tie the other end of the rope to the back of your garrison belt and start walking. When there's no snow, you'd probably be wisest to tie the deer up short so part of its body is off the ground. This reduces the drag of friction between deer and dry grass.

Another alternative is the Deer Drag, a one-man shoulder sling and 8-foot-rope combination. The sling is made of wide belting so it won't cut into your shoulder, and it's colored blaze orange for safety. Just in case you forget how, the package the Deer Drag comes in contains field dressing instructions on the back. Price: $3.29 D & H Products, P. O. Box 22, Glenshaw, PA 15116.

"My heart's in the Highlands, my heart is not here, My heart's in the Highlands a-chasing the deer, | *A-chasing the red deer, a-chasing the roe, My heart's in the Highlands wherever I go."*
—Robert Burns

47

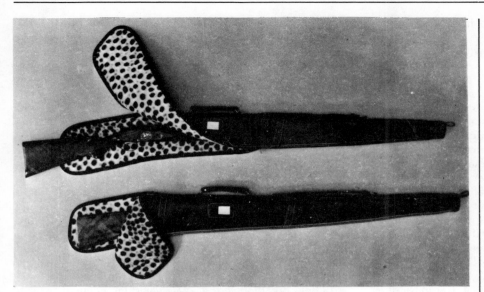

BUFFALO-HIDE GUN CASE

This quality case is built to last as long as the gun it protects. The exterior is tough imported water-buffalo hide, with a heavy-duty handle and adjustable carrying sling. The full-length zipper allows complete drying and cleaning of the interior. Inside, this case is lined with a siliconized pile, and the padding is humidity-resistant. The case may be locked, and it has a loop on the muzzle end for hanging. Available for scoped and unscoped rifles in 40-inch to 52-inch sizes.

Prices: case for unscoped rifle, $60.00; scoped rifle, $65.00. Kolpin Manufacturing, Inc., P.O. Box 231, Berlin, WI 54923.

DEER HUNTING
by Norman Strung

Philadelphia: J. B. Lippincott Company, $7.95.

Norman Strung is a hunter. He is also a writer. Here he has blended together these two talents to give us a book that should be a must for every deer hunter. Strung lives in Montana with his wife, Sil, and I can personally attest to the quality of the wild meat menus served at their house. It certainly gives credibility to his writing a book on deer hunting. He covers subjects from deer management to the use of tree stands. He discusses weaponry and the habits of all North American deer. Real bonuses in this book are the section on butchering deer, and a selection of unusual deer recipes found in the last chapter. My wife keeps a copy in the kitchen.

You will vastly increase your deer-hunting abilities after reading *Deer Hunting* by Norman Strung.

—Dick Weden

BRUSH GUNS

The grizzled Maine hunter and the old Montana rancher will both tell you the same thing: leave your .243 or .25-06 or 7mm Magnum at home when you go after game in the brush. High-velocity pointed bullets, they say, will either disintegrate on the merest wisp of moss or be deflected and fly off over Bald Mountain—in either case, you won't get your game. Some may even tell you that "light" high-velocity bullets will not shoot straight if they even come close to a tree; the projectile will turn simply from the "air resistance" created by its rapid flight. Such hunters always have a story or two to tell about how, after they shot the monster buck, half an acre of thick willow was lying on the ground along with the deer.

Could be. Stranger things happen. The fact is that *any* gun suitable for big game will occasionally bust through the brush and still kill, but most of the arms used by deer hunters for shooting in brush in this country simply won't penetrate vegetation and still kill *reliably*. There have been numerous experiments on this line, and all point to the same thing: while heavier bullets and blunt noses do get through brush better, it takes a *much* heavier and more strongly constructed bullet than is usually advised to do it consistently. For instance, it won't do you any noticeable amount of good to switch from the 150-grain pointed bullet in the .30-06 to the slower 180 roundnose, as is often advised. It won't even do much good to switch from your 130-grain .270 to the 200-grain .35 Remington. There is a difference in performance, yes, but it is surprisingly small, and not enough of a difference to guarantee *reliable* kills.

There are several reasons for this. One is that most bullets used on American game are designed to expand in one way or another—especially the flat-nosed or roundnosed types advised for brush busting—and there hasn't been a bullet invented that will ignore a tree and yet expand on a deer. If it doesn't expand, it generally tumbles. This mushroomed or sideways-pointed bullet has also been slowed by the brush and its chances for good penetration on the game are greatly reduced, so even if you hit what it is you're shooting at, your chances are that it will be merely wounded. I don't know about you, but when I pull the trigger on a game animal I like to feel that there's at least an 80 to 90 percent probability that it will never move from that spot, or at least travel a minimum distance.

This bullet behavior is influenced, too, by the fact that the damn thing probably won't hit where you aimed it if the game is more than a few feet behind whatever the bullet accidentally ticked. Even at ten feet, such suggested brush rounds as the venerable .30-30 have been shown time and again to have the capability of grouping in a pattern more commonly associated with shotguns.

Now you may take all the foregoing with a grain of salt, but the fact remains that the preferred weapon for hunting the African bongo, a very hard-to-find antelope that lives in thick, *thick* brush, is something like the .458 Winchester Magnum shooting a 500-grain solid (nonexpanding) bullet of 500 grains in weight. Now the bongo is about the size of a large caribou or middling elk, nothing near the size of the Cape buffalo and elephant that are normally shot with the .458. If it lived in more open country, most hunters would most likely use something on the order of the .30-06 to hunt them. The reasons for using the .458 are twofold: anything smaller (and soft-pointed) will not get through the thick vegetation and arrive where it is supposed to—that is, at point of aim—and anything smaller will not *kill reliably*. If shooting through brush lowers the effective power of the mighty .458 to that of a medium-game killer, consider for a moment what it might do to your .30-30.

There is no assertion here that the .30-30 is a lousy deer gun. I have killed too many deer with one ever to claim that. And there may seem to be no similarities between a bongo in the Congo and a whitetail in Pennsylvania, but look again. Our Pennsylvania buddy gets a chance to hunt just once a year, and he lays out as big a percentage of his income in doing it as the Houston oil man does on his bongo safari. If our whitetail hunter swallows the malarkey that his uncle in Pittsburgh gives him about chopping wood with the old .35 Remington, he may blow his only chance.

So what should he do? If he's not willing to use a .458 (and I haven't seen too many in the deer woods lately), the best bet might be the .45-70 Marlin described in this catalog. It is a good gun, but in most states it is still legally limited to softnose ammo, which means it won't quite match the magnum's performance. But it is perhaps the best option you have if you insist on shooting through brush and want a conventional rifle. I still wouldn't bet the rent money that it'll blow a cottonwood over and still get the venison every time, but it will probably give a better chance at it than your .30-30.

My first choice in the matter is to miss the brush. This isn't as ridiculous as it sounds. Perhaps the best method of hunting deer in the brush is from a tree stand; certainly more deer are killed from tree stands in timbered country than by any other method. From a stand of ten feet or more in height you can see and shoot down through the brush, instead of having to shoot through a seemingly solid wall of shrubbery. There are still small twigs to contend with, which are often all but invisible in timber even at midday if it happens to be cloudy. A good-quality scope sight is the best remedy for this. Forget what Uncle Elmo said about open sights being the fastest and a scope being slow and clumsy—very likely the last time he looked through a scope was also the first time, along about 1928. I would rate properly mounted modern scopes *faster* in practiced hands than iron sights, as you don't have to try to line up both sights precisely, as you must to shoot accurately with irons at even long woods ranges; you simply put the crosshairs where you want and squeeze. The trick to getting a scope on target quickly is *not* to look through it and then try to point the rifle in the right direction; just keep your eye on the target and insert the gun and scope between you and the game. It takes a little practice to master this technique. With the scope on your gun you are now able to pick out the brush that otherwise would be all but invisible, and any modern round will shoot flat enough to follow that line of sight very closely. Deer hunted from stands are usually not traveling full blast, even if they're driven, and it is generally possible to pick a brushless spot for the kill.

"But what if I jump a deer in thick brush?" you ask. If the brush is very thick and the ranges are short, use a shotgun and buckshot. The nine 00 pellets in the standard 12-gauge load will give you a much better chance of making a clean kill than one hastily pointed bullet, and since there are nine projectiles there's a better chance that some will get through (yes, Virginia, even buckshot can be deflected by brush). Slugs are fair medicine too, but most commercial slugs are cast of fairly soft lead and tend to come apart just as bullets do, though the 12-gauge slugs generally weigh around one ounce (437 grains), which is getting into the right territory.

Action type is important in the brush gun, more so, I think, than the load—whether rifle or smoothbore. I am a bolt-action fan, having grown up in the West, but I'm the first to admit that the bolt gun is too slow, even for an expert, for most brush-hunting situations where a second shot is necessary. The lever gun, in spite of its heritage, is too, especially for the once-a-year hunter, as he tends to take it down off his shoulder just like the bolt gun. The semiauto is best, and the pump a close second, but I feel that the selfloader wins because of its quicker recoil-recovery time and, again, the fact that the once-a-year hunter has to think, Damn, I missed that son-of-a-gun, and *then* jack a round into the chamber of the pump, while the auto hunter just squeezes the trigger. I'm not real crazy about the way some hunters use their autos—I once watched two "nimrods" fire nineteen shots at a mule deer doe before she went down, all in the space of perhaps fifteen or twenty seconds—but even the careful shot needs a second chance sometimes, especially when a bounding deer is his target. My personal first choice for a brush gun is a semiautomatic in the lightest flat-shooting caliber suitable for the game (the lighter the caliber the quicker the recoil recovery time), equipped with a *good* scope of 3x or under.   —J.B.

*"Like Indians, hunters, more than the rest of us, may be com-
muning with nature's Great Spirit."*
—*John Copp,* Psychology Today

49

SAVAGE MODEL 2400

This is a combination gun, a shotgun barrel over a rifle barrel, and would be a reasonable choice for the hunter who wants to cover all situations with one gun. The shotgun barrel could be used with slugs or buckshot for close range shooting and the rifle barrel for longer range. The choices are either .308 or .222 with a 12-gauge; the obvious choice for the big-game hunter is the .308 version, as with proper loads it will take care of just about any-thing smaller than brown bear or moose and elk at the longer ranges. Price: $462.85; weight: 7½ pounds. It has a dovetail system for scope mounting. Savage Arms, Springdale Road, Westfield, MA 01085. —J.B.

RUGER 44 CARBINE

This is a short, light carbine chambered for the .44 Magnum revolver round. In the carbine barrel the .44 puts the 240-grain bullet out at about 1,800 fps, which is OK for deer at woods ranges. While it conforms to the traditional standard of a "brush-buster," it isn't, but the 44's light weight (5¾ pounds) and length of just slightly over 3 feet make it quick. It has a crossbolt safety, which isn't as quick as the tang type, however. It has light recoil and quick-firing capabilities, though, and if you're looking for light weight and an under-100-yard rifle, this is a good choice. It comes in two versions: open-sighted for $172.50, receiver-sighted for $177.50. Sturm, Ruger & Co., Inc., Lacey Place, Southport, CT 06490. —J.B.

H&R 301 BOLT-ACTION CARBINE

For those who might want a bolt rifle for woods hunting, this would be a good choice. It would be a mite handier than standard-size bolt guns where the vegeta-tion grows thick. It has a Mannlicher-style stock with a 20-inch barrel and is cham-bered for the .243, .270, .308, .30-06, 7mm Magnum, and .300 Winchester Mag-num, though why anyone would want a 20-inch barreled gun for either of the mag-nums escapes me, unless they'd simply like to be deaf in a hurry. Big-capacity cases need longer barrels to burn all the powder. The 7mm and .300 probably wouldn't have any more power out of this short tube than the lesser rounds. Actu-ally, the .270 would be a little hampered by it. Weight: 7¼ pounds. Price: $299.50. Harrington & Richardson, Inc., Industrial Rowe, Gardner, MA 01440. —J.B.

WINCHESTER 94

This is the brush gun by which all other brush guns are defined. While the 94 is slower in repeating than auto or pump guns, it is still reasonably fast. Its greatest virtues are its length and weight: 38 inches and 6 pounds. It is not easily scoped, how-ever, and the issue open rear sight is not the most rugged. If you want one you should give serious thought to a good re-ceiver sight. It is chambered for the .30-30 and the .32 Winchester Special. Both are equally good killers, though it is easier to get ammo for the .30-30, and both are equally short-ranged, 200 yards being about their limit even for a very good rifle-man. The regular 94 with straight grip and full-length magazine costs $130.95; there is an "antique" version with half-length mag-azine and pistol-grip stock for $140.95, available in .30-30 only. Winchester-West-ern, 275 Winchester Avenue, New Haven, CT 06504. —J.B.

H&R ULTRA-AUTOMATIC RIFLE

A very good choice for woods hunting, the Harrington & Richardson semiauto is available in .243 and .308 Winchester. It has a "modern" stock with rollover cheek-piece that is one piece, which should help accuracy. Weight is 7½ pounds, which might be just a little bit heavy for some hunters, but it is not excessive. Barrel length is 22 inches and overall length 43½ inches, which again is just a bit long for some woods hunters. Price: $249.50. Har-rington & Richardson, Inc., Industrial Rowe, Gardner, MA 01440. —J.B.

BROWNING BLR

BLR stands for Browning Lever Rifle. This gun is a combination of traditional and modern design for lever rifles. While it has a clip magazine and is chambered for high-pressure cartridges such as the .243, .308, and .358 Winchester, it has an outside hammer and a two-piece stock. The forearm is partially attached by the old metal ring as found on the 94 Winchester; such a system doesn't do much for the ac-

curacy potential of the BLR, especially for repeat shots as the barrel expands and presses against the tightly held fore-end. There is also a strange projection from the front of the fore-end, evidently to simulate the under-barrel magazine of the older lever guns. Why it should be there is strange indeed, as it serves no function.

Nevertheless, the BLR is a good gun for woods hunting, being chambered for modern rounds. The .358, in particular, is a hard-hitting, fairly flat-shooting round suitable for anything in North America within 200 yards. Barrel length is 20 inches, overall length under 40 inches, weight about 7 pounds, and ejection is to the side so its easily scoped. Price: $262.95. Browning, Route 1, Morgan, UT 84050.

—J.B.

MARLIN 1895 .45-70

This is as close as we come to having the traditional brush gun. The .45-70 factory load shoots a 405-grain softnose flat-point bullet at 1,330 fps and 1,590 foot-pounds of energy at the muzzle, or about three quarters of the energy of the popular 6mm rounds. Nevertheless, I wouldn't hesitate to use this load at reasonable ranges (out to about 150 yards) on elk or moose, while I would certainly be hesitant about using my .243 at any range on one of the big deer. The big slow bullet of the .45-70 comes as close as anything that any American hunter would use to being the "brush gun," in that it would be less likely to be deflected by brush, and the Marlin 1895 has the traditional lever-action design that American hunters go for, though it's practically unknown over the rest of the world. The lever action is thought of as being "fast" in terms of repeat shots by the average hunter, though it is measurably slower than the slide or semiauto, and an expert with a bolt gun is probably faster than the once-a-year hunter with a lever; the opening sequence of the old *Rifleman*

TV series has convinced a whole generation of hunters that the lever will sling lead almost as fast as a machine gun. Be that as it may, the 1895 is a good rifle for most woods hunting, with side ejection that allows low, central mounting of a good low-powered scope. It weighs 7 pounds unloaded, a good weight for fast handling, and has an overall length of 40½ inches, which is a couple of inches shorter than the average bolt-action rifle. While the .45-70 is a satisfactory round for most shooting in its factory form, the ready-made load is fairly weak. It's made that way so as not to blow up old trapdoor Springfields (and is even recommended for "replica" trapdoors) and Remington rolling-blocks, which were made in the last century for black powder pressures. The 1895 will take considerably hotter loads, and a great many handloading manuals give data specifically worked up for it. The Speer Manual No. 9 gives as a maximum load 52 grains of 3031, which results in just

under 1,800 fps with their 400-grain flat-point, which is comparable to the factory bullet. This really doesn't do much for the rainbow trajectory, but it does more than double the energy of the bullet! Energy levels are at just about .270–.30-06 range, but the heavy bullet provides a certain amount of bone-breaking and penetrating ability that the smaller-caliber rounds don't have. If you do decide to handload for an 1895, remember to work up your loads carefully and don't start with the maximum, and *don't* use any of these loads in a trapdoor Springfield or any similar arm. A load of this power just might do the old arm some damage, as well as the shooter!

The Marlin 1895 retails for about $195.95, which includes a leather carrying strap on detachable swivels. The butt plate is semitraditional in form and fairly small; if I were going to be shooting this gun with anything heavier than the factory load, I'd spring for a recoil pad. Marlin Firearms Co., 100 Kenna Drive, North Haven, CT 06473.

—J.B.

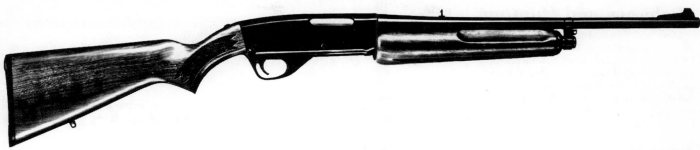

SAVAGE 170 PUMP

This is an inexpensive slide-action rifle for woods hunting. It is chambered only for the .30-30 and comes in two versions, rifle and carbine. There really wouldn't be any reason to select the rifle version, as the .30-30 gains nothing in performance by the 3½ extra inches of barrel over the 18½-inch carbine version, and the shorter gun would be quicker-handling. The .30-30 may not be the best deer cartridge in the world, but it isn't the worst. Perhaps its best aspect is that it has relatively low recoil, making for fast repeat shots. The carbine weighs 6 pounds, the rifle 6¾, and the price for each is the same: $129.00. Savage Arms, Springdale Road, Westfield, MA 01085. —J.B.

Remington 742.

REMINGTON 742 AND 760

The 742 is a semiautomatic big-game rifle, the 760 a pump. Both are of essentially the same design, the only difference being that the 742 is operated by gas and the 760 by hand. Both come in rifle and carbine versions, the rifle with 22-inch barrel, the carbine with 18½-inch. The rifle version weighs about 7½ pounds and is available in flat-shooting rounds such as the .243, 6mm, .270, .280, .308, and .30-06. The carbine weighs about 6¾ pounds and is available in .308 and .30-06. I can't really see selecting the .30-06 in this barrel length, as its velocity would be cut down to about that of the .308's, because its powder capacity is too big to be efficiently handled in this short a tube. The .308 would probably have just about as much velocity and somewhat lighter recoil. I'd really like to see this version in .243 or 6mm, as these rounds would be fastest of all for repeat shots and wouldn't suffer enough velocity loss to make any practical difference at even long woods ranges. Be that as it may, the carbine is a very good woods gun and the .308 is a very good cartridge for it. I have heard that some of these guns, in both versions, can be very accurate, but I haven't found any that will come close to a good bolt gun, even after tuning and careful handloading, though they will all kill deer neatly out to 250 yards or so if held right, and that is about all that will be asked of them. Both are available in two grades, the regular auto costing $239.95 and the deluxe $259.95; the regular pump is $209.95 and the deluxe $229.95. The carbine is available only in the regular version. Remington Arms Co., Inc., 939 Barnum Avenue, Bridgeport CT 06602. —J.B.

NAVY ARMS SIAMESE MAUSER

Built on a Mauser-copy action, these guns feature the .45-70 cartridge. Available in two styles, the rifle with 24-inch and 26-inch barrels and pistol-grip stock, and in carbine style with 18-inch barrel and straight grip, this gun would be a very good choice for woods shooting of *any*thing, especially with good handloads, as the bolt action will take pressures beyond other types. It is still essentially a shorter-range weapon, and the straight military bolt handle would have to be altered for normal scope mounting, as well as the action being drilled and tapped, but a good receiver sight or forward scope mount could easily be fitted. These are well-finished arms and have good open-style sights. Price for any model is $150.00. Navy Arms Company, 689 Bergen Boulevard, Ridgefield, NJ 07657. —J.B.

Highways and Hunting

Deer and those who hunt them are unlikely benefactors of the 55-mph speed limit. Highway kill reports indicate that the lower speed limits are giving motorists more time to see animals in the road, and the deer more time to get off the highway, resulting in more deer than ever when hunting season rolls around.

Man, weather, and dogs, in that order, are the greatest controlling factors in deer populations.

Will-o'-the-Wisp Whitetail

The Savage Arms Company once conducted an experiment to ascertain hunter's ability to see deer versus the whitetail's ability to elude detection. They stocked 7 bucks, 14 does, and 18 fawns in a one-mile fenced area.

Six experienced hunters brushed through the area during a four-year test period. The best time for spotting a buck was 51 hours afield. Does and fawns were easier; the best time established on them was 14 hours.

Timely Whitetail Advice

The sportsman should never attempt stalking the Virginia Deer [whitetail] unless he has nerves of steel, is strong, active, and an untiring walker. Not only the greatest walking powers are required in stalking, but it becomes a tiresome gait, as stooping and not unfrequently crawling on the ground for a long distance is necessary in order to reach a particular spot, unseen by the deer. Deer stalking is simply man versus brute; and requires all the strength, craft, and coolness of the man, before he can lay low the deer, who is possessed of a much keener sense of smell, immense speed, excessive nervous organization, and is ever on the alert to circumvent its human foe.

—Charles Hallock, 1877

SHOTGUNS

Big-game hunting is thought of as rifle territory, but in fact there are circumstances under which the shotgun becomes an equal and perhaps a better weapon. In some areas shotguns are actually the only legal firearm for big game.

There are two types of loads that can be used in shotguns for big game: buckshot and slugs. The difference between the two is that buckshot is simply large shot that is used just as in bird hunting, usually in situations where the game is moving, and has the range limitations of shot; slugs, on the other hand, are single projectiles which are often used in guns specifically designed for them, with rifle-type sights. Their game-killing capabilities and accuracy give just about double the range of buckshot.

In using buckshot the hunter should be aware that the effective range is around 40 yards at the maximum, and that the shot's penetration capabilities further limit it to deer-sized game. It is most effective in a choked shotgun, as a minimal spread of the shot pattern is desired, in order to put as many of the shot into an area as possible. There is evidence, however, that the most effective choke for the big shot may not be full but a more open type, such as modified, as the large shot tends to be deformed when passing through the tight full barrel because they "flow" less easily than smaller shot. This deformation makes the shot curve in flight, and fewer pellets will reach their intended destination. Individual guns react differently with various loads, however, and should be tested by shooting at a target, which will help to determine point of impact as well. Don't waste time figuring percentage patterns as in birdshot; the most effective load will be the one that consistently clusters the most shot in the center of the pattern.

Modern buckshot loads are more effective than they used to be, the plastic shot collar having worked its wonders here as well as with birdshot; also both Remington and Winchester loads now use a granulated plastic filler in between the packed pellets in order to lessen deformation. The largest size commercially available, 00 buck, has long been advocated as the only one to use on deer-sized game, but in actual practice anything from No. 1 up will do as well, as at short ranges the greater pattern density of the smaller shot will cancel out any difference in performance. The 3-inch 12-gauge magnum load has an advantage over lesser loads in that it holds more shot, but it may not work out as well in some shotguns. Again, the hunter should determine what works best in *his* gun; if the 3-inch 00 buck loads are giving sketchy results at best, and the 2¾-inch No. 1 load clusters all its shot in a tight little pattern, by all means use the lighter load, as it doesn't matter how power-

"The earth gets tired of being exploited. A country wears out quickly unless man puts back into it all his residue and that of all his beasts."
—Ernest Hemingway

53

FOR BIG GAME

ful a load is if it doesn't hit anything. The buckshot hunter should always be aware of his limitations, too. While buckshot can kill at 40 yards, that is stretching it some; 30 yards is a better limit. And once you shoot, keep shooting. The shot, while there are more of them, won't pulverize tissue as will rifle bullets, but they don't kill nearly as well, either. A follow-up shot may save you a long tracking job.

If slugs are legal and ranges may be more than 40 yards, the slug gun is a better choice. The 12-gauge load, in essence, is a .72-caliber bullet weighing from 380 to 450 grains, depending on load. It may not shoot clear across the pasture, but at ranges up to 75 yards it will get the job done. Bob Brister, the shooting editor of *Field & Stream* magazine, once killed a Cape buffalo with slug loads. This isn't advisable, but the fact that he did it indicates that slugs will consistently take any American hoofed game at the shorter ranges. I don't know if I'd want to tackle an Alaskan brown bear with one, but for woods black bear they would certainly be an excellent choice.

The special shotguns on the market designed for big-game hunting are all designed to be used with slugs. They have short—under 24-inch—barrels that have no choke or are choked I.C. (improved cylinder) and are equipped with open sights and possibly sling swivels. The open choke may help perpetuate the myth that slugs will be inaccurate in a choked barrel, and perhaps even harm the choke. This simply isn't so, as modern slugs are designed to be shot through any barrel, and indeed, just as with buckshot, any individual shotgun can be efficient with slugs. They may or may not be, but just because a gun has a full choke doesn't mean it *won't* be accurate.

Be that as it may, the short-barreled unchoked guns are on the average more accurate. The nonchoking helps, to be sure, but perhaps as important is the fact that the shorter tubes are stiffer. Shotgunning with slugs and benchrest shooting may seem to be unrelated, but benchresters, in their unending quest for the ultimate in accuracy, have long known that short tubes are more accurate than long ones, as they vibrate less. Some slug barrels are slightly undersized too, in some manufacturer's lines, and so fit the slightly undersized slugs better (the slugs are made that way to go through chokes). These short guns are also handier and quicker-pointing in the thick woods than long-barreled duck guns.

Slugs are accurate enough to need sights, groups of 3 to 6 inches being not uncommon at 50 yards, and while open sights are OK, a good, clear scope of under 2½x is quicker and allows the hunter to see better in the dim light conditions often found in woods hunting. The fastest sights of all,

perhaps, are optical sights like the Weaver Quik-Point that furnish a large, usually orange dot of light as an aiming point. These must be used with both eyes open, and the dot seems to be suspended in the air; a field of view equal to that of open sights results, while the eyes don't have to refocus from sight to game. In spite of the fact that shooters are supposed to use all scopes with both eyes open, many do close the off eye, and even if it isn't closed the necessity of concentrating on an enlarged image through the master eye often reduces the power of the other eye so that, in effect, it sees nothing. A low-powered scope minimizes this, and an optical sight eliminates it; either is an advantage in woods hunting.

Again, the hunter should test various loads through his gun to see what they can do. Very often one make of slugs will give a definite accuracy advantage.

Slugs are not long-ranged, both because of the low muzzle velocity and poor projectile efficiency, and even if they are accurate enough, 100 yards is a very long shot, as their trajectory is decidedly rotund. Seventy-five yards is a better limit. Energy drops off rapidly too, so the heavy 12-gauge slug is preferred. And slugs, despite their great weight, are not the perfect brush-mowing machine, so don't go blasting away at any and all deer seen dimly through the willows. Slugs are also just about impossible to use in double guns, as the two barrels will almost never group to the same point of impact. Keep to the single-barrel weapons, and you'll have a shotgun for big game far superior to the buckshot-loaded weapons; if it is an autoloader or pump with a good, low-powered scope you'll have a quick-firing, powerful gun that for all practical purposes equals the rifle at woods ranges.

—J.B.

FRANCHI SLUG GUN

This is the deer-hunting version of the Franchi lightweight automatic shotgun, so it is very light in weight, approximately 6 pounds in the 12-gauge version. It comes with sights (open) and a cylinder choke; the barrel (as are all Franchi shotgun barrels) is chrome lined. Barrels are interchangeable; chamber is 2¾ inches. Also available in 20 gauge. Its light weight makes it a very good choice. Price: $279.95. Imported by Stoeger Industries, 55 Ruta Court, South Hackensack, NJ 07606. —J.B.

MOSSBERG 395S SLUGSTER

Bolt-action woods guns have one big fault: they're slow on the repeat shots. This one has one big virtue, though, in its price. It costs $84.95, with a 24-inch 12-gauge barrel chambered for the 3-inch magnum. Also includes a sling and swivels. O. F. Mossberg & Sons, Inc., 7 Grasso Avenue, North Haven, CT 06473. —J.B.

REMINGTON 1100 DEER GUN (SEMIAUTO)

This has the standard 22-inch barrel for slugs and is choked improved cylinder, as some gunmakers believe that the IC will shoot slugs more accurately (or at least as accurately) as no choke at all. The IC choke will also handle buckshot passably well. This gun is equipped with what appear to be the same open sights that come on Remington's rifles, and they are very good sights, being rugged and precisely adjustable. A doubtful feature is that it is available in 20 as well as 12 gauge, as the 20-gauge slug is simply not nearly as good for deer as the bigger bores. Be that as it may, the 20 will still kill deer and perhaps might make a good gun for short-range bird-shooting as well. The 1100 has switchable barrels and so is not limited to deer hunting; extra barrels run about $65.00 for plain or $90.00 for ribbed, depending on gauge and length. Chambers for the deer gun are 2¾-inch for both gauges, which cuts down on the effectiveness of buckshot loads. Price: $264.95. Remington Arms Co., Inc., 939 Barnum Avenue, Bridgeport, CT 06602. —J.B.

HARRINGTON & RICHARDSON MODEL 162

This is a break-action single-shot 12 gauge with a 24-inch cylinder barrel for slug shooting. Repeat shots are for all practical purposes impossible, especially under woods conditions, but it is very light in weight (5½ pounds) and inexpensive. It has a fully adjustable peep rear sight along with the front sight. Cost is low—$62.50—but the recoil might be tremendous, even with 2¾-inch shells (it's chambered for 3-inch magnums!) so recoil-shy shooters might think twice before using one. From Harrington & Richardson, Inc., Industrial Rowe, Gardner, MA 01440. —J.B.

SAVAGE MODEL 30 SLUG GUN (PUMP)

This is an inexpensive ($144.50) slug gun. It comes with a 22-inch barrel with open sights, chambered for the 3-inch Magnum 12-gauge load. It is listed as "slug bore" for the choking, which is cylinder. The Model 30 is a rugged gun, so don't be put off by the price. I've been using a 20-gauge bird model for three years now and haven't had a speck of trouble. It weighs 7¼ pounds, which is an OK weight for a woods gun; with a low-powered, light scope it would weigh just about 8 pounds. It is a take-down model, and the barrels are switchable, so you can use it for birds too, by just buying an extra barrel. Plain barrels run $29.20, while those with ventilated ribs are $58.35. A good, solid gun. Savage Arms, Springdale Road, Westfield, MA 01085. —J.B.

" 'Roughing it' . . . I dislike the phrase. We do not go to the green woods and crystal
waters to rough it. We go to smooth it. We get it rough enough at home."
—Nessmuk

55

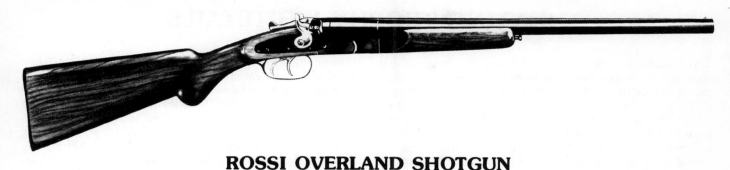

ROSSI OVERLAND SHOTGUN

This is a semireplica type of gun, with external hammers and 20-inch barrels. Its available in 12 and 20 gauge, both 3-inch chambered, and might make a good choice for close-range buckshot shooting, as well as riding shotgun on the Cheyenne stagecoach. Weight: about 6½ pounds. Price: $175.00. Imported by the Garcia Corporation, 329 Alfred Avenue, Teaneck, NJ 07666.   —J.B.

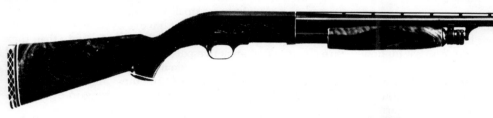

ITHACA DEERSLAYER

This is the Model 37 pump gun with slug barrel. It is especially bored for factory-rifled slugs (slightly under usual bore diameter) in either 20-inch or 26-inch barrel length. It has the usual open sights. Weight is 6 pounds for the 12-gauge and 5¾ pounds for the 20, both with 2¾-inch chambers. Price: $243.95. Ithaca Gun Co., Inc., 123 Lake Street, Ithaca, NY 14850.   —J.B.

HUNTING TROPHY WHITETAILS

By George Mattis

You might have taken many whitetails in your time, but somehow the trophy buck you bagged one memorable deer season stands out as the highlight in all your many trips afield. Maybe it was just a fluke, but you try to justify your reason for intercepting this prince of the forest, and you hope to duplicate the feat. One thing is certain. If you expect to take trophy bucks with any degree of regularity, you cannot trust to mere chance. You have got to hunt in the areas the prize animals are known to frequent.

Hunting a specific animal does not differ greatly from your usual hunting where you hope to chance upon any legal deer. Since your hunting grounds are more limited when trying for a predetermined quarry, you naturally take the time and patience to study the animal's behavior pattern.

Once you learn, either by personal observation or through reports, that a handsome stag hangs around a certain area, you get what information you can as to how frequently he is seen, at what hours, and exactly where. A whitetail is a creature of habit, and he usually sticks closely to his home base even though he might stray off a bit on occasion. The prospective trophy hunter will want to learn all he can about his buck. And there is no better way than to study the animal's habitat in advance of the deer season.

One can piece up considerable information on the habits of his hoped-for trophy in the quiet of the woods before the invasion of hunters. Once the animal's tracks are found, they can be compared with other deer slots in the area and can be recognized wherever found.

The buck rubs of such a stag will be on bigger trees, over an inch in diameter, not on pliable small saplings. There should be dirt pawings nearby, and these will plainly show at least one imprint of the animal's forefoot. This should be the clincher.

Several big buck rubs and dirt pawings in close proximity indicate that the buck spends much of his time here. Since these are usually found at the edges of fields, forest openings, or old logging roads where the deer commonly browse, look for trails leading off from these areas. They should be investigated since they take you to the whitetails' resting grounds, or beds. Often the beds, especially of sage old bucks, are found on hillsides from where the resting animals can detect any threat to their safety.

There could be more trails leading to other feeding grounds, and these should all be investigated. Often, too, there are pockets of very dense thickets to which the whitetails might retreat if they are much harassed, as by hunters.

It is a fact that old veteran bucks, the kind that have escaped the meat pole for several deer seasons, have long learned to live with a low profile. They will stay put in a very limited area so long as they are not molested. And very often their hideaways are in some odd thickets—along a road or near a farm or small village.

The cagey old fellows might have arrived at a stage in life where they are more concerned about their safety than they are about taking an active part in the rut. By remaining cool and staying put in some small covert, they avoid being overtaken in big drives where they might panic and blunder into a stray hunter while attempting to evade others.

The lone hunter, whether he takes a stand on some strategic point or still hunts the habitat of a trophy buck, will not unduly harass his quarry. His purpose is to probe the likely spots slowly without sending the animals off into reckless flight, for he will want to continue hunting here.

There is always that happy fact that, should the hunter not be favored with an interception of his trophy buck, his chances for taking a lesser animal here are as good as anywhere. This knowledge alone warms the heart of the hunter, who does best afield when his spirits are high.

George Mattis, author of *Whitetail Fundamentals and Fine Points for the Hunter,* is a Wisconsin writer, wildlife photographer, naturalist, and active outdoorsman who studied journalism at the University of Wisconsin.

Killing Them with Kindness

Feeding deer hay can kill them with kindness. Deer are primarily browsers. Their summer diet consists of leaves and fruits, and in the winter they live on twigs and branches. When they suddenly switch to other foods, like hay, the natural bacteria in their stomach are incapable of digesting this new substance. There have been countless documented cases of deer dying from starvation . . . with a full stomach.

Line-up for Better Hunting

Here's a quick way to identify well-used deer trails and a prime spot for a stand: just stretch a length of six-pound-test monofilament across the trail, about knee high.

If the line is broken the next time you return to the spot, chances are good that a deer is using the trail. Remember to pocket the mono and dispose of it back at camp. Songbirds might try to use it when building a nest, and they could strangle themselves.

Urban Sprawl and the Sportsman

The National Wildlife Federation reports that urban spread is gobbling up rural land at the current rate of 3,500 acres *daily.* If this rate continues, and all indications are it will, we will have lost 34 million acres of woodlots, pastures, and wilderness by the year 2000. The best time to acquire key wetlands, upland habitat, and big-game wintering areas with sportsman's dollars is now!

*"The grey dawn is breaking;
the horn of the hunter is heard on the hill."*
—Julia Crawford, 1835

57

FRED BEAR TREE STAND

The Bear tree stand is locked into a tree trunk via a chain and a brace below the stand that has a sharp-pointed end. The end digs into the tree trunk, and the chain prevents the stand from leaning away from the tree.

The stand is put in place by way of a pole, and it's reached by ladder. There is some difficulty in getting up and over the rim of the stand. Two pieces of advice when you use this stand: practice setting it up and getting aboard before you use it, and carry it and the associated tools you'll need in a backpack.

The stand measures 14 by 25 inches and it is unusually sturdy. It also does less visible damage to trees than the Baker stand.

I would recommend some sort of safety harness, so you can lean out and around should a deer come down a trail you didn't expect him to. This stand would also be good for duck hunting in swamp areas when added height would open up more shooting area. Price: $49.95. Bear Archery, Route 1, Grayling, MI 49738. —F.S.

There were 500,000 whitetails in the United States in 1900. Today the U.S. herd is estimated to be over 2 million.

BUCK ROPE: THE EASIEST WAY TO DRAG A DEER

The Buck Rope is a 1,200-pound-test poly rope that is woven into an adjustable harness. Two adjustable coils of rope join a third, single strand with a snap clasp on the end. When you down a deer, snap the clasp around his neck, throw a dally around his nose, and drape one coil around each shoulder. Your body pulls in a straight line, and you can use your upper chest weight as leverage to tug the carcass over especially difficult spots. Both your hands are free to pull you forward or carry your gun, as the case may be.

Easier yet, this dragging system adapts to two. Stand abreast of your hunting partner, and each of you throw a coil around your outside shoulder. Lean into the pull like a draft horse, and you can move a trophy buck with ease and comfort.

The Buck Rope can also be adapted as a safety belt up in a tree stand, it can be used to raise and lower your gun up into a tree, and it could be used for a dozen other things in a survival situation. You hear the claim a lot, but in truth this is one piece of equipment that I wouldn't be without during deer season. Price: $2.79. Cabela's, 812 13th Avenue, Sidney, NE 69162.

A Matter of Sportsmanship

Many sportsmen, and good ones too, take great exception to still-hunting, and some are "down" on the man who silently and carefully watches through the forest upwind for hours and hours, ultimately coming across a deer track, following it up again for hours and hours, finally creeps up to 100 or 250 yards of the deer and kills it, and lastly, by a short cut, finds himself fifteen miles away from home or camp, with every likelihood of having to sleep in the forest all night. Is not this sportsman, by all the laws laid down, even by the most fastidious of men, entitled to his game?
—Charles Hallock, 1877

BELT ON TREE STEPS

Hunters are getting hassled more and more about the damage they do to trees on their way up to a stand. "BOTS" (short for "belt on tree steps") anchor a step peg to a tree trunk by way of a nylon web belt with a clasp. There are no holes, scrapes, or pokes to mar the trunk, and each step is tested to 1,000 pounds. Price: $8.95 each. BOTS, Inc., Opp, AL 36467.

Screw-in Tree Steps

If you own your favorite deer-stand tree, one of the easiest ways to get up in it is with threaded tree steps. They screw into the trunk (and actually don't do much damage) and provide a safe, secure step. Four steps, $8.69. Cabela's, 812 13th Avenue, Sidney, NE 69162.

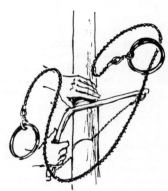

Flexible Pocket Saw

These little pocket saws really work. They're excellent survival/emergency items, and they are *the* tool to use in conjunction with climbing tree stands when limbs get in your way. Available in: 20″, $1.98, or 35″, $2.98. Wildwood Products, 1433 North Water Street, Milwaukee, WI 53202.

RUBBER-CUSHIONED CLIMBING DEER STAND

The Fox Squirrel climbing deer stand works on the same leverage principles as most other devices of this kind. It is different, however, in that all points of tree-trunk contact have a rubber buffer. This makes the stand quiet as you go up and causes no damage to the tree. Seats, climbing aids, carrying straps, and the like are available. We haven't tested it though. Price: $27.95. Dye Sheet Metal Products, Inc., P.O. Box 1664, Athens, GA 30601.

Sex in the Woods!

This product, appropriately called Buck-Mate, is billed as an irresistible buck getter, thanks to "Sex-A-Lure," a secret ingredient that smells like a doe in heat. The 1¼-ounce bottle comes with a leak-proof cap. If the product works as well, and in the same manner, as the manufacturers claim, this nonleaking top is a safety feature. If you were unaware this stuff was dripping in your pocket and you took a walk in the woods, you could get into serious trouble.

As a matter of fact, the bottle comes with a warning, to wit: "Don't open this bottle till your bow is strung or rifle is loaded. It works fast!" Price: $4.95. Kolpin Manufacturing, Inc., P.O. Box 231, Berlin, WI 54923.

Original Indian Buck Lure

One day while I was bow hunting from a tree stand, I watched a doe work her way toward my position. When she hit the trail I had used, she stopped instantly, lowered her head, and then raised it, plainly alert. She stomped her front feet, snorted, and stomped again. After thirty seconds of this, she turned and bounded away.

At that point, I became convinced that scents can do some good, not because they'll necessarily lure deer to you, but because they help make you smell like something other than a human. Indian Buck Lure is the stuff I've used the most . . . mainly on the soles and stitching of my boots. Several deer have crossed my trail since that day, but they haven't bolted. Is it the lure? Who can say for sure? But I've become a believer. Price: $2.69. Cabela's, 812 13th Avenue, Sidney, NE 69162.   —N.S.

Non-Scent Eliminates B.O.

Here's a whole new concept in hunting scents: no scent at all. These are alfalfa-based chlorophyll tablets you take daily (four to six recommended). Start them three days before you plan to go hunting, and continue taking them for however long you're afield. They don't stop perspiration, but the manufacturers claim you will be deodorized.

It's difficult to predict what effect this will have upon the deer and the bear, but you'll probably be a lot more popular around hunting camp, come the third or fourth day without a shower. With Non-Scent, your hunting buddies will love you in December as they did in May. Price: $4.95. Non-Scent, P.O. Box 1381, Whitefish, MT 59937.

Deer Call

Will a deer come to a call? Sometimes. I have never seen a call draw a deer from far away, like a duck or goose call can. But when there's a deer nearby, a call will often pique his curiosity to a point where he'll seek the sound out. Strangely enough, I've drawn as many deer to me with a dying rabbit predator call as a deer call, though the predator call was virtually always being used out of deer season, so mine wasn't really a reliable test.

Olt's Clarion deer call is made of black walnut and has a reputation for unusual quality. It's just under 6 inches long, and weighs 3½ ounces, so it carries easily in your pocket. Price: $6.95. P. S. Olt, Pekin, IL 61554.   —N.S.

Deer Hunter Soap

This product disguises human odor with the smell of oil of anise, the same stuff used to spice up the plastic worms used for bass fishing. When you're done bathing with Deer Hunter Soap, you are fragrant, though it's hard to say if this particular fragrance is a help or a hindrance afield. Price: $1.50. Marco's Enterprises, Escanaba, MI 43829.

Apple-Scented Deer Lure

If you don't relish the risk (or odor) of walking around the woods smelling like a salty old buck or a doe in heat, this pressurized Deer Lure has the comparatively pleasant scent of apples. Price: $2.25. Duxbak, 825 Noyes Street Utica, NY 13502.

DOUBLE GUN CASE

Big-game hunters sometimes take both a rifle and shotgun. A two-gun case will give you a free hand. Two separate padded compartments accept two assembled guns. The full zipper has two tabs, so the case can be opened from either end. Other features include canvas duck exterior, humidity-absorbing padding, a lint-free liner, and a reinforced carrying handle. Price: $40.00. Kolpin Manufacturing, Inc., P.O. Box 231, Berlin, WI 54923.

The Sweet Smell of Success

Buck lures and deodorants are designed to mask your distinctive human odor when you're after deer. The next time you come upon a lucky hunter with a fresh kill, try using this natural "lure."

Cut the musk glands from the inside hind hocks of the dead deer and carry them in the breast pockets of your hunting jacket. Leave them there all season, and every time you don you coat you'll have screened your man smell with that of a deer.

When you're not hunting, hang the jacket in a garage or in the open air; those musk glands will do some funny things to m'lady's haberdashery. When the season's over for you, throw the glands away and get the jacket dry cleaned.

AMERICA'S GREAT OUTDOORS
edited by L. James Bashline and Dan Saults

Chicago: J. G. Ferguson Publishing Company, $19.95.

This book is noteworthy in several respects. First, it was compiled as a Bicentennial project of the Outdoor Writers Association of America, an especially well-qualified group to judge and gather the finest examples of outdoor literature to come out of our 200-year history. Second, all the profits from this book go to a scholarship fund that's earmarked for budding outdoor journalists and naturalists. But most important, this work presents outdoor writing as literature. There is very little how-to contained between the covers, and less kill'em-'n'-eat-'em. What is printed here is a collection of perceptions of our place in this, our land, that focuses upon a rich wildlife and outdoor heritage as the vehicle.

Some of the authors anthologized might be expected: Aldo Leopold, Teddy Roosevelt, and Zane Grey, for example. Some come as a mild surprise: George Washington, Thomas Jefferson, Ralph Waldo Emerson, and Walt Whitman. All have a common denominator, however, in that their selected writings evoke the special relationship that has always existed between Americans and the great outdoors.

Artwork is given due recognition as well, via 54 illustrations by such famous names as Audubon, Catlin, Wyeth, and Maynard Reece. This dimension makes it a beautiful book as well as long-overdue recognition of outdoor writing as a distinct literary genre. May be ordered direct from OWAA, 4141 West Bradley Road, Milwaukee, WI 53209.

ALL ABOUT DEER HUNTING IN AMERICA
edited by Robert Elman

New York: Winchester Press, $10.00.

Here twenty of America's greatest hunters share the secrets of their deer-hunting successes. The book covers every region, every technique, every type of sporting arm, and every huntable variety of whitetail and mule deer. Here are indispensable tips and suggestions on gear and arms, finding and bringing down your deer, and preparing game for the kitchen and trophy room. Population and harvest figures are included for all parts of the country.

STURDY SEAT DOUBLES AS GEAR BAG

Gokey's Pack Stool doubles as a portable seat and a place to stow or carry gear. The "seat" is a heavy-duty water-resistant canvas suitcase, with zipper closures and interior dimensions comparable to an airline flight bag. The suitcase is stitched to opposing legs that scissor-close, and there are two canvas carrying straps at the top; a good gadget for big-game hunters or waterfowlers whose hunting plans include blinds or stands. Price: $13.95. Gokey's, 21 West 5th Street, St. Paul, MN 55102.

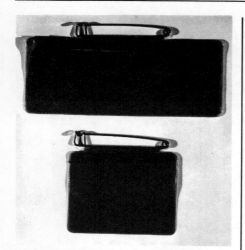

HUNTING LICENSE HOLDERS

Many states require that you wear a license tag on your back, but none of them bother to make a tag that would last longer than five minutes in modest brush if you just pinned it in place. Kolpin makes license sleeves that pin to your back and display your tag through clear plastic. Available in 9″ by 3½″ $.80; or 4″ by 5″ $.75. Kolpin Manufacturing, Inc., P.O. Box 231, Berlin, WI 54923.

HOPPE'S HUNTER'S SEAT AND DEER DRAG

This is a nylon rope equipped with a vinyl seat that is hung from a tree trunk to provide a quick, protable seat for a hunter. Supports 300 pounds. It also can be used to drag deer with the seat portion of the drag across the hunter's chest, which gives a wide support area and more comfort than smaller drags. Price: $10.95. Penguin Industries, Inc., P.O. Box 97, Parksburg, PA 19365.

Pocket Gun-cleaning Kit

A clean rifle is an accurate rifle that's also free of malfunctions, but, let's face it, you can haul just so much stuff along on a hunting trip, and the average gun-cleaning kit takes up a lot of space. The Pocket Rifle Cleaning Kit comes in a 4½″ by 3½″ by 1″ package, and it contains premoistened patches, disposable cloths, and a pull-through cleaning tool that coils up. Price: $4.95. Loner Products, P.O. Box 219, Yorktown Heights, NY 10598.

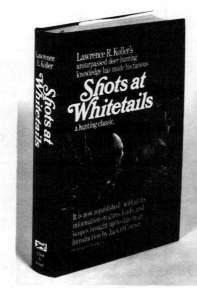

SHOTS AT WHITETAILS
by Lawrence R. Koller

New York: Knopf, $12.50.

Since its original publication more than twenty years ago, *Shots at Whitetails*—the first of Larry Koller's many books on guns and hunting—has become the deer hunter's bible. Now republished after the author's death with updated technical information (rifles, loads, and telescopic sights) in the introduction by Jack O'Connor, it is as instructive and invaluable as when it was first written. It tells the reader everything about hunting deer: the woodcraft of hunting, the organization of the hunt, the place of archery in deer hunting, dressing the buck, preparing venison for the table, taxidermy, hunting equipment, sportsmanship and safety in the woods, equipping the hunter's camp, and, above all, the actual technique of hitting the buck.

WHITETAIL: FUNDAMENTALS AND FINE POINTS FOR THE HUNTER
by George Mattis

Manhasset, N.Y.: Outdoor Life Books (44 Hillside Avenue), $9.95.

Mattis's book has become a classic in its own time for several reasons. Primarily, it's because Mattis is an independent thinker. Rather than attempt an all-inclusive tome about whitetail and whitetail hunting, he writes (with conviction) about how he prefers to hunt them. For example, he summarily dismisses large drives as unsuited to those reasons why he is in the woods. He doesn't exactly call it unsporting, and points out that it's a damn successful technique, but hunting with crowds just doesn't fit in with his perception of the sport. This editorial attitude partially sets the book apart from strict how-to and encyclopedia. You think about the hunter as well as the hunting.

This same attitude is reflected in his inclusion of things on the periphery of hunting—songbirds, plant types, small game—that might not have much to do with bagging a whitetail but that have everything to with the hunting experience.

Finally, the book does what it purports to do: it educates. There is here, indeed, a granite education in whitetail hunting that's bound to profit the beginner and expert alike. This combination of sense and sensitivity make it *the* book to read if you're ever going to read about hunting America's number-one big-game animal.

"There is a pleasure in the pathless woods,/ There is a rapture on the lonely shore . . . I love not man the less, but Nature more."

—Byron

61

RATTLING UP BUCKS

by Stan Meseroll

I've watched the waterfowler toot on a wooden caller and turn flock after flock of high-flying brant, then coax them down to a set of factory-made, plastic imitations on the water less than 60 feet away.

More than one fox, of course, has been outwitted by a cassette PA system, and everything from a cedar box to the wingbone of a real bird has been used to lure a lovesick turkey to within gunshot range. I know one Wyoming hunter who uses a piece of ordinary garden hose to whistle up bugling bull elk. Mimic a moose during the rut, and he'll come charging to do battle.

But what about deer? How can you corral a crafty whitetail with a counterfeit call? Commercial deer calls, when properly used, can sometimes bring an excited buck on the run. Some deer hunters claim that a loud, squawling predator call will spook a bedded buck out of thick cover, too. But by far the most successful method for "calling" buck deer is "horn rattlin' " or, more properly, the ramming or rattling of deer antlers together to imitate bucks fighting over a female. It can be so successful that why the technique isn't used more widely is one of those small mysteries of the hunting world.

A buck stakes out his own territory and will fight off any others who come courtin' on his home ground. Sometimes he'll wander from his own backyard into another's territory, hoping to run down a doe. Defending warriors and invading interlopers invariably lock horns, and that clanking sound of clashing antlers is a signal for war. Like any paramour dedicated to protecting his love, a buck will come to the sound on his home ground because he imagines two other swains have invaded his domain and are fighting. Or, being a gregarious playboy, he may hear two fighting next door and rush over hoping to take on the winner, or perhaps to sneak off with the doe while the two competitors clash for her favor.

A buck drawn to the sound of rattling antlers may rush to battle with hell-bent fury, or he may circle and silently sneak in, suspicious and wary, to size up the situation. How fast or slow a buck comes depends often upon his age and whether he's in full rut or not. The best rattling time is at the peak of the rut. Weather, too, may influence his battle charge. On windy days, the rush to rattling will slow to a walk, if there's any rush at all. Rattle antlers on a still, crisp morning, however, and your chances of drawing a buck are excellent. Early morning is best; at or near dusk is a good time too.

Find a rubbing tree or three, or better still a scrape, and you'll have a good rattling stand. How you rattle doesn't seem to be as important as what you rattle. Some of the more practiced rattling aficionados like to use two complete medium or heavy sets of antlers almost identical in size and shape and relatively "green"—not old and chalky. But finding two sets of matched 10-point racks, for most, is no easy chore. One well-balanced, reasonably heavy, dark set of 8- or 10-point typical whitetail antlers will make good "rattlers." Light-colored antlers are not very resonant. Saw the antlers from the skull, remove the brow tines and any crooked or small extra points, and rasp or file the rough spots.

When it's time to rattle, don't be timid. Whack 'em! Try to visualize a real buck battle; then simulate that fight. Strike the inside curve of one antler against the curved back of the other. Then fit the tines of one antler into the tines of the second and rattle them hard and loud. Continue the rattle, but diminish the din as you do. Swish the antlers through the brush, pound the ground, rap them against a tree. Then stop and wait a few seconds. If you get no response, begin over again. If a buck does respond, some hunters continue to rattle, lightly, until they coax the deer to within shooting range.

Rattling up bucks is best known in the brush country of Texas, but it can work almost anywhere, especially where you find a high ratio of whitetail bucks to does. Try it and see. Once you call one up, you'll become a rattlin' convert.

Stan Meseroll heard the call of the wild seven years ago and moved from New York City to Glenville, West Virginia, where he publishes three newspapers and edits *Deer Sportsman* magazine. When he's not hunting whitetail or ruffed grouse, he free-lances for all the major sports magazines.

BAKER CLIMBING TREE STAND
AND ACCESSORIES

When you're hunting whitetail, getting up above your quarry isn't just one thing, it's everything. Four out of my last five whitetail fell prey to this tactic, which says a great deal about its effectiveness and about my hunting habits, since I began using a portable climbing tree stand made by Baker.

The device works on a leverage principle. An edged collar goes around the trunk of a tree, and it's braced down to meet the outer edge of a platform. The platform, too, has a sharp inside edge, so that when you put pressure on your heels, the upper and lower edges work in opposite directions and bite into the tree trunk, securing the platform in place.

The platform has webbing for your feet. You climb facing the trunk. When you draw your feet under you, pressure is relaxed on the edges and the platform moves up. It's a lot like shinning.

Baker is the granddaddy of climbing platform manufacturers. Their standard tree stand is made of aluminum and exterior plywood, and it folds up into a package roughly the size and weight of a steel folding chair. The platform comes with a carrying strap, and while it's a little bothersome getting through brush to your chosen tree, its credits far outweigh this minor inconvenience.

For reasons I have yet to understand, the metal trim on a Baker Tree Stand is left au naturel. The shiny aluminum should be primed with acetone and then painted with flat camouflage shades. Contrary to popular myth, whitetail do look up now and then, and they're quick to spot the stand's gray glint.

Baker makes another stand, about twice as large as their standard tree climber, called the Pro Hunter. Because there's more room up there, it is a more comfortable and reassuring perch, but it's a hassle to get through the woods and to your tree. Look into this model if you have a semi-permanent location where you can leave the stand up for several days.

Baker's hand climber is a welcome alternative to ascending a tree via shinny-power. It works on the same principle as the stand, it has a good hand grip, and with it you can pull yourself and your stand up a tree with about half the effort and in half the time required for shinning. It, too, should be primed and painted before using, and when aloft make sure it's securely anchored in place when not in use. The climber has a habit of clattering down around your ears at critical moments if you don't.

There are several other accoutrements made by this company for tree-stand hunting: a seat, a carrying strap, and a safety belt, which need no more comment than their existence. All in all, a well-conceived and made product that's a tremendous aid when hunting the wily whitetail.

Standard Tree Stand, $49.95; Xtra large, $79.95; Hand climber, $15.95; Seat, $5.95; Strap assembly, $3.95; Safety belt, $8.95. Baker Manufacturing Co., P.O. Box 1003, Valdosta, GA 31601.

Dazy Deer Call

If nothing else, the folks at Funk are painfully honest, because they're quick to point out that they don't have the slightest idea why their deer call works. They're pretty adamant about the fact that it *does* work, though, so you might give their call a try.

It operates on a vibrating rubber-band principle: you blow in a slot and the rubber raps against the wooden sides at high speeds, creating a bleatlike shriek. The call comes with extensive instructions and folksy advice on where to sit, how to call, and how to be a safe hunter. The funny thing is, it's damn good advice, and if you follow it to the letter, you'll be way ahead of 95 percent of the hunting crowd who will probably be bumbling around the woods. Price: $3.00. Funk Manufacturing Co., P.O. Box 129A, Route 2, Newville, PA 17241.

KUHN'S STUDIO

"The old hound wags his shaggy tail, / And I know what he would say:
It's over the hills we'll bound, old hound, / Over the hills, and away."
—George Meredith

63

BIG RACK
by Robert Rogers

Corpus Christi, Tex.: Outdoor Worlds of Texas, $10.95.

This is a complete rundown of the whitetail pictures and stories of Texas Boone and Crocketts, from 1892 to 1975. It also includes the widest spreads, heaviest antlers, and official Boone and Crockett scoring instructions.

ROPE LADDER

While there are a lot of trees in the forest, the chances of finding one with low branches for climbing, and a high branch large enough for a comfortable stand, are pretty slim. The Baker Manufacturing Co., markets a 15-foot-long rope ladder that will get you up high in a hurry.

The ladder has oak steps connected by 1,200-pound-test poly rope. It comes with a 20-foot throw line and long ends on the bottom of the ladder, securing it to a tie-down.

Aside from obvious applications, this ladder would allow use of a climbing portable stand in trees that are too branchy to climb by conventional means. Price: $10.95. Baker Manufacturing Co., P.O. Box 1003, Valdosta, GA 31601.

LEO WITT

WARREN & SWEAT SELF-CLIMBING TREE STAND

We all know about climbing deer stands. This one qualifies as a climbing sit. You buckle into a chair and step into a separate platform. The principles of climbing are essentially the same as with other stands. The chair and footrest operate independently of each other, locking against the trunk of a tree on a leverage principle. Stand on the platform and you relax leverage on the chair, which goes up with your body. Sit in the chair and it locks into the tree, allowing you to draw your legs up under you for another step upward.

This stand is tested for a 600-pound load, the two parts secure together for easy carrying, and the whole outfit weighs 13 pounds. It is made of tempered aluminum, heat-treated hardware, and marine plywood.

It is available in kit form for $55 or unpainted (though otherwise complete) for $65. Warren & Sweat Manufacturing Co., 4121 Aldington Drive, Jacksonville, FL 32210.

THE BEST THIRST QUENCHER

Hunting in rugged country or hauling your game out gets to be hot, sweaty work, and you soon develop a burning thirst. But problems arise when you gulp down water. Your body doesn't absorb it fast enough and it lies in your stomach like a football.

To avoid this discomfort, carry a film canister of powdered Gatorade, made by Stokely-Van Camp. When the powder is added to water, the good-tasting lemony beverage that results can be immediately absorbed by your system, replacing important body salts lost through perspiration as well.

HEAT SEAT FOR LONG WINTER WAITS

Fidgeting around while you're on stand is a sure way to spook a deer heading your way, but it's awfully hard not to when your fanny is frozen. Polar Heat Seats are waterproof pillows, with a synthetic foam fill that not only insulates well but feels as if it generates a heat of its own. They come with a snap clasp to hook onto a belt loop and are available in straight fluorescent orange or in a flip seat, with one side a camouflage pattern for duck hunters who often have long winter waits too. Price: $4.00. Kolpin Manufacturing, Inc., P.O. Box 231, Berlin, WI 54923.

THE WORLD OF THE WHITE-TAILED DEER
by Leonard Lee Rue, III

Philadelphia: J. B. Lippincott Company, $8.95.

This picture-and-text study of the white-tailed deer in his natural surroundings contains some of the most detailed and revealing photographs ever made of these beautiful camera-shy creatures.

Following the seasons, the book takes the reader through a full twelve months in a deer's life and gives a great deal of information about the white-tailed deer which is not generally known. For instance, what do deer eat in winter? How fast can they run? How high can they jump? Do they migrate? Are there more deer today than in Revolutionary times?

The author, who has doubtless taken more deer photographs of higher quality than any other American naturalist, has captured the deer's world in minute detail in breathtaking close-ups of bucks, does, and fawns feeding, resting, and playing. We see them under the pressures of the hunting season and in all kinds of weather, and one especially rare photograph shows a pair of bucks fighting.

Pittsburgh, Pa.: Carnegie Museum (4400 Forbes Avenue), $15.50.

The Boone and Crockett Club is an organization of hunters dedicated to the conservation of big game and to recording the biggest and the best of each recognized species.

While their commitment to conservation, research, and habitat preservation is on an equal footing with their record-keeping interests, it is the Boone and Crockett record book that grabs the limelight. When you get "one for the books," this is the place your trophy will be recorded.

The correct title of the book is *North American Big Game*. Its 403 pages catalog

NORTH AMERICAN BIG GAME
by the Boone and Crockett Club

the grandest representatives of each game species taken by hunters. Individual trophies are ranked within separate species and classes; a trophy's place among the ranks, its measurements, the name of the successful hunter, the place it was taken, and the current owner of the head of horns are given.

In addition, there are 47 photos of the

highest-ranking trophies. These are eye-openers, and this hardcover is well worth its price if, just once, when your neighbor comes in with a spindly 8-point and asks you if you think it will "make the books," you can show him "the book." For further insult, you can proceed to thumb through the official scoring charts, which explain how to measure and score each recognized species.

For your own personal reading and information, there are also articles on hunting experiences, trophy care and preservation, and what Boone and Crockett is doing to preserve and enhance North America's big-game population.

SPEER BULLETS

Speer recently introduced the Grand Slam bullet, a controlled expanding type. It has a two-part core, the harder lead-alloy rear half being cold-swaged into the jacket and crimped around the base (to keep it from separating from the jacket on impact) and then the soft lead front half of the core being injected on top of the rear half as molten metal. This serves to bond the two cores together and also has a tendency to bond the front core to the jacket. The Grand Slam also has a heavy cannelure to aid core retention. In tests (both on game and controlled substances) the Grand Slam has shown excellent performance, retaining about 75 percent of origi-

nal weight, about on the level of Nosler bullets. It is available only in .270, 7mm, and .30 calibers at the moment, in 130/150, 160/175, and 165/180 weights respectively, with a protected-point softnose design (nose flattened at the tip slightly) to prevent deformation in the magazine. The only price info I could come up with is that it will retail at around $9 to $10 per box of 50, or about what Noslers run. It should be an excellent heavy-game bullet, and I hope it will be offered in the future in other bullet weights.

Speer's regular hunting bullets, priced at $6 to $8 per 100 in common calibers, are excellent for most hunting. I've used

their 105-grain 6mm extensively and have found it the best on the market for long-range shooting of big game in the 6mm rounds. Their regular bullets are all Hot-Cor types (core metal injected as a molten liquid instead of cold-swaged as in most bullets), which helps retain the core, though it isn't foolproof. I've had Hot-Cor bullets come apart just like other types, though not as often. Sample prices, per 100: 6mm-.243/105, $6.25; .270/130, $7.10; .30/180, $7.45; .338/275, $10.20. Speer, Inc., 1023 Snake River Avenue, Lewiston, ID 83501.

—J.B.

COLORADO CUSTOM BULLETS

Instead of giving these bullets a hard jacket and tough lead-alloy core so that they'll hold together, the Colorado Custom people give them a pure copper jacket and pure lead core; both are softer than normal bullet materials. The theory behind this is that both core and jacket will bend instead of breaking. One of their virtues is that they won't shatter and send bits of jacket and core through good game meat. I probably wouldn't have noticed this in the testing I did of the bullets if it hadn't been suggested to me by one of the heads of the company, but it seems to be true. The two big-game animals I've taken with CC bullets aren't perhaps a complete test in the strict scientific sense, but both instances impressed me. The first was a buck pronghorn at about 275 yards; a 100-grain CC 6mm bullet from my .243 hit him just in front of the diaphragm and angled forward through the lower spine and exited just behind the far shoulder blade (he was standing angling away from me). Try as I might, I couldn't find any

trace of bullet material. The bullet shattered the spine but didn't come apart, and it penetrated a good 2 feet of muscle, bone, and hide. The other animal I got was a buck mule deer; again, the bullet exited, going from side to side through his ribs, so I didn't have a chance to recover it, but no bullet material was found. This was with a 130-grain .270 bullet.

These must be handloaded, but they seem to be excellent bullets for most big-game hunting, from my experience and other hunters'. I haven't found them to be quite as accurate as some other hunting bullets, but they are accurate enough for most big game (they were accurate enough for a pronghorn at 275 yards). Groups run 2 to 2½ inches in my .243, which will do just about 1 inch with most other bullets; this still is adequate for most game situations.

Colorado Custom bullets are also available in heavier weights as well as the standard sizes. In 6mm, for instance, they make a 110-grain semi-spitzer and a 120-

grain roundnose. Either of these might be a good choice for woods black bear hunting, giving a degree of bone-breaking capability and penetration not found in standard .243-diameter bullets. Colorado Custom bullets also cost just a bit more than standard bullets, but not as much as some other controlled-expansion types. They are also not available on most dealers' shelves, and can't be shipped to anyone without a federal firearms permit, but they are worth the hassle and price. Some sample prices, per 100: .243-6mm/100, semi-spitzer soft point, $10.20; .243-6mm/120, roundnose soft point, $10.20; .277-6mm/130, semi-spitzer soft point, $10.20; .277-6mm/180, roundnose soft point, $11.40; .308-6mm/180, semi-spitzer soft point, $11.40; .308-6mm/250, roundnose soft point, $13.80. For more information write: R. C. and Bob Brooks, Colorado Custom Bullets, P.O. Box 215, American Fork, UT 84003. —J.B.

CALIBER	CARTRIDGE
257 ROBERTS	
264 WIN. MAG.	
270 WIN.	
280 REM.	
7mm REM. MAG.	
7mm MAUSER	
30 CARBINE	
30-30 WIN.	
30 REM.	
30-40 KRAG	
30-06 SPRINGFIELD	
300 SAV.	
300 H. & H. MAG.	
300 WIN. MAG.	

Cartridge illustrations approximate size.

REMINGTON BULLETS AND AMMUNITION

The Remington Core-Lokt bullet is a very reliable, controlled-expansion type. The jacket at the tip is thin for reliable expansion; it thickens greatly toward the middle of the bullet, then thins toward the rear, so the core is essentially locked into the rear part of the jacket. The Core-Lokt is also cannelured at the heavy point of the jacket to further discourage separation of the core. It is available both as a reloading component and in Remington's factory loads.

The Bronze Point, available only in 130-grain .270 and 150- and 180-grain .30, is Remington's other big-game bullet. It has a metal wedge protecting the point; this wedge drives down through the lead during expansion. Remington Arms Co., Inc., 939 Barnum Avenue, Bridgeport, CT 06602.

—J.B.

WINCHESTER
ARMS AND ACCESSORIES

WINCHESTER BULLETS AND AMMUNITION

Winchester produces two types of bullets for big game: a standard-type softpoint for game of deer size, the Power Point, and a controlled-expansion type, the Silvertip. The Silvertip's point is covered with a harder metal both to delay expansion and to protect it from battering in the magazine during recoil. It is a good bullet but has a slight reputation for being resistant to expansion at longer ranges. Each is very accurate and is available both as components for reloading and in Winchester's factory ammunition. The Silvertip is a good load for some smaller game where minimal meat destruction is wanted, such as javelina and wild turkey; I know several Montana turkey hunters who use the 130-grain .270 Silvertip load. It is also, I think, the best factory load for bigger game (such as elk and moose) available for the .270. Winchester-Western, 275 Winchester Avenue, New Haven, CT 06504. —J.B.

QUIK AMMO POUCH

The Hunter Company makes a useful ammo pouch for big-game hunters. There are three models to choose from, each made of suede cowhide. All three pouches are worn on your belt and contain individual cartridge pockets that hold shells seven to a row. Two sides fold against each other, a little like a wallet, and are held fast by a snap closure. Models include space for fourteen shells in a double row, space for seven shells with a license pocket and knife sheath, and space for fourteen shells with a knife sheath. Prices: $10.70 to $13.95. Hunter Company, 3300 West 71st Avenue, Westminster, CO 80030.

FEDERAL AMMUNITION

Very good ammunition—some of the Federal loads are the most accurate I've ever seen. Their .270 loads match anything I can brew up by handloading. Of special note are their .30-06 loads using the 165-grain and 200-grain Sierra boattail bullets. Starting out at 2,800 and 2,550 fps respectively, they give higher energy levels and flatter trajectory than any other '06 factory loads of their class. If I did my big-game hunting with an '06 and factory loads, I'd definitely use these in place of the standard 150/180 grain loads that are advised for deer and larger game. While the Sierra bullet loads don't start out quite as fast (the 150 is listed at 2,910 and the 180 at 2,700) they catch up fast, and drift less in the wind. Let's hope that Federal brings out more boattail loads in the popular calibers.

Federal ammo also comes boxed with convenient plastic ammo holders. There are two in each box, each holding ten rounds, and they may be worn on your belt or stuck inside most shirt, jacket, or jeans pockets. They keep the ammo undamaged, clean, and reasonably available. They also keep it from rattling.

Federal Cartridge Corp., 2700 Foshay Tower, Minneapolis, MN 55402, or see your local dealer.

—J.B.

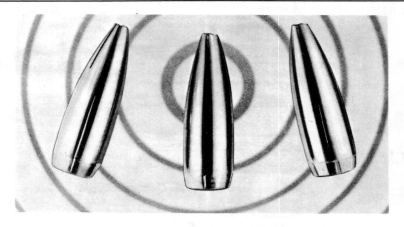

SIERRA BOATTAIL BULLETS

Other companies are starting to produce hunting-style boattail (tapered heel) bullets, but Sierra has been making them in most hunting calibers for a long time. They are excellent bullets for long-range shooting, as the boattail design is the most efficient ballistically, giving about a 5-percent advantage in most cases, at least according to Sierra's published figures. There is some argument as to whether the tapered-heel design is actually much more effective than the flat-base bullets at the supersonic (faster than sound) velocities at which hunting bullets always travel in modern long-range calibers. I am convinced that, while it wouldn't be noticeable in most hunting situations, for long ranges (past 300 yards) the boattail types offer an advantage, both in trajectory and wind-bucking ability. I have used the 130-grain boattail .270 for a number of years and have probably taken more big game with it than with any other bullet in any caliber, and it shoots flatter at long range than any other bullet of its weight and caliber. I have noticed some tendency of the boattail bullets to shed their jackets on impact, particularly if they happen to be used at close range, possibly because the non-square base of the jacket doesn't grip the core as well, but this has never affected their killing ability on deer-sized game.

The latest Sierra boattails, a 250-grain, .338 and a 300-grain .375, feature cannelures that may help retain the cores better. Federal factory .30-06 ammo is available with 165- and 200-grain Sierra boatail bullets, and these are both cannelured. I have no experience with this load, and so I can't say if it holds together any better than the standard bullet. Some hunters have used the 165-grain on elk and report it does well if the shots are properly placed. I have used the non-cannelured 165 in the .30-06 handloaded, and it gives the flattest trajectory at 400 to 500 yards of any '06 load I've ever used. Sample prices, per 100: .25/117, $7.10; 6.5mm-.264/140, $7.55; .270/130, $7.65; .308/165, $7.95. Sierra Bullets, 10532 South Painter Avenue, Sante Fe Springs, CA 90670.

—J.B.

"Go fish and hunt far and wide day by day—farther and wider—and rest thee by many brooks and hearthsides without misgiving."

—Walt Whitman

67

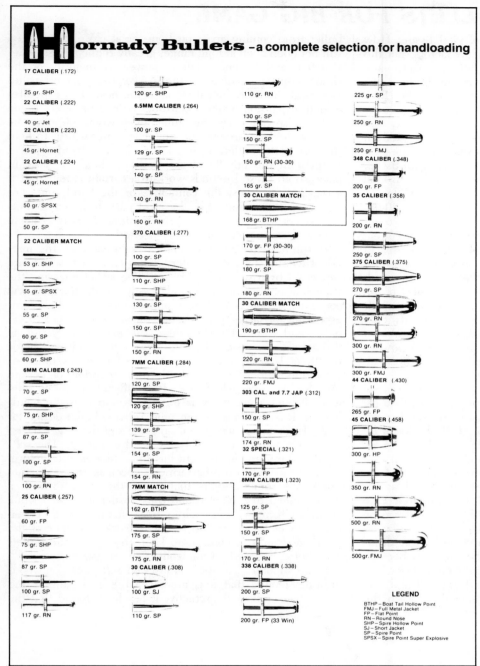

Hornady Bullets – a complete selection for handloading

17 CALIBER (.172)
25 gr. SHP
22 CALIBER (.222)
40 gr. Jet
22 CALIBER (.223)
45 gr. Hornet
22 CALIBER (.224)
45 gr. Hornet
50 gr. SPSX
50 gr. SP
22 CALIBER MATCH
53 gr. SHP
55 gr. SPSX
55 gr. SP
60 gr. SP
60 gr. SHP
6MM CALIBER (.243)
70 gr. SP
75 gr. SHP
87 gr. SP
100 gr. SP
100 gr. RN
25 CALIBER (.257)
60 gr. FP
75 gr. SHP
87 gr. SP
100 gr. SP
117 gr. RN

120 gr. SHP
6.5MM CALIBER (.264)
100 gr. SP
129 gr. SP
140 gr. SP
140 gr. RN
160 gr. RN
270 CALIBER (.277)
100 gr. SP
110 gr. SHP
130 gr. SP
150 gr. SP
150 gr. RN
7MM CALIBER (.284)
120 gr. SP
120 gr. SHP
139 gr. SP
154 gr. SP
154 gr. RN
7MM MATCH
162 gr. BTHP
175 gr. SP
175 gr. RN
30 CALIBER (.308)
100 gr. SJ
110 gr. SP

110 gr. RN
130 gr. SP
150 gr. SP
150 gr. RN (30-30)
165 gr. SP
30 CALIBER MATCH
168 gr. BTHP
170 gr. FP (30-30)
180 gr. SP
180 gr. RN
30 CALIBER MATCH
190 gr. BTHP
220 gr. RN
220 gr. FMJ
303 CAL. and 7.7 JAP (.312)
150 gr. SP
174 gr. RN
32 SPECIAL (.321)
170 gr. FP
8MM CALIBER (.323)
125 gr. SP
150 gr. SP
170 gr. RN
338 CALIBER (.338)
200 gr. SP
200 gr. FP (33 Win)

225 gr. SP
250 gr. RN
250 gr. FMJ
348 CALIBER (.348)
200 gr. FP
35 CALIBER (.358)
200 gr. RN
250 gr. SP
375 CALIBER (.375)
270 gr. SP
270 gr. RN
300 gr. RN
300 gr. FMJ
44 CALIBER (.430)
265 gr. FP
45 CALIBER (.458)
300 gr. HP
350 gr. RN
500 gr. RN
500 gr. FMJ

LEGEND
BTHP – Boat Tail Hollow Point
FMJ – Full Metal Jacket
FP – Flat Point
RN – Round Nose
SHP – Spire Hollow Point
SJ – Short Jacket
SP – Spire Point
SPSX – Spire Point Super Explosive

HORNADY BULLETS

Hornady bullets have a good reputation for penetration and expansion on heavy game, at least for a conventionally constructed bullet. I have used Hornadys of various calibers and weights for quite a bit of big-game hunting, and haven't yet had one separate (core and jacket come apart), though there often isn't much left of the base if bone has been struck. I am positive that they will do for most situations, however; I hit a running whitetail this year through the shoulder blade and spine with a 150-grain .270 Hornady spire-point at about 200 yards and found the last third of the bullet, core intact, under the far shoulder blade. This is good performance indeed for a conventional bullet; it had penetrated at least 4 to 5 inches of bone, not to mention muscle, and held up well. If you are not a handloader, Hornady bullets are available in their Frontier brand of cartridges in the more common big-game calibers and weights. As I write this, Hornady has just announced a new 165-grain boatail hunting bullet in .30 caliber; this design and weight of bullet is the most effective I've found yet for long-range shooting in the .30-06. Hornady bullets are very accurate, too; I can usually put five of the 150/.270s into 1¼ inches at 100 yards. Hornady Mfg. Co., P.O. Box 1848, Grand Island, NE 68801. —J.B.

BITTERROOT BULLETS

These bullets have pure copper jackets, just as the Colorado Custom bullets do, but the cores are soldered to the jackets to prevent separation. 90-percent weight retention is common, which is better even than Nosler bullets. The process involved is expensive (the cost per bullet is 30–45 cents!) and they are not as accurate as some bullets, but for very large game they might be a good choice. Some sample prices, per 20: .270/130, $6.00; 7mm/160 $6.00; .30/200 $7.00; .338/250 $8.00; .375/325 $9.00. Bitterroot Bullet Co., P.O. Box 412, Lewiston, ID 83501. —J.B.

BULLETS FOR BIG GAME

Bullets kill through the disruption of vital tissue. How well they do this depends on a great many factors, not the least of which is the construction of the bullet. In fact, many hunting experts hold that, next to where the bullet goes, bullet construction is the most important factor in the effectiveness of a certain rifle/cartridge combination.

To understand why a bullet is built a certain way, we must first understand what it is supposed to do. Modern bullets for use on big game are of the expanding type—essentially they start to turn inside out on impact with tissue, forming a "mushroom." This greatly increases their frontal area, and the path of tissue destruction is much wider. A .308-inch-diameter bullet, for instance, fired from a .30-06, will commonly expand to two or even three times its original diameter, depending on other factors. This is the great advantage that modern rounds have over the older black-powder types. In the last century bullet expansion was minimal, if indeed it took place, but bullets were of much larger diameter to begin with, over .40 caliber most of the time. A modern bullet travels through the air at a much smaller diameter, under .30 usually, and expands only when it strikes game. This small bullet diameter, combined with higher velocity than was possible in the black-powder rounds, extends the range of the weapon while at the same time inflicting a wide, quick-killing wound.

The most common bullets used today are simply a metal cup—called a "jacket," usually of a copper-zinc alloy known as gilding metal—surrounding a lead core. In hunting designs the jacket is left open at the front of the bullet in either a soft- or hollow-point design to allow the bullet to expand. The jacket serves two purposes: to control the expansion to a certain extent and to protect the lead from the friction of the barrel. This simple design is satisfactory in most big-game hunting. It has certain flaws, though. One is that expansion is not fully "controlled," in that it can be either more or less than desired. At close range or when striking heavy bone it may overexpand and even disintegrate; this reduces its penetration. The core may become separated from the jacket, again reducing penetration. Ideally, the bullet should expand over its front half and stay together in the rear. A jacket heavy enough to keep the bullet from coming apart on bone or at close range often will not open at all at long range, greatly reducing tissue destruction and lessening killing power. A majority of the simple cup-type bullets on the market today have heavier jackets at the base than they do at the nose; this expedites frontal expansion while retarding rear expansion. Some makers also cannelure the bullet, even when crimping the neck of the case around the bullet isn't necessary, to hold the core in the bullet, or they leave a heavier band of jacket material in the middle of the bullet to hold the core in place. Both these methods work to a certain extent, but if expansion goes past the cannelure or the band, the core may separate anyway. For the most part, however, bullets of this construction are fine for hunting deer-sized game where extreme penetration isn't needed.

In the late 1940s a new bullet design came on the market. Invented by John Nosler, it has two cores which are separated by a wall in the jacket. The jacket covering the front half of the bullet expands easily, while the rear half continues to penetrate. This is an extremely reliable design, especially for larger game. I have never seen it fail to expand, and while at short ranges the expanding part may disintegrate occasionally, the rear half always holds together. Unfortunately, it costs about twice as much as conventional bullets, and, with the exception of certain Weatherby loads (which are often difficult to obtain anyway), it isn't available in factory loads and must be hand-loaded. It is acclaimed as our most reliable bullet design for really large game, such as elk, moose, and the larger bears.

There are various nose types on the market. The soft-point is the most reliable but has some tendency to deform when subjected to the battering of recoil in the magazine. There are some designs that cover the lead tip with a harder metal to protect it and thus ensure accuracy, while another alternative is to solder small strips of metal on either side of the magazine box where the shoulder of the cartridge comes in contact, to keep the tips of the bullets from being battered on the front of the magazine.

Some shooters use the roundnosed soft-point for woods hunting, feeling that it is more reliable in expansion and will not be deflected. Actually, it has been found that the

This expanded steel jacket of a 33-calibre rifle was extracted from the beef about four inches from the surface, the lead of the bullet passing through, leaving a three-inch rent where it passed out

"If the deer like to go there, I thought, I had better take a look. I have often noticed that a deer's taste in scenery and solitudes is very much like my own."
—Aldo Leopold

69

diameter of the lead tip where it meets the jacket has more to do with reliable expansion than point shape, and as either type can be easily deflected on brush there is really no reason to put up with the ballistic inefficiency of a round or flat point unless you have a gun with tubular magazine. (This type of magazine can't be used with pointed bullets as the sharp tips can set off the primers of the shells in front during recoil.)

The hollow-point is less reliable in expansion, especially at long range, and is often not as ballistically efficient.

More and more companies are bringing out hunting bullets with boattail (tapered) heels. This design is more ballistically efficient than flat-based bullets, though not greatly so, and is sometimes desirable for long-range situations. It also drifts less in the wind, in addition to shooting flatter and arriving with more energy. I have found some tendency for boattailed bullets to shed their jackets, more so than flat-based bullets, probably because the non-squared base doesn't grip as well, and so I'm rather doubtful of their use on game larger than deer—unless they're of a controlled-expansion design such as the Nosler.

If a good, controlled-expansion bullet is used, there really isn't much difference in performance between two weights. For many years, for instance, it was advised to use 130-grain bullets in the .270 for deer and 150-grain bullets for elk and moose. I have used both these bullets in Nosler design and can't see any difference in expansion or penetration, at least not in practical terms. The reason heavier bullets were used a generation ago is that the slower velocity inhibited expansion, increasing penetration. Heavier bullets usually had heavier jackets, too. But today there is really no reason to use a 220-grain bullet in the .30-06 for most game (with its moon-shaped trajectory) when a good 180-grain Nosler will do the same things in terms of penetration and expansion and shoot flatter as well. I would much rather use a well-constructed bullet of even 150-grain weight in the '06 on elk than a doubtful 220-grain.

In conventional bullets it is still wise to select the heavier-weight bullet for larger game because the 150-grain, for example, in the '06 is usually lighterjacketed than the 180-grain. If you stick to factory loads, the heavier weight would be an advantage on large game in most cases. At any rate, modern bullets are fairly reliable, and you'll never be too far wrong.

—J.B.

TED WARD

COMPACT TEN-SHELL CARRIER

Carrying rifle shells in your pocket isn't the best for accuracy. The tips of the bullets can get bent or nicked, which affects their flight. Carry your bullets in the box they came in, or use a shell pouch.

Cabela's sells a simple folding cartridge case. You wear it on your belt, and it opens like a wallet, exposing ten shells within easy reach. Price: $2.95. Cabela's, 812 13th Avenue, Sidney, NE 69162.

Slings and Sling Swivels

A sling is one of the most important accessories for the sporting rifle. It aids in carrying the gun and, properly used, helps steady it in aiming.

Slings come in three basic styles: military, strap, and wide. The military sling has a loop which is used in steadying the gun; the arm is put through the loop and braced against the forearm. The strap, which is a simple beltlike piece of leather, can be used in the "hasty sling," where the arm of the shooter is essentially wrapped in the sling and then used to brace the forestock of the rifle. The wide sling can be used in the same way but is much wider in the part of the sling that fits over the shoulder, which helps in carrying heavy rifles.

The slings are attached to the gun by means of swiveling-loops of metal. In most rifles they are attached to the butt stock near the "toe" of the stock, and just in back of the fore-end tip. These can be permanently attached, but in their most popular form there is a base which attaches to the rifle, to which the swivel can be easily attached. In this form the sling is easily removable, which is sometimes an aid in thick brush. Also, one or two slings can be used on a number of rifles with this system.

For special guns, the front swivel is sometimes attached to a magazine tube or to the barrel just in front of the fore-end tip, by means of a band. On rifles of heavy recoil this is preferable, since the front swivel, if mounted on the fore-end, can hurt the fore-end hand during recoil.

It's a good idea to epoxy the bases of the swivels into the stock, even if the screws seem secure. When attached this way, there is little chance they will come loose; if they do, it rarely does anything beneficial for the gun.

Shotgun Sling

If you're a casual shotgunner for big game, or don't want to mar your scattergun with sling snaps and swivels, Eddie Bauer catalogs an all-leather shotgun sling that adjusts to fit any firearm. Suede lined to prevent slipping off your shoulder. Price: $11.00. Eddie Bauer, 1737 Airport Way South, Seattle, WA 98134.

Packmayr Quick Detachable Flush Sling Swivels

Instead of having a stud that projects from the stock to which the swivel is attached, these sling swivels are inserted in a base that is below the line of the stock. You give the swivel a 90-degree twist, and you're set. They give a very clean appearance both to the swivel and to the unslinged rifle on display. Prices: from $6.50 to $8.50, depending on style. Pachmayr Gun Works, Inc., 1220 South Grand Avenue, Los Angeles, CA 90015.

Michaels of Oregon Slings and Sling Swivels

These people have quick-detachable swivels for every kind of rifle, ranging in price from $4.50 to $8.95 per pair. They also market swivels and bases by themselves, for those rifles that already have bases or for people who want to use a sling and swivel set on more than one rifle.

They also have nondetachable swivels, at $1.75 a pair for bolt-action models and $6.95 for tube-magazine rifles. They have slings of all three types in prices from $5.50 to $10.50. Michaels of Oregon Co., P.O. Box 13010, Portland, OR 97213.

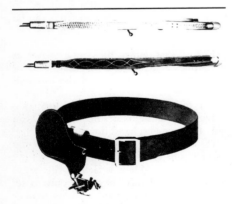

Safariland Slings and Ammo Pouch

Safariland's slings are both wide types. One is smooth and stitched, the Model 84, for $13.95; the other, the Model 85, is available plain or basketwoven, for $11.95 and $13.95 respectively. Safariland also makes the handy Swivel Cartridge Pouch that loops onto your belt and can carry a number of any size cartridges; price is $6.95. Safariland, 1941 South Walker Avenue, Monrovia, CA 91016.

Wide, Western-style Rifle Slings

Wide rifle slings are advantageous in two respects. First, they distribute the weight of your rifle more evenly across your shoulder so the load is more comfortable to carry. Second, their enlarged surface contact area makes the load stay put. Your rifle is less likely to slide out of place when both your hands are busy dragging a deer than it is with slick, narrow military slings.

The American Sales and Manufacturing Company makes a number of these Western-style slings that are suede-lined, nylon-stitched, and fully adjustable. They'll also personalize your sling by hand stamping your name into the sling leather (names to thirteen letters only, so Theophilius Glutenschnable, beware). Typical price: around $13.00. Send $1.00 for a complete catalog. American Sales and Manufacturing Co., P.O. Box 677, Laredo, TX 78040.

Bianchi Rifle Slings

The Bianchi "Cobra" slings are, with one exception, wide-type slings, 2¼ inches at their widest, with 1-inch ends. There are seven wide models, from $11.95 to $15.95, in plain, stitched, and basket-weave styles with ammo pouches available in each style. The Model 67 Hunter is a nice light carrying strap, at $7.95. Bianchi, 100 Calle Cortez, Temecula, CA 92390.

If you have troubles with your rifle sling slipping off your shoulder, sew a large top-coat button an inch above the sleeve/shoulder yoke seam.

"Whether 'tis nobler in the mind to suffer
The slings and arrows of outrageous fortune . . .?"
—*Shakespeare, Hamlet*

71

OPTICS FOR THE HUNTER

There are two types of optics for the hunter: those that aid in aiming (telescopic sights) and those that are used in spotting game or targets. While there are a great many hunters who will never feel the need for a binocular or a spotting scope, almost everyone can make use of a scope sight.

Any optical instrument is in some ways a compromise, and so it is with scopes. A basic telescope, which is what most scopes essentially are, has a minimum of three lenses, and the interaction of these lenses determines to a great extent what compromises must be made, given the intended use of the scope. The first lens in the front of the scope, the one nearest the target, is the objective lens: it forms the primary image, which is upside down. The next lens takes that image and rights it, and so is called the erector lens. The last lens is the eyepiece, on which we see this erected image. The reticle of the scope, whether crosshair, dot, post, or some other version, can be placed either between the objective and the erector lenses or between the erector and the eyepiece.

These three lenses are all made and placed, in a good-quality scope, to minimize distortion in the image. This is where compromises come in, as adjustments necessary for one type of image distortion, such as line, do not always agree with other adjustments, such as color. The technical aspects of the corrections involved do not really concern the shooter; he must be aware, however, that it takes quality design and manufacture to bring this about. In a cheap scope the image may be clear in the middle of the eyepiece but muddled on the outside. Look for an image clear to the edges of the field of view.

The quality of the lenses also determines how clearly the image is going to be defined. The great virtue of a scope in absolute terms is not its magnification but its definition, its ability to resolve detail. For instance, if we are looking at an object with the naked eye at 400 yards and all we can tell is that it is a brown object about 4 feet long—it might be a deer and it might be a log—it makes little difference if we use a scope of poor definition even if it magnifies the object 10 times. The brown object will still be just a brown object. A good-quality scope of even 4x often has better definition than a cheap one of twice the power, and hence is a better instrument in aiding the eye.

The size of the objective lens has something to do with this image quality, but in all good scopes the objective is much bigger than needed for good definition because of another factor: relative brightness. This is a commonly misunderstood aspect of scopes; a great many shooters are under the impression that a scope "gathers light" and that is why the hunter can see better with it under dim light conditions than he can with the naked eye. Light-gathering is an optical impossibility; there is no way that more light can come out of a scope than went in, and in fact any optician will tell you that it is an impossibility for light to pass through any kind of glass without some actual loss. The reason we see better with a scope in dim light is, again, definition; in effect we are that much closer to the object. Nevertheless, if the objective isn't of a certain minimum size, the eye can't get all the light it can use, particularly in dim light. The size of the exit pupil of the scope, which in effect is the amount of light coming out of the scope, in relationship to the human eye, determines how bright a scope will be in relative terms. If you divide the diameter of the objective lens in millimeters by the power of the scope, you will have the size, in millimeters, of the exit pupil. As it is the area, rather than the diameter, of the exit pupil that determines relative brightness, we square this number. For example, a 6x scope with an objective of 30mm has a relative brightness of 25; 30 divided by 6 is 5, and 5 squared is 25. If we increase the size of the objective to 42mm, the relative brightness is 49; 42 divided by 6 is 7, and 7 squared is 49. Thus we have nearly doubled the relative brightness while only adding about 25 percent to the lens diameter, and we should get twice the light.

The one thing that throws a monkey wrench into this whole rather boring set of numbers is that the human pupil can only take advantage of an exit pupil of 5mm, which results in a relative brightness of 25, as the human pupil itself is only about 5mm across when dilated to its largest, in dim light. This means that the 6x scope with the 42mm objective is in practical terms not any more efficient than the smaller scope.

At the other end, any objective smaller than 30mm in a 6x scope will result in a poor image under adverse light conditions. If you look through a 6x scope with an objective of at least 30 mm and then through a .22 scope of the same power, which usually has an objective of half that size, you may not see any difference at midday when light conditions are at their best and the pupil of your eye is narrowed. Looking through both the scopes at sunset, though, when your pupil has dilated to its full 5mm, the image of the larger scope will still be fairly bright, while that of the .22 scope will have a washed-out image of low contrast.

The position of the eye behind the eyepiece at which the full field of view is visible is called eye relief and is expressed in inches. This position actually is where the exit pupil's relation to the eye is at its optimum; this is why your eye must be so much closer to the small-objectived .22 scope than to the large-lensed big-game scope. This small eye relief is why you shouldn't use .22 scopes even on rifles of .243 recoil, as the kick of the gun will stick the eyepiece of the scope in your eye. There is theoretically an advantage to scopes that have a larger objective and exit pupil than is necessary for relative brightness, in that the position of the eye is not so critical to pick up the entire field of view. In practical terms, however, such scopes need higher mounts, which takes the cheek of the shooter off the stock and makes positioning more difficult.

Another factor which determines how much light gets to the eye is the coating of the lenses. As stated before, there is always some loss of light when it passes through glass; this is not strictly true, as it is actually the passage of light from air to glass that reduces the light, at around 5 percent per surface, or 10 percent for each lens. Even more important, air-to-glass transmission also serves to scatter light,

reducing contrast. Actual image efficiency in a three-lens scope can be as low as 60 percent. Coating the lenses helps this; the technical aspects of coating involve wavelengths of light, molecular bombardment, and any number of other aspects that only confuse the average shooter (especially me!) and are not really important. What is important is that the shooter be aware of it. You can actually see this coating as a color, anything from yellow to purple, on the surface of the lenses. Cheap scopes will often have only the two visible lens surfaces coated, leaving at least four other surfaces uncoated, in order to fool the unsuspecting. The only way to make sure that all the surfaces are coated, and that the coating is properly applied, is to buy quality instruments.

Parallax is another aspect of scopes that is misunderstood. If when your scope is clamped in a vise with the reticle on some object in the distance, there is an apparent reticle "movement" on the object when you move your head back and forth while looking through the scope, you have parallax. This occurs when the primary image formed by the objective lens—or the erected image of the erector lens, depending on where the reticle is located—is not in the same plane as the reticle. This will happen at some distances with all scopes, as the plane of the image varies with the distance to the object being viewed through the scope. In scopes used for big-game hunting, however, any parallax is so small as to be unimportant. In scopes of more than about 6x, provision is usually made for parallax adjustment, with the exception of variable scopes up to the 3x-to-9x range. (Actually, parallax is nonexistent *if* the eye is perfectly centered behind the scope, which in practical terms doesn't happen very often.) In reality, parallax is only important to the target and varmint hunter, and the scopes he uses are usually adjustable for it. A hunter intending to use a scope for long-range varmint hunting should be sure any instrument he buys of over 6x has this provision. With the better big-game scopes parallax is minimized, and with adjustable scopes it can be eliminated at the desired distance.

Scopes should be focusable, and if they aren't don't buy them, as one of the great virtues of scopes over iron sights is that there is no need to focus and refocus your eyes on two or three different objects. Even a scope with a clear image can be focused improperly—the reticle may not be instantly clear, and time is lost because the eye must focus on it. Look through the scope each time you adjust the focus until the reticle is sharp the instant you look at it.

The scope must be rugged, especially the big-game scope, as there are always small accidents that occur. I blush to confess some of the things that have happened to my scopes, but with very few exceptions modern scopes can take very hard knocks without changing the point of impact. I once slammed a scope in a car door with no apparent damage. The only time I've had a scope fail me in the field is once when the mounts came loose, so it wasn't actually the scope. I did see a reticle snap when a hunter fell on top of rifle and scope, but the rest of the scope was undamaged and the reticle cost only $5.00 to repair. Iron sights would have certainly been mashed just as badly in that accident. Good scopes are incredibly rugged, as well as being fogproof and dustproof, so that you'll never have to clean the

*"No man is fit to be called a sportman wot doesn't kick his
wife out of bed on a haverage once in three weeks!"*
—Robert Smith Surtees, Handley Cross (1843)

73

insides of the lenses. When the outsides of the lenses get dirty, *don't* take out your handkerchief and wipe them off! The only delicate part of a scope is the lens coating, and when you wipe it off with your handkerchief you simply grind the grime into the coating, creating permanent scratches that will never come out and that will be worse than dirt for the image. Carefully brush the dust away with a camel's-hair brush (available for a tiny amount of your hard-earned cash at an art or camera store) and then, if anything is left such as water spots, use a lens fluid—available at the same camera shops—and lens tissue to remove it, being careful not to get any of the fluid around the edges of the lens where it can affect the sealing substance.

Perhaps you have noticed that I've emphasized *quality* in everything concerning scopes. It is the only way the layman can be sure he's getting his money's worth. A $25.00 special and a $125.00 scope of the same power may look the same, and any difference in clarity and brightness may be unnoticeable in bright light, but there is a difference—in the precision lenses, in the coating, in the sealing—that will eventually mean the difference on a hunt someday. Actually, you can get a quality hunting scope of 2½ to 4x for around $40.00 to $60.00 which is an engineering miracle. If you treat it right it will last as long as your rifle, perhaps longer.

The choice of the scope depends on the game you're hunting. I generally prefer fixed-power scopes for most shooting, for a number of reasons. Most variable scopes do not have provision for parallax adjustment in the hunting sizes of up to 3 to 9x, and their objectives are usually 40

mm or under, usually less, and so you not only have a certain amount of parallax at higher powers (which is *accentuated* by higher powers) but you may not have the relative brightness you need. Variables larger than this have parallax adjustment, but the objective (and indeed the whole scope) is so large that it becomes clumsy on a big-game rifle. If you buy a combination varmint gun, say a .243, and put a 3 to 9x on it, you may not be getting the top-end aiming precision you need in varmint hunting. This is not to say that modern variables are not good, as they've long since licked the old enlarging-reticle and changing-impact faults, but for the ultimate in optical efficiency you might opt for two scopes on your two-purpose gun: a 3x or 4x for big game and an 8x or 10x for varmints, and switch them according to season. It won't cost much more, either.

There used to be arguments raging back and forth about the pluses and minuses of the various reticles. The basic types were the dot, post, and crosshair; the first two were supposedly better for aiming in dim light and the crosshair for precision shooting. With the advent of the thick-and-thin type of crosshair, where either heavy posts give way to a finer central intersection or the crosshair tapers toward the center, these arguments are pretty well done for. The thick-and-thin reticle offers a sure aiming point in both dim light and long-range conditions. Even the claim that a dot or a flat-topped post offers a type of range estimator (by using a reticle of a known size against a target of a fairly closely guessed size) is equaled by the new crosshair. The distance from the tip of the thick part of the crosshair to the intersection provides the same principle.

The optics involved in binoculars and spotting scopes are basically the same as those involved in scopes, though there is usually a prism that works in conjunction with the lenses to enable the tube to be shorter for a given size of binocular or scope. In effect, the light is "bent" in the manner that you might bend a rod to get it to fit in a given length.

The most commonly used binoculars in this country are of the porro-prism type, which can easily be differentiated from the roof-prism type in that porro-prism glasses give a "dogleg" effect to the barrels of the binocular, while roof-prism glasses use straight tubes. Roof-prism glasses can be somewhat lighter and more compact, but the wider-spaced objective lenses of the porro-prism type provide a greater degree of depth perception, which is where a binocular has an advantage over a telescope. There is no optical advantage in terms of brightness or definition in one type over the other.

Both tubes in a binocular must point in precisely the same direction. This collimation is necessary or severe eyestrain and headaches will result if the glass is used for any length of time. A bad case of misalignment will be obvious in that the two images seen through the glass will not merge at all, but in a subtle case of noncollimation the eyes can adapt to this to a certain extent, and the image will appear to be all right even though eyestrain will result over a period of time. If there is the slightest "funny" feeling in the eyes when looking through a binocular, reject them. A cheap glass, too, can be collimated at first but easily come out of whack.

The most common size of binocular, and the most recommended, is 7x35; the 7 is the power and the 35 the size of the objective lens. These glasses are usually fairly light and yet of usable power, but under circumstances where binoculars are essential to finding game a higher power is advisable. A great many people shy away from larger glasses, having been told that anything stronger can't be held sufficiently steady, especially when you may be looking for an object as small as a deer's ear. Perhaps this is true for the football fan, who is holding the glass with one hand in order to hold his beer with the other, but for the rifleman who is used to holding things steady even a 10x glass can be useful. For any serious glassing the hunter should sit or lie down, bracing his elbows either on his knees or the ground, and hold the binocular with both hands. If the neck strap is adjusted so that it can be tightened by the shooter's hands while holding the glass (usually a matter of having the strap short enough to just fit over the head) and used like a shooting sling, this will aid in steadying the binocular.

Pocket-sized binoculars are very popular but, like .22 scopes, do not have objective lenses large enough for efficient viewing in dim light. They are OK for most casual use, but, where a glass is really needed, weight and size should be disregarded to an extent. A glass that is *too* small is useless and weighs much more than the empty space it's as good as.

As noted above, objective size, just as in scopes, must go up with power in order to have relative brightness usable in dim light. The standard is objectives 5 times the size of the power. Thus, a 10x should have 50 mm objectives.

Spotting scopes are useful and are almost a necessity at times in rough country, where the ability to size up a trophy a mile away can save a hunter a hard day's walking and climbing. A scope of 15x is the minimum, and 20 to 30x is much better. Anything over 30x becomes less useful, because of mirage, in most hunting situations. Variable spotting scopes are available, and models with changeable eyepieces for different powers, but—as with variable rifle scopes—often you run into problems with these at higher powers. A tripod of the small folding type is a necessity with spotting scopes; most scopes are now threaded for camera tripods, and if one doesn't come with the scope there are many excellent tripods on the camera market.

The key word in optics is, again, *quality*. There are many features in good optics that aren't apparent to the average shooter, but they are there, and they are worth the price if the product is going to get more than casual use. —J.B.

LYMAN 6X Scope
LYMAN SCOPES

The Lyman people are the only scope makers we know of who will admit (through their prices) that it costs no more to manufacture a 4x scope than a 2½x. Their 2½x, 3x, and 4x models all cost $84.95 and are well worth it. Their 6x is $99.95. They also have two hunting-type variables, a 1¾ to 5x and a 3 to 9x. The 1¾ to 5x should cover most big-game hunting situations; it is priced at $114.95. Lyman hunting scopes are available in crosshair, thick-and-thin crosshair, post-and-crosshair, and various sizes of dots for reticles. All are of the same high quality as the famous Lyman receiver sights.

Lyman Products for Shooters, Route 147, Middlefield, CT 06455. —J.B.

REDFIELD WIDE-ANGLE LOW-PROFILE VARIABLE SCOPES

If the latitude of a variable scope appeals to you, Redfield incorporates this feature with a low profile and wide-angle effect. Five types of reticles are available, along with Accu-Range, a distance-judging system. The cheapest wide angle variable, 1¾x to 5x, sells for $128.00. The most expensive, a 3x to 9x variable with Accu-Range, sells for $180.40. (The symbol *x* next to a scope's magnification number stands for the number of times normal vision is multiplied. A deer would appear four times larger viewed through a 4x scope than viewed with the naked eye.)

Redfield, 5800 East Jewell Avenue, Denver, CO 80222.

WILLIAMS SCOPES

These people make what is perhaps the best all-around big-game scope. It is a 2 to 6x variable which is only 10¼ inches long and weighs only 10 ounces. It has enough power (6x) for just about any situation and enough field of view (60 feet at 100 yards) for any situation. The upper-end power isn't high enough to require a parallax-adjustable objective, and its weight and bulk are small enough for any rifle. Price is $124.95. Williams also makes other scopes of various powers, both fixed and variable, all very good.

Williams Gun Sight Co., 7389 Lapeer Road, Davison, MI 48423. —J.B.

*"Poets sing and hunters scale the mountains primarily for one
and the same reason—the thrill to beauty."*
—Aldo Leopold

75

BUSHNELL RANGEMASTER SCOPE

The Rangemaster system is one which enables the shooter to hold the crosshairs of his scope right on his target at any range up to 500 yards—and hit it. A scale is attached to the elevation-adjustment knob on the scope—you just set the scale for whatever range you think you're shooting at and go to it. I tried a 6x Banner model on my .243. My normal practice is to sight this rifle in at 250 yards, as the trajectory is flat enough to disregard up to that range and a bit beyond; as I felt that any animals sighted under that range would possibly be too nervous to allow use of the Rangemaster system, I sighted in the same way with the Bushnell scope, then cranked the knob up to 400 yards and shot three rounds from the bench at a 12-inch bull measured 400 yards away. Result: three shots in the bull. I then set the scope back down to 250 and shot at that range again; the bullets printed right back where they started. Since then I've flipped the scope up and down quite a few times and the adjustments are *positive*, which is a necessity in a system like this. The Rangemaster comes with three calibrated cylinders and one blank one (for nonstandard loads) which are used depending on caliber and type of load. I used the No. 2, which is recommended for the 100-grain Winchester factory load. I was using a 105-grain handload at about the same velocity; it made little practical difference.

All Bushnell scopes come with their Multi-X reticle. A handy feature of this type of reticle—four posts pointed inward to fine intersecting crosshairs—is that it can be used as a rangefinder. On the 6x model I tested, the distance between the tip of the heavy post and the intersection of the crosshairs covered six inches at 100 yards, twelve inches at 200, eighteen at 300, and so on. Suppose a big buck mule deer is standing off in the distance. If the distance between his brisket and his back as seen through the scope just about fills this post-to-crosshair distance, he's probably just about 300 yards away, as a big buck will measure about 18 inches through the body (a doe won't, and neither will an antelope, but a big buck will). So we set the Rangemaster at 300 and down he comes, if we hold steady and squeeze right. If he fills only three quarters of the space in the scope reticle, he's around 400 yards off. Again, set the Rangemaster, and if the wind isn't blowing a howling gale and you've done your practice shooting you should have him. The Rangemaster system is a good one, and coupled with the Multi-X reticle it should be a great help to the long-range rifleman. It isn't a cure for the shooter who doesn't practice with his rifle and it doesn't judge the wind, but it is a good system.

Rangemaster is available in both the Scopechief and lower-priced Banner lines, in fixed-power scopes from 4 to 10x, in variable from 1½ to 4x to 4 to 12x, priced from $64.95 to $118.50. Write Bushnell Optical Co., 2828 East Foothill Boulevard, Pasadena, CA 91107.

—J.B.

REDFIELD ROYAL . . . MAGNUM PROOFED

The Redfield Royal, a 3x-to-9x variable scope with a 4-plex reticle, is especially designed for heavy rifles in the 7mm mag to 358 Norma mag class. The scope is specially constructed to withstand magnum recoil, and there's an extra half inch in the eye relief. This prevents the rifle from coming back and clouting you above the eye with the top edge of the scope, a malady among magnum-power fans that's referred to as the "half-moon effect." Redfield Royal, $142.90; with Accu-Range, $157.90. Redfield, 5800 East Jewell Avenue, Denver CO 80224.

Leupold Scopes

A very good line of hunting scopes, available in 2x, 3x, 4x, and 6x in fixed models, and 1 to 4x, 1½ to 5x, 2 to 7x, 2½ to 8x, 3 to 9x, and 3½ to 10x in variable models. Prices range from $72.50 to $102.50 for fixed powers and from $118.50 to $188.50 for variable types.

Two scopes are especially worth noting. The 2x model is a long eye-relief type for forward mounting on the Model 94 Winchester and other rifles where mounting directly over the receiver is not possible because of ejection or other problems. (It is also used on handguns.) Eye relief is 8 to 18 inches, compared to the 3 to 3½ inches for most big-game scopes. The 3½ to 10x and one of their two 3 to 9x variables are also available with parallax/focusing objectives of 40mm, so parallax and relative brightness are not the problems they can be in most variables. Weights run about 15 ounces, a bit heavy for some hunting, but if you want a variable for a combination varmint/game gun, these are as good as any on the market.

Leupold is the company that pioneered the thick-and-thin crosshair back in 1962. They call it the Duplex in the four-post version and the CPC in a tapered-crosshair type. These, along with the regular crosshair and the dot reticles, are available in all except the top-of-the-line Gold-Medallion variable series, which is available only with the Duplex.

Leupold scopes have one of the clearest, sharpest pictures on the market, and can be highly recommended. Leupold & Stevens, Inc., 600 Northwest Meadow Drive, Beaverton, OR 97005.

—J.B.

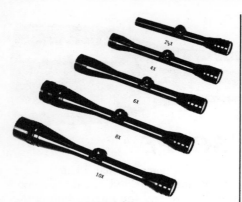

REDFIELD TRADITIONAL SCOPES

These are standard fixed scopes, with no wide-angle effect. Tubes are made of light but strong anodized aluminum, and the scopes are "magnum-proofed," which means that while the wallop of a 7mm magnum might ring your bell, it won't bother the scope.

The 4x scope is probably the most traditional of them all. For all the modern improvements in optics, this one stands tall as the hunters' favorite. It has a 4-plex reticle and sells for $83.40. Redfield, 5800 East Jewell Avenue, Denver, CO 80224.

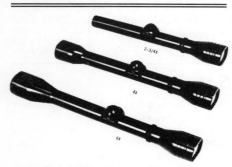

REDFIELD LOW-PROFILE WIDEFIELD

This is a fixed-power scope with a wide-angle effect for a larger viewing area through the scope. Its low profile means you can get closer to your rifle stock with your cheek, and thus in a more stable shooting position. The scope is available in five types of reticles and in 2¾x, 4x, and 6x magnifications. Price: $103.00 to $145.70, depending on magnification and reticle type. Redfield, 5800 East Jewell Avenue, Denver, CO 80224.

Tasco Scopes

This company has long been known for low-priced optics (they import from Japan), though recently they've been offering some more highly priced items. If you are looking for a mid-priced scope, you will not be disappointed. Their lower-priced items all are moisture-sealed, completely coated, and feature their 30/30 (thick-and-thin) reticle with a good rundown of how to use it as a range-finding aid. I have had a Tasco 3 to 9x on a .243 for several years, mostly for big-game hunting, since at the top range, like many variables without parallax/focusing objectives, parallax is a problem. The 32mm objective doesn't have the best relative brightness either when the scope is turned up over 6x. For the 3 to 6x range it is excellent, however, and this takes in most big-game hunting. The cost is about half of what some other scopes cost. The only difference between it and higher-priced scopes (including Tasco's own more expensive items) is a slight definition loss, but it isn't enough of a difference to matter in most big-game hunting. I paid $60.00 for it. Their low-cost 4x32 is $49.95; they sent me a sample of this to look over. It is a good, solid all-around hunting scope. Its definition was very good, and the only problem I had with it was that the adjustments weren't always positive, but that happens with many scopes twice its price. Their top-of-the-line products are equal to almost any. Tasco Sales, Inc., 1075 Northwest 71st Street, Miami, FL 33138. —J.B.

Swift Mark I Wide-Angle Scopes

These scopes are notable in that they give you a round viewing area rather than the squarish "TV screen" common to other wide-angle scopes. Your field of vision is increased by as much as 60 percent, and you are thus less likely to lose your target when you slam your gun to your shoulder for a fast snap shot.

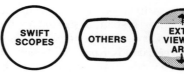

Other Mark I features include one-piece tube construction, anodized exteriors, quad-raplex reticle, waterproofing, and fully coated lenses. Model 651—4x, 32mm (views 37.3 feet at 100 yards); model 656—3 to 9x variable (42.5 feet to 13.6 feet at 100 yards). Price: $65.00. For further information write: Swift Instruments, Inc., 952 Dorchester Avenue, Boston, MA 02125.

Weaver Accu-Point

This sight for shotguns is essentially a low-profile tube, not much higher than most bead-type sights. It must be drilled and tapped to fit the forward end of a ribbed shotgun (it won't work unless your barrel has a rib).

Available light is gathered in a red sighting point; however, you cannot see that point unless the gun is lined up on target. The long hollow tube that leads into the sighting point blocks it from view unless you're looking directly down the inside.

When you can see the red light (assuming you or your gunsmith has properly sighted the gun in during installation), your shot pattern will center around the point covered by the light.

The Accu-Point is a very workable system, enhanced by its simplicity. Its low profile requires no special cases, and it doesn't interfere with more conventional means of shot-gunning, should you choose to ignore the presence of the site. It works equally well with bird loads or deer slugs, and it's most reasonably priced at $14.95. W. R. Weaver Co., 7125 Industrial Avenue, El Paso, TX 79915.

DARST-IRELAND PHOTOGRAPHY

QWIK-POINT FOR SHOTGUNS AND RIFLES

The Qwik-Point sight gathers available light in an upper tube and, through a prism system, projects a dot in the middle of an O-shaped ring that you look through. The sight is adjustable for windage and elevation, and there is no magnification.

The advantages of this particular sight lie in a relatively unobstructed view of what lies in front of the barrel. It's virtually impossible to lose a dodging deer or dipping goose in the sighting device, especially if you shoot with both eyes open. It's also relatively foolproof in terms of malfunction, and it won't fog or get clogged by snow.

Mounted on a shotgun or rifle, the Qwik-Point is a little on the bulky side, and if you're used to a delicate balance in your guns, you'll find your favorite shooting iron barrel-heavy. The biggest hassle is casing a gun. Rifles aren't much of a problem, but try to locate a case for a long-barreled duck or goose gun that will accept a scope!

Still, we can't help but accentuate the positive. For long-range scattergunning and whitetail deer in heavy brush, a Qwik-Point is a real asset.

Available for big game rifles, .22's, and shotguns. Price: $39.95. W. R. Weaver Co., 7125 Industrial Avenue, El Paso, TX 79915.

AIMPOINT ELECTRONIC GUNSIGHT

Ever since Normark brought out the Singlepoint sight around eight years ago, the spot-of-light concept in gunsights has grown in popularity and been steadily improved upon.

This class of sight resembles a standard scope, but it does not magnify an image. Rather, it creates an optical illusion whereby a red dot appears to be projected out beyond the rifle, seemingly hanging in midair. When correctly sighted in, the dot covers the gun's point of impact.

This sighting system has several advantages, including quick tracking ability under brushy or low-light conditions. Since it may be used with both eyes open, the shooter's vision is not limited to the narrow tunnel of a scope or distorted by a rear sight that is always out of focus. You see everything in front of you, game and/or people, making the system safe, efficient, and fast-aiming.

The Aimpoint Electronic gunsight is the newest entry into this field. Rather than using gathered light to project the dot, electricity provided by two small batteries generates the pinpoint of light. The intensity of the light is adjustable too, so you can match its brightness to any light condition.

The sight is trim in size and weighs about as much as a conventional fixed scope. The dot it projects covers 12 centimeters at 100 meters, about the same as the intersection of fine crosshairs.

The Aimpoint would surely be a great help for anyone hunting under brushy conditions, including slug-and-buckshot scattergunners, and even has a place among wingshooters. I've long used point-of-light sights on shotguns for long-range waterfowling and have found it extremely helpful when teaching lead to beginning shotgunners. Take an Aimpoint and a box of clays and you'll soon have the rankest amateur busting birds with amazing regularity. Price: $200.00 from ADKO Industries, Inc., 2428 Grand Avenue, Baldwin, NY 11510.

—N.S.

Bushnell Binoculars

Bushnell has a complete line of binoculars in various grades, compact, standard, and wide-angle—all sorts of models, all very good. Many of them are equipped with Bushnell's Insta-Focus system, wherein focus can be smoothly, quickly changed, much more rapidly than in standard-focus glasses. Prices run from $50.00 or so in the economical Sportview line to around $200.00 in the Custom line. Most are porro-prism types, but they have a few roof-prism glasses for those that prefer the trimmer lines. Bushnell Optical Co., 2828 East Foothill Boulevard, Pasadena, CA 91107.   —J.B.

Bushnell Spotting Scopes

Bushnell makes a variety of spotting scopes in both variable and fixed-power models. Perhaps the best choice for the hunter might be the Sentry fixed-power model in 20x. It's rare that you need much more power than this, and the hunter usually puts a premium on light weight. The Sentry weighs 25.4 ounces, to which Bushnell's excellent, simple tabletop tripod ($5.95) adds 10 ounces. Price for the Sentry is $99.95. Bushnell Optical Co., 2828 East Foothill Boulevard, Pasadena, CA 91107.   —J.B.

Tasco Binoculars

Tasco imports a complete line of porro-prism binoculars at competitive prices. The popular 7x35 is priced at $119.95, a 10x40 at $139.95. I've used a 7x35 Tasco for the past couple of big-game seasons in a wide-angle model; it has perfectly clear optics and I've never had the slightest eyestrain with it. Tasco Sales, Inc., 1075 Northwest 71st Street, Miami, FL 33138
—J.B.

8x Binoculars That Fit Your Shirt Pocket

If you've got a lot of climbing or walking to do, a pair of standard-sized binoculars is a pain in the neck. Redfield's 8-power sportsman's binoculars weigh 5.4 ounces, and, folded, they're just slightly larger than a pack of cigarettes. They include individual eye focus, a 20mm objective diameter, and neoprene eye cups that shield out random sun rays. Price with carrying case: $97.90. Redfield, 5900 East Jewell Avenue, Denver, CO 80224.

TASCO SPOTTING SCOPES

I tested a sample of Tasco's inexpensive ($59.95) 22T 15 to 45x Zoom Spotting Scope. It is a compact scope, very light (under 1 pound) that includes a light yet very practical little tripod. Its definition isn't up to some $200 scopes, but I was able to spot .270 bullet holes in a target 300 yards away on an 85-degree day with enough wind to make mirage a problem. Its 40mm objective lens would hamper it at the higher powers, but in the most useful range for hunting, 20 to 30x, I had no problems. Tasco Sales, Inc., 1075 Northwest 71st Street, Miami, FL 33138.—J.B.

To End Scope Blackout of Game

If you've ever seen an animal with your naked eye and then can't seem to find it in a scope, don't feel alone. Low light conditions and the confusing patterns caused by magnification can make the image transition tough, if not impossible. But take heart. A neat gadget helps get your scope right on the animal before you look through the lens.

Called simply a Sighting Device (this name will take on a more distinctive ring in time), this is a blade and buckhorn-type one-piece sight that clips over the top of a scope tube. It's adjustable by a pretty primitive method; you get your crosshairs on a point at 100 yards, then bend the "device" with pliers until it, too, is on that point. But it does its job well. If it's aimed in on something you can see without a scope, that object will be somewhere near the middle of your scope's field of vision, so long as you keep the rifle steady. Price: $4.90. Redfield, 5800 East Jewell Avenue, Denver, CO 80224.

"Up the airy mountain | We daren't go a-hunting
Down the rushy glen | For fear of little men."
—William Allingham, The Fairies

79

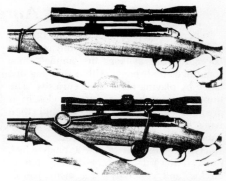

RANGING, INC.

Ranging, Inc., makes a line of optical rangefinders that are useful to sportsmen. Probably the most useful is the Rangematic 1000 MK5, with its 50 to 1000-yard capacity. These are coincident rangefinders with two ocular cells. You look through a monocular attached to the rangefinder, turn a dial until the two images coincide, and then read the distance off a scale. No, they're not absolutely accurate, but they're close enough for use in varmint or long-range big-game hunting. I brought one along on an antelope hunt this fall, and it told me that the buck I got was about 280 yards away, when I would have sworn he was closer to 350, which brings up one of the interesting features of these rangefinders—they teach you how wrong you usually are. I've found that most people overestimate range by a good margin; four out of five will call 300 yards 400. I don't carry the Rangematic on all hunts simply because it's too bulky for many situations (it's about a foot long in its carrying case), but I estimate range much better since I've started using it. Ranging also makes other sizes, down to an optical "tape measure" that indicates distances from 6 feet to 100 feet. Prices range from $19.95 for the tape measure to $44.95 for the 1000 and its metric companion, the 1200. Ranging, Inc., 90 Lincoln Road North, East Rochester, NY 14445. —J.B.

KA-RAM-BA SCOPE LENS COVERS

These lens covers are the fastest to remove. They are constructed of two rubber disks that fit snugly over the ends of the scope. Simple and foolproof, they're held firm and fast by two rubber bands connected to the covers, and covers and banding are in turn secured either to the scope itself or to the rifle forearm.

To clear the scope of its covers, you just flick up the rear cover with your thumb and the whole assembly flies off. It's that quick. Price: $4.95 (indicate type and make of scope). Durfee & Deming, Inc., 7160 Southwest Scholl's Ferry Road, Beaverton, OR 97005.

[The hunter] needs to prepare an attention of a different and superior style—an attention which does not consist in riveting itself on the presumed, but consists precisely in not presuming anything and avoiding inattentiveness. It is a "universal" attention, which does not inscribe itself on any point and tries to be on all points. There is a magnificent term for this, one that still conserves all its zest of vivacity and imminence: alertness. The hunter is an alert man.
—José Ortega y Gasset, *Meditations on Hunting*

WHERE GAME ABOUNDS

As things stand at present, the country where game most abounds is that which is now, or has lately been, infested by hostile Indians. The red fiends know enough to preserve their game from excessive and continual persecution, and it is where the white man dare not go that it is found most abundant and most unsuspicious. The Indians are the only real preservers of game in the West.
—Charles Hallock, 1877

SPRING-LOADED LENS COVERS

These Supreme lens covers are spring-loaded so they snap up and away at the touch of a button. Air-tight and light in weight, they're hinged to their mount, so there's no time wasted in putting them in your pocket to shoot, and no lost covers. Price: $7.50 (advise make and model of your scope). Butler Creek Corp., Jackson Hole, WY 83001.

An antelope can run at speeds up to 60 miles per hour; day-old juveniles have been clocked at 25 mph.

Antelope

Where antelope are numerous, but the prairie is too level to afford the requisite cover for the stalker, the animals may sometimes be brought within shooting distance by playing upon their curiosity. The hunter approaches his game as closely as possible without alarming it, and then lying flat on the ground elevates a flag, handkerchief, arm or leg. This soon attracts the attention of the animals which proceed toward him, not directly but in circles, and generally with many pauses and halts. Sometimes they will turn and run off as if quite satisfied, but before they have gone far, will circle round and advance again, approaching a little nearer than before. This continues for some time, and with care, the game may be brought within three or four hundred yards, but rarely nearer. The task requires more patience than most hunters possess, and is only to be recommended to a man who is very hungry, or very tired of "sow belly" and anxious for fresh meat.

—Charles Hallock, 1877

WINTER RANGE

Public acquisition and protection of key big-game wintering ranges and yards is of primary importance if we are to preserve maximum game populations. These wintering areas usually amount to 5 percent or less of the animals' summer range.

BRUSH BEATING FOR BLACKTAILS

By Jim Martin

The Rocky Mountain mule deer is traditionally the *numero uno* trophy for big-game hunters throughout the West, but when it comes to a venison-in-the-pot animal I'll take the Columbian blacktail (*Odocoileus columbianus*). It's smaller than the big-racked mule deer of the sage country, but the blacktail is a clever and challenging target.

Many other California deer hunters also enjoy the blacktail, as a check of the annual deer kill reports will reveal. Mendocino, Tehama, Trinity, Humboldt . . . names of counties which always rank high on the annual deer-take tally, all lie within the blacktail's range, which extends along the coastal mountains from Oregon south to Santa Barbara and throughout the western slopes of the Cascade and Sierra Nevada ranges. The bulk of all deer killed in California each season are the black-tailed variety.

I've enjoyed hearing many a campfire yarn recounting blacktail hunting adventures, good and bad, and will admit to contributing a few tales myself. In a showdown of those strategies which have led to success, one tactic stands out—brush beating. No matter where or how you choose to hunt the elusive blacktail, you had better be prepared to get out and work the brush if you hope to be successful.

The Columbian blacktail is a creature of the dense conifer forests and oak- and brush-covered hills which blanket much of its home territory. The deer spend much of their time in the thickest undergrowth available, especially when alarmed. Any hunter who hopes to spot a target should plan his strategy around ways to spook the deer into the open.

Beating the brush is never easy. Often it calls for picking your way through heavy tangles of scratchy scrub oak, manzanita, and pestiferous poison oak. You will most likely encounter steep hillsides where footing is treacherous and impassable cliffs which must be circumvented. Daytime temperatures in many parts of the blacktail's range may reach 100 degrees, especially during the early deer season.

Brush beating calls for teamwork in which shooters are stationed at vantage points along a canyon rim or at the edge of an opening, while others are dispatched to enter the undergrowth with instructions to hoot and holler, toss rocks, and otherwise make noise that will cause the deer to move out. Frequently the beaters never see most of the deer they push ahead of them, and seldom will one get an opportunity for a good shot. So when we set up a drive, the "bird dogs" are usually those members of our party who have already bagged a buck.

Even the most conscientious brush beating is unlikely to pay good dividends unless the shooters are stationed at key points where they have an opportunity to get a shot at a buck when he moves into an open area. Targets will generally be moving, either at a slow trot, which is the pace of a deer not unduly alarmed, or on the flat-out bounding run of a badly frightened buck. Frequently, a legal buck will be moving in company with several does, a situation which calls for proper judgment and good marksmanship.

Some of the best country for hunting blacktails is in the numerous burned-over areas found in the national forests or on rangelands administered by the Bureau of Land Management. A check with a local ranger station or BLM office will often provide maps and information on where to hunt.

Productive blacktail hunting is also available on some of the timberlands and tree plantations belonging to private lumber companies, particularly in areas in which the undergrowth has been thinned in conjunction with the conifer release programs designed to encourage rapid growth of more marketable timber. Hunting regulations will vary from firm to firm, so be sure to check with the lumber company whose lands you wish to visit for current information.

One of my favorite areas for hunting blacktails is in the oak-covered hills and canyons east of Red Bluff, an area which is the winter range of the Tehama deer herd. Public hunting is allowed on the state-owned wildlife area at Paynes Creek, and this receives heavy pressure. Much better hunting is available on the Dye Creek Preserve, a 100-square-mile cattle ranch which offers deer hunting on a fee basis. Details about the various hunting programs can be obtained by writing to Dan Patten, Game Manager, Dye Creek Preserve, P.O. Box 308, Red Bluff, CA 96080.

Jim Martin is Western Field Editor for Outdoor Life *magazine. His work in that capacity, and as a free-lance photojournalist, has found him prowling around the hills of the far West for several decades.*

"Tiger, tiger, burning bright / In the forests of the night,
What immortal hand or eye / Could frame thy fearful symmetry?"
—William Blake

81

BINOCULAR AND SPOTTING SCOPE FEATURES

Most binoculars have a central focus adjustment (between the lens barrels) for one eye and an adjustment for the other eye on the eyepiece, as two eyes rarely focus just alike. The easiest way to use them is to focus one eye with the eyepiece adjustment and then use the central focus.

A handy feature to look for if you wear glasses is rubber eyecups that can be folded back. The standard eyecup distance is fine as long as the cup butts up against the eyelids, but the field of view will be severely restricted for the eyeglass wearer if this deep a cup is used. Most binoculars have this fold-back feature, but if you do wear glasses make sure, as otherwise you'll be forced to take your glasses off every time you use the binocular.

It's just about imperative that spotting scopes have a means of attaching a tripod. Most of the better makes are threaded for standard camera-type tripod screws. Scopes of over 10x need this; under that power, a pair of binoculars is better for most hunting uses. —J.B.

CURIOSITY KILLS

When you're on a deer stand, you can improve your odds for a prime buck if you'll give the whitetail something to look at besides you.

A shiny slip of aluminum foil hung from a tree will attract a deer's attention to a point where the animal will concentrate on it instead of you, often standing to watch or slowly advancing toward the object for minutes at a time.

To make this trick work, however, *you* will have to be uncommonly sharp-eyed. The deer will move so slowly that it will be hard to see.

See-through Scope Lens Covers

These sound—and look—like a good idea, but beware of a long shot taken with your scope's lens protected by a layer of clear plastic. The slightest bend or bulge in the plastic will cause the point of impact on a sighted-in scope to change as much as 3½ inches at 100 yards. In addition, the plastic lowers resolution and contrast, so it's more difficult to pick out an animal against its background and to determine detail, such as if a deer is wearing horns.

See-through scope covers are OK for close-in snap shots, but for long-range shooting either remove them before sighting or consider using one of the fast-clearing covers that expose the scope's lens.

New Scope Features

All modern, quality big-game scopes have features that a couple of generations ago were rare: constantly centered reticles, internal adjustments, and moistureproof sealing. These are things so taken for granted today that many younger shooters aren't even aware of the problems hunters experienced before these scopes existed.

Most scope manufacturers offer a variety of reticles: post, dot, crosshair, and the newest type, the thick-and-thin crosshair. This involves four thick posts that point toward the center of the scope; these decrease, sometimes gradually and sometimes abruptly, into fine center crosshairs. These have become popular because they incorporate the advantages of coarse and fine aiming points. They are usually standard equipment and the other types can be had mainly as options. Some manufacturers offer only this type of reticle.

Most manufacturers also offer both standard (round) and wide-angle scopes. Expect to pay a few dollars more for the wide-angle feature.

All modern scopes for big-game rifles have 1-inch tubes. Most are constructed of aluminum; if they are of other construction it will be mentioned. Weight must go up with power: most 2½x and 3x scopes weigh about 8 to 10 ounces, 4x's about 9 to 11 ounces, 6x's 10 to 12 ounces. Variable scopes will be dimensioned about the same size as a fixed-power scope halfway between their highest and lowest powers: a typical 3 to 9x will be about the size of a 6x and, because of the extra lenses, weigh a couple of ounces more. —J.B.

PRONGHORN PROWESS

by Gabby Barrus

People from all over the world now hunt yearly for one of the West's most sought after big-game trophies. With an array of scientific names the likes of *Antilocapridae* and *Antilocapra americana*, this wild little creature has captured my admiration and a great deal of respect in my efforts to outsmart it. Better known to most as the pronghorn antelope, this unique little animal has been my backyard wildlife neighbor for more than a quarter of a century. I have shared these many years with the pronghorn in its infinite Wyoming domain and profess to know it as well as most.

The pronghorn is a matchless animal, the only one of its kind in the world. Its speed is legendary, and its eyesight is almost unmatched. With these credentials, this little speedster will often provide the hunter searching for a challenge more than he has bargained for.

The ultimate for most antelope hunters is to take a better-than-average trophy. The patient hunter, willing to study his quarry—its habits, the terrain to be hunted, and the use of proven tactics—is a logical contender for success.

Stalking is the most enjoyable method of hunting a trophy buck antelope. The hunter will be matching his skill against eyesight more powerful than his own, even through a rifle scope. Extreme care should be exercised to avoid unusual movement in stalking and glassing situations. It is not uncommon for a watchful doe to detect something unusual half a mile away.

If time is available, arrive in the area early to scout the hunting country. Pronghorns, like other game animals, are creatures of habit. With adequate food and water, a herd of pronghorns will not leave the immediate area unless forced to do so by weather or unusual pressure.

My binoculars and spotting scope have been standard equipment in my search for an unusual specimen. I dislike the more powerful glasses, since I am almost constantly scanning the desolate home of the pronghorn, and my 7x35 Bushnell and Swift glasses have given me excellent service.

It would be difficult to calculate the miles a good spotting scope has saved me in judging a trophy animal. Borderline cases of evaluating can be quickly determined with my 25-power Bushnell scope. Look for the following in judging a buck: note the coal-black face, a customary identification of a mature animal, then double the six-inch length of his ears. If his horns extend beyond, you are examining a head worthy of serious consideration. The more powerful scope will also let you appraise horn length, massiveness, and length of the prong with less chance of alerting the animal.

Opening day of the antelope season doesn't excite me in a search for a trophy buck. The early rush of hunters will often foil a well-planned stalk. Once the herds scatter, more careful planning can be initiated. But all planned trophy antelope hunts should be scheduled before early November, because the pronghorn annually sheds part of his horns. The black outer sheath, goal of the trophy hunter, drops off, leaving only an inner core.

Many of the large bucks become loners. These crafty trophies seek out the spacious valley floors, which places them beyond rifle range. Also look for them on big open ridges where they have unlimited vision.

One productive way to bag a pronghorn is to make use of a waterhole that the animals visit regularly. Carefully construct a blind. Normally, antelope will seek water in mid-morning and late afternoon.

Most antelope hunting will be in open country, where a long shot is a possibility. The flat-shooting rifle is the best medicine. In the past five years the .270, .243, and 25.06 have been the most popular antelope rifles in my section of the West. My advice is to zero a pronghorn rifle in at 200 to 225 yards. Without a doubt, more big-game ammunition is used up on this prairie phantom than any other of our western animals.

A full-grown buck will weigh a little over 100 pounds. His great speed, along with his keen vision and the vast real estate in which he roams, offers the hunter no easy target. The best advice is to equip the firearm with a 4x or variable power scope and then spend hours tuning up for the hunt. For sport, fine meat, and a great challenge, the pronghorn fills the expectations of the most selective hunter.

Gabby Barrus has been a hunter and guide in Wyoming for thirty-five years and a writer and photographer for ten years. He is Associate Editor (Hunting) for *Gun Week*.

"Three jovial huntsmen, and a-hunting they did go;
And they hunted, and they hollo'd, and they blew their horns also."
—Anon.

83

The American pronghorn is the only horned animal that sheds its horns.

ALL FOGGED UP

If your scope fogs on the inside, you either have an inferior scope or the gas seal has been broken. Quality telescopic sights are filled with gas (usually nitrogen) and sealed against moisture.

If your scope fogs on the outside, it's caused either by a rapid change in barometric pressure, or temperature, or both. You can avoid fogging by storing your rifle overnight at the same temperature you'll be hunting in on the next day (for example, in a car or outbuilding rather than in a heated cabin).

SCOPES FOR BIG GAME

The use of telescopic sights when hunting big game is not usually tied to the need to see a small or distant target better. Magnification is not the prime virtue of a big-game scope; the ability to see better in dim light (when big game is usually most active) and the instant focus of the sighting point on the target outweigh any considerations of magnification, as big-game animals are large and usually not shot at extreme ranges.

An argument formerly raged over the virtues of the 2½x and the 4x scopes. At one time these were just about the only types available for big game. The 2½x was recommended for woods shooting, and the 4x for long ranges. The primary difference between the two is in the field of view. A typical 2½x will have a field of about 40 feet at 100 yards, a 4x of about 26 to 28 feet; these figures are for standard scopes of typical objective lens size and shape. Theoretically, it is easier to find a bounding deer at short range with the large field of the 2½x than with the 4x. To a certain extent this is true, but a practiced shot using a scope of 4x on a gun with a high comb—to support the shooter's cheek in proper alignment with the scope—can usually get off an aimed shot quicker than a once-a-year shooter using a 2½x on a rifle stocked like the typical woods gun: with a low comb for lining up with the open sights. This is not to say that the 4x is the equal of the 2½x for woods hunting—it's just that other factors are perhaps more important.

A large field of view is desirable, but not at the expense of other things. Recently there has been a trend to enlarge the field of view of scopes by giving them a TV-screen-type eyepiece or enlarging the objective lens. The TV-screen eyepiece enlarges the field of view laterally and so may be some help in game running to the right or left, but not uphill. I have seen some scopes of this sort, too, that have faked the supposedly larger field of view by simply cutting off the top and bottom of the sight picture. You actually end up with less field! A larger ocular lens will give a larger field of view all around, so that a 4x with a large rear end might have the same field as a 2½x of standard measurements. The catch to this is that often the wide-field 4x must be mounted higher on bolt rifles, and even on some rifles of other types, and must be larger and slightly heavier. In quick-shooting situations where the large field of view is desirable, the scope should be mounted low for quick alignment with the eye and should be as small and light as possible. There is no advantage in the extra magnification at quick-shooting ranges, either, so the enlarged-eyepiece 4x is actually at a disadvantage with the standard 2½x. I have used all three types of scopes and have yet to see any marked advantage in the field in any over the standard type. If you are buying a new scope, it might not hurt to get a TV-screen type, but don't expect miracles from it.

For woods shooting a light scope of 3x or less is best; for very close-range situations, under 50 yards, under 2x is even better. A good reticle that shows up plainly in dim light is a big help in brush and timber. The dot, post, and thick-and-thin crosshair are all good types for this shooting, but the crosshair can be used for more precise shooting at longer ranges too.

The 4x has long been considered *the* big-game scope for all-around and open-country shooting. Its magnification is enough for most situations, while the field of view is large enough for running shots from about 30 to 40 yards out. The 4x is also reasonably compact. I feel the 3x might be a bit better as an all-around choice, however, since it is usually at the closer ranges that the hunter begins to feel uncomfortable with a scope. The 3x is better for woods situations and provides enough power for all but extreme ranges. You can't go very far wrong with either, however.

In the situations in big-game hunting where power is really needed in a scope, the 6x is it. For long-range pronghorns, for picking a brown bighorn from a brown hillside, for precisely placing a shot on a mule deer at 300 yards, the 6x has a definite advantage over lesser scopes. Its 20-foot field of view limits its applications, but in a well-stocked rifle surprisingly close-range shots are practical. I have killed more than one running deer at under 100 yards with my 6x-scoped .243 and have never felt handicapped.

The 6x is about as high as the big-game hunter should go in power for most hunting, however. It is as much power as he can use in compact scopes and retain good relative brightness. Anything bigger needs a large objective, and also a parallax-focusing objective. This means higher mounts, weight, clumsiness, and expense, as well as reduced field of view.

There are good variable scopes for big-game hunting on the market. I can't really recommend anything with a top power of much over 6 for a purely big-game rifle, however. The best are in the 1½-to-4x range, as they are light, compact, and cover most hunting situations. A 2½ to 7x might be useful for the long-range hunter, but parallax can be a problem if you go any higher. Some shooters select 3-to-9x scopes and try to use the higher setting for spotting game. This is clumsy at best and dangerous at worst: if a hunter on the opposite slope sees you pointing your rifle at him he might not take it kindly. A pair of binoculars offers better spotting, and a good pair combined with a 3x scope won't set you back any more than a 3x to 9x of equal quality, either.

Actually, this whole discussion of what power to pick is by no means absolute. I have used the three most popular powers—2½, 4, and 6—for all kinds of hunting. I have used the 6x in woods hunting and the 2½x in situations where most of my shots were sure to be over 200 yards; if there is any situation in which the power becomes a hindrance it is when the scope is *too* powerful, but if your rifle is correctly stocked and you've practiced with it you'll rarely foul up a shot. The first deer I ever shot fell at a range of 30 *feet*, to a rifle with a 4x scope.

There is another kind of optical sight on the market that is not strictly a scope, but it's not an iron sight, either. It involves a bright aiming point, usually orange, and must be used with both eyes open. There is no magnification, just a big orange dot to be put on the target. Some woods hunters

say these are the fastest of all, as they have the unlimited field-of-view of iron sights and the quickness—since the eye does not have to focus on different points—of the scope. Their one disadvantage compared to the scope is that they do not provide better definition, which is an aid in dim light.

For the hunter with one all-around big-game rifle, I believe a 3x or a low-range variable is the best choice; the multigun hunter can match his gun and sight to the situation. For either hunter, though, there is a scope on the market to fit his needs.

—J.B.

Back in the bad old days before every Tom, Dick, and Harry—including the hermit in the woods—got a fancy new spyglass on Old Betsy, there were any number of difficulties involved in equipping a gun with a scope. Scopes were fairly good instruments, even then, and the guns were fine; it's just that they weren't conceived of as belonging together. Back before 1930 or so, lever-action guns were much more popular than they are today, and the favorite Winchester 94 ejected its empties straight up through the top of the receiver, making central mounting of a scope impossible. Bolt guns, just then coming into general use, had bolt handles that made low, central scope mounting impossible too, though side mounts, high mounts, forward mounts, and all sorts of strange things were used to combat this if the shooter didn't want to get the shape of the bolt handle changed. The wing-type Mauser safeties on many bolt guns, too, made scope mounting difficult. Few guns were drilled and tapped for scope mounting, and Rube Goldberg devices that used existing slots and holes on the gun were invented so that the average gun owner could mount a scope himself without a trip to the gunsmith. Scopes came in all shapes and sizes, so a gun owner usually had to use a mount made by the manufacturer, which as often as not wasn't the greatest of engineering marvels. In short, the situation was haphazard at best, and many shooters came to distrust scopes and mounts in those days.

Today the shooter is much better off. Gun catalogs may still proudly proclaim the fact that their arms are drilled and tapped for scope mounts—which may sell a few rifles to the innocent in the outback—but the fact is that since World War II there haven't been many rifles left undrilled by the factories. Mounts and screws are pretty well standardized too, and just about all the scopes used in big-game hunting have 1-inch tubes, so that any standard mount can be used. There are a few daring and devil-may-care manufacturers who are willing to admit that most of their products will be graced by glass sights in top mounts that make the iron sights unusable, and these manufacturers leave the open sights off the barrels of their guns. There is even one American company and several European firms that machine bases for scope mounts right onto the receivers of their guns.

The insistence that American shooters have for open sights on guns that are scoped is, in some instances, rational, but I have known two shooters in the past few years

"A man may not care for golf and still be human, but the man who does not like to see, hunt, photograph, or otherwise outwit birds or animals is hardly normal."
—Aldo Leopold

85

SCOPE MOUNTS

who, when asked why they still had the front sight still on their scope rifle when the rear sight was missing (it had been removed, in both cases, by the person who mounted their scopes because it interfered with the objective lens of the scope), were practically reduced to nervous wrecks when they realized they'd been traipsing around in the wilderness for years without benefit of backup sights. The fact that neither had ever bothered to shoot the guns with the open sights to see if they were reasonably sighted in, and that they'd never had the slightest trouble with the scopes, didn't matter.

The reliability of modern scopes is amazing, but, in spite of the fact that shooters have better mounting systems today than ever before, there is still room for improvement in the mounts. Applied correctly, with a screwdriver that fits and some kind of goop such as Loctite or linseed oil on the screw threads to prevent them from vibrating loose, there is really no need to worry about them, but there are ways in which they could be made even more reliable. The built-in base on the receiver eliminates one connection and makes the mount more reliable (most mounting systems involve a base that must be screwed to the rifle in order that the mount have something it can be attached to). The Ruger 77 bolt rifle, alas, is the only American arm with such a feature. Bases also add expense, anywhere from $2.00 to $15.00. The mounting systems common today also use little 6-48 screws that, while fine for open and receiver sights, aren't the best possible holding fixtures for something with the mass of even the lightest scope. Most mounts try to make up for this by using a lot of screws, but—like the rifle-to-base-to-mount system—this simply provides you with more things that can work loose. Larger and fewer screws would be better, but it is doubtful that this will ever happen, since the industry is so standardized. All this goes simply to point out that most mounts aren't perfect, but are OK if care is used in applying them.

While there are a number of mounting systems available to the hunter, there is only one basic type that should concern him. This is the receiver-based mount, either with two bases, one on each end of the receiver, as in the Weaver type, or a one-piece base that "bridges" the receiver, as typified by the Redfield JR. Whichever base is used, there are two rings that fasten onto the scope and then to the base or bases. This type of mount will do for 99 percent of the hunting situations in the world.

A type of mount fast becoming extinct for hunting purposes is the adjustable mount. These were in use when a great many scopes didn't have internal adjustments; there are very few hunting scopes of this type sold today. In its most common form, the adjustable mount involved opposing cones and could be used with scopes of varying tube diameters.

A type of mounting system occasionally used for ultra-long-range varmint guns is the target type. It involves a base on the receiver and one on the barrel, in order to support the long and heavy target scope better. The target mount is coming into disrepute even among certain target shooters, as the base on the barrel has a tendency to interfere with barrel vibrations in a way that can't be easily controlled. There are modern, internally adjustable scopes of over 20x now available that can be totally receiver-mounted. These are becoming popular among target shooters, and there is really no reason that even the zaniest varmint hunter can't be satisfied with a system like this.

There is another general class of mount, which includes side mounts, see-through mounts, quick-release mounts, and swingaway mounts, that gives the shooter reasonably quick access to auxiliary iron sights on his rifle. In spite of the fact that modern scopes are extremely reliable, there are good reasons for wanting a system like this: for example, when a wounded animal may have to be followed up and finished at close range, or when making an extended trip with only one rifle, or possibly when hunting in very wet country. A great many hunters who will never see any of the above-mentioned situations use mounts of this type, since the mounts make them feel secure and happy.

There is one other type of mount, which uses a long eye-relief scope in front of a rifle's receiver. This is most commonly used on the Winchester 94 to get around the problem of top ejection, though whether it has any advantage over a side mount on such a relatively short-ranged gun is open to doubt. It will also make a gun somewhat muzzle-heavy, which isn't really a good idea on a woods gun like the 94.

All in all, the low, central-mounted scope will do extremely well, and unless the hunter is absolutely sure he needs another type of mount he should stick to the standard receiver-mounted base-and-ring system, as it gives the quickest sighting and is the most reliable.

—J.B.

An antelope head is worthy of a mount if its horns are twice the size of its ears. If they approach three times the size of the ears, the head might make the record books.

MARBLE'S "GAME-GETTER" CATALOG

This 20-page catalog is put out by one of the oldest sporting goods firms in the country. Ask Grandpa about Marble's "game-getter" gun someday. It was a weird kind of collapsible shotgun contraption, banned by the Feds because the gun didn't conform to their ideas about sawed-off shotguns. Anyway, it's a collector's item now (with proper permits, of course).

Marble's currently catalogs a wide variety of sights (mostly iron, but of every imaginable variety) and gun-cleaning accessories and a limited number of sensible-looking knives. It's not a terribly interesting catalog to read, but they're thorough in what they handle and have a reputation for old-time quality. Free from Marble's, P.O. Box 111, Gladstone, MI 49837.

Williams Streamlined Top Mount

Instead of having a base to which the mount is attached, as with most scope mounts, the bottom half of the rings is the base in this mount, eliminating at least two screws. The streamlined top mount is also a slightly slanted type, which by simple reversal can accommodate just about any scope. Its one disadvantage is that it can't be transferred to rifles other than the make it is made for, as can mounts of more normal construction, but it is a good-looking, solid, light mount. Price: $14.50. Williams Gun Sight Co., 7389 Lapeer Road, Davison, MI. 48423.

Leupold Bridge Mount

The Leupold STD rings and base interchange with the Redfield JR and SR systems. Rings are available in three heights and cost $16.70. Bases, available for most popular rifles, cost $10.50. Leupold & Stevens, Inc., 600 Northwest Meadow Drive, Beaverton, OR 97005.

Griffin & Howe Scope Mounts

This custom gunsmithing firm also makes some very good scope mounts. The side mount has the reputation of being one of the best around. It consists of a side mounting plate, the top of which is a male dovetail; the ring base slides onto this and is tightened by two levers. This is a quickly removable rig, making iron sights easily available. There are two styles, one which positions the scope to the side of the receiver, and another which puts the scope over the receiver. Price: $52.50. Griffin & Howe, Inc., 589 Broadway, New York, NY 10012.

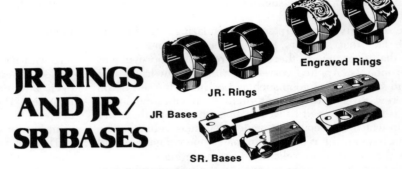

JR RINGS AND JR/SR BASES

REDFIELD JR MOUNT

Bridge mounts supposedly give an added measure of strength and reliability to a mounting system, as they form a "bridge" from the front of the receiver to the rear. This is probably true, but any real advantage over two-piece bases in most field situations might be hard to prove.

The Redfield JR is the most popular bridge mount around. It is made out of steel, so it is very strong, but it weighs more than aluminum and aluminum-and-steel mounts. It is a good, solid, precise mount and, if extra strength is needed, is well worth it. Actually the JR is simply a base, since the good-looking Redfield rings (blessed with hex-head screws) will fit the SR two-piece bases as well.

Bridge mounts do have one rare quirk. Occasionally the holes for mounting will be slightly out of line, either on the base or the rifle, or perhaps a combination of the two, and when the screws are tightened down the receiver can actually warp slightly. This is nothing you can see, but it can cause all sorts of weird accuracy problems. If your gun is stringing its shots or giving any other strange accuracy indications, and nothing else can be found wrong, suspect the mount. Take the scope off the mount and then tighten down first one end of the mount and then the other. If there is any discrepancy, such as the end of the mount that is not screwed down being even 1/16 inch off the receiver, you must shim the mount to eliminate the strain on the receiver which surely results when the base is tightened. This is rare, but when it happens it can be very exasperating. I have a .243 that drove me nuts with this problem.

Price for the JR base (and the SR) is $12.00, and the rings are $17.80, in three heights. Engraved rings are available for $33.00, and extension rings for $24.00. Redfield, 5800 East Jewell Avenue, Denver, CO 80222.

"The hunter knows that he does not know what is going to happen and this is one of the greatest attractions of his occupation."

—*José Ortega y Gasset*

87

TASCO SEE-THROUGH SCOPE MOUNT

Tasco's Quick Peep rings put the scope high and have holes through the mounts under the scope so that the shooter can use iron sights as well. They fit standard Weaver bases and are good, solid mounts. I got to try a sample and had no problems. The split rings are tightened by a screw on each side, so there shouldn't be any problem with torque twisting the crosshairs of the scope out of line during mounting. Price: $12.95. Tasco Sales, Inc., 1075 Northwest 71st Street, Miami, FL 33138.

—J.B.

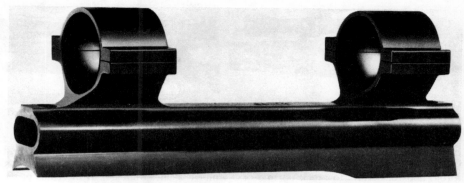

SEE-THROUGH SCOPE MOUNTS

Scope mounts with either the "O" ring see-through feature or a design that holds the scope offset are available through Marble Arms. Either mounting system allows you to use your open sights for those close-in quick shots when scopes are likely to blank out.

See-through mounts are made for virtually every brand of firearm, and both the O-ring and the offset cost $20.00. Marble's, P.O. Box 111, Gladstone, MI 49837.

SCOPE MOUNTS FOR SHOTGUNS

Some shotgunners like to use a 2x or lower magnification scope when they're after deer with slugs. If that's your druthers, Redfield makes a special mount for scattergunners that matches up with their FR scope rings. Price: $7.80. Redfield, 5800 East Jewell Avenue, Denver, CO 80224.

MOUNT FOR WINCHESTER 94

The venerable 94 with top shell ejection has a few flaws, one of the more notable being that it won't accept a common scope mount. Redfield makes a special mount for this gun for $19.90 that offsets the scope just enough to clear a flying cartridge. Redfield, 5800 East Jewell Avenue, Denver, CO 80224.

Bushnell Mount Rings

These rings fit on the standard Weaver bases that can be bought at almost any hardware store for a buck apiece. They tighten up with hex-head screws (allen wrench of the proper size provided), and so even the klutziest home mechanic doesn't have to worry about tearing up the screw heads. They also provide a certain amount of windage adjustment in the mount. With most rings that fit Weaver bases, when you get the rig all set up and for some reason the scope won't adjust enough to be sighted in (which happens now and then when the mounting holes are out of line on the rifle), you have to shim the bases. With these mounts a simple reversal of one of the mounts, which one depending on which way the scope should go, will give about a foot of windage adjustment at 100 yards.

Another virtue of these rings is that they are the lightest that we've yet found and yet are rugged enough for most hunting. A total ring-and-base weight of 2½ ounces is about 1½ ounces lighter than standard Weaver rings, about 3 ounces less than Redfield or Conetrol two-base mounts, and 5 to 6 ounces less than most bridge mounts. These differences may not seem important, but the hunter of mountain game who wants the lightest rifle possible is concerned with such matters and should give these mounts a good looking over. Price: $11.95. Bushnell Optical Co., 2828 East Foothill Boulevard, Pasadena, CA 91107.

—J.B.

Conetrol Mounts

These are used on many custom rifles, as they are among the most streamlined and elegant of mounts. The rings have no projections or screws to break up line or curve, and the bases are precision products (available in either bridge or two-piece) well suited to the best of rifles. The Conetrol people also claim that they support the scope better on heavy-recoiling rifles, as both rings are attached to the base in the same solid manner, but even

with the most precise machining one ring is certain to bear more than the other, and in practice there simply may not be that much of an advantage, as the rifles of really heavy recoil use the smallest scopes as a rule. The rings fit into holes in the bases with a pair of opposing cone-tipped screws holding them there. By adjusting these screws, windage can be finely tuned in both front and back rings, and by loosening one of the cone screws on each mount,

the scope can be lifted from the bases and replaced with no loss of zero if so desired (if iron sight use is needed, for example, or if the scope is going to be transported separately on a trip, as might be desirable on some airlines). The bases are available in three grades, Huntur, Gunnur, and Custum, and range in price from $9.95 to $14.95, with split rings ranging from $6.45 to $9.95. Conetrol Scope Mounts, Highway 123 South, Seguin, TX 78155. —J.B.

Weaver Mounts

These are the workingman's mount: cheap, reliable, and plain. Ten dollars or thereabouts will get you a set of Weaver rings, and the bases only cost a buck each. You can buy them at just about any hardware store that sells ammo, and the screws and construction are simple enough for even a fumble-fingered and slightly unmechanical shooter to install with a reasonable degree of success. There are a couple of quirks that they have, however, that confound people. The rings are basically ring clamps, and when tightened they tend to twist the scope out of perpendic-

ular, so a rifle that had the scope's crosshairs sitting nice and square with the rings loose will be all cockeyed when they are twisted down. A surprising number of people just leave them that way, apparently assuming that crosshairs were meant to be crooked, and such shooters probably can't shoot worth a damn anyway, so they don't notice the inaccuracy that results. The easiest way I've found to install them is to start with the crosshairs perpendicular, then notice how much out of line they are after clamping the rings down; by loosening the rings again and

turning the scope just that much out of line, the crosshairs will usually be close to square when you tighten the screws down again. Usually. Some days nothing seems to go right. The other bothersome thing about the rings is that the screws are very soft, and the heads easily torn. The best solution is to get a small screwdriver and grind or file the tip until it fits the screw head perfectly. Once you get them on, they are fine, reliable mounts. W. R. Weaver Co., 7125 Industrial Avenue, El Paso, TX 79915. —J.B.

PACHMAYR SWING MOUNT

Every year I see a few hunters with high, see-through scope mounts on their rifles. The rationale for this type of system is that you can use the scope for long shots and the open sights for close snap shots. I feel sorry for these people, as they're missing the best parts of both types of sight. A properly mounted scope is equally as fast, under most conditions, as open sights, except at extremely close range where the whole of the target can't be seen. Mounting the scope up so high with the see-through mounts only makes the scope slower and sighting more difficult, as the shooter must juke his neck around like a feeding goose to get the proper alignment. The iron sights are no better off in such an arrangement, as their greatest virtue, that of an unlimited field of view, is cut off by the scope mount. These mounts came about, I believe, because many people consider scopes delicate and unreliable. I must confess that I don't even have iron sights on most of my rifles, as I found long ago that today's scopes are usually more rugged and reliable than the cheap iron sights found on most factory

rifles; the open sights only tend to get caught on things, so off they go. But for some situations, such as hunting in wet weather or in country where either a long shot or an extremely close shot may be necessary, there is a need for the instant availability of either scope or iron sights. The Pachmayr people make the best arrangement on the market for this. Their Lo-Swing top mount puts the scope low and centrally over the bore (no compromise side-mounting) and yet it can be swung away in an instant to make the iron sights available. On a rifle to be used on dangerous game I wouldn't have any other mount—if, indeed, I decided a scope was necessary. And, unlike quick-detachable mounts, you don't have to look for someplace to keep the scope—it rides right along there on the rifle, ready to use. It costs $35.00 and is guaranteed to maintain alignment no matter how many times it is swung over. Pachmayr Gun Works, Inc., 1220 South Grand Avenue, Los Angeles, CA 90015.
—J.B.

"IRON" SIGHTS

You'd be hard put to find any truly iron sights on today's market. The closest you might come would be steel, but a great many nonoptical sights are made of aluminum, plastic, or other materials. We call all of them iron sights, simply as a generic term.

There are two basic types of iron sights: the open sights that come with most factory rifles and the "peep," or receiver, sights. Open sights are usually blade- or bead-front sights that the shooter visually aligns with a notch in the rear sight in order to line up his weapon. Receiver sights are simply rear sights that involve a hole through which the shooter "peeps" in order to line up the front sight.

Open sights are more common than peep sights, as they come on most factory rifles. Peep sights were originally designed as a better long-range sight than the open type, but generally today the hunter who wants a better sight than the factory provides buys a scope.

The common open sights have few applications today wherein they would be superior to either peeps or scopes. Their most glaring fault is the fact that it is an optical impossibility to focus on three objects of varying distance—rear sight, front sight, and target—at the same time. In a steady position a shooter practiced with open sights can place his shots on big game fairly well out to 200 yards or so, perhaps farther, but the light must be good. The use for which they are most often advocated—that of shooting running game at close ranges—is not really all that well suited to their limitations. In a hurry-up situation, a shooter doesn't have the time to focus and refocus his eyes on the sights, as he can when shooting at stationary objects, and as a result exact bullet placement (which is hard to accomplish on running game anyway) is difficult. The greatest virtue of open sights is their virtually unlimited field of view (which is why people consider them "fast"), but to take advantage of this they must be used with both eyes open. Sad to say, a great many shooters were taught by their dad or their uncle or whomever to "squinch" their off eye when shooting. When only one eye is used, part of the field of view is blocked by the sight and the barrel, and for the hunter shooting at running game headed uphill, which is fairly common, the sight will effectually block view of the target, as the game must be "led" just as in shotgun shooting. Even shooters who have learned later in life to shoot with both eyes open are apt to squinch in the excitement of hunting. Open sights, too, are not the best choice for the dim light often encountered in

woods hunting and are impossible to use in early morning or late dusk lighting.

Probably the best application for open sights is in very close-range shooting, under 50 yards, such as when following up wounded, dangerous game that might charge. There are very few people who regularly get involved in adventures of this type in the United States, however.

If you insist on open sights, and many do as they are lighter and less bulky than scopes (though not any more so than peeps), there are a few things to look out for. The rear sight should be as compact as possible, in order to cover up as little of the target as is practical. The "buckhorn" rear sight that was in vogue a number of years ago is sometimes recommended by old-timers, though their rationale remains a mystery as the sight has two ears that stick up on either side of the sighting notch, effectively blocking a great deal of the view of the target. The rear sight should also be precisely adjustable for windage and elevation. The common notched wedge used for elevation adjustment on cheap open sights is not satisfactory, as each notch amounts to at least 3 to 4 inches of adjustment at 100 yards. A sliding sight that is tightened with a screw is best. A bright arrow or triangle indicating the center of the sight is an aid in precise aiming. The front sight can be either a flat-topped post or a bead. Beads have some tendency to reflect light more on one side than the other under certain conditions, and unless the bright aiming point is really needed many shooters prefer the post.

One facet of open sights is that the farther they are separated the more accurate they will be. Open sights 15 inches apart, as is common on today's rifles, allow much more error than the ones 30 inches or more apart on Great-Grandpa's muzzleloader. Even $1/32$ inch of misalignment with the 15-inch sighting radius can cause a missed shot, while the same error with the 30-inch spacing would be only half as critical. This phenomenon is the basis of the long-held belief that longer barrels are more accurate. When scope sights came into general use, eliminating any sighting advantage in the long barrels, it was found that short barrels are more accurate on the average, as they are stiffer, at least in modern centerfire rifles. Grandpa's gun, too, had an advantage in that the sights were farther away from the eye, causing fewer focusing problems. In modern short-barreled guns some shooters prefer to place the rear sight *closer* to the front sight. The sighting radius is shorter, but the rear sight is in better focus with this arrangement, aiding in more accurate pointing, especially in snap-shooting.

Open sights must be rugged. A funny thing I have noticed is that a great many people who refuse to use peep or scope sights, saying they are too "delicate," have cheap .22-type open sights on their guns that can actually be almost blown out of synch. If you decide you need open sights, get *good* ones. I would still hesitate to say that open sights are more rugged than today's peeps and scopes, unless you plan to bang your gun around on rocks.

Peep, or receiver, sights are a very good compromise between the inaccuracy of open sights and the bulk of a scope. People who don't like peeps are usually confused by the aperture. They are under the impression that a tiny aperture is needed for accurate shooting, and they are stymied in their attempts to get a shot off quickly with such a sight. Unless you plan to be taking only long-range shots at stationary game (where a scope would be the choice), an aperture of at least $^1/_{10}$ inch is better, and for close-range shooting even larger holes can be used, as the eye naturally centers itself at the strongest part of the light. I have shot many groups of 2 inches and under with a .30-06 equipped with a ⅛-inch aperture, at 100 yards. Even this size aperture has an aiming precision of at least that of open sights with a $^1/_{16}$-inch rear notch, as peep sights are mounted on the receiver and have a sighting radius of about twice that of most open sights. In reality, because of the eye's tendency to center itself, the aiming precision is greater. The peep has another advantage over the open sight in that the shooter only has to focus his eyes on two points, the front sight and the target, and the front sight is in fairly good focus anyway. The peep also has a field-of-view advantage over the open sight in one way, in that the rear sight doesn't block any of the target.

The shooters who say they can't use peeps have generally only tried them once, perhaps on someone else's gun (just as scope-haters do), and the type of sight may have been a target variety or the gun may not have fit. Each type of sight is different and must be approached differently. A driver wouldn't attempt to use his car, with its low clearance and long hood, as he would a four-wheel-drive pickup, but that in effect is what a lot of shooters do with different types of sights. The man used to open sights will be confounded by the peep and look *at* it instead of through it, just as he will first put his eye to a scope and then try to pick up the target. As most of us start our shooting careers with open sights, there are adjustments to be made in using any other system, but that does not mean the other systems are inferior.

Good receiver sights are rugged and precisely adjustable. They are usable in a driving rain, and they are good for most open country shooting out to 250 yards on big game. They do not have the dim light capabilities of scopes, but they are lighter and more compact, and the hunter who places a premium on handiness and weight might seriously consider them. If I wanted a rifle to take on a long trip in the wilderness, I would definitely equip it with a peep as an auxiliary sight to a scope. —J. B.

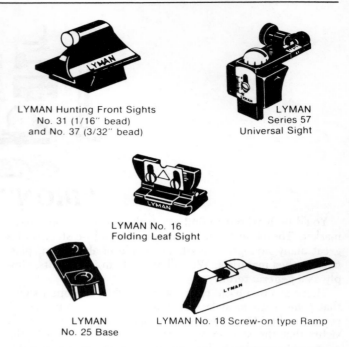

LYMAN Hunting Front Sights
No. 31 (1/16″ bead)
and No. 37 (3/32″ bead)

LYMAN
Series 57
Universal Sight

LYMAN No. 16
Folding Leaf Sight

LYMAN
No. 25 Base

LYMAN No. 18 Screw-on type Ramp

LYMAN IRON SIGHTS

Just about 100 years ago the Lyman company started making their receiver sights, the first practical "peep" sights for hunters. These were a great improvement over the open sights then available. William Lyman, who developed their receiver sight, also improved the bead front sight by giving it a flat face, thus cutting down on irregular reflections. The Lyman company is still the number-one producer of iron sights in the United States today.

Their Series 57 and 66 receiver sights (both the same sight, essentially, the 57 for bolt actions and the 66 for flat-receivered pump, lever, and auto guns) are fine hunting sights, having audible ¼-minute clicks for adjustment and a quickly removable slide. The slide is a handy feature on any gun that has the receiver sight as a backup sight in conjunction with a low-mounted scope. The base of the receiver sight doesn't interfere with the scope, and if the switch in sights is desired the scope is removed and the slide dropped into place. A rifle with such a feature could use a trap butt plate for storage of the slide. The Lyman sight comes with two disks, one of hunting aperture and the other target. The hunting disk is of .093 size, or almost $^1/_{10}$″, and the target .040. Price: $22.50.

Lyman also makes a folding-leaf rear sight for those who like this type. It will fold flat and not interfere with the objective lens of a scope, yet will flip up when needed. This costs $4.50 and is available in various heights. They also sell a base for this sight for rifles that aren't dovetailed; the base is mounted with two 6-48 screws and runs $3.50.

The flat-bead Lyman front sight is available in $^1/_{16}$-inch and $^3/_{32}$-inch beads and in two widths (to fit different ramps) and costs $4.50. Ramps of the screw-on type cost $6.00. Lyman Products for Shooters, Route 147, Middlefield, CT 06455.

" 'Unting fills my thoughts by day, and many a good rui. I have in my sleep."
Robert Smith Surtees, Handley Cross (1853)

91

INEXPENSIVE SHOTGUN SIGHT

If you're a casual shotgunner for deer, or own an expensive shotgun, the Slug Site might be for you. It is a one-piece front-and-rear sight combination that attaches to any shotgun receiver or barrel without screws or tapping.

A tough adhesive bonds the Slug Site to your gun, yet it can be removed when it's time to shoot birds without any damage to the steel of the blueing. The device is "sighted in" by bending the front sight blade up, down, or sideways until you're on target. Once properly adjusted, the Slug Site should get you into a 4-inch group at 50 yards.

There are probably more deer missed than are taken in shotgun-only hunting areas, and the majority of those misses may be laid on the barrels of guns that have no sighting system. This site is cheap insurance that it won't happen to you. Price: $5.00. Slug Site Co., Whitetail Wilds, Lake Hubert, MN 56459.

Williams Iron Sights

These people make two types of open rear sights, a dovetail-mounting type that tightens with a screw, instead of having to be driven into the dovetail, and their Guide model, which is mounted with two screws and involves a sliding ramp. The Guide model is available in four blade types, including the shallow-V favored by African hunters.

Williams also makes a ramp-front sight, with a bead in heights from 1/8 inch to 9/16 inch, and the Guide receiver sight, which mounts in the rear scope-mounting holes in most rifles and is a very compact receiver sight. It, like the Guide rear sight, adjusts by means of a sliding ramp.

Prices for the Williams products: dovetail rear, $5.35; Guide rear, $6.75; ramp front, $5.75; Guide receiver, $9.35. Williams Gun Sight Co., 7389 Lapeer Road, Davison, MI 48423.

WORDS ABOUT WHITETAILS
by Jim Bashline

For a teenage lad in northcentral Pennsylvania, hunting whitetail deer during the first two weeks of December was no small matter. The fortnight of legal hunting for antlered bucks was planned, rehearsed, and discussed with all of the seriousness that customarily accompanies such momentous undertakings as the invasion of Europe or filling out a fly-tying order to Herter's.

For Potter County kids of hunting license age, to return to school after a day or two of quietly condoned hooky and announce that they had placed a tag on *their* buck was a badge of honor. Unlike the kids who grow up in urban atmospheres, we small-town teenagers almost had to hunt in order to be accepted by our peers. Perhaps I would have hunted anyway. I can never be sure. But I certainly am thankful I had the chance to grow up in a community where kids had time to be kids and where hunting, fishing, and all of the good outdoor rewards were commonplace.

In spite of the number of deer in our part of the world, my first five deer seasons were nothing much. I managed to claim a couple of deer, but my first buck with honest-to-goodness antlers didn't come until I was seventeen. The feelings and chest-beating pride are easily recalled, but quite honestly I didn't learn to respect the whitetail as the great game animal it is until many years later. The anticipation of seeing a well-antlered trophy as I top the next knoll is still the driving force behind my annual deer hunts. But be he spike-horned or a perfectly formed eight-pointer, the whitetail buck has got to be the smartest creature that exists in North America. Whitetails have been pursued earnestly by primitive and modern hunters with such diligence that it seems logical to expect them one day to pass from the scene. Yet the whitetail survives and—yes—thrives, right at the doorstep of the nation's largest metropolises. Warren Page once told me that one of the largest whitetail

bucks he'd ever seen was spotted on a New Jersey hilltop on a clear evening as the lights of the Empire State Building could be seen on the horizon.

While it is true that the finest trophies, as a group, seem to come from a special pocket of farmland in southern Saskatchewan, the Boone and Crockett record book is well laced with smashing good heads that came from all over the map. Like the old cliché about gold, trophy whitetails are where you find them. One could be in any backyard.

There are no secret methods that I know of that will make anyone a better finder of record-class heads. They are a matter of good luck plus a small measure of good management. For the most part, hunters lay down their license money and hit the woods on opening day. Today's busy world doesn't allow much time for the study and dedication required to produce what could honestly be called an "expert" whitetail hunter. The hours are too precious. Therefore, the best time to go deer hunting is whenever you can.

The hunter can, however, control some things. Thirty-two years of whitetail chasing have put three major points into sharper focus for me:

• In hard-hunted areas (like most top whitetail country) don't be despondent if you fail to score the first day or two. Big bucks are big because they have outwitted many an opening-day license buyer. After the smoke clears away, the deer calm down a bit and the solo hunter who pussyfoots along upwind and keeps his eyes open will be amazed at how many deer he sees.

• For some species of small game, the best hunting technique may be fast walking and equally fast gun handling, but for whitetails, on foot or horse—move slow. A turtle's pace is just about right, with both eyes constantly scanning the immediate area as well as the far horizon. The high-stepping hunter who huffs and puffs from one ridgetop to another covers a lot of ground but he doesn't see much game. He's too busy worrying about mileage.

- Know your firearm. I mean really know it. Handle it a lot before deer season and be able to push the safety into firing position without looking down at the gun. Practice shooting from all sorts of positions, since deer will pop up at the darndest times and the classic kneeling and prone positions are seldom useful. Make sure that your rifle is well sighted in and that you have confidence in it. No super-demolishing magnum cartridge will kill a deer with one shot unless you put that bullet into the heart/lung area or break the spinal column.

All right, I know that you've probably read those three admonitions several times before, but once more won't hurt. Reading them and then applying them are two entirely different things. I know. I break rule number two almost every year and end up spooking what I'm sure is the biggest buck in twelve counties. After watching the bouncing white flag disappear into the hemlocks beyond, I curse myself for not being more attentive to my own advice.

If the hunting gods take pity on you and you happen to be out on that ideal day of days, here's what you'll find. A soft carpet of half-melted snow is beneath your feet (excellent tracking and very quiet). A mild breeze blows *from* the direction you intend to hunt (the deer don't smell you or hear you). The light will be behind you with just enough overcast to kill your all-black silhouette, and—if you're very, very lucky—no other hunter will be within a square mile. Oh, yes, I almost forgot, a 40-degree temperature would add the final touch to such ideal conditions, just cool enough for easy walking but not warm enough for heavy sweat to form.

If you are ever fortunate enough to be in the woods when all those conditions prevail, you are indeed a blessed deer hunter. I keep waiting and hoping for that day to occur. In the meantime I'll take pot luck just as you do and try to make those three personal rules pay off.

Hundreds of experienced big-game hunters with trophy rooms full of assorted horned and antlered species have echoed the same thoughts about whitetails: "No more elusive big-game animal exists than the North American whitetail deer." Amen . . . in spades.

Jim Bashline is an outdoor writer and photographer who lives in Pennsylvania, our greatest whitetail state. He is Outdoor Editor of the *Philadelphia Inquirer* and Associate Editor of *Field & Stream* magazine.

The whitetail's white tail is highly valued by fishermen, who use it to make bucktail jigs and flies. Never throw a tail away; someone is sure to have a use for it.

BIG-GAME SKINNING KNIFE

A skinning knife should have a relatively short (4-to-6-inch) blade, a wide blade profile, and a bluntish tip with a large forward cutting area where the edge sweeps up to meet the point. Most of the cutting is done with this part of the knife. Beware, however, of so-called skinners with very sharp points. Unless you're a pro at skinning they're sure to puncture the hide as you work, rendering large sections of skin useless for tanning or taxidermy.

Buck Knives sells one of the best designed skinning knives in the country for $20.00. If you're into taxidermy, they also have a "trophy set" that combines their skinner with a caping knife in one sheathed package ($33.50). Their caping knife is a short-bladed one-piece knife used for delicate fleshing and skinning chores, such as around the ears, eyes, and nose of a big-game trophy head. Buck Knives, Inc., P.O. Box 1267, El Cajon, CA 92022.

Beauty in Simplicity

The clean lines of this knife speak softly of quality and common sense. The V-grind is easy to sharpen, the in-line point a style compromise that suits this blade to gutting and skinning. Blade, 5½ inches; knife, 10 inches overall. Hardwood handle. Price: $18.50. Western Cutlery Co., 5311 Western Avenue, Boulder, CO 80302. —N.S.

SKINNING SIMPLIFIED

The next time you have to skin a large animal, buy or borrow a couple of vice-grip pliers. These are pliers with an adjustable bite that lock down hard onto the surface they're gripping and stay there when you take your hand away. They make an ideal "handle" for pulling cold, slippery hides from a carcass and cost about $8.00 at your local hardware store.

"In works of labor or of skill / I would be busy too,
For Satan finds some mischief still / For idle hands to do."
—Isaac Watts, "Divine Songs"

93

THE BIG-GAME KNIFE

The big-game knife is a little like a wheel. It is simple in principle—a blade and a handle—yet infinitely complex in the many variations of design, construction, and application.

There are, however, some definite guidelines that can be laid down for a practical game knife. The first is size. Choosing a knife that is too big for comfortable carrying or accurate handling is perhaps the most common mistake made by big-game hunters. If you'll be gutting a deer or similar-sized animal (antelope, sheep, mountain goat), there's no need for a blade longer than 5 inches. The biggest of big game—moose, elk, and large bear—requires no more than a 7-inch blade. A blade longer than this becomes unwieldy and hard to control as you work with it, and it doesn't wear well on your hip.

Handle size is important too. A handle much shorter than 5 inches won't fit comfortably in your grasp.

A hunting knife should be tough, and that's where construction comes in. The blade should have a rearward extension, called a tang, that is cast or drop-forged from the same blank of steel. The handle is affixed to the tang. A tang that reaches through the handle to the butt and is then capped by a pommel makes for the strongest knife.

The type of steel the blade is made from rates as the heart of a knife. If the steel is soft, the knife will take an edge easily, but it will loose that edge during the simplest cutting chore. Steel that is too hard requires special sharpening tools that you wouldn't carry afield and that aren't normally found at home.

There is a way to determine the hardness of knife steel, called the Rockwell Hardness Test (RC for short). Most hunting knives test out to an RC between 56 and 60, and it's agreed that an RC of 58 is just about right.

The effects of blade shape, especially at the tip, is almost as widely misunderstood as knife size. Long, slender, wicked-looking tips are inherently weak and often break when subjected to the rigors of cutting cartilage and breaking soft bones. Upswept tips—those that rise above the straight line of the back of a knife—will cut into visceral material as you gut an animal, spilling stomach contents over the meat, which to put it mildly makes your steaks taste kinda funny.

The most practical blade designs will find the point in line with the knife back or dropped slightly below the back. In addition, the blade should be strong, thick, and unbending, with a flat, unsharpened back so you can guide the sweep of the edge without cutting your hand.

The most practical edge for a hunting knife is called a "dropped V." This amounts to a flat blank of steel ground on each side to form a V on the very edge. This type of edge is the strongest and least likely to nick or chip. How acutely that V is ground determines how sharp the knife can be honed, but remember, the more acute the edge, the less strength it will have and the more prone it will be to crumble under stress. As a rule of thumb, an edge that can be sharpened to 24 degrees will possess both strength and all the keenness you'll need to field dress an animal efficiently.

Several other features of big-game knives deserve mention. The so-called "blood groove," a long hollow ground into both sides of the blade, really has nothing to do with blood. It makes the blade stronger by increasing the surface area of the steel. A heel on a big-game knife—a notch cut into the sharpened edge before it touches the handle—usually ends up interfering with the cleaning process by hanging up in meat or folds of hide rather than cutting them. A choil, a cutout to accommodate your finger on the back of the blade, affords more delicate blade control, but it isn't needed so much afield as at home when you're skinning a carcass or caping out a big-game head for mounting. Graceful, sculptured handles look attractive, but the more suited they are to being held in one position, the less comfortable they will be in another position, and field dressing requires up cuts, down cuts, and side cuts at some point in the process.

Rather than an artistic expression or a conversation piece, a big-game knife should be chosen for what it really is: a tool. Look for practical lines, strong construction, and quality steel, and you'll have found a friend you can count on whenever you take to the woods.

CUSTOM-MADE HUNTING KNIVES

In the past decade, the custom hunting knife has taken its place alongside the engraved rifle or shotgun as a functional sports item that is also a personal adornment. The truly custom-made knife is virtually all hand-made by a skilled artisan and may conform either to his design or to yours.

They are not cheap. A small (5-to-6-inch) knife with minimal engraving is practically a bargain at $75.00, and $125.00 rates as a fair price for a well-wrought big-game knife.

Because these knives are not made in large numbers or widely distributed, most knife makers are unknown to the sporting public at large. The *Catalog* staff has endeavored to compile a list of the best custom knife makers. Should you wish a custom knife of your very own, these are the folks we recommend you contact, along with a few personal observations on cost and quality.

—F.S.

CUSTOM KNIFE MAKERS

John R. Applebaugh
Thunderbird Custom Knives
912 South Second Street
Blackwell, OK 74631

W. P. Bagwell
P.O. Box 869
Vivian, LA 71082

Ralph Bone
The Bone Knife Co., Inc.
806 Avenue J
Lubbock, TX 79401

Lew Booth
Booth Custom Cutlery
16 Cypress Terrace
Boonton, NJ 07005

Roderick Choppee
Daves Knives, Inc.
P.O. Box 148
Airway Heights, WA 99001
(this guy is great)

J. Nelson Cooper
P.O. Box 1423
Burbank, CA 90515

Dan Denneby
Dan-D Knives
P.O. Box 4479
Yunia, AZ 85364

T. M. Dowell
T.M.D. Knives
139 Saint Helens Place
Bend, OR 97701
(works part-time but puts out
   good stuff, copied Loveless lines)

Clyde Fisher
Fisher Custom Knives
Route #1, P.O. Box 170M
Victoria, TX 77901
(good prices)

Heinrich H. Frank
Mountain Meadow Road
Whitefish, MT 59937
(engraver and pocketknife maker)

Bucher Gascon
P.O. Box 398
Brusly, LA 70719

Thomas M. Enos III
Route 1
Winter Garden, FL 32787

Lloyd Hale
3305 Barkwood Road
Texarkana, TX 75501

D. E. Henry
Star Route
Mountain Ranch, CA 95246

George H. Herron
920 Murrah
Aiken, SC 29801
(part-time, possibly going full-time)

Gil Hibben
P.O. Box 3914
Anchorage, AK 99501

Cubby Hueske
Cubby Hueske Knives
4808 Tamarish
Bellaire, TX 77401
(part-time maker)

La Don Johnston
2322 West Country Club Parkway
Toledo, OH 43614
(part-time, but Dixie Firearms
   sells his stuff)

Walter Kneubukle
W. K. Knives
P.O. Box 327
Pioneer, OH 43554

James B. Lile
Route 1, Box 56
Russellville, AR 72801

William F. Moran, Jr.
Route #5
Frederick, MD 21701

Jim Mustin
Cajun Handmade Knives
P.O. Box 149
Liberty, MS 39645

Ralph W. Prouty
Prouty Custom Knives
5240 Southwest 9th Drive
Portland, OR 97221

Jim Pugh
Pugh Made Knives
917 Carpenter Street
Azle, TX 76020

R. H. Ruana
P.O. Box 574
Bonner, MT 59823

A. G. Russell
Morseth Knives
1705 Highway 71 North
Springdale, AR 72764

Blackie Sewell
Collins Brothers Knives
593 Westminster Drive NE
Atlanta, GA 30324

Corbet R. Segman
Star Route #1, P.O. Box 3
Red House, WV 25168

William J. Sonneville
1050 West Chalet Street
Mobile, AL 76608

Bernard Sparks
Dingle, ID 83223

G. W. Stone
Stone Knives, Inc.
703 Floyd Road
Richardson, TX 75080

Zack Knives
Don Zaccagnino
P.O. Box ZACK
Pokokee, FL 33476

Frank Centofante
P.O. Box 17587
Tampa, FL 33612
(part-time)

Harvey Draper
Draper Blade, Inc.
519 East State Road
America Fort, UT 84003

Merle Seguine
Box 989
Juneau, AK 99801
(he puts out a great knife)

Howard Lemery
P.O. Box 98
Knoxboro, NY 13362
(part-time, good knife)

A. G. RUSSELL KNIFE CATALOG OF CUSTOMS AND COLLECTIBLES

One of the best-known custom knife makers in the United States, A. G. Russell, publishes a catalog of knives. The featured merchandise reflects quality and custom lines. Aside from Russell's own creations, there are hunting knives by Morseth, Hen and Rooster, Gerber, Buck, Boker Tree Brand, and Puma. He also lists associated materials such as do-it-yourself knife kits, sharpening stones, and books about knife history, manufacture, and care.

Several unusual services are also offered by the Russell firm. One is a knife collector's club. For $5.00 you get a membership card and a monthly illustrated mailing of collector's knives and their prices. Russell also makes appraisals of existing collections and functions as a kind of clearinghouse for handmade knives.

Knife makers consign their products to the company, which in turn prints circulars illustrating and describing the knives on hand. These circulars are then sent out periodically. Given the long waiting lists for true custom handmade knives, this is one way to get a knife by someone like Loveless, Horn, Lake, Hale, or Henry pronto.

For further information on this service and others, or a Russell catalog, write: A. G. Russell Co., 1705 Highway 71 North, Springdale, AR 72764.

SMITH AND WESSON OUTDOORSMAN

A sensibly styled, general-purpose hunting and camping knife. Notable features include a contoured handle, dropped point, and a hollow handle interior reached by a screw-on pommel that makes an ideal place for matches, string, fishhooks, and other survival gear. Has 440-series stainless-steel blade.

Overall length, 10 inches, blade length, 5½ inches. Weight, 10 ounces. All in all, this looks like an excellent design and a high-quality product. Price: $45.00. Smith and Wesson Co., 2100 Roosevelt Avenue, Springfield MA 01101.

The Classic Hunting Knife

Those things called "hunting knives" have become trendy of late, with points sweeping up, and sweeping down, and sculptured handles and stuff. While there's something to be said for the knife as art, there will always be a need for a knife as a proven functional tool.

Case Cutlery's No. 364 SAB is a classic of the genre, a pure hunting knife of the type that's graced sportsmen's hips since before Grandpa's day. Features include a short clip point, blood groove, dropped V-grind, and a leather handle. You can argue all day about fine points, but you can bet your poke that this kind of knife will get the job done. Price: $13.50. Case Cutlery, Bradford, PA 16701.

Track Bonecracker

One of the hardest jobs that faces a big-game knife is splitting an animal's pelvic bone. The Track Bonecracker is designed with that job in mind. Aside from standard features that make it an admirable gutting and skinning knife, the Bonecracker has a 2-inch-wide chisel-back feature that you can hammer on (this is the easiest way to get through a pelvic bone).

The blade is of high-carbon/nickel vanadium steel and has a satin finish. The handle is Micarta with carved finger grooves. A good knife for all big game. Price: $74.95. Ithaca Gun Co., Inc., 123 Lake Street, Ithaca, NY 14850. Free catalog.

WYOMING BIG-GAME KNIFE

The Wyoming Big-Game Knife is truly one of a kind. As a matter of fact, folks have trouble identifying it as a knife. It looks more like a pair of brass knuckles with a can opener built in.

The primary blade is shaped like a shark's fin. It is used for skinning, slicing, and cutting breast cartilage. The secondary, opposing blade is really a gutting hook. Make an incision into an animal's stomach cavity, insert the gutting hook, and pull. The stomach walls open up like a zipper. The handle, with fingerholes, fits

Bowie Knife

We include this knife under mild protest. It is emphatically *not* a hunting knife. But everybody knows about Bowies, and someone is bound to ask, "How come it's not mentioned?"

In fact, it should rightly be included in the section on collectibles and antiques. It is a classic of American design and ingenuity that surely has a place in the sportsman's world—on his wall. True, it helped carve out frontier living 150 years ago, but the contemporary outdoorsman has little use for a blade that big. In the words of a friend, "Bowies are too big to gut game and too small for profitable logging." Price: $35.00. Western Cutlery Co., 5311 Western Avenue, Boulder, CO 80302.   —J.B.

comfortably in your grasp and is more sensitive than a conventional handle. The blades are also replaceable. This is truly a revolutionary idea, and it works! Price: $13.95. Wyoming Knife Corp., 115 Valley Drive, Casper, WY 82601. Free catalog.

Ensign Knives

The Ensign Company makes what is called a one-piece big-game knife. My reaction the first time I saw one was the same as most people's: Where's the handle? Essentially the one-piece knife is a flat piece of steel with a blade formed and a flat handle. Once you get used to its looks it's not bad at all. The knife I looked over was their drop-point design, the SDP. It takes a nice edge—the blade is 3½ inches long, about right for most hunting—and the handle is texturized for a nonslip grip, as well as having a serrated section where the thumb comes in contact

with the knife. This "handleless" design allows the knife to lie closer to the body when carried in the black leather sheath that is provided, and, like the flat handles on many folding knives, it allows a certain amount of control that is missing with round-handled knives. The most important aspect of the knife, however, is that the design lowers costs, so a quality knife is available for $12.50, postpaid. This includes the sheath. They also make a swept-point design, the SSP, for the same price. Ensign Co., Gunnison, UT 84634.

—J. B.

Tips on a Folding Big-Game Knife

Folding big-game knives are "in" at the moment, but before you buy, consider this: a folder can never be as strong as a traditional one-piece hunting knife. Then, too, a folding knife capable of gutting big game must be large, not really suited to pocket storage. In fact, most of them come with a belt sheath, just like one-piece knives. Finally, they're hard to keep clean of meat, fat, and hair.

If, however, a folder is a must on your list, here are a few tips on buying one. Choose a knife with only one blade. Multi-bladed folders are weaker than single-bladed knives; the more blades that hinge on the bolster pin, the weaker the knife will be. Get a positive locking device on the blade to prevent it from closing on your hand should you inadvertently use the blade the wrong way.

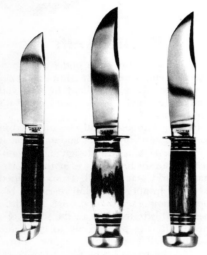

Marble's Hunting Knives

Clean lines and hand manufacture at reasonable prices characterize the Marble knife line. Other features worthy of mention include: extra-large handles so they heft well with gloves on, high carbon manganese steel, and a full tang that extends from the blade back to the pommel. The slightly dropped tip, V-grind blade bevel, and broad blade make these real working knives. They come with leather sheaths.

Top: 5-inch Hunter with tigerwood handle, $26.00; middle: 5-inch Stag Hunter with stag handle, $44.95; bottom: 4-inch Campcraft with leather handle, $15.95. Marble's, P.O. Box 111, Gladstone, MI 49837. Free catalog.

Sod Buster

This single-bladed folder includes a straight-back blade, making it a good combination gutting/skinning knife. It is available in chrome-vanadium or stainless steel, with or without a lock-open feature.

The standard Sod Buster measures 4⅝ inches closed, the junior measures 3⅝ inches closed. Prices: $12.50 to $21.00; leather sheath, $3.50. Case Cutlery, Bradford, PA 16701.

The Apollo line of hunting knives is made of rust-proofed steel coated with Dupont Teflon. This gives the blade a non-stick easy-sliding surface which is easy to maintain and keep clean. Apollo handles are made of a nonstaining synthetic material. They have molded finger grips and a nonslip surface, and the handle material is bonded to the knife tang. Sheaths are formed from heavy-duty plastic, and they're molded to the contours of the knife blade.

These knives are especially well suited to hunting in humid climates and around salt water, and they are useful in the preparation of a carcass for butchering because they are easy to keep clean.

Three sheath models make up the Apollo line: the Ranger, a general-purpose knife with a straight back, the Cape Skinner, and the African Hunter, a typical "hunting knife" with a clip-type blade. Price: $12.00. Jet-Aer Corp., 100 6th Avenue, Paterson, NJ 07524.

Apollo Knives

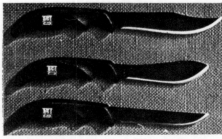

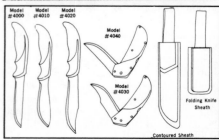

"Better to hunt in fields, for health unbought,
Than fee the doctor for a nauseous draught."
—John Dryden

97

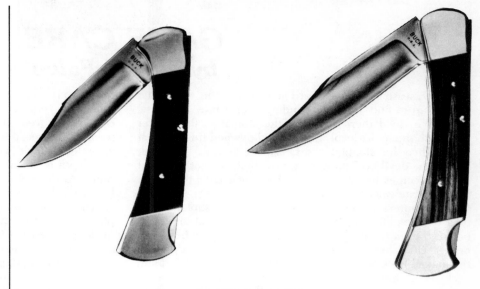

Powder River Folding Knife

Here's a very interesting and practical big-game folder. It opens on the butterfly principle, which makes for an exceptionally strong blade hinge. The hinge itself is a sturdy nut-and-bolt-like assembly, and, indeed, the knife will break down into its component parts—all of which are replaceable! This makes for a few other unusual features in a folder. It can be thoroughly and easily cleaned, broken or chipped blades can be quickly replaced by you, and any lost part can be ordered from the manufacturer.

I haven't tried this knife out personally, so I can't speak of steel, sharpness, or heft. But the blade shape looks perfect for a big-game knife, and the manufacturers claim a super-sharp edge that lasts. All in all, I'm sending for one. If it's an inferior knife with a lot of bugs that doesn't catch on, it will become a collector's item. If it's as good as is claimed, it has to be the best folding knife on the market. Price: $32.00 (with leather sheath). Wyoming Knife Corp., 115 Valley Drive, Casper, WY 82601.

Buck Folding Knives

Famous for its line of folding knives, the Buck company also features a line of standard sheath knives, sharpening products, pocket knives, and a small Hunter's Axe. Their motto is "Famous for Holding an Edge," and indeed they do. I've carried a Folding Hunter for the last three big-game seasons and have field dressed as many as four deer without even having to touch up the blade. This knife folds up small enough to fit in a pocket (4⅞ inches). The folding Ranger is a similar, smaller model which folds into 4¼ inches. I also like the squared handle of the folding knives—it gives me an idea of where the edge of the blade is pointing even when I can't see it, such as when I'm working inside a deer's body cavity. The same sort of feel isn't possible with round handles. The folding Hunter is probably their most popular model and retails for $22.00, which includes a belt sheath, but the best bet for the deer hunter would probably be the Esquire model, featuring a drop-point blade and folds into 3¾ inches, which retails for $18.00. They also have a good little free booklet, called "Knife Know-How," that you can get by writing to them. Buck Knives, Inc., P.O. Box 1267, El Cajon, CA 92022. —J.B.

PROTECT MEAT FROM BLOWFLIES

If you hang a carcass while the weather is warm, there are two ways to keep the flies off the meat. If you can get the carcass over 12 feet off the ground, flies will not be a serious problem. A somewhat simpler solution is to cover the meat with netting or cheesecloth, something that will allow breezes to cool the carcass and keep flies out. Deer Bag, $0.99. Cabela's, 812 13th Street, Sidney, NE 69162.

LITTLE LIFTER HOIST

This block-and-tackle hoist weighs less than three pounds, yet it will lift up to 1,000 pounds. It's handy for getting *big* game (like elk or moose) up off the ground and for moving heavy loads short distances. It is not all simple to use, however. The lines have a habit of twisting, and should the blocks flip over inside the coils of line, it takes a Houdini to unsnarl the crisscrosses and get the lifter back in efficient working order. Price: $11.49. Cabela's, 812 13th Avenue, Sidney, NE 69162.

Apollo Folding Big-Game Knives

These folding hunters come in two blade styles: the Scout, with a straight back, and the Rancher, with a clip point that drops down to meet the tip. Both are 5¼ inches long in the closed position.

These knives have a locking device and synthetic side plates, with Teflon-coated blades. The purchase price includes a plastic sheath. Price: $17.00. Jet-Aer Corp., 100 6th Avenue, Paterson, NJ 07524.

GAME CARE
by Joe DeFalco

A few seasons ago, I heard a shot on the ridge and walked up to find a hunter standing over a fine, fat young buck. We stood there admiring the animal as the hunter told, with dramatic detail, how he had downed this, his first deer. Then he stopped short, looked at me, and said, "What the devil do I do with it, now that I've got it?" That question comes to many hunters each year after they have fired the fatal shot.

Most hunters do not realize that if you have shot a trophy buck or intend to have the head mounted, special care must be given from the moment the deer is killed. The head and neck region should be carefully protected while dragging the animal back to camp. The sooner the trophy (head and neck) is in the hands of a taxidermist, the better your chances are of getting back a mount that you will be proud of. The flavor of the meat, also, in most cases, depends on the manner in which it is field dressed. All this has to be kept in mind as you prepare to field dress your deer.

A deer should be dressed out in the exact spot in which it was downed. Dragging causes hemorrhaging. Run your fingers down the breastbone of the deer until you reach the first part of the soft upper belly. At this point, just below the breastbone, insert the point of your knife. Penetrate the skin completely, about ¼ inch or so, but not so deeply as to cut the intestines. Make a small cut of approximately ½ inch . . . and step back. Most of the time gas will escape from the deer with a hissing sound. This gas sometimes has a foul odor.

After all the gas has escaped, reinsert your knife and extend your incision the whole length of the belly wall down to the pelvis. If the belly wall is pulled toward you and the sharp edge of the knife is faced away from the intestine, there will be little chance of cutting these intestines, but be careful of your own fingers! The intestines will then be exposed and will fall out of the belly. Put your hand over the cavity and over the liver. Pull down on the liver, which lies mostly on the right side of the deer. This will expose the diaphragm, a smooth muscle that separates the chest cavity from the abdominal cavity. Cut the diaphragm where it is attached to the lower ribs, in a circular manner. Place your hand into the chest cavity and over the heart. Pull down firmly on the heart. Now, with your knife go as high as possible into the chest cavity up to the neck region. Cut across the windpipe (trachea) and the feeding tube (esophagus), which lies behind the windpipe. Gradually cut all the attachments of the heart and pull out the chest contents. Detach the heart and liver and put them into a polyethylene bag.

The attachments of the intestines to the back wall of the deer are either pulled loose or cut. The kidneys (bean-shaped) will be easily seen and removed. They too are put into the plastic bag. Do not cut the neck to bleed the deer, as the blood will drain out when the deer is hung. The in-

testines are now only attached to the body by the rectal tube. It is very important that this tube be completely and cleanly removed. Below the base of the tail, the opening (vent) of the rectal tube will be seen. This should be widely encircled (3-inch diameter), with the knife deeply inserted to a depth of at least 5 inches. Encircle at least two or three times. At this point, put your hand inside the deer and pull firmly on the rectal tube. It may be loose, but if it remains attached, cut around the tube from inside to release it completely. As you can see, the new opening that has been made is at least 3 inches in diameter and will serve as a drain when the deer is hung head high.

At this point, step behind the deer and tilt it away from you in order to drain as much blood out of the cavity as possible. This should be done quickly, as blood congeals rapidly. Your deer is now properly field dressed.

With the price of meat today, most smart hunters will learn the right method for game care. It pays big dividends in the long run.

Good Hunting!

Joe De Falco rose to fame as a deer hunter in New York's Catskill Mountains. His lectures on game care have drawn traffic-snarling audiences. He regularly hosts his own sports show on TV, the *Outdoorsman*.

"The mountain sheep are sweeter, / But the valley sheep are fatter;
We therefore deemed it meeter / To carry off the latter."
—Thomas Love Peacock

99

BUT WE AIN'T GOT NO MOOSE
by Jerome Knap

When I was a young fellow, still in my early twenties, I served a stint as a forest ranger in some of northern Ontario's best moose country. One fall afternoon, three or four weeks into the moose season, I was driving down a logging road in my government pickup when a scarlet-clad hunter jumped out of the bushes and excitedly flailed his arms about.

"Boy, am I glad to see you!" he shouted excitedly. "I just shot a great big moose over there!"

"Congratulations," I answered, "but what's the problem?"

"The problem is I don't know what to do," the hunter stammered. "I've shot deer before, but no one told me how big a moose was. Can you come and show me what to do? And maybe take a picture of me with the moose? I'd be glad to pay you." Excitement was rushing through his veins. The man's hands shook like poplar leaves in an autumn breeze.

"Yeah, I guess I'd better show you what to do," I replied, shaking my head. "Payment won't be necessary."

The first problem was to find the moose. The man in his agitated state couldn't remember exactly where to look, but eventually we found it. It was a young bull, not at all big as bull moose go. Even the rack was small, but it had nicely shaped, even palms.

The second problem was to find the rifle. While trying to take a picture of the dead moose, the man had laid his rifle down and couldn't remember where.

I finally located the rifle, some 30 feet from the moose by a pile of slash. After emptying the magazine, I posed the hunter and his .300 Weatherby with the moose and took several pictures with the camera the man was carrying. In fact, he insisted that I shoot the whole roll just to make sure one photo would turn out.

Next I dressed the moose, while the hunter marched around saying, "This animal is bigger than a horse."

While I was dressing the moose, I found out that the hunter was a farmer from Indiana and that he'd had a bumper corn crop. As a result he'd decided to take a holiday—a moose hunt—and had driven to Ontario the day before. He'd heard that the northern Ontario woods were full of moose, and now he knew they were. Next year he'd bring along a couple of friends.

"How are you going to get this moose home?" I asked him.

"Oh, I have a car on a side road up a ways."

"Once this moose is cut up and wrapped you'll be able to get it into your car," I replied.

"Are you kidding?" the Indianan replied. "I'm taking this moose back whole! I want everybody back home to see him."

Well, I suggested that perhaps he rent a U-Haul trailer in Hearst or Kapuskasing and haul the moose home that way. I also suggested that a couple of ten-dollar bills would probably get a tractor with a fork lift from a nearby logging camp to load the moose into the trailer. With that I left to go about my business.

Returning a couple of hours later, I found the Indiana moose hunter on the logging road with a tractor, a fork lift, and a couple of lumberjacks just finishing a bottle of Old Moose Hunter. The moose was tied onto the roof of a big late-model Buick.

The animal hung over the roof on all sides. There was no way that it would stay on for the ride down the logging road, let alone the trip to Indiana. But even worse, the weight of the moose had completely flattened the Buick's roof.

"Well that was a stupid fool thing to do," I said in slightly more colorful language. "It'll cost you two or three hundred bucks to have that roof fixed."

"Don't worry about that, son," came the reply. "In Indiana we got lots of Buicks, but we ain't got no moose."

Jerome Knap lives and writes in moose country, near Guelph, Ontario. He's a frequent contributor to outdoor magazines and sits on the board of directors of the Outdoor Writers Association of America.

WHAT WILL IT WEIGH IN THE FREEZER?

To determine the amount of edible meat on a cleanly killed carcass, subtract one pound from each four pounds of field-dressed deer.

A word as to knife or knives. These are of prime necessity, and should be of the best, both as to shape and temper. The "bowies" and "hunting knives" usually kept on sale, are thick, clumsy affairs, with a sort of ridge along the middle of the blade, murderous-looking, but of little use; rather fitted to adorn a dime novel or the belt of "Billy the Kid," than the outfit of the hunter.

—Nessmuk

KNIVES
by Ken Warner

New York: Winchester Press, $10.00.

This book is all about knives for sport and utility—how they are designed, how to make them, and how to use them. The Eskimo would starve without his flensing knife, and the Gurkha would be a push-over without his kukri. The modern outdoorsman, usually only minutes away from an electric carving knife and other comforts, is not so dependent on the edge he carries—yet he carries it, and of all outdoor accoutrements, the good knife is perhaps the one he values most. Partly this is because a knife can be handsome to look at and pleasant to handle—a well-crafted tool. But it is also because a knife in knowledgeable hands is a true equalizer. The sportsman's knife makes him master of his environment—backyard or backveld. This book explains design and construction of both commercial and home-crafted knives, establishes standards for judging their quality, and describes their use in detail.

AN ENCYCLOPEDIA OF KNIVES
by Norman Strung

Philadelphia: J. B. Lippincott Company, $12.50.

Most hunters have a drawer full of knives. Many of these were purchased with little or no attention paid to the purpose of the knife in the first place. Careful thought would save us all a pocketful of change as well as a mess of unused knives.

Norman Strung's book, *An Encyclopedia of Knives*, would probably have saved this pocket full of change *and* let us face the purchase of a knife with more knowledge. He covers the manufacturing of knives and the sharpening and care needed to keep the knife in proper condition. He describes outdoor knives used by hunters and fisherman, butcher knives for the home butcher, and food knives and general household blades such as chisels and pocket knives.

As the title states, this is a reference book and should be used as such. No hunter is without a good knife. Neither should he be without *An Encyclopedia of Knives*.

—Dick Weden

"Hunting doesn't degrade an animal. It's not as bad as what we do to our domestic animals; they become more debased as they become suited to our purpose."
—Patrick Hemingway

101

BUTCHER TOOLS AND KNIVES

A few years ago, Congress saw fit to enact legislation to protect the consumer from impure meats. Perhaps these laws did the public at large some good, but they also did big-game hunters some bad. The way the laws were conceived and written, game animals and domestic animals had to be processed and even cooled out, in separate facilities. This had the net effect of making it more difficult to get your deer cut up, and it became a lot more expensive. A lot of butchers simply bowed out of the game processing business. Those who stayed had to rebuild their facilities, and the cost was passed on to you. To give you some idea of the difference in prices, in 1965, you could have your deer cooled, skinned, cut, wrapped, and frozen for 9 cents per pound if you shopped around. Today, the going rate is 27 to 30 cents per pound for the same service . . . if you can find someone to do it.

There is a better, cheaper way, and that's to do it yourself. The basic tools aren't expensive—knives, cleavers, saws, and the like. More sophisticated machinery and furniture (meat choppers, grinders, and chopping blocks) require a much larger investment, but they might be worth it if you can get several of your hunting partners to chip in. You might even consider going into the butcher business yourself on the Q.T. I know of a couple of enterprising folks who do custom cutting in their kitchen or garage at 17 to 20 cents a pound, and they clear in the neighborhood of $10.00 an hour!

To be a basic butcher, you'll need four tools.

- *A meat saw.* This looks like an overgrown hacksaw. It has a highly tempered blade and specially tuned teeth for cutting through bone. Like a hacksaw, its blade is replaceable. If you buy a meat saw, make sure the manufacturer sells blade replacements (order a few with the saw), since the blade is brittle and breaks fairly easily. Like all cutting tools, it will eventually become dull, and the hard steel isn't worth the time it takes to sharpen it. If you don't want to hassle with a meat saw, a fine-toothed crosscut carpenter's saw will get the job done, but it will dull quickly, so you'll have to learn how to sharpen a crosscut.

Use your meat saw to cut the deer in half by following the back line from tail to neck, use it to cut off legs and the small pieces of bone in the middle of round steaks, and use it to cut the bones in roasts.

- *A cleaver.* Cleavers come in weights from ½ to 5 pounds. I like a 2-to-3-pound cleaver for deer, a 4-pound cleaver for elk and moose. Use a cleaver (with much vigor) to chop ribs free from the carcass and then to reduce them to cooking-sized squarish chunks for your barbecue. After you've cut the back meat into chop-sized chunks with a slicing knife, use the cleaver to cut through the bone and separate the chops. The easiest way to do this is to lay the edge of the cleaver against the bone and then hit the back of the cleaver with a leather mallet. You can use a 16-ounce claw hammer, but eventually you'll break shards of steel off the back of the cleaver, and they're hard to chew.

- *A boning knife.* These knives have long, slender blades, with a stiff back. They are used to separate meat from bone—to filet it, if you will. You will find use for two boning knives; one with a 5-inch blade and one with a 7-inch blade.

- *A butcher knife.* This is really a bad term; I can think of no other tool in the cutlery realm that is kicked around more. So let's define this knife as having a blade between 10 and 14 inches long, with a depth of at least 1½ inches between back and edge. Like boning knives, I like to have two of these butcher knives while I work, one with a short blade and one with a long blade. I use the short blade on chops and roasts, the long blade on large steaks.

—N.S.

BAJA CAMP SAW FROM DICK CEPEK

This is a handy little saw that looks ideal for *big* big-game hunters, those guys that go after elk and moose and mammoth and need something more substantial than the old sheath knife to cut the beast up into smaller pieces. It's built like a big pocket knife and locks solidly in place. Price: $5.95 postpaid. Dick Cepek, Inc., 9201 California Avenue, South Gate, CA 90280.

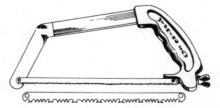

Super Saw Cuts Wood and Bone at Home and at Camp

This product belongs to the "why didn't somebody think of this before?" class. It is a collapsible bow-type saw with replaceable blades. Two blades come with the saw, one for wood and one for bone. The entire unit breaks down into an 11½-by-2¾-inch package that fits into a leather carrying case that may be worn on your belt (weight, 18 ounces).

No, we don't feel that this would replace a butcher's meat saw at home, because the short stroke of the blade would make it difficult to saw a carcass in two. But all things considered, if you can afford just one saw for camp and meat cutting, this looks like the one. Price: $24.00. Wyoming Knife Corp., 115 Valley Drive, Casper, WY 82601.

CUTTING BLOCK

This hardwood cutting block, 8⅝ by 10⅛ inches, has the butt ends of wood blocks as a surface. You won't make splinters as you slice. It comes with a small boning knife and a magnet which holds the knife to the side of the block. Price $15.50. L. L. Bean, Freeport, ME 04033.

TOUCH-UP STONES

As the knife cuts hide or meat, hide or meat cuts knife. Any material will eventually dull a knife. At that time, you can restore its edge to razor keenness with a touch-up stone.

Three stones are packaged in a clear plastic pouch: a square stone for knives and arrowheads, a round stone for axes, hatchets, and machetes, and a hook honer with a groove for fishhooks. Price: $2.50. Worth Co., Stevens Point, WI 54481.

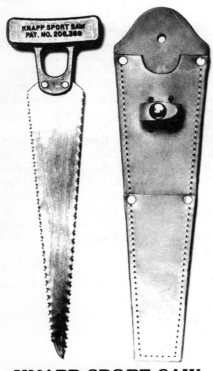

KNAPP SPORT SAW

This is an excellent tool for on-the-spot quartering of large game. The blade is one piece (nonfolding), 10½ inches long, with teeth on both sides. One set of teeth is fine for thick bone, the other coarse for cartilage. The T-shaped handle rests in the palm of your hand, and your middle finger goes through the hole in the center, so you can bring a lot of pressure to bear as you saw up and down.

It comes with a leather belt sheath that also has a pocket for a 6-inch- or smaller-bladed hunting knife. Price: $10.95. Cabela's, 812 13th Avenue, Sidney, NE 69162.

IF YOU CAN'T SHARPEN A HUNTING KNIFE

This tool is guaranteed to give you a perfect edge every time. It is a clamplike device that elevates the back of a knife blade to whatever angle you wish. Rest the edge of the knife and the clamp underside on a stone, and move the blade into the grit an equal number of strokes on each side. A blade-to-stone angle of 12 degrees will create an edge sharp enough to shave with (may not be used on knives less than ⅝ inch from back to edge).

Buck Honemaster, $5.00. Buck Knives, P.O. Box 1267, El Cajon, CA 92022.

Heavy-duty Game Shears

If you have trouble swinging a cleaver accurately, here's another way to trim legs and wings off gamebirds, rabbits, and squirrels. These sturdy, stainless-steel shears have large, cushioned finger holes so you can exert a lot of pressure. They can be used against a flat surface, too, so you can bear down with both hands. The short blades assure maximum leverage. Also useful on hides, frozen foods, and other hard-to-cut items. Price: $9.95. Super Game Shears, 79 West 1st Street South, Salt Lake City, UT 84111.

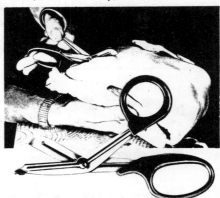

Leather Mallet

This tool consists of a heavy pot-metal ring that holds a concentrically wound 3-inch strip of rawhide. It's normally used to strike chisels, but it's also handy when cleaving meat. Tap the cleaver on the back with the mallet to make accurate cuts without the inaccuracy inherent in a haymaker swing. Price: $10.20. C. S. Osborne Co., Harrison, NJ 07029.

"Alone far in the wilds and mountains I hunt, / . . . Kindling a fire and broiling the fresh-kill'd game. / Falling asleep . . . with my dog and gun by my side."
—Walt Whitman, "Song of Myself"

103

Whetstones

Smith Cutlery has an entire line of Arkansas (Novaculite) whetstones available. All four grades of Arkansas stone—Washita, soft, hard, and black hard—are available in numerous sizes from 3-by-1-by-¼-inch pocket stones on up to 12-by-2-by-1-inch bench stones, with combination stones, paddlestones, bench stones mounted in cedar, hard Arkansas stone files, and fish stones (for sharpening hooks) made also. The best all-around stone is the soft Arkansas. It is reasonably fast cutting (though not as fast as the Washita) and yet can produce a razor edge with light pressure. I used a Smith soft Arkansas pocket stone to touch up my arrow razorheads this season. These pocket-sized stones are excellent for carrying in the woods, but for home use a bigger stone would be advised, such as the Hard Arkansas/Washita combination stone, which is 4 by 1 by ½ inches. The Washita (softest) grade is the best stone I've found yet for putting an edge on the super-hard knife blades put out by the Buck company. Smith also makes an excellent honing oil. Smith Cutlery and Whetstone, 262 Central, Hot Springs, AR 71901.
—J.B.

Pocket Hoist 500

This is a small (2-pound) hoist that consists of a spool on which is wound a steel belt. Power is by a crank. It will lift 500 pounds 12 feet, and there is a warning click that sounds when the support level is reached. Price: $46.00. Cam-Gear Industries, P.O. Box 1002, Kalispell, MT 59901.

Simple Hunter's Hoist

This hoist is more than powerful enough to hang a big deer high. Although the mechanical advantage isn't great, I view it as a kind of plus; 10-to-1 and 20-to-1 hoists have so many lines that it's almost impossible to keep them clear. Price: $9.00. Precise Imports, 3 Chestnut Street, Suffern, NY 10901.
—F.S.

Butchering Tip

Wrap all cuts of meat tightly in a good grade of butcher paper (one side lined with plastic), tape it closed, then wrap it once again. Meat will keep up to two years in a freezer protected this way.

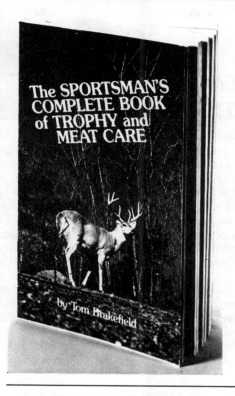

KNIFE-SHARPENING SERVICE: BARGAIN USED KNIVES

L&M Grinding serves restaurants and butchers in the New York area, and in that capacity they also buy used knives. This is a super source for bargain-basement prices on professional knives and butcher tools, and they'll put a razor edge on any knife for $.75 to $1.50, plus postage. L&M Grinding Service, 39-20 61st Street, Woodside, NY 11377.
—F.S.

SMALL BONING KNIFE

The slender, short (4½-inch) blade on Case's No. 307 boning knife is ideal for delicate butchering jobs, such as separating joints, boning out hams and haunches, and trimming bloodshot meat from bullet holes. Carbon steel blade, and synthetic, sculptured handle. Price: $6.00. Case Cutlery, Bradford, PA 16701.

THE SPORTSMAN'S COMPLETE BOOK OF TROPHY AND MEAT CARE

by Tom Brakefield

Harrisburg, Pa.: Stackpole Books, $8.95.

What to do after your hunting trip has produced a magnificent specimen you want to preserve as a trophy and proper in-field care of an animal to assure maximum enjoyment of the meat at the table—these are the subjects of this book. The aim of the author is to help any hunter become a more complete sportsman by learning to handle the animal between the field and the table. Big-game butchering, small game, game birds, and fish are all covered in the book. Photos and diagrams, some of his own trophy room, give hints on ensuring satisfactory results from a taxidermist, and Brakefield suggests secondary trophies that are within anyone's range. He includes ideas on keeping trophies clean and attractive for many years. An excellent book to round out the hunter's reference bookshelf.

GAMBRELS

Gambrels look a little bit like a clothes hanger and are used to hang game for skinning and quartering. They're handy in that they keep the animal's feet spread-eagled while you work with a knife or saw.

We tried this gambrel on two deer, and it worked fine. However, it did wilt a little when we put the pressure on the frozen hide of a calf elk. Price: $7.45. Baker Manufacturing Co., P.O. Box 1003, Valdosta, GA 31601.

SHARPENING STEELS

The proper function of a knife steel isn't sharpening in the true sense. In order to sharpen a really dull knife, economy of motion dictates that you go through a series of very coarse to fine abrasive grits until you have honed a keen edge bevel. At this point, the steel is brought to play to impart that final brilliant sharpness that shaves hair.

Steels are also useful as a touch-up medium. They will return that sharpness, for a while, to a properly beveled edge that has been dulled by normal cutting.

A sampling of knife steels would include the following:

- *Steelmaster*. A sheath-and-steel combination constructed so the 5-inch steel locks into the metal sheath by way of a cam, the sheath then providing a handle. This is an uncommonly abrasive steel, capable of light sharpening as well as touch-up. Price: $12.00. Buck Knives, P.O. Box 1267, El Cajon, CA 92022.

- *Moonstick*. The moonstick is a solid dowel of compressed aluminum oxide, with a handle and a belt sheath. Because it is round, it is somewhat easier to maintain a regular blade angle-to-stone orientation than with a flat steel. A disadvantage to the moonstick afield is that it must be cleaned with a household abrasive cleanser like Ajax when a gray metaling sheen indicates clogged pores in the material. But you can touch up ten or twelve knives before this is necessary. Price: $6.50. Case Cutlery, Bradford, PA 16701.

- *Gerber Steel*. This is a compact, flat-surfaced steel with rounded edges that can be packed in your pocket or on your belt. It is most effective at sharpening when you bear a lot of pressure on the knife edge, which in turn makes it hard to maintain blade to steel orientation. Price: $14.00. Gerber, 14200 Southwest 72nd Avenue, Portland, OR 97223.

Where to Buy Butcher Tools Locally

You can usually find butcher tools in the hardware departments of stores around farm country. In the big city, look in the Yellow Pages of your phone book under Restaurant Supplies. You can also inquire at any restaurant as to where they get their supplies.

LARGE BONING KNIFE

This 6-inch blade is made from high-carbon steel, the steel generally agreed upon as best by professional meat cutters. The hardwood handle is secured by three sets of compressed rivets. A good knife for big boning jobs: neck, shoulder blade, backstrap, and so on. Price: $3.75. Old Forge Cutlery, Bradford, PA 16701.

CLEAVERS

A 2½- to 3-pound cleaver is sufficient for most big-game butchering jobs. Koch makes 40- and 45-ounce cleavers, with hardwood handles and an RC of 55, for $9.90 and $11.00 respectively. Koch Supplies, 1411 West 29th Street, Kansas City, MO 64108.

STEAK SCIMITAR

Here's the kind of knife that will lop off steaks and chops in smooth, even slices. The ten-inch blade and scimitar tip, properly sharpened, will cut its way through a ham-sized round steak in two strokes or through a loin chop in one. Carbon steel blade, hardwood handle. Price: $10.95. Case Cutlery, Bradford, PA 16701.

Butcher Saw

A good bone saw is the one prerequisite to processing your own game. You can cut meat with kitchen knives, but getting through bone with any blade other than one specifically designed for this purpose either makes a lot of work or ruins your saw.

Koch catalogs a standard butcher saw with a 25-inch replaceable blade, 12 teeth to the inch: a bargain, considering the jobs it will do. Saw, $10.00; extra blades, $9.00 per dozen. Koch Supplies, 1411 West 29th Street, Kansas City, MO 64108.

MEAT GRINDER

If you do a lot of butchering, you'll benefit by owning a meat grinder. Venison burger is great in a meat loaf, in spaghetti sauce, or grilled over coals in the backyard.

You can buy a hand meat grinder at most hardware stores. This clamps to a table and cranks out ground meat by muscle power.

With a little ingenuity, you can also power a hand meat grinder. Eli Spannagel, inventor, entrepreneur, and Montana rancher, has made a classic. With the addition of a few universal joints, a drive shaft, a ½-hp electric motor, and the transmission out of an old Fiat, he created what must be the first—and probably only—meat grinder with four forward speeds and reverse. The meat really flies as you go through the gears, and if the knives get clogged you can always back up.

If you really want to be professional, commercial-grade powered choppers will convert 5 pounds of venison to hamburger per minute. They are expensive, but you can often get a group of friends to chip in on the price. Motorized meat grinder (⅓ hp motor), $259.00. Koch Supplies, 1411 West 29th Street, Kansas City, MO 64108.

"Now I see the secret of making the best persons.
It is to grow in the open air and to eat and sleep with the earth."
—Walt Whitman

105

CHOPPING BLOCK AND CUTTING BOARD

You shouldn't cleave meat on the kind of wood surface that's found on most workbenches and tables. As you chop away, you cut into the wood and across the grain and end up with wood chips and splinters in the meat.

Butcher blocks are specially constructed so the butt ends of hardwood planks serve as the cutting surface. This won't splinter because you cleave into the wood grain rather than across it.

Butcher blocks are very expensive because hardwoods are so dear. For example, an 18-by-18-inch maple meat block costs $130.00 plus shipping (105 pounds). A 30-by-30-inch block costs $266.00 (250 pounds).

If such an investment is too steep for you, look into two other possibilities. The next time a big old hardwood blows down in your neighborhood, cut a cross section of trunk, sand down the surface, and oil it with olive oil. It's a perfectly good block, and it's free.

Another possiblity is a plastic block. Trade-named Durasan, this styrene/thermoplastic resin is tough enough to stand up to heavy cleaving. When it gets badly scarred, you can restore a smooth surface by melting the nicks and cuts with a propane torch. It costs $18.95 per square foot, and a 1-by-2-foot piece is large enough for cleaving deer-sized game. Both maple and Durasan blocks from Koch Supplies, 1411 West 29th Street, Kansas City, MO 64108.

SMOKING WILD MEATS

Smoking wild game makes for a distinctly different and delicious class of foods, and it isn't all that difficult. You'll need a smokehouse, of course, but these can be simple affairs: just some kind of small enclosure that may be vented, an old hotplate, and a frying pan. Put wood chips or sawdust in the pan, turn on the hotplate, close the door, and you've got a working smoker.

A far more sophisticated smokehouse may be constructed from an old steel-lined (not plastic) refrigerator. Dig a pit two feet from the door, and sink a large bucket or small garbage can that has been fitted with an air intake pipe, a damper, and a smoke pipe. Run the smoke pipe underground, then up into the refrigerator. Install a vent pipe, with a damper, on the top of the fridge.

Build a roaring fire in the pit, load it up with hardwood of your choice, and cover the top of the pit. You'll be able to regulate heat and smoke through adjustment of the intake and exhaust dampers. To check the temperature, mount an oven thermometer in the refrigerator door so the spike extends into the smokehouse.

Meat should be brined before smoking. Mix pickling salt with warm water until no more salt will dissolve. Another old-timey test is that your brine is ready when it will float an egg.

The length of brining time will determine saltiness. Most people seem to like a 12- to 24-hour brining period. If you like food lightly salted, brine 12 hours. If you like a lot of salt, brine 24.

Like brining, smoky flavor will be determined by the length of time foods remain inside the smoker. I'd say I have middling taste for both smoke and salt, so I brine for 18 hours and smoke for 24 hours at 120 degrees. The finished product is not "cured"—that is, able to be kept without refrigeration—but that's what I have a freezer for. Traditional smoke-curing is time-consuming and the refrigerator method is quick, effective, and virtually hassle-free.

Use common sense when you smoke. The procedure I list here works on things like three-pound deer roasts and moose tongue. For tiny antelope chops, shorten the brine and smoke time; for a haunch of venison lengthen it. The woods suitable for smoking all have different flavors, so experiment with several kinds to find the taste that suits you best. My favorites are hickory, apple, black cherry, and alder, in that order, though virtually any hardwood may be used for flavoring.

Remember, too, that you can impart a delicate hint of smoke to meats and cheeses simply by storing them in a well-crusted, aromatic smokehouse for two or three days. Do this when the weather is cool.

—N.S.

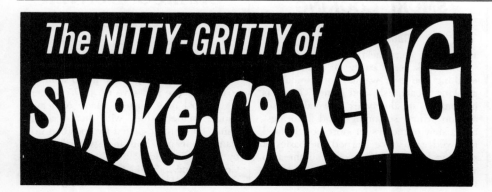

SMOKE-COOKING BOOKLET

If you want a quick course in smokehouse cooking, Luhr Jensen publishes a 16-page booklet that gives you all the basics on brines and the smoking techniques and times for all manner of fish and game, cheeses, beans, and domestic meats. A good primer for beginners who want to start slow and easy. Price: $0.25. Luhr Jensen, P.O. Box 297, Hood River, Ore 97031.

Chunks of Hickory and Mesquite for Serious Smokers

If you're into smoking heavy (smoking meats and fish, that is), you probably have a naturally fired wood smokehouse made out of an old refrigerator or some such thing. And you probably have a hard time locating a selection of aromatic woods (everybody's got chips and sawdust, but serious smokers want chunks!).

Cabela's sells hickory and mesquite chunks at $12.19 and $13.79 for 27 pounds, respectively. It's a little steep, but you can stretch out these hardwoods by soaking them overnight in water and then mixing them half and half with a dry hardwood that's easy to come by in your area (I use applewood). Cabela's 812 13th Avenue, Sidney, NE 69162.   —N.S.

WILDLIFE HARVEST GAME COOK BOOK

edited and published by John Mullin

Goose Lake, Iowa: Arrowhead Hunting and Conservation Club, $3.50 (spiral bound).

Favorite recipes of the licensed game breeders and licensed hunting resorts in North America have been compiled by John Mullin. These members of the North American Game Breeders and Shooting Preserves Association are more knowledgeable about game propagation, nutrition, processing, and cooking of wildlife than any other group. The book covers more than enough recipes for ducks, venison, partridge, pheasants, quail, squirrel, rabbit, wild turkey, doves, turtle, and wild boar, to name some, as well as side dishes, soups, and desserts to keep cooks busy for years.

OUTERS PORTABLE SMOKEHOUSE

This "portable" smokehouse is powered by electricity, so there are some definite limitations on its portability. Smoke and heat are produced by way of hardwood sawdust in a metal pan which is heated over coils. Three racks nest in a 2-by-1-foot-square sheet-metal "house." Just put your meat or fish on the rack, sprinkle a half pound of sawdust on the pan, close the door, and plug it in. Price: $38.44 for the smoker, a recipe booklet, and 2 pounds of hickory sawdust. Outers Laboratories, Inc., Route 2, Onalaska, WI 54650.

LIQUID SMOKE

Commercial smokehouses use liquid smoke, the condensed distillates of hardwoods like hickory. You can flavor your coals with this stuff and make a hickory flavor out of any hardwood available. Price: $5.95 per gallon. Koch Supplies, 1411 West 29th Street, Kansas City, MO 64108.

SMOKE COOKING
by Jack Sleight and Raymond Hull

Harrisburg, Pa.: Stackpole Books, $6.95.

This book could easily be retitled "everything you ever wanted to know about smoking meats, fish, and game." There is information on the types of wood to use, and on brines, seasonings, and flavorings, and a slew of recipes for store-bought food and wild game. We learned the basics of smoking from this book, and all the info worked well in practice. If you want to get into smoking, start here.

THE VENISON BOOK: HOW TO DRESS, CUT UP AND COOK YOUR DEER
by Audrey Alley Gorton

Brattleboro, Vt.: Stephen Greene Press, $2.95 (paper).

This book remains the most compact, complete authority on the subject. With the central theme that deer is a delicacy and not just a trophy, this book is a clear, crisp guide to handling venison with today's methods and equipment. Where to shoot, woods-dressing the kill, getting it home, whether to hang, how to skin, where to cut for chops and steaks, freezing, canning, curing, cooking—*The Venison Book* gives the how and why for every step from woods to table.

COMPACT CHARCOAL-SAVER GRILL

This compact 7-pound grill is designed for use by camper, four-wheel drive, and trailer owners where space is at a premium. After cooking, close lid to snuff out coals for reuse and save up to 75 percent of charcoal now wasted. Made of heavy-gauge welded steel with heat-resistant paint, the chrome-plated two-position grill stands on its own built-in legs. Grill size: 8 by 15 inches. Price: $29.95, postpaid. Dick Cepek, Inc., 9201 California Avenue, South Gate, CA 90280.

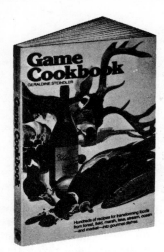

GAME COOKBOOK
by Geraldine Steindler

Chicago: Follett Publishing Company, $4.95 (soft cover).

With food costs rising everywhere, not only can you save money by preparing game dishes economically but you can make every meal a gourmet's delight. Covering everything from soup to fish, this volume gives easy-to-follow directions for field dressing big and small game, birds, and other animals for the table or freezer; covers the making of variety meats, burgers, garnishes, sauces and stuffings, appetizers, and what to do with leftovers. Includes recipes for home-baked breads, pancakes, vegetables, unusual fish dishes, and desserts; and designates which recipes are suitable for camp cooking, using ingredients found in camp kitchens or trail packs.

Other Sources of Wild Game Recipes

• *The Joy of Cooking* by Rombauer and Becker has some excellent pheasant and fowl recipes.

• *The New York Times Cookbook* by Craig Claiborne gives you a taste treat with the recipes on Hassenpfeffer, goose, and venison.

• Julia Child's *Mastering the Art of French Cooking I* has excellent recipes on ducks with fantastic sauces. One caution: this book requires a lot of cooking experience.

• *Cooking Wild Game* by Zack Hanle has helpful hints on the cooking and preparation of wild game. Especially good for cooking grouse, quail, and venison. —P.S.

Son of Hibachi™
PATENT PENDING

DOUBLE PORTABLE BARBECUE

The most ingenious idea since the invention of the barbecue

SECOND-GENERATION HIBACHI

When hibachis first hit the market ten or so years ago, they enjoyed immense popularity because of their practicality: They afforded draft control and thus some control over the heat of the coals; they were compact; and, made of cast iron, they would not rust or rot out from corrosion. Best of all, coals were held suspended above the bottom, so they caught quickly, fanned by circulating air. Now a second-generation hibachi, dubbed Son of Hibachi, promises to be as revolutionary today as the first was then.

The two cooking surfaces, totaling 170 square inches, are hinged in the middle, allowing the unit to fold up into a tidy package that can be carried in one hand. This folding feature also sets the scene for two other improvements; a "blast furnace" effect that gets coals glowing even faster than the original hibachi, and a means to extinguish coals when you're through cooking. Close the Son up tight, and coals are starved of oxygen and quickly suffocate. You can use the coals over and over again—up to five times, according to the manufacturer.

The stove is also self-cleaning. The contained heat in the closed hibachi incinerates residual foods and sterilizes the grates. Ash tumbles into the drawered bottom compartment and is easily removed.

The one claim we must clarify, however, is that this unit may be used as an indoor cooker or space heater. True, it can be safely used to cook in a fireplace, with the flue open, or on a range with an exhaust fan that is vented to the outside. But without flues or venting, even in a relatively porous tent, you're running a terrible risk of carbon monoxide poisoning when you heat or cook with charcoal. Its heating features should be reserved for relatively open conditions: in a duck blind, lean-to, or deer blind. Price: $19.76. H.C.I., Son of Hibachi, P.O. Box 13520, Portland, OR 97213. —F.S.

HERTER'S CATALOG

The Herter's catalog is surely the most complete listing of goods, gear, garb, and garbage for any hunter or fisherman. Just about everything you either wanted or dreamed about is gathered in these 350 pages (about one eighth in color) of quaintly written copy and photographs.

Reading a Herter's catalog is always a treat. Aside from slightly strange syntax, there's the matter of superlatives. Everything is the "best" quality, and that's where the copy begins. To indicate succeeding levels of excellence, more superlatives are added until you get things like "Herter's Super-Deluxe Model Superior Shell Type Flying Goose Field Decoys # D 433FWO." On the order blank, you are allowed 2¾ inches of space to write that in.

As to quality—well, we've been burned once or twice, but they're good about replacing defective equipment free of charge, and 95 percent of their stuff is a cost/quality bargain. Another incredible thing about this outfit: If you don't send enough money because of a price rise or something, they send you the goods anyway and bill you with the nicest form letter that essentially says, Please pay up. The amount may seem small, but when you add everyone else who owes us small amounts, we'll have to discontinue this service if you don't. And they've been doing that for the fifteen years we've dealt with them.

If I have any real ax to grind with Herter's, though, it is about this "new" catalog. Up until two years ago, they issued an even bigger catalog (about 500 pages) that was filled with all kinds of extraneous stuff that was really fun to read, like George L. Herter's personal advice on what to do in the event of a nuclear attack, and the suggestion that if you're having head problems you should try firing your psychiatrist and buying a Herter's Teddy Bear, and the information that the Herter's diamond merchant in South Africa was a Lutheran. At least such great stuff lives on in George's books (all listed in the Herter's catalog, and I highly recommend them). Price: $1.00 (refunded upon a purchase of $10.00 or more). Herter's, Inc., Route 2, Mitchell, SD 57301.

WOOL:
STILL TOPS IN THE WOODS
WHEN YOU'RE AFTER BIG GAME

There's a lot to be said for "miracle fabrics": yarns and weaves of petro-chemical threads like Dacron, nylon, and rayon, but none of them alone can match the qualities of natural wool in the woods. Two characteristics of this material make it tops for stalking and standing when you're after big game, and they're of equal importance. Wool stays warm when it's wet, and it's as quiet in the brush as an owl in flight.

Because individual wool fibers are water repellent, and because they maintain their loft under virtually all conditions, a wool cap, jacket, or pants can be soaked in a drenching shower and will still retain your body heat, not quite as efficiently as if the material were dry, but a little more efficiently than Dacron II or PolarGuard and infinitely more efficiently than a down, cotton, or other natural-fiber fill. Wool is also less absorbent than other natural materials. Water quickly drains out of wool, where it is retained in fills like cotton, Kapok, or open-celled foam.

Wool's quiet in the woods is unmatched. Canvas, ripstop nylon, and other synthetics squeak like chalk on a blackboard when brush scrapes by. Cotton, brushed denim, and corduroy are reasonably quiet when it's dry, but if you have any snow at all, or get your pant legs wet in cold weather, ice bells out the bottom of the legs, and they scrape, scratch, and whistle with each step. With wool pants, ice forms little broken beads rather than a frozen wall. Your footsteps stay quiet.

Admittedly, wool is not the most efficient insulator, so when you're after deer or elk and it's bitterly cold, you might be wise to wear a down vest underneath a wool mackinaw, and long johns under your wool pants. When it's that cold, you're not likely to get wet anyway. And there is a narrow range of substitutes that are nearly equivalent in quality: a synthetic knit with a Dacron II fill, for example. But for all-around outerwear when you've got big game in your sights, wool is still tops in the woods.

"The writing style of George Leonard Herter is by far the best of any North American author, living or dead."
—H. Allen Smith

109

DOWN VEST

Down vests are worth more than their weight in warmth, and that's why they're ideal in and out of doors.

Afield, they'll give an unlined wool jacket or shirt an extra boost from underneath, and they're just what's needed to keep the chill off your shoulders in a drafty hunting cabin or chilly tent. This vest is reversible, blaze orange on one side, tan on the other. Price: $29.00. L. L. Bean, Freeport, ME 04032.

WOOL CRUISER-STYLE JACKET

This is the kind of hunting outerwear that looks good both afield and as casual wear. It is 100 percent wool, and extra heavy (24-ounce fabric) to withstand cold, windy, wet weather. The shoulder-cape cut helps drain water away from the garment. Eight pockets in all, plus a wall-to-wall game pocket (unlined) in back. I've worn one of these for years and love it. Forest green or red/black plaid. Price: $67.50. Eddie Bauer, 1737 Airport Way South, Seattle, WA 98134.

BUFFALO SHIRTS

These traditional hunting shirts are pure wool and come in red and green plaid. They have extra-long shirttails so they won't pop out of your pants, and button-down flap pockets. They may be worn as a shirt in cold weather, or a jacket when it's cool. Price: $11.75. Woolrich, Inc., Woolrich, PA 17779.

Heeksuede Shirt

The name is as intriguing as the cut of this all-cotton imitation-suede shirt. The upper patch pockets have button flaps; a good-looking shirt afield or by the fire. Price: $10.50. Woolrich, Inc., Woolrich, PA 17779.

WARM BLAZE-ORANGE VEST

For safe hunting when the weather's too warm for a jacket but too cool for a shirt, Woolrich's Bounty vest is just the thing. It's Acrilan on the outside and quiet. Inside it's lined with a sheepskinlike acrylic pile. It includes a zipper closure and patch pockets along with a knit collar. Price: $8.75. Woolrich, Inc., Woolrich, PA 17779.

Why Do Hunters Wear Red Suspenders?

To keep their pants up, just like firemen.

These classics of the one-line joke are the old button-hole type with adjustable brass tabs. They're extra-long (44-inch) elastic, and when worn in conjunction with a belt they'll keep the weight of a hunting knife, shell pouch, and drag rope from riding down on your hips. When bird hunting, they make wearing heavy upland field pants more comfortable.

They're also available in green, should you grow weary of people asking you why firemen wear red suspenders. Price: $2.95. Bob Hinman Outfitters, 1217 West Glen, Peoria, IL 61614.   —F.S.

Explorer Shirt

This is a wool-blend shirt with a heavy weave that can be worn as a jacket or a shirt. It's warm, comfortable, and versatile, and it carries lots of outdoorsy charisma. Available in bobtail for exclusive outerwear or with a long tail for when you want to tuck it in. A really good all-around garment. Price: $13.75. Woolrich, Inc., Woolrich, PA 17779.

FOAM FILLS . . . A MATTER OF FULL BUBBLES

Foam fills, essentially a thin layer of what is commonly known as "foam rubber," is often used to line and insulate jackets, boots, heavy jumpsuits, and fishermen's waders. It's an efficient insulator that works on the same principle as every other means to keep you warm: tiny bubbles inside the material trap air, and it is that trapped air which keeps you warm.

However, there are two types of foam fills, each with very different characteristics. Open-celled foam has interconnected air chambers. In other words, viewed under a microscope, each little bubble would have a break in its walls that connects with another bubble. This type of foam is advantageous if compactability is your primary concern. Because the bubbles are interconnected, when you crush open-cell foam, it will reduce considerably in volume.

But those same open cells readily accept water. They are comparable to a sponge, and clothing and footwear lined with this stuff gets soggy as fast as a sponge and dries about as quickly. Open-cell fill also becomes a repository for perspiration and odor.

Closed-cell foam means just what the name implies. Each little bubble is complete and doesn't "leak." In fact, this is the kind of fill used in flotation jackets and vests, outerwear that both keeps you warm and keeps you afloat should you fall into the water. So a rule of thumb—if compactability is of the utmost importance, open-cell foam insulates as well as closed-cell foam. But given the average activities associated with hunting, you'd be wiser to choose closed-cell foam fill for jackets and footwear.

THERM-A-REST SELF-INFLATING AIR MATTRESS

This is a three-quarter mattress with an inner core of open-celled foam. An airtight nylon twill cover is bonded to the foam. The cover has an air inlet/outlet valve. When you roll this mattress up, you open the valve and, as you crush the foam, the air escapes, making it almost as compactable as a conventional air mattress. To "inflate" the mattress, you just open the air valve. The foam recovers and sucks in air, inflating itself.

The mattress measures 19-by-47-by-1½ inches inflated, and 20 by 4 inches rolled up. When I tested this mattress it seemed as comfortable as much bulkier closed-cell foam mattresses, and warmer than equal-sized air mattresses. Aside from duty during sleep, this is an excellent way to wait for a deer on a cold morning, as you can stretch out and use it against your back to break the wind. I also use it on the seat of my car on cold mornings. A good buy. Price: $29.00. Cascade Designs, 568 1st Avenue South, Seattle, WA 98104.   —F.S.

"But I reckon I got to light out for the Territory ahead of the rest, because Aunt Sally she's going to adopt me and sivilize me and I can't stand it. I been there before."
—Mark Twain

111

HUNTER-ORANGE VEST

Many states require that 400 square inches or more of hunter orange be worn when you're afield. The simplest way to satisfy this requirement without buying an all-weather hunting wardrobe is to wear a light orange vest over whatever clothing it takes to be comfortable.

The most inexpensive of these vests are plastic, and they're hardly a bargain. They crack and split when it's cold, and pop and snap when hit by twigs. Another problem with plastic is that it doesn't breathe. Substantial amounts of moisture gather around your shoulders when you're climbing or walking hard. As a result, you get a chill when you rest or take a stand.

Synthetic vests made from soft nylon material make much better safety jackets. The material breathes, it stays soft in the coldest weather, and it is relatively quiet (though it does tend to *whisssh* when brush scrapes by).

If you're handy with a sewing machine, you might also consider making your own vest. Fluorescent cotton-weave cloth can be bought through most fabric shops for around $7.95 a yard (one yard should make 3 vests of 400 square inches or more in total area). The plus with this stuff is that it is completely noiseless. Scrap pieces may be used to band hats, to mark the backs of gloves, or to decorate the mane and tail of a mountain horse.

Bob Hinman Outfitters catalogs a 700-square-inch soft nylon vest with a fast-locking Velcro closure that satisfies the legal requirements of every state. One size fits all. Soft nylon safety vest, $3.95. Bob Hinman Outfitters, 1217 West Glen, Peoria, IL 61614.　　　　　　　—P.S.

REFRIGI-WEAR FOR COLD, COLD WEATHER

If you're a cold-weather hunter, or one of those poor souls whose hands and feet are always cold, look into the line of garments made by Refrigi-Wear.

They are designed specifically for cold weather, with a layer of Kodel polyester fiberfill sandwiched between nylon duck. Along with clothes, these folks also make gloves, mittens, booties, boots, and insulated underwear, all suited to Arctic conditions.

Pictured here is a blaze-orange hunter's special with leg zippers, imitation fur trim around the face, a storm-sealed front zipper, and adjustable waist. Price: $117.00. Refrigi-Wear, 71 Inip Drive, Inwood, NY 11696. Free catalog.

Lightweight Parka

Opening day of the deer season countrywide usually dawns on a crisp morning that warms into a sunny afternoon. For those days afield when heavy jackets are too heavy, a light sweatshirt-type parka is just right. Kolpin's Thermal Parka is lined with polyester foam, and it comes with a hood and drawstring. Fully buttoned up, it will keep you warm down into the low 20s. Throw back the hood, open the nylon zipper at the neck, and you'll be comfortable in 50-degree sunshine. Parka includes two large pockets up front, stretch waistband and cuffs, and it's water repellent. Available in blaze orange or camouflage, sizes small through extra large. Price: $28.00. Kolpin Manufacturers, Inc., P.O. Box 231, Berlin, WI 54923.　　　　　　—F.S.

Eddie Bauer Catalog

Eddie Bauer is the daddy of down as far as retail outlets are concerned. He was the first to perceive the public interest in and need for down sleeping bags, jackets, underwear, and the like, and he is still one of the most dependable suppliers of quality down garments.

The Bauer catalog also lists conventional outerwear and bags, boots, hats, socks, shirts—just about any garment you'll ever

need for hunting and shooting. There are some peripheral products for the outdoorsman, such as knives, tents, and binoculars, but basically this is a clothing catalog.

While the prices he quotes aren't cheap, you do get what you pay for, which is a fair deal anywhere. The catalog has approximately 100 pages, in color, and is issued four times a year, free. Eddie Bauer, 1737 Airport W, Seattle, WA 98124.

DOWN WARMTH WITHOUT THE WHOOSH

The Buckmaster hunting coat and high-bib coveralls combine down warmth with quiet in the woods. The outer shell is made of a soft, yarnlike synthetic that won't snap, zip, pop, or crackle when you brush by branches, and the garments are filled with a total of 17 ounces of down.

The jacket includes a synthetic fur stand-up collar, knit cuffs, detachable fur muffler, fur-lined "handwarmer" pockets, and a two-way zipper with a snap-over wind flap. The snap closure is detachable so it will handle a hunting knife and tow rope, and the jacket has epaulets for nonslip carrying of a slinged rifle. A snap-on down hood is optional with this jacket.

The bib coveralls are made of the same quiet fabric, and they include a front zipper and leg zippers, so you can get them on without having to take off hunting boots. The straps at the shoulder, leg, and waist are all adjustable for a snug, comfortable fit that will keep out the worst northern winds and cold.

Both garments come in blaze orange and are available in sizes from small through extra large. Buckmaster jacket, $71.00; Buckmaster coveralls, $60.00; optional hood, $13.00. Stearns Manufacturing Co., P.O. Box 1498, St. Cloud, MN 56301. —P.S.

WOOL COAT FOR WOODS OR LEISURE

This simply styled wool coat wears equally well in the woods or during other leisure pursuits. It includes a zipper front, a rear "lunch pocket" (which I suspect translates as an unlined game pocket), and snap cuffs. It's available in blaze orange or red and black stag plaid. Price: $38.00. Duxbak, 825 Noyes Street, Utica, NY 13502. —P.S.

STAY WARM WITH PLASTIC FOAM

Cold-weather hunters of any persuasion can profit from the insulating qualities of plastic foam. This material is so effective that it seems to generate a heat of its own when it's in contact with your body. A few but by no means all of the possible applications of this synthetic include the following:

- Use a plate-sized piece of foam to sit on when you're in the blind or deer stand.

- If you're camping, or hunting on your back in a lay-out boat or slit trench, put a large piece of foam between your back and the ground or boat bottom.

- If your feet are apt to get cold, trace the outline of your foot on the plastic trays that hold meat and produce sold in the supermarket. Cut out the tracings and slide them into your boots.

- If your hands get cold, carry plastic foam packing chips or "peanuts" in your pockets and grasp them barehanded inside your pockets.

INSULATED COVERALL

Coveralls make for good cold-weather hunting clothes because they don't have as many openings as jacket/pants combinations for cold air to seep in. They're also pleasant as outerwear because when you take them off you take accumulated dirt, blood, and icy cuffs off with them.

This garment is lined with polyester foam. Along with standard features, it has side access to underneath clothing, an elastic waistband, and zipper closures at the calf for easy on and off, and it's available in green, camouflage pattern, and blaze orange. Price: $50.00 (plus $3.00 for blaze orange). Duxbak, 825 Noyes Street, Utica, NY 13502. —P.S.

Frostline Kit Clothing

This Colorado company enjoys wide popularity and a good reputation among backpackers for their kits. For a most reasonable price, they send you all the top-flight materials needed to make sleeping bags; rain ponchos, tents, and jackets, with easy-to-follow plans. You take up needle and thread (or, better, sewing machine) and do the rest, at considerable savings. Typical kit prices include: down vest, $16.00; down jacket, $31.00; down bag, rated to −10 degrees comfort range, $64.00 Free catalog. Frostline Kits, 452 Burbank Street, Broomfield, CO 80020. —P.S.

Have your clothes fitted for hunting. Select a good cassimere of a . . . no-colored
neutral tint, like a decayed stump, and have coats, pants, and cap made of it."
—Nessmuk

113

Camouflage Clothing for the Rifle Hunter?

You bet. They're de rigeur down South, and they're even practical in northern states where you're required to wear blaze orange.

While it's true that deer can't see colors, they can discern relative light intensities on a gray scale. Blaze orange registers pretty bright on that scale, and a full suit of the stuff against a dark background would surely be noticeable. With a set of light camouflage coveralls pulled over your hunting clothes, and a pull-on blaze orange vest, you're a lot harder for a deer to see.

One other nice feature: coveralls keep your regular clothes clean when you've got to mess around with mud or blood. Pants, $11.50; jacket, 12.50. Duxbak, 825 Noyes Street, Utica, NY 13502.   —P.S.

CATSKILL HUNTER'S REVERSIBLE

One of the hassles with blaze-orange hunting clothing is that you don't really want to wear it for leisure. That dazzling orange makes you feel, well . . . conspicuous. This wool-blend hunting coat has blaze orange on one side, and a comparatively sedate wool plaid on the other. Includes patch pockets, a heavy-duty zipper, and a game pocket. Price: $39.00. Woolrich, Inc., Woolrich, PA 17779.

INSULATED WOOL OUTFIT

This has our vote for tops in the woods. The wool blend material is water-repellent, mothproofed, and quiet. The coat has an insulated lining, muff, and patch pockets and a game pocket. Colored traditional hunter's red-and-black plaid. Jacket, $28.75; pants, $18.50. Woolrich, Inc., Woolrich, PA 17779.

Eight-Point Barrier Hunting Outfit

This blaze-orange Acrylan knit is as quiet as wool in the woods and is insulated with down for extra warmth. Jacket includes a two-way zipper, four large pockets, and a detachable down hood. Pants include side zippers so you can get them on over boots.

Of special note is a detachable waterproof game bag. Not only will it carry a deer heart and liver, it zips completely open so you can use it to sit on, enjoying both insulation against cold snow and protection against wet. One of snow hunting's seemingly unavoidable downers is a wet butt. This feature solves that problem nicely.

Pants, $47.00; jacket, $71.00. Woolrich, Inc., Woolrich, PA 17779.

It had already begun on that day when he first wrote his age in two ciphers and his cousin McCaslin brought him for the first time to the camp, the big woods, to earn for himself from the wilderness the name and state of hunter provided he in his turn were humble and enduring enough. He had already inherited then, without ever having seen it, the big old bear with one trap-ruined foot that in an area almost a hundred miles square had earned for himself a name, a definite designation like a living man:—the long legend of corncribs broken down and rifled, of shoats and grown pigs and even calves carried bodily into the woods and devoured, and traps and deadfalls overthrown and dogs mangled and slain, and shotgun and even rifle shots delivered at point-blank range yet with no more effect than so many peas blown through a tube by a child—a corridor of wreckage and destruction beginning back before the boy was born, through which sped, not fast but rather with the ruthless and irresistible deliberation of a locomotive, the shaggy tremendous shape. It ran in his knowledge before he ever saw it. It loomed and towered in his dreams before he even saw the unaxed woods where it left its crooked print, shaggy, tremendous, red-eyed, not malevolent but just big, too big for the dogs which tried to bay it, for the horses which tried to ride it down, for the men and the bullets they fired into it; too big for the very country which was its constricting scope. It was as if the boy had already divined what his senses and intellect had not encompassed yet: that doomed wilderness whose edges were being constantly and punily gnawed at by men with plows and axes who feared it because it was wilderness, men myriad and nameless even to one another in the land where the old bear had earned a name, and through which ran not even a mortal beast but an anachronism indomitable and invincible out of an old, dead time, a phantom, epitome and apotheosis of the old, wild life which the little puny humans hacked at in a fury of abhorrence and fear, like pygmies about the ankles of a drowsing elephant;—the old bear, solitary, indomitable, and alone; widowered, childless, and absolved of mortality—old Priam reft of his old wife and outlived all his sons.

—William Faulkner, *The Bear*

[Grizzly] bears are, in our estimation, contemptible creatures, not fit for food. Their diet is too varied. In the spring they dip up ants' nests and devour the eggs and inmates, catch frogs, and eat with relish any carrion that can be picked up. The summer is devoted to the untir-

A Questionable Trophy

ing pursuit of mice and beetles, and a huge creature weighing a thousand pounds gives his whole time and energies

to the capture of such game as this. When the berries and nuts are ripe, the bear's food is delicate enough; but, although we have occasionally been obliged to eat bear meat or go hungry, we would vastly prefer good tough government mule.

—Charles Hallock, 1877

BLACK BEAR HUNTING
by Bob Gilsvik

Getting a black bear in your rifle sights depends largely on finding a concentration of fresh sign, tracks, trails, and droppings, selecting a vantage point downwind, and then waiting it out. In some areas, blueberry patches and oak groves are fall hotspots.

Tracks are often the most difficult sign to find. The broad, padded foot of the black bear leaves little indentation except in mud and sand. The front footprints usually show more clearly. If you can find a clear hind footprint, here are some observations you can make based on the combined measurement of the widest and longest part of the pad: less than 6 inches indicates a cub, over 10 inches an adult male. In a Washington state study, no female collected had a combined length-plus-width pad value equal to 10 inches, whereas 86 percent of the males 4 years or older had pad values of 10 inches or more.

Studies show that black bear cubs may be self-sufficient when as young as five and one-half months. Cubs of a sow bear killed in September will survive and go into hibernation that winter. Snow and cold have nothing to do with a bear's hibernating except as they affect the bear's food supply. Bear dens are not as cozy as legend would have it—a poor den can be 34 degrees below zero inside. A bear is so well protected against cold, however, that it could curl up outside and sleep under a heavy insulating blanket of snow.

If you fail to get a bear during the fall hunting season, some states and provinces offer a spring season. Hotspots in the spring are creeks filled with spawning suckers. Suckers will spawn in shallow riffles, water only a few inches deep. This makes it easy for bears to catch them. A water temperature of 55 degrees will start the fish running.

Some hunters worry unduly about trichinosis, the man-originated disease sometimes contracted by hogs or bears

when they eat man's leftovers. It is preventable by thorough cooking and, if contracted, is a treatable disease. Curiously, the danger of trichinosis is very low in heavily hunted areas, because there is a good chance a bear so afflicted will be killed by a hunter and the disease not spread. In a wilderness area, however, the bear may die a natural death and as many as a dozen bear feed on the carcass and contract the disease.

If there was a great deal to fear from black bears, Lynn Rogers of the Department of Ecology at the University of Minnesota probably wouldn't be around. Rogers, working toward his Ph.D in ecology with a wildlife minor, is possibly the best-known expert in the field of the black bear in the United States. During a recent six-year study, he gained a wide variety of data from 756 captures of 252 individual black bears in Minnesota.

"I crawled into the den, put my head on the mother bear's chest, and tried to time her heartbeat," he casually told a group of us. "All of a sudden, she raised her head and looked at me eyeball to eyeball. Her heart had been going at about eight beats a minute, but it was doing 250 by the time I got out of there—and so was mine!"

Contrary to old myths, the bear doesn't snarl fiercely and display an awesome array of teeth, Rogers says. When it's mad, it slaps its front feet down hard while running and "huffs and puffs." But Rogers maintains that it will usually stop 15 to 20 feet away, turn around, and run in the opposite direction. He admits there are exceptions.

Bob Gilsvik is a free-lance outdoor writer who lives in Grand Rapids, Minnesota. His articles have appeared in all the major outdoor magazines, and he has written two books.

"We are not hunting targets. We are seeking to take a living creature that certainly deserves the best we can deliver."
—Keith Schuyler

115

The black bear exhibits color phases that include chocolate, cinnamon, dark brown, and buff.

A bear has no clavicle, the bone which serves to keep the shoulder blades apart. The lack of this bone is responsible for the bear's shuffling, rolling gait, and the fact that bears have difficulty running downhill.

A stand of beech trees is a great place to set up a stand for black bear. Bruins love beechnuts, and they're not alone in their addiction. At one time or another, beech groves are attractive to turkey, ruffed grouse, and squirrels as well.

Smokey the Bear just might have been the richest animal on four legs. He earned over one million dollars in royalties for the use of his name.

A bear's age is determined by examining cross-sections of his teeth, much like a tree's age can be determined by its annual rings.

FISHNET UNDERWEAR

The principle of this wide-mesh underwear is ventilation and transfer of moisture to outer garments when the weather is warm. When it's cold, the mesh traps static air next to your body. It is ultimately trapped air, not layers or weight of clothing, that keeps you warm. Shirt and drawers, $4.99 each. Cabela's, 812 13th Avenue, Sidney, NE 69162. —F.S.

DID HE WEAR WOOL OR DOWN?

[At the point] chosen for the morning's shoot, there was a hut that had been built of blocks of ice to afford us a little shelter against the terrible wind that would come at daybreak—that icy wind which tears the flesh like a saw; that which cuts into one like the blade of a knife; pricking like a poisoned arrow, twisting like pincers, burning like fire.

—Guy de Maupassant, *Love*

L. L. BEAN CATALOG

The folks from L. L. Bean are downeasters all, and the gear featured in their catalog reflects the spare, tight-lipped practicality that is characteristic of the region.

This is a place where you can still get "tin pants," plain old tight-weave canvas brushcutters, that whistle, squeak, and snap but will turn back briers as well as any synthetic-fronted pair of field pants. They also have the boot that made Bean's, the Maine Hunting Shoe, and a hundred other items that are favored by knowledgeable outdoorsmen because they've withstood the test of time.

Another telling thing about this outfit is what they omit. They don't catalog a lot of those tacky glasses with grouse decals, or bird miniatures, or pins for m'lady. They carry a little bit of that stuff, but their stocks are limited, and, like everything else in their catalog, even this is high quality.

The Bean catalog is issued four times a year, and it's around 100 pages long. They also have a store that's open 24 hours a day, 7 days a week. Free catalog, L. L. Bean, Freeport, ME 04033.

THE LOWDOWN ON DOWN AND SYNTHETICS

What's the difference between down and a synthetic fiber fill in sleeping bags and outdoor clothing? Well, for starters, the best down fill boosts the price of a garment from 50 to 100 percent when compared to a synthetic fill. And there's a lot more.

Down achieved its fame because it is the most effective of all the natural insulators, better than wool, cotton, kapok, or feathers. The reason it works so well is that small pockets of stagnant air are what really trap warmth in and keep cold out, and, viewed under a microscope, a single piece of down would look like the head of a dandelion gone to seed. A handful of these pieces of down create thousands of little air pockets. Pound for pound, down is the best insulator, and it is the lightest insulator for the warmth it traps.

It is also compactable. The "dandelion head" can be crushed to the relative size of a pinhead and held there. When pressure is released, it returns to its original form and insulating capabilities.

All down is not the same, however. Prime northern goosedown is considered to be the best. Other down may be from ducks or inferior domestic geese and less effective at insulation. Another fault with down is that it mats when it's wet, compacting in the moisture, and not recovering until it dries.

Synthetic fibers like Dacron II and PolarGuard fiberfills are inventive attempts to recreate natural down. Pound for pound, synthetics insulate nearly as well as down, but they compact only about half as well. A down sleeping bag capable of keeping you warm in fall weather will fit into a bag about the size of a basketball. A similar synthetic bag would fill a pillowcase.

Any synthetic's biggest selling point, though, is directly related to this uncompactability. It won't mat when it's moist, so it stays warm when it's wet. This is an important consideration when you're hunting, since fall weather typically includes ample doses of rain and wet snow.

DOWN UNDERWEAR

Beware of down underwear. As a rule, hunting is reasonably strenuous activity, and down just gets too hot. But if you'll be sitting in bitter cold, and not doing a lot of walking around, down underwear is the way to go. These Upperdowns and Longdowns are insulated with northern duck down. The top has knit collar and cuffs, and the bottoms have an elastic waist, zip fly, and knit cuffs. Upperdowns, $24.25, Longdowns, $21.25. Woolrich, Inc., Woolrich, PA 17779.

DACRON 88 INSULATED UNDERWEAR

This is a solid foundation for a day in the cold, and then some. The jacket boasts a knit collar and zip-up front, with a fly over the zipper. It has a bi-swing back for freedom of movement, and a 3-inch extension "back warmer" that snaps to the pants. Not only will you find this type of jacket comfortable underwear; it's just the thing to throw on over house clothes when you have to step outside for a few minutes. In terms of sheer use, my insulated underwear tops probably see more time on my back than conventional jackets.

The pants include a knit crotch piece (like a bi-swing back, if you don't have this, every time you make an exaggerated movement, like stepping *way* up, it will stop you in your tracks and frustrate the hell out of you), and snaps to attach them to the jacket.

In my humble opinion, this class of insulated underwear is the workhorse. There are warmer kinds and prettier kinds and better quality kinds, but for the money these can't be beat. Prices: $32.50 for suit, $22.00 for jacket alone. Duxbak, 825 Noyes Street, Utica, NY 13502.

—N.S.

TWO-LAYER UNDERWEAR

One of the best things that ever happened to me was that someone left some Duofold underwear at my house. This underwear is among the warmest I've ever worn. Cut for either men or women, it is constructed in two layers. The outer layer is a blended virgin wool (25 percent wool, 65 percent cotton, and 10 percent nylon); the inner layer is 100 percent cotton, which prevents the wool from itching. This inner layer absorbs the moisture from your body. It then transfers this moisture to the outer layer, where evaporation takes it away. Price: $8.85. Duofold, Inc., Mohawk, NY 13407.

—P.S.

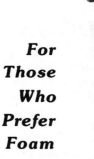

For Those Who Prefer Foam

The one advantage of foam is that wind can't blow through it. But this does create condensation problems, since it acts as a barrier to evaporation. Foam is best when you're sitting, not working, in the wind for a long time.

This underwear set is insulated with 3/32-inch Scott polyester foam. It has a fly over a full front zipper and a knit collar and cuffs. Price: $21.80. Duxbak, 825 Noyes Street, Utica, NY 13502.

COTTON THERMAL UNDERWEAR

When you need underwear that will cut the chill of a mid-fall morning but won't overheat you in the day, use cotton. It's warm when the weather is cool, yet it will absorb and transpire perspiration. In extremely cold weather, cotton long johns and tops, worn under fiberfill-insulated underwear, will absorb perspiration and keep the insulated underwear clean. Price: $6.80. Duxbak, 825 Noyes Street, Utica, NY 13502.

UNDERWEAR
FOR THE OUTBACK

Suiting up with the traditional long winter underwear when it's cold is a lot smarter than piling on extra outer clothing. Ounce for ounce, underwear will insulate your body better than outerwear, and with less bulk and greater freedom of movement.

At what point you'll need long handles is better left up to you; some folks retain heat better than others, and there's also the matter of what you'll be doing. Speaking for myself, I'd never don any kind of special underwear if the temperature was around 30 and I planned to be stalking all day. But if I were going to take up a stand, I surely would want extra protection from the cold.

Cotton long johns are the least efficient insulator. This isn't to say they're inferior, just that they are the garb to choose if you want a little extra warmth. As a rule of thumb, they're the kind of underwear I'd choose for posting in 40-degree weather or walking the hills when it's around 25 and a little on the breezy side.

Fishnet underwear is the next warmest. This stuff is wide-mesh, like a fishnet, and is worn right next to your skin. Cotton underwear should go over it for the greatest warmth, the theory being that air is trapped in the pockets between the cotton and your skin.

There's some debate about which is warmer, waffle-knit underwear or fishnet underwear. My body says that waffle-knit is. This stuff, too, should be worn next to your skin, under cotton underwear.

Wool (in case you haven't guessed, I'm heavy on wool) underwear rates next in my book, but be forewarned; some people find it intolerable to wear. It's itchy and scratchy; in fact, this might be part of the reason why it's warm—it irritates your skin. It might also be worth noting that hives have the same effect, which might explain all the jokes about Grandpa being sewn into his wool long handles in November, never to emerge until April. Once you get accustomed to the stuff, you don't want to go through a break-in period again.

Synthetic fiber fills are warmer yet, and, like wool, they retain a large percentage of their capabilities when they're wet. When you don this type of underwear, you should wear cotton underneath it to absorb perspiration. This keeps the synthetic underwear cleaner and you a bit more comfortable. The nylon-weave outer cloth can feel cold against your skin.

Down underwear is the warmest of all, but it should be worn only under the coldest conditions—so cold, in fact, that the game probably won't be moving anyway. If you get down wet from rain or perspiration, or even from wet snow dripping off the trees, it mats and makes a poor insulator, and it's difficult to get dry. When you use down underwear, you should have cotton next to your skin for the same reasons that it should be worn with synthetics.

—N.S.

Always break in a new pair of boots before an extended hunting trip. The easiest, most painless way to do this is to make a practice of wearing them around the house and yard and on short walks to the store. You can accelerate the break-in process by warming the boots in a hot, sunny place, or a low-temperature oven, and then taking a short walk in them wearing wet, bulky socks.

DUNHAM DURAFLEX BOOT

This company made the first waterproof leather boot, a state of grace achieved by a dry-tanning process. Features include: all leather waterproof uppers, foam insulation, leather lining, cushioning underfoot, and a lug sole that is bonded to the uppers.

Model No. 7615 is available with or without insulation and a safety steel toe. Price: $80.00. Dunham Co., Brattleboro, VT 05301.

GAITERS FOR DEEP SNOW

If you're hunting in deep snow, or like low-cut boots and want to protect your ankles from seeds and such, use a pair of gaiters. They make for a shinglelike covering over your boot top and keep your pant legs dry without the weight of high-top boots. Price for 16-inch gaiters, $12.50; 7-inch gaiters, $5.50. L. L. Bean, Freeport, ME 04033.

INSOLES THAT WARM COLD FEET

Polar Comfort insoles are made of a flexible foam material that's lined with cotton on one side. They help keep your boot dry, and the foam insulates the bottom of your foot from the boot sole. One size fits all shoes (trim them with scissors). Price: $1.85. Kolpin Manufacturing, Inc., P.O. Box 231, Berlin, WI 54923.

ROYAL RED BALL RUBBER FOOTWEAR

This company makes quality rubber footwear in both insulated and noninsulated models. Of special note is their variety of lacing and buckling systems and boot-top heights. They've really got boots for every use or hunting condition.

Oneida. This is an insulated boot, with a full lace. If you really need a lace boot in rubber footwear, fine, but I've found that, even tightly laced, my foot slops around a little inside, and they're a pain to lace and unlace, since the rubber grabs the shoelace as you tighten down. Consider a rubber boot with an easy-on-and-off lacing system. If you already have, and still like a lace boot, the Oneida costs $32.00.

Morgan. This boot has a top lace that is threaded through three opposing eyelets only. It's easy to get on and off and comes in two top heights, 12 inches and 16 inches. The 16-inch top is great when you'll be hunting around swamps or shallow streams; those extra 4 inches really let you get around. The Morgan is available in insulated and noninsulated styles, $33.10 for the former, $25.40 for the latter.

Premier. An insulated boot with a zipper closure and a 12-inch top, it holds your feet every bit as snugly as a lace boot, and goes on and off with ease: $32.00.

Traileaze. Easy to get into and out of, it then cinches tight around your calf with a buckle closure. It also has an adjustable top strap for a super-snug fit. Insulated, it has a 15-inch top. Price: $34.20.

Calhoun. A top-lace boot with a 12- or 16-inch top, this style has a hobnail sole design that won't pick up snow or mud, so it's the perfect boot for wet snow. Price: $25.10. Royal Red Ball, Naugatuck, CT 06770.

PROTECTION FOR THE COLDEST WEATHER

This boot consists of two parts. An outer layer of PolarGuard-lined nylon uppers and a Sorel rubber boot with a walking heel make up the outer part. Inners are heavy felt liners. This combination makes for the warmest of all footwear.

A tip: buy this boot with two sets of liners and use them on alternate days, allowing each pair 24 hours to evaporate the accumulated moisture of perspiration. Sorel boots, $31.50; extra felt liners, $5.95. Cabela's, 812 13th Avenue, Sidney, NE 69162.

THE MAINE HUNTING SHOE

If you hunt over soggy ground, these are the boots. The chain tread is sure-gripping. Prices run from $24.00 for the 6-inch height to $40.00 for the 16-inch calf height. These boots are available in brown or tan uppers (except for the 14- and 16-inch styles, which come in brown only), in whole sizes from 3 to 14 in D and EE widths, 5 to 14 in FF. There's also a ladies' Maine Hunting Shoe in 9-inch height with tan top for $27.50. Innersoles are available for use in either cold or normal weather, depending on the style of the sole, and with leather or steel shanks for the amount of foot support desired, priced from $2.50 to $4.60. L. L. Bean, Inc., Freeport, ME 04033.

"The long-distance runner is paid by the snap of a white thread across his chest. You are paid by the picture at your feet."
—Terry and Renny Russell

119

For warm feet while you wait, always kick or wipe any snow off the top of your boot. As snow melts, it uses up tremendous amounts of heat energy—heat that it will collect from your foot if you leave the snow there.

MOUNTAIN HIKER

If you'll be hunting the high country in warm weather, this 6-inch-high mountain boot combines cool comfort with solid traction. It includes a padded sweater collar, a garrison back for strength, and a ski-flap tongue closure to keep out duff and dirt, plus Vibram lug sole and heel, Goodyear wilt, and speed laces with Alpine hooks. If you're caught in a snowstorm, these boots work fine in snow if you wear them with gaiters. Price: $63.50 (Style 825). Red Wing, Red Wing, MN 55066.

INSULATED HIGH-TOP

If you'll be hunting around high mountains, bitter temperatures, and deep snow, you'll need insulated high-top leather boots to keep your feet warm and dry. These boots boast speed laces for easy on and off and ¼-inch foam insulation. Vibram soles mean good traction. Price: $67.50 (Style 855) Red Wing, Red Wing, MN 55066.

BIG-GAME BOOTS

Much ado is made about fitting boots to your feet. Of course, it's important that your footwear be comfortable, but unless you have a history of foot and/or ankle trouble, any boot of reasonable quality in your proper size should feel good once it's broken in. "Breaking in" a boot is simply a matter of the leather's working and forming around the contours of your foot and adjusting to the way you walk. In terms of fit, then, the important thing is to break that boot in long before hunting season by wearing your big-game footwear whenever it's practical. Lacing up a pair of brand-new boots on opening-day morning makes blisters by noon close to a sure bet.

Fitting your boots to the weather and the terrain you'll be hunting is more a matter of choice, however, and one that deserves more appraisal than it's commonly given.

To start at the bottom and work up, soles and tread design are interrelated. A very hard sole will not grab as well as a soft sole, and a smooth sole will give you less traction than a sole with a tread pattern. For example, a smooth leather sole, like the kind commonly found on cowboy boots, is probably the worst choice you could make in a hunting boot. Not only is the sole slippery, the high heel makes for unstable walking conditions that are compounded by the lack of ankle support.

While the worst boot for hunting can be described easily, it's impossible to identify the best boot, because different treads and boot types are designed for different conditions.

The Vibram or heavily lugged sole is a great gripper around the mountains. In fact, it achieved its popularity first among mountain climbers because of the sure footing it provides around hard rock, loose shale, and hard-packed earth. It is not a good gripper on wet snow or in mud. The cleats get clogged, and the soles act like skis. They are also difficult to clean and track dirt and snow with them wherever they go.

Chain or ribbed cleats are an all-purpose tread for the varied conditions you'll meet during a big-game season. They work best on a soft to medium-hard rubber or composition sole. In general, the softer the sole the better the boot will grip, but the quicker the sole will wear down.

Hobnail patterns, round cups of rubber or composition material that protrude down from a flat sole, are the best performers on mud or snow. Their design is such that they'll release any accumulated snow or mud as you flex the boot while walking.

On most boots, the heel is separate from the sole. A few boots are designed so the heel and sole are one. A one-piece heel-and-sole combination makes for surer footing on flat ground and, for the most part, quieter walking because your weight is more widely distributed. In steep, hilly country, especially if it's muddy or snowy, a heel will brake a lot of slips and slides that a one-piece sole won't.

At one time or another, a big-game hunter could have use for boot uppers made of leather, rubber, or a combination of both.

Leather uppers are the most popular, because leather "breathes," allowing a transfer of moisture from around your feet, through the material, and into the air. Excess moisture will chill your feet when it's very cold, and it will contribute to blisters in warm weather. When the weather is from 25 to 40 degrees, and it's rainy or snowy, or when you know you'll be slogging through swamps or through shallow water, an all-rubber hunting boot is the only kind that will stay truly waterproof. "Waterproof" leather boots are far more moisture resistant than conventional leather uppers, but they will eventually leak. Rubber boots, so long as they are sound, will not leak, but they will accumulate considerable condensation from the inside.

Low-cut "hiker's" boots are lighter than high-top boots, and they are cooler in warm weather. High-top boots afford a bit more ankle support if you have weak ankles, and they keep snow, duff, and plant seeds away from your ankles. There is seldom any justification for a leather boot higher than 9 inches. You may want higher rubber boots if you know you'll be hunting around deep water.

—N.S.

LEN RUE, JR.

THE BEST MOUNTAIN BOOT

by Leonard Lee Rue, III

I was taking photos of a young billy goat high in the mountains of Glacier National Park in Montana. These mountains are often referred to as the alps of North America, and the comparison is a good one. The high, snow-capped peaks, the almost vertical mountain walls, the wide, sloping, glaciated valleys, the unlimited carpets of fantastically beautiful wildflowers, and the good supply of wildlife—such as mountain goats, bighorn sheep, moose, deer, and grizzly and black bears—make this area a photographer's paradise.

The goat had evidently found a mineral lick because he had been slurping on a hollow in the rocks with all the enthusiasm of a child with a soft ice cream cone. The mineral lick had anchored the goat, so after locating him the picture-taking was easy. After about twenty minutes and one hundred photographs, the goat turned, walked over to the face of the cliff, went over the edge, and disappeared. I know that goats don't fly, but that goat just disappeared. Another thing I know is that when goats move out across the kind of sheer cliff face that this one retreated to, I don't follow them.

I do not do sheer rock climbing. I have no desire to climb where you have to use pitons and ropes and prayers. I'm all for the prayers but forget the pitons. I have just taken lessons in rappelling so that I can, if the occasion arises, at least work on hawk and eagle nests, but my main interest in being in the mountains is to photograph the wildlife living there, and the sheer rock faces don't offer much.

I do do a lot of work in the mountains, because my favorite photographic subjects are the wild sheep of North America. In fact, my greatest desire is to have the chance to photograph the Marco Polo or argali sheep of Asia. I have climbed after Dall sheep in Alaska, Stones in British Co-lumbia, bighorns throughout most of the Rocky Mountains, and desert sheep in Arizona and Nevada.

The two most important pieces of equipment that are needed to photograph wild sheep in their native habitat are your camera and your boots. Or perhaps I should say your boots and your camera, because without the best in foot-wear you are not going to be able to get your camera within working distance of the sheep.

For all the years that my son, Len Rue, Jr. (also a wildlife photographer), and I have been working in the mountains we wear only the Chippewa Shoe Company's mountain boots. We have found that the Chippewa's Kush-n-Kollar boots are the most rugged, most comfortable, most dependable boots that we can obtain anywhere at any price. These boots are built to last, and they do; our first boots had to be discarded after ten long years of really rough wear. Our boots shape themselves to our feet and are as comfortable as bedroom slippers, and this is important when you have to wear the boots for some of the fourteen- to sixteen-hour days we put in.

Ruggedness is great, comfort is a must, but the real test is how the boots perform in the mountains. All I can say is that our Chippewa boots have never let us down. The Vi-bram lug soles will hold on sheer rock angles where you can no longer stand. You may lose your balance, but the boots won't slip. And that's what climbing in the mountains is all about. When our lives depend upon our boots, we depend upon our Chippewas.

Leonard Lee Rue, III, is a naturalist and wildlife photographer living in Blairstown, New Jersey. He has written 14 books and over 650 articles, and he has taken 250,000 photographs in his pursuit of wildlife with a camera.

"For [hunting] footgear, two pairs of heavy yarn socks, with rubber shoes or buckskin moccasins. In hunting, 'silence is gold.'"
—Nessmuk

121

AN OVER-THE-BOOT BOOT FOR LONG COLD WAITS

If your feet are prone to get cold when you sit for long periods, you might try wearing Sport Boots.

They are an over-the-boot boot made of expanded polystyrene. The top of the boot hinges in the front, you put your booted foot inside, and the top closes like a clamshell, held in place by a nylon strap. There's a polyurethane foam collar at the top of the boot to seal off warm air.

These are not boots for long walks (though you can hobble about in them) or tap dancing, but for long cold waits they sure look like they'd keep you comfortable. Price: $8.99. Sport Boots, Inc., P.O. Box 652, Route 6, Easley, SC 29640.

CLIMBER BOOTS FOR HORSEBACK HUNTING

Climber boots are the preferred footwear of linemen and loggers, and they have a place around a big-game camp if you do a lot of hunting by horseback. They have a high heel that rides well in a stirrup, yet the boot toe, sole, and heel are wide and stable for sure-footed walking. In addition, they lace up tight, providing plenty of ankle support. If desired, these boots may be fitted with Vibram soles by a cobbler. Price: $58.95 (Style 917). Red Wing, Red Wing, MN 55066.

WELLINGTON BOOT

All your time around camp won't be spent hunting, and you'll make your leisure hours a lot more pleasant if you don't have to lace up a pair of hunting boots every time you want to go outside. The Wellington-style boot pulls on and slides off as easily as slippers, and won't take on water if you have to slog through deep snow. They're also good-looking and stylish enough to wear with sports clothes at home. Price: $48.95 (Style 866). Red Wing, Red Wing, MN 55066.

WARM, DRY FEET START WITH WARM, DRY BOOTS

Everyone knows that if your feet are wet and you're sitting, not forcing circulation and warm blood out to your toes, your feet will get cold. But an awful lot of people don't realize that there are varying stages of "wetness." It's pretty obvious if your feet are soaked after having gone in over your hip boots when you didn't see the drop-off, or after slogging around after deer all day in a wet snow, but just plain dampness that results from perspiration can cut your footgear's efficiency by 50 percent.

Always start the day with warm, thoroughly dry boots. When you're on an extended hunting trip, the only way you can assure they'll be dry the next morning is to drive out or absorb the moisture they've collected from the day before.

When you're not around electricity, don't hang leather boots over a fire or heater or they'll dry from the outside in, which turns boots hard and causes them to crack. Just set them in a warm part of the room rather than a cold outside entrance. Two old-timey tricks work well. If your boots are no more than damp, stuff them with wadded paper and keep them warm. If boots are soaked through and through, fill them with heated whole grain like wheat, oats, corn, or rice. In both cases, the material inside the boot draws moisture to it. The combination of dry grain and heat soaks up moisture like a sponge.

If you're around electricity and household appliances, a vacuum cleaner with the hose reversed, so it blows rather than sucks air, will dry the inside of a boot in less than an hour. A hair drier is twice as fast, because it blows warm air. You can also use special boot driers, shaped like a foot,

that plug into a 110-volt outlet. They're warm enough to dry a pair of thoroughly soaked boots overnight, yet they don't get so hot that they'll damage rubber or leather. And they're made of aluminum, so they won't rust in all that moist heat. Electric Boot Driers, $14.95. Bob Hinman Outfitters, 1217 West Glen, Peoria, IL 61614.

DRY TAN vs. OIL TAN

Leather boots may be tanned in one of two ways. An oil tan is the conventional technique. Special oils keep the leather soft, supple, and lustrous. While it sheds water, an oil-tanned boot is never so water resistant as a dry-tanned boot. Leather that's been dry-tanned is usually the main component of hunting boots that are "waterproof."

STANDBY SEALER

Any kind of wild or domestic fat makes for a good standby waterproofer for oil-tanned boots if you find you've left your commercial moisture sealant home. Get your boots bone-dry and warm (around 100 degrees). The fat should be warm too, just below the temperature where it starts to melt. Rub the fat liberally along all seams and welts—any place water might enter. Coat smooth leather with a modest amount of fat. Keep the leather warm by hanging the boots over a stove or source of heat, or storing them up high where heat collects. The leather will gradually absorb the fat. Continue applications until no more fat is absorbed.

HERTER'S MINK OIL

If you have a good pair of oil-tanned boots such as those put out by Red Wing, an oil-based waterproofing is the best; a silicone type simply will not penetrate the leather. Mink oil is the classic type, and Herter's offers it at a good price: 98 cents for 3½ ounces, $1.69 for 8½ ounces. It doesn't necessarily waterproof, since eight hours in wet snow will eventually let some moisture through, but for most hunting it is a highly practical treatment, anything short of rubber-boot conditions being easily handled. The application will be the most effective if you set your boots next to warmth, which helps expand the pores slightly and aids in penetration of the oil. Two or three feet from a good hot wood fire is close enough. Dogs are also really intrigued with the smell (yes, it really is mink oil from real mink fat). Herter's Inc., Route 2, Mitchell, SD 57301.

BOOT WATERPROOFING SPRAY

Dry-tanned leather boots require a silicone-based spray rather than grease or oil. This pressurized spray keeps leather soft and dry, and it eliminates mildew as well. Price: $2.00. Duxbak, 825 Noyes Street, Utica, NY 13502.

THE WILD SHEEP IN MODERN NORTH AMERICA

Jackson, Wyo.: Teton Bookshop (P.O. Box 1903), $10.50 (soft-bound).

The Wild Sheep is essentially textbook/research material, rather than a popularly written treatise on sheep hunting. It catalogs material presented by wildlife managers from the western states at a workshop on sheep in Missoula, Montana. All states with a sheep population are represented, as well as Canada and Mexico. Topics discussed include sheep management, current status of sheep, population movements, and the effects of domestic livestock, hunting, and transplanting upon wild sheep.

It isn't a book you can curl up with next to a crackling fire, but as an argument-settler and sourcebook, it's the most up-to-date in America. Also includes a fold-out map, showing sheep herd locations, species, and whether they are sustaining, transplanted, remnant, or captive.

TIMBERLAND WATERPROOF BOOTS

These are 9-inch waterproof boots with lug soles, insulated to −20 degrees. They are four-line stitched with nylon thread and are equipped with brass eyelets and D-rings. They are said not to require breaking in. Price: about $65.00. Timberland Co., P.O. Box 370, Newmarket, NH 03857.

WATERPROOF BOOTS NEED SILICONE

Leather boots that have been waterproofed (dry-tanned) should not be greased or saddle-soaped. If the waterproofing needs a shot in the arm, use only silicone-based boot treatments.

BOOTLACE BLESSING

Tuck an extra bootlace in your pocket when you're after big game. Aside from its obvious use in case a lace you're wearing breaks, you can use it to construct a tripod emergency shelter, to repair a broken gun sling, to tie your gun in place on your shoulder so both hands are free to drag a deer, to tie a tag to a deer or elk, and to satisfy a hundred other needs that might arise during your day outdoors.

"You don't go hunting to kill, you go hunting to hunt . . . there are hunters and there are killers. To the true sportsman, the kill is an anticlimax."
—Fred Bear

123

STONE SHEEP HUNTING
WITH
3,000,000 PEOPLE

by Sheila Link

"How would you like to hunt Stone sheep in British Columbia?" asked Bud Morgan. Bud, a film producer for ABC TV, had interviewed me sometime earlier about doing a hunting segment for the *American Sportsman* program. He'd been searching since then for an area and a game species that would make a good program for the *Sportsman's* first attempt at using a woman protagonist.

"That sounds great—I'd love to!" I answered. As simply as that, one of the most memorable adventures of my life began.

Hunting for me has always been a *total* experience, not merely a chance to stalk and hopefully take a desirable animal. I thrill to beautiful country, to the personal challenge of a tough adversary, and I enjoy the casual camaraderie of congenial hunting partners. This TV hunt should, I thought, combine all those elements to a high degree.

Stone sheep are one of North America's finest big-game trophies; British Columbia encompasses some of the wildest, most spectacular scenery to be found anywhere; furthermore, having such a hunt recorded on film would enable me to relive it over and over.

The following eight weeks were spent in a flurry of preparation. I began gathering clothing and equipment and also embarked upon a rigorous schedule of calisthenics, hiking, and target shooting.

Despite my keen anticipation of the adventure, I was concerned about two possible problems. First, I realized that the TV crew would necessarily direct their efforts not toward a quality *hunt* but to getting a film with a successful conclusion. Would I, I worried, be faced with compromising my personal standards of sportsmanship? I had, after all, agreed to help make a film.

My second worry was even more personal: How would I perform when the "moment of truth" arrived? Could I make a clean, sure, swift kill when I was surrounded by spectators and distracted by the knowledge that every move I made was being recorded by a camera?

As much as possible, however, I pushed these concerns to the back of my mind and concentrated instead on being well prepared.

Things certainly started out well. I found the TV crew, individually as well as collectively, very congenial. The hunting camp, situated on Nevis Creek, was both attractively rustic and very comfortable. Everyone there—wranglers, guides, the cook, and the manager—all made us feel most welcome.

Roaming the high country of the Northwest is a delight in itself, but it is also a lung-bursting, muscle-straining, heart-pounding challenge. The days are long, too. We were on the trail by seven or seven thirty each morning and didn't get back to camp until after ten at night. It would have been exhausting except that it was so exhilarating!

Sheep aren't *easy*, which is why they're so highly regarded by serious sport hunters. These hardy mountain dwellers are blessed with incredible eyesight, equal, it's said, to a 10-power scope. In addition, they can cover seemingly impassable real estate with remarkable speed. The pleasure of hunting these handsome animals is exceeded only by the thrill of actually getting a good ram.

We hunted very hard for three days before sighting rams, then planned our stalk for the fourth day. I didn't sleep very well that night. My worries about the TV crew wanting to "guarantee" a film weighed on my mind, along with concern over my ability to keep cool and competent under pressure.

Climbing up the far side of the mountain where we'd spotted the rams took the better part of the day. When we finally hauled up onto the ridge I was totally enervated—until, suddenly, we again saw our prey. A herd of eleven rams was slowly working its way toward us.

"Remember now," the director told me, "don't fire until you get my signal."

We sat or lay around, resting, for about two hours; then the three cameramen slipped into the locations they'd already chosen.

The sheep were out of sight when guide Jim Mullin and I eased into a small flat crevice, but they soon appeared again, this time on a broad, grassy promontory below us. The best ram was in the exact center of the herd, with a young one just beside him. To avoid any chance of hitting the youngster, we decided to take one almost as good as the big fellow, a darker animal off to our right.

"Any time," Jim whispered. I set the crosshairs for a heart shot, squeezed the trigger—and got a misfire! Gently easing back the external hammer of the lever-action .308, I re-set my aim, squeezed again, and the rams bounded away—except for the one I hit, which fell off the promontory, dead.

Both my fears, I'm happy to report, were groundless. We'd had a completely honest hunt, and when we finally found a good ram I was able to nail him with a single well-placed shot.

Sheep hunting, in my books, is the greatest, for it combines everything a good hunt should have: a beautiful setting, a tough, challenging adversary, and a truly handsome and impressive trophy.

Sheila Link has had a lifetime love affair with the outdoors and enjoys everything from whitewater canoeing and backpacking to fishing and—most of all—hunting. In addition to writing, she's an instructor of outdoor skills and also teaches wilderness survival at the NRA school near Raton, New Mexico.

SHEEP AND SHEEP HUNTING
by Jack O'Connor

New York: Winchester Press, $10.00.

The sheep-hunting book, by the number-one sheep hunter in the world. If you have any inclination at all toward hunting mountain sheep, perhaps you should not buy this book, as it will turn that inclination into a passionate desire.

This book deals mainly with the North American varieties of wild sheep—the bighorn, desert, Stone, and Dall—though it examines other types found all over the world. Each type is described thoroughly as to habits, habitat, and means of hunting. There is an enormous amount of sheer biologial information in this book, which I suppose proves again that the very best hunters not only care very much about the game they hunt but know an awful lot about it too.

There are also chapters devoted to equipment—clothing, optics, rifles, and so on—as well as judging trophies. There is also a chapter on the Grand Slam aspect of sheep hunting, in which O'Connor laments the immoral and illegal hunting that has sometimes occurred in the quest for all four of the North American sheep, while at the same time considering that perhaps he and other writers have had a small part in the popularization of sheep hunting that brought about those abuses. I do not think he should blame himself even slightly, as anyone who can share with others his love of sheep and sheep country in the manner that O'Connor does in this book has probably done an immeasurable amount of good, not only for sheep and their situation but for the cause of all hunters, or anyone else who cares about the wild places of the world. —J.B.

SHEEP

The successful pursuit of this species requires the exercise on the part of the hunter of the utmost patience and deliberation: no animal is more shy and wary than the Bighorn, and if it receives the slightest hint of the enemy's presence, it is up and away, not to be seen again. No tyro in still hunting will succeed in securing one of these vigilant climbers, and we have seen many a hunter of experience who had yet to kill his first mountain sheep.

—Charles Hallock, 1877

EDDIE BAUER, INC.

ARCTIC TROOPER CAP

In cold weather—or when you might run into it—the trooper-style hat is tops. It's comfortable when the weather is just cool when worn with the flaps up. When it's cold, turn down the flaps, and your ears, neck, and forehead are protected.

The crown is insulated with goose down, the flaps with mouton lamb. Hidden drawstring adjusts the hat to a perfect fit. Price: $21.00. Eddie Bauer, 1737 Airport Way South, Seattle, WA 98134.

VISOR ARCTIC CAP

If you prefer a bill on your hunting cap, this one has it, and warmth as well. The crown is down, protected by water-repellent nylon. Synthetic fur earflaps can be turned down to keep your ears and neck warm in the coldest weather. Price: $15.95. Cabela's, 812 13th Avenue, Sidney, NE 69162.

HUNTER-ORANGE HAT COVER

If you like to wear a cowboy or fedora-style hat afield, you can convert it to a safe hunter orange with a hat cover. The nylon blaze-orange shell slips over the crown of the hat, and it can be adjusted through a Velcro tape fastener to fit any size crown. Price: $1.50. Bob Hinman Outfitters, 1217 West Glen, Peoria, IL 61614. Free catalog.

REVERSIBLE JONES CAP

The Jones-style cap is a practical favorite among hunters of all persuasions. This particular cap reverses from blaze orange to a camouflage pattern, making it a good choice for the all-around hunter who enjoys the woodlands, the wetlands, and archery too. Price: $6.50. Duxbak, 825 Noyes Street, Utica, NY 13502.

THERMAL WATCH CAPS

A watch cap is the ultimate in head warmth when worn in conjunction with a hood. These caps boast a heavy thermal knit for maximum insulation and come in either wool or acrylic yarns. Colors available include orange, olive, and camouflage patterns. Price: $3.75. Wigwam Mills, Sheboygan, WI 53081.

"They ain't screwin' our sheep, they're eatin' 'em."
—*Comment heard during a sheepmen's meeting regarding the
possibility of sterilizing coyotes as a means of control*

125

THE CRUSHER

The Columbia Crusher (that's the hat, not the guy wearing it) is a 100 percent oiled-wool floppy-brim hat that just plain feels good to wear. It will keep the rain, sun, and snow out of your eyes, and it sheds water well, yet it's breatheable. When you don't want to wear a hat, just roll it up and put it in your pocket. It will return to shape when you want to wear it again. Available in tan, black, red, and green. Cabela's, 812 13th Avenue, Sidney, NE 69162.

DICK CEPEK, INC.

AUSSIE ARMY HAT

The Australian Army hat with its turned-up brim is known the world over. It has an interesting history that blends fact, fiction, fancy, and symbolism.

Initially, Australia was a kind of penal colony. British criminals and personae non gratae were sent there to open up this new land. Tied up with this notion of undesirability is bastardy, which, legend has it, is indicated by left-handedness. The bar sinister is one historical vestige of this. It appears on the family crests of illegitimate children who were the issue of titled parents. It is essentially the mirror image of the regular family crest, with the bar slicing through the middle of the figures from left to right rather than right to left.

Strangely enough, an unusual number of Aussies were left-handed, and they shot left-handed. The turned-up side of this broad-brimmed hat allows you to lie along the cheekpiece of a rifle stock without knocking the hat off your head. You can own all that symbolism and history and the hat that goes with it for $24.95. Dick Cepek, Inc., 9201 California Avenue, South Gate, CA 90280.

HATS FOR BIG-GAME HUNTERS

There's an old and true saying that goes, "If your feet get cold, put on a hat." Heat rises, and the top of your head amounts to one of your body's greatest radiators. But hats for big-game hunting should be chosen with more in mind than just staying warm. Different styles of headgear evolved to satisfy some specific needs.

- Cowboy hats are popular for hunting out West. They're OK early in the hunting season, when it's not too cold, and great for warding off rain, snow, or a strong sun, but their wide brim is bad news when you're hunting afoot in heavy brush. You spend half the day picking up your hat.

- Peaked baseball-style caps stick to your head better than a cowboy hat, and they keep it warmer too. They're good for cutting down the glare of the sun and perfect for hunting in the rain. They fit well under a slicker hood and the peak directs drops of rain away from the end of your nose.

- Jones-style caps, with a narrow, turned-up brim in the back and along the sides, are good all-around hats for mild to cool weather. The turned-up brim directs drops of water out to the peak of the cap, and they don't collide much with brush.

- Wool watch caps are the most practical headgear in very cold weather when you'll be wearing a hood. Most other hats are so thick and bulky that they won't fit well inside or allow you to cinch the drawstring tight around your face. Watch caps are also handy because they tuck away in your pocket.

- Trooper caps, with fur earmuffs that tie across the top of the hat, are the warmest headgear of all. With the earflaps down, they keep the back of your neck warm. The bills of these caps also turn down to protect your forehead.

There are many possible variations on these basic hat themes. For example, a good friend of mine likes to wear a floppy old fedora. It stays on his head well, and he sits on it when the ground is damp or snowy and also uses it as a kind of rifle rest when shooting from a prone position. One of my favorite hunting hats is a tam o'shanter. You can direct the brim any way you wish and thus ward off sun, wind, or driving rain. When it's very cold, you can pull it down over your ears, and when it's warm you can carry it in your pocket.

The main thing is to choose headgear that matches the conditions under which you'll be hunting. Just about any hat will keep your head warm, but it takes some thought to pick the right hunting hat.

—N.S.

GLOVES FOR BIG-GAME HUNTING

Although there's a good argument for cold being just plain cold, when it comes to your hands it's better to discuss gloves in terms of three kinds of cold.

Let's call the first kind "morning cold," meaning the frosty temperatures and damp air that are commonly associated with early morning hours around the beginning of a hunting season. This kind of cold has an edge, but one that's easily cut by a light pair of finger-fitting gloves. As far as feel is concerned, a supple leather or buckskin glove is about the most sensitive, but it's a poor insulator. A close-weave synthetic glove with a leather or nylon trigger finger will be warmer and reasonably sensitive to things like trigger pull and removing scope caps. A leather glove lined with fleece, wool, or synthetic yarn will be the warmest of all and the least trigger-sensitive.

Which one is the best choice for you is largely a function of your circulation. But consider one other thing—how you carry your gun. If you're used to encircling the receiver, or even the stock and forearm, you'll essentially be holding onto an ice cube, and your hand or hands will get a lot colder, and need a heavier glove, than if they were free of solid contact. So one thing to remember about your hands is that they'll stay warm with light gloves if you'll use a rifle sling.

Wet cold is the second condition. It arises when you're hunting during a cold rain or snow, or even on a clear day when the snow is melting. You're bound to touch the wet snow at some point, and your gloves will get wet. There's nothing that will keep your hands dry under these conditions. Even rubber gloves won't because your hands will perspire and they'll get wet from the inside. The best protection under these circumstances is a pair of wool knit gloves. Wool retains heat when it's wet. It's also wise to carry a second pair of gloves in your pocket, so that if the weather turns suddenly cold (and it often does after a heavy rain) you'll have a dry pair of gloves to put on.

Biting cold, the kind that finds the thermometer hovering in the teens all day long, is best counteracted with mittens. When each finger is housed separately in a glove, even though they're protected by leather, wool, or cotton, there's much greater heat loss than when they're all together, because of the ratio of hand surface that's exposed to the cold. Admittedly, mittens are bulky and awkward, but shooting mittens, with either a slit in the palm or a tailored trigger finger on your shooting hand, allow you to get off a surprisingly quick shot once you get used to them. The exposed trigger finger is the fastest shooting, but they're colder than a slit palm. These mittens are usually leather, heavy wool with a leather palm, or synthetic weave with a down fill. The down-filled mittens are the warmest, but you should only use them in the coldest weather, when there's no possibility of snow melting on them and wetting them. They'll lose virtually all their warmth if they get wet. Which brings us to another point about gloves and warm hands: If you must handle snow, make sure all of it is brushed off the glove as soon as you're done. Residual snow, especially in the palm, will eventually melt from the heat of your hand.

WARM WATER IN YOUR POCKET?

Scotty Handwarmers operate on a chemical process: put in two teaspoons of water, squeeze, and you have six hours of hand-warming heat. They can be used up to ten times before a refill heating unit is needed. There are other sizes of this product, such as body warmers and belts. The hand warmer costs $3.99, the hot pad $5.99, the body warmer (essentially a belt with pads), $8.99. Refill unit is $3.39 for hand and body warmer, $4.99 for hot pad. Scotty Manufacturing, Inc., 14139 21st Avenue North, Plymouth, MN 55441.

DEERSKIN MITTENS WITH TRIGGER FINGER

Of all mitten materials, deerskin has the most sensitive feel. These gloves are lined with polyester fleece, so except for bitterly cold conditions you won't have to wear liners with them. Price: $19.50. L. L. Bean, Freeport, ME 04033.

CATALYTIC HAND WARMERS

Supplant your body or hand heat with a catalytic hand warmer. You'll stay much warmer with one of these chugging away in your pocket or hand. You fill them with hand-warmer (or lighter) fluid, touch off the burner, and when the flame dies down it's ready to go for up to twelve hours.

Warning: Keep them in a soft felt case, rather than bare in your pocket. They get so hot that they can raise a nasty welt, and you won't know it's happening.

There are many sizes to choose from, and one particular model is self-starting. We haven't tried that one yet, but it sounds like a good idea. The other warmers are kind of a hassle to start when your hands are numb, so as a rule you should touch them off before leaving home. With this self-starting feature, you'd save fuel. Price: $6.50. Aladdin Laboratories, 620 South 8th Street, Minneapolis, MN 55402.

"The Nation behaves well if it treats the natural resources as assets which it must turn over to the next generation increased, and not impaired, in value."
—Theodore Roosevelt, 1910

127

PALM-SLIT MITTS IN DOWN AND LEATHER

Eddie Bauer catalogs two excellent mittens for cold weather. If there's any chance you'll be around water, his cowhide Shooting Mitts, with a wool liner, would probably be the better choice because leather is water repellent. For really cold temperatures, try his Sports Mitts, insulated with goose down and with an outer covering of nylon.

Both gloves have palm slits for trigger access (specify right or left hand.) Shooting Mitts, $10.50; Sports Mitts, $19.95. Eddie Bauer, 1737 Airport Way South, Seattle, WA 98134.

THERMAL GLOVE LINER

The ultimate protection for your hands when worn inside a pair of mittens. Warmth-retaining Milanese silk lining plus foam insulation is sure to keep your hands warm on the bitterest days. Price: $12.25; Refrigi-Wear, 71 Inip Drive, Inwood, NY 11696.

DAN OWEN

WOOL GLOVE

This knitted wool glove will keep your hands warm when the weather gets soggy. It has a deerskin palm for a sure grip, a sensitive touch, and long wear. Price: $8.00. Duxbak, 825 Noyes Street, Utica, NY 13502.

ELECTRIC SOCKS AND MITTENS

Electric socks and mittens have always struck me as a super idea that has never panned out in practice. Way back in the late 50s I bought my first pair of electric socks in hopes that they'd be the answer to the numbing cold of 28-degree salt water and ice on the Great South Bay. They were . . . for about two hours. Then they went on the blink and never worked again.

So far, the strength of half a deer and duck season has convinced me that someone has finally come along with a trouble-free heating system. Timely Products Corporation's Lectra-Wear (socks and mittens) have delivered reliable, cozy performance, but before you run out and buy any brand, realize that they are subject to certain limitations.

A normal pair of socks takes a beating in the course of a day afield, a beating that comparatively fragile electric socks will not endure. They are not designed for a lot of walking, but rather for sitting while you wait for that deer or duck to go by. During the test period, if I had a long distance to walk to my stand or blind, I carried the socks in my pocket and then put them on upon arrival. Ditto the mittens, and I took them off and donned my regular pair if my hands were

to come into contact with water.

This isn't as much of a hassle as it might seem, and in fact it's good, sound practice even with standard socks and gloves. Walking and movement create perspiration, and damp clothing will chill you. Don perfectly dry duds when periods of extreme activity are over, and you'll stay a lot warmer with or without a supplementary heat supply.

Another tip: You don't have to keep the juice flowing every second you're afield. Snap the batteries on, warm your extremities, then turn them off until you start to feel cold again. This extends the life of the alkaline batteries, which aren't cheap.

Electric socks and mittens aren't a panacea. They have limited applications in special situations and to some extent must be treated with kid gloves, if you'll excuse the pun. But as an alternative to foot-stamping, finger-flexing, numbing cold and the givaway fidgeting that discomfort brings, they're well worth the price. Socks (sizes 7 to 13), $10.95; mitts (red or green, with right- or left-hand shooting slits), $17.95. Timely Products Corp., 210 Eliot Street, Fairfield, CT 06430. —N.S.

SILK UNDERSOCKS

If you have problems with blistered feet after a long hunt, one way to avoid this painful problem is to wear pure silk socks next to your feet. The slick, smooth material eliminates friction between your foot and footwear and it helps carry moisture away from your skin to outer stockings. Silk socks, $3.95 a pair (white only). Bob Hinman Outfitters, 1217 West Glen, Peoria, IL 61614.

QUILTED BOOTIES

Kodel polyester fiber fill forms a barrier between inner socks and outer boot that keeps your feet warm. Booties have an elastic ankle band to ensure a snug, toe-warming fit. These booties have insulated cushioned soles and look like they'll keep the coldest feet warm. Price: $6.50. Refrigi-Wear, 71 Inip Drive, Inwood, NY 11696.

A SYSTEM FOR YOUR SOCKS

When you're afoot in the woods, a good pair of socks become as important as any other wearing apparel. They not only keep your feet warm, they keep them comfortable: free from blistering and binding.

The standard hunting sock is a high-top wool sock. Pure wool is best, though they require a lot of care, such as washing them out every night and drying them blocked and in a cool spot so they won't shrink. Because of all this hassle, and the primitive facilities at most big-game camps, you might prefer to use a wool/synthetic combination. Most "washable" wool socks share these materials. You'll still have to keep these socks clean by washing them, or bring several fresh changes of socks (dirty socks don't insulate well, and your hunting partners won't appreciate them either), but you can soap, rinse, and dry them without kid-glove handling.

As the weather gets colder, you can always add a second pair of wool socks if your feet get icy, but first consider two things. If two pairs of socks create an overly snug fit in your boot (you have to fight to get the boot on, and you can't wiggle your toes), whatever warmth gained by that extra layer of wool will probably be lost by restricted circulation. If your foot is going to stay warm, blood has to circulate throughout. Another factor that might be cooling your tootsies is moisture or perspiration. If your socks are damp when you take them off in the evening, instead of wearing two pairs of wool socks, use a pair of Wick-Dry socks under your wool socks. These Wick-Dry socks are smooth on one side and look like a terrycloth towel on the other. They function just like a lampwick, transferring moisture away from your foot. There's one other advantage to Wick-Dries: They'll keep the outer sock cleaner longer, so you don't have to hassle with washing it so much (you'll have to wash the Wick-Dries, but they're even easier than wool/synthetics.

If you have a history of blisters, consider wearing silk socks next to your feet. They're smooth and slick and act as a kind of lubricant between your foot and the boot insides.

One kind of sock not to wear are those crazy things with "fingers" for your toes, like a glove. I can't imagine how or why they were invented, except as a joke. Your toes will always stay warmer when they're together, like fingers inside a mitten, because they warm each other.

While booties and felt inserts aren't exactly socks, they deserve some kind of mention, and it seems most logical here. In principle, the more insulation you fit around your feet, the warmer they'll stay. But don't forget that matter of circulation. A boot that fits you properly with one pair of socks will never fit right with a pair of booties added.

If you have constant trouble with cold feet, buy a special pair of hiking boots for cold weather that are fitted to whatever combination of booties and socks you need to be comfortable, but underneath all those layers of down, foam, or felt, you'll still be wise to wear wool or Wick-Dries next to your skin.

BEAVER SOCKS

These were the standard hunting socks twenty years ago, and you can't go wrong with them today. They're 50 percent wool, 10 percent cotton, 40 percent synthetic, retain heat when damp, and are washable. Price: $2.10. Duxbak, 825 Noyes Street, Utica, NY 13502.

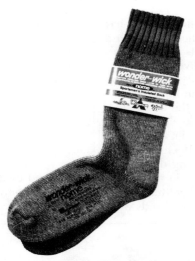

THERMAL WICK-DRY SOCKS

Here's a neat combination for cold feet—a wicking feature incorporated into a thermal knit. They're 65 percent acrylic, 25 percent wool, and 10 percent nylon. Price: $4.25. Wigwam Mills, Sheboygan, WI 53081.

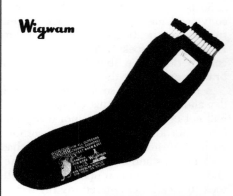

TWO LAYER SNOW-MOBILE THERMAL SOCKS

These socks were designed for snow-mobiling, one of the coldest sports there is—for your feet. A moisture-repelling inner layer of yarn wicks perspiration to the moisture-absorbing outer layer. A terry stitch creates air pockets for thermal warmth. Length: 12½ inches. Price: $4.25. Wigwam Mills, Sheboygan, WI 53081.

WOOL THERMO SOCKS

This 100-percent-wool sock is listed as medium weight, but a special thermal knit pattern makes for exceptional warmth. Price: $3.75. Wigwam Mills, Sheboygan, WI 53081.

HEAVYWEIGHT WOOL SOCKS

For those who like a heavy wool sock, these Klondikes are 90 percent wool and 10 percent nylon. They are of an extra-heavy knit and are fully cushioned from toe to rib top. Price: $5.95. Wigwam Mills, Sheboygan, WI 53081.

PLASTIC SOCKS: A NEW THEORY OF WARMTH

All that's ever been penned regarding foot warmth may be summed up with the following caveat: "Your foot must breathe!"

Then along comes a new theory that contradicts everything you've always believed. In practice it's an airtight plastic "sock" (big baggies also work) worn over wick-dry socks, inside your boots.

Actually, it is not a contradiction but rather an extension of the wicking theory. If your foot breathes, some heat must be lost in the process. If it does not breathe (and surrounded by plastic, it won't), that amount of heat will be retained. With modern wicking socks, the moisture is transferred out and against the plastic, not your foot, so your feet actually stay dry.

We've played around with this but haven't tested it sufficiently to say good or bad. It appears to work best when you have two or more pairs of socks on your feet, but we've noticed one inherent flaw. Your boots should never be tight, because lack of circulation becomes a factor in cold feet. Yet if boots are loose or just comfortable with plastic socks, you do a lot of sliding around inside, and it makes for tricky walking. We all agree it's a technique that's worth looking into, though. Foot Guard plastic socks, $0.29. Wigwam Mills, Sheboygan, WI 53081.

BAMA SOCKS

This product is a kind of compromise that falls between socks and felt boot inserts. Thicker than socks, though not formed like a shoe, they are of the down or Dacron "booty" genre. They have a "wick" feature: an inner lining of Acryl fleece to insulate the foot and an exterior of cotton tricot to absorb moisture.

I found them a very good insulator, worn over a pair of Wick-Dry socks and inside a pair of chest waders. We duck hunted on open salt water from sunup to sunset, and the temperature dropped from 35 to 21 degrees. By the time we left, it was making ice. My feet felt cool when I sat for long periods, but they never became uncomfortable. The Bama looks well-made enough to last about a season, even if you do a lot of hiking, and I've got a hunch that with the addition of a light leather sole, an old pair of Bamas would make a dandy slipper for hunting camp. Price: $4.95. Bob Hinman Outfitters, 1217 West Glen, Peoria, IL 61614.

—N.S.

CABELA'S CATALOG

The Cabela catalog numbers in the neighborhood of a hundred pages, about half of which are in color. It is issued semiannually. The spring/summer issue is primarily a fishing catalog, the fall/winter issue a hunting catalog.

We give these folks high marks as a retail outlet on several counts. First, they have a good, representative selection of products that touch most corners of a hunter/shooter's interest. With a few exceptions, you can thumb through this book and come up with all you'll ever need to hunt big game, upland game, waterfowl, or whatever.

Second, their selection of wares comes close to ours. Not that we're the ultimate authority, but we have had a chance to evaluate objectively a lot of products, and in more instances than mere chance would dictate, when we select a brand to feature because it is exceptional, it will also appear in Cabela's.

Third, in our research we are privy to wholesale and jobber prices that manufacturers charge. It wouldn't do any good to list them, since you won't get goods at those rates anyway, but checking Cabella's prices against what they probably paid for the goods they're listing, they're hardly price-gouging. In short, these folks know what hunters need, they know quality, and they are reasonable.

Free catalog: Cabela's, 812 13th Avenue, Sidney, NE 69162.

WORLD'S FINEST QUALITY SPORTING GOODS

THE GUIDE: A-WALL TENT FOR COLD CAMPING

This tent is the classic used by guides, outfitters, and anyone else with a lick of sense who will be camping for long periods of time in cold weather. Standard features include white canvas for a bright, cheery interior, a sod or dew cloth, to seal out floor drafts, a zippered door, a zippered ridgepole opening, a zippered rear window for ventilation, and an asbestos stovepipe shield for a wood-burning stove. Options available include a tent fly, a snap-in floor, jointed upright and ridgepoles.

These tents come in sizes from 8 by 10 feet to 16 by 20 feet. Sixteen-by-20-foot tent, $551.60. Colorado Tent and Awning Co., 3333 East 52nd Avenue, Denver, CO 80216.

TUFTED AIR MATTRESS

This is the kind of air mattress that will feel most like the bed you left at home and consequently will probably afford the best night's sleep. Includes a "Measure-air" safety valve. Guaranteed for 18 months. Dimensions, 30 by 74 inches, weight, 4½ pounds. Price: $36.60. Colorado Tent and Awning Co., 3333 East 52nd Avenue, Denver, CO 80216.

SHEEPHERDER WOOD-BURNING STOVE

This is the most practical way to beat a large tent. These stoves are made of 22-gauge steel with reinforced corners. The firebox takes 12-inch logs, and the stove has an oven for baking. The stove includes a set of telescoping stovepipes for ease of transport (stove weight, 22 pounds). Price: $50.00. Colorado Tent and Awning Co., 3333 East 52nd Avenue, Denver, CO 80216.

GENUINE GI ISSUE

A MOST BASIC NEED

If you've never been confronted with a choice between pine cones, crisp leaves, or your shirt tail as a substitute for toilet paper, you either have uncommon foresight or chronic constipation.

This 3-by-5½-by-¼-inch heavy paper envelope answers the call for toilet tissue and solves the problem of carrying a cumbersome roll. Each package contains 100 sheets. You might get as much as a nickel a sheet from your buddies if you barter up until the last moment. Price: 15 cents per package. Dick Cepek, Inc., 9201 California Avenue, South Gate, CA 90280.

"Let us be thankful that there are still thousands of cool, green nooks beside crystal springs, where the weary soul may hide for a time, away from debts, duns and deviltries."
—Nessmuk

131

PROPANE CATALYTIC HEATER

A catalytic heater means safe heat for a tent, cottage, or even in a duck blind. Primus's Duo-Flow 6-inch has a 6,500 BTU capacity and throws heat in two directions. Its metal case stores three disposable cylinders, or the unit may be used in conjunction with refillable propane bottles. Primus-Sievert, P.O. Box 502, North Haven, CT 06473.

ULTI-MATE CAMP KITCHEN

Propane has one big advantage over white gas, and that's instant lighting. There's no pumping or prepping required for light or heat. Primus's Ulti-Mate camp kitchen is a propane-fueled light and cookstove combination that's powered by a central gas bottle. Large capacity propane tanks also hook up to this system. Price: $102.95. Primus-Sievert, P.O. Box 502, North Haven, CT 06473.

Explorer Propane Lamp

This backpack-weight propane lamp lights at the strike of a match and throws as much light as a 100-watt bulb. They're great around camp for 2 A.M. trips to the outhouse and for fast light first thing in the morning before gas lanterns are pumped and the fire stoked. Price: $2.50. Primus-Sievert, P.O. Box 502, North Haven, CT 06473.

COLORADO TENT AND AWNING CO. CATALOG

This company makes and markets material for the mountain hunter. The pages of their catalog list things like big A-wall tents that you can heat with wood-burning stoves, panniers and pack saddles for horses, and even covers for covered wagons. They'll also make tents or any canvas gear to order.

One remarkable feature of this outfit is that they discount their catalog prices 25 percent when they don't have a dealer in your area. Good stuff, well made, at reasonable prices. If you need something that's made out of canvas, start looking here. Free catalog: Colorado Tent and Awning Co., 3333 East 52nd Avenue, Denver, CO 80216.

STAG HIMALAYAN: BELOW-ZERO COMFORT RANGE

This bag is insulated with a full 5 pounds of prime goose down in slant baffle construction, with a water repellent 10.38-ounce army duck cover and a cotton lining. Inside the bag is a zip-out 24-ounce virgin wool blanket plus an extra wool shoulder blanket.

The bag has a full-length, heavy-duty No. 10 Delrin zipper with two-way sliders and double weather protection from an outside storm flap and an inner down-insulated weather flap. A drawcord at the top allows closing the bag in around the shoulders.

Finished size of the king-sized Himalayan is 41 by 85 inches. Total weight, packed inside its duffel, is 25 pounds.

The Stag Himalayan is recommended only if you'll be encountering extremely cold temperatures, such as might be found late in the season at high altitudes in the Rockies. It is *not* recommended if you plan to get there by backpack. Price: $275.00. Hirsh-Weis, 5203 Southeast John Creek Boulevard, Portland, OR 97206.

KELTY DAY PACK

This is a good pack for the day hunter—narrow enough so it doesn't hang up on brush yet roomy enough for binoculars, spotting scopes, rain gear, ropes . . . just about anything you might want to tote up to timberline.

Features include a separate easy-to-reach compartment for clothes, a teardrop shape to dampen bouncing and shifting of loads and to facilitate passage under low-hanging brush, and accessory strap holders. Available in red and blue. Price: $24.00. Kelty Pack, Inc., P.O. Box 639, Sun Valley, CA 91325.

If you can't afford a long stay at hunting camp, or if you'll be hunting with a small party, Wildwood's Wrangler tent (10 by 12 feet) is large enough for comfort, small enough to be heated with a catalytic stove, and goes up and comes down fast. It includes an outside support system, a sewn-

Wildwood Tent for Weekenders

in floor, and reinforced stress points. The tent is made of tan poplin, and the floor is

a heavy-duty drill. It's not recommended for wood-burning stoves.

Wildwood lists a whole slew of quality canvas items and camping products in their free catalog. Wrangler tent, $249.00. Wildwood Products, 1433 North Water Street, Milwaukee, WI 53202.

Wood-burning camp stoves are built of relatively light sheet steel so they can be moved easily, but that same lightness usually finds them burning through the

SAVING A STOVE

bottom after a few years' use. You can prolong the life of your camp stove by lin-

ing the bottom with two inches of dry sand before starting your fire. The sand also helps the stove hold heat through the night.

McCULLOCH POWER MAC 6 CHAIN SAW

The Power Mac 6 is a lightweight chain saw that packs heavy-duty performance, a combination that makes it a perfect companion around a hunting camp. For $179.95 you get a 2-cubic-inch engine, a 14-inch bar, chain brake, and an automatic oiler. This kind of saw is perfect for cutting camp wood and building makeshift furniture, and it will do double duty for home firewood. Because it's so easy to carry, it's also ideal for clearing trails. My Power Mac was once instrumental in getting two six-point bull elk out of the woods and into a pickup truck. They were shot in an incredible tangle of peckerpole pine, and the only way out was via a chain-sawed trail straight down the fall line.

A few words of caution about power saws, though: Remember that you can't use them in most wilderness or primitive areas. Also, these small saws require a lot of care in order to function properly. Packing an intricate mechanism into such a small, light frame means a loss of some heavy-duty dependability. Check the tightness of the chain after each half hour of use, and touch up the teeth after each cord of wood. Always keep a spare spark plug handy, and strip the saw down and clean out the sawdust after every five hours of use. If you don't, the accumulated dust will act like insulation, the air-cooling feature of the saw will be shortcircuited, and the engine will overheat. Price: $179.95. McCulloch Corp., 5400 Alla Road, Los Angeles, CA 90066, or your local McCulloch dealer.   —N.S.

TREE HANGER AND LANTERN FOR OUTSIDE LIGHTING

It's better to light just one little candle than curse the darkness, but if you're stumbling around outside in the pitch black, you'll find a double mantle gas lantern with a tree hanger is better yet. The tree hanger has an adjustable chain, so it can be used around trees, limbs, or posts. Aside from lanterns, the hanger can be used for a mirror, foodstuffs, or clothing—anything you might want to get up off the ground. Best of all, it requires no nails.

A double-mantle gas lantern is the backbone of any camp or cottage lighting system. It throws enough light to illuminate a 20-by-20-foot room and burns for about 8 hours per filling. Lantern hanger, $3.00; double mantle gas lantern, $25.00. Coleman, 250 North St. Francis, Wichita, KS 67201.

SLEEPING BAG SENSE

Here are a few things to remember when buying a sleeping bag specifically for a hunting trip.

- Square-bottom or "rectangular" bags are the least constraining and the most like your bed at home, but they contain a lot of unused space that your body will have to heat. Semirectangular bags are a cross between a tight-fitting mummy and a rectangular bag. They have a lot of foot room but not much wasted room. Mummy bags are form-fitting and the most saving of body heat, but most people can't get used to sleeping in a cocoon. They also take up the least packing space and should be the least expensive, since they use the least material.

- Zippers should be heavy-duty and be encased in a flap or snapped closure. Without some sort of protection, a lot of cold will transfer through the zipper. A full zipper means the bag can be opened to lie flat. This makes airing the bag out a breeze and means you can use it as a comforter at home on cold nights. A double zipper that opens from each end is a plus too. On unusually warm nights you can open the bottom as wide as it takes to create a draft that will keep you comfortable.

- Batts—tubes or boxes of sleeping bag fill—should be constructed so they overlap. When batts are simply stitched through from one side to the other, they mat the material in the stitching and insulating properties are lost.

- No part of a sleeping bag should be waterproofed. It must breathe so that body moisture can escape from the bag. Use ground cloths under you and tents over you to keep dry.

THE OFFICIAL HUNTER'S PERSONALITY TEST

by Chuck Durang

What makes a hunter? Are you suited to follow the Call of the Wild, or would you be better off making potholders? The ideal "hunter personality" is a rare blend of manual dexterity, physical endurance, mental delirium, and pemmican that until now has been impossible to detect without Trial by Ordeal.

But now the magic of modern psychology can help you determine, *right in your own home,* whether you are the type who should be hip deep in snow, carrying a lot of heavy stuff in pursuit of an animal without the common decency to turn sideways . . . or the ignoble stay-at-home, doomed to spend the winter indoors before a roaring fire, drinking brandy and suffering a lapful of amorous female.

Gentlemen, load yours pens and *answer vigorously:*

1. I would rather be (a) Teddy Roosevelt, (b) Fonzie, (c) left alone.
2. Some of my favorite things are (a) high tides, warm woolen mittens, and Muhammad Ali, (b) three-day weekends, chocolate-covered hard-boiled egg on a stick, and the Tydee Bowl man, (c) Mount Rushmore, Mount Whitney, and Raquel Welch.
3. I often travel by (a) bus, (b) yak, (c) night
4. I am most enraged by (a) guerrilla warfare, (b) Democrats, (c) Howard Cosell.
5. My fondest memory is of (a) *Lassie Come Home,* (b) the Dole-Mondale Debate, (c) a Big Mac.

Okay, take a break. Light 'em up if you got 'em. You get the idea, right? We'll find out if you're a hunter, by Natty Bumppo we will. Forge on—*choose decisively:*

6. My idea of an evening on the town is (a) getting stiff in the joints, (b) getting stiff in the joints, (c) all of the above.
7. I would rather (a) fall off a log, (b) buy Butte, Montana, (c) not.
8. I sometimes wish I were (a) Tony Orlando, (b) Dawn, (c) stronger than dirt.
9. If I had my life to live over, I'd (a) dream the impossible dream, (b) not, (c) live it as a blonde.
10. I would most like to be marooned on a desert island with (a) Ratso Rizzo, (b) the Shah of Iran, (c) the Cincinnati Reds.

See, some of them are really tough choices, right? Okay, it's the home stretch. *Select with vim:*

11. I would like to go (a) skin diving, (b) bananas, (c) to Muskogee.
12. I wish (a) the sun would set on the British Empire, (b) my brother-in-law would move out, (c) I could find a broad who can play pinochle.
13. I am versed in (a) karate, (b) voodoo, (c) running.
14. I am good at (a) ax-throwing, (b) making my own bed, (c) none of the above.
15. I am (a) the second coming of Liberace, (b) a stone's throw from being a heartbeat away, (c) tired of this test.

That's it. Send your answers, written on the back of an envelope, gum wrapper, or bathroom door, to the publisher of this book. It'll serve him right. Better yet, grade your own test. All (a) answers are right and all (b) answers are wrong. No (c) answers count. Exception: if facing West when taking this test, vice versa. Count each right answer as 5 points, and each wrong answer as 5 points. If you scored 100 or better, you should be locked up.

Chuck Durang works as a logger in the Mojave Desert. His hobbies include raising catfish and restoring antique cuckoo clocks.

CAMP AXES

Axes are the traditional wood cutter around hunting camps, but it's a tradition you should question. You can cut firewood far more efficiently with a light bow saw, or better yet, a chain saw. Axes are useful under certain conditions, however. They'll split sawed wood, they're great for lopping off limbs, and they are efficient at light cutting, so long as you can get through the log in two swipes, one on each side. If it takes more chopping than that, you're probably wasting energy better spent with a saw. Axes are also useful hammers for pounding tent stakes and nails; consequently, the most useful camp ax will be single-bitted. The flat-back feature of a single-bitted ax also allows the head to be used like a wedge when you can't split a thick log with one stroke.

Camp axe: 3¼-inch blade, head weight 2¼ pounds, 27-inch overall length. Price: $10.00. Precise Imports Corp., 3 Chestnut Street, Suffern, NY 10901.

FRONTIER CAMPWARE

A porcelain finish on steel utensils is traditional camp cookware. It cleans up fast, it won't break, and all the plates, cups, and pots can be put on the stove for warming or reheating.

General Housewares Corporation manufactures a camp kitchen full of pots, pans, kettles, skillets, plates, and cups. Sizes range from a cooking kit for two up to a 24-cup coffee pot and a 12-inch skillet should you like to hunt with crowds.

Sample prices: 10-inch dinner plate, $1.50; 12-inch skillet, $5.75. General Housewares Corp., P.O. Box 4066, Terre Haute, IN 87804.

9-piece set in reuseable carton

ROLLAWAY TABLE

This 3-foot-square table rolls up into a 7-by-36-inch carrying duffel for easy packing into the outback. It has a weatherproofed wood slat top and sets up as easy as a conventional card table. Useful for gas cookstoves, washbasins, and card games after the day is done. Price: $39.95. Dick Cepek, Inc., 9201 California Avenue, South Gate, CA 90280.

Sims Collapsible Wood-Burning Stoves

These stoves are designed with the horse packer in mind. The assembled stove measures 15 by 13 by 22 inches and breaks down into a suitcase-sized package weighing 36 pounds (stovepipes included). Also available as an option is a hot-water tank that attaches to the back of the stove, affording a ready hot-water supply around camp for washing faces and dishes. All in all, an efficient camp stove and a great idea that fits equally well on horseback or in the trunk of a car. Free brochure. Price: $75.00. Sims Stoves, Lovell, WY 82431.

"The slapjacks are a solid job of work, made to last, and not go to pieces in a person's stomach like a trivial bun."
—Charles Dudley Warner, quoted by Nessmuk

135

PHOEBUS 625 CAMP STOVE

This stove bridges the gap between ultra-light backpacker stoves and two- and three-burner propane or gasoline stoves. Features include excellent fuel-economy/heat-output ratio and dependable performance in cold weather. A good bet for a camp backup stove or for backpack hunting in cold weather. Price: $38.00. Precise Imports Corp., 3 Chestnut Street, Suffern, NY 10901.   —F.S.

BASE CAMP TIP

The plastic lid from a 2-pound coffee can fits snugly onto the base of most gas lanterns, providing a nonskid, nonscarring surface and a handy place to store extra mantles and repair materials.

TIPS ON TENTING

A hunting camp under canvas is a different way of life from what you might have remembered during midsummer. The most immediate change will be that unless you're in a warm climate, or in the middle of a bad-luck warm spell, you'll be spending most of your nonhunting hours inside.

For all practical purposes, this means you can forget about lightweight "mountain tents" of the backpacker variety. They are handy to store gear in (which also must be kept undercover), and they may be used on an overnight backpack hunt early in the season, but for long-range, comfortable living and sleeping, look to a large tent of canvas or cotton drill material.

If your camp-out will be of short duration, let's say less than five days, you can get by comfortably with 30 square feet of tent floor space per person. If you'll be camping/hunting for longer than that, increase that floor space to 40 square feet. Part of the reason is the extra provisions, clothing, and equipment you'll need to support a long stay, but an equally important part is a kind of territorial imperative. The longer you camp out, the more room you'll need to get along with your hunting pals and feel comfortable.

A tent with a floor is fine for short stays, but it's a pain in the neck to keep clean, and it won't stay dry because of tracked-in snow and wet. If you object to good old dirt underfoot, throw down a canvas tarp for a floor. You can roll it up, toss it outside, and clean and dry it there.

A tent without a floor should have dew flaps. These are a skirt or apron, sewn just above the bottom of the walls. You pile dirt on these dew flaps and thus eliminate drafts across the floor. Another wise choice is a tent with white or bright-colored walls. They'll throw a lot more light at night than old olive-drab "army" tents, and you won't have to use lamps during the day. In general, they make for cheerier living, too.

For short trips, any one of the modern propane- or white-gas-fueled catalytic heaters should keep you toasty inside. But when using a large tent on long trips, you'll find a small wood-burning "sheepherder stove" worth its relatively light weight in Arab oil. Fuel is no farther than the nearest deadfall, so you needn't bring gallons of gas or bottles of propane. Your cooking and heating unit is one, so you gain even more compactability. Most remarkable, there is something about the heat, smell, and crackle of a wood stove that makes it an indescribable joy to behold, after you come back from a long day on windy mountain ridges and prop your feet up next to the oven. Next to your trophy buck or bull elk, the fondest memories of your hunt will be that simple stove.

Other creature comforts will help too. In fact, given the limits of reason, the more homelike furnishings you can incorporate into big-game camp, the happier you'll be. You should have a table and chairs for every hunter, and a set of shelves for the cook. Two washbasins, one with clean water and one with soapy water, are the only way you'll keep dishes clean, and it will be far more pleasurable if those washbasins can be kept full on a table of their own. Cots round out the basic hunting camp interior. Actually, sleeping on a cot is not quite as warm as sleeping on the ground because air can get under you, but with a stove things should stay pretty warm anyway. And the biggest advantage of a cot isn't really in the sleeping, it's in the storage space it provides underneath.

—N.S.

CAST-IRON COOKWARE

Despite all the modern miracles of Teflon, aluminum, and Pam, none of them can compare to the magic of a meal cooked in a cast-iron skillet. They're heavy, so they're not exactly pack-in items, but as cookware in a permanent camp they're unbeatable. Cast-iron cookware has perfect heat distribution and long heat retention, and you can clean up with a paper towel.

Kit includes dutch oven, 10½- and 8-inch skillets, and a 19-inch pancake griddle. Price: $29.95. L. L. Bean, Inc., Freeport, ME 04033.

SOTZ CORPORATION

Splitting Maul for Camp Firewood

The wide flare from edge to back on a splitting maul wedges wood apart on impact. Conventional "trail" or "woodsman" axes often stick into the butt end of the log.

The Sotz Wood-Splitting Maul is a beast of a tool, with a 20-pound head and a pipe handle threaded into the head. It will never break, and it wedges apart even big hardwoods. Price: $15.70. Sotz Corp., 23797 Sprague Road, Columbia Station, OH 44028. —F.S.

CHARTER ARMS
SKACHET

CUTTING   SKINNING   HAMMERING

CHOPPING   FIELD DRESSING

WHATSIT? A SKACHET

This tool is a little hard to classify, since it's a jack-of-all-trades, incorporating features of a knife, a hammer, and a hatchet. We tested one, and as is normally the case with such multipurpose gadgets, it doesn't really cut as comfortably and efficiently as a top sheath knife, nor is it as good a chopping tool as a hand hatchet.

Still, it is capable of all the work it is advertised as doing, and packing that much performance into a 14-ounce package is noteworthy in itself. Actually, the place we found it most useful was around a tent camp, for trimming and pounding stakes, making fuzz sticks, and using as a back-up knife.

All in all, a worthwhile investment for the hunter/camper. Price: $15.95. Charter Arms Corporation, 430 Sniffens Lane, Stratford, CT 06497.

ROCKY MOUNTAIN GOAT HUNT
by Dick Miller

I got my goat in two days, which has to rate as some kind of a miracle when you consider the odds against it. First, I was fresh out of Wisconsin and was unfamiliar with mountain hunting. Second, a mountain goat is a permit animal in Montana, and licenses are drawn by lottery. You stand about a 40-to-1 chance of getting a goat permit. Finally, I could only afford three days' time to hunt, and any wise man would set aside three weeks.

Well, maybe a "miracle" isn't exactly correct, because there were a few things I did right. The first was to con Bob Morton into coming along. Bob is a good friend and part-time guide who knows the Spanish Peaks wilderness area where we were to hunt. Next was getting up into goat country as early as possible the day before the season opened, so we could do a lot of glassing. That's what really turned the trick, because we had a herd spotted before the sun went down and at least had an idea of where we'd be going the next morning.

It snowed that night, which was lousy luck. It made climbing tough and spotting the white goats nearly impossible. But we started climbing in the dark and struggled our way up through shale rock and thin air until we felt we were above the herd. That was another "right" thing. It took extra energy, and it was a chancy play, but when the sun came out we saw the goats below us.

They were 400 yards away, and I wanted a closer shot, but as we inched toward them I started a small rockslide and the goats started moving. I picked out the biggest horns I could find and connected on the second shot. I still wasn't all that lucky, though, as the goat slid a ways, then

dropped off a cliff and fell 50 feet, breaking off a horn that was never found.

If I'm ever lucky enough to draw a permit again, I'd do things a little differently. For one thing, I would get in shape for those high altitudes (a friend who accompanied us got altitude sickness), and I'd budget more time for the hunt, so that if it snowed I could wait for it to melt. I'd also wait for a better place to drop the goat, though surprisingly enough the meat wasn't that torn up when we butchered him out.

Dick Miller talks a lot about luck, but his deeds belie his words. Since the goat hunt, he's successfully hunted antelope, moose, elk, and deer. Not bad for a "dude" from Wisconsin.

WALT HODGES

"Recreational development is a job not of building roads into lovely country but of building receptivity into the still unlovely human mind."

—Aldo Leopold

137

HOW TOUGH ARE ELK AND MOOSE?

by Erwin A. Bauer

Living as I do on the boundary of the National Elk Refuge in Jackson Hole, Wyoming, I spend every winter with about 8,000 elk and several hundred Shiras moose, the two largest deer living on the face of the earth. What never fails to amaze me is how tough, durable, and absolutely tenacious these two mammals are. The winters are brutal, lasting for at least five months, and the temperature frequently falls below zero for weeks at a time. In addition the snow is deep—often so deep that humans can travel across country only on skis and snowshoes.

Still the survival rate of the elk and moose is extremely high. Whenever a storm strikes, the moose simply bed down until it blows over. I've found them nearly covered over under deep drifts, with only their noses exposed, but apparently none the worse for the weather. When the storm breaks, the moose survive on a simple diet of willow tips and alder that they are able to reach on long, powerful legs. It is true that springtime finds even the finest specimens in deplorable shape—emaciated, their hair falling out. But with warmer days and new green growth, most recover to grow big and sleek again.

It is possible throughout the winter to "drive" right among the massed elk (on the Refuge) in a horse-drawn sled. One day on such a ride I noticed that one huge bull had one antler broken off, while the other antler had been neatly drilled, near the base, by a bullet during the hunting season just passed. The mushroomed slug of some unlucky hunter had obviously knocked off the missing antler. But can you imagine what an impact that must have had on the elk? Only an incredibly tough animal could have survived it.

It is true that nowadays the elk of the National Elk Refuge manage to exist in winter only by freeloading. Their traditional migration routes southward to former wintering ranges have been blocked off by the town of Jackson and by cattle ranching operations. So it is necessary to feed them with hay and alfalfa pellets, a practice which concentrates all the elk in herds far too large for their own good. Crowding spreads disease and viruses. The elk are more susceptible to everything from mange to pneumonia, especially toward the tag end of winter. It is sad to see some die slowly in the intense cold, after which the carcasses are eaten by coyotes, ravens, and eagles.

But as I said, elk are super-tough. At worst the overall mortality is rarely more than 5 percent and during late April most of the vast herd migrates again to the high country to produce another generation of this splendid game animal.

HONDA GENERATORS

Courtesy of your friendly neighborhood motorcycle people, you can now, with the mere addition of a 40-pound EM400 portable generator, watch the Sunday afternoon football game while you are up in the Colorado Rockies on your elk hunt. On color TV! This little unit puts out 400 watts of AC power through a 55 cc 4-stroke engine. The half-gallon tank (gasoline) will operate the generator for about four hours. It has a recoil starter, is about the size of a portable TV, and retails for $300.00.

While the EM400 would be the most practical for a horse camp (it has enough capacity to run some electric lighting and cooking stuff at the same time), Honda has other generators suitable for more permanent camps that put out from 1,500 to 5,000 watts (enough to run a heater and meat

cooler, plus lighting and cooking). Prices range from $450.000 to $1450.00. The largest are electrically started, and the very biggest is mounted on wheels, since it weighs 423 pounds. American Honda Motor Company, Inc., P.O. Box 50, 100 West Alondra Boulevard, Gardena, CA 90247.

FIBERGLASS PREFAB CABIN

This modular fiberglass cabin boasts 423 square feet of floor space, and it's maintenance-free inside and out, since there's no wood used in the structure whatsoever. Along with clean lines and clean living, it also carries an amazingly low price tag: $4,500.00. Modular Structures, P.O. Box 318, Bala Cynwyd, PA 19004.

The Aristocrat

These cabins are precut, much the same as a log home, and shipped broken down. The walls amount to 3-or-4-inch-thick semirounded cedar boards that interlock.

The smallest shelter made by this company is 320 square feet and the largest is in the 2,000-square-foot range. Prices cited are by the square foot: 3-inch walls, $9.90 per square

MODULAR VACATION HOMES

Nobel Homes, based in Orlando, Florida, markets vacation and permanent homes built on the modular principle. They are prefabricated and shipped to the building site, then pieced together like building blocks. These homes arrive completely furnished, with all wiring, plumbing, and the like.

While these homes are not the least expensive on the market, we have it on excellent authority that on a cost/quality basis they're one of the best deals in the United States. Free brochure. D. M. Knoebel Corp., 3748 Bengert Street, Orlando, FL 32808.

PAN ABODE CEDAR HOMES

foot; 4-inch walls (for unusually hot or cold climates), $11.40 per square foot.

Illustrated brochure, plus a packet of sample floor plans, $2.00. Pan Abode, 4350 Lake Washington Boulevard, North Renton, WA 98055.

LOG RECREATION HOMES

If you're ever in the market for a mountain hideaway and hunting camp at a most reasonable price, look into a prefabricated log home. Building with logs has a lot going for it. There is no need for baffling, insulation, or interior or exterior siding. The log is your wall, inside and out, and six inches of wood makes for quite an insulator.

Maintenance is low, too. Exterior protection is more than provided by a coat of easy-to-apply stain, and bothersome chinking is not necessary, so long as the logs are tongue-and-grooved. As each log is laid up, a narrow strip of insulation is bedded between the upper and lower log. Once in place, the seal between the two is airtight.

Best of all, costs are low. The human effort involved in harvesting, dimensioning, and grooving enough logs for a sizable home is far less than that required to produce the two layers of planed lumber, studding, papering, insulating, and siding required for a standard frame structure. In other words, your basic building materials are cheap. Then, too, they are so simple to erect that you can do it yourself.

Prefabricated log homes are sold in kit form. Plans and materials are numbered. You place log 123 on side A, followed by 124 on side B and so forth, and walls, windows,

and doors begin to take shape, just like the Lincoln Log toy houses you built as a kid. If you don't want to tackle the building chores yourself, most prefab suppliers will build your home for you, at a cost of between one third and one half over the purchase price of the basic home kit.

Costs for a do-it-yourself log home vary according to the amount of rooms and floor space you want. Examples of some current prices: $5,513.00 for an 18-by-26-foot bare-bones cabin, and $20,053.00 for a 44-by-40-foot two-story, four-bedroom home. For more detailed information write: Northern Products, Inc., Bomarc Road, Bangor ME 04401 (East Coast) or Lumber Enterprises, Star Route, Gallatin Gateway, MT 59705 (West Coast).

"Be sure of three things when you buy a place; your water, your neighbors, and your land, in that order."
—Joseph Wolny

139

MINI-MILL
LUMBER-MAKING CHAIN SAW ATTACHMENT

THIS IS HOW IT WORKS:

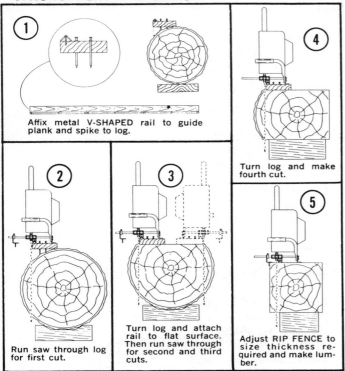

1. Affix metal V-SHAPED rail to guide plank and spike to log.
2. Run saw through log for first cut.
3. Turn log and attach rail to flat surface. Then run saw through for second and third cuts.
4. Turn log and make fourth cut.
5. Adjust RIP FENCE to size thickness required and make lumber.

MILL-DIMENSIONED LUMBER FROM LOGS WITH A CHAIN SAW

Build your own hunting cabin or camp with dimensioned lumber you mill on the spot. The Mini-Mill is a remarkable gadget that clamps a chain saw down tight in a jig. You nail a light steel rail to a log, and the jig and saw follow the rail, cutting off slabs and squaring up the round log into beams or planks. There are larger jigs for larger jobs. This tool and this concept have built shelters in the outback throughout the world. It's used by the U.S. Forest Service, the Red Cross, and others. Free brochure and catalog of various attachments, chains, sharpeners, and jigs for do-it-yourself lumber. Mini-Mill, $49.50. Granberg Industries, 200 South Garrard Boulevard, Richmond, CA 94804.

BUY YOUR OWN HUNTING CAMP

Because game-rich land is by its very nature far removed from civilization, buying a piece of wilderness or an abandoned farm is far more reasonable than, say, a lot that fronts on Miami Beach.

A few sample prices that we've looked into include the following: An upstate New York farm, with buildings in livable condition, a stream on the property, and 75 acres of rolling meadowlands, costs $32,000. A three-room summer cabin on an acre of Forest Service ground, near a stream, and with road access in central Montana (the land lease expires in fifteen years, and it will surely be terminated, at which time the cabin will have to be removed or destroyed), is $4,500; 20 acres in the Arkansas Ozarks, no water or access roads, though legal access is part of the deal, is $2,000. And 35 acres of prime goose and duck hunting on irrigated rich farmland, right on the Yellowstone River in eastern Montana, with road access, is priced at $20,000. We're not advertising these places. As a matter of fact, they'll surely be snapped up by the time you read this.

But they do prove one point and suggest another—that owning some kind of hunting camp is within reach of many of us, and that buying a piece of the rock is one answer to the current posting crunch.

How do you go about finding a potential hunting camp? By far the best way is to shake the bushes and talk to local residents. It takes time, but eventually you're bound to find the kind of place you're looking for, at a price you can afford. Don't get discouraged when everyone tells you that local land is going for $2,000 an acre. That may be what *they* value their land at, but "they" aren't everybody.

Realtors also have listings of lands, but they get a commission on the purchase price. If Jake Smith wanted to sell ten acres of land at $100 an acre, and the realtor he went to thought he could get more, he'd convince Jake to raise his price, which is all fine and good; that's free enterprise. But still, land listed by realtors tends to be either inflated in price or commanding top dollar.

Wilderness lands are also advertised through the mail. These lands are generally either submarginal farm or grazing lands that have been sold for taxes or logged-over tracts of timber that are unsuitable for modern management methods. We would never recommend buying any land sight unseen, but you can eliminate a lot of personal, time-consuming investigation by way of letters.

For example, you can ascertain things like the presence or absence of streams, lakes, or roads, mileage to the closest town, total acreage, liens and the nature of titles, and, of course, purchase price. That saves a lot of work right there. Here are some other things you might want to ask about:

- If there's no water on the land, how much does drilling cost per foot, and how deep must you go for water?

- Are there good building sites on the land, specifically, an acre on less than a 4 percent grade that is above the 100-year floodplain?

- If you're close to a river, is the river subject to flooding in the spring or ice gorging in the winter?

- What is the nature of the ground cover on the land (pasture, mature timber, swamp, second-growth timber, logged bare, or rocky)?

- Are there any unusual natural phenomena peculiar to the locale, like intolerable insects, incredibly deep snow, or deer so thick that you can't keep a lawn in (you should be so lucky)?

Once you've posed these questions, and their answers satisfy your dreams and your pocketbook, then you can go and look for yourself. By all means *do* go and look for yourself unless you can afford to throw the purchase price away. In real estate as in most other goods, the rule is caveat emptor: let the buyer beware!

The following list is not an endorsement of these mail-order land dealers; it's just included as a place for you to start asking.

Surplus Lands
P.O. Box 19107
Washington, DC 20036

Blackburn Real Estate Co.
Mountain Home, AR 72653

United Farm Agency
612 West 47th Street
Kansas City, MO 64112

Government Lands
421 Center
Lewiston, NY 14092

Strout Realty
P.O. Box 2757
Springfield, MO 65803

American Land Disposal
P.O. Box 730-C
Holland, MI 49423

Timber Resources, Inc.
P.O. Box 4246
Spokane, WA 99202

West Real Estate Agency
2728 Murray Avenue
Pittsburgh, PA 15217

National Associated Properties, Inc.
P.O. Box 1322
Coeur d'Alene, ID 83814

A & P Properties
P.O. Box 14028
Spokane, WA 99202

Canadian Estate Land
286 Lawrence Avenue West
Toronto, Canada

The gradual destruction of the Moose is a matter of history. . . . The being with the skin and clothes of a white man, who in one winter butchered seventy-five of them for their hides alone, leaving their meat to pollute the air, still flourishes on the upper waters of the Passadumkeag in Maine. His memory deserves to be execrated more than him who burned the celebrated temple of antiquity, for destroyed temples can be rebuilt, but exterminated species cannot be recreated. —Charles Hallock, 1877

CONVERSION KIT

One of the most efficient and economical stoves around is an "Alaska" stove, made from a 55-gallon oil drum. The basic materials are cheap, and the stove can be stoked with 3-foot logs, fueling a fire that will last 24 hours.

The basic materials for conversion include: legs, stovepipe flange, door assembly, draft control, and nuts and bolts. The kit comes with a full set of instructions (you supply the barrel). Price: $24.95. Sotz Corp., 23797 Sprague Road, Columbia Station, Ohio 44028.

Headstones to Mark Your Departure to the Happy Hunting Grounds

Watertown Monument Works specializes in gravestones with an outdoorsy touch. If you want to be remembered as a hunter, you can have things like a moose splashing through the water, a dog on point, flying ducks or pheasant, or Canada geese in a cornfield carved in granite, to mark your final resting place. Write: Watertown Monument Works, P.O. Box 130, Watertown, SD 57201.

THE HUNTING HYPOTHESIS
by Robert Ardrey

New York: Atheneum, $10.00.

This book (by the same man who did *The Territorial Imperative* and *African Genesis*) might well be retitled "Let Us Hunt." It is an eloquent defense of hunting and the hunter, with a lot of popular scholarship to back it up.

The author argues that man is man, not chimpanzee; that we have evolved after millions and millions of years of killing to eat, and that it is nothing to be ashamed of.

Like Paul Shepard, he views agriculture as the real threat to the survival of animals, not the hunter, and he contends that unless we keep alive the hunting spirit, the human species might not survive the next ice age. An excellent book with lots of ammunition if you enjoy shooting down antihunters at cocktail parties.

COZY HUT PORTABLE CABIN

This is an exceedingly well-thought-out shelter that might become as popular as pickup campers in the years ahead. The shelter comes packed in a box that is small enough to fit in the bed of a pickup and light enough to be carried by two men. Part of the secret of its lightness and trim packaging is that the "box" it comes in is actually the corner sections of the cabin.

It takes twenty to thirty minutes to erect, and no tools are needed. The finished shelter measures 79 inches square, affording enough interior room to sleep four (in bunk beds).

The shelter is insulated with 3 inches of foam on the floor and 1½ inches of foam on the walls and roof. It is made of aluminum, so there's no upkeep, rust, or rot. The shelter comes with a roof vent, a screen and solid door, windows, and a keyed lock and night latch. A 12-volt lighting system is standard, but a 110-volt system may be had as an option.

At present, some other optional features are being developed. By the time you read this, you'll also have available a shipping pallet that converts into a foam-mattressed bunk bed, floor hole kits for ice fishing, kits for connecting two huts together, a lightweight transport trailer, and a shipping pallet that converts into a picnic table. Price: $1,288.00. Foam-Alum Manufacturing Co., 426 Old Wire Road, Springdale, AR 72764.

20-minute erection from crate

THE ROUND HOUSE FROM RONDESICS

The "round house" concept in home building makes sense on two counts. It is easily prefabricated, constructed, and structurally sound, and it affords a clear-span interior so you can put walls and rooms wherever you want them, without concern for bearing weight.

Rondesics is one manufacturer specializing in this type of structure. They have a free, informative kit that contains floor plans (with artist's conceptions) for eight of their dwellings, and a basic description of how these homes are put together.

Also included is a "home planning template" that consists of cut-outs of furniture, walls, appliances, doors, windows, and so on, and outlines of interiors. You pick the interior size you want, cut out the appliances and appurtenances you want, and then play house, shuffling things this way and that until you have created your dreamhouse. Send them the plan and they'll tell you how much it will cost. A hunting cabin of 336 square feet can be erected for $7,500, and a cabin of 509 square feet for $9,500. This includes no appliances, but the cabin will be weatherproofed and sealed.

Don't be put off by the notion of living in unfamiliar dimensions when you're used to a square house. I lived in a round house for a week and found it spacious, charming, and great outdoor-oriented living because of the panoramic view. Write Rondesics Leisure Homes Corp., 527 McDowell Street, Asheville, NC 28803.

—N.S.

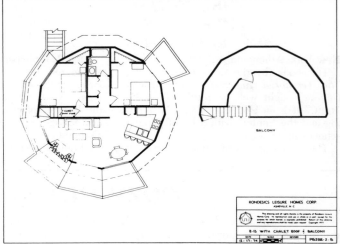

When one is hunting, the air has another, exquisite feel as it glides over the skin and enters the lungs. The rocks acquire a more expressive physiognomy, and the vegetation becomes loaded with meaning. But all this is due to the fact that the hunter, while he advances or waits crouching, feels tied through the earth to the animal he pursues, whether the animal is in view, hidden, or absent.

—José Ortega y Gasset,
Meditations on Hunting

Maps

Maps are more than just a way to find out where you are and how to get back. The hunter who knows the terrain has a big edge over the guy who doesn't. When you're aware of creeks, coulees, gulches, gullies, and hollows, you've got good leads on where to look and where the game will go when it's pressed.

The easiest way to get a map of the area you're hunting will probably be to buy one from a sporting goods store near the place you'll be hunting. Most of these folks stock U.S. Coast and Geodetic Survey maps of their region, which they sell for a buck. You can also buy these direct from the USCGS, but unless you know what quadrangle you want by the time you get done figuring it out you'll be a blithering idiot and will have spent three times what the map cost in postage.

The U.S. Forest Service also has maps of the public lands they administer, although they are not nearly so detailed as USCGS maps. They are helpful, however, in identifying public and private lands, in narrowing down quadrangles, and for identifying prominent landmarks. Again, if you don't know what you're looking for, your best bet is to stop into a Ranger District Headquarters and go through what

"Go light; the lighter the better, so that you have the simplest material for health, comfort and enjoyment."
—Nessmuk

143

FREE MAP GUIDES FOR HUNTERS

Topographic Maps—Silent Guides for Outdoorsmen is an 8-page booklet with some great tips on how to find better hunting through the use of topographic maps. It includes the procedure for cloth-backing a map so it lasts longer in your pocket or pack.

Topographic Maps is a 23-page booklet that explains how to read topo maps, what the data they contain mean, including map scales, control surveys, and symbols, and how to order them. A must if you want to order topo maps direct, or if you don't know how to read one. Free from U.S. Geological Survey, Map Information Office, Washington, DC 20244.

FOLDING SVEN SAW

Also known as a "bow" or "buck" saw, this type of hand saw is the most efficient of all the manual wood cutters. The Sven saw has the additional advantage of folding up into its own handle for ease of transport. Replaceable blades. Price: $8.99. Laacke & Joys, 1433 North Water Street, Milwaukee, WI 53202.

CANTEENS

If you ever want to carry drinking water with you, Oasis makes a wide variety of canteens, one of which is bound to suit your drinking tastes. Styles range from 1-quart polyethylene bottles to pancake-shaped belt flasks and include the round Western-style canteens with the fuzzy cloth on the outside that keeps the water inside ice-cold when it's wet (sizes 2 to 4 quarts). Prices: $4.25 to $8.50. M. E. Shaw & Sons, P.O. Box 31428, Los Angeles, CA 90031.

THE TENDER CARNIVORE AND THE SACRED GAME
by Paul Shepard

New York: Charles Scribner's Sons, $9.95.

This is not the kind of book you curl up with on a stormy winter night. In some places it is heavy, even laborious reading (it was originally a Ph.D. thesis), though generally its academic weight isn't crushing. To Shepard's way of thinking, it's the agriculturist who is the bad guy, and the only way up and out of the mess we're in is to reestablish hunting and gathering societies . . . by turning the entire United States west of the Mississippi into a hunting preserve.

THE WHITE EARTH SNOWSHOE GUIDEBOOK
by Tom Hallatz

Saint Cloud, Minn.: North Star Press (P.O. Box 451), $3.50 paperback, $5.00 hardcover.

This is an all-around guidebook for selecting snowshoe equipment, and includes a history of snowshoeing along with tips on use. The author is a *Chicago Tribune* photo editor and snowshoes in Wisconsin.

BACKPACKER STOVE

A compact one-burner stove can be used to cook a full meal when you backpack into big-game country. Around a permanent camp, it will get your morning coffee done a lot faster than a wood-burning stove—in about the time it will take to stoke the firebox and get the morning chores done. Sportster Stove, $20.00. Coleman, 250 North St. Francis, Wichita, KS 67201.

and Charts

they have. Costs for these maps run from freebies to 50 cents.

The Bureau of Land Management's maps are comparable to Forest Service maps. One notable exception is a map series currently under way that precisely identifies public and private lands and indicates access. These are a tremendous help to the hunter, since landowners out West don't have to post their lands against trespass—you have to get permission whether they're posted or not—and they often buffalo the public off public land, claiming it to be their own. With one of these maps in hand, you got 'em cold

when someone tries that trick. At this writing, these maps cost 75 cents, but there are only limited areas that have been so mapped.

For further information write:

U.S. Geological Survey, Map Information Office, Washington, DC 20244.

U.S. Forest Service, Department of Agriculture, Building E, Rosslyn Plaza, Rosslyn, VA 22209.

Bureau of Land Management, Department of the Interior, 1800 C Street NW, Washington, DC 20240.

—N.S.

WALT HODGES

THE BACKPACKING HUNTER
by Sam Curtis

Grizzled horse packers have a way of peering down from their saddles in disbelief when they see a hunter who carries his camp on his back. But the backpacking hunter is no longer a strange phenomenon. When you finally get that sheep or goat permit, you may discover that carrying your own gear to the lofty haunts of the big billies is the only way to get it there. Even when hunting deer or elk, your bank account can't always afford the cost of a horse-packing outfitter. So toting your own camp into big-game habitat might be your only option.

Successful backpack hunting is a combination of proper gear, careful logistics, and lots of sweat. In addition to the usual lightweight backpacking gear, such as down sleeping bag, nylon tent, stove, and freeze-dried food, there are several other items of equipment that should be given special attention. An aluminum pack frame with a pack bag is a must. The bag should be easy to remove, allowing you to convert the pack into a modern version of an old-fashioned pack board. It's on this frame that you'll lash your halved or quartered game, so bring along about 50 feet of nylon cord for the job. To make things more secure, add a tubular aluminum shelf to the bottom of the frame to keep the load from slipping. These shelves are sold as pack accessories by most backpacking suppliers.

The pack bag itself will undoubtedly be nylon and annoyingly noisy when whacked by twigs and branches. For this reason, you may want to fashion a makeshift pack cover out of some old pieces of cotton or flannel. It doesn't have to look pretty or fit particularly well, but it will let you move quietly through the brush and can double as a protective game bag.

Before you carry any game out, you'll have to do some rudimentary butchering. Along with your hunting knife, a saw is indispensable. Some people halve or quarter their game with a hatchet, but a saw is lighter to carry, does a neater job, and damages less meat. Either a triangular folding saw or a sheath saw will work, but the sheath type has smaller teeth and is closer to a regular butcher's saw.

A final equipment consideration is your boots. When carrying heavy loads on your back, you need more foot support than usual. Also, in mountain goat country, lugged soles add an ounce more traction. Both these features come together in a regular leather hiking boot. But you may also need protection from the snow. This can be achieved by giving your hiking boots a liberal coat of paste sealer (carry some in your pack too) and by wearing knee-high snow gaiters. The best gaiters are canvas since they're porous and won't let moisture condense on the inside. To keep them from being too noisy it's wise to cover them with wool. Other fabrics will absorb water and freeze easily.

When it comes to logistics, there are several things to keep in mind. You have to use common sense about how far you can pack out the game you're after. You might easily be able to pack a mountain goat five miles by yourself, but to get an elk one mile, even with help, could be a multi-trip, multi-day affair. Be realistic about the weight you'll have to carry through the kind of terrain you're in, and set some boundaries beyond which you won't hunt.

Once you do get something down you'll have to make at least two trips—one or more to pack out the game, one to pack out your gear. Take the game first. If you get tired or a storm comes up you'll want to have food and shelter available out in the bush, not back at your vehicle. Also, unless you are positive about the location of both your tent and the game, take compass readings to mark their location. A piece of colorful clothing hung from the branch of a tree near the game can save a lot of wasted wandering around.

One more thing. When you pack out that trophy headgear, hang it upside down on your pack frame and festoon it with color. You'll have enough work to do without dodging bullets.

Sam Curtis is a well-known authority on backpacking and a regular contributor to *The Backpacker*, *Backpacking Journal*, and *Camping Journal*.

"You can always tell an old soldier by the inside of his holsters and cartridge boxes. The young ones carry pistols and cartridges: the old ones, grub."
—George Bernard Shaw, Arms and the Man

145

COMPRESSED FREEZE-DRIED FOODS

Hunters and campers have long been aware of the advantages of freeze-dried foods: light weight, ease of preparation, and about half of it actually tastes good! Mountain House has added yet another feature to their freeze-dried line: they compress their freeze-dried foods, so they take up an absolute minimum of space. Their "menu" of available foods reads like a restaurant and includes predictable fare like stews and spaghetti as well as uncommon campfire dining like shrimp creole and freeze-dried ice cream.

Such a variety in lightweight dining is surprisingly reasonable, too (2 rib eye steaks, $5.00; vegetable beef stew for four, $5.10), and as long as you keep them in an airtight container, they have a long shelf life. Free customer catalog (menu/price list) from Oregon Freeze-Dry Foods, Inc., Albany, OR 97321.

Various absurd stories are told by hunters of the wonderful power assessed by mountain goats to leap from great heights and light safely on their horns. That these tales have no foundation in fact, anyone who has ever examined their skull will readily comprehend. The species is also said to prefer death to capture, a statement which is on a par with the one just referred to. If one of these animals throws himself over a precipice, it is not to spite the hunter, but because in his fear, he has taken an unusually dangerous leap or selected some path where the foothold is too precarious even for such a sure-footed climber as he.

—Charles Hallock, 1877

AIR MATTRESS FOR BACKPACKERS

Grizzled backpackers will tell you that air mattresses aren't nearly as efficient as an Ensolite pad, and in a way they're right. Air mattresses are actually pretty cold in cold weather, but if you're used to sleeping on a regular mattress at home, they're the only way you'll get a comfortable sleep on a weekend hike.

Of the air mattresses I've used, far and away the best one for backpacking is the Air Lift, manufactured in Berkeley, California. It's a fresh, new concept in air mattresses, a tubular-sectioned case, made of heavy-duty nylon, that accepts individual plastic "sausages" that you blow up one at a time. There are nine of these air tubes to a mattress, and it takes one good breath to blow each one up in the three-quarter mattress. The tubes, if they puncture, can be repaired with Band-Aids. The Air Lift comes in two sizes, a three-quarter mattress for $10.50, and a full-width mattress for $18.50. My solution to the cold problem? I take along a three-quarter Air Lift and put a light Ensolite pad over it. It's plenty warm and like sleeping on a cloud. Sierra Designs, 4th and Addison Streets, Berkeley, CA 94701.

—N.S.

SLEEPING BAGS I'VE USED AND LIKED

Coleman. Their Dacron II fiberfill semi-mummy is the best buy we've come across. It lacks some niceties, and it's a little on the bulky side, but it's warm, comfortable, and cheap. Coleman Company, 250 North St. Francis, Wichita, KS 67201.

Comfy Cordillera. This is a bag with the niceties that the Coleman lacks. Full, heavy-duty zipper with zip-together bag features if you can handle romance after a full day of hiking the hills. It's semi-mummy and machine washable. An excellent buy, but more expensive than Coleman. Comfy, 310 First Avenue South, Seattle, WA 98104.

White Stag. Their top-of-the-line fiberfill bags are very well made and surprisingly compactable. These bags cost around $50.00, but they're the warmest I've found for their weight. They also have a two-way zipper so you can get good ventilation on warm nights. You get both quality and a wide comfort range with this one. Hirsh-Weis, 5203 Southeast Johnson Creek Boulevard, Portland, OR 97206.

Sears. Sears is a "middlin' " outfit when it comes to sporting goods, sleeping bags included. I've used their Hillary down bag for a number of years now and have been fully satisfied. There's nothing innovative about the bag, nothing remarkable, but it keeps me warm and it doesn't fall apart. Like the product, the price is middlin' too—not cheap, not excessive, but fair. In fact, I'd go so far as to say that for the person who knows nothing about outdoor equipment, you could buy exclusively from Sears and not get stung. But you'd be middlin'. Sears, Dept 703-40-15, Sears Tower, Chicago, IL 60684.

—N.S.

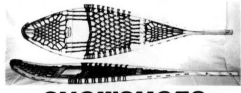

SNOWSHOES

If you'll be hunting in heavy snow, snowshoes are usually better than skis. While skis are faster, and to some extent easier to use, they don't wind through timber well.

The biggest problem with snowshoes is generally your conditioning. They require that you walk slightly spraddle-legged, and after a full day in the woods you develop a pain in the groin muscles known as *mal du raquet*, which is also a favorite joke among guides in Canadian hunting camps.

The shoes least likely to transmit this ailment are those that are narrow and allow you to walk closest to normal. The Canadian Cross-Country, sold for $32.00 by Cabela's, and the Pickerel, $46.00 from L. L. Bean, are both shoes of this style. Cabela's, 812 13th Avenue, Sidney, NE 69162; L. L. Bean, Inc., Freeport, ME 04033.

Note: Snowshoes are usually sold without rigging (shoe bindings). Bean sells these for $7.00 a pair.

WATER TREATMENT KIT

If your hunting camp has a questionable water supply, purify the water with this Environmental Protection Agency approved kit. The components nest and lock together, and the whole package weighs a pound, so it can be packed on your back if you're walking. Good for up to 1,000 gallons of water. Price: $16.00. Palco Products, P.O. Box 88, Slatersville, RI 02876.

FREIGHTER PACK FRAME

This pack frame was especially designed to haul heavy loads, and as such it makes for an ideal companion for the pack-in hunter. It is heliarc welded for strength under stress, and it has tapered shoulder straps and an all-around padded hip band. Of special note is the removable shelf in the rear. This feature allows any number of heavy, bulky items to be lashed directly to the frame, so this is the most practical way to pack out quartered game.

The Freighter pack frame mates up with several styles of pack bags, both three-fourths and full. Pack frame, $32.00; pack bags, $15.50 to $59.50. Camp Trails, P.O. Box 23155, Phoenix, AZ 85063.

CAN OPENER

Next to matches, a can opener can be a great help in case of an emergency. Most can openers are big and bulky, but the Burnham Brothers are selling the original G.I. issue can opener for 25 cents. It can be folded and carried in your wallet or worn on your key chain. Write: P.O. Box 100A, Marble Falls, TX 78654.

THE NEW COMPLETE WALKER

by Colin Fletcher

New York: Knopf, $10.00.

While there may be another book by the same title, this one deserves to be subtitled "The Backpacker's Bible," if for no other reason than that I've seen so many packers carry their copy with a reverence akin to that of a circuit preacher for his Bible.

Fletcher has a unique combination of qualifications for writing a book of this type. He's walked thousands of miles with a pack on his back (through wilderness, not down a paved highway), he is an experimenter and innovator with a keen, critical mind, and he is a good writer, with a genuine sense of humor.

You may assume his advice on equipment and backpack techniques is tried, tested, and sound. The book is an excellent primer for any kind of backpacker or backpacking, and it's just good reading.

R.E.I. (Recreational Equipment, Inc.) for Backpacking Gear

If you're into backpack hunting, or backpacking at any time of the year, R.E.I. has just about anything you might want, and a unique sales policy.

The outfit is a co-op. You pay $2.00 to join, and then you must buy over $5.00 worth of goods annually to keep up your membership. You are then paid an annual dividend based on purchases. Through the period 1970 to 1974, R.E.I. returned over $5,600,000 in dividends to its members.

R.E.I. has a free 100-page catalog with all kinds of equipment and backpacking/mountaineering tips, along with a co-op membership application. Worthwhile reading, worthwhile joining. R.E.I., 1525 11th Avenue, Seattle, WA 98122.

SAWTOOTH TENTS FOR BACKPACKING

When you compare quality, cost, and performance, Browning's Sawtooth II and Sawtooth III mountain tents are unbeatable.

They include a waterproof floor that goes 8 inches up the wall, full nylon mesh coverings to bug-proof doors and windows, vents at critical points to reduce condensation, and a fly. Without a fly—essentially a tarplike second tent drawn tightly over the roof of the enclosed tent—the tent would either leak from rain or drip from the inside because of consensation.

The Sawtooth II measures 5 by 7 feet and weighs 5 pounds, with poles and stakes. It costs $74.95. The Sawtooth III weighs 6 pounds, 12 ounces with poles and stakes and measures 6 by 8 feet. It costs $94.95.

Either tent is perfect for backpacking, or as a storage shelter around a permanent big-game camp, though you'll probably be happier living in the larger tent if you encounter inclement weather on your hunt. Browning, Route 1, Morgan, UT 84050.

"When you're lost, fire three shots in quick succession, every three minutes. If all you have is a bow and arrow, you're probably a born loser."
—Anon.

147

THE ROCKY MOUNTAIN GOAT
by Bill McRae

America's greatest game animal? Hardly! But as I consider the roster of large mammals that inhabit this continent there is none for which I have more respect than the mountain goat, and there are none more apt to furnish a never-to-be-forgotten hunting experience.

The goat has one great talent, one thing that it does better than any other animal in this hemisphere, or perhaps on the earth, and that is its ability to climb. This gift it owes to wolves, grizzlies, and maybe even primeval men, who in the distant past drove it to some of North America's sparest lands. There it flourished, and continues to do so. The mountain goat alone has a home range so rugged and remote that it hasn't been affected by the advances of civilization. In fact, the range has actually been enlarged through some very successful transplanting programs.

Here are some tips for the hunter who plans to test his mettle, to say nothing of his legs and lungs, in the goat's beautiful domain.

Get in shape! For God's sake, man, get in shape! This is good advice for any big-game hunter, but it is extremely important for hunting goats.

Hunt early in the season. Do this in spite of the fact that the later you kill your goat the more luxurious his coat will be. The reason is that snow can effectively close goat country to human travel, and snow also makes the goat about as hard to see as a black horse at midnight.

What makes a good goat cartridge? I firmly believe, with a few obvious exceptions, that any big-game cartridge in use today will effectively kill any animal around if the bullet is placed well. However, for their size goats are unbelievably tough, and when you add the fact that wounded goats have a nasty habit of falling off cliffs, a magnum cartridge is in order. I use a 7mm Remington magnum.

Footwear is also important, and Vibram-soled boots are a must. But unless you have a lot of time to break them in, don't buy the European-style climbing boot that has recently become so popular with backpackers in this country. They are foot killers. I've gone that route a couple of times and always wind up going back to my Browning waterproof Vibram boots.

There are, however, a couple of items of mountain climbing gear that the goat hunter would do well to adopt. The first is an ice ax. They make great walking sticks, are an aid to balance, which is often precarious in goat country, and can be used to chop steps in ice or frozen ground. Second, it's a good idea to carry about 100 feet of 5/16-inch nylon climbing rope. It could be needed to lower a dead goat off a ledge or get one's self out of a bad spot.

I've hunted goats on several occasions and spent a great deal of time photographing them, often at hand-shaking distance, but I think that the most astonishing experience is to sit with binoculars and watch while a goat, at dizzying heights, nonchalantly picks its way along what appears to be, and nearly is, a vertical cliff. Life in the wild is always precarious, but only the mountain goat lives continually on the borderline of the impossible.

Bill McRae is a wildlife photographer of international reputation and a regular contributor to *Field and Stream*, *Sports Afield*, and *Outdoor Life*. His favorite subjects are sheep and goats.

THE BIG-GAME HUNTER'S SURVIVAL PACK
by Anthony J. Acerrano

You're going big-game hunting. You've sighted in that polished magnum and are shooting groups the size of a silver dollar. Your boots are comfortably broken in and you've coated them liberally with Sno-Seal. You're all ready to go.

Well, almost.

There's one essential matter no hunter should overlook: his safety. Big-game hunting takes a nimrod through thick backwoods, up remote draws, and over high ridges. In such places it's easy to become lost or injured, and without the proper gear and know-how such mishaps can turn into tragedies. But by taking the following precautions *before* the hunt, you can stack the odds in favor of a safe and happy trip.

First, get a firm idea of the potential emergencies that can confront a big-game enthusiast, and learn what to do if they arise. For this, there are a number of good books on survival available in libraries and bookstores. My own recently published *Outdoorsman's Emergency Manual*, available from Winchester Press, contains information on most aspects of emergency and survival, with a special section devoted entirely to hunting dangers. Byron Dalrymple's *Survival in the Outdoors*, published by Dutton, is another good reference.

Next, prepare a small pack of emergency essentials and plan to wear it while hunting. The Amigo, by Camp Trails, is a triangular day pack that fits snugly and comfortably on your back, without interfering with hiking or shooting. An orange or yellow pack is your best choice for protection from other hunters.

Inside the pack, you should stock the following:

- A topographical map of your hunting area. These can be obtained by writing the U.S. Geological Survey. For maps of regions east of the Mississippi, write the USGS, Washington, DC 20244; west of the big river, address USGS, Federal Center, Denver, CO 80225.

- A functioning compass. I personally like the Leupold lensatic compass, which can be purchased for a few bucks at any sporting good store. Another popular model is the Silva Huntsman, a compass mounted on a flat, cardlike base.

- A spool of 60-pound or heavier monofilament fishing line. Any brand will do. It takes up a tiny corner of your pack and provides line for emergency lashing, snares, and fishing.

- Signaling equipment. This includes a signaling mirror and loud police whistle. There are many brands of both, but all have the same basic design. The mirror can be purchased at most sport shops; the whistle at drug and hardware stores.

- Fire equipment. A Metal Match carbon stick is inexpensive and good insurance for starting fires. Also carry a *plastic* waterproof match case of any brand filled with kitchen matches. These plastic cases cost about a dollar and won't freeze or rust shut the way metal containers do.

- Shelter. A Versa-Tarp, 8 by 12 feet, weighs only 2¾ pounds and can be rigged into a good emergency shelter. Lighter but less effective is a 4-by-8-foot Space blanket.

- Food. Pack along a crush-proof box of your favorite chocolate bars and beef jerky. If you prefer commercially prepared rations, Rich-Moor's Quick Energy and Meat Bars are a good bet.

- First-aid kit. Cutter's Camp Pack first-aid kit includes the necessary essentials, plus a snakebite kit, and folds into a billfold-sized package.

That's a basic emergency pack. With it and some survival know-how, you're ready to face most of the hardships nature's likely to throw in a big-game hunter's way.

Anthony J. (Tony) Acerrano is a free-lance journalist and hunter and an expert in survival techniques.

COMPASSES YOU CAN WEAR

If you have trouble maintaining your bearings, keep a compass out in front of you at all times and keep checking your direction. The pin-on compass can be worn outside your jacket; just look down for a reading. The tape-on compass will stick to a gun, bow, or the handlebars of a trail bike. The regular compass has a ring for a thong attachment.

All compasses are rust resistant and waterproof and come with an unbreakable crystal. They have agate jewel bearings and are available in luminous or nonluminous dials. Prices: pin-on, $6.49; Standard revolving, $5.95. Marble's, P.O. Box 111, Gladstone, MI 49837.

MAGNESIUM FIRE STARTER

This product is the newest improvement in the "metal match" concept. It consists of a small bar of magnesium with a flintlike sparking insert on one side of the bar. You scrape the magnesium with a knife until you have a pile of magnesium shavings, then ignite the shavings with the flint.

The thing that sets this product aside from others of its kind is the magnesium. It burns at 5,400 degrees F (the blue part of a match or candle flame is around 600 to 800 degrees). Such searing heat is sufficient to raise just about any combustible to kindling temperature, even to dry out wet twigs or tinder. Price: $4.95. Doan Machinery and Equipment Co., P.O. Box 21334, South Euclid, OH 44121.

"Nine men out of ten, on finding themselves lost in the woods, fly into a panic, and quarrel with the compass. Never do that. The compass is always right."
—Nessmuk

149

CONVENTIONAL SNAKEBITE KIT

There's some disagreement among medical authorities as to what treatment is best for snakebite, so the druthers are up to you. This conventional kit includes a sterile cutting tool and tourniquet, housed inside a rubber vial that converts into a suction device. Price: $3.95. Cutter Laboratories, 4th and Parker Streets, Berkeley, CA 94710.

THE QUALITY COMPASS

The Suunto RA-69 DE Wayfinder compass is the one we hear most recommended by folks who should know. It packs an awful lot into a breast-pocket-sized package: all standard conversion scales for map proportions, a metal step recorder, a magnifying glass, luminous points, and a declination offset. It is ruggedly built and easy to read day or night. Price: $18.95. Precise Imports, 3 Chestnut Street, Suffern, NY 10901.

—F.S.

WAIST PACK FOR THE WALKING HUNTER

If you'll be spending a full day afield, this waist pack will carry your lunch, shells, binoculars, and any survival gear you want to tote along. It's available with loops that go over your belt or with its own adjustable web belt. Price: $10.50. Kolpin Manufacturing, Inc., P.O. Box 231, Berlin, WI 54923.

STOCKING UP FOR SURVIVAL

Bird shooters and big-game hunters both run the risk of someday finding themselves in a survival situation. The time to prepare for it is now, by removing the butt plate of each of your guns and filling the drill hole with survival gear. Wooden matches or throw-away butane lighters wrapped in tissue, a length of string, and aluminum foil wrapped around bouillon cubes will make for a basic survival kit.

SPACE BLANKET

The space blanket principle is one of the many spinoffs of the research done for the U.S. space program. This is a very thin sheet of material that measures 56 by 84 inches. It does not insulate like conventional blankets and sleeping bags but, rather, reflects up to 90 percent of your body heat back at you.

It is light and compact enough to fit in a glove compartment or game pocket, and aside from obvious survival use it's also great as a ground cloth, or when used as a warmer on a stand. Price: 2.95. Cabela's, 812 13th Avenue, Sidney, NE 69162.

SCRIPTO RESERVOIR LIGHTER

Reservoir lighters hold fuel in two stages. The base of the lighter is a see-through reservoir that holds an ounce of lighter fluid. The contents of the reservoir are released in small quantities to the upper stage by depressing a button. This upper stage contains a lifetime wick, a flint and wheel, and a flint reservoir that holds three extra lighter-type flints.

An advantage of this kind of lighter is that you can always see how much fuel you have. Full, the lighter is good for around 1,000 lights, and the fuel and flint may be removed from the lighter and ignited separately in case of malfunction.

This lighter is affected by water. If you get a thorough dousing, water will enter the upper chamber and the flame will not strike. But it dries out in about a half hour if you open the lid, fill the chamber with fresh fuel, and keep the lighter warm next to your body. Price: $5.95, from drug and tobacco shops.

CRICKET BUTANE LIGHTER

Disposable butane lighters are good for around 1,000 lights, and fuel and flint are sealed in the unit. They ignite easily, and the flame may be adjusted for intensity. It leaves the lighter in a jetlike stream, so the flame may be directed into the tinder and kindling.

When this lighter is very cold, the fuel will not vaporize well and the flame might not ignite. However, if you place the lighter next to your body for fifteen minutes, it will warm the fuel and strike flame. If this lighter is to be used exclusively as a survival tool, secure the fuel release lever with tape so it can't be inadvertently depressed. This lighter has the important capacity to fit inside the stock of most rifles and shotguns.

Gillette Cricket Lighter, $1.19, in drug and tobacco stores.

REEL USEFUL

Just plain string has a thousand uses around camp, and it can save your life in a survival situation. The Mechanical Fisher Company's Automatic Fishing Reel holds 50-plus yards of 60-pound-test fishing line. Under normal conditions, the line may be used to replace a broken shoelace, as a clothesline to dry a pair of wet socks, or to hang foodstuffs out of the reach of mice, squirrels, and chipmunks.

In a survival situation, you can make a tripod of limbs by tying the ends of three branches together. Place boughs around the limbs and you have a tepeelike shelter from the wet and the wind.

Sure, you can get all this done with a ball of strong twine, but this product goes a lot further. The "reel" is more than a receptacle for line. It is equipped with a spring, lock, and trip mechanism, so a tug on the business end will cause the reel to rewind automatically. Bait a hook, tie the reel to an overhanging branch, and a biting fish gets caught. Make a snare, set it along a game pass, and small animals can't back out of the loop because of the constant tension. Price: $15.80. Mechanical Fisher Company, P.O. Box 703, Little Rock, AR 72203.

FREEZE-A-BITE SNAKEBITE KIT

Current thinking on the treatment of poisonous snakebite questions the wisdom of the old tourniquet, slash, and suck routine. It's pointed out that the dangers of cutting tendons, muscles, and the resulting blood loss, along with gangrene, which may result from loss of circulation, balance or outweigh the dangers of snakebite (very few people have actually died of snakebite).

The recommended treatment is to chill or freeze the bite area, thus reducing the potency of the venom and slowing its spread, until the victim can reach competent medical care. The Freeze-A-Bite snakebite kit contains all the stuff you'll need to do just that, including instructions on how to use it. Price: $11.95. Dow Safety Products, Turner Street, Cleveland, MO, 64734.

MULDOON STUDIO

LIFE-TOOL SURVIVAL TOOL

The Life-Tool is a classic example of good things in small packages. A screwdriver, can opener, file, knife, compass, signal mirror, and wire stripper are engineered into a flat piece of stainless steel with no moving parts! It is small enough to be carried unnoticed in your wallet. You'll forget it's there . . . until the day you need it, which to my way of thinking is this remarkable gadget's greatest asset.

The Life-Tool comes with a vinyl case that holds the tool and an illustrated instruction manual. Price: $12.95. Allison Forge Corp., P.O. Box 404, Belmont, MA 01178.

SURVIVAL KNIFE

The true survival knife is the ultimate jack-of-all-trades. Aside from conventional cutting chores, it is also adapted to combat or to use as a hunting weapon (you can make a spear out of one by lashing it to the end of a lance).

Smith and Wesson's No. 6030 is a high-quality knife with a 440-series stainless-steel blade. "Survival" features include a double quillon (or guard) for hand protection during combat, a sharpened false edge on the back of the knife for deep penetration and/or cutting an opponent on an upthrust, and a hollow handle with a threaded pommel cap for access. The interior of the handle holds fishhooks, matches, water purification tablets, and the like. Price: $50.00. Smith and Wesson Co., 2100 Roosevelt Avenue, Springfield, MA 01101.

"In the night, imagining some fear,
How easy a bush is supposed a bear!"
—Shakespeare, A Midsummer Night's Dream

151

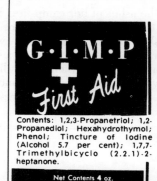

BUT WILL IT MAKE A GOOD MARTINI?

GIMP—yes, that's right, GIMP—First Aid and Antiseptic Healing Solution is an old-time cure-all that's useful around camp or in your car. You can use it for just about anything that ails you: minor cuts, scratches, burns, abrasions, skin irritation, insect bites, leeches, chapped hands, windburn, as an aftershave, for athlete's foot, simple ringworm, dry scalp, and loose dandruff. Price: $1.98. GIMP, Box 7243, Kansas City, MO 64113.

WHAT HAVE BANDANNAS GOT TO DO WITH BIG GAME?

They're a lot more than hankies. Bandannas are close to the most versatile articles of comfort you can ever carry. Wear them around your neck like an ascot, and they'll keep you warm. When it's hot, soak them in cool water, and wear them around your neck or like a headband. They'll keep you cool.

Should a sudden storm blow in, you can wear them around your ears, babushka-style, to prevent frostbite. Wear them bandito-style when it's bitter cold to warm inhaled air. And they also work as emergency bandages, towels, and fire starters. Price: $2.50. Duxbak, 825 Noyes Street, Utica, NY 13502.

Heavy Cutting   Skinning

Light Cutting   Cap Lifter

SURVIVAL KNIFE IN BELT

This product is especially noteworthy because it fits into the class of survival gear that you'll carry automatically, so it will always be there when you need it.

The buckle of the belt forms the handle (it is also designed to lift bottle caps, which could be involved in a survival situation), and the blade of the knife slips into a sheath inside the belt.

The knife blade is canted to fit stomach contours and is available in double- or single-edged models. The single-edged blade would be the better tool. The blade is made of 440c stainless, an excellent steel for knife blades, and the belt is real leather, 1 11/16 inches wide. Specify waist size and color (brown or black) when ordering. Price: $30.00. Bowen Knife Company, Route 3, P.O. Box 3245A, Blackshear, GA 31516.

These know that nature is stern, hard, immovable and terrible in her unrelenting cruelty. When wintry winds are out and the mercury far below zero, she will allow her most ardent lover to freeze on her snowy breast without waving a leaf in pity, or offering him a match; and scores of her devotees may starve to death in as many different languages before she will offer a loaf of bread. She does not deal in matches and loaves; rather in thunderbolts and granite mountains. And the ashes of her camp-fires bury proud cities. But, like all tyrants, she yields to force, and gives the more, the more she is beaten. She may starve or freeze the poet, the scholar, the scientist; all the same, she has in store food, fuel and shelter, which the skillful, self-reliant woodsman can wring from her savage hand with axe and rifle.

—Nessmuk

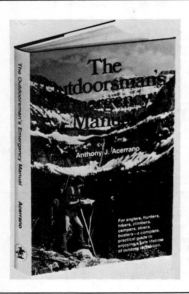

THE OUTDOORSMAN'S EMERGENCY MANUAL

by Anthony J. Acerrano

New York: Winchester Press, $10.00.

This is a new approach to safety and survival in the outdoors, and the best I've seen. It is excellent by virtue of three things. First, being new, it includes up-to-date, modern advice, applicable to the probable situations hikers, packers, and hunters will find themselves in. The emphasis is off things like bough shelters and on things like having the good sense to carry a plastic tarp with you in the first place.

The second reason that this is an excellent book is because Acerrano personally tested and evaluated the majority of survival techniques mentioned in the book. For example, the fire-a-gun-into-tinder method of fire starting is ignored because he couldn't get it to work reliably.

Thirdly, he debunks a lot of survival myths perpetrated by word of mouth and outdated publications. If you think that food eaten by birds is safe for human consumption, that streams always lead to civilization, or that frostbitten hands should be rubbed with snow, better stay home until you've read a copy of this book.

I could remember . . . one time in a hospital with my right arm broken off short between the elbow and the shoulder, the back of the hand having hung down against my back, the points of bone having cut up the flesh of the biceps until it finally rotted, swelled, burst, and sloughed off in pus. Alone with the pain in the night in the fifth week of not sleeping I thought suddenly how a bull elk must feel if you break a shoulder and he gets away and in that night I lay and felt it all, the whole thing as it would happen from the shock of the bullet to the end of the business and, being a little out of my head, thought perhaps what I was going through was a punishment for all hunters. Then, getting well, decided that if it was a punishment I had paid it and at least I knew what I was doing. I did nothing that had not been done to me. I had been shot and I had been crippled and gotten away. I expected, always to be killed by one thing or another and I, truly, did not mind that any more. Since I still loved to hunt I resolved that I would only shoot as long as I could kill cleanly and as soon as I lost that ability I would stop.

—Ernest Hemingway, *Green Hills of Africa*

ELK

"The antlered monarch of the waste." How applicable is this term to the stately elk, the giant deer of the forest, the plains and the mountains of North America. Standing as tall as a horse, bearing a superb pair of antlers worthy to adorn any baronial hall, with senses than which no keener can be found among all our varied examples of animal life, and a form faultless in the grace and symmetry of its outlines, the Wapiti justly holds the first place among the game animals of our continent.

—Charles Hallock, 1877

*"Old hunters have a saying, that a band of Elk when fairly
started, will not stop until they have crossed flowing water."*
—Charles Hallock, 1877

153

BUGLING UP
A BULL

by Dave Wolny

There is nothing in this world that can compare to the bugle of a bull elk on a frosty morning in the high country. It is lonesome, sad, and frightening, piercing the wilderness. It sticks in your mind like that day you were playing in the school yard and your mom hollered.

Well, that big bull is hollering, and his harem knows where they belong. There's no women's lib in his domain; he's the boss, or the cow gets a sharp horn in her butt.

The bull elk will breed his harem for maybe a month to six weeks; then he'll leave and bunch up with the same bulls he fought with earlier. But during the times he's got wives, he's always spoiling for a fight, and you can trick him into coming to you.

Elk start bugling around the first full moon in September. You can buy a bugle at a local sporting goods store, but old-timers like to make their "elk whistle" out of bamboo or a piece of plastic pipe. You whittle the whistle notch and plug with a pocket knife and then tune it until it sounds like an elk. If you don't know what an elk sounds like, you've got problems, but you're probably not an old-timer anyway and would be just as well off to buy one.

An elk bugle has two notes. One low, like the wind blowing across the mouth of an empty beer bottle, and one high, like blowing across a .30–30 cartridge case, but more wheezy. You make the notes by blowing soft, then hard, with one hand over the open end of the whistle. It takes some practice to keep from making three notes, which will clear every decent elk out of the country, so work on your call before going hunting.

Again, it helps to have heard a bull before, just so you know who's answering. I once listened to two damn fool hunters bugle themselves into each other. At least they could see straight, because nobody got shot as far as I could tell. But if you blow it right, that bull will get hot and come to you. I've had one 25 yards away, scraping the ground and uprooting sagebrush with his horns. He was hot!

For about a month, the bull will protect his harem of four to eight cows, or as many as he can fight for, and the bugle will work. After that, they head for the roughest, meanest country around, and that's where the smart hunter should go too.

Dave Wolny has guided hunters in Wyoming and Montana. He is now a rancher and proprietor of the Greater Gallatin Gateway Spelling Bee, Literary Guild, Marching Band, Timing Association, and Cottonwood Canyon Camping Club, Unlimited.

A GOOD GUIDE IS A HUNTING PARTNER

by Dick Weden

"Gee, what a great guide we had in California. He knew more stories than any guy I've ever met. And shoot . . . he could hit a beer can at two hundred yards and never once miss."

Charlie had just returned from a hunting trip to California and was ecstatic with the great job the guide had done for them. They were picked up promptly at the airport and provided with comfortable accommodations and good food during their week's stay in the West. I asked Charlie how he had fared with the hunting. "Not a thing," said Charlie, "the deer weren't moving and we couldn't even find any tracks." I quizzed him as to how much looking they had done, and he allowed that Charlie had gone out each day in his pickup truck to look for deer signs. He had called his buddies each night to see if they had seen anything. The reply was always the same—"Zilch."

This may have been a good trip for Charlie, but I'd have scratched that guide from my list post haste. I have been skunked myself. But never once have I left with the feeling that I personally did not give it all I had, or that my guide had not worked his butt off trying to provide me with as many opportunities as possible to get my game down.

A guide can't be all things to all people. However, the guide that can come close to meeting these criteria is going to provide his "sport" with good hunting and a good time as well. Personally, I would have felt better to have been in the pickup with the guide. Not only are two pairs of eyes better than one, but this particular guide might have been off punching cows when he should have been looking for deer.

Webster defines a guide as "one who directs and instructs." Although I doubt Webster had a hunting guide in mind when he put together his dictionary, he sure came close to a perfect definition for a hunting guide.

The guide I have used for my Western hunting trips is my idea of what a guide should be. He shall remain nameless here, as overpublicizing his abilities might make it more difficult to engage him for my annual fall trip. I will, however, refer to him as Norm.

First of all, he is friendly and a pleasure to be with. He hunts *with* me, and that is more like hunting with a buddy. This eliminates any employer-employee feeling that might exist. He does *not* hunt *for* me. This, more than anything else, would bother me. If I can't shoot it, I don't want it. Although we do a lot of scouting from a pickup truck, we brush out all possible haunts on foot where deer might be bedded down. This we also do together.

He believes in preparation. Tomorrow never breaks without a plan for the day's hunt. This is figured out the night before and usually results from what we have encountered that day. I remember an antelope hunt we were on together. We had spotted a small herd late in the afternoon; they were a long way off and on an adjoining ranch. We could have made a play on them, but Norm felt it wiser to let them bed down for the night, get permission to hunt that ranch, and give it a try in the morning. While asking for permission from the rancher we were also given valuable help in getting to where the animals were. That night we diagrammed the area on paper and organized the plan to use in the morning. This preparation paid off as we had our antelope down shortly after sunrise.

A good guide must be enthusiastic and be able to greet each new sport with a positive attitude. I have gone through many dry days, but this guide has never let me get discouraged. He is quick to point out that "we know the deer are here and it is just a matter of finding them." This lets you approach each day with confidence and keeps you working hard to find your game. Three years ago I got my deer twenty minutes before sunset on the last day of the season. It would have been easy to quit early that day, but Norm kept me going with "just before sunset is a great time to jump a big buck."

Frequently, while stomping the hills, he will stop at a deer track and ask me which direction the deer had been going. Together we will carefully examine the track and decide the direction of the deer. Without making an issue out of it he is teaching me something I did not know. His subtle approach extends to the flora and fauna, and even to the history of the Indian tribes that once roamed the area. This is a real bonus for me, since the more knowledge I have, the more I feel a part of the whole scene and can start to figure things out for myself.

Lastly, a guide will be what you make him. If your real interest is hunting, your guide will feel this and usually work hard for you. If, however, your main desire is just getting away from it all, and this is more important than the desire to hunt, the guide will detect this attitude and allow you to goof off.

I remember a Florida fishing guide who was asked by his sport to bring him in early so he could get to the bank to cash some traveler's checks. From there the sport decided he needed a haircut, to be followed by a trip to the post office. When it came time to settle up for the day's fishing, the sport was dumbfounded when the guide charged him for a full day. In his slow Southern drawl he answered, "Hell, we fished all morning and this afternoon I guided you to the bank, the barber shop, and then to the post office. That comes out to a full day."

Dick Weden is a Dover, Massachusetts, sportsman who has hunted and fished from northern Quebec to Costa Rica, and an occasional contributor to outdoor magazines.

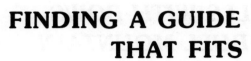

FINDING A GUIDE THAT FITS

by *Russell Tinsley*

If we are to put much stock in the adage that "luck is preparation meeting opportunity," then securing the services and know-how of a competent big-game guide is indeed serious business. You must have total confidence in his ability to produce. Even if your hopes go unfilled, the ultimate compliment your guide receives is, "It wasn't your fault, you gave your best." Keep in mind the guide has an ego too. He dislikes failure.

But to me this concept is a bit too sterile. Basically you hire a guide to put you on game. Nonetheless, there is too much emphasis on the win-or-lose proposition: Get your game and the hunt is a success; don't kill your game and it is a total failure.

I shop for a guide very carefully. Some people, who have read my letters asking other customers of the guide for a reference, claim I am more interested in a psychoanalytic profile than I am in his game-finding ability. Not so. But I do admit to putting great emphasis on the fellow's personality.

One person responded to a letter with: "A helluva good guide; all business, no fun and games; with him the hunt is everything and I do mean everything." That turned me off. This man would be my constant companion for more than a week. We would share the failures and successes together. The intermesh of our personalities was most important.

I've had some good hunts and bad hunts. The quality of the trophies hanging on my wall has nothing to do with it. A game head is more than a symbol of success. I enjoy the memories which go with it.

Dan Conoly, Jr., and Alex Kibler, two friends of mine, ventured deep into the British Columbia wilds in search of Dall sheep. An early snowstorm kept them imprisoned in a tent for six straight days. "Thanks to our good-natured guide, we were able to keep our sanity," Dan recalled. "We were disappointed by the way things turned out, but still I think back on that hunt with a lot of nostalgia. You've got to experience a few of those setbacks to really enjoy the successes."

Yes, something like that brings out either the best or the worst in people. There is no way of telling how individuals will react to certain situations, but you can hedge on the odds by knowing beforehand something about your guide's personality. I count a few guides among my best friends. And the cement of friendship has to be more than just a man's ability or lack of it in his chosen profession.

A guide is a pretty good judge of people. It doesn't take him long to realize how far he can go without offending someone. Like George Clover of Jackson, Wyoming. We were camped high in the timbered mountains not far from Yellowstone National Park. It was after dark and we were around a campfire, relaxing our tired muscles with some bottled tonic and grilling steaks. George told me about a tragic hunt he'd had with another Texan the season previously. It was a morbid story. The poor chap had suffered a fatal heart attack in camp so they immediately carried the body on horseback to Jackson. There, according to George, another problem was encountered. The Texan was huge, six foot five, but the largest casket in town was just six feet long.

I was caught up in the web. "What in the world did you do?"

"Gave him an enema and shipped him home in a shoebox." And everyone around the fire suddenly doubled over with laughter.

I'd been had, but good, yet of all the memories I treasure about that hunt, those story-telling sessions around the campfire are among the most vivid.

Gene Ramos and I exchanged almost constant barbs while prowling the rough high country of the big island of Hawaii in search of wild goats and turkey gobblers. After a few hours I told him he wouldn't know a billy goat if he saw one; he countered that he could find goats all right, but the problem was getting one close enough for me to hit. All this in fun, mind you. But it sort of broke the tension as we searched the lava flow crevices where crafty goats might be hiding out.

Later, when he dropped me at the Kona Surf hotel hanging on the edge of the incredibly blue Pacific, we were both laughing at the day's developments. Yes, I had gotten a trophy goat and a long-bearded turkey tom, but these were just icing on the cake.

Ramos was still laughing as he drove away. I well remember his last remark: "You Texans are all a bunch of crazy bastards."

The way he said it, I couldn't be offended. Strange as it might seem, I know a compliment when I hear one.

Russell Tinsley is outdoors editor of the *Austin* (Texas) *American-Statesman*, has written eight books on outdoor recreation subjects, and has published more than 1,000 magazine articles in addition to contributing to numerous anthologies.

HORSE PACKER'S DIRECTORY

A 208-page book called *Adventure Trip Guide* lists every pack outfitter in the United States. Also included with each listing is information on the types of trips offered. An awful lot of these outfitters are summer trail/ride/dude ranch operations, but there's more than enough hunting outfitters to justify buying the book if you'd like a horsey hunt. Price: $2.95. Adventure Guides, Inc., 36 East 57th Street, New York, NY 10022.

GUIDE DIRECTORIES

The National Rifle Association (NRA) publishes a directory of guides and outfitters in the United States and Canada. It is called *Denali* and lists services offered and the kind of guiding operation involved (such as horse-pack hunt, pickup, tents, or cabins). Price: $5.00. National Rifle Association of America, 1600 Rhode Island Avenue Northwest, Washington, DC 20036.

Irrgang's Directory to North American Guides and Outfitters is a new enterprise that we know little about, other than that they contacted us close to press time. The first year they will publish is 1977, and their material claims they'll list guides from twenty states and ten provinces, along with a bow-hunter index, license fees from states and provinces, big-game species and seasons in all areas listed, and a directory of all state and provincial game commissions, outfitters' associations, and tourist information centers. Price not available. Write: Irrgang's, P.O. Box 17, Listie, PA 15549.

BULLS WITH BOWS ON BULL MOUNTAIN

Bull Mountain Outfitters offer an intriguing opportunity if you've ever wanted to hunt elk with a bow. The area in which they guide is open to hunting elk by bow alone, but the hunting season lasts through Montana's rifle season, which adds up to about two and a half months of opportunity. In addition to elk, Mike Murphy and Steve Cole also guide archery hunts for deer and antelope and rifle hunts for both species during the gun season.

Their hunting area lies 80 miles north of Billings, Montana, and amounts to 100 square miles of leased land, give or take an acre. Accommodations amount to a lodge and bunkhouses, transportation is by pickup or horse, depending upon circumstances, and rates run $70–$100 daily. Write Bull Mountain Outfitters, P.O. Box 191, Musselshell, MT 59059.

IF YOU WANT A WESTERN HUNT. . . .

Try writing to one of the following organizations. They represent most of the licensed guides and outfitters in their respective states.

Idaho Outfitters and Dude Ranch Association, P.O. Box 95, Boise, ID 83701.

Montana Outfitters and Dude Ranch Association, P.O. Box 382, Bozeman, MT 59715.

Montana Outfitters and Guide Association, P.O. Box 1158, Livingston, MT 59047.

Wyoming Outfitters Association, P.O. Box A-1, Jackson, WY 83001.

STATE DEPARTMENTS OF FISH AND GAME

Nearly every state licenses guides through its fish and game department. These departments then compile a list of all those individuals holding licenses, and they'll forward that list upon request. It is seldom more than just names and addresses, but it's as good a place to start as any.

Alabama: Game and Fish Division, Department of Conservation, 64 North Union Street, Montgomery 36104

Alaska: Department of Fish and Game, Subport Building, Juneau 99801

Arizona: Game and Fish Department, 2222 West Greenway, Phoenix 85023

Arkansas: Game and Fish Commission, Game and Fish Commission Building, Little Rock 72201

California: Department of Fish and Game, Resources Agency, 1416 Ninth Street, Sacramento 95814

Colorado: Division of Game, Fish and Parks, Department of Natural Resources, 6060 Broadway, Denver 80216

Connecticut: Board of Fisheries and Game, State Office Building, Hartford 06115

Delaware: Division of Fish and Wildlife, Department of Natural Resources, D Street, Dover 19901

Florida: Division of Game and Fresh Water Fish, Department of Natural Resources, 620 South Meridian, Tallahassee 32304

Georgia: State Game and Fish Commission, 270 Washington Street Southwest, Atlanta 30334

Guam: Division of Fish and Wildlife, Department of Agriculture, Agana 96910

Hawaii: Division of Fish and Game, Department of Land and Natural Resources, P.O. Box 621, Honolulu 96809

Idaho: Fish and Game Department, P.O. Box 25, Boise 83707

Illinois: Department of Conservation, 102 State Office Building, Springfield 62706

Indiana: Division of Fish and Game, Department of Natural Resources, 608 State Office Building, Indianapolis 46204

Iowa: Fish and Game Division, State Conservation Commission, 300 Fourth Street, Des Moines 50319

Kansas: Forestry, Fish, and Game Commission, P.O. Box 1028, Pratt 67124

Kentucky: Department of Fish and Wildlife Resources, State Office Building Annex, Frankfort 40601

Louisiana: Wildlife and Fisheries Commission, 400 Royal Street, New Orleans 70130

Maine: Department of Inland Fisheries and Game, State Office Building, Augusta 04330

Maryland: Fish and Wildlife Administration, State Office Building, Annapolis 21401

Massachusetts: Division of Fisheries and Game, 100 Cambridge Street, Boston 02202

Michigan: Department of Natural Resources, Mason Building, Lansing 48913

Minnesota: Division of Game and Fish, Department of Conservation, 301 Centennial Building, 658 Cedar Street, Saint Paul 55101

Mississippi: Game and Fish Commission, 402 High Street, P.O. Box 451, Jackson 39205

Missouri: Game Division, Department of Conservation, P.O. Box 180, Jefferson City 65001

Montana: Fish and Game Department, Helena 59601

Nebraska: Game and Parks Commission, State Capitol Building, Lincoln 68509

Nevada: Department of Fish and Game, P.O. Box 10678, Reno 89510

New Hampshire: Fish and Game Department, 34 Bridge Street, Concord 03301

New Jersey: Division of Fish, Game, and Shellfisheries, P.O. Box 1809, Trenton 08625

New Mexico: Department of Game and Fish, State Capitol, Santa Fe 87501

New York: Fish and Wildlife Division, Department of Environmental Conservation, 50 Wolf Road, Albany 12201

North Carolina: Wildlife Resources Commission, P.O. Box 2919, Raleigh 27602

North Dakota: State Game and Fish Department, 2121 Lovett Avenue, Bismarck 58501

Ohio: Division of Wildlife, 1500 Dublin Road, Columbus 43212

Oklahoma: Fisheries Division *or* Game Division, Department of Wildlife Conservation, 1801 North Lincoln, Oklahoma City 73105

Oregon: State Game Commission, P.O. Box 3503, Portland 97208

Pennsylvania: Fish Commission, P.O. Box 1673, *or* Game Commission, P.O Box 1567, Harrisburg 17120

Puerto Rico: Division of Fisheries and Wildlife, Department of Agriculture, P.O. Box 10163, Santurce, San Juan 00908

Rhode Island: Division of Fish and Wildlife, Department of Natural Resources, 83 Park Street, Providence 02903

South Carolina: Wildlife Resources Department, P.O. Box 167, Columbia 29202

South Dakota: Department of Game, Fish, and Parks, State Office Building, Pierre 57501

Tennessee: Game and Fish Commission, P.O. Box 9400, Ellington Agricultural Center, Nashville 37220

Texas: Parks and Wildlife Department, John H. Reagan Building, Austin 78701

Utah: Fish and Game Division, State Department of Natural Resources, 1596 W.N. Temple, Salt Lake City 84116

Vermont: Fish and Game Department, 151 Main Street, Montpelier 05602

Virginia: Commission of Game and Inland Fisheries, P.O. Box 11104, Richmond 23230

Washington: Department of Game, 600 North Capitol Way, Olympia 98501

West Virginia: Department of Natural Resources, 1800 Washington Street East, Charleston 25305

Wisconsin: Department of Natural Resources, P.O. Box 450, Madison 53701

Wyoming: Game and Fish Commission, P.O. Box 1589, Cheyenne 82001

HOW TO BOOK A BIG-GAME HUNT

Book early is our advice or, more precisely, begin looking early. Guides usually like to have their sports lined up with deposits in hand by mid-June. This is as it should be. Nobody ever became a millionaire by being a big-game guide, but guides can at least make a decent wage if they fill every day of a relatively short season with clients.

January is about the right time to start research. You surely have some idea of the kind of game you'd like to hunt and the general section of the country in which you'd like to hunt, so, with that decision made, write either the State Chamber of Commerce or the State Fish and Game Department, or both, requesting information on licensed guides.

Depending on your energy, pick between three and ten of the outfits listed and write them each a brief letter requesting information on their services. What you get back should give you a pretty good idea of what kind of a package they're offering and how much it will cost. This should narrow the field to a handful that deserve serious consideration.

Once you reach this point in negotiations, it's very important that you get everything down in writing, from the number of hunters that accompany each guide to who supplies the toilet paper. Here's a sampling of specific questions to ask:

- What are the accommodations?
- Is it a horseback or pickup-truck hunt?
- What are you expected to bring?
- How many hunters per guide?
- What percentage of success did last year's hunters have?

- How much does the hunt cost, and are there any sur-charges involved with a kill?

There are no "right" answers to these questions, but the response you get should say something about the fairness of the price being charged. For example, a bunkhouse type of arrangement with gourmet dining should cost more than a tent and campfire cooking.

Generally, a hunt that involves horses will be more expensive than one where you ride around in a truck, especially if you have to pack into camp. The logistics of supplying a wilderness camp by horseback, wrangling horses and hunters, and getting game out are quite complex.

First-class hunts should require you to bring your gun, personal items, and a sleeping bag, no more.

Two hunters per guide should be maximum. There are exceptions, but two hunters are all that one man can adequately handle on a typical hunt.

Success percentages give you some idea of how hunters fared last year. The higher the success ratio, the better your chance is the assumption, but figures can lie (and liars figure). It's been my experience that most camps average 25 percent success on elk, 75 percent on deer, and 50 percent on other big game. If figures cited are markedly higher, double check. You might have found a super guide, but you might also have found an exaggeration.

Costs for a hunt can run between $100 and $1,000 per week, depending on the package offered. At the high end of the scale, you should expect a lot for your money: top-flight accommodations and food and close personal attention. The $100 rate usually represents a "drop camp." This arrangement simply means that you'll be packed into a camp and then left pretty much on your own for a week. Again, there's nothing wrong with this. In fact, money aside, I'd prefer a drop camp, as I enjoy going it alone and learning about my quarry from the ground up. But cost should reflect your outfitter's investment in goods and services.

One other aspect of a guided hunt deserves mention. This is the so-called "guaranteed hunt." This usually means no game, no pay, but look into that "guarantee" very carefully, as it could be a hint of a rip-off. For example, one fellow I know booked into one of these hunts for a week and learned the "guarantee" was that he could stay around camp, hunting on his own, for the rest of the season or until he got his game. This might be satisfactory to some, but he could only afford a week off work, and so he felt cheated.

Get it all down on paper, including some opinions of others. Before you send a deposit (usually 10 to 25 percent of the cost), ask your prospective outfitter for the names of a few former clients. Write to them and ask for a brief appraisal. Basically, do they feel they got their money's worth?

There is much more at issue than whether they—or you—got their game. Weather conditions, migratory patterns, and just plain luck all play a part in hunting, and there really is no guarantee that you'll score. If there was, it wouldn't really be hunting. But if the individual you're considering comes across as the kind of outfitter who'll do his honest best to make you comfortable and guide you to a shot, and who's only charging you his costs plus a decent wage for himself, you've found a top guide, and you'd better get your deposit in his hands before he's all booked up.

—N.S.

A GUIDE CRITICIZES
SOME OF HIS CLIENTS
by Eli Spannagel, Jr.

If I had to pick the most common fault among the 150 or so out-of-state deer hunters I've guided, it would be their unwillingness to hunt the way I hunt.

People come to my Montana ranch from the Midwest and as far away as New York, and they bring their ideas about how deer should be hunted with them. It's kind of hard to argue with a guy who might have spent $1,000 in hopes of getting a big buck, but hunting methods that work in one section of the country don't necessarily work in another.

The biggest pain in the neck is the type of firearms most hunters show up with. If they live east of the Mississippi, I can bet my bootlaces they'll show up with a 30-30 or 30-.06. I always suggest a .270. You need this flat caliber for the long across-canyon shots we often get. Another fault is their reluctance to take a long shot. Out here 300 yards is nothing, but the average hunter has never practiced those ranges, and he's afraid and nervous to try. I'm about at the point where I insist hunters spend an hour or so shooting targets before I take them hunting. This is not very popular, as they are anxious to get going, but I find it really helps in making that first shot count.

Believing your guide is another thing. I once got a hunter a standing shot at a mounting-class muley at 100 yards. He refused to take it because he couldn't see horns. I had seen them all right, and the hunter finally did too . . . at 300 yards and running on the other side of the canyon. It was especially frustrating because I'd hunted with this guy for four days, and he'd already botched two other chances.

I'll admit that hunters are human, and they can make mistakes, and I've never come down on a client for an honest one. I've made them too. But the guy who hunts against his guide instead of with him isn't just mistaken, he's a damn fool.

Eli Spannagel, Jr., is a Montana rancher and guide who lives near Forsyth, Montana.

TRAVEL TIP

Tie a short length of international orange plastic tape to the handles of your baggage. They'll show up fast in claim areas, and you'll reduce chances for a case of mistaken identity.

CARIBOU

One of the many unanswered questions about the environmental impact of the Alaska pipeline is the effect it will have on caribou migrations. A similar pipeline in the Soviet Union has nearly put an end to annual migrations there. Should the animals refuse to cross the line, they will be blocked from a huge amount of their natural forage range.

There was nobody around but me, nobody else in the world but me and a million animals and a thousand noises and the bright sun and the cool breeze and the shade from the big trees that made it cathedral-cool but a lot less musty and damp and full of century-old fear and trembling. I got to thinking that maybe this was what God had in mind when he invented religion, instead of all the don'ts and must-nots and sins and confessions of sins. I got to thinking about all the big churches I had been in, including those in Rome, and how none of them could possibly compare with this place, with its brilliant birds and its soothing sounds of intense life all around and the feeling of ineffable peace and goodwill, so that not even man would be capable of behaving very badly in such a place. I thought that this was maybe the kind of place the Lord would come to sit in and get his strength back after a hard day's work trying to straighten out mankind.

—Robert Ruark, *Horn of the Hunter*

SEASON OF THE ELK
by Dean Krakel

Kansas City, Mo.: Lowell Press, $14.95; paper, $9.95.

This is a coffee-table book with a lot more than good looks going for it. The author spent a full year photographing and following the great elk herds in and around Jackson, Wyoming. The result is a sound education, in word and picture, of the elk's annual cycle, from epic migrations to calving time.

True, it is more of an elk's life history than a hunting yarn, but half of successful hunting lies in understanding your quarry. Reading this book is a beautiful way to get that part of your hunt started.

ELK

There are five times as many elk in the United States today as there were in 1910. Current populations are estimated at 300,000.

BURNHAM ELK CALL

This is a difficult elk bugle to master, but it has a superb tone—that same reedy snort that sends chills up your back on moonlit September nights in the mountains. It comes in two parts for ease of carrying: the whistle and reed and a latex hose extension for depth of tone. Price: $6.95. Burnham Brothers, Marble Falls, TX 78654.

ELK CALL

This elk call—black and red plastic, 7 3/8 inches long, 2 ounces—is recommended for beginners. It's one of the easiest on the market to handle, since it resists falling off on that third, elk-spooking note. Remember, you've got to chop off the high, reedy whistle of the second note if you're going to bring a bull in close. Price: $6.95. P. S. Olt Company, Pekin, IL 61554.

BEAR AND ELK IN WASHINGTON

Ron Moore's Western Enterprises offers bear and elk hunting from April through November. Bear are hunted in the warmer months, generally over bait through June and then with hounds for the duration of the season. Elk hunting is an October/November pursuit, with about 50 percent of the elk hunters also getting a crack at a bear.

All in all, this sounds like a well-run though woodsy operation. Moore's brochure comes across with a folksy kind of honesty that has a peculiar eloquence. Good reading, and when you're done you just know what to expect. I'd sure book him, and he's got good rates: guaranteed bear hunt, $375; seven-day elk hunt, $525; all other hunts, $75 per day. Contact Ron Moore, P.O. Box 176, Kalama, WA 98625.

—N.S.

JARRY PATTERSON

BUGLING EXPERT

If you'd like the thrill of bugling up a bull elk, give Ken Smith a toot. In one of his favorite pictures he's holding up nine fingers that indicate the number of bulls he called in to his clients last year. That, folks, is some accomplishment!

Ken hunts the Idaho Primitive Area out of Challis, Idaho. Travel is by horseback, and his camps are located 15 to 20 miles from any airstrip, so if you're not used to the saddle, plan on eating off the mantel your first night at camp.

Along with elk, during and after the bugling season, Ken also hunts sheep, goats, deer, and cougar, and bear with bait and dogs.

Rates start at $850 for a week and go higher, depending on the length of your stay and the species (or combination of species) hunted. Contact Ken Smith, P.O. Box 27, Challis, ID 83226.

LION AND BEAR WITH HOUNDS

The JP Bar Ranch specializes in mountain lion and bear hunts with hounds. Hunts run five to seven days, and lodging is either in camper trailers or tents, depending on where the game may be moving. At no time are there more than twelve hunters in camp. Transportation is provided either by four-by-four or horse, again depending on the game. All goods and services provided except your sleeping bag, personal effects, and weapon. Archers and muzzle loaders are as welcome as long-rifle hunters.

Typical rates for a seven-day hunt are as follows: lion, $450 plus $450 at kill; bear, $300 plus $300 at kill. Special April hunt available. Contact Jarry Patterson, 1076 Twenty Road, Fruita, CO 81521.

PHONE 207 528-2131

EST. 1947

Katahdin Lodge & Camps
(10 MILES NORTH OF PATTEN ON ROUTE 11)

HUNTING   BEAR   DEER   BOBCAT   FISHING

Finley K. Clarke

Registered Maine Guide   Benefactor Member N.R.A.

R. F. D. 1   Smyrna Mills, Maine   04780

KATAHDIN LODGE & CAMPS: BEAR, WHITETAIL, AND MORE IN MAINE

This sportsman's camp is located in northern Maine, and one of the more telling aspects of the literature they send out regards summer vacations. "We do take a few summer vacationers, but remember, this is a hunting and fishing lodge."

They specialize in black bear over bait from the beginning of May to the end of November and have a high success rate (in 1976, 177 adult bear were sighted by hunters and 51 were taken). Rates for bear hunters are about $300 weekly, including guides.

In November, these folks also entertain deer hunters ($200 weekly, no guide), and again their success ratio is well above the state average. They also have hunting for grouse, woodcock, snowshoe rabbit, fox, and bobcat.

The lodge borders 3,500 square miles of wilderness, so there's plenty of room to roam. There's free literature on the hunting, fishing, and accommodations at Katahdin, and it's unusually thorough and exceptionally well-written. Contact Finley K. Clarke, R.F.D. 1, Smyrna Mills, ME 04780.

"A wild bear chase didst never see? / Then thou hast lived in vain. / The richest bump of glorious glee / Lies desert in thy brain."
—*Abraham Lincoln, The Bear Hunt*

161

RAMSHORN LODGE

ROUTE No. 1 - BOX 228 B
SALMON, IDAHO 83467

ELK HUNTING AT IDAHO'S RAMSHORN LODGE: BARGAIN RATES

Here's a super deal for the guy who likes to go it on his own. For $280, you get a week's worth of food, lodging, advice, and transportation. Ramshorn Lodge is at the gateway to the Idaho Primitive Area, and the package they offer is basically this: Each day you are given information on where the game may be found by way of a scout. You never hunt the same area twice, unless you request it.

Depending on the area and the location of the game, you might be given a horse, a four-by-four, or a pair of hiking boots. You will be hunting that area with three others, and the lodge limits their hunters to sixteen. There are no guides.

Hunting season runs roughly from September 14 through November 24. This really sounds like a challenging way to hunt some beautiful country. Contact Ramshorn Lodge, Route 1, P.O. Box 228-B, Salmon, ID 83467.

CARIBOU IN NORTHERN QUEBEC

The Quebec Eskimo Indian Outfitters can best be described as a tribal coalition/coop, aided by the Canadian Government, that has set up a series of hunting and fishing camps in northern Quebec. Two lodges specialize in caribou hunting, the Ikalu Caribou and Char Camp and the Whale River Caribou and Salmon Camp. Both posted a phenomenal 100-percent kill in 1976, which has to be some success ratio!

Accommodations aren't very plush (plywood cabins, four people to a room), but what do you expect from a hunting camp? The numbers seem right—twelve to sixteen hunters per camp.

Species hunted include Ungava and Barren Ground caribou, and should you score early, you can hunt for ptarmigan or fish for char and lake trout. Eight-day hunt, $935.00 per person. Contact Den Austin, P.O. Box 520, Rawdon, Quebec J0K 1S0.

SHEEP, GRIZZLY, AND BROWN BEAR IN ALASKA

Trophy class Dall sheep and brown and grizzly bear are Larry Rivers's specialty. He hunts sheep in the Brooks Range and bear on the Alaska Peninsula.

Camps consist of large, heated A-wall tents, and each hunter has his own personal guide. It might be pointed out that while this is the most expensive way to go, it is also the most profitable both for game and for an education.

Transportation between camps is by aircraft, and the rules of fair chase are strictly adhered to. Seasons run roughly two weeks in May for bear and five weeks in August and September for sheep. Other species available include moose, caribou, wolf, wolverine, and black bear.

The prices of these hunts are determined by the length of your stay and the type of game you wish to hunt. They would run somewhere between $1,500 and $5,000 for up to twelve days.

Larry Rivers has an excellent poop sheet that he'll send you on request. It clearly outlines camp conditions, the kind of hunting and terrain to expect, and costs. This appears to be a first-class outfit that delivers first-class hunting. Contact Larry Rivers, P.O. Box 107, Talkeetna, AK 99676.

FAIR CHASE

LARRY RIVERS
P.O. BOX 107
TALKEETNA, ALASKA 99676

Registered Guide and Outfitter
Alaska Hunting, Fishing, & Photography

RIFLE SCABBARD

Whether you're hunting from a modern trail bike or Old Paint, you'll need a receptacle for your rifle. These expanded-vinyl soft scabbards are lined with red pile to protect the bluing on your gun, and they have six tie rings so they can be secured in any position, to just about any kind of transportation. No-scope scabbard, $20.00; scope scabbard, $23.00. Kolpin Manufacturing, Inc., P.O. Box 231, Berlin, WI 54923.

TAXIDERMY TIPS

By John Bleth

The majority of trophy hunters are business or professional people who love to hunt to relax from the pressures of their professions. The desire to escape from civilization, to enjoy the solitude and the beauty of the outdoors and wilderness area, is essential for happiness. My brother-in-law, for example, has made several trips to Africa and British Columbia and has many trophies that he has acquired over the past several years. He is building a special home in order to enjoy his many beautiful trophies. He says, "I just want to come home from the day's pressures, sit down, relax, and relive all my hunting experiences." This explains why the taxidermist plays a big part in the life of a hunter.

It is very important to find a taxidermist who is a real artist and will make the trophies lifelike. But the taxidermist cannot do it all. Proper care of the animal as soon as it is killed is also important. Be sure to find out how to cape the trophy properly, or have someone along who knows; many trophies are ruined by ignorance of proper care. You cannot always depend on the guides, either, as I've had some of my work devastated by guides and skinners from different parts of the world. It just doesn't make sense to pay huge prices for hunting trips and then have a ruined cape or horns eaten up with bugs to show for it. So the best solution is to inform yourself and then supervise to make sure the job is done right.

When heads are skinned out properly, make sure there is plenty of salt put on them. If you cannot get them to the taxidermist soon, they should be frozen if at all possible. Do not salt if there are facilities to freeze. Use at least two plastic bags and freeze as soon as possible. Do not let them spoil before freezing. That has happened more times than I care to remember. I really prefer to do my own skinning at no extra charge, if this is feasible.

For proper care of the mounted heads, to keep them looking lifelike, use a damp cloth and wipe in the direction that the hair lies. If the heads are very dusty or oily, such as heads displayed in bars, it takes a special cleaner, which can be purchased from your taxidermist. Heads of deer, antelope, or sheep should *never* be cleaned with a vacuum cleaner. A damp cloth will do the trick. With proper care of your trophies, they will last for many years.

John Bleth is a taxidermist living near Lewistown, Montana. He's done a lot of work for me, and it's all been excellent. His address is 1311 West Water Street, Lewistown, MT 59422.
—F.S.

TYPICAL TAXIDERMY COSTS

RUGS
Black bear rug, with open mouth: $225 (yearling) to $300
Grizzly: $250 to $450
Bobcat, fox, and coyote rug, with open mouth: $175
HEADS
Deer: $155 to $165
Antelope: $145 to $155
Goat: $155 to $165
Sheep: $175
Elk: $250 to $350
Caribou: $250 to $350
Moose: $300 to $550
Buffalo: $300 to $550
OTHER
Badger: $155
Raccoon: $155 to $165

PRESERVING SNAKESKINS

1. Skin the snake carefully by making a straight cut through the middle of the belly from the jaw to the end of the tail.

2. Scrub the back of the skin with steel wool and white borax until all meat and fat are off.

3. Let cure overnight, then paint the front and back of the skin with a solution of equal parts of glycerin and wood alcohol (methanol).

4. When dry, apply a second coat and the skin is ready to mount, on either a hat or a board. The finished skin can be either sewn or glued to fabric.
—F.S.

TAXIDERMY GUIDE
by Russell Tinsley

Chicago: Follett Publishing Company, $3.95 (soft cover).

No more will you have to try to convince doubting friends of the size or beauty of "the one you didn't keep." Using the techniques described in this practical handbook, you can convert that animal, bird, or fish into an interesting and attractive trophy. Based on the professional techniques developed by famous Texas taxidermist Lem Rathbone, this illustrated volume shows how to achieve lifelike results. Includes tips on making rugs and novelties such as gun racks and lamps, how to display horns and antlers, and more. Gives details on the art of sculpturing and casting, formulas for making your own materials, and sources of supply.

TAXIDERMISTS WE HAVE TRIED AND LIKED

J. M. Self, 3721 East 7th Street, Panama City, FL 32401.
Earl Locke, Jackrabbit Lane, Belgrade, MT 59714. (Bargain rates and quality work.)

Jack Atcheson, 3210 Ottawa Street, Butte, MT 59701.
Lentfer's, 215 West Park Street, Butte, MT 59701.
Wayland Adams, 1213 Shelly Street, Clinton, OK 73601.

Kulis Freeze-dry Taxidermy

This process preserves an animal (or part of an animal) simply by removing all moisture by freeze-drying—just like for your coffee. Its advantages are that the hunter or his guide has no need to cape out the trophy—it is simply frozen and sent off—and that if in the future you decide you'd rather have an erect deer mount, instead of the sneak mount you got, all you have to do is send it back and they'll redo it in the new pose! The only artificial parts of the new mount are the eyes; they are of glass, just as in regular taxidermy.

Taxidermists will tell you that their biggest problem is in fixing up skins and capes where the hunter goofed with his knife, or skins that weren't properly taken care of. Now even the most inept knife handler can have perfect mounts.

Prices for shoulder mounts of big-game animals run from $125 for a whitetail deer to $3,100 for an elephant, with most running $175 to $400. Crating runs from $30

to $65 for most common species. Full mounts are also done, which run from $475 for a javelina to $24,000 for a total elephant. Rugs run $300 to $600, approximately. They also do small game and fish, as well as lamps, stools, gun racks, and so on. Kulis Freeze-Dry Taxidermy, 725 Broadway Avenue, Bedford, OH 44146.

BUYING A TRAIL BIKE

So a trail bike sounds like a good idea to you, huh? Well, before you buy one, just make sure that you're allowed to use one wherever you plan to hunt. There are an awful lot of private and public lands where they're verboten, and several states prohibit their use in conjunction with hunting.

If all checks out, here are a few things to consider. The most attractive bikes in terms of cost versus use will probably be machines that are capable of double-duty: as hunters in the hills and as an alternative means of transportation around home. The problem is that the more suitable a bike becomes to road use, the less suitable it is to the back country. For example, big BMWs and Harley Hogs cruise like Cadillacs down the open road, but you'd have to be a fool to try and jockey one around on anything beyond a hardpack surface. On the other end of the spectrum, Tote Goats are very able vehicles in the outback, but they're noisy, slow, and uncomfortable riding when you crank them up to 25 mph.

There are of course, a whole bunch of suitable bikes between these two extremes, but the rule of thumb still holds true: The better the road bike, the poorer the trail bike. And here are a few other features to consider.

• Horsepower or cc displacement needn't be high in a trail bike. They're geared low enough to handle about any load the frame will carry. They go slow, but in situations where you need that kind of pull, you wouldn't want to be

going fast anyway. Low horsepower also means minimum gas consumption, a greater roving range, and light weight—a very important matter. Sensible trail-bike motors run 90 to 125 cc's or 5 to 8 hp. On the open road, 125 cc's might get you up to 60 mph with a tail wind.

• Tires will perform best off the road when they are knobby or cleated, wide, and soft (around 3 to 5 psi). They will perform best at high speeds (and contribute to high speed as well) if they are narrow, smooth, and hard. Take your choice; the treads, patterns, and tires are there for sale at any cycle shop.

• Weight is a most important factor, as you're bound to encounter conditions where the bike has to be manhandled around some obstacle. The power of the bike may often be used as a helper during the operation. As a matter of fact, the times I've actually had to lift a bike off the ground, up and over something, have been rare, but they do occur. I rate the limits of reasonable maneuverability at around 250 pounds. I find a bike of 150 to 200 pounds a definite advantage.

• Accessories or accouterments are more bother than benefit on the trail. Things like automatic starting, lights, mirrors, and batteries add weight and just make for something else to go on the fritz. You're best off without them in the outback, but they'll probably be required by law if you want to use the cycle as a street machine. —N.S.

SXT 125 BY HARLEY DAVIDSON

For those who prefer a roadworthy trail bike, the SXT 125 is powered by a 123-cc engine. It has a five-speed constant mesh transmission, with a low gear ratio of 29 to 1. Electrical equipment includes a 12-volt alternator and battery and a head lamp, taillight, stoplight, signals, and horn.

Ground clearance is 8.6 inches, and the gas tank holds 2.8 gallons, both features indicating freedom to range. The dry weight of the SXT 125 is 216 pounds.

All in all, this looks like a good bike for both off-road and on-road use, a reasonable compromise if you want a bike that's more than a hunting machine. Price: $799.00. Harley Davidson, 3700 West Juneau Avenue, Milwaukee, WI 53201.

A Super Trail Bike by Rokon

If you're looking for a pure trail machine, the power and traction of this Rokon is hard to beat for climbing hills. The key to this machine's mountain-goat ability lies in a system that throws power to both wheels. Add this "two-wheel-drive" feature to big soft (3½ psi) tires and 185 pounds dry weight, and you have a trail machine that not only climbs 45-degree slopes but one that coasts over bogs and hard-crusted snow as well.

Other Rokon features include a 134-cc Chrysler two-stroke 10 hp engine, automatic transmission, front disk brakes, Forest Service-approved spark arrester on the muffler, ground clearance of 15 inches, and a fording depth (for water crossings) of 24 inches.

Worthy of special note are a power take-off system whereby (with special implements) these bikes may be used to run a 12-cubic-foot trailer, a spreader, a rake, a moldboard plow, a three-point hitch, a 1,500-watt alternator, an agricultural fogger, a double gangharrow, and a cultivator, and a hose, pump, and reservoir

package that converts this bike into a go-anywhere mini fire truck! Free brochure. Price: $1,495.00. Rokon, Inc., 160 Emerald Street, Keene, NH 03431. —F.S.

YAMAHA TRAIL BIKE DT100D

The Yamaha trail bike zooms along with a sensible combination of features, light weight, and one of the lowest list prices around.

The bike is powered by a gas-saving 97cc engine with a magneto and kick starter. Its five-speed transmission should provide more than enough low-range power to grind up hills, yet sufficient speed to make time when trail conditions permit. The gas tank holds 1.9 gallons, and while it's hard to judge consumption under trail conditions, that should afford a minimum range of around 25 miles and a maximum range well over a hundred.

Ground clearance is 7.9 inches at the lowest point, which is enough to get over the average rock or log. Should you have to leave the bike to lift and heave it over or around a deadfall, two people can easily handle its 176 pounds. Price: $540.00. Yamaha USA, 6620 Orangethorpe Avenue, Buena Park, CA 90622.

"The ethics of sportsmanship is not a fixed code, but must be formulated and practiced by the individual, with no referee but the Almighty."
—Aldo Leopold

165

FORD F-150 4X

This short-wheelbase pickup is well suited to rugged off-road conditions. The 117 inches between front and rear axles means it has a small turning radius and the ability to traverse deep gulches and gullies without hanging up on the front or rear bumper.

The flare-side box makes for easy access to gears inside, and the 360 V-8 engine and four-speed transmission add up to a powerhouse that will pull you out of or over just about any obstacle you'll encounter.

An interesting addition to Ford's 150 series is their Mono-Beam front suspension—a combination of coil springs and steering linkage shock absorbers that supposedly make for a much smoother ride than other four-by-fours. Spend a couple of hours pounding around the bush with a conventional suspension, and you'll appreciate the potential of this innovation. Four-

bys are marvelous machines, but, brother, do you take a beating on broken terrain! F-150 4X suggested retail price: $5,343.05. See your local Ford dealer.

JIMMY CASA GRANDE

Of all the recvee styles there is no combination that teams relative comfort with off-the-road mobility like a camper on a four-wheel-drive truck. GMC's Casa Grande option is right up at the head of this particular class of hunting wheels.

Go power with a Jimmy starts with options that include things like power steering and full-time four-wheel drive. Living space amounts to a fiberglass-and-plastic camper that is an integral part of the vehicle. The camper has a pop top for a low profile to get you under low branches, to cut down wind resistance on the highway, and to keep the center of gravity low. Interior appointments include: two-burner lpg stove, ice box, 5-gallon water tank, stainless steel sink, dinette, and sleeping room for up to four. Suggested retail price: $10,537.00 from your local GMC dealer.

Subaru Combines Economy and Four-Wheel Drive

Subaru's four-wheel-drive station wagon amounts to a tidy package indeed. Aside from the obvious advantages of a four-by, it incorporates gas economy (25 to 30 mpg) with the lowest four-wheel price tag in the business (around $4,000).

The vehicle rides like a dream when compared to the stiff suspension of larger trucks and wagons, and standard equipment includes a manual transmission, reclining front seats, tinted glass, a flow-through vent system, rear window defogger, and front disk brakes.

The faults inherent in this vehicle are derived from the same qualities that make it attractive: its size. A big man will feel cramped in the front seat, especially if he's wearing heavy clothes, and the rear compartment—even with the rear seat folded down—is too short for comfortable sleeping.

In terms of off-the-road mobility, the Subaru's traction and tracking ability is excellent, but the wheels won't fit into the trails blazed by larger vehicles. It has only 8 inches of clearance under the rear differential, and the wagon's climbing ability exceeds the motor's muscle to drive it.

The Subaru is not an all-terrain vehicle, but it's sure worth looking into if you're a hunter who likes to go beyond the range of two-wheel-drive vehicles and who needs a second car that has to satisfy your pocketbook and your wife.

GMC SUBURBAN

The GMC Suburban with four-wheel drive looks like a good choice for the heavy-duty hunter with things to do around town.

With the rear seat removed and the second seat folded down, there's 144 cubic feet of interior load space—plenty of room for a complete canvas camp. Should you want more convenience and fewer appointments, these dimensions allow enough room for a double bed. Around town, with rear seat installed, there's seating for nine passengers and groceries, and it's good looking enough to please the distaff side of the household. It has the traction to go in all kinds of weather.

GVW ratings range from 6,200 to 8,400 pounds with up to 3,190 pounds of pay-

load—a lot of wild meat in anyone's book. Factory-installed trailering packages allow you to tow up to 14,500 pounds, and coupled with a travel trailer the combo should provide a great cure for wanderlust. Unhitch your trailer by lake, stream, or seaside, and you're free to hunt just about anywhere you please. Suggested retail price: $6,260.35 from your local GMC dealer.

FOR FOUR-BY-FOUR BUYERS

The purchase of a new four-wheel-drive vehicle amounts to a substantial investment, but as a four-by owner for some twelve years, I can attest to their worth. They have gotten me into and out of some prime hunting territory and have cut the drudgery of deer and elk drags by incalculable miles.

But just buying a rig that throws power to all four tires doesn't necessarily mean that you've got the most maneuverable machine on the market. There is no one consistently "best" brand. Annual model and design changes (and their consequences when you're off the road) shift mobility back and forth among brand names and even among body styles. So here's a quick consumer's guide to consider when buying a four-by:

• Settle on the body style you want—pickup, van, suburban, or Jeep—and then test what's available in the field.

• Buy late in the model year, if for no other reason than you can talk to owners who bought early and can learn about possible lemons.

• Remember that narrow-track vehicles are generally undesirable. They will not fit into the tracks made by four-bys with conventional-width axles, and you're virtually always breaking a new trail in mud, sand, or snow.

• Get an engine with lugging power—the ability to deliver substantial power to your wheels at low engine rpm's. An engine that will not lug is bound to die under critical conditions, such as climbing the last ten yards of a steep hill or getting stuck in the deep mud that you didn't realize was at the bottom of the draw. Engines that must be revved up to deliver power also are the most likely to break traction.

• Consider an automatic transmission in a four-by, especially if you're new at off-the-road driving. An automatic transmission in the hands of a beginner is far less likely to break traction than a standard shift. However, experts generally prefer standard transmissions in their rigs. You have more precise control over the power being thrown to the wheels, and there is beauty in simplicity when you're off the road. That's another thing to consider. Spare appointments in your four-by, devoid of hood-filling options, make for a vehicle that's easy to fix yourself—no small matter in a rig that by intent and design is regularly going to be miles from mechanics.

• Off-the-road mobility can be gauged by how well a vehicle tracks going uphill on a slick surface. If a four-by constantly fishtails in the hands of an experienced driver, with the rear wheels falling out of alignment with the front wheels, that rig is not going to be any great shakes in the outback. The best performers will stay in line, even though all four wheels are turning slowly, slowly in the muck.

—N.S.

BORN FREE SUPER COACH

Here's an interesting recvee for the well-heeled hunter. The living unit comes with its own set of rear wheels, which help carry a load and appointments equivalent to a motor home. But, unlike a motor home, it has a jacking system that lets you remove the camper from the truck in less than five minutes. Then you can use your pickup to roam at will.

The Born Free catalog has a full break down of costs, options, and a Test Report and Testimonial Booklet which includes all kinds of upbeat praise from owners for this camper. Several horror stories tell of rolling the whole rig down embankments or off cliffs, with the camper coming through without much more than scratches—and sometimes less than that. The unit evidently is built like a tank.

Still another interesting customer service: the Born Free folks will help you sell your old recvee or will try to find you a used Born Free if you don't want to buy new. Base price: $9,750, FOB. Dodgen Industries, Humbolt, IA 50548.

AVERAGE RECVEE RETAIL PRICES

If you're considering buying a recvee for your hunting trips, here's an average of what you can expect to pay.

Travel trailers	$5,901
5th-wheel trailers	7,684
Camping (tent) trailers	2,091
Truck campers	2,534
Pickup caps	331
Motor homes (large)	19,644
Motor homes (van)	11,241

Well,
Have we guys learned our lesson?
You bet we have.
Have we learned to eschew irresponsible outdoorsmanship, to ask advice, to take care and to plan fastidiously and to stay on the trail and to camp only in designated campgrounds and to inquire locally and take enough clothes and keep off the grass?
You bet we haven't.
Unfastidious outdoorsmanship is the best kind.

—Terry and Renny Russell, *On the Loose*

For Sale: the Piltdown Zephyr

This custom-built hunting vehicle boasts design features seldom found on Detroit production models. Lovingly crafted from a 1948 Buick, the encumbering hood, fenders, rear seat, and trunk have been removed by expert hands and a cold chisel.

Ample power is delivered via a straight-8 engine and three-speed standard transmission, with a welded differential that drives both rear wheels and makes it interesting and fun when you turn a corner. This is a progressive hunting vehicle. Since getting it into reverse is kind of tricky, it's virtually impossible to regress. Make us an offer. The Editors.

WINNEBAGO'S SPORTSMAN'S DEN

We all want our own hunting hideaway, with gun and rod racks, soft padded furniture, a bar and kitchenette, beds, a small bath, and even a green-felt gaming table for a few rounds of poker after the day's shooting is over. Well, if you put wheels under that dream, you've got a good approximation of Winnebago's Sportsman's Den model motor home. This luxury vehicle is rated as a Minnie Winnie, but at nearly 25 feet it's bigger than many standards. Its plush accommodations include the aforementioned gun storage, gaming table, and watering hole, along with sleeping and eating facilities for four and one of the roomiest bathrooms on wheels.

The living unit is carried on a Chevy chassis and is powered by a 350-cubic inch engine. Optional equipment includes a 100-volt AC generator, AM/FM stereo radio and tape player, air conditioning, and cruise control. Interiors are color-coordinated and are available in a choice of shades that includes Cactus, Sage, or Inca Gold.

If you ever wanted to get away from it all, in style and surroundings that complement the sporting life, this is one way to do it. Price: $19,186.00, from Winnebago Industries, Forest City, IA 50436, or from your local Winnie dealer.

AIRCAT AIRBOATS

Airboats are the most practical of hunter transportation around swampy areas, and the Aircat 14/200 is noteworthy in that its manufacturer, Hurricane Fiberglass, claims it needs "no water—just dew!"

The four-cylinder Continental engine drives the boat at a sizzling 60 mph, and it has a payload capacity of 900 pounds. The hull is a catamaran-style, so it performs reasonably well in a chop. The boat and motor run $7,050, and you can add an extra $575 for the trailer if you plan to use it at times other than dewy mornings or rainy days. Otherwise I assume you can dock the boat on your front lawn and start from there.

Hurricane Fiberglass makes a whole bunch of other airboats ranging in price from $2,450 to $7,950, and they also sell airboats in kit form or piece by piece at considerable savings. One practical alternative to the expense and, to some extent, the limitations of a "pure" airboat is their Swamp Cat, an air-cooled VW-powered propeller and cage that will bolt to a standard johnboat in "25 minutes or less." It will drive a 14-footer at speeds up to 25 mph over as little as 2 inches of water. At $1,850 this could be a good investment for river-bottom deer hunters and waterfowlers anywhere.

Aircat puts out a comprehensive catalog that's kind of folksy, funky, and slick all at once. The graphics are good

and so are some of the ideas, such as using an airboat instead of a snowmobile when hunting around shifting ice. Hurricane Fiberglass Products Corp., Box 8, Lake Hamilton, FL 33851.

HUSTLER ATV

Back in the early 70s it seemed as though everyone was making an all-terrain vehicle. They were promoted as the ultimate off-road transport, combining the features of bikes, four-bys, and snowmobiles in one impossible-to-stop machine.

The field of ATV manufacturers has thinned considerably since then, reflecting the truth of the matter: they are as limited as any other kind of ORV, and perhaps more than most, because low ground clearance makes rocks and logs formidable barriers; unless they have a dozer-track-type conversion, they bog down in deep uncrusted snow; and they are plodders afloat and downright dangerous when the water gets rough.

There is one area, however, where they excel, and that is in the swamps. They will pull through soupy mud, ford small ponds, and ride smooth and fast over boggy mire that would suck in each footfall.

If an ATV fits your hunting plans, the Hustler provides a good profile of what to look for. It was one of the first ATVs

to be manufactured, and it's still alive and well. That says something about both product excellence and customer satisfaction. The vehicle seats four, which translates to two hunters and their gear. (A two-seater never has enough room for what you want to bring unless you go alone.) The body is seamless polyethylene, reinforced with 10-gauge channel steel. Thus it is less likely to develop leaks and it can take a beating.

Positive power is delivered to all six wheels via individual chains. Some ATVs have idlers in the middle; some drive each set of wheels with a single chain. Idlers have no pulling power, and a single chain invites breakdowns.

There's also a long list of comfortable options for this machine—things like gun racks and winches and cargo racks that suggest an ATV that's made with hunting in mind. And when you compare prices with competitors, you'll discover they're reasonable in that department too. Price: $2,695.00. Hustler Corp., Jonesboro, AR 72401.

"As all trails do . . . it branched . . . grew dimmer and slimmer, degenerated to a deer path, petered out to a squirrel track, ran up a tree, and ended in a knot hole."
—Nessmuk

169

JET POWER UNITS FOR OUTBOARD MOTORS

Boats—at least big boats—aren't usually required for hunting, so we decided it would be beyond our scope to cover them. We did feel, however, that among boat-borne hunters there's probably strong interest in jet power, since it allows you to run in extremely shallow water.

The most highly recommended manufacturer of outboard jet power units that we could track down is Specialty Manufacturing Company, which makes units for all major outboards, starting at 18 horse (lower hp jets aren't practical, as you lose up to 50 percent efficiency with a jet) and up to 135 hp. An excellent free catalog describes this product and the uses to which it's best suited. Prices: from $390.00 to $530.00. Specialty Manufacturing Company, 2035 Edison Avenue, San Leandro, CA 94577.

SOURCES OF JET BOATS

You'll get the best performance out of a jet unit if you mate it with a special hull—essentially a light shallow-draft hull with a wide, flat bottom. The following folks make boats that are especially well suited to jet propulsion.

Glen Wooldridge
913 Southwest H Street
Grants Pass, OR 97529

(If you're handy with tools, Glen has full plans for a 16-foot fiberglass/plywood jet boat for $7.50.)

Smoker Craft
Smoker Lumber Company, Inc.
New Paris, IN 46553

Gregor Boat Company
355 M Street
Fresno, CA 93721

Alumaweld Boats
4665 Crater Lake Highway
Medford, OR 97501

Valco Company
5733 East Shields Avenue
Fresno, CA 93727

Monark Boats
P.O. Box 210
Monticello, AR 71655

Ouachita Marine Corp.
P.O. Box 420
Arkadelphia, AR 71923

Hewes Marine Company
Route 1, Municipal Airport
Colville, WA 99114

JEEP CJ-5

The CJ-5 is the traditional workhorse of the Jeep line; the vehicle that everybody thinks of when you say you drive a Jeep.

Two noteworthy improvements have been made on this short-wheelbase, go-anywhere four-by: the gas tank has been better protected against punctures from road rocks, and a wide-tracking axle is available as an option. It's one option I heartily endorse, as most CJs won't fit into the tracks left by other vehicles in sand, mud, or snow unless you equip them with reverse rims. This costs you gas, traction, and energy because you must then fight the wheel.

Other options of interest to the hunter include front disk power brakes and a manual or automatic transmission. Price: $4,399 (open body). Jeep Corporation, 27777 Franklin Road, Southfield, MI 48034.
—N.S.

Jeep Wagoneer

Here's luxury in a four-wheel-drive vehicle and a reasonable compromise when one half of the family wants a pleasure car and the other wants a weekend hunting rig. Aside from niceties like automatic transmission and power brakes and steering, the Wagoneer features optional air conditioning, cruise control, power rear window, seat trim in Brampton Plaid fabric, bucket seats, and a vertical mount inside the spare tire carrier. The Wagoneer is powered by a 360 V-8, and a 401 V-8 is optional. Quadra-Trac full-time four-wheel drive is standard. Price: $6,966. Jeep Corporation, 27777 Franklin Road, Southfield, MI 48034.

FORD BRONCO

The Bronco is classed as a small 4WD, like the Jeep CJ-5, Toyota Land Cruiser, and International Scout II, though it is a bit wider-tracked than those vehicles, making it more stable on sidehills but harder to squeeze through small spaces. Although I chose mine as a combination hunting vehicle and car, it leans toward the serious hunting vehicle side. It has a smoother ride than many 4WDs due to Ford's suspension system, which some say is a bit soft for serious back country use. I use mine mainly on roads (though some are really rough), preferring not to tear up the back country, and have had no trouble with the suspension. (If you are bound and determined to use a 4WD to get you everywhere, you'll run into problems.) There is also a two-person back seat available as an option. I have it and use it quite a bit. It comes out and goes in with four bolts—a five-minute job—and even with it in I can fit two big deer between the tailgate and the seat.

The Bronco is definitely not a luxury vehicle, though it is by no means uncomfortable to drive. Optional power steering (which I advise for any four-wheel machine), front disk brakes, and a turning radius that rivals any of its competitors make it easy to handle (it's great in downtown traffic too, with marvelous visibility) and fun to drive. It has a three-speed standard shift on the column or an optional automatic, along with a standard two-speed transfer case (there are at least two popular makes of 4WDs that only offer a two-speed transfer case as an option!). I have the standard transmission in mine, mostly because my wife is still intrigued with clutches after finally having learned to use one after ten years of driving. For much four-wheeling an automatic is nice; you don't have to shift all the time and have an instant low gear simply by tromping on the pedal. The stick on the column is very handy, much more so than the floor types, if you prefer a standard shift. The only engine available is the small-block V-8, the 302, which gives ample power to the light Bronco even in heavy mud or snow. The six-cylinder that used to be available as an option was severely hampered by smog-control devices, and so it was dropped. The V-8 gives good mileage, however, along

with the power: about 18 mpg when cruising at 55. Its only fault is that it needs unleaded fuel, but when I found two or three places where I could get the unleaded stuff in Jordan, Montana—which is the most isolated spot in the lower 48—I ceased to worry. The standard fuel tank holds only 12 gallons, with a 7½-gallon spare tank available as an option. Even with this tank you don't really get enough capacity for back-country situations; instead I ordered a 13-gallon spare tank from a specialty firm. The 25 gallons is enough for most situations with the good rough-country mileage of the Bronco (10–12 mpg), though there is still room for another tank if you feel you really need it.

The spare tire is mounted inside the tailgate and takes up valuable interior space unless you get the outside-mounted swingaway rack as an option. Lock-out hubs are standard, with Warn hubs available as an option. The Bronco is equipped with a steering stabilizer that is adequate for the largest tires you can get as options. These are Firestone L78-15s, which are excellent snow-country tires but which are a bit narrow for sand and mud (though I have done some mudding with them and haven't had serious problems). If I wanted a Bronco for a snow-country vehicle, I would definitely get these; but if you intend to travel in sand or mud, get the standard (car) tires and then substitute wide tires. If you do mount big tires, you'll have to enlarge the rear fender cutouts and mount an additional steering stabilizer (kits for both are available).

The Bronco is a good hunting vehicle for small parties, and while you might not want to take your wife to the opera in it, it's a pretty good car, too. There are two models—a station wagon and a pickup—but I really wouldn't consider the pickup, as the bed is only about 4 feet long. The station wagon is legally a car, not a truck, so you can register it without having to pay any extra tax. Base price runs $4,000 or thereabouts, but with the options I got (which were nothing fancy) mine was $6,400. This pricing is pretty standard for four-wheel-drive machines. Because each will be used in a different way, manufacturers offer a bare-bones model and let customers add what they want.   —J.B.

"If you view hunting as getting out and shooting game as fast as you can and getting back home—maybe you shouldn't be hunting!"
—Tony Acerrano

171

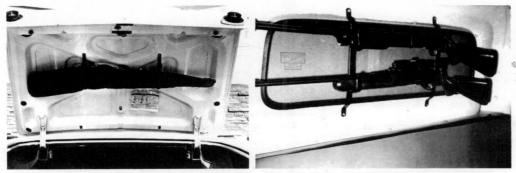

ANGELO GUN RACKS FOR VEHICLES

This outfit makes gun racks that reflect the easy Western (and especially Texan) approach to hunting and guns: namely, that you're allowed to carry anything just about anywhere you want to. A sampling of the places you can carry guns with special racks includes:

• Underneath your trunk lid. This should be perfectly legal in any state, and the spring straps are made for cased guns. Racks bolt or rivet to the inside of the trunk lid, and three guns can be carried this way inside the average trunk. Price: $4.95 each.

• Propped with the muzzle upward on the dashboard of your car. Includes clip-type mounts for muzzle (on the dashboard) and stock (on the floor). Price: $6.95.

• Between the seats of bucket-seat-type cars, Jeeps, Scouts, etc. This one props the gun muzzle up, with the barrel pointing toward the rear. It takes two guns. Price: $28.95.

• Across-the-dashboard racks for most hunting vehicles (pickups, Jeeps, etc.) one- and two-gun models. Price: $3.95 to $7.95.

• Propped with the muzzle downward on a standard one-piece front car seat (holds two guns). Price: $24.95.

• Suspended from a standard seat back, so that the guns rack in front of the rear seat (no holes or bolts needed); two cased guns or three uncased guns. Price: $9.95.

• Suspended from the springs of the seat, so that the gun rests across the front bottom of the seat (no holes or bolts needed). Price: $10.95.

• And a variety of racks that ride in the rear windows of pickup trucks or the side windows of station wagons. Some of these can be locked. Price: $5.95 to $7.95.

One word of warning: carrying an uncased gun in these racks will wear the bluing off the barrel after a lot of traveling. The racks are covered with protective plastic, but dirt, dust, and grime get between the barrel and the racks. I've tried lining the racks with felt, cotton cloth, and carpet, but it still happens.

Write: San Angelo Company, P.O. Box 984, San Angelo, TX 76901. Free catalog available. —N.S.

HANDYBOY PLIERS

If you're accustomed to carrying a full set of tools with you whenever you're around machinery that could go on the fritz, read something else. If you don't carry tools, keep reading, because this gadget can save a lot of blood, sweat, and tears. It amounts to a standard slip-joint pliers, with a small crescent wrench on the end of one handle and a screwdriver on the end of the other. As a kind of jack-of-all trades, it is a master of none, but it will usually suffice to pull a worn sparkplug on an outboard, adjust a cranky carburetor on your four-by, or tighten a loose scope mount.

A tip: you're never going to carry one everywhere you go, so buy enough to stow a pair in every vehicle, boat, or hunting camp you own. Price: $8.95. Dick Cepek, Inc., 9201 California Avenue, South Gate, CA 90280.

BLOOD SPORT
by Robert F. Jones

New York: Simon and Schuster, $27.95. This is a most unconventional hunting yarn involving a mythical, mystical trip taken by a father and his son up a nonexistent river called the Hassayampa.

The basic conflict involves the son's allegiance, which vacillates between his father and Ratnose, a bandit king who rates as one of the most likable, despicable villains since Gollum in the Lord of the Rings trilogy (both books are sort of the same genre).

There is a lot of killing of men and game, and a little pornography, and it's all in good clean fun. If you like good, practical literature, this book isn't for you, but if you like to speculate, and daydream about the impossible, and appreciate the kind of ultimate truth that can only be illustrated in fairy tales, you won't put *Blood Sport* down.

GET AWAY FROM IT ALL . . .
WE MEAN REALLY GET AWAY

Have you ever been on the way to the top of an 8,000-foot mountain and dreamed of a chair lift? Or lusted after a patch of public land set square in the middle of posted, private land where there is no access? Or been on a two-week wilderness hunt where secretly you wished for an easy chair and martini or ice cream or the inanities of network TV? Then by all means look into the Heli-Home. It is *the* answer to your prayers.

The heart of the Heli-Home is a Sikorsky S-58 helicopter powered by a Wright 1,525-hp radial engine. The cockpit has all those electrical goodies that pilots have come to know and love.

Interior appointments include sleeping for four, electric refrigerator and range, 40,000 BTU furnace, hot water heaters, bathroom with shower, wash basin, and toilet, air conditioner, refreshment bar, color TV, and an AM/FM stereo and tape system. Also standard is an attachable awning with a screened enclosure for mosquito-free living atop Mount Airy.

One other standard feature is an electro-mechanical sling for airlifting exterior cargo. Speaking as one who, on several occasions, has downed a 600-pound elk or moose ten miles from the nearest trail, that's a nice feature too. Price: $400,000.00. Winnebago Industries, Forest City, IA 50436.
—N.S.

WHERE TO FIND BOAT LABELS AND (FUNKY) FISH AND GAME

The Dyer Specialty Company can help you with numbers, letters, fish, game, flags, signs, and witticisms in stick-on decals. Costs run from 29 cents for individual letters to $2.99 for letter packs that are used for making signs. The Sportcals—fish, game, cows, etc.—are $1.29. Dyer Specialty Company, Inc., 9901 Alburtis Avenue, Santa Fe Springs, CA 90670.
—J.B.

J. C. Whitney Automotive Parts and Accessories Catalog

Here's a source for just about any gadget, gimcrack, or option you might want to install on your hunting vehicle or recvee. The catalog includes spare gas tanks, skid plates, electric winches, front tire carriers, CB equipment, recvee furniture and appliances, and a thousand other items to customize the wheels you use in the wilds. The catalog costs a buck, but you get a one-dollar credit on your first order. J. C. Whitney & Co., 1917–19 Archer Avenue, Chicago, IL 60680.

DICK CEPEK, INC.

ROOF RACK

This heavy-duty rack, made of high-quality steel, is suited for packing into the back country and will carry over 1,000 pounds of camping gear or game. Designed to fit 4WD Toyotas, Broncos, hard-top Jeeps, etc., or vans and buses. Installation is easy; no holes need be drilled and the rack mounts in 60 seconds by three bulldog clamps on each side. It's 55 inches wide and 71 inches long. Price: $79.95. Dick Cepek, Inc., 9201 California Avenue, South Gate, CA 90280.

KOLPIN MANUFACTURING, INC.

Under-the-Seat Gun Case for Cars and Pickups

Protect your gun and keep it out of sight with a front seat gun case. It fastens virtually anywhere—at the base of a seat, to the springs under a seat, or to exposed springs behind a pickup seat. The full-length zipper has two pull tabs, so you can remove a gun from either end. The lint-free green corduroy lining is water-repellent, and the padding guards against moisture. One size (52 inches long) fits most guns, scoped or not. Price: $21.00. Kolpin Manufacturing, Inc., P.O. Box 231, Berlin, WI 54923.

In still-hunting, swear yourself black in the face never to shoot at a dim, moving object in the woods for a deer, unless you have seen that it is a deer. In these days there are quite as many hunters as deer in the woods; and it is a heavy, wearisome job to pack a dead or wounded man ten or twelve miles out to a clearing, let alone that it spoils all the pleasure of the hunt, and is apt to raise hard feelings among his relations.
—Nessmuk

SKIP GANDY

A TOP TOW ROPE

Whether you've got the family flivver or sure-footed four-by, you should always carry some sort of tow rope on a hunting trip. Four-wheeling in the outback carries an understandable risk of getting stuck, but even chance snowstorms or just pulling off to the side of the road in unsuspected sand or mud has found me up to my hubs.

The traditional towing medium is a chain, but chains have no give at all. Draw it up slowly and the towing vehicle often breaks traction before it gets you moving. Draw it up fast, and the resulting yank can be damaging to your vehicle and you.

A rope with some give, so that it stretches like a rubber band, is a much better idea. It softens the tug and acts like a catapult, multiplying the towing power of another vehicle by three to four times.

One way to achieve this effect in a pinch is to tie an old tire between two tow chains. A more practical way is to carry a Snatch-"Um"-Strap, a 30-foot tow cable with plenty of give engineered into it. Includes reinforced eyelets that won't let go when you throw the power to them and a carrying case. Price: 20,000 pound test, $29.95; 36,000 pound test (for heavy recvees), $59.96. Dick Cepek, Inc., 9201 California Avenue, South Gate, CA 90208.

Revolutionary Way to Get Unstuck

Ducks are lovers of wetlands, and duck hunters, being lovers of ducks, often find their vehicles up to their hubs in mud or sand. In the past the only way to get out of this kind of a bind was to find a friendly four-by owner and hail him for a tow, or go through the laborious process of jacking up all four wheels, filling in the holes, and then backing out.

If this kind of thing happens to you more than once a season, it might pay to look into the Bull Bag, an ingenious and effortless way to get your wheels up high when they're caught in the middle of no-

where. It is a reinforced air bag which stores in a flight-size tote bag and weighs 7 pounds. Unfold it, slide it under the stuck vehicle, hook up the provided hose to the exhaust, and in a minute or so it will raise the wheels of the vehicle up and out of the mire. You still have to fill in the holes, but there is no jacking hassle at all.

The Bull Bag is capable of lifting 3,000 pounds. It has a check valve that prevents overexpansion and keeps the bag full when the engine is turned off. Price: $49.95. Dick Cepek, Inc., 9201 California Avenue, South Gate, CA 90280.

TIRES

If you get a vehicle for hunting, especially a 4WD, tires mean the difference between getting back home, getting unstuck, or even getting around.

There are two types of tires for back-country vehicles: flotation and what might be called standard. Flotation tires are essentially tires that have a wider-than-normal track (up to 12 inches or more). This keeps you from sinking out of sight in sand or some types of mud. For the desert- or swamp-traveling hunter these are good choices. For snow, however, they have some disadvantages. For one thing, driving in snow is different from driving in sand or mud; instead of floating over the top, you sink in. I haven't run into snow yet that will support a vehicle; instead of flotation tires you'll want something that will dig in and bite. Flotation tires tend to ride up in snow, and instead of biting they spin. Their design isn't the best for slippery hills either. Most wide tires have rounded edges, which won't bite into snow or ice crust. I have seen flotation-equipped 4WDs actually slide sideways off an icy hill. Again, in snow the tires should go through, not stay on top, and wide tires rob you of some of your power as the engine must work harder to push them through the snow. This is particularly true of hard-crusted snow.

Essentially, you must first decide where you are going to use your vehicle and then get tires. If you get flotation tires, you must get wider wheels, which are an additional cost, and you may have to widen or cut out your fender wells. Power steering is also a must for serious use of wide tires, as they are almost impossible to control with standard steering. A device called a steering stabilizer is also advised. This clamps onto your tie rods and dampens the side-to-side jerking of the wheels as they go over rough terrain. In spite of all these disadvantages, in some situations wide tires are a necessity, as smaller-tracked rubber will simply sink down. Wide tires, too, will give you better tracking (keep you going toward where you want to go) in sand and mud.

For snow somewhat narrower tires with sharp "edges" are advised; these are not power-sapping in deep snow and give you bite, both in uphill traction and lateral control (slippery sidehills). I have found that a tread about half the size of the wheel diameter is very good for this type of use (I have 8-inch-wide tires on my 15-inch-wheeled Bronco), which is still larger than most stock tires. Power steering is still wise, especially in deep snow, but you probably won't need to cut out your fenders or buy wide wheels. Studs, where legal, will help traction.

Standard bias-ply tires are best for most back-country use, as they have much sturdier sidewalls than radial tires. There are tougher radials coming onto the market now, however, especially designed for tough, back-country use;

these give the better mileage of radials along with a somewhat quieter ride.

When choosing a tread, remember that those macho-looking deep lugs will give more grab, sure, but they are also noisy and not really necessary in most situations. They also heat up the tire in highway use, increasing wear. A medium-size tread is the best choice for all but extreme driving.

There is no such thing as an all-around tire, though some come reasonably close. Some people keep two sets for their vehicle just as they do for their standard car: one summer (wide) set and one winter (narrower) set. If you decide you need flotation tires, look into the Dick Cepek catalog reviewed in this book. It will tell you what you need to know.

—J.B.

A Jack for All Trades

If your sporting life customarily carries you off paved roads, you should have a heavy-duty jack. The High Lift Jack is a device of many trades that's a direct descendant of the wagon jack carried by pioneers on their way to the West Coast.

It is virtually fail-safe. As the lift elevates, it is locked firmly in place by a crossbolt that passes through a series of holes in the steel supporting member. The 3-foot handle also affords great leverage, so it's easy to raise heavy loads; the jack has a 3½-ton capacity. It will lift a vehicle up to 48 inches high, and at that nosebleed altitude, it is more stable than a conventional bumper jack with its load barely off the ground.

The real value of this product, however, is that the lifting face can be slid under a bumper that is nearly touching the ground. You can be up to your axles in mire and still get a purchase on your vehicle without having to dig in. Another remarkable feature: with the addition of a tow chain and either a few cooperatively placed trees or a dead man, the jack can be used like a winch to pull a vehicle out or like a dozer to push a car sideways back onto a road.

High Lift also makes a rip-off-proof Loc Rack for their jack that mounts on any flat surface (like the inside of a pickup bed or a flat bumper). Price: $34.95 for the jack; $7.95 for the locking device. Dick Cepek, Inc., 9201 California Avenue, South Gate, CA 90280.

We fear what we don't know: . . .
Learn wildness and you don't fear anything. / Except people afraid.
—Terry and Renny Russell

175

DICK CEPEK CATALOG

This catalog, ostensibly anyway, deals in wide tires for off-road vehicles. I'm not sold on super-wide tires for every kind of terrain. (Cepek deals and drives in southern California. I'd like to get him and a set of super-wides on a slippery Montana sidehill sometime when the temperature is about 10 degrees below and an ice crust is building on top of the snow. I think he'd agree then that something that would dig in and bite instead of "float" would be a little better under the vehicle.) The catalog also includes tips on how to take care of tires, a lot of good vehicle accessories, advice on back-country camping (mainly desert), and lots of useful outdoor equipment: fishing, hunting, camping, clothing. There's even a canteen for your pet. And a great deal of it is "Baja-proven" by the Cepeks themselves. All in all, entertaining, educational, and full of good deals. You get it free. Dick Cepek, Inc., 9201 California Avenue, South Gate, CA 90280.
—J.B.

DISCOUNT CBs

By spot-checking prices from mail-order houses around the country, we found that some real bargains can be had from Sight and Sound Camera and Audio Exchange. A sampling of a few sale prices (which, of course, could change with time): Hygain Hy-range 1A, $99.00; J.I.L. 604, $100.00; Pioneer KP 500, $136.00. This outfit also has some super deals on cameras, if you like to record your hunt on film. Sight and Sound Camera and Audio Exchange, J. M. Fields Plaza, Route 46, Parsippany, NJ 07054.

ADAPTS WHEEL HUBS TO WINCH PRINCIPLE

The Unstucker isn't really revolutionary. The idea's been around for a long time, but to my knowledge these are the first folks to offer a rim winch commercially.

The device begins with a special adapter that is bolted to the rim lugs on both rear wheels. You just leave the adapter there. When you get mired in muck, mud, snow, or sand, you dig out the rear wheels so you can get at the adapters, and you lock a drum to them. The drum looks very much like a wheel rim without the tire, and it accepts a steel cable, which locks in place. You attach the cable to one drum, run the cable around a tree, dead man, boulder, or some other immovable object, and then attach the cable to the other drum. Drop your vehicle in gear, and it pulls itself out as the line winds up tight on the drum. Rated capacity: 8,000 pounds. Price: $95.00 (a real bargain compared to the price of a winch). Sports Innovations, Inc., 5301 Edina Boulevard, Minneapolis, MN 55435.
—N.S.

OFF-ROADER TIRE

This excellent flotation tire is experienced off-roader Dick Cepek's own design. It is available in either $^{14}/_{32}$–15 or $^{14}/_{32}$–16.5 in load range B or C, and the tread is a full 12 inches. The tread is fairly quiet but sure-gripping. For four of the 15-inch tires and Cepek's special wide-spoke wheels (another excellent design) you have to pay $479.95, but you get a lot for your money. As in mounting most flotation tires, it's not the tires themselves that are expensive; it's having to get new wheels to mount them on.
—J.B.

RUMBLE SEAT

Here's a safer way to store your guns and other hunting equipment out of sight as long as you own a Blazer or have a 48-inch clearance between wheel wells of your vehicle. This seat is good-looking and is constructed of a heavy-gauge steel. The back rest of the seat will hold up to three rifles in its Plastisol-coated steel rack. There is also an underseat storage area for such things as binoculars, cameras, etc. The steel-pin Medico cylinder lock is supposed to be unpickable. Price: $438.00 plus shipping (175 pounds). Security Chest Division, P.O. Box 5497, Roanoke, VA 24012.
—P.S.

RAY JEFF'S CB-740 40-CHANNEL SET

An adjustable squelch control clears out extraneous noise for static-free reception. Adjustable on-off volume control turns on the unit and sets volume in one operation. A horizontally deflecting SRF meter monitors the strength of signal transmitted and shows the strength of the signal received. The SRF meter and channel indicator are lighted for easy night readings.

The CB-740 can also be used as a PA system. There is a built-in jack for an optional external speaker. A plug-in microphone and keyed power cord with in-line fuse are other features. The unit operates from any 12-volt DC power source, negative or positive ground. Price: $149.95. Ray Jefferson, Main and Cotton Streets, Philadelphia, PA 19127.

The Sporting Goods Directory

If you're an equipment freak—and if you bought this book, you probably are— *The Sporting Goods Directory* is an excellent supplement to *The Complete Hunter's Catalog.*

It is divided into three parts. The first part, and the longest, is an alphabetized listing of equipment by genre. In other words, if you were interested in a camp saw, you would look under "Camping" until you came to the S's, and there you'd find eleven alphabetized names of people who make saws. You then turn to the next section, easy to find because its pages are color-coded, and look up the address of each firm. The last section, again color-coded, is an alphabetical listing of products and the pages on which those products may be found. Again, this listing is generic, not by brand name.

It's a great reference source that's help-ful when you want to trace down some specific product you saw afield but you don't know where to buy it. Once you find the original manufacturer, he can tell you where the nearest retail outlet for his product is located.

In many ways *The Sporting Goods Directory* isn't as thorough as *The Complete Hunter's Catalog.* There are no pictures, prices, or explanation/evaluation of equipment. Then, too, it lists only major manufacturers of sporting goods. You won't find either the Funk Manufacturing Co. or good old Floyd Zongker listed. But between the two books you'll have a reference source that includes nearly everyone who makes anything relevant to hunting and shooting in the United States of America. Price: $5.00. Chas. C. Spink & Son, St. Louis, MO 63166.

WESTERN SEAT COVERS WITH GEAR POCKETS

These seat covers are made of strong, Western-looking saddle blanket material, and they lace into place without bulges or bumps. Of special note are the gear pockets along the front of the seat. These pouches will hold three glove compartments' worth of odds and ends, and there is another pocket behind them that accepts a rifle or a shotgun. This pocket wouldn't abrade bluing like window racks, and it keeps the gun down and hidden from view. Available in six colors. Price: $39.95. Empire Corporation, 8777 Brighton Road, Adams City, CO 80022.

CAMPER FOLLOWING ROLLER GUIDES TO TRUCK BED HEIGHT. ENTERING TRUCK ON ROLLER GUIDE-NOTE-NO TRACKS IN BED OF TRUCK OR GEARS TO BIND.

Aldropp Camper Unloader

This is one of the slickest rigs for pickup campers that I've ever seen. It allows you to drop the camper from the bed in less than five minutes, affording you a comfortable permanent campsite and a hunting vehicle free from the encumbrance of a heavy, high load.

The unloader is essentially a frame that goes around the bed of the camper unit. This frame rolls on guides into the bed of the pickup truck, allowing it to slide in and out easily. Power is provided by cables and a winching system that may be cranked by hand or with an electric motor that plugs into a 12-volt system. With this system, there's no need to mess around with jacks. The camper unit goes on straight every time, too. Price: $299.00. Aldropp, 1364 Wilshire Place, Stayton, OR 97383.

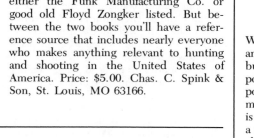

Deluxe and mobile radio

THE BEST CB?

According to a quick check with local truckers who surely have a lot of CB exposure, their strongest recommendation was for the Johnson 323. They said in the same breath, however, that the cheaper Johnsons didn't compare with the same price competition. In the $100–$200 range they seemed to like Lafayettes.

The 323 is a fully solid state radio with twenty-three channels. There is built-in electronic speech compression for increased range. A crystal selectivity filter offers maximum interference rejection. The illuminated meter shows transmitter output and received signal strength. This CB also has built-in public address function. It is supplied complete with mounting bracket, microphone, power cable for 12-volt DC (plus or minus ground) operation, and complete instructions.

Johnson is also the only company making CBs exclusively in the United States, if you like to buy American. Price: $249.95. Johnson, Waseca, MN 56093.

—N.S.

TRUCK WINCHES

If you're planning to four-wheel it into real outback, consider installing a winch on your hunting rig. A few guidelines: buy a winch with pulling power equivalent to the weight of your vehicle and, unless special circumstances dictate otherwise, buy an electric winch. They're cheaper in the long run than the power take-off/driveshaft/winch combination required for a unit driven by a truck engine, and the motor need not be running to operate an electric winch. This is an important feature when you're fording streams. If you don't remove the belt from the engine fan and the water gets deep, the fan will drench and drown the engine, and there will be no getting out save a tow from another vehicle or an electric winch.

The Ramsey Winch Company has a complete line of light- to heavy-duty winches, electric and motor-driven, including winch kits and accessory items like power take-offs, tow ropes, winch cables, and worm-gear speed reducers. Approximate cost for getting into the winch business: $300–$500, depending on pulling capacity and how much work you do yourself. Ramsey Winch Company, Box 15829, Tulsa, OK 74115.

Part II
UPLAND GAME

UPLAND GUNS

An upland shotgun is used on upland game. Simple, isn't it? Not really, as upland game varies from the few ounces of quail to the possibly 20 pounds of turkey, and the ranges run from almost point-blank to over 50 yards.

Actually, any shotgun can be an upland gun, even a 10-gauge weighing 12 pounds or more. But the traditional idea of an upland gun is of a light, open-choked arm, easily carried over hill and dale, quick to point at rapidly flushing game, and usable at short to medium ranges. For 90 percent of the upland hunting in North America this is a good choice.

A hunter could conceivably use just one gun for all upland game, especially if it had interchangeable barrels, a variable choke, or screw-in choke tubes. There are advantages to this system: it's economical, you need only get used to one gun, and your wife won't be rolling her eyes toward the ceiling every time you mention another gun, asking you where on earth you plan to keep it. (This last is perhaps the biggest argument for the single upland gun.)

But a better system, if you have the money and a gun-tolerating wife, is to have at least three guns: a short-range weapon for thick cover (particularly ruffed grouse and woodcock); a medium-range gun for more usual, open upland situations (such as pheasant); and a long-range gun, used on the days when the ringnecks are flushing wild or when you're looking to put as many shot as possible in a gobbler's neck.

This still leaves a big area, so let's put some limits on our upland gun. An upper weight limit of 7½ pounds is a good idea, as this gun is going to be carried a good deal; 7 pounds would be even better, since Americans aren't as practical as Europeans and refuse to put slings on their shotguns. Let's also eliminate the .410 from consideration,

at the risk of offending all the .410-lovers in the universe. Its heaviest loading is OK at the shortest of ranges for the smallest of game, but that's it. You'll simply be handicapping yourself in most situations by using one. Let's eliminate the 10-gauge and the 3-inch 12, too, as they simply aren't chambered in many light guns, though I have seen days when a magnum 3-inch 12-load would have come in handy on long-range pheasant or sharptail grouse. Its practical advantage over the 2¾-inch magnum load might not be apparent, however.

What do we have left? The 28, 20, 16, and 12. The smallest, the 28, has a couple of advantages in upland hunting and a couple of disadvantages. The advantages are that in most models it is very light and, because it has a relatively mild load, the recoil is negligible. One of the disadvantages is that even in the heaviest of handloads it is limited to 1 ounce of shot, and so it is essentially only a short-range weapon. The other problem is that the shells are hard to get and aren't often stocked in a variety of loads. Some people say that the short range isn't a disadvantage, as they can get the light gun "on" the bird much sooner than they can with heavier arms, but what about the days when the birds are flushing wild?

The 20-gauge is my personal favorite as an upland gun. Most 20s are now chambered for the 3-inch shells, which hold 1¼ ounces of shot, giving them a measurable range increase over the 28. You can also use 2¾-inch shells in most of these guns, giving them added versatility. The shells are much easier to get than 28s—they're stocked just about anywhere you can find shot shells—and you can get 20s about as light as you'd want, many off-the-shelf models running 6 to 6½ pounds. With its light weight and versatility (rarely does an upland hunter need more than 1¼ ounces of shot), it makes a very good choice as a short-to-medium-range gun.

The 16 offers just about as much versatility as the 20. Unfortunately, you'd be hard put to find one on today's market. Since the 3-inch 20 came out, overlapping the 12-gauge's performance, the 16 has gone steadily downhill in popularity. The shells are sometimes even harder to get than those of the 28, except in other parts of the world. If you plan to do most of your hunting in Africa or Germany, it would be the number-one choice; in America, unless you already have a good 16 or can pick one up at a steal, it is not a practical arm.

The 12 is and always has been first choice in America for any kind of scattergunning. With this gauge's enormous array of guns and loads, it will cover everything from quail to turkey and beyond. Its one disadvantage is that it is usually heavier than the other guns, 7 pounds being about the bottom line, though there are lightweight 12s on the market that go below this. The 2¾-inch chamber will do for all upland hunting, and usually guns with this chamber are slightly lighter than 3-inch-chambered models. It would be the first choice for a longer-range upland gun.

There are really only three types of action that the serious hunter should consider: double, pump, and semiauto. Each has advantages and disadvantages.

Many upland gunners pick the double gun, whether side-by-side or over-under, because it is generally somewhat muzzle-light in balance, at least more so than the other guns, and tends to point quicker in upland situations. There is also the benefit of two chokes instantly available. This advantage, I think, is somewhat overplayed. If you are hunting in thick cover, the tighter barrel is somewhat of a handicap; in more open country, if birds are getting up at the fringe of range, you are either going to be crippling birds with the open barrel or be limited to a one-shot weapon. In many situations the two-choke idea is handy, but not as often as many folks believe.

The double is limited to two quick shots. Again, double-lovers claim that's all you need. I am a double fan myself, but there's been more than one time when I've wished for another shot or two to finish off a wounded pheasant. Most doubles come these days with single triggers. I may be nuts, but I simply don't swoon over these mechanical wonders, possibly because I grew up shooting double triggers and never felt handicapped. Twin triggers give me the instant choice of choke when it's needed and allow me to change my mind in mid-shot if another bird gets up closer. The biggest objection to double triggers is that they change the length of pull (butt plate-to-trigger length), which supposedly screws up a shotgun's shootability. This has always seemed strange to me, as most of my double guns have two triggers that can easily be reached without changing hand position; the others are reachable with a shift of only about ⅛ inch. I have no objection to single triggers if the selection between barrels is easily done with the safety, but on a great many models this isn't so, and a nonselective single trigger is, to me, stupid. Why shoot a double gun at all if you can't select the barrel?

The biggest advantages of doubles are their muzzle-light qualities and their easy handling of reloads. With the cost of

factory shells what it is, any hunter who shoots a lot might well consider the doubles, as they'll chamber and extract just about any reload. Here again, I differ with many other double-lovers, as I prefer simple extractors instead of selective ejectors; that way I retrieve all my empties instead of leaving a good many in the weeds (you'd be surprised at how hard it is to find even a bright red shotgun shell in tall grass).

There have been all kinds of arguments concerning the merits of the over-under and the side-by-side. Most of these arguments are purely aesthetic, as many are for both types of double guns over other actions. The only real difference is that side-by-sides, in factory models, are generally somewhat cheaper than over-unders (either type is going to cost a mint in custom, top-of-the-line grades). Some people cannot handle the side-by-side twin tubes; they are used to pumps and doubles with their single-sighting plane. These people prefer the over-under. Balance and handling qualities are similar in both arms.

The all-American shotgun is the pump. It is the cheapest quick-repeating shotgun on the market and will digest most loads with more ease than the auto. It has more shots than the double, but with the magazine (usually a tube through the forearm) fully loaded, it is somewhat more muzzle-heavy than some people like for quick pointing. A great many models are available with interchangeable barrels (as are autos and some expensive doubles), so the hunter can change choke and barrel length. A pump is less susceptible to weather than the auto, and there are many, many models to choose from. The biggest objection I have to many pumps, even some fairly expensive ones, is that they often employ the crossbolt-type safety in the trigger guard. This has always seemed a clumsy place to put a safety, and I've never gotten used to it, even after using them for years. I can't see where the economical advantage over the tang safety occurs, because I have an under-$100 pump in my rack that has the tang type.

Autos have this same safety fault to a degree. Their biggest advantage, on the other hand, is that in gas-operated models they dampen recoil somewhat, which is an aid to recoil-shy shooters or those who use heavy loads in light guns. It helps all of us in getting off a faster repeat shot. Most autos, however, will not operate with the same variety of loads as will the double or pump, thus cutting down on their versatility.

Unless you select a shotgun with interchangeable barrels or a variable or screw-in type of choke, you'll be limited to a single choke in pumps and autos or two in doubles. If I had to choose one choke for all my upland hunting, it would definitely be modified, and I'd use spreader loads for close ranges. If you hunt mainly in brush or other short-range terrain, improved cylinder is the choice on a factory gun. One choke that isn't available for most bird model guns (though it is fairly standard on slug guns used for deer) is straight cylinder, which actually isn't a choke at all, since there's no constriction of the muzzle. I find it superior to improved cylinder for brush and forest grouse hunting; its wider pattern catches birds that otherwise might be wounded. Ranges in this type of shooting are often measured in feet, not yards. I have a 20-gauge pump that

*"Come out, 'tis now September, the Hunter's Moon's begun,
And through the wheat an' stubble is heard the frequent gun."*
—Anon.

179

started out in life as a 28-inch modified but is now a 23-inch cylinder choke. I shortened the stock a little, too; this is heresy to most shotgunning purists, but in brush situations your gun has to be fast, and you are often in strange postures. Precise gun fit (usually measured under ideal conditions) often results in a stock that is too long for quick handling. I usually use a length of pull of 14 inches, but this brush gun has a 13-inch length. These modifications, both barrel and stock, also lightened the gun some to a little over 6 pounds loaded. At the present time this is about the only way to get a cylinder gun unless you're willing to use a deer model, which is often heavier than necessary and is normally only available in 12 gauge. Part of the reason that factories won't make cylinder guns is that there is a myth involving straight bores that says that "blown" patterns—patchy, uneven types—will result. Nothing to it, especially with today's ammo. My gun gives nice, even patterns with most loads, and I've even checked it out with old-style paper-and-felt wad loads and it's still good. Another factor concerning such guns is that many shooters don't believe they'll hit as hard as longer-barreled guns. This was valid in black-powder days, but smokeless loads attain full velocity, for all practical purposes, in 22-to-24-inch shotgun barrels. There might be a few fps difference, but you'll never notice it. And such guns are by no means limited to brush shooting. I've used mine for early season pheasant and sharptail, and out to 30 yards it is much more deadly than any tighter-choked gun, simply because it's easier to hit with. I've made a couple of triples with it on sharptails—something I'd only done once before in my life. If you wish to modify a gun in this way, take it to your gunsmith; he'll know how to install sights and make any other modifications necessary.

Full choke is rarely needed in most upland situations, but when it's needed, it's really needed! When the pheasants are getting up on the edge of range, when the sage grouse are really wild, there is nothing like a full barrel and maybe even some magnum loads. But there is no need to select a full barrel for most upland hunting; in fact, you'll be handicapping yourself if you do. If you are involved in much hunting in open country (like the Western plains), you might consider a second barrel or changeable choke for those situations that occasionally demand a full choke.

The upland gunner, like all scattergunners, should pattern his gun to make sure that it does what he wants it to do. Chokes are by no means absolute, and many shooters have found that modern shot cup loads will tighten a pattern considerably. If you buy an improved-cylinder gun that patterns modified or even tighter, it won't help you in those short-range situations. And just because Winchester's loads do the job for you in a certain shot size, don't believe Remington's will necessarily do the same and vice versa.

The biggest piece of advice that could be given to any upland gunner is not to overgun or overchoke. A heavy, tightly choked shotgun will only handicap you when a bird flushes from under your feet. An oft-repeated mistake for a shotgunner is to go to a tighter-choked gun after he's wounded or missed a few birds. More often than not, he needs a more open choke instead. Even the straight cylinder barrel will kill at most upland ranges if the shooter does his part.

—J.B.

ALL ABOUT SMALL GAME HUNTING IN AMERICA
edited by Russell Tinsley

New York: Winchester Press, $10.00.

Small-game animals are the most sought-after quarry of American hunters, and this book brings together the finest lineup of small-game experts in the field. Tinsley, a well-known outdoor writer and hunter himself, has contributed three chapters. Other contributors include Byron Dalrymple, Erwin Bauer, John Wootters, Bob Gilsvik, Geraldine Steindler, Hal Swiggett, Dave Duffey, George Nonte, and Jerome Knap. This who's who of small-game hunting experts shows you how to get more enjoyment and satisfaction from your favorite pastime and provides you with a wealth of specific, practical advice on how, where, and when to hunt every small-game animal anywhere in North America.

HUNTING UPLAND BIRDS
by Charles F. Waterman

Chicago: Follett Publishing Company, $5.95 (paper).

This is an excellent book—perhaps the most complete rundown of American upland game available (including rabbits and squirrels, in spite of the title). Waterman is an entertaining writer and a practical hunter and shooter, who has little time for some of the more esoteric (and probably mythical) aspects of shotgunning that seem to dominate some shooting books. On everything from doves to turkeys, he gives good advice and entertaining examples.

—J.B.

CHOKE

Choke is nothing more than a slight constriction of the muzzle of a shotgun. It was popularized (if not invented) by one Fred Kimble, a duck hunter, in the last half of the 1800s. How a choke works is something of a mystery. The most popular theory is that it operates on basically the same principle as the nozzle on a water hose; the more you constrict the muzzle (nozzle), the less rapidly the shot (water) spreads after it leaves the barrel (hose). In a shotgun barrel there is a point beyond which, if you constrict it any more, the shot spreads wider again. This optimum level is known as "full" choke. A completely open muzzle, one that is of the same size as the rest of the barrel, is known as "cylinder." The gradations in between have various names. A choke halfway between cylinder and full is "modified"; one halfway between cylinder and modified is "improved cylinder." There are other degrees of choke, but these are rarely seen on game guns. "Skeet" choke can be anything between cylinder and improved cylinder; "improved modified" (commonly used on trap guns) is halfway between modified and full. Europeans have a different, somewhat simpler, system that gives each choke a fractional value of full. Modified, for instance, is half choke, improved cylinder, one quarter choke.

The odd thing about all this is that there is no guarantee that a barrel choked a certain way will shoot a certain way. The accepted way to measure the effectiveness of a choke is to fire a shotgun at a target 40 yards away. A circle 30 inches in diameter is then drawn around the thickest part of the pattern that results, and the shot holes inside the circle are counted. This number is divided by the total amount of shot in the load, and a percentage is arrived at. The standard percentage for a full choke is 70, give or take 5 percent. It would indeed be a wonderful and miraculous thing if every barrel put out by the manufacturers marked "full" gave 70-percent patterns with all loads, but the sad fact is that they don't. And it isn't the manufacturers' fault, either.

For many years there have been certain standards generally followed by the firearms industry as to what constriction constitutes what choke. Here are a few samples of 12-gauge chokes applied by American manufacturers (all figures in inches):

Bore Diameter	Choke	Constriction	Diameter of Muzzle
.730	Full	.035	.695
.730	Modified	.012	.718
.730	Improved Cylinder	.007	.723

Cylinder choke is, of course, no choke at all, or .730 inch all the way through. These standards are pretty strictly adhered to. Theoretically, they result in these pattern percentages:

Full: 65–75 percent
Modified: 50–60 percent
Improved Cylinder: 35–45 percent
Cylinder: 25–35 percent

Obviously, there are no absolutes in choking. These are approximations; in other sources you may find percentages that differ slightly from these.

You can take two guns right off the assembly line, with consecutive serial numbers and for all practical purposes identical, shoot loads from the same box out of them, and as often as not get different patterns—sometimes very different. Why? Nobody knows. It probably has something to do with unmeasurable differences in bore and choke diameter, frictional differences in the barrels, how hard the firing pin strikes the primer, any number of factors. I have seen various guns marked full shoot everything from 50 to 90 percent patterns with No. 6 shot. I have seen the same barrel shoot anything from 55 to 80 percent patterns with different loads.

One of the oldest myths involving choke is that of the dime and full-choked 12-gauge barrels. Supposedly, if a dime won't fit into a 12's muzzle, the barrel is acceptably full-choked. This is because the constriction makes the muzzle end about .695 inch; a dime from my pocket mikes about .700 to .702 inch, depending on which way it's measured. Truly, if a dime won't fit the barrel, it is a full-choked barrel by industry standards, but I have seen dime-tried barrels that shot less than 50-percent patterns, and I have seen barrels that dimes would fit in with room to spare that shot 75-percent patterns.

So why don't the manufacturers rate barrels by their percentages instead of their constriction? It's expensive and still not definitive. They'd have to try every barrel with at least ten rounds, and that would still only give an indication of what that load would do in that barrel. There are custom gun shops that will choke a gun to shoot a certain percentage, but only with one load and then only within 5 percent, as even atmospheric conditions can affect pattern. This process is one of starting with a very tightly choked gun and then reaming the choke out slightly, testing it after each reaming until it's right. Obviously, this is time-consuming and expensive.

Load and the individual gun aren't the only things that affect pattern. A great many guns in 20 and 12 gauge these days have 3-inch chambers but are used with 2¾-inch ammunition also. Sometimes this has an effect on pattern and sometimes it doesn't. I have a 20-gauge double that shoots 2¾-inch shells loaded with No. 6 shot at 55 percent from both barrels. It is choked modified and full. With 3-inch shells it still shoots 55 percent from the modified barrel but 70 percent from the full, again with No. 6 shot. It seems that generally guns shoot more open patterns with short shells in long chambers, but it works both ways.

The size of shot can have an effect on choke. The general idea is that tighter chokes handle large shot better, but again there is no hard and fast rule. Some guns will "prefer" a certain size of shot, giving markedly tighter or more even patterns with one size. In the old days of muzzle-loading, when any gauge from 2 to 32 might be used, shooters often blocked off their muzzle with a piece of cardboard and then tried different shot sizes to see which size fit the best in a one-layer pattern in the muzzle. It was held that this size would pattern the best, and very often it did, probably because there was less deformation to the close-fitting pellets.

Different wads will affect choke. Modern shot cups will often tighten a pattern by as much as 10 to 15 percent over older felt wads. Overshot wads, crimps—everything can have an effect on pattern.

What does all this mean to the shooter? It doesn't necessarily mean that the choke designation stamped on your gun is worthless. More often than not your gun will shoot a load with medium-size shot fairly close to what the manufacturer says it will, but you shouldn't bet on it. If you're a serious shooter, you should find the time to pattern your gun with various loads, using the 30-inch circle and 40-yard range. To spend an afternoon counting pellet holes is a pain to all except masochists, but it will teach you a lot about your gun and put more birds in your bag. A five-shot string is sufficient in most cases, and don't be surprised if your patterns vary as much as 10 to 15 percent with identical loads.

—J.B.

• Pheasants are extremely well suited to harsh northern winters. They can go for ten days without food and show no ill effects.

PHEASANT: OUR NO. 1 EXOTIC GAME

by George Laycock

• A young pheasant will have short tailfeathers and pyramidal knobs rather than sharp spurs on the inside of each leg, and if you hold the bird by his lower bill, it will break. These "birds of the year" have the tenderest meat.

In America the ring-necked pheasant falls into the category of happy accidents, and I seldom see one of these alert, sharp-eyed birds along a fencerow or on the edge of the woods without thinking of Judge Owen N. Denny. Except for the pheasant, Judge Denny would have been forgotten long ago. His story surfaced for me some years ago while I was researching a book.

The judge had risen to high places through the political process and eventually went to Shanghai as U.S. Consul. While in the Orient in the 1880s, he was delighted with a new dish placed on the Denny family table—roast pheasant. Here was a bird that Judge Denny thought America had been unjustly denied.

His was a typical reaction of travelers who do not know much about the complexity with which the varied elements of a natural ecosystem fit together. He decided that God's shortsightedness in this case could be easily corrected. Similar thinking has led to scrambling the wildlife of the world and has brought to America the carp, house sparrow, starling, walking catfish, and a number of other unwelcome foreigners.

But Judge Denny was blissfully unaware of any scientific implications. His experiment came in an age when few people had any concept of the hazards of reshuffling the world's wildlife. His plan was simple and direct. He installed ten wild-caught cock ring-necked pheasants and eighteen females in a big bamboo cage in the hold of the *Isle of Butte* and he shipped them back to his home in Oregon's fertile Willamette Valley, convinced that his good deed was done.

But that first shipment of pheasants had a rough time at sea, arrived in weakened condition, and disappeared from the Oregon scene shortly after they were turned free. Undaunted, Denny dispatched another shipment. These birds prospered as if they were made to order for the Willamette Valley. Within ten years they had multiplied so abundantly that Oregon held North America's first open season on the ringneck. The year was 1891, and hunters took an estimated 50,000 pheasants there.

Word spread quickly. Every state now wanted its share of pheasant brood stock. The birds were at a premium. So grand did the new pheasant look to some sportsmen that America's native prairie grouse were seen as drab and useless by comparison. One of these sportsmen was N. L. Witcher, of South Dakota, where the native prairie chickens were endangered by overshooting. Witcher announced that he was bringing in some pheasants from Oregon and that he would appreciate the favor if all his neighbors would leave them alone so they might prosper and get a good start. These fine birds, he explained, were prolific and hardy. Furthermore, he speculated that if the pheasants were protected until they could get a start, they would "drive out the vulgar native grouse, which are not really game birds."

Whether these imports or others deserve the honor of founding that state's population, South Dakota soon became famous for its pheasants. The first open season was held there in 1919, and within half a dozen years hunters from distant states were beginning to filter into South Dakota as surely as autumn brings on the pheasant season. One official estimated the legal kill between 1919 and 1940 at 20 million birds.

There is scarcely a corner of the country where the pheasant was not planted. But in state after state, saddened sportsmen and wildlife authorities saw these new birds dwindle and disappear. The ring-neck was not adapted to a wide range of habitats, but its success in some cool, fertile farmlands encouraged the importation of other wildlife. Such releases of foreign species in America's fields and waters have almost always been mistakes. Judge Denny just happened to play a lucky hunch, a little game of wildlife roulette where, unbelievably, he came out a winner.

George Laycock is a prolific writer and noted conservationist who lives in Cincinnati, Ohio. He is the recipient of the Outdoor Writers Association of America's Jade of Chiefs Award, given for outstanding work in the field of conservation.

TURKEY GUNS

The turkey is in a class by itself as far as upland birds go. A big tom will weigh three times as much as the next biggest North American upland bird, the sage grouse, and is a hell of a lot harder to bring down.

Many game departments acknowledge the toughness of the turkey by allowing hunters to use rifles as well as shotguns in pursuing it, usually during fall seasons. I must confess that the rifle is my preferred turkey weapon, where legal, because of the eastern Montana turkey country I hunt as much as anything else. Last fall I used a .243 to take a nice hen at about 350 yards across a canyon. This simply isn't a typical turkey situation to most Eastern hunters but is fairly typical of much of the West. Much Western turkey country consists of open and semiopen hills topped by juniper and pine. A shot closer than 100 yards is the exception rather than the rule.

Turkeys take a lot of stopping, especially at long range, where exact shot placement isn't always possible, which is why I prefer the rifle. The regular .22 long rifle simply isn't enough for 15-to-20-pound birds, though the .22 magnum is adequate to 100 yards. It is the minimum turkey cartridge that I'd use; even better would be the old .22 Hornet or possibly the .222 Remington. All three of these cartridges shoot bullets of 40 to 50 grains: the .22 magnum at 2,000 fps, the .22 Hornet at about 2,700, and the .222 at about 3,100. The .222 is about as high as you can go with a factory-loaded cartridge and still have minimal meat destruction at normal turkey ranges. For most turkey hunting (under 200 yards) the Hornet and the .222 will do fine, as will bigger centerfires used with reduced handloads. Special solid-point bullets (nonexpanding) are on the market now in both .22 and 6mm sizes for use in taking fur bearers or small game with .22–250s, the .243 and 6mm, and similar cartridges. These must be handloaded, but they are fine turkey loads at the shorter ranges. For longer ranges the .243 with expanding bullets isn't as overpowering as it might seem. Again, shot placement is crucial if you want to stop a turkey fast, but most bullets designed to expand well on deer will do surprisingly little damage to a turkey. My

.243 handloads for turkey use a 105-grain Speer bullet at about 2,800 feet per second. With facing shots I can shoot the turkey in the middle of the breast; the bullet will simply punch a pencil-size hole going in and ruin only back meat on its way out. On a side shot I aim for the wing butts, which is the classic placement. In any case, I've never lost more than 10 percent of the meat and usually much less. I'd rather waste a little meat and not lose the turkey, because a turkey that gets into brush can be hard to find, especially since dogs aren't usually used in hunting them. That 10-pound hen went over 30 feet after being hit right in the boiler room!

There are two theories as to shotguns and loads for turkeys. One says use the biggest shot you can, such as 2s or even No. 4 buck; the other says use nothing larger than 6s and aim for the head and neck. I would tend toward the small-shot school, since even a No. 4 buck pellet is smaller than a .22 long rifle bullet and not as efficient. Remember, turkeys are usually shot on the ground, with their tough wings covering much of their vitals. A good compromise is to use small shot for the first shot, backed by big stuff in case the turkey doesn't stay down. The 3-inch 20-gauge load would be a minimum, and I think I'd prefer a full-choked pump or auto over a double, simply because I'd want to keep shooting until the bird went down to stay. Two shots might not be enough.

There are several guns on the market that combine rifle and shotgun barrels. These might be the best of all in some situations. A scope is very nice on a turkey rifle for fine placement and shooting in dim light, but a scope would hamper the shotgun barrel. A scope with a side mount, leaving the barrel tops open for shotgunning, might be a good compromise here. Most of these guns, however, have provision for scope mounting only on top and probably would have to be drilled and tapped for a side mount.

Whatever you use, practice with it. A turkey is a tough customer and a top game animal. Missing one is bad enough, but wounding one and losing it is much worse.

—J.B.

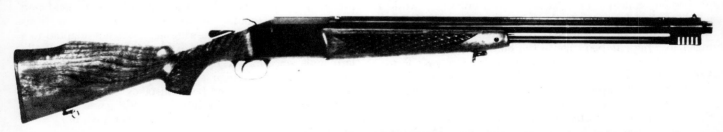

ITHACA TURKEY GUN

The Ithaca-LSA Turkey Gun is just that: something that could be used in just about any turkey-hunting situation. It has a 12-gauge barrel (2¾-inch chamber) choked full over a .222 Remington rifle barrel, both of which are excellent choices for turkeys. It is grooved for a top scope mount, has a muzzle brake, and is equipped with sling swivels. The barrel selector is on the left side of the receiver and has an exposed hammer. As with all combination guns, it's a break-action. Weight is 7 pounds, barrel length is 24½ inches. Price: $384.95. Ithaca Gun Co., Inc., 123 Lake Street, Ithaca, NY 14850.

—J.B.

"The necessary equipments for stalking are a good gun, a turkey call, clothing as near the color of dead leaves as possible, and some knowledge of the habits of the game."
—Charles Hallock, 1877

183

SAVAGE MODEL 24 SERIES

I've had one of these since I was sixteen. It's chambered .22 WRF magnum over 3-inch 20-gauge, and I can't imagine a better all-around small game and bird gun unless you're willing to shell out $1,200 or so for a European drilling. The Model 24 comes in various shapes and sizes—all with a rifle barrel over a shotgun—priced from $89.95 for the field grade, which comes in combinations of .22 and .22 magnum over either .410 or 20-gauge, on up to the 24-V for $462.85, which is a centerfire model featuring either a .222 Remington or a .30-30 barrel over a 20-gauge. The model I have is a 24-B, which has been discontinued, but it's basically just a dressed-up version of the plain 24. The rifle barrel will group inside 2 inches at 100 yards—which is damn fine for any .22 hunting rifle—and the shotgun barrel will down ducks at 50 yards. I've used it not only on ducks but prairie dogs, grouse, partridges, coyotes, rabbits (both cottontail and jack), pheasants, and squirrels. It also would be a dandy turkey gun. The only limiting factor is the single shotgun barrel, but you can't kick much about two guns in one at this price. Especially recommended for a Christmas or birthday gift for the number-one son. Savage Arms, Springdale Road, Westfield, MA 01085.

—J.B.

BROWNING SUPERLIGHT SUPERPOSED

This is a lightweight version of the Browning Superposed O/U shotgun. It is chambered for 12- and 20-gauge shells (2¾-inch chamber) with 26½-inch barrels. Weight is 6 pounds 6 ounces. It has a straight-grip stock and a single selective trigger. It is available in three ascending grades: Grade I ($1,170), Diana ($2,000), and Midas ($2,700). It is also available with extra barrels, prices upon request (probably around 80 percent more than the standard model). Chokes are any combination of all standard chokes, including cylinder, skeet, and improved modified. Browning, Route 1, Morgan, UT 84050.

—J.B.

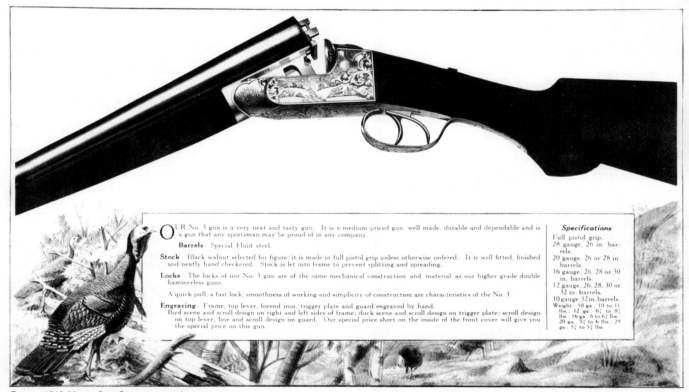

From a 1919 Ithaca Gun Company catalog.

BROWNING B-SS DOUBLE

For the hunter who is slightly less cash-ridden than those who go for the Superposed, Browning also makes a nice side-by-side. Price is more in reach of the average hunter, but still not bargain basement: $354.95. It comes with 26-, 28-, and 30-inch barrels in 12 and 20 gauge (30 inch in 12 only) in the standard combo of modified and full or—in the 26-inch length—improved cylinder and modified. Automatic ejectors. Weights run 7 pounds 3 ounces to 7 pounds 7 ounces, depending on barrel length. For a gun of this quality, one feature seems slightly out of place: the nonselective single trigger. Browning, Route 1, Morgan, UT 84050.   —J.B.

FRANCHI AUTOMATIC SHOTGUN

Famed for its lightweight design, the Franchi is a good choice for upland gunning anywhere. It weighs 6 pounds 4 ounces in 12 gauge and only 5 pounds 2 ounces in 20 and 28 gauge. The lightweight model is chambered for 2¾-inch shells, in barrel lengths from 24 to 28 inches in 12 and 20, and 26 to 28 inches in 28 gauge, with most popular chokings. All barrels are chrome-lined and are fully interchangeable within gauge. Action is adjustable for different loads; safety is crossbolt. Price is $254.95 for standard model in all three gauges. The 20 and 28 models are probably the lightest autoloaders in the world, and they are excellent guns for fast upland situations. Stoeger Industries, 55 Ruta Court, South Hackensack, NJ 07606.   —J.B.

FRANCHI PEREGRINE O/U 451

This is a lightweight O/U, available in 12 gauge only, that weighs just over 6 pounds and comes with two barrel lengths, 26½ and 28 inches. Choke combos are cylinder/improved cylinder, improved cylinder/modified, and modified/full, with the last available only in the 28-inch length. It has a single selective trigger, with the selector on the trigger (one of the clumsiest places to put it), and it is chambered for 2¾-inch shells. This gun has the standard Franchi chrome bores, extractors, and a ventilated rib. Price: $469.95. Stoeger Industries, 55 Ruta Court, South Hackensack, NJ 07606.   —J.B.

ITHACA MODEL 37 PUMP GUN

The Model 37, one of the best known pump guns, comes in various styles and is priced from $189.95 to $349.95. The standard grade—the lowest-priced—is a very good upland gun weightwise. In 12 gauge it runs 6½ pounds; in 20, 5¾ pounds. Barrel lengths are 26 and 28 inches, with 30 available in 12 only. Chamber is 2¾ inches for both gauges. Chokes are improved cylinder, modified, and full. Crossbolt safety. Ithaca Gun Co., Inc., 123 Lake Street, Ithaca, NY 14850.   —J.B.

HARRINGTON & RICHARDSON O/U

This is a 12-gauge gun with 2¾-inch chambers, improved cylinder and modified choking, 28-inch barrels, a ventilated rib, and a single selective trigger. A good choice for an upland gun, though the barrels could be a couple of inches shorter. Price: $335.00. Harrington & Richardson, Inc., Industrial Rowe, Gardner, MA 01440.

—J.B.

"Hunting? Look, you know it ain't no fun if you hit 'em every time."
—Robert F. Jones, Blood Sport

185

ITHACA 600 FIELD GRADE O/U

In 12 gauge with 2¾-inch chambers or 20 with 3-inch chambers, this gun weighs about 6½ pounds. Available in standard choke combos with 26-to-28-inch barrels in 20; 28-to-30-inch in 12. Chrome-lined barrels, selective ejectors, single selective trigger, ventilated rib. Price: $549.95. Ithaca Gun Co., Inc., 123 Lake Street, Ithaca, NY 14850. —J.B.

REMINGTON 3200 O/U

This gun comes with a ventilated rib and standard choke/barrel-length combinations. It is only available in 12 gauge with short chambers. Single selective trigger, automatic ejectors. Price: $695.00. Remington Arms Co., Inc., 939 Barnum Avenue, Bridgeport, CT 06602. —J.B.

WEATHERBY REGENCY O/U

Nice-looking over-under, with tang safety, single selective trigger (selector in front of trigger), automatic selective ejectors, engraved side plates (though it's a box lock), in 20-gauge with 3-inch chamber and 12 with 2¾-inch. Available in standard choke/barrel lengths with skeet, and skeet also available in 26- and 28-inch tubes, which might make for a good short-range shotgun. Recoil pad, vent rib. Price: $799.50. Weatherby, Inc., 2781 East Firestone Boulevard, South Gate, CA 90280. —J.B.

MOSSBERG BOLT-ACTION SHOTGUNS

The first shotgun I ever owned was a Mossberg 20-gauge bolt. I think all I ever shot with it was one cottontail rabbit before hard times and girl friends forced me to sacrifice it for the same price I'd bought it for—$20 used. They are a bit slow on the repeat but are good, solid guns that will take all kinds of abuse and keep working (a good idea for some young hunters, not to mention older ones). They hold two shells in clip magazines and one in the chamber. Prices: $67.50 for .410, on up to $82.50 for 12 gauge; $5.00 extra gets you a C-lect-Choke. O. F. Mossberg & Sons, Inc., 7 Grasso Avenue, North Haven, CT 06473. —J.B.

MOSSBERG PUMP GUNS "T" SERIES

These are good, low-priced pump guns, available in 12, 20, and .410, in common barrel-choke combinations, and with C-lect-Choke; 3-inch chambers. Stained birch stock, fore end grooved. Tang safety (good deal!), which isn't available on many higher-priced guns. Prices: $124.95 and slightly higher. O. F. Mossberg & Sons, Inc., 7 Grasso Avenue, North Haven, CT 06473. —J.B.

REMINGTON 870 PUMP

Fast becoming an American classic, the 870 pump is probably the most popular slide-action today. It comes in a variety of styles and in two not-very-popular gauges—28 and 16—in addition to the regular 12, 20, and .410. Most versions are chambered for 2¾-inch shells, though there are magnum models available. Left-hand ejecting styles in regular models, too. Crossbolt safety. Prices: $184.95 to $264.95 in field grades. Remington Arms Co., Inc., 939 Barnum Avenue, Bridgeport, CT 06602. —J.B.

SAVAGE/FOX DOUBLES

Looking for a reasonably priced double? The Savage/Fox series, which costs from $144.50 to $213.30, might be good bet. They all use the same basic action, though with double triggers in the lower-priced grades. The Fox Model BSE for $213.50 is the top of the line: selective auto ejectors, ventilated rib, single trigger (nonselective). I have a 20-gauge Stevens—the same gun, just toned down. Tang safety, double triggers, simple extractors—just a reliable, simple double. Its one disadvantage is that it doesn't take down easily. All come in 12, 20, and .410 with 3-inch chambers; the Stevens 311 comes in 16 gauge also, which naturally only has 2¾-inch chambers. All are reasonably lightweight, too. The Model B with 24-inch barrels (shown) is a dandy short-range weapon. Savage Arms, Springdale Road, Westfield, MA 01085.   —J.B.

WINCHESTER 101 O/U

Pictured is the 101 field gun, which is available in 12, 20, 28, and .410 gauges. The 20-gauge has 3-inch chambers; the others are standard length. Barrels are 26 inch with standard choke combinations. This gun has one very nice feature: a combined safety and barrel selector. Auto ejectors, some engraving on receiver. Prices: $580 for 12 and 20; $610 for the .410. Winchester-Western, 275 Winchester Avenue, New Haven, CT 06504.

WINCHESTER 37A SINGLE-SHOT SHOTGUN

The standard choice as a beginner's gun, the hammered single-shot break-action is indeed safe, both because of the single shot and the visible hammer. The 37A Youth Model might be a good choice for the beginner, as it has a shorter stock and is lighter than the standard models. It comes in .410 and 20 gauge, the .410 choked full and the 20 improved modified (why? don't ask me!), and costs $69.95. The standard model is available in all standard gauges except 10, with 3-inch chambers in the 12, 20, and .410, all full-choked. Barrel lengths are 26 inches in .410, 28 inches in 28 and 20, and 30 inches in 16 and 12, with 32 and 36 inches being available in 12, too. Price: $64.95. Winchester-Western, 275 Winchester Avenue, New Haven, CT 06504.   —J.B.

GAME CARRIERS

If you're looking for a cheap way to tote home the rewards of a morning's hunt, buy a fish stringer. Chain-type stringers, with their eight safety-pin clasps, are just the right size for large duck, goose, or pheasant heads. Smaller ducks will stay in place if you lock them in place, three at a time. Price: around 98 cents at your local sports store.

If you want to tote your game in style, Old Guide will sell you a duck strap. It is made of genuine leather, hand rubbed with mink oil for softness and luster. It may be slung over your shoulder or carried in your hand, and the strap has a brass ring for hanging up to six birds when you get back to camp. Price: $11.25. Old Guide, 105 Irving Street, Framingham, MA 01701.

"The mellow autumn came, and with it came / The promised party, to enjoy its sweets.
The corn is cut, the manor full of game, / The pointer ranges, and the sportsman beats."
—Byron, Don Juan

187

ANSCHUTZ 1432, 1433, AND 1533

What is a rifle doing in an upland gun section? Well, it's for hunting turkeys. The Anschutz series shown here is essentially the same gun in rifle and carbine configuration. The rifle has a 24-inch barrel and is available in .22 Hornet only (perhaps the very best turkey cartridge that you can get in a factory load), and the carbine comes in both the Hornet and the .222 Remington, which is somewhat more powerful though not overly destructive in factory form on turkeys. Both come with clips, 5-shot in Hornet and 3-shot in .222, and weigh about 6½ pounds. They're both grooved for .22-type scopes and are drilled and tapped for big-bore scope bases. The carbine is available with either a single- or double-set trigger. The rifle comes with bases for detachable sling swivels, the carbine with swivels. Prices: $385 for the rifle; $450 for the carbine. Imported by Savage Arms, Springdale Road, Westfield, MA 01085.   —J.B.

CUSTOM-MADE SHOTGUN

If you have a yen for a scattergun that you can truly call your own, Orvis will custom fit one of their side-by-sides to your specifications. You will be measured at their Vermont headquarters with a Try-Gun, an Orvis shotgun that is broken up into extendable and retractable component parts. The kinds of measurements that will be made are your personal length of pull (the distance from the trigger to the center of the butt), the drop at comb (distance between two parallel lines drawn from the top of the sight plane to the top of the stock's forward grip), the drop at heel (the distance between two parallel lines drawn from the top of the sight plane to the top of the shotgun butt), and castoff (how much the stock must bend to the right or left in order to line up properly with your shoulder and your eyes). Once these measurements are made your shotgun will be machined and molded to your body and your preferences by Orvis's Old World gunsmiths.

Standard features include 12-gauge side-by-side shotgun in 26- or 28-inch barrels or a 20-gauge side-by-side in 25- or 27-inch barrels. Improved cylinder, modified, improved modified, or full choke are available in any combination you wish. Other standard features are 2¾-inch chambers, a matted rib, double triggers, straight- or pistol-grip stock, hand-checkered butt, splinter forearm, and Spanish engravings on a white metal receiver.

Optional features include a single nonselective trigger and extra set of barrels, 3-inch chambers, 30-inch barrels, a Churchill rib, a ventilated rib, a special rare, figured, Spanish walnut stock, a beavertail forearm, special engraving, and your initials, inlaid in gold, on the trigger guard. Prices: standard custom model, $1,250; option combinations to $2,978. Orvis, 10 River Road, Manchester, VT 05254.
—N.S.

Two-Shotgun Case: Ultimate Protection

All-American Shooting Products makes a two-gun case that's virtually indestructible. The outer shell of their hard case is made of thermoplastic with glass-fiber filament added for extra rigidity. The interior of the case is lined with one layer of foam and a fleecy synthetic. Barrels are snugly suspended by molded hangers. Hinges, clasps, and leather strapping are extra heavy

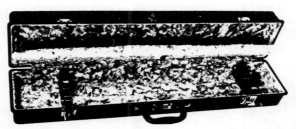

duty in construction, and the lock is a combination type.

Regarding the indestructibility of their product, All-American makes the ultimate claim: Their case will protect your guns, even on the airlines! Price: $169.95. All-American Shooting Products, P.O. Box 1526, Alvin, TX 77511.

HIP HOLSTER

The Hip Holster is a plastic holder for the butt of long arms. It slides onto the belt in the manner of handgun holsters and allows the shooter to use only one hand to support the rifle or shotgun and still have it at a fairly quick-pointing position. This is useful in thick brush, such as when hunting ruffed grouse or whitetail deer, or for a person who's using a call in one hand, or even for a trap or skeet shooter who tires of holding his gun over a long match. Price: $3.00, plus $1.00 for postage. Holster Sales, Delta American Corporation, 320 East 70th Street, Cleveland, OH 44103.

EXTRA-BARREL GUN CASE

Shotguns with interchangeable barrels are deservedly popular with scattergunners, but an extra barrel or two won't fit into conventional gun cases. The Extra-Barrel Gun Case is a padded canvas case that comes with separate pockets for one or two extra barrels. Other features include a full-length zipper, a hang-up loop, and an adjustable leather carrying sling. Lengths: 48 to 56 inches. Prices: single-extra-barrel case, $32.00; two-extra-barrel case, $38.00. Kolpin Manufacturing, Inc., P.O. Box 231, Berlin, WI 54923.

LEADER SIGHT FOR SCATTERGUNNERS

If you have trouble with your lead on a crossing bird, a Leader Sight might straighten out your problems. It clamps to the tip of the barrel and displays two see-through rings, one on either side. The idea is to encircle the bird with one of the rings, and you'll be on target.

There are quite a few variables involved in this system, though, like your distance from the target, its speed, and so forth. Tests indicate that a wise man will spend a few hours with clays before depending on this device to get him more game. Price: $2.98. Leader Sight, Inc., P.O. Box 328, Pembina, ND 58271.

CARTRIDGE ADAPTORS

Sport Specialties, P.O. Box 774, Sunnyvale, CA 94088, makes a series of adaptors that allow owners of the more popular .22- and .30-caliber centerfire rifles to fire smaller cartridges in those guns, such as 22 Long Rifle in the .222 Remington and the .30 Carbine in .30-06 rifles. They are priced at $11.95 postpaid, and no federal firearms permit is required to order them. The following adaptors are available: .22 Long Rifle for the .221 Fireball and .222, .223, .22-250, and .220 Swift; .22 Magnum for all the above except the Fireball; .22 Hornet for the .22-250 and .220; and .30 Carbine and .32 ACP for the .30-30, .308, .30-06, and .300 Winchester Magnum. A good idea for low-recoil, cheaper practice or for small game if you don't happen to be a handloader.

POLY-CHOKE

Some people hate these devices with a passion, saying they bulk up the end of a shotgun barrel, make it look like hell, and destroy its balance. Be that as it may, if you can only have one shotgun and you don't happen to want a Winchester with Winchoke, or if you have an older gun that you want to keep, the Poly-Choke will make a more versatile firearm out of it. It may not be perfect in all situations, but it will be more useful than a single-choked gun. The Poly-Choke comes in two styles, ventilated and standard, for $34.95 and $32.95 respectively. The company also

makes an excellent line of ventilated ribs and, of course, installs everything they make. Poly-Choke Co., Inc., P.O. Box 296, Hartford, CT 06101.

SCRU-WIN CHOKE: CUSTOMIZED CHOKE TUBES BY STAN BAKER

Essentially, this is the same system as used by Winchester in their Winchoke pump and semiauto guns, except that Stan Baker will convert any single-barrel 12 gauge and one barrel of some doubles to the same system. Cost is a minimum of $50, which includes one choke tube and wrench (extra tubes in most borings $10.95), ranging up to $400 for the lower barrel of the Remington 3200 O/U. There are some single barrels that can't be done because they're too thin, but most can; doubles can only be done if the barrels aren't soldered close together. The Winchoke tubes are interchangeable with these. Stan Baker, 5303 Roosevelt Way Northeast, Seattle, WA 98105. —J.B.

CHUKARS: THE CHARM AND THE CHALLENGE

by Clare Conley

I die a little each year and at an alarmingly increasing rate. I reside in Pennsylvania, which, from any point of view—outdoors, hunting, or whatever—is the best state in all the Northeast, but I live in Idaho. What I'm saying is that when I daydream or think back or ahead about someplace I'd like to be, it is always the steep, rocky canyons and rolling plateaus of southwestern Idaho and eastern Oregon.

Many people would wonder about this preference. It is the northern edge of the Western desert; there are few trees—occasional aspen, chokecherry patches, and scattered junipers on the higher elevations. But for the most part it is a mountainous, apparently barren country laced with canyons that have cliffs of red, orange, and black rock that rise at times hundreds of feet. In the bottoms of these canyons are brush-lined creeks. Sagebrush is everywhere, and its pungent aroma fills the air. And when the world is right, cheatgrass grows in abundance. And when the world is wrong, the cheatgrass does not grow.

Why cheatgrass? Because it is the natural grass of that harsh, desert rangeland, and when it doesn't grow, the chukar partridges decline in numbers until they almost vanish from the land. And thus chukar hunting, which I so dearly love and fantasize and dream about, ceases to be practical.

It's not that I have to bag a chukar to be sublimely happy hunting them. It's that although they may outwit me all day in those mountains and valleys, at least they outwitted me all day. They were there. If I said to a New Yorker that I climbed to the top of the Empire State Building every day for a month, he would think I was either a physical culture freak, a nut, or a liar. But it was not uncommon, when hunting chukars, to climb many more feet in a day than just the 1,200 feet of the Empire State Building. And yet we never thought it was particularly impressive. But it does take conditioning and the right equipment if you are to get the most out of chukar hunting and the most out of yourself.

Chukar hunting really began to come into its own in Idaho in the middle 1950s. Curiously, these birds had been planted in the area many years before, but somehow they never seemed to have taken hold. Then, in the '50s, they began to increase in numbers in southwestern Idaho and eastern Oregon. I had grown up hunting birds in Idaho, but it was limited to sagehen, pheasant, mountain quail, and valley quail. I had read about chukar, of course, in the writings of Pete Barrett, Dan Holland, and Ted Trueblood, but largely these articles dealt just with their experiences in hunting chukar, because at the time we were all learning how it was done, and they had had the first exposure to

hunting them in Nevada.

We had many misconceptions. I remember the first time I ever shot a chukar. I was hunting with Hugh Grey, then editor of *Field & Stream,* and Ted Trueblood. Ted, the ranking expert on the bird, having hunted them before, quite honestly believed that they could "throw their voices" in the sense that they made their voices reflect in such a way that they sounded to be where they were not. Time proved that wrong, of course. What was happening was that they would call and then run, and they are notorious runners—much more so than we had ever experienced before. And when approached from below, they always ran straight uphill. There are many stories about chasing chukars uphill, and they are all told with a frustrated fascination.

One of the first pieces of equipment I bought for chukar hunting was a chukar call. Some outfit in Nevada had found out that a plastic squirrel call with the piston-type plunger sounded reasonably like a chukar when operated with the right rhythm. I saw it in a mail-order column and sent for one. It seemed to me that if I could call a chukar to me, it would be a lot easier than climbing a mountain after one.

Items from a 1909 Stevens Arms catalog.

Until that time no one had explored the possibilities of calling chukar. And as it worked out, the outfit that sent the call didn't know a lot about it either because there were no directions. I experimented with my call and tried to determine if it was of any value, because chukars do talk a lot from covey to covey; out of this came a magazine article, the first ever printed on calling chukar.

Of course, chukars aren't stupid. You can't call them to you, or at least I've never heard of anyone that did. What developed was that chukars would answer the call when they were not disturbed. Now, if you are hunting in country that is miles wide in every direction and has mountains and canyons a thousand feet high, it is a help to know where a covey of birds might be. Even in days of their great abundance, the country could just swallow up these birds. So the call proved a tremendous help after I realized that its value was in locating birds, by getting them to answer.

The call that I had in those days was primitive compared to what is available now. Today the best call I'm aware of is made by the P. S. Olt Company of Pekin, Illinois. It has a rubber bellows, which makes the operation of the call easy, and it has a good voice. A second call the Olt Company has that, I have often used for chukar is the valley quail call, which is about the size of a two-inch section of a large pencil. Because it is small it can be carried around your neck. It is operated by blowing through a slot in its side while holding it cupped in your hand. It does require more practice with your breath than does the bellows call, but it has the dual advantage of being usable on valley quail as well. With it I have called valley quail right up to me.

I still must laugh when I think about the mystique that surrounded chukar in those early days. There were a great many full-choke shotguns and magnum-load shells sold for these birds, and a good many hunters believed chukar were harder to knock down than pheasant, which is just not the case. A chukar is about the size of a small hen pheasant. They are good but not exceedingly fast fliers; however, they are fantastic runners. When properly approached, which is by coming downhill or along the sidehill to them, the hunter can get within good shotgun range most of the time. When thirty burst into the air, the hunter is surprised and off balance, and the person who plants his feet before he can shoot has a real disadvantage.

When we finally arrived at the ideal shotgun for chukar hunting, it was an open choke, improved cylinder and modified; probably even cylinder bore and skeet chokes would work well. I liked an over-under with 26-inch barrels in 12 gauge that weighed slightly over 6 pounds. Trap shells were about as good as anything—3-1 ⅛-8.

I guess one of the things I miss most about chukar hunting is the physical challenge that it involves. I wouldn't climb a mountain just because it is there, but I will happily struggle, trudge, crawl, sweat, and fight my way up a mountain if I think there is a chukar on top somewhere. It is the way I am and the way many chukar hunters are. Chukar hunting isn't easy—or at least it shouldn't be.

Under this kind of physical stress, a chukar hunter should keep two things in mind: get in shape first and wear the right boots. Running is excellent, but it bores the hell out of me. So I more often do deep knee bends and repeated rises from standing flat-footed up onto my toes. Work up to fifty deep knee bends and two hundred rises; then get 20 or 30 pounds of weight you can hold in your hands and work up to the same count with that. Then the hills won't bother you—so much.

The right boots are the other secret. Slipping and sliding will tire you out twice as fast. What the correct boot is causes the widest divergence of opinion in chukar hunters. Some like light boots at the sacrifice of sturdiness, and some even like slip-ons. But I am adamant that the most ideal boot is the type now sold for backpacking and mountain-climbing, which is a stiff boot of ankle height, with padded sides, making it easy to bend at the ankle, and Vibram soles. The rigid sole and the Vibram cleats make it easier to get solid footing on steep mountainsides. My current ones are Vasques made by the Red Wing Shoe Company. They fit like a glove and are nearly indestructible.

The only other item of clothing that I feel strongly about is a particular red nylon jacket (the color makes no diference, of course) that is just perfect. When you start out early in the morning cold, it is just enough to keep you warm until the sun comes up. Then, because it isn't bulky, it can be folded up and carried in the game bag of my shoulder-strap-type bird vest. And it is water-repellent enough to get you through a sudden storm when you are a long way from the car. I don't know where to tell you to get one except where I got mine, which was from John Young at the Pensic Corporation, 3141 Monroe Avenue, Rochester, N.Y., 14603. Mention the Conley chukar jacket, and he'll know what you mean.

As I said at the beginning, I live in the West. Unfortunately, it is the West in my mind. But the next time you are climbing in the desert mountains, listening to the call of the chukar, breathing the fresh clean air, and sweating and exulting and dropping from exhaustion on one of those high mountainsides, think of me; I'll be there somewhere—in that valley or on that mountaintop. Somewhere I'm there.

Clare Conley has an extensive background in the outdoors and in outdoor communication. He has been editor of *Field & Stream*, *True*, and currently is editorial director of Popular Publications (*Argosy* et al.). He is a pilot and an expert on the environment and has appeared in guest slots on programs like Johnny Carson's *Tonight Show* and *World of Fishing*. Nice work, Clare, but after reading this we get the feeling you'd rather be home hunting chukars.

UPLAND AMMUNITION

In general, the upland hunter will not have as much use for magnum loads as will the waterfowler. His ranges are shorter, and his game is generally smaller and easier to bring down. There are really only two things that concern him when he buys a box of shells: the size of the shot and the amount of shot (usually expressed in ounces).

No. 6 shot is often touted as the all-around size. It is indeed suitable for most situations, and you won't go too far wrong if you use it. In some places, however, you might want to use a slightly larger or smaller size. I have found No. 4 or No. 5 good for pheasant in certain situations, while Nos. 7½ and 8 are better for our smaller gamebirds, such as ruffed grouse and quail. (Shot size is in inverse order to its number—the smaller the number the larger the shot.)

The *number* of shot makes a difference, too. This is where the weight of the load comes in. I generally prefer 250–300 shot in my loads for most upland hunting, so that my patterns will be adequately thick for good coverage of the bird. This means no less than ⅞ ounces of 7½s, 1⅛ ounces of 6s, or 1½ ounces of 4s. Some shooters use larger shot and fewer, believing in shot size, while some use even smaller shot, believing more in pattern. My selections are fairly middle-of-the-road. I have found that No. 7½ is more effective in 1-ounce-and-under loads than the popular No. 6, as there are too few 6s to kill reliably out to the limits of the shot's penetration capabilities. In other words, I try to match pattern thickness with the range of the shot size's killing power. I have found 7½s to kill well, even on pheasant, out to 35 yards or a bit more, 6s out to 45 yards, and 4s out to 55 yards. But it is necessary to have adequate pattern to take advantage of this. An older hunter I know who always used 4s on everything in his 12-gauge for many years decided as he got older that he needed a lighter gun. He got a .410 and used 4s in it, as he believed in that shot size. There are approximately 170 4s in the standard 1¼-ounce 12-gauge load, while there are only about ninety even in the biggest .410 load and about sixty-eight in the load he used. In spite of the fact that 4s will kill sharptail grouse past 50 yards, he couldn't kill them consistently past 25, and he is one of the finest shotgun handlers I've ever seen. This is an extreme example, but it happens to a certain extent in all loads and gauges.

As an example of shot and load selection, I generally use ⅞ ounce of 7½s in my 20-gauge at the beginning of the sharptail season, when the birds hold tighter. This load is better-killing than the same amount of 6s at closer ranges and doesn't tear up the bird as much. It also recoils less, giving quicker repeat shots—something that is usable on close-flushing birds. Later in the season, when the birds tend to be wild, I use 3-inch loads with 1¼ ounces of 6s; these kill reliably out to 45 yards or so.

Most modern loads have shot cups and chilled (alloyed) shot. Both of these features keep the shot from deforming, and more of it ends up in the pattern instead of across the pasture. Round pellets also carry more energy and penetrate better. Of late some skeet shooters have "discovered" that noncupped loads of drop shot (pure, soft lead) will have wider patterns, and some manufacturers have brought out loads without the cup part of the shell and with soft shot to accommodate them. While these are fine for target shooting and theoretically would give an advantage to the upland gunner at short ranges because of the wider pattern, the shot on the outer edges of the pattern is usually badly deformed (which is why it flies wider) and lacks killing power. If you want a larger pattern without changing choke, you can buy "brush" loads in 12 gauge. These are *hunting* loads; the shot is induced to scatter by means of spacers inside the shot cup. The outside shot is not deformed (at least not as much) as in the target loads and is better for game.

Again, I have generally found—though there are shooters that will disagree—that pattern is more important than shot size to a certain extent. If you are wounding birds on the edge of range, either don't try shots that long or possibly try one size smaller shot, or a heavier load of shot, instead of larger shot. While you may scratch down a pheasant at over 50 yards now and then with big pellets, you will also wound more.   —J.B.

SMALL-GAME GUNS

In America small game is understood to mean the smaller edible mammals: rabbits and squirrels. These and a few local types of small game are hunted with two kinds of weapons, depending on the hunting involved. Shotguns are used on hard-to-hit, usually moving game such as cottontail rabbits jumped in brush; rifles are used on sitting targets, though very often semiautomatic arms are used to take running game.

Small-game animals are not large, most weighing under 2 pounds. It depends on what you define as small game. Some people consider raccoons or jackrabbits small game. In any case, they are not difficult to kill and traditionally are not shot at extreme ranges. A light upland shotgun loaded with No. 6 shot will do for most rabbit and squirrel hunting, while rifles can be of almost any caliber as long as the loads used are accurate enough for small targets and are not overly destructive of meat. Many small-game hunters use their deer rifles loaded with cast-bullet handloads with perfect satisfaction, but the traditional small-game rifle is a rimfire .22.

Twenty-twos are some of the very oldest cased cartridges and have been around since black-powder days. They excel at small-game hunting because they are accurate enough for such hunting, they are cheap to shoot, the report is light, and they destroy very little edible tissue.

Rifles for rimfire cartridges are made in all the popular actions and styles that centerfire hunting rifles are available in: bolt, lever, pump, auto, and single shot. In target rifles the bolt action is preferred, just as in larger calibers. In hunting rifles, any of the standard actions is suitable in terms of accuracy. This means different things to different hunters, but any .22 that can keep five shots in 2 inches or less at 50 yards is doing well enough for most game hunting, though squirrel hunters demand more control when they are trying to head-shoot a fox squirrel at 75 yards.

Probably the bolt and auto .22s are the most popular. Bolt guns are traditional hunting rifles, and a good one will give all the accuracy that is necessary for small game. Autos are generally preferred by those who go after running game. Both styles can be had at very reasonable prices, especially the single-shot bolt gun, the traditional "boy's" rifle.

If you are thinking of a .22 for serious small-game hunting, it would be wise to look the arm over very carefully. Often .22s are thought of as being casual guns for an afternoon of tin-can shooting or for keeping foxes out of the chicken coop. In the cheaper grades triggers are rough and heavy, parts are stampings that can easily be bent or broken, sights are of poor quality, and stocks are of softwood that doesn't hold up well under many hunting conditions. Tolerances are greater than in centerfire rifles, too; rimfires do not produce anywhere near the pressures of big-game rounds, and the manufacturers can get by with less expensive techniques. All these things point to a chance of unreliability (and many small-game hunters take their sport very seriously!) not to mention the fact that optimum accuracy will probably not be present. This is not to say that the lower-priced .22s on today's market are dangerous or even inferior; it simply points out that guns are produced for a variety of purposes. If your purpose is small-game hunting, it might be wise to invest in the very best.   —J.B.

*"Bye, baby bunting, Daddy's gone a-hunting,
Gone to get a rabbit skin to wrap the baby bunting in."*
—*"Gammer Gurton's Garland"* (1784)

193

RABBIT RAP

- The cottontail rabbit is America's number-one game animal.
- A female cottontail rabbit normally gives birth to three to four litters annually. The litters average five young.
- In rare instances the cottontail rabbit can live to ten years of age.
- Ninety-nine percent of all cottontail rabbits live and die within a mile of where they were born.
- When snows are heavy, look for cottontails in willow thickets. Willow bark is a favorite food of bunnies, and it's probably the only meal available.
- A wounded rabbit often crawls into a brushpile or brier patch and dies out of arm's reach. You can often retrieve these "lost" bunnies by breaking a splintery sapling, slipping it into the hide, then twisting the shaft. The rough end will snare an ear or loose skin or fur, and then the carcass can be pulled close enough for you to grab it.
- When skinning a rabbit, take care to

avoid getting hair on the meat; it can impart unwanted flavors. To easily remove any hair that inadvertently adheres to the meat, run the carcass over a gas stove or propane torch flame and then wash the meat to remove the ash.
- A rabbit has a cholesterol level of fifty, which makes it the lowest in cholesterol of all meats. Wild game, in general, is much lower in cholesterol than domestic meats.

The Rabbit Hunter

Careless and still
The hunter lurks
With gun depressed,
Facing alone
The alder swamps
Ghastly snow-white.
And his hound works
In the offing there
Like one possessed,
And yelps delight
And sings and romps,
Bringing him on
The shadowy hare
For him to rend
And deal a death
That he nor it
(Nor I) have wit
To comprehend.
—Robert Frost

Tularemia: The Rabbit Hunter's Disease

Tularemia, also known as rabbit fever, is an infectious disease transmitted by rodents which can be fatal to man. Beware of any bunny that plods along and is an unusually easy kill. Ideally, you should handle these animals with gloves, especially if you have a cut or infected hand. When cleaning the animal (again, this should be done with gloves), pay particular attention to its liver. If it is yellow or white-spotted, the animal is likely to be infected with the disease. Proper cooking will render the meat safe to eat, but it's best not to take chances. Bury the carcass, hide, and entrails.

Field Dressing in a Flick

To field dress a rabbit in a minimum of time and with minimum mess, open the carcass from anus to throat with a pocket knife. Grasp both hind legs in one hand and forelegs in the other, and hold the rabbit so the opening faces the earth. Stretch your legs wide apart and swing the carcass between them hard, snapping sharply downward at the end of the swing. Inertia and centrifugal force will tear the innards free, and the field dressing job is done.

SQUIRRELS

by Pete Czura

It sports no glamorous "rack" and no brilliant plumage. Its mounted form graces only a few sportsmen's dens. Few hunters even list it among the top choices of game they hunt. Yet, as many as seven out of ten hunters admit it was the first game they went after as youths.

What's the name of this game? It's the frisky, sometimes cantankerous and sneaky squirrel, which is hunted in long seasons in nearly every state of the union.

The most prevalent species of squirrel are the gray and the fox (called the red squirrel). There is also a smattering of tree, black, flying, and silver squirrels in scattered parts of our country.

According to Arkansas game department officials, "In terms of number of hunters, the squirrel, both gray and fox, is Arkansas's most important game animal."

Alaska and Arizona boast of year-round seasons on squirrel. Other states that have a longer than average season include Oklahoma, seven and one half months; South Dakota, six and one half months; Kansas, six months; New York, five months; and Nebraska, five months. All other states have seasons ranging from one month up to four.

I won't go into specifics about hot spots, but there is one state I would definitely recommend. During the past year hunters bagged around two and one half million gray and fox squirrels in the Ozark Hills of Missouri. One of the better spots is around Table Rock Lake. According to game officials, this game could easily stand a greater harvest.

The gray squirrel is found principally from the New England States west to the Mississippi River Valley. Its favorite hangouts are in the timbered river valleys, along forested mountain slopes, and in the gently rolling foothills. Fox squirrels occupy about the same terrain except they do not frequent the New England area.

Incidentally, Arizona hunters can add the Abert squirrel to their bag. It is also found in New Mexico and Colorado. Many sportsmen call the Abert one of the handsomest of all squirrels.

Since squirrels are abundant throughout our country, great opportunities are provided for youngsters to cut their eyeteeth on these tricky game animals. Squirrel hunting teaches a tyro sportsman how to be patient and sit quietly, like an Indian, waiting for the furry critter to come out of hiding for a clean shot.

Despite the abundance of squirrels, some interesting challenges are still provided in the way they can be taken. Anything from bows and arrows to .22 caliber rifles, scat-

terguns, pellet guns, and even slingshots are legal.

Some sportsmen prefer stalking their game. During a dry spell it can be murder; your footsteps on dry leaves sound like cracks of a rifle, sending the squirrels into hiding. Of course, if you stalk after a rain, your chances of a silent aproach improve considerably.

Personally, I prefer the sit and wait method. I find a comfortable spot, sit, and rest against a tree and remain still for a while. Usually the curious critters will come out of hiding to present an easy target. Sometimes, if the boogers are stubborn and won't budge out of hiding, I successfully use squirrel calls made by Lohman or Olt to lure them out.

As for weapons, I use either a Daisy Model 881 pellet rifle or an Ithaca BSA Mercury .177 caliber. For a change of pace, I switch to a Saunders Wrist Rocket (slingshot). Best of all, if I miss the first shot with the slingshot, it is so silent the squirrel is not spooked, thus offering me up to as many as four chances.

The bonus from a squirrel hunt comes when you belly up to the table for a tasty young squirrel stew.

Pete Czura is a free-lance photo-journalist who has had over five hundred articles and picture essays published. He is also recognized as one of America's premier wildlife photographers.

Squirrels feed in the early morning just after sunrise, and disappear soon after eight or nine o'clock, retreating to their holes or nests, there to remain during the midday hours. They appear again in the late afternoon to feed, and may be heard and seen playing and chattering together till twilight. —Charles Hallock, 1877

Twenty-two Features

Most of the .22s on today's market are grooved for scope mounting. This system is essentially a dovetail on which scope mounts are clamped, rather than holes drilled for scope-mount screws as in centerfire rifles.

Magazines in .22s are of two main types: clip and tube. The clip type is usually of six- to eight-shot capacity, while the tube holds around fifteen long-rifle shells. The clip type is faster for reloading, because the inexpensive clips can be purchased and loaded before a hunting trip while the tube requires some hassle to get loaded, though once you get it full you can shoot for quite a while.

Twenty-two sights are frequently only very crudely adjustable and are often so rickety that they won't even stay sighted in if subjected to a stiff breeze. This is some-

thing to especially be aware of, since a gun with bad sights is almost as worthless as a gun without them.

Semiauto rimfires are virtually all of the blowback type, where the force of the cartridge is utilized to blow the breech open. These must be kept perfectly clean or they won't operate. —J.B.

Twenty-two Sights

For most serious small-game hunting, scopes are preferable to iron sights. The targets are small, and often the hunter is trying to place his shot in a very small area on a very small target, such as the head of a squirrel. Open sights are adequate for running shots at cottontails, but even here a scope of proper size is not a handicap, and it is definitely an aid in standing shots.

The .22 scopes on the market are quite satisfactory for much shooting, and their prices are reasonable. However, their small objective lenses and their short, critical eye-relief leave something to be de-

sired for some types of hunting. If you feel the need for something a little more suitable for your type of shooting, whether it be running cottontails or hidden fox squirrels, you might consider a big-bore scope. There are mounts that are especially made to mate 1-inch scopes and .22 dovetails, or you can get your .22 drilled and tapped for regular scope bases and mounts. This might cost you a ten-spot, but it is well worth it. And don't be misled into putting a cheap or low-powered scope on your huntin' .22 simply because it's "just a .22." In small-game hunting as well as in var-

minting and big-game hunting, the better you see the better you shoot, especially when you are trying to hit targets the size of a silver dollar at 75 yards. My number-one .22 now has a 3-to-9x big-bore scope on it. At the ranges a .22 is useful—100 yards at the most, often half that range—there is no need to worry about parallax adjustments even at the upper range of this scope, and it lets me aim at just about anything I want. At 3x it is fine for running cottontails. —J.B.

Weaver Tip-off Mounts

These are mounts made to fit 1-inch-diameter scopes (big bore) to dovetailed .22 rifles. They are of standard Weaver split-ring design. Price: $11.95; also available in solid rings for ¾-inch- and ⅞-inch-diameter scopes for $4.95. W. R. Weaver Co., 7125 Industrial Avenue, El Paso, TX 79915.   —J.B.

Redfield Traditional .22 4x

This is a scaled-down version of Redfield's Traditional big-bore 4x (the Traditional line is round-viewed) and is a very nice little scope. Good quality, good optics, with an exit pupil of 5.2mm, which means enough relative brightness for dimlight hunting. Price is $43.60, and you'll need some ¾-inch-diameter rings for them. Redfield makes these, too, as well as .22-type 1-inch rings, for $16.40. These are styled somewhat after Redfield's popular JR-SR big-bore mount system: nice looking. Redfield, 5800 East Jewell Avenue, Denver, CO 80222.

BUSHNELL 4x SCOPECHIEF .22 RIFLESCOPE — #70-3000

BUSHNELL 3x-8x SCOPECHIEF .22 RIFLESCOPE — #70-3100

Bushnell Rangemaster .22 Scopes

The .22 long rifle is a very good small-game round, but it won't kill much beyond its effective hitting range because it has a looping trajectory. These Bushnell scopes are equipped with the Rangemaster system, which eliminates holdover. These are adjustable out to 175 yards, though I would be hesitant to try shots that far with a .22, especially if the wind was blowing. With an accurate .22, however, shots to 100 yards and even a bit beyond might be possible. These come in two models, a 4x and a 3 to 7x, both equipped with hex-head screw mounts. These are very good scopes optically and have better relative brightness qualities than many .22 scopes on the market due to their ⅞-inch objective lens. Prices: $26.95 for the variable and $21.95 for the 4x, with both also available without Rangemaster for $2.00 less. Bushnell Optical Co., 2828 East Foothill Boulevard, Pasadena, CA 91107.   —J.B.

Ruger 10/22 Carbine

This little gun has a unique rotary magazine that holds ten long-rifle rounds, hence the name: 10/22. It handles just about the same as the Ruger .44 magnum carbine. It has an 18½-inch barrel and a folding-leaf rear sight. Weight is 5 pounds. It has an excellent reputation for reliability. Price: standard, $77.50; deluxe, $89.50. Sturm, Ruger & Co., Inc., Lacey Place, Southport, CT 06490.   —J.B.

Four-power .22 Scope for Squirrel and Rabbit Hunters

Four power is relatively high magnification for a .22 scope, but it can come in handy for squirrel and rabbit hunters. Both animals often hide most of their body behind protective cover and peer out at their pursuer with one shiny eye. Such a tiny target requires the kind of precise aiming that a four-power scope provides. Another plus is that such a scope often picks up that shiny giveaway when it is invisible to the naked eye.

The Mark I 600 is a compact, lightweight, four-power scope made for .22 rifles. It has magnesium-coated optics, a self-centering cross-hair reticle, and comes complete with a mount to fit most .22 receivers. Price: $12.50. Swift Instruments, Inc., 952 Dorchester Avenue, Boston, MA 02125.

See-through .22 Scope Mounts

The Ironsighter is a low-profile O-type see-through scope mount that clamps to the grooved receiver of most rimfire rifles. It should be a good, practical mount for the rimfire hunter: fast to pick up moving game and handy for getting the cross hairs on a target under low light conditions or when game is against a look-alike background. Price: $14.95. J. B. Holden Co., P.O. Box 393, Plymouth, MI 48170.

Anschutz .22 Sporters

These are high-class .22 sporters in every sense of the word. Very nice wood, good triggers, and hand checkering. They are available in three versions: the 164 and 164M (magnum) for $189.50 and $204.50; the 54 Sporter (on the same action as their .22 Hornet and .222 rifles) for $313.40; and, pictured here, the 1418 and 1518 (standard and magnum) Mannlicher-style carbine for $269.50 and $284.50. Imported by Savage Arms, Springdale Road, Westfield, MA 01085. —J.B.

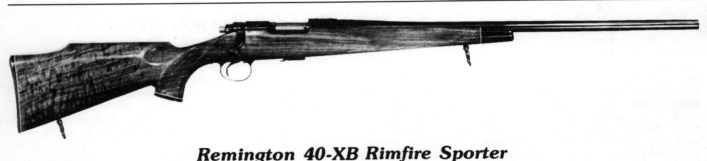

Remington 40-XB Rimfire Sporter

This is a rimfire version of the Model 700 centerfire rifle: same action and stock. It includes sling swivels and is drilled and tapped for scope. For price information write to Remington Arms Co., Inc., 939 Barnum Avenue, Bridgeport, CT 06602. —J.B.

Remington Nylon 66 Autoloader

This is the only synthetically stocked long gun that's ever been a success on the American market. The nylon stock is very tough (Remington's first ads showed it getting run over with a truck), and the nylon parts in the action need no lubrication and will keep working long after metal-made guns clog up and jam with dirt. For long rifle only; 14-round magazine is in butt stock. Available in brown or black. Barrel is 19⅝ inches; weight, 4 pounds. Price: $79.95.

Remington Arms Co., Inc., 939 Barnum Avenue, Bridgeport, CT 06602. —J.B.

Remington 581— For Southpaws

Once again the folks at Remington are looking out for all the left-handed shooters in the world. The Model 581 clip-fed bolt gun is available in left-hand version for $79.95 (regular right-hand for $5.00 less). Barrel is 24 inches; weight about 4¾ pounds. Remington Arms Co., Inc., 939 Barnum Avenue, Bridgeport, CT 06602. —J.B.

"Sitting on a log includes a deal of patience, with oftentimes cold feet and chattering teeth; but [it] is quite as successful as chasing [game] all day on tracking snow."
—Nessmuk

197

Winchester 9422 and 9422M

These are rimfire guns designed to look and handle like the famous Model 94 lever gun. The 9422 is a long-rifle chambered gun, the 9422M a .22 magnum arm. Both are tube-magazined and eject to the side, so scope-mounting low over the receiver is possible (it isn't with the 94). The regular version holds fifteen long rifles, the magnum eleven shells. Prices: $159.95 for the 9422; $164.95 for the magnum. Winchester-Western, 275 Winchester Avenue, New Haven, CT 06504. —J.B.

Winchester 490—Built Like a Big-Game Gun

This was originally designed as a companion piece to Winchester's auto and lever-operated big-game rifles, the 100 and 88. When compared to the two big guns, it is easy to see the similarity of the stock design, the way the action is laid out, etc. The thinking was that a hunter could have both a big-game and a small-game rifle with the same feel. Unfortunately, not many people purchased the 100 and 88, so the .22-caliber 490 is all by itself; the two big guns were discontinued. The 490 is still an excellent gun, with stock dimensions and feel that are man-size and are often more comfortable for adult shooters than many .22 stocks. Clip is five-shot; rear sight is a nice folding-leaf, front a ramp. Price: $119.95. Winchester-Western, 275 Winchester Avenue, New Haven, CT 06504. —J.B.

Stevens 73 Single Shot

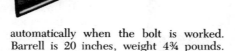

The traditional "boy's" rifle is a bolt-action, single-shot .22. The safety goes on automatically when the bolt is worked. Barrell is 20 inches, weight 4¾ pounds. Price: $39.55. Savage Arms, Springdale Road, Westfield, MA 01085. —J.B.

Stevens 89 Single-shot Lever .22

A good choice for the beginning shooter, this little gun weighs in at 5 pounds with its 18½-inch barrel. It is built to look like a lever-action carbine but is in fact a sort of dropping-block single shot operated by the lever. The exposed hammer easily shows when it's cocked. Price $48.00. Savage Arms, Springdale Road, Westfield, MA 01085. —J.B.

MODEL 72 SADDLEGUN

CHARTER ARMS **AR-7 EXPLORER**

A .22 LR survival rifle for campers, fishermen, backpackers, boatsmen, private pilots, skimobilers, RV owners

.22 long rifle, rimfire caliber semi-automatic survival rifle

Saddlegun-style Magnum .22

Ithaca Gun Co.'s Model 72 is a lever-action saddle carbine chambered for .22 wmrf magnum cartridges. Features include an American walnut stock, a grooved receiver for scope mounting, and a precision rifled 18½-inch barrel. This looks like an all-around .22 that won't dig too deeply into your shell money should you want to do some plinking and that would also perform fair to middlin' on varmints. Price: $159.95. Ithaca Gun Co., Inc., 123 Lake Street, Ithaca, NY 14850.

AR-7 EXPLORER: A .22 FOR ALL SEASONS

This remarkable .22 is dubbed a Sporting/Survival rifle, but it deserves a better title, for it is many more things than that abbreviated name implies.

First, the basic dope. The AR-7 is a semiautomatic carbine that shoots .22 long-rifle ammo from an eight-shot magazine. It is reasonably accurate, considering it has a 16-inch barrel. It will consistently place rounds inside a silver-dollar-sized bull at 50 yards. OK . . . so will most other .22s. So what else is new?

• The rifle weighs a mere 2¾ pounds, making it a practical companion for the hunter/backpacker with small game on his mind who doesn't want to carry a heavy load.

• The rifle has a noncorroding finish and a plastic stock. Except for the steel lining in the aluminum barrel, it will not rust or rot.

• The rifle floats if you drop it in the drink.

• It breaks down into component parts that are carried inside the stock. They take about a minute to assemble. The length of the stock/action package is 16½ inches.

This combination of size, compactness, weight, accuracy, and durability in a rifle frame makes this gun ideal as backup gun for a scattergunning squirrel hunter (it will tuck away in a game bag) or a source of plinking fun packed in an RV, snowmobile, motorboat, ATV, trail bike, or in the aforementioned backpack. It is legal in all states (it does not qualify as a handgun), so it's a good personal protection device as well.

The many shooting possibilities that are crammed into this tidy package lead us to suggest that if you want or need just one .22 for all seasons, this is the one to own. Price: $64.95. Charter Arms Corp., 430 Sniffens Lane, Stratford, CT 06497.

—N.S.

THE J·STEVENS ARMS & TOOL CO. Chicopee Falls, Mass. U.S.A. 1900

SMALL-GAME AMMUNITION

For many years there were only three main types of .22 shells on the market: short, long, and long rifle. The short was the first of the bunch; it uses a shell less than ⅜ inch long and fires a 29-grain bullet at about 1,100 fps muzzle velocity with an energy of less than 80 foot-pounds. The long was brought out to step up the short's power; it uses a ½-inch case and shoots the same bullet at 1,240 fps with 99 foot-pounds of energy. The long rifle went one step further, using the long's case but a 40-grain bullet. The high-speed loading is the most popular for hunting. In most loads it uses a 36-to-37-grain bullet at about 1,300 fps with around 140 foot-pounds of energy.

The long rifle is the most useful of the three for hunting. It shoots flatter, kills better, and drifts less in the wind than the other two. The short is also useful, mainly as a practice round, though in hollow-point form some use it as a pest cartridge or for game shooting where minimal meat destruction is desired. The long has neither of the others' virtues; it is only slightly more powerful than the short, but far less accurate in most guns. It hangs on, I believe, because it looks about as big as the long rifle, (it has the same case). Because it's slightly cheaper, many people believe they are getting just about as much power for a lesser price. My father, who grew up on a Montana homestead where everyone was expected to help keep the larder filled with their .22s, was a great believer in the long, and he always thought I was crazy when I'd spring the extra few cents required for a box of long rifles.

People get into as many arguments debating whether the hollow-point long rifle or the solid point should be used on small game as they do over the merits of the 12 and 20 gauges or the .30-06 and .270. It is all a matter of personal preference, though I have found (after using hollow-points all through my teenage years) that solids pack all the punch needed to take squirrels and cottontails. However, they are not as good on bigger animals such as jackrabbits.

Awhile back, Winchester figured that people were looking for a bit more power in a .22 and came up with the .22 Winchester magnum, an elongated .22 that fired a 40-grain bullet at 2,000 fps out of a rifle, with over 300 pounds of energy. It does indeed shoot flatter and kill bigger game than the ordinary .22s, but I have never been really crazy about it. I owned one for a while but couldn't see where it gave all that big an advantage over the long rifle for most small-game hunting. It is overly destructive with the hollow point, and the solid point doesn't kill well unless it is precisely placed, which is impossible for most shooters past long-rifle range anyway (and is difficult for many at even 40 yards). When it does hit where it's supposed to, it will kill past 100 yards, but I haven't seen the .22 magnum hunting rifle yet that will group well enough to place shots on small game at that distance. It also costs about 6 cents a shot as compared to about 2 cents for long rifles.

The Remington 5mm magnum (.20 caliber) is a small bottlenecked round created with the same idea in mind. It has ballistics slightly better than the .22 magnum, but as of now no rifles are made for it because shooters weren't willing to pay the price for gun or ammo.

Regular .22 ammo is available with two types of lubrication. Actually, one isn't a lube at all but a soft metal plating over the lead bullet. The standard wax- or grease-lubed bullets were always kind of messy, especially when dumped in a pocket, and in recent years the factories seem to have lessened or even eliminated the lube, as I have noticed more leading in .22 barrels lately. A friend of mine who borrowed a .22 was under the impression that you don't have to clean modern .22s (which very often is true); he ran a few boxes through it without a thought. I looked through the barrel one day and couldn't see any rifling for 6 to 8 inches in front of the chamber. It was so leaded I couldn't get a standard .22 cleaning brush in through the breech. This does little for accuracy. For most shooting I prefer the plated bullets; they do not lead the bore and are not as subject to deformation. They do cost just a bit more, however.

Twenty-twos are just like bigger rifles and may prefer a certain brand of ammo over another. Most .22 ammo will group fairly close to other brands, but for serious hunting find the most accurate brand for your gun and stick to it.

—J.B.

Wallet-type .22 Ammo Carrier

This polypropylene case holds thirty rounds of .22 ammo in snap slots and fits comfortably in a back or breast pocket. Price $1.49. Cabela's, 812 13th Avenue, Sidney, NE 69162.

.22 Cartridge Belt

This bandolier-type belt holds fifty .22 cartridges in a single row of stapled loops. Gold finished buckle, 1½-inch-wide leather strap. State small, medium, or large when ordering. Price: $7.20. Burnham Brothers, Box 100A, Marble Falls, TX 78654.

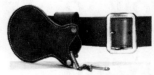

.22 Ammo Pouch

Safariland's No. 73 Swivel Pouch is a leather shell-holder that fits on your belt. It has a steel spring closure that opens when you squeeze the pouch mouth. The pouch swivels at the belt loop, so shells tumble into your hand. Price: $6.95. Send $1.00 for a Safariland catalog. Safariland, 1941 South Walker Avenue, Monrovia, CA 91016.

Hardest-Hitting .22 Ammo?

The Stinger, a standard-size .22 long-rifle bullet, posts some pretty impressive figures to prove it's the hardest-hitting .22 on the market. The maximum velocity of the Stinger is 1,685 fps versus 1,335 fps for its closest competitor. At 100 yards the Stinger drops 3½ inches less than a regular .22 long-rifle. The Stinger may be used in any .22 chambered for conventional long-rifle cartridges. Price: $1.95 per box of 50. Omark Industries, Snake River Avenue, Lewiston, ID 83501.

OL' BOOTS

I was impressed with Ol' Boots. The other, younger dogs ranged far, wide, and fast, but Boots worked with deliberate purpose, using his nose more than his legs. He would go from one plum thicket to the next, in a straight line, knowing that he'd never find quail on the sand flats and in the sparse grass of western Oklahoma. Plainly, he knew where they lived, and he was wise in other ways, too. The Brittany spaniels were constantly gnawing at their pads to extract sand burrs and prickly pear cactus buttons. Boots never stopped once. He knew the places to avoid as well as those to inspect.

He was unspectacular, but something told me to stick with him, so while Carroll, Joe, Bruce, and Wayland kept pace with the faster-moving dogs, I adopted Boots's easy gait. My hunch paid off. In five minutes he locked up tight on an isolated patch of thick shin oak. His tail wagged slowly. He looked at me out of the side of his yellow pointer eyes as I walked up, and I thought I saw him grin.

Suddenly the quail were aloft, a fluttering fountain of feathers. My 20-gauge double spoke twice, and the first bird of the day fell from the frantic covey. Boots was on it in an instant. He picked up the bird and began to chew.

"Boots! Dammit, bring that bird here! Boots!"

I could hear the tiny bones breaking between the nubs of worn teeth.

"Boots!" I walked over to the dog and wrapped my hand around the top of his jaw, pinning jowls against teeth. I squeezed, gently at first. "Boots!"

The dog stopped chewing, but he would not turn the bird loose. I squeezed harder and harder; the dog slowly cocked his head and gave a little whimper of pain, the bird still tight in his jaws.

I squeezed harder yet, and he cocked more, the top of his head now touching the ground. Then he was on his back, and I was kneeling, both of us locked in a convoluted contest over whose bird this was.

"Blow in his nose, blow in his nose," I heard Bruce cry. "He'll drop the bird if you blow in his nose!"

I leaned forward, more contorted yet, and managed to cup my hand over Boots's nostrils. "Poof." The dog immediately relaxed his grip, I relaxed mine, and I had my badly mangled bird. Boots sneezed, shook off, and looked disgusted.

"Shoulda told you," Bruce called. "He eats birds. Damn fine retriever once he's full, though."

—N.S.

HOW TO BUY A HUNTING DOG

If you're serious about having a good hunting dog, approach its purchase as you would a new car or a house. While the initial investment isn't comparable, the eventual investment in terms of time, care, and upkeep will be. However, the returns can be greater than on any Cadillac or country estate.

Never buy any dog on impulse. Your family might adore some cute pup, but resist their imploring. This is the time to be cold and calculating; love and affection come later.

Get a good idea of the kinds of bloodlines that made your prospective partner. I have never been impressed by bench or field trial credentials alone, but that kind of heritage, coupled with parents or cousins or siblings who are demonstrably good hunters afield—who hunt the way you would like to hunt—are the best recommendations I can think of.

There are three ways to buy a dog: as a pup, as a started dog, or as a finished dog. Unless you are an accomplished handler/trainer, I would strongly recommend that at some point you have a pup trained by a professional. My reasons are based on experience. Pups are scatterbrained, cute, calculating, and deceptive. Unless you know dogs, they train you to perform for them instead of the other way around.

I personally prefer buying a started dog, a one-and-a-half- to two-year-old who has a solid foundation in discipline and who has absorbed the rudiments of hunting etiquette. There are two advantages to started dogs: they have been properly trained and you know what you are getting in terms of a hunter. Some pups, even from the best of back-

THE CONDO DOG

by Stu Apte

Way down in Uvalda, Georgia, I came upon a phenomenon which illustrates how adaptable—and downright shrewd—hunting dogs can be when properly conditioned to circumstances.

My good friend there in Uvalda, Hugh McNatt, has a huge plantation, mostly reserved for the quail-hunting pleasure of his multitudes of friends. And like most Southern men of means, Hugh leaves very little to chance. He not only keeps twenty-eight hunting dogs, including pointers, setters, and nonslip retrieving Labs, he arranges for big bunches of pen-reared quail to supplement the vast numbers of wild birds on his property, to assure a good time and a successful hunt for all his friends. Like all perfect schemes, his activity in assuring plenty of quail, plenty of dogs, and plenty of good times has brought forth some interesting, and quirky, side effects. One of these is the "Condo Dog."

Now, condo is a Florida for-short term meaning condominium, a kind of apartment house that has sprouted up all over the Sunshine State and houses any number of families, or people. On Hugh's property in Georgia there is a similar situation, except that there a great number of bird feeders placed along paths and roads throughout the acreage house numbers of planted, pen-raised quail.

His Georgia quail condos are not elaborate; they're simple wood and wire structures containing feed and serving as a place for birds to get in out of the weather to eat and rest. Jeeping down a hedgerow or edging along a pasture, you can spot their tarpaper roofs from some distance. You know

there will be some birds there, if you haven't scored anywhere else. And of course the dogs get to know these locations, too, and never fail to point the birds long before you get there.

One day as I approached another area with my good buddies Flip Pallot and Sandy Morette, we weren't really thinking about shooting penned birds because there were plenty of wild ones around. Suddenly our pointer, Boy, pulled up rock solid in a classic point.

We jeeped up, got out, and walked past the dog, kicking the brush, with shotguns at the ready. Nothing happened. No birds. Yet Boy maintained his statue point. We walked around and around him, trying our best to find the bird, but to no avail. Finally we saw it. His quarry lay right under his stylish nose: not a bird, but a one-foot-square piece of tarpaper, the same kind used on the roofs of the condominiums. Boy had pointed the condos so much that the smell of tarpaper had become the smell of quail to him and turned him into the "Condo Dog."

Another pattern, repeated endlessly in the lives of Hugh's great stable of dogs, produced "Five-Bird Sally." A beautiful setter, Sally had gotten used to the groundskeepers' habit of planting five quail in the feeders, and I imagine that, after having flushed five birds a few thousand times, Sally learned to count.

When Sally pointed at a bird feeder and the hunters flushed the birds and shot, she always expected to see five birds flush, hear five shots, and see five birds hit the ground. If the pattern did not repeat, and only four birds flushed, or four shots were fired, Sally would staunchly keep on pointing until she had to be led off. If, however, the five-bird pattern played out to its end, it caused even worse results in Sally's behavior. Sure that there were no more birds in that feeder, she would race on to the next condominium and wait for the jeep to arrive.

One other training effect was worth noting for the quirk it produced. To mark the many feeders and make them easily visible to hunters not used to the territory, Hugh had his groundskeepers attach gleaming chrome hubcaps to each of the roofs. With those, even the most inexperienced hunters knew which way the next covey was. What Hugh did not count on, it seems, was the effect of repetition and the dogs' willingness to adapt to a pattern.

Now, if you drive into his long, curving driveway and happen to have the same brand of car those hubcaps were taken from, you might just be startled to see a full-grown, blue-ribbon, high-blooded hunting dog take a look at your hubcap and pull itself up into a stylish picture-book point.

grounds, just never turn into good hunters. I might also mention that all my started dogs have become close companions. The notion that you must raise a dog from puppyhood for it to be truly yours is a myth.

Finished dogs are polished hunters. I buy started dogs and finish them, but if you don't have the time, a finished dog is the only answer. Obviously, if you don't have the time to finish a started dog, you won't have the time to train a pup.

The problem with finished dogs, however, is that trainers like to hold on to the good finished dogs through their prime, either for field trials or as advertisements for their offspring. So you usually have to settle for an older finished dog or one who, for some reason, hasn't quite come up to snuff. One source of finished dogs to consider other than established kennels is a game preserve. Quite often they'll finish a good hunter that develops some little quirk which doesn't work out for them, such as killing cripples instead of bringing them to hand live.

A good finished dog will, of course, be the most expensive hunting dog of all, with prime animals bringing up to $1,000. —N.S.

Stu Apte is a pilot for Pan American Airways and a salt-water angler of wide renown. He holds or has held over a dozen world record catches, and he appears frequently on ABC-TV's *American Sportsman* show. He is less well known, but equally expert, in the pursuit of upland game and waterfowl and is one helluva shot.

MEDITATIONS ON A MEAT DOG

There has long been a running argument between dog handlers and hunters regarding the relative merits of field trial training versus developing a practical gun dog.

The conflict is roughly this: the formalized performance expected of a dog in a field trial is often at odds with actual hunting situations. Field trial dogs are expected to range great distances from the handler, to lock in and hold a point forever without inching up, and to make unusually long retrieves on a straight line, no matter what obstacles might be along that path.

While this kind of drive, obedience, and exceptional performance is a beauty to behold and is testimony to the handler's time, knowledge, and patience, does it have all that much to do with hunting? More important, in the handler's desire to develop a dog with "natural" field trial instincts, is this kind of competition breeding out qualities that make for a good hunting dog?

Afield, a far-ranging dog can be more of a liability than an asset. Natural wild birds will seldom hold for long periods of time in front of a dog. They will either run or get nervous and flush before a hunter can walk up on them if the point is thrown 200 yards away. And how about things like the qualities of a dog's nose and an innate desire to work with the hunter, coupled with the brains to figure out how it is done? Or just love for the hunt? How do field trials measure or even develop these traits?

Cast my lot with the meat dog, the lusty hunter who occasionally breaks point or at times shivers and fidgets in the blind as a flock of mallards swing overhead. Give me the dog with the good common sense to retrieve a bird along the path of least resistance . . . to work close to me in heavy brush . . . to stay within gun range in an open field . . . who follows a bird when it moves before I get there. I want that kind of dog for two reasons: he hunts like a partner, not a machine, and he will get me more shots at game, which is the reason for using a dog to begin with. —N.S.

Getting Bowser Down to Business

For most gunners their dog is half pet and half workmate, so there are bound to be times when the "playful pet" half of the dog fails to recognize that it's time to get down to business and hunt. This problem is a cinch to solve if you'll give your dog something to associate with work every time you hunt or train. Snapping a bell to the collar is one possibility, as is a special "work" collar—something to hang around the dog's neck that is immediately perceivable as different by its weight, shape, or smell. Use this during work periods and remove it for play, and your dog will have no trouble recognizing when it's time to get down to business.

BIRD-DOG DUMMY

You can make an effective dummy for a young bird dog out of an old pair of socks. Fill one sock with the feathers of the kind of bird you hunt most, then pull the second sock over the first from the opposite direction. Sew or tie the two socks together. The dummy will smell like a bird, will familiarize the pup with the feel of feathers, and will be soft in the dog's mouth.

KILLER HEARTWORMS

Heartworms are microscopic parasites transmitted by the bite of a mosquito that can cause death in a dog within six to nine months. They were once common only in the South but now occur nationwide. Death results from an accumulation of the parasites in the dog's heart and pulmonary artery, which in turn causes cardiac collapse and severe damage to the liver and kidneys. Symptoms of the infection include shortness of breath, coughing, and weakness, though by the time the symptoms appear, it is usually too late to save the animal. Preventive care is the best cure, including annual checkups and preventive medicine prescribed by a vet, which must be continued on a daily basis until the first frosts of fall put an end to mosquito activity.

*Hunting song**

Black hound and blue hound,
   Faint hound and true hound,
Follow the huntsman
   At break of the day.

Gray hound and white hound,
   Scent hound and sight hound,
Cast for the trail,
   Then sing out and away.

Somewhere the rabbit starts.
   Somewhere a partridge darts.
Somewhere the doe and hart
   Spring from the cry.

Somewhere the fox is still,
   Waiting below the hill,
Nose on his paws until
   Hounds have gone by.

White hound and gray hound,
   Go hound and stay hound,
Lost is the scent now,
   The fox is away.

Blue hound and black hound,
   Turn and go back hound.
Hunting is over.
   And so is the day.
          —Jane Yolen

* This poem was brought to our attention by Sabrina Spannagel, age nine. We couldn't resist its simple eloquence or her excellent taste in poetry.

"Fox-hunting with hounds . . . is one of the purest of sports; it has real split-rail flavor.
. . . The fox is deliberately left unshot, hence ethical restraint is also present."
—Aldo Leopold

203

THE GREATEST HUNTER I EVER MET
by Jack Samson

I doubt if I will ever hunt again with another living thing that shared the same intense love of the sport as a German shorthair pointer I once owned. When he first came into my life—trembling with uncertainty, wetting the floor whenever anyone reached for him, and smelling of that ice-cream-carton-clean odor of puppyhood—he showed few signs of becoming anything special in the hunting field. All ears, frantically wagging rear end, and stub tail, and with paws as big as those of a full-grown springer spaniel, Moshi was only interested in eating constantly and chewing up every piece of furniture in the house.

The name was only meant to be temporary, but it stuck. Having just returned from five years in the Orient as a foreign correspondent covering, among other things, the Korean War for UP (before it became UPI), I spoke fairly fluent Japanese. Moshi—used repeatedly by the Japanese in a telephone conversation—was about as close to "hey, you" as I could come up with for a name.

The ungainly pointer—from good field stock lines—grew like a weed and at the end of the first year weighed almost 70 pounds. From the time I threw the first stick for that pup to retrieve, it seemed as though he knew what the game was all about. He would point robins in the yard, sparrows on bushes, and constantly had his nose stuck in clumps of grass, thickets, or down holes looking for something—anything—to hunt. His first reaction to the sound of a shotgun going off was one of sheer elation, like a small boy hearing his first firecracker on the Fourth of July. The only problem I ever had in his training was to make him hold to a point. He was so intense about hunting that he would try to creep up on the game, after coming to a point, in order to try to pounce on it. After he understood that the gun did a lot better job of bringing down the birds than he could, he would wait until birds flushed. But I never did succeed in training him to stay put after the gun went off. I don't think an anchor chain would have stopped him after he saw a bird get hit. He would not chase birds far that were not hit—perhaps 50 yards before returning with almost a disgusted glance at me—but few wounded birds ever came down within half a mile of where they were shot that they didn't find that big pointer waiting for them. I didn't care. Maybe it wasn't the best form in the world,

but Moshi and I shared such an enthusiasm for the hunt that we really didn't care what anybody thought of his style.

I once watched the big pointer sitting—trembling all over with cold and excitement—waiting for another duck to fly in, having just brought in a full-grown Canada goose through a swift-flowing river filled with ice floes the size of rugs. The gent who owned the black Lab (which had twice refused to breast the river current for the same goose) had just made his first tentative offer to buy my hunting friend. Neither he nor anybody else ever had that much money.

I had trouble keeping the shorthair close to me, that's true. They like to range wide and run fast. But I have seen him come to a sliding stop in midstride and point a covey of scaled quail that was 30 yards upwind from him on a dry, windy day. And by the time I got to him he was still on point, but 10 feet from the covey.

But I think his greatest joy was in decoying crows. He had a special hatred for crows. They are smart birds and always post sentinels. He had spent many a fruitless hour

stalking several dozen crows who were feeding in the middle of a field only to be foiled in his last-second dash by the croak of a sentinel on a nearby tree. And to add to his humiliation, crows would dive-bomb him all the way back across the field, cawing raucously as he made his retreat. I was leaning against an apple tree one afternoon, waiting for mourning doves to pass overhead during the first week of the dove season in New Mexico. I had collected about four birds with the light side-by-side .410, and the shooting was a bit slow. Moshi had decided to range about and look for something more interesting to do than to retrieve my occasional falling dove. I didn't mind. The day was cool, and both the big dog and I were enjoying our own brand of hunting. Idly I watched the pointer stalking his usual bevy of crows, certain how it would all turn out. Predictably, the dog made his last-second charge and just as predictably the crows rose in a black cloud over his head as he slid to a stop, frustrated, amid the furrows of the cornfield. Again the crows dived until he gave up leaping at them and streaked back toward the orchard where I was. A long, winding, dusty farm road ran the length of the orchard and past the tree where I stood. The pointer, certainly not by plan but probably because the footing was more suitable for running, turned and ran down the narrow road toward me. A dozen crows flew just above and behind him, and several kept up the cawing and diving harassment as the big dog approached. I flipped off the safety and, as the pointer streaked by me on the way toward the house, swung ahead of two crows and knocked both end over end to the earth. The look on that pointer's face, after he had come to a sliding stop in a cloud of dust, was incredible. He might just as well have said to me, Cripes, boss! I think we have the makings of a pretty good thing here!

After thoroughly shaking and chewing up his two dead and hated tormentors, the pointer had learned his favorite game. He would make sure I was going to stay put in some hidden spot; then he would start out to find a flock of crows. It might not work every day or even every week, but it worked well enough to make him a very happy bird dog whenever he conned a few crows into chasing him home. The crows finally caught on—toward the end of the winter—when they finally noticed their ranks were becoming somewhat thinned, but the pointer always knew there would be a crop of new, stupid crows each year and that was good enough for him. And each time he succeeded in

bringing the noisy black birds close to me—each time they would hit the ground with a satisfying thud—my hunting friend would sit on his haunches, let his tongue loll out, and actually grin, as only a dog can grin. If he had ever learned to wink, I think he would have done that.

A fool shot that pointer with a .22 caliber short. It entered his back and went into a lung; it took the big dog two days to die. The hole was so tiny that I didn't even know he had been shot and was treating him for a bad cold when he died in his sleep.

Bill Tarrant, one of the best writers I know, said it best: "I've seen men bury their dogs and not be able to stand up to leave the grave. And I've seldom known a man to mention a dog's parting."

Well, I guess there is an exception to every rule.

Jack Samson is editor of *Field & Stream*. A newsman, foreign correspondent, writer, and editor, having contributed to major outdoor magazines and written an outdoor column for the AP for nine years, he was a 1960 Nieman Fellow at Harvard and is the author of half a dozen books on the outdoors.

THE HOMING INSTINCT

Whether your hunting dog lives in a kennel or in your house, he should have a "place." It might be an old blanket or a scatter rug. Our favorite is a 2-by-3-foot chunk of shag carpet, because it cleans easily; just beat it against a tree.

Not only does such a "place" keep your dog comfortable and your house clean. If you take it along on hunting trips, the dog will lie on it just like at home—in the back of a station wagon, in the corner of a duck blind, or next to the door of a motel room.

Call the rug "your place," and the dog will come to learn that "go to your place" means lie down on the rug, wherever it might be. The rug will also prove invaluable should the dog ever become lost. Leave it in the vicinity where you last saw the dog, and he'll eventually home in on it and wait for your return.   —N.S.

Good Visibility for Hunting Safety

This flourescent red collar means other hunters can see your dog easily, even in thick brush. It comes in 13-to-17-inch sizes for $3.25; 19-to-25-inch sizes for $3.95. Sporting Dog Specialties, Inc., P.O. Box 68, Spencerport, NY 14559.

GUN DOG
by Richard A. Wolters

New York: E. P. Dutton & Co., $7.95.

This book describes Wolters's "rapid training method," which the author claims can turn out a good gun dog in a few months with minutes-a-day training. Good, clear photos and writing. The book has drawn some criticism from traditional trainers, however.   —N.S.

Acme Dog Whistles

Called the Thunderer, though it just whistles, this comes in three sizes: small, medium, and large, priced at $1.00, $1.25, and $1.50 each. Cork ball, nickel-plated lanyard ring. Can be heard a hell of a lot farther than your voice. Lanyards, $1.00 each. Sporting Dog Specialties, Inc., P.O. Box 68, Spencerport, NY 14559.

"The mellow notes of the hunter's horn over the hills so clear,
The voices by the breezes borne are the sounds of the hounds I hear."
—*Children's nursery song*

205

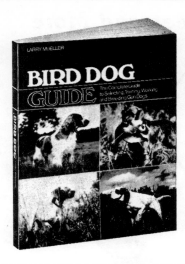

BIRD DOG GUIDE
by Larry Mueller

Chicago: Follett Publishing Company, $6.95 (paper).

This book deals with just about all phases of the selection, training, and care of a hunting dog. It also has info on field trials and transporting dogs and has a directory of dog clubs and organizations. Some of the information is general, as it only could be unless you'd want to end up with a volume the size of *War and Peace*, but the author touches all bases and gives good directions in which to go. Especially recommended for the hunter who is just considering the purchase of his first dog.

BEST WAY TO TRAIN YOUR GUN DOG
by Bill Tarrant

New York: David McKay Company, $9.95.

Bill Tarrant says that dog-trainer-extraordinary Delmar Smith, five-time winner of both the national open and U.S. open Brittany Championships, is the best friend a dog ever had. What would Smith's methods do for your dog, your hunting, your field-trial aspirations? "If you want to train like a pro, you've got to think like a dog," says Smith. Then, in colorful Oklahoma speech, Smith explains exactly how to go about it, and photos by Bill Tarrant illustrate the fine points.

In his earlier horse training, Smith learned the secrets of what he calls "point of contact, repetition, association." He takes the mystery out of how to apply these lessons to dog training and passes along advice on problem situations.

Even if you live in the suburbs or in the city, not ideal places for training a dog, you'll be surprised by how much of the Delmar Smith method you can use. His method gets outstanding results without shouting, stomping, or striking the dog.

TRAINING YOUR RETRIEVER
by James Lamb Free

New York: Coward, McCann & Geoghegan, $8.95.

American Field calls this book "The classic work in its field," and a lot of trainers agree. My one criticism is Free's all-work-and-no-play approach, which emphasizes the "master" in a dog-handler relationship. I prefer dogs that are companions as well as servants, and I have found my "companion" dogs to be capable of understanding and responding to an enormous vocabulary.

CHARLES MORGAN ON RETRIEVERS
edited by Ann Fowler and D. K. Walters

Stonington, Conn.: October House, $17.50.

This is another classic that in many ways is 180 degrees from Free's work. While there is ample information and advice on all sorts of training problems, Morgan's is a more philosophic, subjective approach to training and dogs. Reading Charles Morgan is like talking to an old friend. If dogs were polled, I'm sure they'd choose Morgan over Free 3 to 1.   —N.S.

Other Specialty Books*

• *Spaniels for Sport* by Talbot Radcliffe. New York: Howell Book House, $8.95.
• *Your Vizsla* by John X. Strauz and Joseph F. Cunningham. Fairfax, Va.: Denlinger's Pubs., $6.95.
• *Your German Shorthaired Pointer* by Gertrude Dapper. Fairfax, Va.: Denlinger's Pubs., $9.95.
• *The New Complete Beagle* by Henry J. Colombo and others. New York: Howell Book House, $5.95.

• *The Complete Brittany Spaniel* by Maxwell Riddle. New York: Howell Book House, $9.95.
• *Wing and Shot* (pointers) by Robert G. Wehle. Scottsville, N.Y.: Country Press, $8.50.
• *Training Pointers and Setters* by J. B. Maurice. Cranbury, N.J.: A. S. Barnes & Co., $6.95.

* These books are available from Tidewater Specialties, 430 Swann Avenue, Alexandria, VA 22301.

Tidewater specializes in dog-handling products with a homey touch. Oh, they have a bunch of electric gadgets, but their real standouts are handmade leather lanyards and collars, do-it-yourself whelping box kits, and handmade natural wool sweaters.

The catalog is worthy of special recognition in that it's an artistic departure from the standard slick paper-and-product

TIDEWATER SPECIALTIES CATALOG

photo layout. Products are virtually all illustrated with sketches, and descriptive literature is hand-lettered. It's the kind of catalog that's nice to have around and nice

to look through, reminiscent in tone of the sense of class that goes with landed gentry and Establishment East Coast gunning.

Selected hunting items are catalogued as well (turkey, deer, and duck hunting items, again with the handmade touch) and ceramic coffee mugs with bird prints on the side. Nice things, nice catalog. Free from Tidewater Specialties, 430 Swann Avenue, Alexandria, VA 22301.

Retriever-Trainer Sends Dummy 200 Feet and More

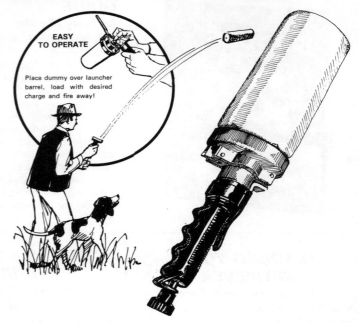

This gadget is a super training device for retrievers. It consists of a soft canvas dummy with a metal female receptacle inside. The dummy fits over a male dowel with a hole in it. The dowel is affixed to a hand grip and firing device that breaks in the middle, a little like a double-barreled shotgun.

Nest the dummy in place, insert a .22 blank in the chamber, latch the firing mechanism closed, and you're ready to shoot. The blank is fired by pulling and releasing a spring-loaded plunger in the handle. Expanding gases pass through the male hole and send the dummy up and away.

It's an invaluable training device, because it throws a dummy much farther than you can by arm (short throws "train" a dog not to range out) and because the dog learns to associate a shot with a retrieve. I used this successfully and quickly to remind my Lab that he shouldn't break at the sound of a shot but should sit, watch, and wait.

A few tricks to the use of this device: the male and female parts must be kept perfectly clean or you won't get optimum range. A light spray of WD-40 on the male part gives you an extra 50 feet. If you hold the trainer with thumb pointing to the rear and your arm across your body, you'll get even greater range, because there is less recoil absorption by your arm. Incidentally, these things do kick (especially with the maximum loads), so get a firm grip and keep your thumb away from the base of firing mechanism. A highly recommended training device. Price: $49.95;

shoulder pad for this trainer, which gives even greater range and accuracy and allows one-hand firing, $29.50. Sporting Dog Specialties, Inc., P.O. Box 680, Spencerport, NY 14559.

ELECTRONIC SHOCKING COLLAR

An electronic shocking collar is a tremendous training aid for several reasons. Most important, corrective punishment is immediate. You push a button on the transmitter, which activates a high-voltage/low-amperage shock from the special collar, and the dog is jolted (the shock is roughly comparable to the spark from a spark plug—it doesn't really hurt, but it sure gets attention). This eliminates chasing the dog or calling it to you, and the resultant time lag that may confuse a dog's association with a certain act's being a no-no.

The second plus is tied somewhat into the first. The dog doesn't associate the punishment with you directly. You don't develop a dog that runs away or cowers when you move to correct it.

Finally, there's no leash to hassle with. The dog is free to run, and, again, there is no association with "now I can do as I please," which often occurs when you remove a leash from a leash-trained dog.

These shocking collars are not without fault, though, and neither are the dog handlers who use them. They can be mistakenly used to teach rather than as a strong corrective measure when a dog is plainly misbehaving. These things don't teach, they punish. And if you use them too frivolously, the dog will either become mean or it will cower and hide every time you work it.

Then, too, some of the cheaper training collars are activated by extraneous radio signals, or they short-circuit when wet. It's fair to project that this kind of random shocking will drive a dog bananas; exactly this technique has been used to create neuroses in rats.

What's the answer? Get the best shocking device on the market and use it judiciously. The one that has been recommended to us most by dog trainers and game preserve operators is made by Tri-Tronics, 7060 East 21st Street, Tucson, AZ 85731. Price: $295.00.

TROUBLES WITH BIRD DOGS . . . AND WHAT TO DO ABOUT THEM
by George Bird Evans

New York: Winchester Press, $10.00.

Subtitled *Training Experiences with Actual Dogs Under the Gun*, this is a how-to book, but it won't tell you how to train bird dogs. It will tell you how to train *one* bird dog—yours. George Bird Evans has been breeding and training his own line of bird dogs—one at a time—for close to half a century. Experience has taught him that no two dogs are alike, and that each dog must be custom-trained for the job he is to do.

Troubles with Bird Dogs is based on case histories of dogs the author has gunned over, loved, and understood, and of dogs and friends who brought their problems to him: problems and solutions considered from the viewpoints of both the dog and the gunner. It is about natural hunters and problem dogs; finished bird dogs and green pups; specialists on grouse, on pheasant, on woodcock, and on quail. Evans also covers bird dog breeding in detail, discussing bloodlines, the complexities of mating, and whelping. And there is plenty of advice on how to keep your dog in top physical and emotional health.

Convinced that the individual bird dog requires treatment as personal as a prescription, and that the gunner's style shapes the style of the dog, Evans offers a training philosophy that blends his own ideas with methods proved effective for as long as a hundred years. His clear, commonsense advice is presented in the engaging, literate style that readers will remember from *The Upland Shooting Life* and his other books. And it's all illustrated with scores of helpful photographs.

In reading *Troubles with Bird Dogs*, you will understand why the author has had a succession of brilliant bird dogs, and why they don't just happen. And whether you're starting a puppy, trying to cope with an unusual bird dog psychosis, or dreaming of that champion in the future or past, you will learn how to develop a dog worthy of the bird.

Starter Pistols for Dog Training

Precise Imports is a good source for a wide variety of starter pistols. Styles include six- and seven-shot revolvers and eight-shot automatics. The revolvers are available in swing-out or break-cylinder types, and all guns take standard .22 crimped blanks.

Precise also catalogs Big Boom cap pistols, which make a lot more bang than the standard kid stuff and accept 12-shot cap rings. Price range: $4.00–$21.00. Free catalog. Precise Imports Corp., 3 Chestnut Street, Suffern, NY 10901.

Sure Cure for Barking Dogs

A barking dog is a nuisance to you and to your neighbors, and it's a hard trait to break. I had one such animal and finally broke him of barking by perching a bucket of water on top of his kennel, with a long rope that led to the house. As soon as he barked, I yanked it and doused him. It took three such experiences and he quit.

A much easier and more reliable way to break a dog of barking is with an antibark collar. These collars contain a battery, coil, and positive/negative terminals. The throat vibrations of a barking dog close the circuit, the electricity from the batteries is upped in voltage as it passes through the coil, and the terminals pressing against the dog's neck release a charge about like that from a spark plug. Dogs get the idea very quickly, for that first bark is usually a memorable cacophony of growls, ruffs, and squeals.

If you have hunting partners with the same problem, you can all chip in on one collar and a dummy collar of the same weight and shape for each dog. After a dog gets the idea that he'll get zapped every time he barks, these dummies usually work as well as the real thing. Prices: Bark-trainer collar, $39.95; dummy collar, $3.95. Relco Products, P.O. Box 10563, Houston, TX 77018.
—N.S.

Bird Launchers for Training Pointers

Bird launchers are containing boxes into which pen-raised quail are put. The box is then hidden in cover, and the dog works it up just like a wild bird. At a manual tug of a lanyard, or a foot trip or electronic signal, the bird is literally launched into the air by a spring device.

Bird launchers are excellent tools for steadying dogs on point and to wing and shot, whether they're pups just learning or older dogs who usually could stand some brushing up at the start of a season.

Tidewater Specialties, 430 Swann Avenue, Alexandria, VA 22301, catalogs an inexpensive bird launcher (quail-sized) that prevents the bird from fluttering when it's inside, thus giving away its position by sound when a dog should be using its nose. It may be activated by a foot trip, lanyard, or the crack of a training whip. Price: $19.95.

Tri-Tronics, 7060 East 21st Street, Tucson, AZ 85731, makes a far more sophisticated launcher, which is triggered by a radio signal from a distance of up to 500 feet away. It may be ordered in quail, pigeon, chukar, or pheasant sizes, and it throws birds 5 to 6 feet into the air. Price: $219.00.

Where to Buy Pen-Raised Pheasants, Quail, etc., for Training

Most shooting preserves either raise their own birds (which they'll sell you) or they can order extra birds for you with their batch. You can get a directory of shooting preserves from the North American Game Breeders and Shooting Preserve Association, ℅ John M. Mullin, Route 1, Box 28, Goose Lake, IA 52750.

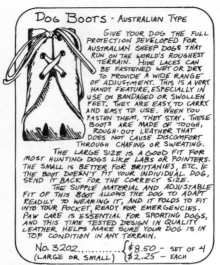

DOG BOOTS - AUSTRALIAN TYPE

GIVE YOUR DOG THE FULL PROTECTION DEVELOPED FOR AUSTRALIAN SHEEP DOGS THAT RUN ON THE WORLD'S ROUGHEST TERRAIN. HIDE LACES CAN BE FASTENED WET OR DRY TO PROVIDE A WIDE RANGE OF ADJUSTMENT. THIS IS A VERY HANDY FEATURE, ESPECIALLY IN USE ON BANDAGED OR SWOLLEN FEET. THEY ARE EASY TO CARRY AND EASY TO USE. WHEN YOU FASTEN THEM, THEY STAY. THESE BOOTS ARE MADE OF TOUGH, ROUGH-OUT LEATHER THAT DOES NOT CAUSE DISCOMFORT THROUGH CHAFING OR SWEATING.

THE LARGE SIZE IS A GOOD FIT FOR MOST HUNTING DOGS LIKE LABS OR POINTERS. THE SMALL IS BETTER FOR BRITTANIES, ETC. IF THE BOOT DOESN'T FIT YOUR INDIVIDUAL DOG, SEND IT BACK FOR THE CORRECT SIZE.

THE SUPPLE MATERIAL AND ADJUSTABLE FIT OF THIS BOOT ALLOWS THE DOG TO ADAPT READILY TO WEARING IT, AND IT FOLDS TO FIT INTO YOUR POCKET, READY FOR EMERGENCIES. PAW CARE IS ESSENTIAL FOR SPORTING DOGS, AND THIS TIME TESTED DESIGN IN QUALITY LEATHER HELPS MAKE SURE YOUR DOG IS IN TOP CONDITION IN ANY TERRAIN.

No. 3202 .... $8.50 - SET OF 4
(LARGE OR SMALL) $2.25 - EACH

Boots and Salve for Footsore Fidos

Prickly pear cactus, sand burrs, shale rock, and sharp stones are all hard on Fido's feet. Keep your dog working and happy with dog booties made of rough-out leather (leather is generally agreed to be better than plastics or rubber since it chafes least and breathes). The hide laces can be fastened wet or dry, a handy feature in case of swollen or bandaged feet. Available in small or large. With the lace adjustment, these two sizes will fit all hunting dogs this side of an Irish Wolfhound. Price: $8.50 for a set of four booties or $2.25 each.

If your dog is just plain tenderfooted, Blue Foot pad toughener will condition the feet. This stuff is also a good antiseptic for cuts, bites, and bruises. Price: $4.00. Both from Tidewater Specialties, 430 Swann Avenue, Alexandria, VA 22301.

Doggie Dooley Destroys Dog Droppings

If you keep your dog in a kennel, or if you have a small yard, this device provides a place for dog droppings. It is a bucket-with-cover container that you bury in the ground. An enzyme converter that you add weekly reduces the droppings to a mulch, which is absorbed by the soil.

Checking with Doggie Dooley owners, we find general agreement that the thing works, *but* that its capacity seems suited to a miniature poodle. If you've got a big, booming black Lab, better buy two. Price: $13.95. Huron Products Corp., 555 Moore Avenue, Bellvue, OH 44811.

Sporting Dog Specialties Catalog

This outfit has about everything conceivable in the dog products line. Besides collars, kennels, training scents, training dummies, training books, vitamins, live-bird release traps, calls, whistles, dog portraits, doghouses, dog clippers, and beer mugs with dog and bird pictures on them, they offer an aerosol "bullshit repellent." There's no guarantee (probably because there are uses to which the spray could be put over which they have no control), but it's supposed to be good for hunters and fishermen, as well as most public figures. Only $1.69 a can or a dozen for $12.95, "for those in real need." The other products in the catalog are all good too. Sporting Dog Specialties, Inc., P.O. Box 68, Spencerport, NY 14559. —J.B.

Canine Carrier

This is a dog carrier that mounts on a trailer hitch. It isn't a trailer, so it doesn't need to be licensed. Made of aluminum with a steel base, it is fully weatherproof and ventilated. It is low enough so that it doesn't interfere with rear-mirror vision and light enough for one man to mount. Prices start at $99.95 for a single dog model and go up to $199.95 for an insulated two-dog model. Quali-Craft Industries, Inc., P.O. Box 21505, St. Louis, MO 63132. —J.B.

DICK CEPEK, INC.

CAR VENTILATOR

If you leave your dog inside a locked car, always crack a window or two to provide ventilation. An unventilated car left in the hot sun can generate interior temperatures in excess of 150 degrees, which can cause death or brain damage to dogs.

The Levergap is an expandable window screen with grooved frames that fits in the top of car windows from 16 to 60 inches wide. It provides plenty of ventilation, while preventing the dog from jumping out. Compressed, it's small enough to fit inside your glove compartment. Price: $13.95. Dick Cepek, Inc., 9201 California Avenue, South Gate, CA 90280.

BIRLAUF & STEEN, INC.

Wikjon Portable Kennels

These are rugged steel kennels that are assembled by means of pipe clamps. They can be ordered either as complete kennels or in pieces, so that you can add on to the kennel. A kennel 4 feet high and 4 by 6 feet on the base runs $146.26 with top. This is made of galvanized pipe and wire. A 4- by 6-foot side panel alone is $28.82. Gates and isolation panels (solid steel) are available also, with the isolation panels costing about twice as much as the wire. All joints are welded, as are the latches on the doors. Rates for shipment run $7.00–$14.00 per 100 pounds, with most around $10.00. (The kennel described above weighs 102 pounds.) Wikjon Industries, P.O. Box 12212, Denver, CO 80212. —J.B.

Ralston-Purina Handbook of Dog Care

This book is put out by the people who make Purina Dog Chow, and though it's not primarily directed toward the hunter, it has some good information in it, especially concerning your dog's diet. It also has some basic obedience-training techniques, a summary of breeds and types of dogs, and other information that may be useful, especially to the beginning dog owner. Of course, it recommends Ralston-Purina products, which is all right as they are excellent, especially their High Protein Dog Meal, which is fine for any hunting dog during the hunting season. There are also eight 5-cent-off-on-dog-food coupons in the back of the book, so you get back the 25-cents-plus stamp that you have to send to *Dog Care Handbook*, P.O. Box 9466, St. Paul, MN 55177, to get the book.   —J.B.

Heater Prevents Dog Water Freeze-up

If you live in a cold climate, you can eliminate the work of breaking ice each morning with the Blue Devil. It plugs into a regular electrical outlet and fits all sizes of bowls and buckets. It keeps water around 50 degrees F and shuts off when the bowl is drained dry. Price: $28.50. Nelson Manufacturing Company, P.O. Box 636, Cedar Rapids, IA 52406.

CHESAPEAKE BAY RETRIEVERS

If you're interested in owning a Chessie, you can find the breeder nearest to you by writing to the American Chesapeake Club, P.O. Box 252, Sussex, WI 53089, for a free pamphlet and list of breeders.

AUTOMATIC DOG FEEDER

If your hunting dog lives in a kennel, here's a good gadget for those times when you're away. The Dog-O-Matic feeder holds 25 pounds of dry dog food that's fed to Fido automatically. The food tray can be cleaned, and the feeder can be used for limited feeding if your hound is an inside dog.

All in all, the Dog-O-Matic stacks up as a good way to get the mess and bulk of dog feeding and food out of the house and into your yard or pen. Price: $39.95. Walnut Hill Farms, P.O. Box 130, Cross Anchor, SC 29331.

Sooper Dooper Pooper Scooper

This aptly named little number is a shovel designed to pick up dog droppings. It works on a scissors principle, with the shovel blades at right angles to the opposing shafts. Handy if you've got a pen or enclosed yard, and a good gift for the man who has everything. Price: $5.95. Scooper Company, P.O. Box 22115, Indianapolis IN 46222.

HUNTING DOG MAGAZINE

There are a lot of dog magazines around, but this is the only one we've been able to find that's devoted exclusively to hunting dogs: bird dogs, hounds, and retrievers. (Huskies and poodles need not apply.) It is also an excellent source for dog training aids, kennel supplies, etc. Price: $9.00 for twelve issues. *Hunting Dog Magazine*, 9714 Montgomery Road, Cincinnati, OH 45242.

Automatic Water Shut-off for Kennel Dogs

Do you feel like Gunga Din toward the end of a long, hot day? Stop carrying water to your kennel; pipe it in and regulate the level with this automatic dog waterer. It shuts off when the trough is full and reactivates when the water level gets low. Comes with a 2½-foot hose that screws into a standard threaded faucet. Price: $6.98. G. Q. F. Manufacturing Company, P.O. Box 8152, Savannah, GA 31402.

Prefab Doghouse

This is a one-piece molded ABS plastic doghouse with a raised floor. The floor has a drain plug, which means you can thoroughly hose down the inside without a lot of hassle.

The house measures 40 by 34 inches and is 22 inches high. The port size is optional; it can be cut for large or small dogs. It is available in green, blue, or yellow, and it will fit into the rear of most station wagons. The company claims it's large enough for a man should you fall into disfavor with your wife. Price: $39.95. Ferguson Manufacturing Company, P.O. Box 408, Richmond, MO 64085.

Dog Training Kit with Special Scents

Get into the basics of dog training with this beginner's kit. It contains a bottle of scent, a training drag, a whistle, and an instruction booklet on how to use all these items.

When ordering, specify the scent you want your dog to know, love, and hunt: pheasant, quail, grouse, rabbit, duck, coon, squirrel, fox, skunk, bobcat, coyote, bear, lion, possum, or mink. Price: $6.95. Cabela's, 812 13th Avenue, Sidney, NE 69162

Stainless Steel Feeding Pans

There are all kinds of clever-looking dog feeding dishes around, most of them designed to keep a dog from tipping them over and most of them impossible to really clean thoroughly. These simple stainless steel pans are reasonably stable, and cleanup is as easy as doing a kitchen dish. Price: 2- to 5-quart sizes, $2.95 to $4.95. Sporting Dog Specialties, Inc., P.O. Box 68, Spencerport, NY 14559.

LEATHER LEADS

These shorter leads are especially useful for early obedience training. In lengths from 12 to 24 inches, priced from $3.50 to $6.00, they are nylon-stitched, with heavy snaps. Sporting Dog Specialties, Inc., P.O. Box 68, Spencerport, NY 14559.

BROWNING KENNELS

This is an idea that's long overdue. Browning, the gun people, are now in the dog breeding and training business. They have kennels located 35 miles north of Salt Lake City, where they'll board or train your dog and where they breed and raise their own champion stock for sale.

Pups and started and finished gun dogs (mostly Labradors) are for sale by mail order, and you get a two-week trial period on started and finished dogs.

Dogs are trained with live mallards and pheasants under actual field conditions on a 640-acre tract of land. Brad Smith supervises the training. Boarding, $2.00 daily; training, $150.00 monthly. Pups and started and finished dogs priced individually. Current price list available upon request from Browning Kennels, Route 1, Morgan, UT 84050.

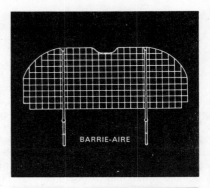

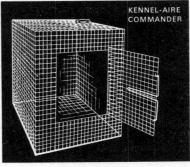

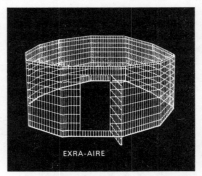

Kennel-Aire Portable Kennels

These folks specialize in foldaway dog kennels—panels of stout wire mesh that hook together to form a box and lie flat when disassembled.

They have about every shape of kennel you can think of—for the back of a station wagon, an octagonal running area, a whelping pen, quadraplex pens, pens that stand up off the ground—and accessory material such as cushions for the bottom of the pen, watertight covers, and steel stakes to anchor pen walls to the ground.

Some typical prices: a 42-inch-high 4-by-8-foot enclosure, $59.75; an adjustable barrier to keep dogs in the rear of a station wagon, $34.95; and a full enclosure 48 by 36 by 24 inches, with a Masonite floor, $63.95. Free catalog. Kennel-Aire Mfg. Co., 725 North Snelling Avenue, St. Paul, MN 55104.

"It is said the bluebird is declining in numbers. . . . But it would not be so if the bluebird weighed three pounds and held well to a pointing dog."
—Joe Linduska

211

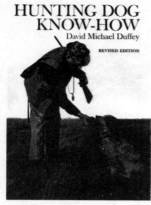

HUNTING DOG KNOW-HOW
and
HUNTING HOUNDS
by David Michael Duffey

New York: Winchester Press, $6.95 each.

Dave Duffey's credentials to discuss both these subjects are as impressive as his Irish wit. In addition to his position as dog editor of *Outdoor Life*, he runs a game breeding farm and dog kennels. Dave spends most of his time with dogs, and these books reflect that kind of intimacy.

Hunting Dog Know-How is an all-inclusive work that offers advice and counsel on the breed that will best suit your tastes and how to train that dog for hunting once you have made your selection.

The author also discusses problems that might arise and how to cure them—the gun-shy dog, blinking, hardmouthing—and with characteristic candor tells you what to do when his suggested training procedures just don't work.

There are a lot of other bits of information and opinion in these pages: the advantages and disadvantages of having a hunter who's also a house pet, the field trial dog versus the gun dog . . . all in all a thorough exposition of what a dog owner needs to know about his favorite hunting partner.

Hunting Hounds is subtitled *The History, Training and Selection of America's Trail, Tree, and Sight Hounds*, and that aptly describes this important work. There has probably been less written about hounds, in proportion to interest in them and use of them, than any of the other hunting dog classes. This book helps fill that void.

All types and breeds of hounds, from beagle to bear and boar dogs, are discussed, including information on the training, selection, and care of each species. A real help if you're a houn' dawg man, and entertaining reading as well.

LONG LEADS

These are made of nylon, ⅝ inch wide and 1200-pound test, for longer distance field training (quartering, etc.) and come in lengths of 9 to 40 feet, priced from $3.75 to $8.95. One end is looped for secure grip, the other is a heavy-duty snap. The nylon makes for light weight, which is helpful because the dog feels unencumbered. Many dogs associate the weight of a heavier cord with the control of the trainer and know when they are under control and when they aren't, which makes for entertaining times if they are prone to chase rabbits, etc. Sporting Dog Specialties, Inc., P.O. Box 68, Spencerport, NY 14559.

Sporting Dog Safety Collar

Made of 1-inch latigo leather and rust-proof rivets, this has a heavy-duty O-ring at the back of the dog's neck—a handy spot to snap a lead or leash to. No D-ring, so there's less chance of the dog's getting hung up on a fence or in the brush. Sturdy enough for the biggest dogs. Sizes 15 through 25 inches, $3.25 each or three for $8.50. Sporting Dog Specialties, Inc., P.O. Box 68, Spencerport, NY 14559.

Small-Game Knives and Pocketknives

These knives rate as small utility knives, tools designed for the dozens of light cutting jobs that arise daily in the field. They should be significantly smaller than a big-game knife; a 3-inch blade is plenty of steel, because a much longer spread between the hilt and the point becomes unwieldy in such delicate chores as gutting birds. To some extent, a one-piece sheath knife fits the hand a little better than a folder, so it is a more precise tool, but there is a lot to be said for the multiplicity of jobs that a three- or four-bladed folder is capable of.

The number and types of individual blades that may be incorporated into a pocketknife are many. Aside from cutting edges of various shapes, there are screwdriver blades, awls, wire strippers, can openers, scissors, and on and on. Whether these blades are worthwhile or are extra weight is strictly a matter of need. If you're mechanically inclined, you'll find use for a screwdriver. If you go camping, you'll praise a can opener.

I can, however, make a blanket recommendation for two cutting blades on a pocketknife. If you attend to them regularly, you will always have at least one edge that's razor sharp. I do prefer different tips on those blades, though, specifically a bluntish "spear" tip on one blade for slicing and a "clip" or "long clip" on the second blade for puncturing.

There's a vast difference in cost between the least expensive and the most expensive pocketknives, and, like most things, you're paying for what you get. Cheap pocketknives will have blades of mild steel or a class of stainless that's too hard to sharpen. The bolster pin, the hinge upon which the blade swings, will usually be soft brass that is crimped or riveted in place. A good folder will have a blade of alloy steel and a nickel or stainless bolster pin, and the pin will be welded or forged to the bolster plate.

These features make the difference between a knife that will take and hold a critical edge and one that won't, and between a blade that will swing firm and true on its pin versus a pocketknife that will disintegrate into its component parts under heavy use.

Quality pocketknives range in price from $6.00 for a tiny penknife to $40.00 for a many-bladed folder. Some of the midrange manufacturers that combine excellence with a fair price include Buck, Case, Queen, Schrade, and Wenger.

—N.S.

BARLOW POCKETKNIFE

The Barlow pattern is one of the most popular ever conceived—popular because it's practical. The long clip (larger blade) is a good heavy-duty carver and whittler or gutter and skinner. The smaller pen blade is suited to delicate work. Both blades are housed in a frame that fits well in your hand or your pocket. Price: $8.75. Western Cutlery Co., 5311 Western Avenue, Boulder, CO 80302.

THE STOCKMAN'S KNIFE

The folding knife pattern called the Stockman is a worthy combination of blades for the bird and small-game hunter, and even for careful cutting chores on big game. The long-clip master blade is perfect for gutting small game and strong enough to sever wing and leg joints. The sheepfoot and coping secondary blades are suitable for fine skinning and cutting chores like the musk glands on deer and the well-attached hide of a squirrel. Price: $15.00. Buck Knives, P.O. Box 1267, El Cajon, CA 92022.

SMALL-GAME SHEATH KNIFE

The 3-inch blade on this sheath knife is a perfect length for cleaning ducks, upland birds, squirrels, and rabbits. It has an interesting and good-looking handle of alternating aluminum and black fiber disks and measures 7⅞ inches overall, with a tubular leather sheath. Price: $9.15. Western Cutlery Co., 5311 Western Avenue, Boulder, CO 80302.

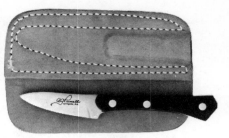

RUSSELL WOODSWALKER KNIFE

This small sheath knife is 6 inches overall with a 2¾-inch blade. It fits well in the hand (most short-blade one-piece knifes don't), and the blade has a conformation that's well suited to delicate cutting chores.

The sheath is unusual in that it's designed to be carried in your back pocket like a wallet. The Woodwalker knife and sheath carries comfortably afield, and it's a good combination for cleaning small game and for caping out trophy game heads. It will even gut a deer if no larger knife is available. Price: $14.00. A. G. Russell Co., 1705 Highway 71 North, Springdale, AR 72764.

Muskrat Pattern

This very simple pattern—two opposing long-clip blades—is an old-time favorite with trappers, who need a razor-sharp edge. Chrome-vanadium steel blades, bone stag handle, and honed edge. Price: $16.95. Case Cutlery, Bradford, PA 16701.

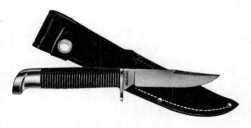

*"Very intensive management of game or fish lowers
the unit value of the trophy by artificializing it."*
—Aldo Leopold

213

SWISS ARMY KNIVES

Swiss Army knives are characterized by a multiplicity of blades and utensils contained within the sideplates. The many patterns available include things like toothpicks, tweezers, saws, scissors, corkscrews, files, can openers, and, of course, a knife blade or two.

The larger, more complex knives are heavy and cumbersome and only carry comfortably in a sheath, so there's always the question, "Do you really need all those blades?" Sam Curtis, a fellow writer and neighbor of mine, has a theory about these larger Swiss models. He senses a kind of camper's machismo inherent in a thirteen-bladed knife and cites one fall evening when he matched a fellow hunter blade for blade in a tingling showdown.

"Well, mine has a saw, does yours?"

"Sure does, and I've got a toothpick too" . . . etc.

Sam says the other guy finally won when he unfolded a combination screwdriver/magnifying glass that Sam couldn't match. Sam had plenty of screwdrivers but no magnifying glass.

If you'd just as soon pass up such nerve-racking contests, there are smaller Swiss Army knife patterns that, in truth, qualify as pocketknives. My favorite is the Tinker, a trim, six-bladed pattern that includes in its small frame two knife blades; a can opener, wire stripper, and file; a large and small screwdriver blade; an awl; and a Phillips screwdriver. This knife does a dozen jobs in the course of a day that would require my stopping to round up the appropriate tool. Afield it has fixed a cranky outboard, adjusted a jeep's carburetor, sewed up a pack strap and rifle sling that had come apart, and cleaned innumerable birds. Prices: $5.00 to $40.00, depending on the pattern. Precise Imports, 3 Chestnut Street, Suffern, NY 10901.

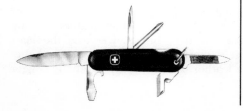

TRAIL CREEK FROM TRACK KNIVES

Somebody's thinking at Track. Here's a light, short-bladed, one-piece knife with a choil and finger cutout in the handle, where it should be. Every other knife I've seen has these in the blade, and they interfere with certain cuts. Choils and finger cutouts promote accurate, delicate blade-work. This knife should be ideal for cleaning small game and taxidermy preparation work.

High-carbon nickel-vanadium steel forms both blade and handle. This is truly a one-piece knife, and it's tough. Price: $39.95. Ithaca Gun Co., Inc., 123 Lake Street, Ithaca, NY 14850.

AMERICAN WILDLIFE BIRD KNIFE

This is a pocketknife designed especially for the bird hunter. It is 3⅞ inches closed, with a turkish clip master blade. This blade is of sufficient length and strength to make cleaning incisions and to sever neck, wing, and leg joints.

The supplementary blade is a gut hook. This blade is inserted into a bird's anal vent and twisted a half turn. The hook snares the intestines. Remove it, and the full length of the intestines, and you have a field-dressed bird.

The American Wildlife knife is available with four game birds depicted on the sideplate epaulet: mallard, Canada goose, wild turkey, and ring-necked pheasant.

The quality of the metals used in blades, bolsters, and rivets is excellent. This is a good-looking, well-made knife at a surprisingly reasonable price: $15.00. Free catalog. Camillus Cutlery Co., Camillus, NY 13031.

BLADE SHAPES

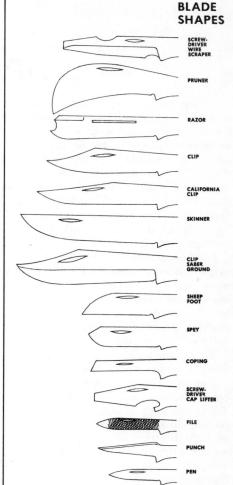

SCREWDRIVER WIRE SCRAPER

PRUNER

RAZOR

CLIP

CALIFORNIA CLIP

SKINNER

CLIP SABER GROUND

SHEEP FOOT

SPEY

COPING

SCREWDRIVER CAP LIFTER

FILE

PUNCH

PEN

CAN OPENER

CUTICLE

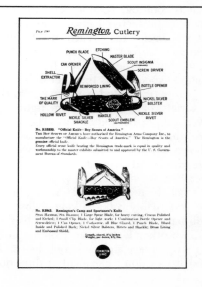

UPLAND CLOTHING

To some extent, upland gunning is simple sport (at least as far as equipment goes). You could easily don the same leisure clothes you wear around the house and yard on weekends and not be too far behind the hunter who has an extensive wardrobe carefully suited to the sport. Yet each item of outerwear has its purpose and, in its own way, makes a day afield more pleasurable. An upland jacket, for example, isn't as central to field hunting as a pair of waders are to decoy hunting, but it is comparable to tennis shorts. You can bat the ball around in slacks, but you feel—and perhaps perform—a lot better in the right clothing.

Field pants are the most important garment you might or might not wear, important because they'll probably get you more game. Conventional weaves of cotton, brushed denim, and wool are too soft and porous to turn back brush and briers. Consequently, when you wear this kind of clothing, you're discouraged from entering these coverts—and that's where the game likes to hole up.

There are three classes of field pants: canvas, canvas-fronted, and synthetic-fronted.

Canvas field pants are the traditional "tin" pants, so-called because they're stiff and noisy and wear a bit like tin. There are a lot of other names for this kind of material—poplin, duck, drill—but it is all very tightly woven cotton, so tight that prickles and spines can't poke through the weave. After they're well broken in, tin pants are comfortable, but it takes a lot of washings and wearing to create this condition of casual grace. During the break-in process they're stiff and hot, so much so, in fact, that if you choose to wear canvas field pants I'd recommend you wash them several times before wearing them.

Canvas-fronted pants are usually more comfortable because the basic garment is usually a light-weave material that is cool and flexible. The front of the pants amount to chaps of protective canvas, and the best pants will also have canvas backs that reach up to mid-calf. Canvas-fronted pants are also moisture-resistant. They won't soak up a light dew, but in heavy, wet brush they will eventually get soggy, especially as they get older.

Synthetic-fronted pants may afford brush protection with a variety of materials, from tight-weave nylon to vinyl or even rubber-backed canvas. The more waterproof the fronts are, the heavier and hotter the pants will be. My all-around choice is a tight-weave, heavy nylon. It's reasonably light, it breathes, and even if it gets wet, it doesn't retain water. Leather, incidentally, is probably the poorest choice of all. It's hot, heavy, holds water like a sponge, and while it will be undeniably good-looking at first, one day in heavy briers will have your trousers looking like a cat's scratching post.

Two other features to look for in field pants are buttons for suspenders and wide belt loops. These pants are heavy, and if you don't like pants riding down around your hips, you'll have to wear a wide belt, suspenders, or, better yet, both.

Field jackets and vests are next in order of importance. These, too, are generally made of a canvas-type material. They include pockets with shell loops and a game bag.

The shell-loop pockets are functional in several ways. They provide shells at the ready for fast reloading, but, more important, they keep them clean and well formed. Generally, this won't be the case when you carry shells in your pocket.

The game bag is the only practical way to tote game. You'll get tired of carrying it in hand (and probably miss some shots), and if you use one of the over-the-belt game carriers that hold birds by the head, you'll bloody your pants leg. Worse, you'll lose a lot of game. Bird heads have a habit of coming off in these, especially if you've wrung their necks, and you never notice them drop if you have more than one kill in the carrier.

If you plan to own just one shell holder–game carrier, you'll probably be best off with a vest. They are cut so that the same garment will fit reasonably well over either a T-shirt or a heavy jacket, so you can use it throughout the season. If you shoot both 12 and 20 gauge, however, you'll probably have to buy two vests. I've never found shell loops that won't stretch beyond the snugness required to hold a 20-gauge shell when you use them to hold 12s.

One important feature in either a vest or a jacket is a lined game bag that can be opened for cleaning. Generally, the most agreeable lining will be cloth-backed rubber, the same kind of material used in fishing boots. If you opt for a jacket, buy one with a soft collar or your neck will chafe.

Hat style is more critical than might be imagined. I've found nothing to surpass a jones-style cap, the traditional upland headgear. This kind of cap can best be described as a sailor's hat with the front of the brim straightened out. The peak shades your eyes from the sun, and the turned-up sides catch seed, leaves, and raindrops that would otherwise go down your neck. Buy one of these caps with ear flaps, and you'll have protection for that quarter on frosty mornings.

Gloves for upland gunning will probably be necessary, even when the weather's only cool. Your shotgun is always in hand, and the cold from the stock, and especially the receiver, will transfer to your hands and numb your fingers. You'll need sensitive gloves, too, for shots are usually fast and snappy, and you'll need feeling in your fingers to get the safety off and find the trigger. Soft leather driving gloves are the most sensitive, but they're also the least warm. For really cold mornings use a wool or synthetic-weave glove with a leather or tight-weave synthetic trigger finger.

"Be happy while y'er leevin,
For ye'r a lang time deid."
—Scottish motto

215

Eddie Bauer "Bone Dry" Hunting Pants

These are pretty handy in the wet brush often encountered in upland shooting and not too bad in wet reeds either. They are made of heavy canvas treated with Martexin (a plasticizing process, evidently) to protect from dampness, while allowing the fabric to breathe. Big, full front pockets and buttoned-flap back pockets; cut full for easy walking. I like them especially for upland hunting; they are a bit too noisy for big game.

Bauer also makes a Bone Dry hunting coat with game bag and shell loops. If you walk around much in damp forests, it might be handy. Coat comes in sizes 38–46; pants in waists 32–44 inches, 32-inch length only. Prices: coat, $36.50; pants, $21.00. Eddie Bauer, 1737 Airport Way South, Seattle, WA 98134.

KELTY RAIN CHAPS

Rain chaps are the answer to dewy or frosty mornings and soggy trouser legs. They roll up into a fist-size ball that is easily stowed in a hunting coat, and they can be slipped on over your pants without first removing your boots. The pair I tested, made by Kelty, were of urethane-coated nylon. It is reasonably tough material that should withstand a season's worth of punishment. The tight-weave fabric also does yeoman duty at turning back thistles and wild rose thorns.

Rain chaps will also be a benefit to waterfowlers if they are without wading boots and a rainstorm hits; ditto deer hunters on stand. They are not the thing for walking up on deer, though, because they're very noisy.

Rain chaps are available in green, red, and blue; medium or large sizes. Free catalog, though it's mostly hiking and backpacking gear. Price: $7.25. Kelty Mountaineering, 1801 Victory Boulevard, Glendale, CA 91201.   —N.S.

COVERT LEGGINGS

These are heavy-duty chap-type leggings that will keep you dry while you buck thick brush. They're made of dense-weave nylon, built to take heavy briers, and are urethane-coated. A pair weighs 7 ounces, and they roll up into a small enough package to carry comfortably in a game pouch. Sizes: 29-, 31-, and 33-inch inseams. Price: $19.95. Orvis, 10 River Road, Manchester, VT 05254.

Full Net Upland Vest

This is a remarkably well constructed and well thought out upland vest that is made of stout, close-weave netting material. The only solid cloth is in its two balloon breast pockets and in the shell-loop backing. There is a full net game bag in back and two front game pockets that may be opened wide or snapped closed. The vest is colored olive drab. It's an ideal garment for dove or duck hunting in very warm weather (I've used it extensively in Mexico), yet it's also practical for just about any other kind of hunting because of its light weight. It fits comfortably over camouflage jackets or heavy upland outerwear, and the netting allows undercolors to show through. Price: $19.95. Columbia Sportswear, 6600 North Baltimore Street, Portland, OR 97203.   —N.S.

An Upland Glove for Cold Weather

This 100 percent wool glove will keep you as warm as any with fingers. The leather palm and fingertips make for a sure grip on the stock of your shotgun, and the index finger and thumb have a special cloth covering that is touch sensitive. Price: $6.00. Duxbak, 825 Noyes Street, Utica, NY 13502.

SHELL BELT FOR SHOTGUNNING

One simple and inexpensive way to keep shells fresh, clean, and at the ready is to hold them in a shell belt. Available in blaze orange or marsh brown. Price: $4.00. Duxbak, 825 Noyes Street, Utica, NY 13502.

Fabric Waterproofing

If the weather is dewy, drizzly, or damp, spray your hunting jacket and pants with this silicone-based waterproofer. It doesn't really waterproof your garments, but they resist water absorption enough to make the effort worthwhile. Price: $1.80. Duxbak, 825 Noyes Street, Utica, NY 13502.

Nylon Chap Hunting Pants

These are the pants favored by Wayland Adams, quail hunter *par excellence*, who uses them all season long in the quixotic temperatures and murderous underbrush of western Oklahoma. They have four pockets, buttons for suspenders, a waterproof front, and a double seat. Like all sensible brush pants, they're faced on the rear of the calf, and they're even cuffed for good looks should you care to wear them to the office (he does on those mornings when the birds hold so well that he can't get home to change). Price: $29.00. Duxbak, 825 Noyes Street, Utica, NY 13502.

PA'TRIDGE VEST

The name is appropriate, because this vest has swatches of blaze orange, front and back, so you can be easily seen in dense partridge cover. Other features include a mesh back for ventilation, a drop-open rubberized game bag, and shell-loop pockets. Price: $27.75. L. L. Bean, Freeport, ME 04033.

Lightweight Shooting Gloves

Claybirders are gloves designed for trap and skeet shooters, but they're also ideal for cool upland mornings. The skin-thin leather transmits near-perfect sensitivity. Capeskin palms and backs with stretch nylon inserts between the two halves assure a tight fit. Two-tone brown or black. Price: $8.95. Bob Hinman Outfitters, 1217 West Glen, Peoria, IL 61614.

VINYL-FRONTED FIELD PANTS

The tough vinyl chaps on these pants are sure to turn back the worst bull briers and catclaws. They're made of cotton army duck, with a double seat, four pockets, and

Convertible Field Jacket for All-Season Hunting

A conventional cut is about the only conventional feature you'll find in this field jacket. It consists of a water-repellent nylon outer shell that may be worn as is on cool days. The shell includes sueded recoil pads on both shoulders, side vents, four patch pockets, epaulets, and shell loops.

When the weather turns cold, this garment has a zip-in lining filled with goose down. It comes with an optional down-filled hood and a zip-on-and-off rubberized game bag. Truly, a field jacket for all seasons. Prices: jacket (with lining), $74.95; hood, $11.95; game bag, $9.95. Cabela's, 812 13th Avenue, Sidney, NE 69162.

suspender buttons, and are hand washable. Price: $27.50. L. L. Bean, Freeport, ME 04033.

IRISH FIELD HAT

If you like to look tweedily British afield, here's the hat for you. It fairly whispers of driving grouse and fitching hares on the moors. Made of cotton polyester fabric, with a bucket-shaped crown and a 1⅞-inch double-stitched brim, you can wear it up, down, around, floppy, stiff, or whatever feels good. You can also carry it in your pocket. Price: $11.50 L. L. Bean, Freeport, ME 04033.

UPLAND HUNTING JACKET

This jacket is typical of field coats favored by upland gunners. It has a zipper-closed expansion game pocket that may be fully opened for cleaning or used for a dry place to sit. Also included are shell loops and adjustable cuffs. Cuffs and collar are corduroy-lined to discourage chafing. Price: $35.00. Duxbak, 825 Noyes Street, Utica, NY 13502.

"[Man] has not created, he has destroyed. Forests are fewer and fewer, rivers dry up, game becomes extinct, the climate is ruined, and every day the earth gets poorer and uglier."
—Chekhov, Uncle Vanya

217

TRAP-STYLE GAME BAG

Warm-weather shooters sometimes prefer the lightness and coolness of a skeet and trap-style shooting harness. This garment includes shell loops, waist pockets that may be used as a game bag, and a rear game pocket. Price: $16.00. Duxbak, 825 Noyes Street, Utica, NY 13502.

CLASSIC HUNTING VEST

This style of hunting vest has long been the standard among upland gunners. It includes exposed shell loops for fast reloading, a button front, and a detachable rear game pocket. Price: $16.00. Duxbak, 825 Noyes Street, Utica, NY 13502.

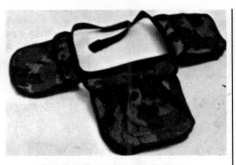

CAMOUFLAGED GAME BAG BELT

As they say in their catalog, this game bag belt from Simmons is "ideal for dove and quail hunters." It will carry birds up higher than loops, is easier to get at than vest bags, appears that it won't bounce around on your legs as you walk. Fits all sizes. Price: $8.50. Simmons Gun Specialties, Inc, P.O. Box 533, Olathe, KS 66061.
—J.B.

HEAVY HUNTING VEST

This heavyweight hunting vest should stand up to long years of hard use. Features include a two-way front zipper, padded shoulder-butt patches, shell loops, and game pockets in front and back (back pocket detachable). Price: $29.00. Duxbak, 825 Noyes Street, Utica, NY 13502.

Handwarmer Pouch

If you find that gloves interfere with your upland shooting, try this handwarmer pouch. Made of brown suede leather, it's worn on the belt, and it will keep an ungloved hand warm while you walk. For greater warmth carry a catalytic handwarmer inside. Price: $7.50. Kolpin Manufacturing, Inc., P.O. Box 231, Berlin, WI 54923.
—P.S.

STAY DRY IN WET WOODS

Hunt in dry comfort when the uplands get soggy with the Go Suit. The waterproof material from which this garment is made is a cotton-knit fabric called Flexnet, which helps to dissipate any moisture from perspiration that forms on the inside. On the outside you're kept dry by shock-cord drawstrings, snap cuffs, and a built-in hood visor that drips water at least 2 inches away from the tip of your nose. That is a plus!

The Go Suit is tailored for men and for women, and it comes in five colors: red, yellow, white, green, and blue. Price: $53.00 for jacket and pants. Royal Red Ball, 8530 Page Avenue, St. Louis, MO 63114.

Light Field Pants

Here's the right garment for early fall when the weather is still warm. Featuring full cut with slightly tapered leg and reinforced pockets, it's not terribly prickle- and brier-resistant, but it's quiet in the woods. Price: $21.95. L. L. Bean, Freeport, ME 04033.
—P.S.

GROUSE SOUTHERN STYLE

by Joel Arrington

The ruffed grouse is a staple game bird in northern sections of the United States, but in the South only a few hardy hunters are interested.

It's a shame. Yankee sportsmen are lucky if they get as much as two hunting months a year, both because of shorter seasons than are offered in Dixie and because some days are just too cold for hunting. Southern hunters get a longer season—up to three and a half months—and have more birds available and more square miles of good grouse range. In North Carolina, for example, the season typically opens in mid-October and expires at the end of February. Most days are huntable because of a relatively benign climate.

The first thing an experienced grouse hunter from the North notices about southern hunting is the rugged terrain. Below the Mason-Dixon, grouse are strictly mountain birds, at home in laurel and rhododendron thickets, or slicks, as the natives call them, and in thick conifers such as white pine and balsam.

The Southern Appalachians are the highest mountains east of the Mississippi River. Because of this rugged terrain, southern birds are little hunted. This pays a double bonus to hardy sportsmen who pursue them—more birds and plenty of elbow room. During the week you are unlikely to see another hunter, even on the public areas which receive most pressure. On weekends there is still plenty of cover for all who may be afield.

Experienced southern grouse hunters study the movements of their quarry. Early in the season, birds are likely to be high on the ridges. Later, when fall cover is gone, they probably will migrate to lower altitudes. Especially on dry or windy days, grouse feed long streambeds on green plant leaves, or "lettuce" as mountaineers say, and on buds. Thick cover in the middle of fields is likely to produce birds—either singles or any number that have grouped for shelter.

There has always been great annual fluctuation in grouse populations. Nesting and rearing success, almost alone among limiting factors, determines the population level. A cold, wet spring is sure to result in few grouse the following season. Predators take a few weak and diseased birds. However, hunting has an insignificant effect on the number of grouse.

Good habitat also can determine the number of birds in a given area. Healthy populations are more likely in second growth—where logged hillsides have grown up in bushes—than in a mature forest with little understory.

Seasoned hunters do not go for grouse until the trees have lost almost all their leaves. Grouse have an uncanny ability to put a tree between the hunter and themselves. The fewer impediments to seeing a flushing grouse, the greater the chance of a hit.

Most experts agree that the ideal shotgun is a light one, that is, one weighing less than 7 pounds. It may be a double, autoloader, or slide action, but it should have a barrel no longer than 26 inches and should be choked improved cylinder. Most shots demand a quick-swinging gun. Size 7½ shot is the universal choice. The distance of most shots is from 15 to 30 yards. You should have a gun that puts as much pattern as possible in that range.

One of the most common mistakes of inexperienced mountain hunters is dressing too heavily. You should dress lighter than you think necessary for the temperature, because walking steep trails can work up a sweat in jig time. A good choice for days with highs in the 50s is light thermal underwear, a warm shirt, and a canvas vest with a game bag. Anyone who carries more than twelve shells is optimistic. In most southern states the daily limit is three or four birds. You have had an exceptional day when you take a limit.

For mountain walking, no item of clothing is more important than boots. Ten-inch rubber-bottom pacs with lug soles are ideal. They protect your ankles from briers, keep your feet dry, and help you get a good grip on steep slopes.

Some of the best grouse hunting is on public lands managed by fish and game agencies. In Tennessee the best are Kettlefoot Wildlife Management Area, near Mountain City; the Unicoi Area, near Johnson City; and Laurel Fork and Tellico areas, as well as the Catoosa Wildlife Management Area, near Crossville on the Cumberland Plateau. In North Carolina the Rich Mountain Section of the Pisgah Game Land and the Standing Indian and Wayah sections of the Nantahala Game Land are excellent. Kentucky's Clinch Mountain Range is also good.

There are no grouse hunting guides in the South. If you do not plan to hunt a public area, it is best to visit hardware or sporting goods dealers in the area you want to hunt and ask them about the location of private lands where permission for hunting may be obtained.

Grouse are a treat on the table. Here is a simple recipe that is widely admired in the mountains of North Carolina:

Cover the skinned and dressed bird (or birds) with water. Season to taste with salt and pepper. Simmer until tender, testing with a fork. Then remove the meat from the bones, discard the latter, and thicken the stock with flour. Serve with wild rice, a tossed salad, a green vegetable, and cranberry sauce.

That's grouse southern style.

Joel Arrington is a free-lance writer and outdoor editor who works for the State of North Carolina. Between his writing duties and his work with the government, Joel has seen a lot of the South and of his favorite game bird, the ruffed grouse.

Upland Hunting Boots

Light weight is the characteristic that's most desirable in an upland boot. For the most part the upland hunter is not confronted with heavy snows or soggy swamps but rather with many woodland miles and with temperatures that may range from morning frosts to midday heat.

You'll generally be most comfortable in a pair of low-cut boots, because they're lighter than high-top boots and allow some air circulation around your ankles. Traction and gripping ability isn't nearly so critical as in big-game country, so most situations will be satisfied by a crepe or soft synthetic composition sole.

One problem the uplander faces, however, that other hunters don't is murderous brush—murderous at least as far as leather is concerned. In certain sections of the country the ground cover is such that a full day afield reduces a shiny, new leather toe to scratched and scarred leather that's been rubbed raw.

For this reason it's wise to buy an upland boot without a lot of prominent stitching and with a lot of leather up front. The sides of the boot also take a beating, so, in general, boot uppers should be stout, with any exterior stitching well recessed or somehow protected. Exposed stitching will tease apart under the assault of briers and creepers, and the seams will part.

Sometimes the nature of the ground cover also dictates a high-top boot. If your hunting habits find you pushing through vines that whipsaw the front of your ankle as you walk through them, high-tops will save both skin and socks. High-tops are also one way to avoid itchy seeds from gathering around your ankles, but if seeds are the sole problem, consider donning a light, cool pair of mountaineer's gaiters over low-cut uplander boots.　　—N.S.

Setter Hightop

This 9-inch-high boot includes a rolled top band that won't cut into your calf and a looper backstay that keeps the uppers up and makes it easy to pull the boots on. The sole is soft crepe with a medium tread, and the uppers are oil-tanned and water-repellent. This is a soft, comfortable boot, best suited to flat or hilly conditions in cool, dry weather. Price: $55.95 (style 877). Red Wing, Red Wing, MN 55066.

Russell Birdshooters

This good, lightweight boot is available in two styles: single vamp, which allows the foot to breathe a bit more and is good for hunting in warm weather, and double vamp, which is essentially another layer of leather in back of the seams which waterproofs the boot (given good waterproofing goop). Both are of true moccasin construction; the top leather runs underneath the foot, preventing those embarrassing moments when the sole comes loose from the leather and your toes poke out. Available both from stock and on special order. Stock price is $47.00 in single vamp, $54.00 in double, for 9-inch boots. W. C. Russell Moccasin Co., Berlin, WI 54923.

Browning Featherweight Boots

The best upland game boots, these are not a waterproof boot, but moisture-resistant enough for most upland situations and light enough to walk around in all day and not feel as though you have exercise weights on every time you take a step. Available with crepe or Vibram soles, with or without German speed-lacing (depending on style), and stitched with rugged Dacron. Prices: $54.95 for HiLand and men's Featherweights; $46.95 for ladies' and jrs'. Browning, Route 1, Morgan, UT 84050.
　　—J.B.

SNAKEPROOF BOOTS

If you know you'll be hunting in snake country, these high-top engineer-style boots are the traditional fang-turners. They are 17 inches high and constructed of chrome-tanned leather. They are a bit on the warm side for hot-weather hunting, but if you get hit by a big diamondback and you're not wearing them, you're in for some sweating anyway.

This company also makes a low-cut snakeproof shoe for use with puttees, a cooler option for hunting in hot weather. Prices: high-top engineer, $79.95; low-cut walker, $39.95. Russ Boot Company, P.O. Box 506, Crawfordville, FL 32327. —F.S.

MEDIUM-CUT UPLANDER

These 6-inch-high boots are a workable compromise between the heat and weight of high-top boots and the seed-collecting tendencies of ankle-high hikers. They include a full crepe sole, water-repellent leather uppers, a sweat-absorbing leather insole, and a rolled top band to keep the boot from cutting into your calf. Price: $44.95 (style 875). Red Wing, Red Wing, MN 55066.

GOURMET GROUSE

Grouse have specific favorites in terms of food. Though their diet is as varied as a gourmet's, chances are good that if you find their dinner table, the birds won't be far away. The list of preferred eats includes strawberries, clover, bunchberries, partridgeberries, wintergreen, wild rose hips, wild grapes and plums, snowberries, blackberries, juneberries, bittersweet, briers, and the buds or fruits of aspen, birch, crab apple, hawthorn, chokecherry, mountain ash, hazel, and alder.

Great grouse coverts often exist no farther afield than the side of the road. Passing cars crush the fruits of nut and acorn-bearing trees, which in turn attracts grouse. Roadsides are also a primary source of pebbles for their crop.

• Ruffed grouse populations regularly go through peaks and declines, usually in a ten-year cycle.

• Sixty to 70 percent of all grouse die between late summer and the following spring, whether they are hunted or not.

• Grouse make it through the winter by burrowing down into snowbanks and sleeping under this white blanket. Temperatures at ground level under 18 inches of snow, have been measured at 52 degrees F warmer than the above-snow air. While this adaptation to their environment allows grouse to survive long, cold winters, it occasionally spells tragedy when freezing rains crust the snow, trapping the birds in bed.

• Ruffed grouse will let a sharp-eared hunter know when they're getting ready to flush. When the birds get nervous, they make a soft popping sound, a little like dripping water. Should you hear this afield, get ready; the air will be filled with feathers in a few seconds.

• You can determine the sex of ruffed grouse by fanning out the tail. Males will have an unbroken black band around the perimeter of their tail; females will have a band that's broken by two brown feathers.

THE
GREATEST
GAME BIRD

by Lee Wulff

You can see ducks and geese coming. Wildfowling calls for judgment, good calculations, and ballistics. Quail flush out in the open. They call for fast reactions and good judgment. Doves are devious, but once one learns to take them, far out before they start their evasive action, much of the difficulty evaporates. Ruffed grouse call for the fastest of reactions and a special sort of instinct, as the bird flashes through the forest, as to when is the right time to shoot. I like them best.

As with so many things in the field, grouse hunting was better years ago. New England covers were better, because the abandoned farms had not yet grown up into solid acres of forest. The apple trees and the berry-bearing shrubs had not yet been strangled for sunlight by the solid spread of leaves from the taller, faster-growing pines, maples, and oaks that have now spread over their heads.

The ruffed grouse are still with us in the coverts of New England, but in few places do they ever reach their old abundance, as in the days when a gunner might flush from fifteen to fifty birds and be lucky to come home with two or three.

We call them "partridge," which is not their true name but was a name given to them by the colonists who came over from Britain, where the true partridge was the bird the landed gentry loved to hunt. They called this similar bird a "partridge," just as settlers in Newfoundland called the ptarmigan they found on the barrens and muskeg a "partridge"—and still do. Just as they called the troutlike fish they found here a "trout," though in truth it was a charr.

Their "partridge," when they first found it in New England, was a pretty stupid bird. Like grouse that have not been exposed to hunting, it sat and looked and was easy to shoot, sitting. But when the gentlemanly hunters among the colonists brought over their bird dogs and, with the hunting ethic of the day, shot them only on the wing, the birds developed a wariness that, combined with their natural flying speed, made them even more exciting than the true partridge had been back home.

The grouse learned to hide under the slightest cover and wait till a gunner had passed before they roared out in curving flight. Whether by instinct or by design, they always seem to fly behind a tree trunk or a stone wall or a mass of pine branches as the swinging gunner shoots. Through the years they learned their lesson well. The wise "partridge" of the New England countryside has given me the best of my bird-hunting pleasure.

Lee Wulff is one of the most recognized sportsmen in America. He is a famed fly-fisherman, who developed both new fly-tying techniques and fishing tactics, including those that led to the capture of a giant tuna on a fly. As this story reveals, he's also a hunter of no small repute. Lee lives in New Hampshire, where, among his many other duties, he also finds the time to sit on the State Fish and Game Commission.

*"Grouse . . . are large birds, of delicate flavor, are swift flyers, often hard to hit, and
above all they give out a strong scent and usually lie well to a dog."*
—Charles Hallock, 1877

221

One way to hunt partridge is to make a plan, based on logic and probabilities, of the terrain to be hunted. This will take you over the ground where the birds ought to be.

Another way is to wander, quite aimlessly, from one red lantern to another. This will likely take you where the birds actually are. The lanterns are blackberry leaves, red in October sun.

—Aldo Leopold

GROUSE AND GROUSE HUNTING
by Frank Woolner

New York: Crown Publishers, Inc., $7.50. This book is about one kind of game bird, the ruffed grouse. Woolner describes habitat, techniques, equipment—everything you need to know about hunting ruffed grouse, including the respect and admiration that the author has for the "king of upland birds." The book is mainly about hunting them in the northeastern United States, which is natural since that is where the ruff is most popular and also where Woolner lives, but when he describes hunting them in other regions, such as the mountainous West, he's right on the mark, too. An excellent book from an honest writer.

—J.B.

NATIONAL HUNTING AND FISHING DAY

With all the enthusiasm for and the benefits derived from things like National Pickle Week and Saint Swithin's Day, why a National Hunting and Fishing Day?

For a lot of good reasons.

Self-advertisement is one. It's an opportunity for sportsmen to be seen and heard in their community, not as the bloodthirsty ogres some claim we are but as folks with a deep and abiding respect for their sport and their quarry.

Education is another. This special day affords an excellent opportunity to teach the nonsporting public things like the principles of good game management, the rules of safe gun handling, and the need to preserve lands for wildlife.

Most important, perhaps, it's a vehicle through which we can reach that group we need most for the survival of our sport: youth. There is no better way to explain the myth of Bambi, that guns are not evil, and that hunting is a vital part of conservation than on a face-to-face basis, at the same time getting sportsmen of the future started on the right track.

National Hunting and Fishing Day falls on the fourth Saturday of September. It deserves your support and participation. Contact your local sportsmen's club, your State Fish and Game Department, or write the National Shooting Sports Foundation, 1075 Post Road, Riverside, CT. 06878, and ask them what *you* can do!

—N.S.

A RUNNING BATTLE OF WITS
by James Tallon

For about a dozen years I have been in a running battle. Oh, it's not one of swords or even pens, but one of wits—my three pounds of gray matter against the one-third ounce of the Gambel quail. And one conclusion I have arrived at, despite what scientists say to the contrary, is that the size of the brain does not necessarily indicate its potency—at least not when it is pitted against the Gambel quail.

Even though I think of this as a conflict, it is one I intensely enjoy; I am in love with my opponents. I get a lift from just seeing them and can watch them and their antics for hours on end. In Arizona desert regions, the beauty of the dawn-sliver and the last trembling finger of the sunset is incomplete without their three-note symphony. On an equal basis, I enjoy hunting (and eating) them.

The first use of my wits is to determine where birds are concentrating. I base this on notes made during the pursuit of other outdoor activities year-round and on past quail-hunting success. For the first three days of the season you can expect this year's birds to be "green"—not in color (for they wear basic maroon) but in experience. You're more likely to down a few then. If they are last year's birds, they'll be less careless, and when you spot them, their legs will be working like pistons in a hotrod at a drag race, turning the birds into immediate blur. This is where the running comes in. It is literal. And it is here that wits become witless. Mine. Running, running, running. "Damn you," I cry, "the object is for you to fly, get into the air." They know me; they know my low frustration response.

I feel that I have "I am not a ground-sluicer" written in facial expressions that Gambel quail understand. They dart out of the brush and run down a well-worn path in plain view. They could have stayed hidden, but they know they have the edge. When they are 60 yards from the muzzle of my shotgun, they dive back into the cover. When I'm at 30 yards, they pop out and run to the 60-yard mark again. Their head plumes look remarkably like the thumb of a hand being held to the nose. I can't take that, so I trip off a hull, to one side, of course, in hopes that splattering shot and the boom of my antique over-under will put them into the blue. On occasions it has worked, but more often than not they're too far down-range for patterns to be effective. Sometimes it spurs the birds into spreading their wings, but they insist on hanging onto the ground with their toenails; they hate to fly.

The past few years I have had my brain (whatever the Gambels have left of it) assisted by the four- to five-ouncer of my Brittany spaniel, Britt. At the beginning of Gambel season his eyes are bright and shiny; at the end . . . aw hell, I don't want to talk about it. Anyway, when he locks on point, the birds give him the bird. They weave back and forth in a high-speed square dance of confusion; they run out of the brush on both sides in an attempt to make him turn both ways at the same time. Once I thought a bird was going to try the old "run under a dog" trick. Frequently they'll saunter out of cover where Britt can see them, and naturally he locks on point. The bird keeps on walking and soon Britt is into his walking point and I am in my walking shotgun stance. Then the bird picks up momentum, and soon we are all running, running, running, with Britt looking over his shoulder at me as if to say, Is this the way we really do it?

Every game has a loser, and much of the time Britt and I are the losers in the Gambel game. But my orange-and-white friend and I work on the law of averages. He gets to retrieve a few birds, and I get to eat a few. The real joy, however, is not in the "getting" but in the "trying to get." And we're out there trying every season. But I'm through trying to outwit these crafty quail. Britt and I are now running a mile a day in the backyard—16½ revolutions. We're going to fight fire with fire.

James Tallon is a free-lance writer and photographer who lives in Phoenix, Arizona. His publication credits extend far beyond the outdoors. As a matter of fact, you might say they cover indoor sports as well, since he's been published in *Playboy*. He also boasts of being the first and only writer ever to get a full refund after taking a course in creative humor.

NO-SWEAT WOODCOCK
by Frank Woolner

Every now and then I hear about some chap who has gunned woodcock for so long that his brain is upside down and his ears have moved around in front of his eyes. Count it pure poppycock. I don't care if my timberdoodle shooting friends *have* long, skinny noses. If their brains are upside down, they sure know how to use them.

Philohela minor, the American woodcock, has become an extremely popular little game bird from Canada's Maritimes over to Wisconsin, thence southward to West Virginia. On wintering grounds in Louisiana, 'doodles are sought after, but never with the dedication displayed by northern sportsmen.

First off, a true aficionado dresses for the game and chooses a shotgun particularly suited to all-day toting in a hot, clutchy covert.

He will need a good bird dog, which may be pointer, setter, Brit, or maybe one of the increasingly popular continental breeds. Whatever the choice, for serious work with woodcock a dog is essential. (Once, believe it or not, I read an *American Rifleman* story that advised shooters to leave all pooches at home. Although a life member of NRA, I privately figured the magazine ought to stick with lengthy features about pot-metal pistols that lost wars for the Russians a hundred years ago.)

Armament in the alders and birch whips may be any shotgun that is light, easy to handle, and open-bored. Choke—or, better said, a lack of choke—is logical, since a majority of pokes will be taken at 20 to 30 yards. Gauge? Anything from 28 up to 12 boasts plenty of clout. Some use the little .410, but I hope the practice is discouraged.

Nines are the ideal shot size, although a lot of folks compromise with 8s where ruffed grouse are likely to provide early season chances in thick woodcock cover. Stick with low-velocity loads: you don't need waterfowl punch in this arena. Ordinary skeet or trap hulls are fine.

Dress light—and tough! There may be frost of mornings, but that stuff burns off quickly under a fall sun. You'll get a lot of exercise fighting the jungle, and it's no fun to get lathered with perspiration. When I get that way, I miss. (It's one of my 1,001 excuses!)

The best pants are light poplin faced with some tougher material to defeat thorny understory. Orvis, L. L. Bean, and a number of other reliable outfitters have them. They are sort of expensive but worth every penny.

My own nice Pendleton shirts never see a woodcock covert, since I expect attrition in short order. Chamois cloth is fine, but on steamy days I favor light cotton. Choose long sleeves and wear featherweight gloves. Ignore this suggestion and you'll come out of the runs looking as if you've just tried to separate a couple of battling bobcats.

An abbreviated shooting vest is most comfortable; all you need is pocket space for a dozen shells plus a small game compartment aft. Choose a baseball-type hat with a brim, and make it blaze-orange fluorescent fashioned of the new soft and porous Acrilan. Of course you haven't forgotten shooting glasses. Light yellow pleases most of us, since they assure contrast.

Footwear can make or break a day. I've always liked the rubber-bottomed pac made famous by L. L. Bean, but light leather, such as the Russell Birdshooter, is grand in reasonably dry going. All-rubber short boots hurt my feetbones; however, they're ideal for the bog-trotter who can abide them.

Now, accoutered like a knight in light armor, you're

WHEN I SAY HUN, I DON'T MEAN ATTILA

by Charles F. Waterman

The Hungarian partridge needs a press agent, and I volunteer. For more than seventy years the Hun has held forth in this country in various stages of anonymity, called "little chickens" by Western ranchers and mistaken for a giant race of quail by wandering bobwhite hunters.

Its beginnings in this country are a little vague, because a number of introductions came at about the same time. A large share of the birds found in the northwestern United States seem to have begun with some plantings in Canada after U.S. introductions were less than successful. But no matter. The "gray partridge" (a more international name than Hun) is the subject of considerable misinformation, because although many northern U.S. shotgunners accept the bird as a target of opportunity, I doubt if more than fifty North American gunners train their dogs and feet specifically for Huns.

The Hun is accused of not holding for pointing dogs, and it's true that the birds run and flush wild at times, but there are days when they fly up your shell vest. In open country, where they're usually found, they can often be watched until they put down again. It's not unusual to follow coveys through five or six flushes. A typical bunch will have about fourteen birds before the shooting starts, and although they may live in grass country where one ridge looks like the next, there are spots where a covey has existed for fifteen years and probably longer.

A fairly wide-ranging dog that's patient about running birds is best, and despite the Hun's love of grain, there are birds that live out their lives in high, dry country where the plow never moves. I prefer the valleys for my Hun trips, but I've found them hale and hearty at 8,000 feet, where they sometimes rest on snowbanks in preference to mountain grasses.

On windy days they may go up in cheeping alarm when you're still 200 yards away, but a typical Hun rise is about 15 yards from the gun. They tend to set their course after they jump, and many shots are at swinging targets. The most ardent Hun-chaser I know uses an improved cylinder and modified double, but there are those who swear by duck guns. I'll take No. 7½ shot and quite a bit of it, preferably at least 1⅛ ounces. Huns usually lack the acceleration of the bobwhite or the ruffed grouse, but they fly through a variety of gears, and though they are sometimes leisurely, there are days when they sizzle.

In the West you top the rise and see the little creek in the draw, and the dogs run the bottom. It probably won't be the skidding stop and the classic freeze of bobwhite country, but more likely an uncertain wariness on the part of the dogs, rolling eyes and nervous quartering. When the birds are found and held in sparse grass, you go up fast, for there's a limit to the Hun's patience. It's no time to take snapshots of your pointer or argue about who stands where when the birds fly. The Hun runs the show.

They squeal and squeak, they tower and turn, and I tend to hurry too much or wait too long. When my gun is empty and I'm gleefully marking dead birds or sadly observing the departing flock, a sleeper leaves like a brown bullet to the surprise of the befuddled dog, while I try to stuff shells in backward.

After that I discover I really didn't mark the bunch very well. I'm not certain just which draw they teetered into, and my dog has forgotten all his training and is chasing the sleeper wildly.

But when I have finally renewed rueful association with my dog and am ready to look for more birds, I am aware that my feet hurt, that it is a mile to the next reliable spot, and that it is getting rather late.

Why didn't I learn about Huns when I was young enough to compete with them?

Charles F. Waterman is one of America's premier outdoor writers and one of those fifty Hun specialists he writes about. He also has the uncommon good sense to live in Florida in the winter and in Montana from trout season through bird season.

---

ready. Just hope that last night's brisk little northwest wind sent legions of tawny flyers down from the north country and that every hot corner is stiff with 'doodles.

Frank Woolner is a writer's writer, who manages to touch and illuminate aspects of our sport that we lesser mortals feel but can't describe. His books on grouse and woodcock are masterpieces of the genre. He lives in Massachusetts and is the editor of *Salt Water Sportsman* magazine.

- The long, slender bill of the woodcock has sensitive nerves at the end which aid in detection of earthworms when thrust underground.
- The spring mating dance of the woodcock finds the male strutting, singing, and spiraling high into the air. If you run to the spot where the bird took off, he'll often alight beside you.
- Late in the season, trading woodcock travel in pairs, so be prepared for a double at this time.
- Woodcock migrations are as spectacular as those of other migratory birds, but because they travel at night they are seldom observed. Daylight hours are spent feeding and resting in traditional coverts, and it's just as well. If it were the other way around, you'd have to hunt them during the dark hours, and they're already impossible to hit in broad daylight.
- To quickly clean woodcock—or any small bird that yields a breast only—lay the bird on its back and stand on its wings. Grasp a leg in each hand and pull steadily and firmly. The skin, crop, head, and entrails will pull free, leaving the drumstick and breast. Clip the legs with shears or scissors.

TURKEY TALK

by Grits Gresham

When the talk turned to turkey, I looked for a way out! As soon as the topic of turkey season dates made the scene, I had a sudden urge to visit the biffy. If the discussion became more specific—"Let's work up a hunt for opening weekend"—it triggered a desire on my part to mix another round. A comparison of the biggest gobbler we'd ever killed? Abrupt splitting headache! Early call tomorrow morning! See you guys later.

There are some things a man just doesn't care to talk about, and in my case it was hunting turkeys. Napoleon had his Waterloo, Nixon his Watergate, but for ol' Grits it was Gobblerphobia.

I'm not a head hunter per se in my big-game hunting. Not that I have anything against a B&C or R&W rack, but I can point with pride to the "representative trophies" on my wall.

So it was with the gobbler bit! For almost a decade I hunted for a gobbler, true, but not particularly for one with a beard dragging the leaves. And toward the end of that era my requirements failed to include even the word representative. All I wanted, in point of fact, was to shoot a legal tom turkey.

Pride has a way of fleeing when faced with the repeated realities of—when I was unable to escape to the biffy, the kitchen, or my bed—"No, I've never shot a turkey."

It wasn't that I didn't try. In Arkansas, in Louisiana, and in Florida I tried, with some of the finest turkey-callers who ever scratched a slate, sucked a wingbone, vibrated a diaphragm, or manipulated a box. On tracts of turkey land where the odds of not killing a gobbler were high, I failed to score—with regularity.

That changed, as I knew it would, when I finally accepted the invitation of Lewis Rush, an Arkansas hunting buddy. Getting a gobbler within shotgun range would be no trick, he assured me. But for my snake-bit turkey-hunting history, I could easily have believed Lewis, since he consistently lured a dozen or two gobblers within *bow range* each season.

Lewis did produce, after being thwarted by my jinx for a couple of days, and I remember it well. "There's a whole flock of gobblers right behind you," came his whispered warning, which followed a kick to rouse me from my dozing. When I rolled to a shooting position, the world turned to running and flying gobblers—about twenty of them—so I shot one with a 2-inch beard.

I was even proud of that. But the day following my newspaper column which outlined the feat, our sheriff served me with an injunction from the district judge. It barred me from participating in further turkey hunts for a period of five years, the penalty for shooting an undersize, uneducated, immature, skinny 12-pound poult.

A few years and no turkeys later the scene shifted to Alabama. With beads of sweat crawling down my nose and several thousand mosquitoes penetrating gaps in the repellent, I touched one off at the beard beyond the screen of dogwood leaves. Well, I had never killed a bearded hen before, but I knew that deficiency had been remedied when I retrieved the flopping bird.

Despite the luck of the draw that has accompanied (plagued?) my turkey hunting, calling gobblers in the spring must rank as one of the rare privileges afforded outdoorsmen. Nobody ever said it better than did Tom Kelly in his book *Tenth Legion*. Two passages, one from the first chapter and another from the last, strike my fancy:

> Not that it is the only yardstick of comparison, but turkey hunting as a cult does have substantial advantages over chasing girls. To adjust a quotation from Lord Chesterfield, not only is the position not nearly so ridiculous but the expense is not so damnable. The pleasure is much less fleeting, and high on the list of its principal advantages is that a gentleman may discuss his conquests afterwards.

The second passage is Kelly's comment about his own actions when, after nine consecutive mornings of working him unsuccessfully, he got a big gobbler within point-blank range.

> I let him walk under the gun, with the safety off, at thirty yards and didn't shoot.
> And ruined it.
> For the past four days that turkey and I had possessed each other—and I had degraded him by letting him go.
> I knew that I had ruined it the minute he was gone, for you may take all the pleasure you choose in losing, so long as you lose. You cannot throw the game.

Pamper yourself. Send your check for $7.50 to Spur Enterprises, 33 Northgate Drive, Monroe, LA 71201, and tell them you want a copy of Tom Kelly's *Tenth Legion*. After you have read this unillustrated, unpretentious volume through in one sitting, which you most likely will do, I'll accept your note of thanks for pointing you toward 109 pages of rare, superb writing.

And you'll know why so many of us in the South head for the woods in the spring.

Grits Gresham is best known as a field host on ABC's *American Sportsman* TV program. He is also *Sports Afield's* shooting editor and is the author of five books about hunting and fishing. He hails from Natchitoches, Louisiana.

• The wild turkey was Ben Franklin's candidate for our national bird.
• As winter approaches, adult toms spend less and less time with hens and birds of the year, and midwinter finds them in small flocks of their own kind.

• The U.S. wild turkey population has quintupled since 1952, with a current estimated population of over 500,000 birds.

For special camouflage clothing, face masks, makeup, etc., for turkey hunting, see the sections on Waterfowl and Archery (III and VI).

HUNTING THE AMERICAN WILD TURKEY
by Dave Harbour

Harrisburg, Pa.: Stackpole Books, $8.95.

Dave Harbour is an excellent deer hunter, archer, and freshwater angler, but if there is one field of popular writing in which he is truly *the* expert, it is hunting wild turkeys.

He has studied and hunted Eastern, Florida, Rio Grande, and Merriam turkeys in twenty different states in the past thirty years and has called or otherwise horn-swoggled hundreds of these birds into bow, gun, or camera range. That kind of savvy adds up to an invaluable education in turkey hunting, an education provided by way of this book.

Topics covered include stalking, calling, camouflage, hunting with weapon or camera, where to go, and where to write for information. There are also some surprising innovations, such as floating for turkeys and the two most important turkey calls out of twenty possible sounds.

DIAPHRAGM TURKEY CALL

This call is a semicircular piece of leather with a small, soft plastic diaphragm midway along the straight edge. You nest this call on the roof of your mouth and apply pressure with your tongue, creating an air lock. As you allow air to escape, the diaphragm vibrates, creating the yelp of a hen turkey with the hots. In some ways this is the most difficult call to master, but in one way it is the best. You can call your heart out with both hands free. There is no movement or losing sight of your target as you lay down your call to take up arms. And in turkey hunting that moment of nonmovement is a big edge. Price: $4.95. Faulk's, 616 18th Street, Lake Charles, LA 70601.

TURKEY BOX CALL

This call, too, operates on the striker principle, but the striker is hinged to the box, so there's less room for human error. It is also one of the few calls capable of making a sound like a tom turkey gobble. You do this by shaking the caller. The striker then scrapes rapidly across the face of the box. Price: $11.00. P. S. Olt, Pekin, IL 61554.

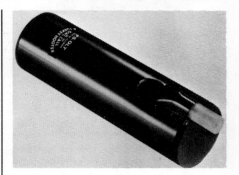

OWL AND TURKEY HOOTER

Don't ask us why, but owls drive turkeys bananas. In the misty chill of a spring dawn, all it takes is one owl hoot and the gobblers start making a racket. This call imitates an owl and thus helps you to locate a gobbler's strutting grounds. Price: $3.95. P. S. Olt, Pekin, IL 61554.

GOBBLER TURKEY CALL

If you want to re-create the sound of a lovesick gobbler, this call is the easiest, most foolproof way to do it. A soft, rubber air chamber puffs air through a reed-type call when you shake the device. Note, however, that the most attractive call to a tom is the yelp of a hen, unless you happen to run across a gay turkey. Price: $9.95. Tidewater Specialties, 430 Swann Avenue, Alexandria, VA 22301.

STRIKER TURKEY CALL

This type of turkey call is tricky to use, but it's very popular among experienced turkey-callers. Sound is produced by drawing a chalked or rosined block of wood across a thin cedar lip. The lip is part of a hollowed-out cedar box that acts as the sounding bell, a little like the body on an acoustical guitar.

In order to get a proper yelp, or rather a series of yelps, you strike the lip smoothly, increasing and decreasing pressure as you draw the wood block across. Unless you've had a lot of practice and are dexterous, it's easy to shriek or squeak (like chalk across a blackboard), which turns everyone off, turkeys included.

Clucking is easier. Just strike the lip light and fast with the block. This makes the nicest cluck in the business (pros call the sounds putts, which is more descriptive). Price: $2.95. Lohman Calls, Neosho, MO 64850.

You Say Your Bird Dog's a Real Turkey?

Good turkey dogs display traits that are in direct opposition to traditional bird dogs. They are expected to break and run when they hit a hot turkey trail and then, upon locating the flock, go dashing into the middle, barking wildly. Understandably, the turkeys scatter. The hunter then finds a nearby hide and tries to call the birds back together, in most cases without benefit of his hound.

BOX-TYPE TURKEY CALL

Dazy's turkey call operates on a striker box principle, but it's considerably easier to master and less likely to hit a sour note.

To call, a rubber slide is moved across the open top of a thin wooden box. The action sets up vibrations; the vibrations constitute the call. By alternating pressure and the pace of the rubber slide across the top of the box, you can re-create a yelp, a cluck, or a whine. The call comes with complete instructions. Price: $7.95. Funk Manufacturing Co., RD 2, Newville, PA 17241.

Wild Turkey Print from Wild Turkey Bourbon

The makers of Wild Turkey bourbon offer a color print of a painting of a wild turkey in flight by Ken Davies. It measures 19 x 21 inches and goes nicely in a den or gun room. If you frame it, hang it, and drink half a bottle of the sponsor's product, rumor has it the bird comes to life. Price: Wild Turkey bourbon, around $12.00 from your favorite vintner; wild turkey print: $2.00. Write P. O. Box 929, Wall Street Station, New York, NY 10005.

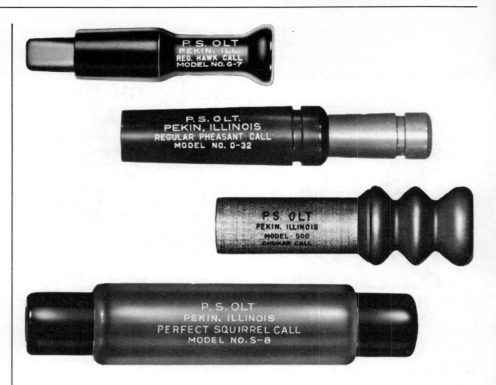

UPLAND GAME CALLS BY OLT

Upland game calls are handy to have afield. While they aren't the attraction that a duck call is to a mallard, they usually elicit a response from game on the ground, which gives you some idea of where they are.

Pheasant Call: This one imitates the cranky cry of a cock pheasant spoiling for a fight. (Another sound that always seems to provoke an answer from a pheasant is a sonic boom, though they're hard to carry around in your pocket.) Price: $5.50.

Quail Call: Use a quail call after the covey rise. Singles try to whistle each other back together again, and they'll answer you about 50 percent of the time. Price: $5.50.

Chukar Call: Chukars are suckers for a call. They're nearly as gregarious as quail and are always looking for company. The one problem you might face using a call in rugged chukar country is catching enough breath to blow one. Price: $4.75.

Squirrel Call: Squirrels are territorial devils, and the threat of an intruder in the neighborhood brings them out of hiding. If you forget your commercial squirrel call, you can re-create the *tchk-tchk-tchk* of a scolding squirrel by clacking the flat of two coins together. Prices: Call, $6.95; two fifty-cent pieces, $1.00.

Valley Quail Call: For calling all variety of Western quail (scaled, Mearn's, California, etc.). Price: $3.95.

Hawk Call: The idea of this call is to frighten game birds into hiding so that they'll hold tight. In most cases this call is useful only if you're hunting with a dog. Alone and afoot, you just about have to step on a close-holding bird to get it up. Price: $5.50. P. S. Olt, Pekin, IL 61554.

"No sport is more delightful than Quail shooting, and there is only one legitimate method by which this bird can be taken; that is over dogs."
—Charles Hallock, 1877

227

BARNYARDS, BOBWHITES, AND BALLET

I have had a long and unrequited love affair with bobwhite quail; long because it was the first bird I ever hunted in earnest, the first game I ever killed with a shotgun. The unrequited part was my fault and decision; I moved from the East Coast to Montana at age seventeen, and there are no quail in Montana. I have hunted them since my youth—every time I got the chance. While there is excitement and pleasure in taking a covey rise in the red clay cottonfields of Georgia or from scattered thickets among the plains of Oklahoma, there is not gut satisfaction. For that you must hear them singing songs of love and mating Caruso-clear on a May morning. Then, in July, you must hide behind the grape-entwined trellis of an abandoned outhouse and count the clutch that scurries and scratches behind a proud, puffy hen. And then, hunting behind a mongrel dog, you must flush that family and the other members that the covey has gathered from who knows where, into a frost-laden morning, and drop a bird more from luck than skill. I can do that no more, but I can still remember.

Bobwhite hunting can be as simple or as complex as you wish to make it. Those early years were spent with a bolt action three-shot Harrington & Richardson 16-gauge, a pair of rubber pacs, and Levi pants and jacket. Today I use a 20-gauge over-under with improved cylinder and modified choke. When the birds are really holding tight, I get the feeling that this might be the one place where a .410 would make sense, but I haven't followed up that theory.

The one thing all bobwhite hunting has in common is that the birds are likely to hole up in and around murderous brush. This dictates either brush pants or chaps and careful selection of footwear. For some reason I have yet to figure out, the brush you'll wade through quail hunting is incredibly hard on leather. I have used boots full seasons in pursuit of ruffs, pheasant, and plains grouse, and put them away still smooth and shiny. But after a day in the quail coverts they look like I've been kicking wads of barbed wire. This suggests two things: don't quail hunt in what you consider dress boots, and look for footwear with recessed stitching, buried well down in the leather. I like Browning Featherweights.

About the only suggestion I have for a hunting vest is that it be made so you can get to the rear game pocket easily. It is a pain in the neck—and the arm—when you have to hammerlock birds into the game bag. When the weather is warm, I've found that the full net vest made by Columbia Sportswear readily accepts birds. When it's crisp, the field jacket with the rubber-lined drop-type game pocket made by Duxbak is my choice (I drop birds in from the inside).

You will be missing a great deal if you hunt quail without a dog. It is not so much a matter of limits as aesthetics. A pair of pointers or Brittanies locked in convoluted postures around a palmetto or plum thicket rivals the swirls and splashes of Van Gogh's wildest masterpiece. To watch the dogs work is barnyard ballet at its best. The walk up to the flush is hunting's most exquisite anticipatory moment.

There are a few tricks that will help a quail hunter at his trade. Watch for ground roosts. These will be round piles of droppings in an area with no overhead cover. They result from a quail's habit of sleeping with its tail pointed toward the center of a circle. (Incidentally, this is the same configuration it assumes when threatened and why a covey seems to rise in all different directions.) The size and frequency of these ground roosts will indicate the size and numbers of coveys in an area.

After the covey rise, you can always locate singles by their whistle. Broken birds try to get together again, and they find each other by calling. There are, however, sporting limits to hunting down singles. The one I use is the 20-percent rule, which translates to taking no more than two birds from a covey of ten, one bird from a covey of five, and no birds other than what I might have downed initially from a covey of four or less. Hunting pressure is another thing that I think can hurt a quail population. When a particular area is hunted hard, the coveys are continually scattered. Quail are obviously gregarious, and they find safety in numbers. If they are not allowed to get back together, single birds become susceptible to predators and bad weather.

Weather is the most critical factor influencing the bobwhite. Heavy, hard-crusted snow that stays on the ground for long periods of time prevents the birds from feeding, and they starve or succumb to maladies associated with malnutrition. You can negate some of the weather's effect by putting out and maintaining feeding stations during winter's worst weather. Unfortunately, not even those measures will see the bobwhite through Montana's murderous winters, so I guess I'll have to be content with occasional trips down South and with memories of a childhood on Long Island.

—N.S.

DOVE AND QUAIL IN MEXICO

Of all the upland gunning I've enjoyed, none has been so consistently excellent as dove and quail hunting in Mexico. In terms of quail, it's not unusual to go through four boxes of shells in a morning. With doves, you could shoot up a case if your arm could take it.

Doves are all over the northern half of Mexico, but I have only hunted them on the West Coast. The largest concentrations of birds begin at Hermosillo, about 250 miles south of the border, and I have found superb hunting as far south as Teacapan, 60 miles south of Mazatlán.

There are three types of dove in Mexico: whitewing, mourning dove, and a large gray dove, a little smaller than a pigeon, whose proper name escapes me. The common way they are hunted is around waterholes and fields of milo or frijole. Establish the flight path they're using and intercept them. Around waterholes it's quite common to combine dove shooting with duck hunting, and its possible to come home with a mixed bag of over twelve different kinds of birds.

The quail shooting is dearest to my heart. Cordoniz quail are the most common and compare favorably with bobwhite, even to their habit of calling to each other when the flocks are split up. They have a reputation of being more prone to run than fly, but I have not found this to be the rule. They will run if you happen upon a heavily hunted area, which is rare, or if they are in very sparse cover, but otherwise they hold as well as a bobwhite.

I have found the best quail hunting in the fields and mountains east of Navajoa, and around Culiacán. Stay away from intensively farmed areas that lack cover around the field borders. Instead, look for small family farms out in the cactus and brushlands. Always ask permission, not that it's expected, but because you'll invariably end up with someone to guide you. These folks know just where the birds are (they are called *choli*), and they have eyes that rival a magpie. They'll spot birds that a dog will miss!

When the day is over offer them part of your bag. This is a courtesy that's much appreciated and even needed on meat-short family farms. A one- or two-dollar tip will make you a friend for life, and you'll probably be asked to stay for dinner.

Without the services of a farmer or his son, you'll probably need a dog. I like to use one anyway, just because they add another dimension of pleasure to the hunt.

If you prefer, professional guides are available for dove and quail, though prices are surprisingly high compared to the Mexican level of economy. One service they do provide, however, is aid in getting your firearms across the border. This is a very complex undertaking, especially now with a major political hassle taking place over land. For information on guides and/or current gun regulations, write the Mexican National Tourist Council, 405 Park Avenue, New York, NY 10022.
                                                                  —N.S.

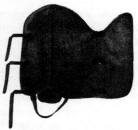

SNAKEPROOF LEGGINGS

Southern and southwestern quail hunters are the most prone to snakebite, because the quail they hunt often hide in brushpiles and under palmettos. Snakeproof boots are one option, but they get awfully hot. A more practical alternative is puttees; they're worn like gaiters or spats.

Burnham stocks two types of snakeproof leggings. No. 215 is a hard-plastic camouflage puttee. It is easy to get on and off, lightweight, and will turn brush and briers. The No. 125 Ranger is a little warmer but more comfortable. It's made of bronze mesh covered with two layers of heavy olive drab canvas and buckles on. Price: $12.00. Burnham Brothers, P. O. Box 100A, Marble Falls, TX 78654.

CHARLEY DICKEY'S DOVE HUNTING
by Charley Dickey

Birmingham, Ala.: Oxmoor House, $2.95 (soft cover).

This is a book for beginners and average hunters, with chapters on the life history of the mourning dove, equipment, how to find a place to hunt, field tactics, how to hit a dove, dressing birds, and recipes. It also has information on white-winged doves and band-tailed pigeons.

BOBWHITE QUAIL HUNTING
by Charley Dickey

Birmingham, Ala.: Oxmoor House, $9.95.

This book is a beautiful blend of fun and fact and quail hunting. Charley Dickey is a gifted writer and a dedicated bobwhite addict who spins wonderfully relaxing yarns with a lesson, and each one either adds to your appreciation of the bird or furthers your knowledge of the sport. Included within these pages is the sum total of Dickey's experience in training dogs, selecting guns, leasing land, hunting the bobwhite, and dealing with the assorted problems that face the modern bird hunter. But most of all it's just good reading.

COLOMBIA DOVE HUNT

The Cauca Valley, near Cali, Colombia, is reputed to have the finest wing shooting in the world. The birds are Andes doves, which arrive in such profusion that they threaten crops. There are no seasons and no limits on these birds, and you can literally shoot until you are no longer physically able to shoulder a shotgun.

Hunting is European style, shooting from stands and blinds. Stands vary daily and follow changes in flying and feeding patterns of the huge flocks. Gunning begins around midmorning, there is a break for lunch, and the day concludes around 3 P.M., or earlier, should you dislocate your shoulder.

Nightly accommodations are in Cali hotels. Breakfast and lunch are provided, but you're on your own for the evening meal, which is just as well, since there are some great restaurants in the city, and the food is both good and cheap (steaks are tops).

You can book into this dove hunt through your travel agent or Braniff Airlines. 4 days/3 nights, around $235 per person plus air fare ($384 from Miami). Estimated total cost, with allowances for sightseeing, trinkets, tips, etc., $650 per person for a week.

A Seat and Cooler for Hot-Weather Hunting

Dove and duck hunters who ply their favorite pastimes in the dusty Southwest or humid South might find Covey's Hunters' Bucket/Seat a cool, comfortable answer to the heat of midday. The "seat" is actually a reinforced cooler with a carrying strap that you can tote to your favorite marsh or field of milo. While you're there it functions as both a seat and a source of cool drink. There's also a shell belt that goes around the top of the canister and holds twenty-five shells. When the shoot is over, use the cooler to carry home your game, cooled down and safe from spoilage. Color, olive drab. Prices: 2-gallon capacity, $14.50; 8-gallon capacity, $33.95. Covey Corp., P.O. Box 978, Holdenville, OK 74848.

DOVES

The mourning dove nests up to six times each year, each nest bearing two eggs. But weather and disease take a terrible toll of the young; hence, parents average only four to six surviving offspring annually. However, in spite of an annual harvest of over 20 million birds, breeding stock has steadily increased over the last twenty years.

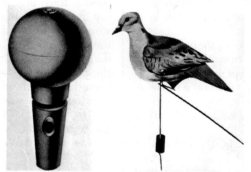

DECOYING DOVES

Ninety percent of America's dove hunters pass-shoot these fast-flying birds as they wing into food or water. It's tough and it's sporty shooting, no doubt, but decoying the birds to you has a charm all its own and a practical side. With decoys you can often start shooting in the middle of the day, when birds are too inactive to warrant pass shooting.

Getting set up in a good place requires that you first find a roosting area. Generally, this means a thatch of thick brush, or a large, well-branched shade tree, close to water. You may either set up while the birds are in the field or run them out of the roost and then set your decoys. They'll be back directly.

You don't need a carefully constructed blind as in water-fowling—just a bush to hide behind. Set the dove decoys so that they can be easily seen. Bare dead branches are ideal. You'll probably need a long pole to do this; a cane fishing pole cut off at the slender tip works. If you want to go first class, con your local power company out of one of those fuse-changing gadgets.

Dove decoys need to be no more than silhouettes. They should have a balancing device akin to those toys you remember as a kid that would perch preciously at a table edge yet never fall off. Calls are helpful, too.

Doves will tolerate shooting for about an hour. Then they'll find another roost where they can rest in peace. Price: balanced dove decoys, $2.00 each; dove call, $4.50. P. S. Olt, Pekin, IL 61554.

READING THE WOODS
by Vinson Brown

New York: Macmillan Company, $2.95 (soft cover).

Wherein lies the pleasure of a day afield? In the kill? If that were the case there would be a thriving market for pen-raised birds and people wouldn't hunt selectively. In just "being outdoors"? You hear that phrase a lot, but if it were taken literally, we'd be happy to sit on the front porch. Rather, hunting is a total kind of experience, a composite of many subtle parts that can best be summed up as an ultimate sense of place.

To be able to read the woods is one of the major composites of that sense. Reading the woods amounts to half perception and half education. You see what is around you, and you interpret it by induction or deduction. The lateral sprouts on bitterbrush indicate that deer fed there last winter . . . tearing pinesap from bruised bark tells of a September velvet rub . . . fresh chews on certain types of browse say that deer have been there recently. It's that kind of savvy which makes for a superb hunter. Beyond the game, it's also a joy to look at a bent tree trunk and to know that the hillside where it grows is slowly creeping down, to identify the scars of an avalanche, to perceive the regular progression of plant and animal life that follows a fire.

The education needed to gain these skills and more rests between the covers of this book. I recommend it highly.

—N.S.

BAGGING THE WILY SHARPTALE
by Patrick McManus

The favorite game of all outdoor writers is the sharptale. The sharptale, if you will note the spelling, is not a grouse with a pointy posterior but, in fact, a sharp tale, which is to say a little story with a point. The point can be on either end of the story or even in the middle, but it has to be there; otherwise the story is not a sharp tale at all but some other kind of tale, most frequently, as old Bill Shakespeare liked to put it, a tale told by an idiot. Outdoor writers generally refer to sharptales as anecdotes and to the other kind as "tales told by idiots."

Outdoor writers use sharptales to keep their hunting-fishing-camping tips to outdoorsmen from bumping up against each other. If it weren't for sharptales, outdoor articles would only be about as long as the verse on a birthday card. An article on How to Catch Lunker Bluegills would say, "Smear a bit of peanut butter on your angleworm." That would be it.

So what the outdoor writer does is to go out and flush a covey of sharptales. A nice plump sharptale would start off something like this: "Old Doc and I hadn't caught a decent bluegill all day. Then it happened. I accidentally dropped a worm on Doc's peanut butter sandwich. . . ." Add a few descriptions of the weather and the landscape—"golden shafts of horizontal sunlight splayed through a scattering of rain-blackened pines"—and the OW has himself an outdoor article.

Thus the OW prowls field and stream, a sport afield with rod and gun in hand, enjoying the outdoor life, but his game as often as not isn't the trophy trout or buck but the wily sharptale.

The best sharptales, of course, are those he flushes out of his own experience, but occasionally, like any outdoorsman, he comes back empty-handed. Then he has to see if his friends have any sharptales he can borrow. Just recently, my old outdoor buddy Retch Sweeney said he had a good story I might be able to use. "A funny thing happened to me the other day," he told me. "I was out fishing with my dad, and old Pop dropped his pocket watch over the side of the boat. Well, it wasn't more than an hour later that I felt something on the end of my line, so I started to reel in."

"Hooked his watch, huh?" I said.

"No," he said. "But I caught a nice perch. Never did see the watch again."

Now that is not a sharptale. That is one of the other kind.

Patrick McManus is probably the best outdoor humorist today. His byline regularly appears along with outrageously funny stories in *Field & Stream,* where he is an associate editor. Pat is also a university-level teacher. He lives in Spokane, Washington.

Bird-Mounting Kit
for
Beginning Taxidermists

If you ever wanted a mounted bird but couldn't afford the prices charged by professional taxidermists, you might consider doing it yourself with an E Z Mount kit. It contains step-by-step instructions and all the preservatives, tools, and fill material you'll need to do a first-rate job. Price: $14.95. Cabela's, 812 13th Avenue, Sidney, NE 69162.

A SAND COUNTY ALMANAC
and
ROUND RIVER
by Aldo Leopold

New York: Oxford University Press, $2.95 and $2.50 respectively (soft cover).

There are two extremes of outdoor literature, the subjective and the objective. Objective literature is characterized by the pure how-to story: how to make a decoy or outfox a whitetail or catch a fish. Subjective outdoor writing gets into the mind and the "why"; it describes those intangibles that make hunting almost a sacred pastime, like the smell of a coffeepot in a duck shack or the feel of snowflakes as you ghost along a deer trail or the sense of pride you feel when your young pup throws its first point.

Aldo Leopold was a unique, one-of-a-kind combination of scientist, hunter, and poet. A Ph.D. wildlife biologist, university professor, and conservation adviser to the United Nations at the time of his death in 1948, he was a man of gifted vision. Within these two works you will find a love of land, conservation, wildlife, and hunting that we are just beginning to perceive and espouse today.

This isn't dry, technical stuff. It's the kind of gut experience any hunter worth the name feels but probably can't express. It is a condemnation of land rape, a celebration of true conservation, and the most literate portrayal of those hard-to-define values a hunter holds most dear that I have ever had the joy to read. And I have never encountered a soul who ever walked in the woods who didn't agree.

The number of Leopold quotes in this book pays homage and testimony to his excellence as a thinker, an outdoorsman, and a man who wants something left of a wild world for future generations.

If you have a yen to read an "outdoor book," you'd do well to start with these. If you've read lots of outdoor literature, you're missing something if you haven't already read *A Sand County Almanac* and *Round River*.

SCHOOL FOR SCATTERGUNNERS

If you're missing birds you know you shouldn't have missed (and who hasn't?), you might benefit from some professional instruction in the art of shotgunning. Orvis offers a three-day shooting school that's designed to satisfy the needs of novices and of experienced scattergunners whose shooting eye has gone astray.

Orvis's instructors are trained in England in the British Churchill shooting technique. Their duties at the school include fitting you for a proper shotgun and coaching you in mounting the gun, in stance, and in swing. They have the latest sophisticated machinery at their disposal for diagnosing your misses: shooting boards, try guns, trap-throwers, and a quail walk.

The quail walk closely duplicates actual upland conditions. Hidden trap machines toss out birds as you walk by; they hold up to six clays and re-create the effect of a covey rise. You also get practice at typical waterfowl pass shooting: fast and slow high incomers, birds that zing from left and right, slow and fast outgoers, and straight-away birds. During all this shooting you're accompanied by an instructor/guide who carefully appraises your performance and suggests corrections when you miss.

Improving your skill as a scattergunner is the core of this course, but you also receive instruction in how to identify good woodcock, quail, and grouse cover and how to improve wildlife habitat, as well as in gun safety and hunter etiquette.

This three-day course is offered twice a week, August through September. Classes start on Tuesday and Friday and conclude at noon on Thursday or Sunday. Tuition includes lodging and all meals from luncheon of the first day through luncheon on the last. Rates are based on double occupancy. Free brochure. Price: $350 per person. Write: Orvis Shooting School, 10 River Road, Manchester, VT 05254.

GAME BIRDS OF NORTH AMERICA
by Leonard Lee Rue, III
Paintings by Douglas Allen, Jr.

New York, N.Y.: Outdoor Life–Harper & Row, $12.50.

Both waterfowl and upland game birds are covered in this book, with the prose of Leonard Lee Rue, III, describing their habits and the beautiful paintings of Douglas Allen, Jr., describing their physical appearance. Also included are seventy-five black-and-white photos. In spite of the fact that this isn't primarily a hunter's book, the dedication and attention to detail and the feeling for the outdoors that every serious sportsman has are there in both the prose and the pictures.

FAST FIELD DRESSING

Field dressing all forms of feathered game is cleaner and easier when you use a gutting hook. These can be fashioned afield from willow, hazel, alder, or a host of other brush types. Cut a twig 6 inches above a fork and right at the fork. Now, trim one leg of the fork ¼ inch from the Y, so the tool resembles a long-shanked fish-hook. Insert the hook in the game's anal passage, twist it slightly, and draw it out slowly. The intestines will follow. Draw them out by hand. The end of the gut lies at the gizzard. Cut the intestine where it is attached to it. When this is removed, the field dressing is complete.

HUNTING AMERICA'S GAME ANIMALS & BIRDS
edited by Robert Elman and George Peper

New York: Winchester Press, $12.95.

This how-to, where-to, and when-to guide by forty top experts covers the continent's big game, small game, upland birds, and waterfowl. Sections are included on gun ballistics, magnum cartridges, hand-loading, sighting-in, shotgunning secrets, gun care, hunting with a muzzleloader, and hunting with a bow.

There are chapters on vehicles, boats, hunting knives, and scopes, and several chapters on dogs. Information of value is included on preserve shooting, dealing with outfitters, cutting red tape on Canadian trips, and planning faraway hunts. Forecasts are based on surveys by agencies throughout the United States and Canada.

WHY ARE SOME BIRDS EASIER TO PLUCK THAN OTHERS?

Two factors influence the ease with which feathers are removed from a game bird: the age of the carcass and how the bird was killed.

Birds will be easiest to pluck immediately after they're killed, when the carcass is still warm. If you like to eat fresh-killed birds, get after the feathers as soon as you can—while you wait for more ducks in a blind or as soon as you get home from a pheasant or quail hunt.

If you like to hang or age birds, there will be a period when feathers are difficult to remove. Let the bird hang until the feathers just above the tail pull loose easily. This is the time when it will be easiest to pluck and is also a reliable sign of a properly aged bird.

How a bird is killed is purely a matter of luck. One of a bird's defenses is the ability to release its feathers. This is an escape mechanism; a fox pounces on a pheasant's tail and gets a few long feathers for dinner. If you hunt with a dog, you will doubtless have seen cripples do the same thing; your dog makes a pass for the bird and then coughs feathers for half an hour.

It is possible for a pro to kill a turkey or a chicken in such a way as to make them release their feathers, usually by inserting a needle or sharp knife into the brain. Occasionally, a stray shotgun pellet will trigger this same mechanism. When it happens, feathers can be removed with little more effort than peeling a banana.

RINGNECK! PHEASANTS AND PHEASANT HUNTING
by E. C. Janes

New York: Crown Publishers, $8.95.

Janes has here put together a book of pheasant-hunting techniques, pheasant natural history, pheasant ecology, guns, loads, recipes—and a strong plea for pheasant-hunting conservation—that is bound to please and inform John W. Ringneck's admirers everywhere. Here is the full story of the pheasant's successful immigration to America, through a description of modern game farm techniques and pheasant-rearing principles.

CLEAR-CUTTING AND WILDLIFE

by George Reiger

Clear-cutting is like one of those good news–bad news jokes. It is good news when done in limited stands on level ground where new habitat for different species of wildlife is created. It is bad news when done over vast areas on steep slopes where silt and poisonous minerals run off to destroy trout streams and salmon spawning grounds.

The U. S. Forest Service doesn't like the verb clear-cut, with its implication of a devastated landscape unfit for man or beast. "Even-aged forest management" is the phrase professional foresters use. To quote a recent Department of Agriculture booklet on the matter, "Even-aged management is a system of growing, harvesting, and reproducing trees in stands of timber that are essentially the same age. Each year, small areas of mature trees are harvested and reforested with young trees. About 1½ percent of all National Forest acreage is harvested and regenerated each year by this method."

When described this way, few people could complain about clear-cutting. Yet clear-cutting is increasingly symptomatic of another facet of modern forest management unfavorable to wildlife, and that is monoculture: the growing of one tree species to the exclusion of all others. Every year in my home area of the Southeast, countless oaks and beeches are girdled and wasted to make room for the faster growing, and hence more profitable, loblolly pine. Such dense stands of pine are planted that, even when mature, the forests provide far fewer homes and food for game species such as bear, deer, turkey, and squirrel than the hardwood stands the pines replaced.

The secret of wildlife abundance is habitat diversity. Section upon section of even-aged timber of one species is a biological desert compared to the same region recovering from a clear-cut and overgrown with legumes and shrubs, forbs and berries, and seasoned with such brush-loving wildlife as quail, rabbit, and ruffed grouse.

The way to improve wildlife yields in forestry management is to provide as many "edges" as possible. An edge occurs wherever one type of habitat touches another. Besides providing water, a stream running through a forest provides "edge" in its diversity of unique plant forms, which in turn support a diversity of insects, birds, and mammals. Similarly, a power-line right-of-way or a logging road creates edges through mature forests where grouse and turkey come to sun and deer browse on the succulent, low-growing forage. Diversity is further enchanced if the power line or road is zigzagged to create points of cover thrust into the clearings. Ideally, restricted clear-cutting provides a checkerboard pattern through wooded country where brushy acres alternate with stands of forty-year-old trees, where openings of ten-year-old scrub oak and chinquapin are found in mature forests a century old.

The hunter becomes an essential part of the forest and wildlife management scheme when he praises good management where he sees it and reports infractions where he finds them. Other than hunters, few people spend much time afield, and if we don't step forward to cite someone for clear-cutting too steep a forest slope or for encroaching on protected scenic or wilderness areas, we are nullifying our responsibility as concerned citizens.

Federal law protects trees growing near national forest streams to keep water temperatures cool and to prevent siltation from logging operations. Sometimes, however, loggers can be careless (let's give them the benefit of the doubt and avoid the word greedy), and stream banks are denuded or the protective tree line cut so thin as to be practically worthless. Only legal action brought against the wrongdoers will make better (more thoughtful) loggers of them and their successors, so we can have better forests and improved wildlife management in the future.

George Reiger is conservation editor of *Field & Stream* and Washington editor of *Audubon*. He has written and contributed to many books on the outdoors, and most recently he and his wife, Barbara, published *The Zane Grey* (Outdoor) *Cookbook*.

Hunter Preserve Packages and Hunter Etiquette

Here's a sampling of the kinds of hunts offered by shooting preserves and what's expected of you.

The Walk-up Hunt is a typical upland bird hunt. Quail, pheasant, or chukar are stocked in a naturally wooded area and pointed by a dog. If the bird holds tight, the guide goes in and flushes the bird. This is an extremely dangerous but necessary practice and a time when everyone in the party should be safety conscious. A tight-holding bird may fly anywhere: between you and the guide or between other members of the party. For this reason it's customary for one hunter to walk in with the guide and take the single or covey rise first. Other shooters should hold their fire until the bird is lined out and well away from the party.

Mallard Pass Shooting finds mallards flying from their feeding area to water. You hunt from a blind that intercepts their flight path. Generally, no more than two shooters hunt from one blind.

Turkey Hunting involves calling in birds. You hunt from a blind. If you are adept at the use of a call, you do the talking. If not, your guide will.

The Circle Shoot is of British origin and simulates driven birds. Pheasants and mallards are released from a tower or a hilltop in groups of one to three birds. Shooters encircle the release point and gun from eight stands. The stands are located well away from the release point and are usually hidden from one another.

Sowhatchet Plantation: Quail Southern Style

Sowhatchet Plantation is a 13,500-acre hunting preserve and club. It is intensively managed for all species of native game (quail, dove, duck, and deer), and hunting there is on a membership ($500–$1,500 per year) or daily ($100 per day) basis.

Most quail hunting is done from four-wheel-drive vehicles and on foot. The clubhouse is a large, old, southern-style mansion, with fireplace, front porch, and a sense of leisurely living.

One interesting note: Sowhatchet specializes in group corporate entertainment, with food and lodging facilities for up to twenty people. Sounds like a neat place to throw an office party. Contact Mr. David

Morris, Sowhatchet Plantation, P.O. Box 606, Bostwick, GA 30623.

TRY A SHOOTING PRESERVE HUNT

Urban sprawl has gobbled up the fields and coverts that once lay at the outskirts of our large cities, and finding a place to hunt gets more difficult each year. One alternative to this plethora of shopping centers and posted signs is a preserve hunt.

Shooting preserves amount to large tracts of private farm and woodlands that are stocked with game. Typical species include quail, pheasant, chukar, mallard duck, and turkey. You pay a fee to hunt there, either on a daily basis or by the number of birds taken.

While this might sound like blasting up a barnyard, it isn't. Birds are bred for wild characteristics, and they come busting out of cover at speeds appropriate to humble even the best shots. I once hunted the Homosassa Hunting Preserve in Homosassa Springs, Florida, with the late Ernie Lind, a superb trick and exhibition shooter. Admittedly, Ernie did better than I, but he managed to miss a few. And he regularly popped 2-inch-square wood blocks out of the air with a .38 pistol. That's got to say something about bred birds as sporty, tough targets.

Preserves are also just a nice way to get away from the big city into open fields and to know that you're going to get some shooting. More recently, I'd been staying in the suburbs of New York City, and I was invited on a quail hunt at Spring Farms, near Sag Harbor, on Long Island. I'd forgotten how beautiful the rolling woodlands were on the East End, and as we hunted, a flock of over a thousand geese passed overhead. Good music . . . how sweet it was!

It was a good afternoon. We bagged nineteen birds and got to know the owner of Spring Farms, Dave Schellinger. Dave's a big, burly guy who takes obvious and deserved pride in the quality of his birds and of the hunting at the farms. His operation is a good yardstick of quality in a shooting preserve.

Between the lands that he owns and those he leases, Spring Farms totals 500 acres. There are never more than five parties hunting at one time, so you don't keep bumping into other hunters. The toughest part of his job is raising fast-flying birds, but his success was obvious that day. We flushed a covey of wild birds and could not differentiate between them and his stock when we worked out the singles. His dogs, all Brittanies, were bird-wise and obedient.

Spring Farms books two half-day hunts: pheasants (ten birds) for $120 and quail (twenty birds) for $140. If you want to use your own dog and don't need the services of a guide, he knocks $20 off that price. Up to four people may hunt in a party. Contact Spring Farms, P.O. Box 966, Sag Harbor, NY 11963.

—N.S.

Shooting Preserve Directory

For a list of shooting preserves that are open to the public either on a membership or daily fee basis, write John M. Mullin, Information Officer, North American Game Breeders and Shooting Preserve Association, Route 1, Box 28, Goose Lake, IA 52750.

Part III

WATERFOWL

IT ISN'T RAINING RAIN, YOU KNOW . . .

Stuttgart, Arkansas, has long been famous as one of the best places in the Central Flyway to hunt ducks, but the town achieved a new distinction the day it rained frozen ducks. A passing flight of birds was caught in the violent updraft of a thunderstorm, which swept them to high altitudes where temperatures were well below zero. The ducks froze and dropped to earth.

Ironically, the incident occurred the day before duck season was due to open. Sympathetic authorities allowed any holder of a hunting license and duck stamp to "harvest" four of the birds.

HUNTING HIGH

"It was in the afternoon on a slow day. I was hunting alone and I had gotten tired of calling and looking for birds, so I just started looking at the things around me. It was real quiet. I was watching bugs . . . on the water, and they were making very regular ripples on the surface. I kept on watching them and got kind of fascinated or something, and then all of a sudden, it was like 'bing!' just like that, I got the sensation that those ripples weren't just on the pond, but that they were spread out everywhere. I mean it was like the whole world was rippling together. I felt a kind of intense feeling, like being real warm, and I found myself really getting off on those bugs. And I don't fool around with dope or anything like that."

—Anonymous waterfowler, Delevan Refuge, California

SHOOTING HOURS

As a rule of thumb, when you can first make out detail—individual leaves, branches, bullrushes, and such—it will be one half hour until sunrise.

PLANT CROPS THAT HOLD AND ATTRACT WILDLIFE

Certain types of plants are especially attractive and beneficial to wildlife. Ducks, for example, relish sago, wild rice, pondweed, and wild celery. Quail go bananas over ragweed. Wildlife Nurseries, P.O. Box 2724, Oshkosh WI 54901, specializes in over forty varieties of these food and cover plants. Free price list and advice are available on what to plant for your favorite wild critter.

What the Wild Goose Knows

The distinctive V of migrating geese plays an important part in flight. The lead bird "breaks" the air, and current discontinuities travel down the edges of the formation, making the flying easier for birds in the rear. The lead position is usually taken by the strongest birds in the flock, who frequently trade places to share the work.

MIGRATION SECRETS REVEALED

Researchers at Cornell University have found that birds are acutely sensitive to atmospheric changes, enabling them to predict weather and favorable winds. They also respond to polarized light, which means that they can locate the sun and use it as a guide even on a cloudy day.

The Canvasback Curse

Of all waterfowl, none are valued so highly or seem so cursed as the canvasback, at least in terms of survival. A quick look at some of the qualities and habits of this bird explain why:

• Cans are generally agreed to be the best-eating duck that flies; hence, they're eagerly sought after to the point of being singled out.

• They are ready decoyers and will approach a well-set rig with abandon.

• Their nesting areas are valued for agricultural lands.

• Their nesting habits make them easy targets for predators and make them uncommonly susceptible to the effects of drought.

• Broods regularly exhibit a dispropor-tionate sex ratio, with males outnumbering females more than two to one.

• To the untrained eye, female canvasbacks resemble several other types of common waterfowl. What's worse, females have a habit of tolling to blocks inside the male, a course which normally carries them closest to hiding hunters.

FLYING HIGH

On July 9, 1962, a Western Airlines Electra hit a mallard duck over Nevada at an altitude of 21,000 feet.

If there are crows around your blind, watch them in flight. If they dip or swerve from their typically straight path, they're seeing you, and ducks probably will, too.

Virtually every species of duck or goose has some part of its feathery anatomy that is of value to the fisherman; wood duck, mallard, pintail, and Canada goose are especially prized as a source of feathers for flies. So get to know a flytier (if you're not one yourself). You can probably engineer some kind of feathers-for-something-else trade and make a good friend in the bargain.

There are over 10,000 muscles in a wild goose the sole purpose of which is the control of feather actions.

Canada geese are the longest lived game bird, with documented records of birds in captivity having lived seventy years.

WATER CHILL FACTORS

Late-season duck hunters seldom realize that cold water makes for a grim ally. Whether you can swim like an otter or are buoyed by the best life jacket, your survival time is severely limited as the water temperature decreases. Note, too, that salt water freezes at about 27.5 degrees F.

Water Temperature (degrees Fahrenheit)	Time (in hours) to Reach Exhaustion or Unconsciousness	Probable Death
70–80	3–12	3–indefinite
60–70	2–7	2–40
50–60	1–2	1–3
40–50	½–1	½–1½
32.5–40	¼–½	¼–1½

WITNESSING WHIFFLES

One of the most spectacular waterfowl sounds you'll ever hear is called whiffling. The word is an apt description of the noise made by the wings of geese and ducks as they lose altitude in a hurry. They accomplish this rapid descent by sideslipping, much like a piece of paper fluttering to earth. Pilots call this trick "dumping air."

Whiffling is most common after birds pass over a popular area for hunters and into some protected sanctuary like a preserve or large expanse of water. When large flocks of big birds such as Canada geese whiffle down on a calm day, the rush of wings comes close to the roar of a jet plane.

"Black duck and mallard . . . fly around forever before they make up their minds to stool. Broadbill . . . just bare their breasts and take what's coming."
—Billy Schneider

237

WATERFOWL GUNS

Shotguns for waterfowl are traditionally heavier and longer of barrel, and they use more and bigger shot through tighter chokes than upland guns. To a certain extent this is a valid premise, as ducks and geese are normally larger than most upland birds and have a tougher layer of feathers and fat that is sometimes hard to penetrate. They are often shot at longer ranges, also, though not as often as some people believe, and in windy weather, which has an effect on shot size and choke selection.

There are actually three main types of waterfowling: jump shooting, decoy hunting, and pass shooting. The jump shooter very often is better off with a gun that might be called an upland type; he'll be carrying it quite a bit and needs a relatively quick-handling weapon, with a fairly open choke, in order to point it quickly at flushed ducks. A light pump, auto, or double-choked modified—or, in the case of the double, improved cylinder and modified—would be a good choice for this kind of hunting.

Decoying can be both a long-range and a short-range proposition. Ducks over decoys are just about the best place to use a double gun in many shooters' opinion; normally, you'll get one shot at fairly close range with the open barrel and then a longer shot with the tighter barrel as the ducks flare. Here again, a light upland gun would be suitable in most situations, but light weight is not necessary since the gun won't be carried too far. However, an overly heavy and long gun can cut down on efficient handling in decoy situations.

Pass shooting is where the traditional duck gun comes into its own. Long, heavy barrels choked tightly not only will reach out to the traveling birds but will give a longer sighting plane—aiding in more precise pointing at long shotgun ranges—and will tend to "follow through" better than short tubes. Heavy loads are normally used in pass-shooting guns, so gas-operated semiautos are favored by many because of the recoil-reduction factor.

I would eliminate the .410 and 28-gauge guns from consideration as waterfowl weapons. They simply don't shove enough shot out the barrel for many situations. The 20-gauge is a good minimum, preferably with 3-inch chambers. The shorter shells are good on decoying birds and in jump shooting, especially early in the season, but later on, and in pass shooting, the 3-inch shells have an edge. The 16 is just about as good; the only problem is the availability of ammo.

The 12- and 10-gauges are the traditional waterfowling weapons, especially in magnum configurations. There is nothing like a 10-gauge on geese, for instance, or a 3-inch 12. Both these shells hold enough shot in the big sizes (No. 2 and up) to be effective on honkers at ranges over 50 yards. For many years the 3-inch 12 would have been perhaps the better choice, because the 10-gauge factory loads were never updated with shot cups and star crimps as were the more popular 12 loads, and actually the 2-ounce 10 magnum load would hardly ever put as much shot in a pattern as the 1⅞-ounce 3-inch 12. The new 10 loads, however, are equipped with shot cups, though some still have roll crimps and are more effective, though very expensive. In truth, except for the handloading goose hunter, in most areas the 10 doesn't exceed the 3-inch 12's potential except in one area: steel shot loads. Lead poisoning is a reality in some areas, because shot from years of gunning is being ingested by waterfowl. Steel shot, which is not as ballistically efficient as lead, has become the legislators' answer in such areas, and many gunners are considering the 10 for such shooting, because it gives an edge with the light shot.

Waterfowl come in about as many sizes as other game, from little teal to huge honkers, but in reality a shooter with two guns is well equipped. A lighter, more open-choked arm for jump and decoy shooting in 3-inch 20 gauge or standard 12 and a magnum in either 12 or 10 gauge for pass and goose shooting should fill anyone's needs. Actually, unless you do a lot of goose gunning, the lighter gun is entirely practical for most shooting. Geese are an entirely different matter, as a run-of-the-mill Canada will be three times as large as the average mallard and much tougher to bring down. There are some shooters who use small shot and light loads on geese and try for head shots, but this is usually only possible at fairly close ranges. On the public areas where most of us do our goose gunning, this simply isn't possible much of the time. Shots at 50 to 60 yards are common, and nothing less than 1½ ounces of No. 2 shot will consistently down geese at that range; more is better if you can handle the recoil.

The windy conditions that waterfowlers often face have an effect on choke and load. If the wind is really howling, you should consider using full choke, even over decoys, or perhaps shot one size larger, as it is astounding how the turbulence can blow the shot around.

The biggest mistakes shooters make in selecting waterfowl guns, just as in most shotgunning, are overchoking and overloading. Unless you are really sure you need that heavy 10 or 3-inch 12, you'll be much better off most of the time with a smaller weapon with a more open choke. —J.B.

THE WATERFOWLING PIECE

by Clair Rees

There have probably been more lies told about what kind of gun makes the best "waterfowling piece" than anything else in modern hunting history. Perhaps "lie" is too harsh a word—most of the experts (real or fancied) who profess to prefer one particular gauge/choke/action type of fowling piece for gunning ducks and geese truly believe that they have the answer. And they carry that answer to others with true missionary zeal.

Try telling a lover of full-choked 12s that you can take as many teal as he can over decoys—and *you* use a skeet-choked 20,—and I'll guarantee you an argument. As a matter of fact, you can spot a group of dedicated waterfowlers at any cocktail party; just follow your ears to the loudest, most boisterous discussion in the room, and if duck season is about to begin, is just over, or is in full swing, I'll give you two to one the arguing parties are hunters.

When it comes to guns and loads, duck and goose hunters can argue for days on end. Hours at a time can be spent over the choice of shot size alone, and when talk turns to gauges or chokes, the clock is forgotten entirely. Of course, the reason these nimrods spend so much time and effort arguing over their choices is that they have widely differing opinions. And the fact that each may be equally successful in keeping his larder stocked with duck or goose indicates that each does well with the particular gun and load he has chosen, whatever that choice might be.

I have my own firm opinions regarding the ideal waterfowling gun, but I'm going to keep them to myself. One of the reasons for my modest reticence is that my opinions have a tendency to change, and I've embarrassed myself too often in the past. The last time I recommended a modified-choked 12-bore pump as the last word in armament for all-around waterfowling, the close friend who subsequently took my sage advice wondered out loud about the dedication I showed to a 20-gauge auto the following season.

The fact of the matter is I've killed ducks with everything from a 28-gauge skeet gun to a full-choked magnum 10, and my geese have fallen to almost equally varied armament. And the pellets I've plucked from succulent brown-roasted breasts on my dinner plate have ranged in size from 2s to tiny 7½s.

Almost any shotgun can be used to hunt waterfowl effectively. The trick is to be aware of the limitations of whatever gauge/choke/shot combination you choose (and they all have their limitations), and observe those limitations whenever you take a shot.

A skeet-choked 20 or 28 will kill cleanly with a mere ⅞ ounce of No. 7½ shot, as long as your aim is true and you don't stretch your range beyond the 30-yard mark. And when ducks are decoying well, you'll have plenty of 30-yard targets to choose from. (Forget the .410, whatever the range.)

Millions of web-footed meals have been collected with full-choked 12-bores over the years, and a gunner so armed can drop birds at 40 or 45 yards, provided he knows his business. But the same nimrod would be smart to pass up extremely short-range shots (that his skeet-choked friends would love) and hold his fire until his shot charge has a chance to open up. And remember, heavier shot is generally more effective at longer range, while the denser patterns afforded by smaller pellets are excellent for close-in work.

What makes the best waterfowling gun? The shotgun you have in your closet right now—or that new gun that felt so good when you hefted it in the store last week. Just be sure you shoot a few patterns into some butcher paper and know what that gun can do before you head for the duck blind. Then, if you handle your end of the job, you'll kill ducks with the best of them.

Clair Rees is a full-time writer who specializes in firearms and hunting. His byline regularly appears in *Guns and Ammo*.

ITHACA AUTOMAG

This is the gun that breathed new life into the 10-gauge shell. It is a three-shot automatic, ponderous to behold and built like a tank.

The Automag is a remarkable gun in several ways. It has a marvelous balance that reflects itself in a superb fit and easy swing. For all its 10-pounds-plus weight, it jumps to your shoulder and tracks a moving bird like an upland 20-gauge. The mighty recoil of the powder and shot packed into a 3½-inch hull has also been tamed; I would compare the amount of kick to a standard 12-gauge side-by-side when it's loaded with 2¾-inch magnums.

Personal testing with the new power piston Remington shells found the Automag's range to be an impressive 85 yards. I put four pellets into the body outline of a goose with plenty of penetration. The tamed recoil also allows fast second and third shots if you miss the first. In many ways it is the answer to a goose hunter's prayer.

I did find, though, that even factory-fresh shells oc-

"Anyone who regularly kills his limit of black duck is either lying or doing something illegal."
—Overheard in North River, Massachusetts

239

STANDARD SHOTGUN FEATURES

There are three principal chokes provided on factory shotguns by American manufacturers: improved cylinder, modified, and full. In addition, these standard chokes are usually matched with certain barrel lengths. Improved cylinder barrels are normally 26-inch long, modified 28-inch, and full 28- and 30-inch. In double guns the improved cylinder/modified and modified/full combinations are standard, with the IC/M usually in 26-inch barrels and the M/F in 28- and 30-inch lengths. Some manufacturers also make full-and-full 30-inch barrels.

Most shotgun stocks are of walnut, though a great many of the cheaper grades are of walnut-finished hardwood. Sights are usually a simple bead on the front of the barrel; two beads are used on upper-price models that are ribbed (a sighting plane extending the length of the barrel), with one bead in the middle of the rib in addition to the front bead.

Chamber length is becoming more standardized. The common gauges—.410, 20, and 12—all are available with 3-inch chambers, with almost all .410s having this feature and 90 percent of the 20s. However, there are just about as many 2¾-inch chambered 12s on the market as the 3-inch models, as the long 12 shell is thought of as being a long-range waterfowl round and fairly specialized. The other gauges—28, 16, and 10—when you can find them, are always of one length in new guns. The 28 and 16 are 2¾-inch; the 10 is 3½-inch, though in used guns you may find a shorter 16-gauge chamber now and then (European chambering) for which special shells are needed, so beware. Some older 10s may be chambered for the 2⅞-inch shell.

There are two main types of safeties: tang and crossbolt. Crossbolt safeties block the trigger and are very simple and inexpensive, which probably is why they are on so many guns. Tang safeties may block either the trigger or some other part of the firing mechanism, such as the striker; they are commonly found, strangely enough, only on very inexpensive or expensive guns. They cost a bit more to manufacture but are much handier than the crossbolt type, because they are naturally under the thumb when the gun is put to the shoulder. The crossbolt is located behind the trigger in the trigger guard and is sometimes adaptable to left-hand use. If it isn't, and you're left-handed, it can be extremely clumsy.

Another thing to watch out for if you're left-handed is the bolt release on pump and auto guns. Sometimes it can be triggered by the left-handed shooter when he grasps the weapon naturally, releasing the locking mechanism. Under these conditions the gun won't fire, which can be downright frustrating.

Autos are of two main types, recoil- and gas-operated. In recoil-operated guns the barrel moves, giving the main impetus for the action's work. Gas-operated guns "bleed" off a little of the gas created by the powder's ignition to work the action. The gas-operated gun is becoming extremely popular, both because it lessens recoil by spreading it out over a longer period of time (it becomes a push rather than a kick) and because gas guns very often will handle a greater variety of loads than recoil guns. Recoil-operated guns are somewhat more reliable, however.

If you buy a double gun with a single trigger, there are a couple of considerations. One is barrel selection. Single triggers fall into two categories: those with the selection button in the trigger guard and those with the selection incorporated with the safety. The safety-selection type is much quicker but not as common. Nonselective triggers simply fire the more open barrel first. Another thing to watch for in single triggers is the switchover system, which is what connects the trigger to the second barrel for the repeat shot. If it is recoil-operated and the first round is a misfire, it won't kick over to the second barrel. A mechanical switchover will fire the second barrel no matter what.

Twin triggers on double guns are usually situated for right-handed shooters: the front trigger is on the right and the rear to the left, which makes it relatively easy for the right-hander to manipulate them. The left-hander can make do, but it involves some contortions that are not always a great aid to accurate shooting.

One thing to look for on magazine guns is easy access to the magazine tube. If you are going to be using the same gun on waterfowl and upland game, you'll have to put a plug (a length of dowel) into the magazine for waterfowling to keep the magazine capacity at two shells. If the magazine is difficult to break down and plug, you'll cuss every time you want to go waterfowling.

—J.B.

10-GAUGE

casionally jam as they're fed from the magazine to the chamber. Reloads, unless they're letter-perfect, just won't work, nor will shells shorter than 3½ inches. A design feature that I don't care for requires that the bolt-release mechanism be tripped in order to load shells into the magazine. When the birds are flying fast and furious and you're trying to reload, it's annoying unless you're used to guns with this peculiarity. But all in all, Ithaca's Automag is a real breakthrough: a gun that's both a pleasure to shoot and

a sure way to bag more geese.

Available in Supreme, Deluxe, and Standard Grade. Standard features include vapor-blasted blue-black nonglare finish on barrel and receiver, nonglare oil finish on stock, and interior mechanisms identical to the more expensive grades. Prices: plain barrel, $399.95; vent, $449.95. Ithaca Gun Co., Inc., 123 Lake Street, Ithaca, NY 14850.

All-Around Auto for a One-Gun Guy

If you can afford just one gun and like an automatic, look into the Model 1000 made by Smith & Wesson. It's the kind of versatile firearm that makes you wonder why it hasn't been put out before. The receiver accepts all popular barrels and lengths from a 22-inch slug special to a 30-inch full choke chambered for 3-inch mags! The manufacturer claims the gun performs equally well with all 12-gauge loads except field loads, which are not recommended.

Stock and fore end are American walnut, and the safety is a crossbolt type. The Model 1000 with a 30-inch barrel measures 50 inches and weighs 8 pounds. Magazine capacity is three 2¾-inch shells or two 3-inch mags. Price: $307.95. Smith & Wesson Co., 2100 Roosevelt Avenue, Springfield, MA 01101.

WINCHESTER 1200 WITH WINCHOKE

Winchester's 1200 shotgun is the successor to the famous Model 12 slide-action shotgun, which is now available only in Trap Grade. The 1200 and the 1400, its semiauto cousin, both feature Winchester's new Winchoke system, which is a choke-changing principle accomplished by threading choke cylinders into the muzzle of the gun. The cylinders are barrel-diameter and scarcely noticeable, unlike changeable-choke devices that constrict the choke by a twist of a ring or knob, which are bulky and alter the gun's balance. Each Winchoke-equipped gun comes with three cylinders: improved cylinder for close range shots, modified for medium ranges, and full choke for long shots. The 1200 with Winchoke is $164.95, or $184.95 with the ventilated rib; the Model 1400 is $209.95, with, again, $20.00 more for the rib. The best choke-changing arrangement yet on the market. Winchester-Western, 275 Winchester Avenue, New Haven, CT 06504.

BROWNING AUTO-5 SHOTGUN

The most recognized, if not the most popular, semiauto shotgun has to be the Browning Auto-5, with its blocky receiver which says "Browning" to everyone that looks at it. One of the best semiautos, too, with the quality that is standard in the Browning line. It comes in 12 and 20 gauge in various models, including a Buck Special with rifle sights for deer hunting, starting at $399.95. Extra barrels in various chokes run from $69.50 to $138.95, depending on length, choke, and if it's plain or ribbed. The one thing wrong with the Auto-5 is that it has the safety behind the trigger instead of on the tang, like any civilized shotgun should. Still, it's a beautiful gun. Browning, Route 1, Morgan, UT 84050.

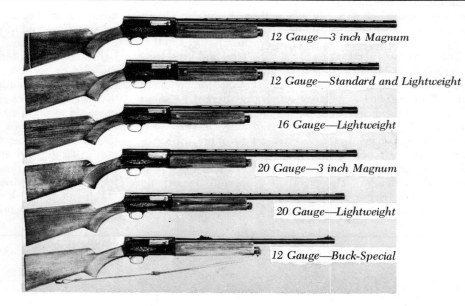

12 Gauge—3 inch Magnum

12 Gauge—Standard and Lightweight

16 Gauge—Lightweight

20 Gauge—3 inch Magnum

20 Gauge—Lightweight

12 Gauge—Buck-Special

Browning 2000 Gas Auto

Browning brought out this gas-operated semiauto at the request of a great many people who wanted a lighter-kicking Browning auto shotgun. The gas-operated feature and the weight (minimum 7½ pounds) make this a very good choice for the waterfowler who wants to use the heaviest loads. The gun comes in both 2¾- and 3-inch chambered models (all barrels are interchangeable). Choke choices are full and modified in 3-inch barrels or cylinder to full in 2¾-inch chambers. The safety is the crossbolt type. Browning also makes a 20-gauge 2000 that comes with 2¾- or 3-inch chambers in 26- and 28-inch barrels. Prices: $374.95 for 12 and 20 ventilated rib models; a plain-barreled 12 runs $354.95. Browning, Route 1, Morgan, UT 84050.

—J.B.

*"Those days when we shot seventy-five birds apiece from a battery and had to quit because
we either ran out of shells or our arms got too sore . . . those were the days, boys."*
—Joe Steigerwald, gazing seaward from Sedam Point, 1973

241

Harrington & Richardson Single-Shot 10-Gauge

If you yearn for the punch of a 10-gauge but don't have a pocketful of cash, Harrington & Richardson sells a single-shot 10 for around $65. It is a break-open with an exposed hammer and automatic ejection.

It might be worth noting that in practiced hands a single-shot automatic eject can be loaded and fired just about as fast as a bolt action, which costs considerably more in this gauge.

The gun is flawed in two respects, however. First, it has a 36-inch barrel, which is simply too long; it makes for clumsy swinging, it won't fit most gun cases or gun racks, and there's really not a lot to be gained in pattern or velocity once you pass 30 inches of barrel. It is also light, which finds it kicking like a mule with a 3½-inch magnum load.

Harrington & Richardson also makes a bolt-action three-shot shotgun, available in 10- and 3-inch 12 gauge for around twice the price. It has the same unwieldy barrel as the single shot, but it is considerably heavier and thus more comfortable to shoot. Harrington & Richardson, Inc., Industrial Rowe, Gardner, MA 01440.

ECONOMY O/U AND 10-GAUGE GOOSE GUN

This over-and-under shotgun (Model 7712) offers some unusual features for its low price. It is available in 26- and 28-inch barrels, with improved cylinder/modified and modified/full chokes. Both barrels are chambered for 3-inch mags. The gun has a single selective trigger and extractors. Barrels, chambers, and chokes are chrome-lined, and the stock is walnut.

While I haven't used this gun, the 26-inch improved cylinder/modified barrel with field loads would be an ideal upland gun. With 3-inch mags it would make a superb duck gun, and it would even pass for geese. A good buy at its suggested list of $299.90.

This company also markets a whole bunch of other shotguns and rifles at very reasonable prices. They have exposed hammer side-by-sides, enclosed hammer side-by-sides, and trap and skeet guns in assorted grades.

Another gun that I haven't tried but that interests me is their 10-gauge goose gun. It sports 32-inch full-and-full barrels and accepts 3½-inch magnum shells. At a suggested list of $249.90, this just might be the cheapest two-shot 10 on the market.

All in all, this company strikes me as a real sleeper. Their products appear well made, and their models seem designed to fill gaps major manufacturers ignore. Prices are right, too. Free catalog. Universal Sporting Goods, Inc., 7920 Northwest 76th Avenue, Miami, FL 33166. —N.S.

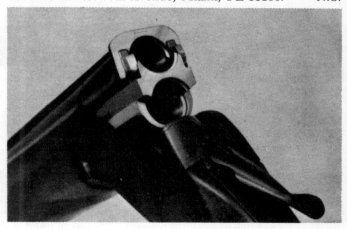

Pride of Spain 10-Gauge Side-by-Side

The POS side-by-side is typical of a whole bunch of imported shotguns (usually from Spain) that were the only 10s available for a long, long time. They sport standard extractors, 32-inch full-and-full barrels, and weigh 10½ pounds.

The worksmanship exhibited rates fair if you're into things like engraving and perfectly fitted stocks, but the shootin' iron itself is eminently serviceable. I've had one for many years now, and there is no sign of the action loosening or the stock cracking. A daft friend of mine once tried overloading his 3½-inch shells to stretch his killing range. The earth-shaking blast spun him around and drove the POS's action back into the stock, but otherwise the breech and barrels remained sound.

Like all singles and side-by-sides, the simple firing mechanism virtually never malfunctions, and the gun accepts all but the most malformed reloads—no small consideration given the cost of shells these days. Price: around $300.00 from sporting goods dealers or Harry L. Moss & Sons, 418 Park Avenue South, New York, NY 10117. —N.S.

Iver Johnson Silver Shadow—Reasonably Priced O/U

This is a well-made, functional over-under. In 12 gauge only it is available in 26-, 28-, and 30-inch barrels, with improved cylinder/modified, modified/full, and full/full chokes respectively. Weight is about 7½ pounds with 3-inch chambers. It

is available in two models, a double trigger for $252.95 and a single (they don't say whether it is selective or not, so it probably isn't) for $272.95. There are no specs in their info on ejection/extraction, so probably it is just plain extractor-equipped. Nevertheless, you are going to look far and wide for an O/U at this price. The barrel-length/choke combinations are good, and the double triggers are hard to find today and, I think, preferable. An excellent value. Iver Johnson's Arms, Inc., 109 River Street, Fitchburg, MA 01420.
  —J.B.

BROWNING CITORI O/U

This is the more affordable Browning O/U. Price for the field gun is $439.50. Comes in 12 or 20 gauge with 26-, 28-, and 30-inch barrels and a ventilated rib. Your choice of chokes is either modified and full or improved cylinder and modified for 26- and 28-inch lengths, or modified and full and full and full for the 30-inch tubes. The 30-inch tubes come in 12 only. All models have 3-inch chambers. Weights run from 6 pounds 11 ounces for the 26-inch 20 to 7 pounds 13 ounces for the 30-inch 12. Ejectors are automatic selective, the trigger is a single selective, and it is combined with a tang safety. Browning, Route 1, Morgan, UT 84050. —J.B.

FRANCHI 500/520 GAS AUTOMATICS

The Franchi 500 and 520 shotguns are regular and deluxe versions of the same gun. Both come with ventilated rib, chambered for the 2¾-inch 12, in 26- and 28-inch length barrels in the three standard chokes. Four-round magazine. Prices: $289.95 for the 500; $369.95 for the 520, which has an engraved receiver. Stoeger Industries, 55 Ruta Court, South Hackensack, NJ 07606.

REMINGTON 1100 MAGNUM AUTO

This gun comes in 12 or 20 gauge with 3-inch chambers and a 30-inch full-choked barrel. A 28-inch full or modified barrel is available in 20 gauge. Weight is about 7¾ pounds, which, along with the gas system, makes recoil very tolerable. Also included is a recoil pad. Comes in two models: plain, $264.95; ventilated rib, $289.95. Again, just a plain old crossbolt safety. Remington Arms Co., Inc., 939 Barnum Avenue, Bridgeport, CT 06602.

MARLIN SUPERGOOSE 10: BOLT-ACTION HONKER

Big gun! This is a repeating shotgun (bolt action is slow but with practice fast enough for much waterfowling) that weighs 10½ pounds. Barrel length is 34 inches, choke, of course, full, chambered for 3½-inch 10-gauge shells. Comes com-

plete with sling that makes it handy to lug around. Capacity is three shots: two in clip and one "up the pipe." For the goose hunter willing to use the 10 and wanting more shots than a double but not wanting to lay out the cash for an Ithaca auto, this would be a good choice. Bolt action makes it good choice for reloads, too, which makes sense, with 10-gauge shells selling for about $12.00 a box. Price: $149.95. Marlin Firearms Co., 100 Kenna Drive, North Haven, CT 06473.

MARLIN 120 PUMP GUN

This is a fairly heavy (7¾-pound) pump gun chambered for the 3-inch 12-gauge magnum. You can get the standard barrel-length/choke combos and a 40-inch(!) full choked barrel. If you miss your goose with it, you can always reach up and trip him. Comes with ventilated rib and crossbolt safety; barrels are interchangeable. Price: $183.95. Marlin Firearms Co., 100 Kenna Drive, North Haven, CT 06473.

"There's a bit of advice that I think I heard twice, and it's worthy of hunters attending.
If you're aiming to kill, hit your bird in the bill instead of attempting upending."
—Anon.

243

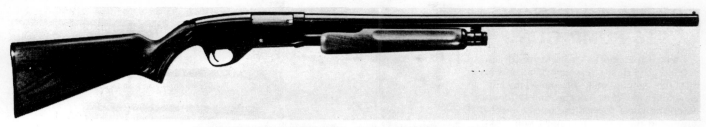

SAVAGE MODEL 30 PUMP GUN— REASONABLY PRICED SLIDE WITH GOOD FEATURES

I have one of these in 20 gauge and can't say enough about it. For the price—$136.50—I don't think you're going to find a better gun on the market. Not only does it have a tang safety, something that many—hell most—more expensive guns don't have, but it has interchangeable barrels and is chambered for 3-inch shells in the three common gauges, 12, 20, and .410. Weight is reasonable, about 6¾ pounds for my 20. Rugged action. I've had no problems with mine in the three years I've used it, and I've used it more than many hunters do in ten seasons. Savage Arms, Springdale Road, Westfield, MA 01085. —J.B.

WEATHERBY CENTURION AUTOMATIC

This is the supermagnum rifle people's shotgun. What is mildly surprising is that it is a fairly conservative-looking gun, something that Weatherby rifles aren't. This might imply that shotgunners are more conservative than riflemen. Might not, too. Anyway, it's gas-operated with a crossbolt safety, nice wood, recoil pad, standard choke/barrel lengths, 12-gauge only, 2¾-inch chamber. Weight with 30-inch barrels is 7 pounds 12 ounces, which definitely does not make it a featherweight upland gun but primarily a waterfowling weapon. It would have been nice if they'd have made a 3-inch magnum model. Still, it's well worth the price: $289.50. Weatherby, Inc., 2781 Firestone Boulevard, South Gate, CA 90280. —J.B.

WINCHESTER 21 S/S

This one will cost you a packet of folding money. Available only on special order, it is built to your specifications: barrel/choke, stock dimensions, fancy checkering, on and on into leather-covered recoil pads and gun cases with gold inlaid initials. In three grades: custom, pigeon, and Grand

American. The gun shown is the Grand American. Write Winchester-Western, 275 Winchester Avenue, New Haven, CT 06504.

SPEED-UP CROSSBOLT SAFETIES

If you haven't figured it out yet, none of us can be counted as fans of crossbolt safeties. However, this gadget might temper our disdain. It appears to be nothing more than a way to enlarge the button, thereby making it easier to feel, see, and use. It should be "safer," too, as it would be easier to tell whether the safety were on or off. It's available for most makes of rifles and shotguns (specify your type). Price: $3.49. Herter's, Inc., Route 2, Mitchell, SD 57301.

SMITH & WESSON 916 PUMP GUN

I tested this gun last fall and was disappointed. The slide release mechanism is in just the wrong spot for me (I'm left-handed), and about half the time I shouldered the gun I tripped the release mechanism and the shot would not go off. Taking the gun down I discovered that the hole for the bolt which pins the firing mechanism inside the receiver had not been centered properly, and there was a hairline crack on the outside of the hole. I returned the gun and found the same problem with the replacement.

Now the real reason for my disappointment: the gun fit me like a glove and had marvelous features for the price—a ventilated rib, a tang safety, and 3-inch chambering in a 28-inch modified barrel (a combination I've come to believe is the best one for duck hunting in places where you might get a crack at a goose). If those two faults were corrected, I'd call this the best pump buy on the market, especially since the newest 916 models also have an interchangeable barrel feature. Price: $138.00. Smith & Wesson Co., 2100 Roosevelt Avenue, Springfield, MA 01101.
—N.S.

AMMO FOR WATERFOWL

Waterfowl have slightly different ammo and shot size requirements from other winged game. They are protected not only by thick feathers (which get thicker as the season wears on) but by more fat and muscle than upland birds of equivalent size. You will need larger shot and more of it in many waterfowling situations, especially those concerning geese.

While 7½s are OK in many early-season situations, 6s are usually even better, and if I had to pick one size of shot for all duck shooting, it would probably be 5s or 4s. Geese need good-size shot to penetrate both bones and a larger body. Anything less than No. 4 is taking a chance, even at decoy ranges, that penetration will be insufficient. This is probably the best choice for the smaller geese. For Canadas a minimum of No. 2 is better, with BB being used in very large capacity hulls like the magnum 12 and 10.

Remember, you must have enough shot to adequately cover the bird. Hunters who use buckshot loads and try to knock down geese past normal shotgun ranges are the worst example of poor pattern, as well as of poor conservation and sportsmanship.

Because of the physical characteristics of waterfowl, good shot performance is needed, and so shot collars and plastic wads become of paramount importance. In the future we'll probably see granulated plastic used as a filler in waterfowl loads just as it's being used for buckshot loads now.

The biggest news in waterfowl ammo right now is steel shot. Mandatory in certain heavily hunted areas because of the problem of lead poisoning of ducks and geese caused by the ingestion of lead shot, steel shot eliminates the problem but isn't nearly as efficient ballistically as lead shot and can cause crippling when it's used at ranges beyond 40 yards. Also, it can damage some gun barrels, since it is harder and doesn't "flow" as easily through the choke as lead shot. Unless your manufacturer specifically states that your gun can be used with steel shot, you shouldn't try it. In the future we're likely to see more and more shotguns built with beefed-up choke sections to handle this.

Elmer Keith, the gun writer, feels that if we outlawed any shot smaller than No. 3, we'd eliminate the lead poisoning problem, because heavier shot sinks through the mud on lakes and rivers, below where waterfowl can take it in as they feed. I haven't seen any statistics on this, but it seems like a more reasonable solution—if it works.

Just as in any shotgun work, sometimes one load will work better in your gun than any other. The three things to remember are shot size, amount of shot, and good performance from *your* gun.
—J.B.

WATERFOWLER'S GUN CASE

One problem unique to waterfowling is how to protect your gun. Conventional soft cases absorb moisture in the marsh. Hard cases are bulky, and if you ever get the spongy liner wet, it will take days to dry it out.

Old Guide makes a soft, rubberized nylon case, reinforced with natural leather. It is waterproof and unlined—ideal temporary protection from wet dogs, salt spray, and marsh mud. One word of warning: this is a car-to-blind-and-back case. Since it is waterproof, condensation will build up on the inside and rust your gun if you store it there permanently. Price: $13.95 (indicate gun length when ordering). Old Guide, 105 Irving Street, Framingham, MA 01701.

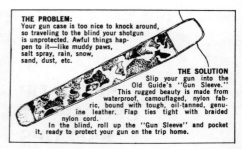

"Some day my marsh, dyked and pumped, will lie forgotten under the wheat, just as today and yesterday will lie forgotten under the years."
—Aldo Leopold

245

REMINGTON'S NEW 10-GAUGE AMMUNITION

This stuff is really the ticket for the serious goose hunter. Because of the law of supply and demand, 10-gauge shells were never improved upon like more popular 12-gauge loads. Consequently, a 12-gauge 3-inch magnum was a better deal than a 10-gauge, performance, cost, and availability of shells and kick taken into account.

The introduction of Ithaca's 10-gauge magnum changed all that. In the wake of revived interest in this gauge, Remington improved their old loads, adding a Power Piston shot cup inside and a 6-fold Venko crimp outside the hull. The results are impressive.

Using old No. 2 loads (my reloads and year-old factory loads), my pattern faded beyond the "four pellets to a goose's body" concentration at between 65 and 70 yards.

(It's generally agreed that four or more pellet hits are needed to bring a bird down.) With these new loads I got that kind of concentration at 80 to 85 yards.

Penetration was similarly improved. Old loads reached from page 80 to 100 in a phone book. Pellets from the new shells clustered around page 130, and a few of them drove on to page 150. These tests were made at 75 yards.

Good news, too, is that Remington sells these shot cups as a reloading component. At $11.00 to $14.00 a box, depending on the generosity of your local sporting goods store, these shells aren't exactly cheap. Remington Arms Co., Inc., 939 Barnum Avenue, Bridgeport, CT 06602.

—N.S.

Killing Cripples

All waterfowl, but especially diving ducks, are difficult to kill when crippled because of their protective habit of swimming low on the water and diving. Standard 4s and 6s do not have a dense enough pattern to regularly hit these birds in the head at 40-yard ranges, so carry a few 7½s or 8s for this purpose.

Don't worry about blowing birds apart at close ranges. They're probably a lot farther than you think, and your pattern will only connect with their back, neck, and head, which are hardly the most edible parts of the bird anyway.

Simmons Camouflage Gun Finish

For those duck and/or varmint hunters who don't give a damn about fancy-looking guns and don't want the bulk and hassle of camouflage tape or cloth, Simmons will do a nice, even camouflage job on your favorite marsh shooter for only $25.00. Simmons Gun Specialties, Inc., P.O. Box 533, Olathe, KS 66061.

HOW TO KEEP YOUR POWDER DRY

Used U.S. Army ammo cases with gasket-lined lids make excellent gear carriers for waterfowlers. The 50-caliber case keeps three boxes of shells, lunch, gloves, and your duck call together and dry, and the boxes double as a seat in the blind. They come in a wide variety of other sizes, large and small, and may be purchased from military surplus stores.

SUPER TOUGH FLOATING GUN CASE

Here's maximum protection for your waterfowling gun: a preformed "turtle-tuff" exterior that you can jump up and down on, and even drive a car over, without damaging it or the gun inside. Should you drop it in the drink, the gun case floats—again, with a gun inside. Foam-lined interior, with acrylic fur pile. Marsh olive in color for easy hiding. Price: $40.00. Gun-Ho, 110 East 10th Street, St. Paul, MN 55101.

TAKEDOWN CASE

Save space by carrying your shotgun broken down. This takedown case accepts barrels up to 34 inches long and includes a wrap-around full zipper and lined and pad-ded interior. Price: $20.00. Kolpin Manufacturing, Inc., P.O. Box 231, Berlin, WI 54923.

KOLPIN MANUFACTURING, INC.

HEAVY-DUTY CAMOU SOFT CASE

Kolpin makes a reinforced soft gun case in camouflage colors that should last many a duck season. Features include a waterproof exterior, humidity-proof padding, corduroy lining, a padded carrying handle that wraps around the full case, a full-length zipper, and a reinforced rubber crown.

The wrap-around handle is less likely to break than simple sewn-on handles, the waterproofing will protect a gun even in heavy rain, and the full zipper allows the case to be thoroughly dried when you get home. Price: $17.00 (Kolpin has other cases, too). Send $1.00 for a 36-page color catalog. Kolpin Manufacturing, Inc., P.O. Box 231, Berlin, WI 54923.

RUST PREVENTIVE FOR HUMID CLIMATES AND SALTY WATERFOWLERS

Rust is a gun's greatest enemy, and its effects are the most pronounced in warm, humid climates or when hunting around salt water. Under these conditions there is virtually no way to prevent rust except by constant attention; that means cleaning all exposed parts and your barrel after each use and then protecting the metal with a rust inhibitor.

Sheath rust preventive is a silicone-based liquid that drives moisture out of metal pores. It is polarized so that it continues to cling to metal in all weather. It neutralizes the acid from fingers and removes prints, and it is nongummy, so it won't freeze up in cold weather.

A tip: apply this stuff to warm-to-hot metal, and it will be even longer lasting.

Sheath Polarized Rust Preventive: aerosol can with extension tube for hard-to-reach places, $1.75; 4-ounce spout can of liquid, $1.00; Sheath "wipes" of impregnated cloth for use afield, $1.10 for package of ten. Birchwood Casey, 7900 Fuller Road, Eden Prairie, MN 55343.

Shell Tote Bag

Duck hunting has some peculiar requirements, and one of them is how to carry your shells. If you pocket them or wear them on a belt, they could drown you. If you store them in their boxes, the boxes break apart from dampness. Then, too, a chance goose or a long pass shot suggests that you tote along several loads.

One way to satisfy these needs is via a shell tote, available in cowhide for class on the trap range or black expanded vinyl for hunting around water. One tote carries four boxes of shells. Prices: cowhide tote, $14.00; vinyl tote, $6.30. Kolpin Manufacturing, Inc., P.O. Box 231, Berlin, WI 54923.

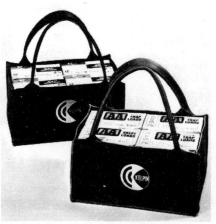

KOLPIN MANUFACTURING, INC.

ALL ABOUT WILDFOWLING IN AMERICA
edited by Jerome Knap

New York: Winchester Press, $10.00.

Drawing on the knowledge of more than a dozen experts, as well as on his own extensive experience, Jerome Knap has indeed assembled a book that tells "all about" wildfowling. From Mexico to Canada, from the Atlantic to the Pacific—and everywhere in between—local techniques and regional specialties are described in absorbing detail. Other chapters give timely information on decoys, bird calling, dogs, apparel, cookery, and more.

*"First it rained and then it blew
and then it frizz and then it snew."*
—Sign on Barnegat Bay duck hunter's shack

247

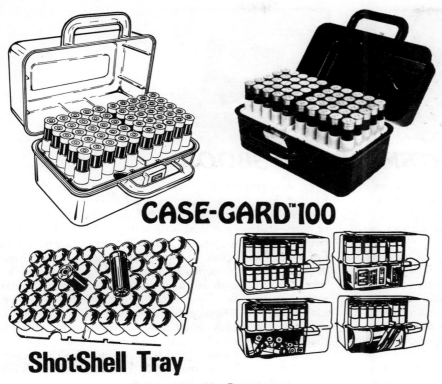

CASE-GARD™100

ShotShell Tray

Shotshell Organizer

A handy carrying case in the duck blind or on the trap range, this shell organizer is a hinged polypropylene box measuring 7 by 9 by 11 inches. It has space for two trays that hold fifty shells each in individual collars. If you use only one tray, you then have room for shooting accessories like calls and a Thermos or shooting glasses and ear protectors. Shells are poised within easy reach, and you can file them: goose loads to the right, duck loads to the left, etc. Available in 12-, 16-, and 20-gauge sizes. Price: $6.49; extra trays, $1.45 each. Cabela's, 812 13th Avenue, Sidney, NE 69162.

INSURANCE AGAINST SHELL BOX BREAKAGE

If you've ever had a damp shell box break as you picked it up (and what waterfowler hasn't), you'll appreciate the value of this gadget. It's a light, plastic reinforcer for a box of shells, with a ring on each side to hold your next load. Keep your duck loads in the box and a pair of deuces or BBs in the rings for a chance goose.

The reinforcer also clips onto your belt, making it doubly useful for when you go skeet or trap shooting. Price: $1.49 each; four for $5.00. John Hall Plastics, P.O. Box 1526, Alvin, TX 77511.

SHELL HOLDER

- Made of strong, high density polyethylene
- New size
- Easily clips on belt, waist or pocket
- Holds one box of shells and two extras
- $1.49 each or four for $5—Postpaid

THE COMPLETE WILDFOWLER
by Grits Gresham

New York: Winchester Press, $8.95.

Who wouldn't like a graduate course in wildfowling with a man who has been called the best duck shot in America? Grits Gresham is an all-round sportsman, as viewers of his *American Sportsman* television shows and readers of his best-selling bass-fishing book already know. However, he brings to wildfowling a special talent and passion in addition to his master's degree in game management and a quarter-century's experience in marshes and blinds throughout North America. And in this sound, readable, and up-to-date book, he reveals his own secret tricks and considered opinions about what counts and what works in duck and goose hunting and why.

Above all, this is a practical book for the

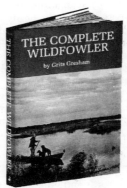

practical hunter. The historical perspective is there, and so are the hard ecological facts, but this is no nostalgic treatise on the way things used to be, or dry statistical analysis of migratory trends. Rather, it is a down-to-earth, step-by-step education in everything you need to know to hunt waterfowl in North America today, from dogs and decoys to snipe-shooting techniques.

MISTY MORNINGS AND MOONLESS NIGHTS
by Norman Strung

New York: Macmillan Company, $9.95.

The cover of this book indicates that this is a waterfowler's guide, and a waterfowler's guide it is. Norman Strung is to waterfowling what Admiral Rickover is to the atomic submarine. He has hunted ducks and geese all his life, starting with his youth in New York and continuing throughout his adulthood in Montana. He has now shared his knowledge and pleasures with the rest of us.

Strung covers all facets of waterfowling, from the making of decoys to the designing of goose pits. He discusses waterfowl identification and the construction of duckboats. He describes the effect of weather on the habits of ducks and geese. He leaves little yet to be learned.

A friend with the best-laid-out duckboat I have ever seen has a watertight compartment for his copy of *Misty Mornings and Moonless Nights*. What more needs to be said?

—Dick Weden

SPORTSMAN'S LOGBOOK

One thinks of hunting as an active sport, yet there is a passive side to it as well. The double you downed with one barrel, the day at deer camp when you lost your shirttail, the first rabbit your son shot with your old .22 . . . what would hunting be without memories?

American Sporting Journals publishes a hunting logbook and a waterfowling logbook at $10.95 each. They are 100-page record books bound in durable leatherette, with pages permanently bonded to the cover. A sampling of entry columns in the hunting book includes species taken, location, gun, load, and dog. The waterfowling book includes a special place on each page for keeping annual migratory bird stamps.

The value of these logbooks, of course, rests with you. But if you have the discipline to make regular, detailed entries, the rewards will be incalculable one, five, or ten years later, and perhaps they will even be profitable. In waterfowling, for example, there's a good chance you might spot a set of parallel conditions—wind direction, location, time of year—that regularly adds up to top gunning. But beyond being the door to possibly better hunting, it's just a lot of fun to read and recall your past experiences. A good friend of mine from Massachusetts keeps the most detailed logbook I've ever seen. It's a joy to read, like a good hunting yarn. For example, the first time I ever hunted geese with him I used a 10-gauge 3½-inch mag with a scope, armament that plainly awed him. Concluding his entry for the day, he wryly observed, "No wonder there is a steel shortage in the country, and lead poisoning in the marsh!" American Sporting Journals, P.O. Box 228, Route 1, Plainfield, IL 60544.

A HUNTER'S FIRESIDE BOOK/MOSTLY TAILFEATHERS
by Gene Hill

New York: Winchester Press, $7.95 each.

This review is not about books, it's about a writer. Whenever you meet Gene Hill, whether he is in a business suit or a field jacket, he looks as if he has just returned from a sleety day of hunting on a Scottish moor. He is ruddy, weatherbeaten, and rough-hewn, yet of a firm handshake, a gentle eloquence, and abiding confidence. If I were to cast *Lady Chatterley's Lover,* he'd be my first choice for the gamekeeper.

His work reflects an uncommon sensitivity, the religious implications of donning a gunning vest and duck call lanyard in the predawn, and the enormous sadness of the present that couples with the infinite joys of the past when one puts a favored hunting dog to death. Yet he is always in perfect control. When a duck call becomes a phylactery, it is not an absurdity. When he toasts the past with heavy, heady bourbon by the grave of his dog, you shed a tear, but it is not maudlin. It is a peculiar celebration that only a man who has loved a hunting dog can understand and only a gifted writer can communicate.

Gene Hill is that rare combination of superb outdoorsman with the perceptions of a poet. He writes like he is, and I can think of no higher commendation for his work. 　　　　　　　　　—N.S.

SUCCESSFUL WATERFOWLING
by Zack Taylor

New York: Crown Publishers, $8.95.

The boating editor of *Sports Afield* knows about things other than boats—and two of them are waterfowl and writing. This book will give vicarious pleasure to the dedicated waterfowler and build a desire in those who are not. It is complete, from descriptions of the how and where of waterfowl hunting to boat designs, decoys and decoy patterns, and equipment, and includes the final enjoyment, waterfowl cookery. Written in an amiable style, the book is well illustrated with photographs and detailed drawings that are easily understood.

THE OUTLAW GUNNER
by Harry M. Walsh

Cambridge, Md.: Tidewater Publishers, $8.50.

Dealing with the ways, the wiles, and the days of the market hunter before and after market gunning was outlawed in 1918, this is a fascinating work, a historical work, that records and illuminates the mechanical and human devices that led to bags of 300 and more ducks per day.

Aside from its documentary value, there's a permeating sense of understanding and perhaps even admiration for the market gunners of old—who would risk life and limb in a mere shell of a scull boat, following a flock of ducks over ice-caked open waters for twelve hours or more—and these two factors make this a highly readable book—almost a novel. Not that Walsh condones illegal activities; he's plainly a committed conservationist. But his words and pictures show the bravery of the market gunner as well as his unsporting practices.

All in all, the book is an intriguing chunk of Americana that makes for great reading, especially if you're a waterfowler.

"Whereas I write a poem by dint of mighty cerebration, the yellow-leg walks a better one just by lifting his foot."
—Aldo Leopold

249

Wood Duck Box

Wood ducks are among the most striking of our waterfowl, and one of our most vulnerable to the encroachment of civilization. As houses are built and new fields are plowed, the hollow trees they need for nesting are destroyed.

Do a woody and yourself a favor by installing a wood duck box near the shores of a pond. You can build one at home (plans are available free from Ducks Unlimited, P.O. Box 66300, Chicago, IL 60666) or you can buy one ready-made, with complete instructions on how and where to install it. Price: $10.95. Cabela's, 812 13th Avenue, Sidney, NE 69162.

Gray's Sporting Journal

This magazine deserves special recognition because of a thing called quality. Other outdoor magazines are how-to and catch'em-kill'em-and-eat'em oriented, which is fine and right and serves a valid purpose. But *Gray's* focuses on those rewards for outdoor pursuits that go beyond the catch or the kill. When you read *Gray's* you get to know people, places, game, and the smell of gunpowder. You get good, entertaining reading, heavy paper, and photos and artwork of sunsets, sleety-gray duck mornings, and elk tracks in snow.

Someone once defined *Gray's* editorial approach as a "me-and-Joe-went-fishing magazine, with the emphasis on 'went.'" OK. But I would add "with class." Price: seven issues a year for $18.50; back issues (they're worth it), $3.00 each. *Gray's Sporting Journal*, 1330 Beacon Street, Brookline, MA 02146.   —N.S.

DUCKS UNLIMITED

Ducks Unlimited is a nonprofit organization dedicated to the enhancement of waterfowl populations across North America. It accomplishes this goal by buying and leasing key nesting grounds in Canada and wintering grounds in Mexico and develops these lands for the greatest waterfowl good.

A typical DU project would include leasing a Canadian marsh or bog, then diking it in such a way that water levels, shorelines, and edge areas are maximized for nesting opportunities. The dike also functions as "water insurance" in times of severe drought. Through this kind of effort, DU has stabilized and, in some cases, increased waterfowl populations and marsh-associated wildlife, too.

DU membership is $10.00, for which you also receive a subscription to *Ducks Unlimited Magazine*, a bimonthly publication dealing with all aspects of waterfowl and waterfowling. The artwork alone in these magazines justifies the cost of membership.

If you've ever shouldered a shotgun in a marsh or thrilled to the whistle of wings sailing out of a gray dawn, you already belong to DU in spirit. Make it official by sending them a contribution of $10.00—or more. Ducks Unlimited, Inc., P.O. Box 66300, Chicago, IL 60666.

DUCKS OF THE MISSISSIPPI FLYWAY
by John G. McKane

St. Cloud, Minn.: North Star Press, paperback only, $2.98 and $4.95 (deluxe).

This book, with paintings by Ernest Strubbe and Ken Haag, identifies and shows the ranging areas of the ducks of the Mississippi Flyway. General info on feeding and nesting patterns is given.

—J.B.

DUCK PLUCKERS, STRIPPERS, SUCKERS, SOAKERS

A noted philosopher once suggested that you can never know the heights of pleasure without also experiencing the depths of pain. When you think about it, the guy was probably right, and this observation doubles in spades when the duck hunt is over and it's time to clean those little devils. It almost makes you wish you'd been skunked. There are many ways to pluck a duck, and unfortunately none of them is painless.

Dry plucking is time-consuming, but in some respects it involves the least hassle. To dry-pluck a bird, cradle it in your lap (preferably out of doors, where flying feathers won't be a nuisance), and yank small hanks of feather from the carcass. It will go much quicker if you use both hands. After you have picked the bird as clean as you can, scorch the remaining feathers with a propane torch.

To wet-pluck a bird, heat a tub of water to around 190 degrees. You'll have the right temperature when you can dip your finger in the water three times in succession and on the fourth get the feeling that you're cooking. Add some detergent (½ teaspoon per gallon) and stir. Immerse the bird (or birds, depending on the size of the tub), and stir for 30 seconds. If the wing feathers come off easily, the bird is ready to be stripped. Get it done as soon as the bird is cool enough to handle. Feathers should come off in big, wet globs. Do not leave the birds in the water; too much "cooking" will set the feathers, and they'll be tougher to remove than before.

Paraffin plucking requires a cursory dry plucking. Then you immerse the carcass in melted paraffin wax. You can use cooking-type paraffin or a special plucking paraffin marketed by Herter's (Route 2, Mitchell, SD 57301; 5 pounds for $2.49).

Dunk the carcass enough times to build up a wax layer on the bird. The feathers will come free when you peel away the wax. The peeled paraffin may be remelted and reused; the feathers will float to the top, where they can be skimmed off. Paraffin plucking is the most reliable way to remove pinfeathers (undeveloped, hard-to-grab, replacement feathers, usually found on birds early in the season).

Mechanical duck pluckers all work on the same basic principle: a core of rubber with supple, sticky "fingers" is set to spinning by an electric motor. The soft rubber clings to the feathers and tugs them free as the fingers whirl around.

The McKendree Duck Picker (1893 Del Moro, Klamath Falls, OR 97601), is a rubber core and fingers mounted on a shaft. The shaft fits an electric drill, which supplies the power. While this system is a cut above dry plucking, it isn't flawless. You either need two people—one to hold the

drill firmly and one to hold the duck—or you must build some kind of solid chuck to hold the drill. Since there are no guards or braces, the McKendree tends to draw the bird into the wheel and can tear skin. Because there is no vacuum device, feathers fly. The majority of them fall to your feet, but you'll still have a substantial amount of down wafting through the air.

One thing this product does have going for it is price. At $15.00 it's the cheapest plucker on the market. And if you're handy with tools, you could surely build a housing around it and adapt the housing to a conventional canister vacuum cleaner, ending up with a close imitation of professional plucking machines that cost twenty times as much as the McKendree.

The Orvis plucker is notable in that the plucking device comes with a motor and it's housed, so you have a receptacle for feathers and control over the bird. It does not have

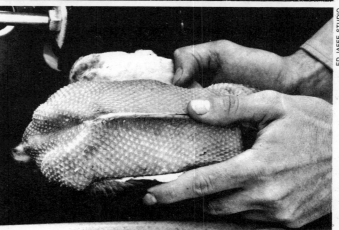

a vacuum device of its own, but it is adaptable to any kind of house vacuum cleaner that uses a hose. As complete duck pluckers go, the price is reasonable ($199.00 from Orvis, 10 River Road, Manchester, VT 05254).

"There was a young lady named Eva, who had an affair with a beaver.
The result of this mate was a brace of baldpate, two canoes, and a golden retriever."
—Anon.

251

The Magna Duck Stripper is a heavy-duty plucker with a fiberglass housing. It makes most sense for duck hunting clubs, shooting preserves, or a bunch of gunning buddies who get lots of birds. Its electric motor drives the plucking attachment, and a vacuum device with a reusable bag connects to it. The vacuum part also may be used as a boot drier. (Price: $395.00 from Magna American Corp., P.O. Box 90, Highway 18, Raymond, MA 39154.

It might be worth mentioning that these soaks, suckers, and so forth also work on upland birds, but because their skin is more tender than that of waterfowl you will need a gentler touch. —N.S.

L. L. Bean Coastal Black Duck Decoys

Down Easters are both pragmatists and traditionalists, and these decoys speak of both. They're oversized so they can be seen from across a Maine bay; they're cork, keeled and heavy so they'll ride well in a stormy, windswept sea; and the heads are hand-carved from solid white pine and hand-painted.

They are a solid, serviceable decoy and more. In their hand-crafted and slightly stylized lines there emerges a suggestion of the decoy as art and of waterfowling as more than shooting a duck. Sure, you might pull as many birds with a Styrofoam block, but you sacrifice a little soul by doing it. These decoys are a little chunk of waterfowling as an ideal, which to some of us is what the sport is all about. Black duck, mallard (also available as field decoys); pintail, canvasback, goldeneye, and bluebill (all suitable for a mantle, incidentally). Price: $9.00 each or 3 for $26.50. L. L. Bean, Freeport, ME 04033.

TRENDecoys

These decoys are made of foam-filled plastic and are something of a boon, since they're unsinkable should they mistakenly get in the way of a charge of No. 4s.

The manufacturer claims the paint is bonded to the plastic in such a way that it will never crack, chip, check, peel, snag, run, or go down at the heels, and a season's banging around in my decoy bag seems to bear out that claim. These decoys are very good at holding their paint.

Although they are counterweighted, I had trouble with the Canada goose decoy's blowing over in a wind, and it wouldn't right itself once it tipped. Otherwise, I would consider the block well made and of

Black Duck Magnum

Pintail

Black Duck

Redhead

Canvas Back

exceptionally strong construction. Time will have to tell, but I doubt there will be many broken head or bill problems with this brand.

TRENDecoys come in a full variety of species (including teal and coot) and in both field and water styles. Prices range around $30.00 per dozen for life-sized duck floaters and $58.00 for a dozen floating geese. They also have magnum-sized ducks in limited species. I would rate these as good decoys at a fair price. TRENDecoy Co., 1663 North McDuff Avenue, Jacksonville, FL 32205. —N.S.

HERTER'S FOAM DECOYS

These decoys are made of plastic foam and are keelless, so they pack relatively flat. They're interior-weighted and self-righting. The body conformation is right, the paint job good, and the head attachment system just about flawless. A long eye bolt is threaded through the body into a tough plastic receptacle in the bottom of the head. It is rare that these heads ever break or slip their thread. If they do, Mr. Herter catalogs extra heads, so they can be repaired.

This same system and construction is common to all Herter's Durlon decoys. The only flaw I've found in virtually all foam decoys is that they scar easily, revealing bright white blotches. But they take paint as easily as they scar. All in all, Herter's makes a great decoy for the money. Prices: oversized mallard, black, pintail, redhead, canvasback, and bluebill, $29.95 per dozen; standard-sized, same species, $18.95 per dozen. Herter's, Inc., Route 2, Mitchell, SD 57301.

Herter's Field Goose Decoys: Best Buy

Herter's makes two styles of field goose decoys, full-bodied and shell. The full-bodied decoys are made of the same foam material as the floating decoys, and they are well proportioned and well painted. They are a pain in the neck to carry around because of their bulk, but they are beautiful decoys. If you've got a private pit site where you can leave your stool, they make a lot of sense.

Herter's shell-type decoys are comparable to every other shell-type on the market save for two things, price and what can be best described as a "wing adapter." These shell decoys will accept a snap-on extended wing that gives the goose that wears one the appearance of flight. Eli Spannagel, Sr., has used these in fields along the Yellowstone River and swears they bring in more birds. Whether or not they do, they can't hurt.

The full-bodied decoys are available in Canada and snow goose. The shells come as Canadas, snows, or blues. As with Herter's duck decoys, the price is sure right; dollar for dollar they're the best decoys on the market. Prices: full-bodied, $54.50 per dozen; shell type, $29.35 per dozen; flyers, $4.97 each. Herter's, Inc., Route 2, Mitchell, SD 57301.

Carry-Lite Magnum Decoys

The Carry-Lite line features oversized decoys made of a semihard rubber material that will bend and dent and return to its original shape without breaking. Their most innovative feature is the Aqua-keel, a hollow tube slung under the body which fills with water and stabilizes the decoy. This eliminates the need for lead weighting and thus reduces the carrying weight of the blocks. The keel may also be used as a receptacle for decoy line.

These molded decoys have a pebbly surface, with every feather detail present in three dimensions. This cuts down glare from splashed water but, on the negative side, will hold ice like a vice. The colors are fast, and the decoys don't need painting often, but their overall conformation is a little off on some species. (For example, while their broadbill looks puffy, and good, their mallard and Canada goose look ornate, as if the guy who designed them used to build Gothic cathedrals.) Price: $54.00 per dozen from your favorite sports store or from Carry-Lite, 3000 West Clarke Street, Milwaukee WI 53245.

CF-10

T-36

P-1

H-100

M4SM

G&H
DECOYS INC.

M-4M

M4

G&H Duck Decoys

G&H floating decoys are made from blow-molded, high-impact polythylene, and feather detail is molded into the body. They are generally good in proportion and detail and include realistic touches like glass eyes. Also of note is the variety of species and styles in the G&H line: mallard, black duck, pintail, bluebill, and two kinds of teal. Mallards and black ducks are available in feeding or alert head postures and in full-bodied field decoys. Price: $46.50 for a dozen mallard decoys. Free catalog upon request. G&H Decoys, Inc., P.O. Box 937, Henryetta, OK 74437.

"When a flock of bluebills, pitching pondward, tears the dark silk of heaven in one long rending nose-dive, you catch your breath at the sound."

—Aldo Leopold

253

OTTER MALLARD FIELD DECOYS

These are full-bodied plastic foam decoys with innovative features. First, the steel legs are carried inside the body in a plugged hole. Second, the round underbody can be removed, and the field decoy becomes a water decoy.

Nice ideas, but they haven't been perfected. The plug tends to pop out in transit, and you have to fish it and the decoy legs out of the bottom of the bag. There are problems with the heads, too. They're plastic foam as well and don't hold their anchor screw after a lot of use.

Conformation of the body isn't bad, the paint job is good, and birds come to them freely. But I wouldn't recommend this particular model for anything but a rig that's set once or twice a year and left alone. Prices: Floating magnum (oversized) decoys (mallard, black, and pintail and Canada, snow, and blue goose), $48.00 per dozen; field decoys, same species, $56.00 per dozen; standard-sized floaters (mallard, black, pintail, canvasback, redhead, and bluebill), $30.00 per dozen. Otter Decoy Company, Mediapolis, IA 52637.

G&H GOOSE DECOYS

Floating/Field Goose Decoys

If you're a goose hunter who builds blinds on land and sea at different times of the season, look into the field and floating convertible decoys made by G&H. They are traditional plastic nesting stool, but with the addition of a special keel and bottom board insert they can be quickly converted to water decoys.

This product is also noteworthy in the variety of species available. Floating field decoys may be purchased in Canada goose, snow goose, white-fronted goose, or in blue goose. G&H goes so far as to offer blue goose decoys in juvenile or adult feather plumage, and head attitudes include both feeding and alert postures. Prices: shell decoys, $53.50 per dozen; keel insert, 3.20 each. G&H Decoys, Inc., P.O. Box 937, Henryetta, OK 74437.

QUACK DUCK AND GOOSE DECOYS: INDESTRUCTIBLE, INNOVATIVE

Quack decoys are made of a heavy, rubberlike material that is comparable to removable auto floor mats. They have an air vent, and you can crimp 'em, crush 'em, or sit on 'em, and they return to shape. If you hit them with shot (not a full blast at close range, just a few stray pellets), they self-seal. Colors are impregnated into the material and don't come off. After a full season, the decoys I tested were in perfect shape.

They ride well in the water and maintain good balance. They have a keeling system that acts as a receptacle for your anchor line and a snap-on anchor. Quack anchors are the best-holding snap-ons in high winds.

Because of the type of material used in their construction, these decoys lack some of the finer detail I've come to appreciate in a decoy. The paint jobs are also a bit on the light side, and colors are overly bright. I'd still rate them high, however, because of their indestructibility and balance. It's a good decoy for those who don't want to spend a lot of time caring for stool.

In this same vein, Quack markets what they call their Premium decoy package, which is a complete kit: decoys, lines, weights, and even a bag for any species or size waterfowl they manufacture. They are also a source for nesting goose decoys and silhouette heads (using silhouette heads allows one man to carry many more stool than would be the case with solid heads). The one thing Quack decoys are not

is cheap. Prices: life-sized duck, $49.95 per dozen; super magnums (goose and duck), $99.95; field shell decoys (mallard, black duck, and all geese), $49.95, or $44.95 with silhouette heads. Quack Decoys, 4 Mill Street, Cumberland, RI 02864.

—N.S.

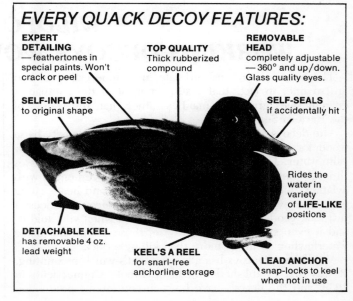

EVERY QUACK DECOY FEATURES:

EXPERT DETAILING
— feathertones in special paints. Won't crack or peel

SELF-INFLATES
to original shape

TOP QUALITY
Thick rubberized compound

REMOVABLE HEAD
completely adjustable — 360° and up/down. Glass quality eyes.

SELF-SEALS
if accidentally hit

Rides the water in variety of **LIFE-LIKE** positions

DETACHABLE KEEL
has removable 4 oz. lead weight

KEEL'S A REEL
for snarl-free anchorline storage

LEAD ANCHOR
snap-locks to keel when not in use

Cheap Goose Decoys

Bankrolling a big spread of goose decoys gets to be rich man's sport in a hurry, but you can cut costs to 20 cents a block by using lath and tarpaper.

Use a heart-shaped pattern with two feet from the cleft of the heart to the point for normal-sized stool, three feet if you want oversized stool. Trace the pattern on common roofing tarpaper and cut out the "heart." Overlap the lobes of the heart and staple them together and you have a good imitation of a goose's body; paint it to suit the species you're hunting.

The head can be nothing more than a piece of lath driven through the cleft and into the ground (which also anchors the body in place). If you desire greater detail, cut a head and neck silhouette from quarter-inch exterior plywood with a jigsaw.

These decoys can be carried flat or stacked.

AND NOW . . . FLYING DECOYS!

Ever notice how birds always seem to be about as soon as you step out of a blind? It's more than chance—ducks and geese are attracted by movement. Of course, as soon as they detect the movement as that of a hunter, they're going to go the other way. But how about if that movement proves to be a reasonable facsimile of a duck or goose flying around?

Sports Innovations makes kites that resemble ducks, geese, and sandhill cranes. They're built on the delta wing design that's so popular with kids on March days, and they work best when flown with 20-lb monofilament line for kite string. The mono is invisible, and it's usually attached to a fishing reel, which is handy for "landing" your decoy or flying it on a windless day. Just set the decoy 100 yards from your pit, and when a flock approaches,

reel furiously. The decoy will climb aloft in a dead calm.

The kites can also be made to resemble whiffling birds. Open the bail on a spinning reel or throw a conventional reel into free spool, and the kite flutters back and down to earth like a sheet of paper.

When ordering, specify the bird type and species you want (such as Canada goose, snow goose, or mallard duck). Price $18.95 per kite. Sports Innovations, Inc., P.O. Box 385, Wichita Falls, TX 76307.

MARTHA ROHL

WILDFOWLER:
WORKING DECOYS WORTHY OF COLLECTION

These decoys are the ultimate in commercial stool and are so fine, in fact, that I suspect most of the company's current sales grace the mantles rather than the waters of the Eastern Seaboard.

The decoys are fashioned from select heavy-density balsa wood for perfect buoyancy and performance in rough or calm water. The heads are fastened with a dowel that passes through the keel and body, and all parts are cemented with aviation glue. Each block is hand-painted, and heads come with glass eyes. The finished product is a decoy that doesn't just look good; it rides well, it feels good when you hold it, and it even speaks, albeit softly, of those things that make waterfowling so much more than killing a duck.

Wildfowler Decoys has a history that's worth recounting. It was first established in Old Saybrook, Connecticut, in 1939, and the decoys have been in continuous production

since then. They are considered to be among the finest working decoys made today, a fact that's lent further credence by a string of first- and second-place ribbons from national decoy contests, including several awards for Best Machine-made Decoy in Show. An even higher recommendation, to my way of thinking, is the number of old Wildfowlers you still see in spreads around Long Island.

Wildfowler decoys are available in just about any species you might want, though some are special-order items. Another special-order feature, if you're a real traditionalist, is hollow pine bodies. The repressed artist in you will also find release with their decorative decoys, available finished or unfinished. Prices: working duck decoys, about $15.00 each; geese and brant, about $22.00 each. Wildfowler Decoys, 3 Shore road, Babylon, NY 11702. —N.S.

"The three most nostalgic sounds in the wilderness: the howl of a coyote, the cry of the loon, and the lonesome call of Canada geese."

—Anon.

255

1. Mold Preparation

2. Filling Mold

3. Cooking, Heating and Cooling

4. Finishing Steps

5. Attaching Heads

6. Painting

DO-IT-YOURSELF DECOYS

The most satisfying spread you'll ever hunt over is one you've made on your own. If you're into wood carving or know of a source of pressed cork, these are two natural materials that make superb stool. If you don't have the talent, time, or materials for such traditional blocks, look into the decoy kits made by Decoys Unlimited. This company sells a whole bunch of split molds of waterfowl species. The head mold and the body mold are separate items.

To make a decoy, first fill the split mold, held together by bolts, with a powdered expandable plastic compound. Then immerse the mold in boiling water. It takes about thirty minutes for the plastic to expand fully and another ten for the mold to cool sufficiently for the decoy to be removed.

When first formed, heads and bodies will have irregularities where the two mold halves come together. These must be smoothed out with sandpaper or a rasp. Heads are attached to the bodies by a combination of epoxy and a long lag bolt with an eye on the end. Ultimately, this eye receives the decoy line.

Once the epoxy sets up, the decoy is ready for painting. If you have two molds (so one may be prepared while the other is being boiled, then boiled while the first is setting up), you can turn out two decoys an hour.

The cost of an individual decoy varies with the amount of material you buy at one time and the number of decoys you turn out. The molds never wear out; once you've bought them, each decoy you make reduces the per-decoy price. A sampling of mold (head and body) and material prices: magnum mallard mold, $51.00; goose mold, $56.00; brant mold, $46.00; expandable plastic (30 pounds makes between twenty and thirty decoys, depending on body size), 95 cents per pound up to 110 pounds; over 110 pounds, 80 cents per pound.

Species and decoy types include both field decoys and floating decoys in Canada goose, snow and blue goose, brant, mallard, black duck, teal, gadwall, baldpate, bluebill, canvasback, redhead, and pintail. Free catalog. Decoys Unlimited, P.O. Box 69, Clinton, IA 52732. —N.S.

USE FIELD DUCK DECOYS

Field goose decoys are an old item in the waterfowler's bag of tricks, but field duck decoys are rather new. They're an excellent idea, one that adds a natural touch to a field goose spread and extra action from the mallards they draw in.

They're also most effective for hunting over water when the blind is located near a bar, a sloping shoreline, or very shallow water.

When field hunting, use only mallards, as they are about the only species of duck that will decoy freely on land (you might see a pintail come in, but rarely). Around water, use either black ducks or mallards, depending on what kind of bird is in the majority on the flyway. If you're hunting

diving ducks, such as the broadbill, and you want to use field decoys, you'd better go hunting with someone else. Diving ducks virtually never walk around on land.

You won't need many of these blocks in the field or on the water. I never rig more than six, and three seem to get the job done. When goose hunting, set the decoys away from the spread of geese, as geese harass ducks and keep them away from their private feeding grounds. —N.S.

PAINTING DECOYS

I consider myself a pretty dedicated waterfowler, which means I'm out on the marsh at least ten times a year, and each of those "times" usually adds up to two or three days of hunting.

In the course of setting, bagging, and transporting blocks (not to mention those telltale shot marks in my stool that are so hard to defend among friends), they get pretty banged up and shabby looking, and I generally have to paint or touch up each decoy at least once a year.

I prefer to do this about midseason, because a new coat of paint makes for a colorful decoy, and ducks are not very colorful at season's start. Early in the fall they are coming out of eclipse plumage, a condition of mottled feathering that's nicely matched by a slightly banged-up decoy. By the time my bright decoys are retired in January, they've achieved that worn state of grace for next year.

Decoys should always be painted with a flat paint. Whether you use an acrylic or oil paint seems to make no difference, as long as it is flat and for exterior use. In fact, I prefer acrylics, because they dry so fast. You can get through all your blocks in a day and be done with it.

There are several tricks to mass-painting decoys for functional rather than decorative use. Start with the color that predominates the block, and slap on that shade. Don't be too exacting about contrasting color lines in this step. Precision takes time, and you get the same result when you wait to be precise about adjoining colors in the succeeding steps. For example, the oyster gray on the side of a drake mallard can sluff over onto the dark wing area. If you're careful about painting the wing on, you get as good a result as if you'd done both operations with coloring-book care.

Use a relatively large (1-to-1½-inch) brush for broad, bold areas, and small (⅛-to-¼-inch) artist's brushes for details like speculums, bill nails, and collars.

I believe in using some suggestion of feather detail. There are two easy ways to get this rough, textured look. For fine detail, such as on the head of a black duck or hen mallard, first paint the head a slightly darker brown than would be normal. Allow this color to dry, then cover it with a light brown. While the light brown is still wet, score it with a fine-toothed haircomb in the same direction that the feathers would lie. The dark will show through the comb marks, and the result will look like fine feathers.

For larger feather detail, such as on the back of a drake scaup or on the breast of a hen mallard, mix contrasting acrylic paint with oil paint and beat it well. For example, for the drake scaup you'd use a flat black oil base with an oyster-gray acrylic. The oil-base paint will break up into tiny globs in the water-based acrylic and will paint on like tiny polka dots. After the acrylic has dried (about thirty minutes) the oil-base paint will still be wet, and if you take a soft rag and gently wipe the decoy surface, again in the direction that the feathers would lie, this will create a great imitation of gray and black feathering.

If you know how to mix colors, you can buy a basic flat shade from your local paint store and then tint it with coloring oils to achieve the colors you need for the kinds of decoys you're working with. A much shorter cut, and in some ways more economical of money as well as time, is to buy decoy painting kits. Parker Paint Company sells mallard, pintail, black duck, canvasback, scaup, and Canada goose kits for around $9.00. They include numbered diagrams that explain what color goes where on the decoy. While the kits are advertised for one to two dozen decoys, they go a lot farther than that when you're touching up blocks that are already painted. Parker Paint Company, P.O. Box 433, Green Bay, WI 54305.

—N.S.

DECOYS OF THE ATLANTIC FLYWAY
by George Ross Starr, Jr.

New York: Winchester Press, $17.95.

"Whether you hear decoys referred to as stools, blocks, tollers, or 'primitive American wood sculpture,' the stimulus to the imagination should be the same, because it's fun to hold a bit of history in your hand." So states Dr. George Starr in introducing this remarkable labor of love, the fruit of more than a quarter-century of collecting decoys, of thinking and talking about them and the craftsmen-gunners who fashioned them, of making them, and of gunning over them along his beloved Massachusetts South Shore and all the way up and down the coast.

Decoys of the Atlantic Flyway is a masterpiece of original research, connoisseurship, and plain storytelling. The book has three parts. The first, "Decoy Art and History," explains the background of decoy making from the market-gunning era when decoys were considered merely a utility to more recent times when they were recognized as an art form, and describes the construction methods of the decoy makers. The second, "Stick-up Decoys," is about the nonfloating imitations—geese, crows, pigeons, and especially the shorebirds that have now passed almost completely from the gunning scene. The third and largest part, "Regional Decoys," is a geographical-historical survey, running from Maine to North Carolina and from the earliest origins of decoys to the present day.

More than 350 decoys, all from Dr. Starr's collection, are shown in George Dow's stunning photographs; more than 60 of the decoys are in full color—masterful carvings from the workbenches of Joe Lincoln, Elmer Crowell, Lothrop Holmes, the Ward brothers, the Cobbs of Virginia,

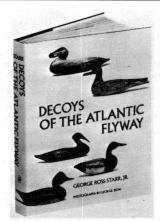

and scores of other makers, known and unknown. Dr. Starr has tracked down the history of most of the decoys, and the accounts of his feats of decoy detection and acquisition are one of the fascinations that make this the most important contribution to decoy literature in many years.

"It'll be good duck weather in three days; the new moon's layin' on her back, and the cup will fill with water. Then we'll have a storm."
—The late Tom Sicard, in conversation

257

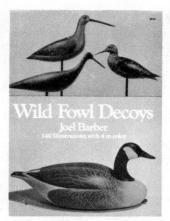

WILD FOWL DECOYS
by Joel Barber

New York: Dover Publications, $5.00.

Joel Barber, one of America's preeminent authorities and collectors, calls decoys "floating sculpture," and in this authoritative book he evokes their special charm and beauty.

There are 140 plates, four of which are in color, showing models of all varieties of North American duck decoys and some European ones for comparison, historical methods of fowling and fishing, equipment, and scale working plans, materials, and instructions on how to construct your own decoys. The author also tells how to recognize the locality from which a decoy comes, how to identify the various well-known makers, and other valuable information on collecting and decoy making as an art form.

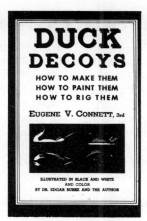

DUCK DECOYS, HOW TO MAKE THEM, HOW TO PAINT THEM, HOW TO RIG THEM
by Eugene Connett, 3rd

Brattleboro, Vt.: Steven Greene Press, $9.50.

This book rates as something of a classic, and if you're into making your own decoys, it's one of the best resources available today. Connett includes patterns for all major species (bodies and heads that are easy to copy) and detailed painting instructions, right down to how to mix each color and where to apply it. It's also interesting reading, because it reveals the special kind of gunner who views waterfowling as equal parts of craft and art.

Carrying Decoys

For all the aprons, racks, and boxes that have been devised to help get a decoy spread from car to blind, nothing yet beats two burlap sacks tied together. Make the ties by bunching material from both bags around a round rock. Then cinch up the material tightly below the rock with decoy line and a strong knot. Fill each bag with an equal amount of stool, and sling it over your shoulder. If you wish, you can carry four bags in this manner and still have your hands free to carry a gun and a Thermos of hot coffee.

HERTER'S GRAPPLE DECOY ANCHOR

If you're interested in grabbing bottom, ounce for ounce this is the best decoy anchor made. I've left my rig out overnight on a hard mud bottom in 60-mph winds and had all my stool the next morning, though when I did eventually pick up, I had to kick some anchors free with my foot. This is, incidentally, a steel anchor and is relatively light, so you don't have quite so much weight to lug across the marsh. There are two drawbacks: the grapple hooks really tear up the decoys when you carry them in a bag, and they snag decoy line like a . . . well, grapple. Prices: 12 standard anchors, $5.17; extra large, $8.97. Herter's, Inc., Route 2, Mitchell, SD 57301.   —N.S.

"TANGLEFREE" ANCHORING SYSTEM

This anchoring system utilizes an oval plug of lead and a smooth, slick, soft-vinyl plastic line. The anchor is drilled and notched so you can snap the line firmly to the lead without any knots.

It's a marvelous system in many ways, the most important being that you can pile decoys in a bag or duckboat without winding them up. Just bunch them together, lines tangled like spaghetti, and when you single them out, no line hangs up in another. It cuts setting-out time in half and cuts pulling-in time even more. And you don't even have to get your hands wet.

If there is one flaw in the system, it is that the anchors will not dig in and hold well in a blow. And they'd be impractical to use with the 150-odd decoys required for a big open-water gunning spread. But for shooting in marshes, protected waters, and on bluebird days, they eliminate most of the disagreeable work associated with decoy hunting. Prices: 500-foot plastic anchor line, $19.98; "Tanglefree" anchors, $11.76 per dozen. Waterfowl Supply Company, 173 Scenic Drive, Concord, CA 94518.

OLD GUIDE DECOY ANCHORS

These are the traditional "oval-with-ears" decoy weights that are still favored by open-water and tidal gunners for their holding power. They're still cast from virgin lead (most of these anchors are steel nowadays). They hold extremely well and are also noteworthy in that the decoy line can be wrapped around the anchor, for quick setting of a large rig, or around the decoy. The line may then be held firmly in place by slipping the anchor over the decoy's head. It's about the only way to avoid tangles when you're bagging keelless decoys. Prices: ½-pound weight, $9.50 per dozen; 1-pound, $14.25 per dozen. Old Guide, 105 Irving Street, Framingham, MA 01701.

DECOY SETS ON WATER

Specific decoy patterns could fill a whole book and, as a matter of fact, they have. If you're interested in the multitude of possible patterns, either my book *Misty Mornings and Moonless Nights* or *Duck Decoys and How to Rig Them* by Ralf Coykendall outlines specific spreads.

There are, however, two basic patterns that are standards of the sport. The "I" formation is best for puddle ducks. This finds loose groups of between four and nine blocks strung out in a line. Leave breaks in the grouping of 15 to 20 feet for landing areas, and make sure those landing areas are within good gun range. The "I" set may be rigged anywhere ducks are trading: in a cove, cut, or along a shoreline. It works especially well on a point.

The fishhook pattern is the only set to use for divers if you're hunting from shore, and it works well on open-water layout rigs, too. When you're hunting from shore, you must rig this on a point. The pattern is just what the name implies—a fishhook shape, with the bulk of the blocks at the bend of the hook. The hook shank or tail of the decoy spread should lead seaward, and as you get farther and farther away from the blind, blocks should be spaced wider and wider apart. Diving ducks will pick up this tail and

follow it in to the main concentration of decoys. They will usually land on either side of the bend, where most decoys are gathered, so keep this area in good gun range.

Even more important than a letter-perfect spread is the blind or duckboat's relationship to that spread. You've got to pay attention to two things: (1) the wind must be at your back, and (2) the set should be made so the bird's approach does not have it looking down your gun barrel as it lands.

To satisfy these two requirements for puddle ducks, it's usually best to have a wind that quarters you, blowing on either shoulder. Place the lead decoy so it appears to be looking past the blind rather than right at it, and tolling birds will do the same.

When rigging a fishhook pattern, the critical trick is to set it so landing birds are looking at open water, not the shore. Divers are shore-shy, and they'll be reluctant to set down unless they have a lot of open water ahead of them. This is the reason why a fishhook must be rigged on a point. Again, the wind must be quartering the point or coming across it. Generally, I've found that it isn't very important to find a lee (calm water) for diving ducks, but it is attractive to puddle ducks.
—N.S.

ZONGKER DECOY WEIGHTS

These decoy weights are cast from lead. A heavy *x* graces the bottom of an eyed shaft. At the base of the grapple there is a small slot which receives a heavy rubber band. The rubber band is used to hold wrapped line in place on decoys whose keels also serve as a spooling place for line (for example, the G&H decoy). They don't hold quite as well as a grapple anchor in a really heavy blow, but on the aforementioned decoys they're super, since they eliminate line tangling. Prices: 5-ounce star decoy anchor, $7.00 per dozen; 8-ounce, $8.50 per dozen.

There's an interesting sidelight to Zongker weights. I had assumed the brand name to be some marvelous stroke of promotional onomatopoeia. I mean, when you drop a lead weight, it goes "zonk," right? Wrong. They are made by Floyd Zongker, Zongker Lead Casting Company, P.O. Box 35037, Tulsa, OK 74135.
—N.S.

OLD GUIDE DECOY LINE

This stout, braided nylon decoy line, comparable to parachute cord, looks as if it would test out around 300 pounds. It's colored dark green, with a coarse braid to resist knot slippage.

Although pull strength of these limits isn't really needed on a decoy, the thickness of the line helps deter Gordian snarls at 5 A.M. Prices: 1,000-foot spool, $16.95; 400-foot spool, $8.95. Old Guide, 105 Irving Street, Framingham, MA 01701.

OLT'S DECOY LINE

This is interesting stuff in that it is sand-colored, rather than green, and for this reason useful if you rig out over light-colored bottoms. It is woven of a hard, coarsely braided nylon that holds knots well, though it is a little on the thin side and it does snarl. Price: 100 feet, $2.00. P. S. Olt, Pekin, IL 61554.

HERTER'S DECOY LINE

Herter's rates this decoy line at 200 pounds, but having used the stuff I wonder about that. It is dark green, about ⅛ inch in diameter, and soft. It tends to slip knots and snarl, but it is rotproof, serviceable, and a hundred times better than string you scrounge around the house. Price: 100 feet, $1.10. Herter's, Inc., Route 2, Mitchell, SD 57301.
—N.S.

"Who alone in our modern life so thrills to the sight of living beauty that he will endure hunger and thirst and cold to feed his eye upon it? The hunter."
—Aldo Leopold

259

DECOY BAGS

There have been many devices designed to tote decoys across the marsh, but to date I've found nothing better than a common bag . . . or perhaps I should say an uncommon bag.

Allstate-Campbell has a 36-by-38-inch product simply called the Decoy Bag. Made of synthetic netting, it is rotproof, strong, and won't absorb water and make the load even heavier. It also includes a drawstring closure. Price: $4.95. Allstate-Campbell, 5141 Lakeland Avenue, Crystal, MN 55429.   —N.S.

DEAD DUCK TRAINER

This replica of a greenhead mallard made of soft, pliable plastic trains a dog to spot floating dead ducks on water. It's also great for fooling your neighbors. Just string a few of them on your game carrier on days when you're skunked and they'll never know the difference. Price: $3.95. Neumann & Bennetts, Inc., P.O. Box 1497, Klamath Falls, OR 97601.

PLASTI-DUK TRAINERS

Ideal dummies to start a pup on, these are made of a pliable plastic that floats and come in a progression of different colors. White is used to start, because the dog will be able to see the dummy. You then go to a shade of gray so that the dog will be able to pick up the scent before sight. Fluorescent is used later for blind retrieves. Price: $3.95. Neumann & Bennetts, Inc., P.O. Box 1497, Klamath Falls, OR 97601.   —P.S.

Duckhunter's Poem

in the fall when the ducks flew
and skim ice edged the lake
he would feel the feathers
along his back as he stretched,
as if his arms were duckwings
thrumming distances in themselves.

in dawn with the sun glare
off the ice i would watch him
walking down to the water
and wonder at the keenness
he was feeling.
                    sometimes
he almost danced down
with rainbows glancing
off his slick feathers.

after we'd shattered the shining
thin ice along the shore
with the boat he would call
as we moved. he'd speak to the ducks
as their shadows angled
along their morning paths.
their voices rested softly
in his mouth
as i would wishing say:

please give me feathers too.

—John Barsness

DUCK CALLS

There are an awful lot of duck calls for sale—I don't think I'd be too far off base if I said 200 different makes, styles, and models—so let me pass on a few words about what to look for in this confusing and competitive field.

The most popular and practical call is the mallard call. It produces the loud "quack" that most people associate with a duck. Surprisingly enough, not all ducks quack; in fact, relatively few do. But the quack call is popular, because it speaks the language of two of the most sought-after ducks, the black duck and the mallard.

Another reason for its popularity is that it's adaptable. In practiced hands the mallard call can be made to chirr, to gabble, and to issue a kind of warbling, guttural growl, thus imitating a large range of sounds that are appealing to most species of waterfowl.

Other calls are really specialty calls. Indeed, if you know you'll be gunning nothing but broadbills, use a diving duck call, or if wood ducks are the only birds around, use a wood duck call. But for the elusive "average" day and "average" duck hunter, you're best off to carry a mallard call and to learn how to use it to its broadest effect.

There are two qualities to assess in a mallard call. You should be able to blow it hard, loud, and clear without the reed's breaking into a squeak. You'll need that range and volume for the highball call, when a black or mallard is passing far away and you want to call attention to your spread.

The second quality is responsiveness of the reed at a low pitch. The reed should activate at the slightest puff of your breath. This allows you to reproduce those myriad other calls of shelldrake, bufflehead, gadwall, teal, shoveler, and diving ducks, as well as the low, reassuring quack that puts the final touch of invitation out to an incoming mallard.

How do you learn to use a call properly? The quickest way is to go with people who already know and have them teach you. You can also learn a great deal on your own by going down to the local marsh or duck pond and listening to the conversation there, and you'll pick up some savvy by osmosis while you're hunting. Instructional records, sold by most of the call makers, are extremely helpful in that they teach you what call to use at what times and what the basic calls should sound like. If you don't have a friend who's a good caller, they are a substitute. They are not a substitute for exposure, experience, and practice in a real hunting situation, however. Expert callers are made, not born, and the only way you'll make that category is by putting time and effort in at a duck blind.   —N.S.

THE MALLARD CALL

by Joel M. Vance

Over the years my efforts to call in wily greenheads have been met with derision the likes of which haven't been seen since a former President said, "I didn't know anything about it."

Most of that derision has come from my hunting companions, whose kindest comment to date has been to suggest that I take my hail call and enter it in the next International Camel Flatulence Competition.

In the meantime, shut up.

I remember frost-shrouded mornings at the Dalton Cutoff, an oxbow lake capriciously created by the Missouri River in one of its kinder moments. It was 1 foot of water, 6 feet of gumbo (which is mud with guts), lying 3 miles south through endless bottoms of corn and soybeans. My dad and I hunted the Cutoff. We rowed a mile to our blind. Outboard motors were a luxury that sowbelly-and-beans Missourians didn't enjoy.

The johnboat broke ice all the way. I packed an antique doublebarrel just this side of a caplock that weighed about what I did and fungoed my shoulder unmercifully. But it was the 1950s, and ducks were everywhere. We'd dump a few decoys, not bothering with fancy hooked patterns or tip-up feeders or anything else, for frills weren't necessary. These were the glory days, and they likely will not come again. You don't raise mallards in what John Madson calls "canned potholes" (grain bins).

Neither my dad nor I knew enough about duck calling to be dangerous, but we had fun and I miss those fading days and I miss him, a sign of sentimentality, ecological conscience, nostalgia, and love realized all too late.

My dad always let me call and never criticized my efforts. He didn't know any more about it than I did but had enough sense not to show it. With the simple-minded assurance of adolescence, I was sure I was a virtuoso of the vibrating reed, and very occasionally I was. Today's mallard seems to be a brighter duck, and calling him in is far more difficult than it was in those far-off days when pimples were a larger problem than arthritis.

Today's greenheads aren't easily lured by noise from a piece of wood that, when blown into, produces a sound useful for summing up baseball rules to myopic umpires or getting your sweetbreads crushed in roadhouses.

There was one morning—perhaps it was all the mornings we cased our guns, half asleep, and followed the bouncing yellow headlights of our rattly old Ford to the Cutoff—when my dad and I stashed the boat before dawn and listened to the clamor of thousands of ducks just rousing in the marsh. We heard a creaking rush of wings over the rip-gutted blind, and finally, in false dawn, we picked out the blurred, silhouetted birds eddying through a sky goldshot by the rising sun. We faced east, sharing a sunrise and companionship.

A distant undecided gang of fifteen mallards was looking for a home, and I started to call. "Tell them you love them," my dad whispered. The birds bent and came our way, curious, willing to be convinced, soothed by whatever magic had crept into my caller. I had sense enough to shut up, and we crouched low, hoping nothing untoward showed. There was a swish overhead—one pass—and we peeked to see the birds, wings set, turning into the wind. It was too quick, and they broke their landing pattern, shuffling to keep altitude, to take another look at this not-quite-right place. They made another swing, a little too high. The tension deepened. We felt their suspicion, their indecision. Another feathery hiss and they were behind us, over the pin oaks. "If they swing in front, take 'em," Dad said.

Then they were above the blocks, setting into the wind, their bright orange legs reaching for the tiny wavelets of the muddy old Cutoff. And we leaped up, and I emptied the old doublebarrel, missing with the first shot but dropping a drake forty yards out and going straight up. "Great shot!" my dad exclaimed, squeezing my arm, his eyes shining.

And that's what I remember most about mallard calling.

Joel Vance is a frequent contributor to outdoor magazines. He graduated in 1956 from the Missouri School of Journalism and has worked on newspapers and with the Missouri Department of Conservation.

*"And of all these things the Albino Whale was the symbol.
Wonder ye then at the fiery hunt?"*
—Herman Melville, Moby Dick

261

ESPECIALLY FOR WOOD DUCK HUNTERS

Woodies aren't much attracted by a conventional duck call, but they'll pile into this one. It produces the nasally squeal of the drake.

If you get a drake woody, remember to save the lemony-colored barred feathers that lie where the wings join the body. They're highly prized by flytiers, who will surely reward your generosity with a box of shells or a few flies come fishing season. Price: $8.95. Faulk's, 616 18th Street, Lake Charles, LA 70601.

OLT DR 115 DUCK CALL

Here's a new concept in duck calls: two reeds. A heavy reed over the low-tone reed keeps it from vibrating so fast that it squeaks. With this tone-distortion check, it's possible to have a very soft and responsive low reed. I've heard this call once, and it sounds great to me, though the test was in my living room not the marsh, and I can't speak for the ducks. Price: $9.95. P. S. Olt, Pekin, IL 61554.

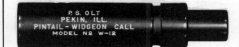

PINTAIL-WIDGEON CALL

Pintail and widgeon whistle and squawk rather than quack. If either of these birds trades through your area in heavy numbers, you'll present a more inviting spread if you talk to them in their own language. Price: $5.50. P. S. Olt, Pekin, IL 61554.

GAME-CALLING INSTRUCTION RECORDS

These records afford some sound basics in the art of game calling. Individual platters instruct you how to talk to mallards, geese, diving ducks, crows, squirrels, predators, and moose. They're also kinda fun at parties. Slip a moose call into the record stack at your next social function, and watch your friends' reactions. Price: $7.95 each. P. S. Olt, Pekin, IL 61554.

DIVING DUCK CALL

The call of a diver is a cross between a croak and a quack. This Big Water Call has a long range, and it works on bluebills, redheads, and canvasbacks. Price: $7.50. P. S. Olt, Pekin, IL 61554.

SCOTCH DUCK CALL

This innovative call produces a perfect *chucka-chucka* feeding call every time. You hold it by the wooden call, shake it, and the rubber diaphragm puffs air across the reed. You can remove the wooden call from the diaphragm if you want to call by mouth. Price: $7.95. Scotch Game Calls, 60 Main Street, Oakfield, NY 14125.

OLT A-50 CANADA GOOSE CALL: BEST IN THE BUSINESS

If you've got Canadas in your sights, this is the call to use. The tone is musical, not flatulent as most other calls are (especially on the first or low note). In addition, the call is marvelously responsive, though a bit trickier than most to master. It takes some practice to keep from blowing a goose-turning-off three-noted call.

Aside from melody, I favor this call above all others, because it's the one call that can be feathered and belled with your hands. Thus one man can produce the sounds of a whole flock of gabbling, excited geese. Price: $8.95. P. S. Olt, Pekin, IL 61554.

COMBINATION DUCK AND GOOSE CALL

A kind of inverse proportion exists for sporting goods to the effect that the wider application a particular product has, the less excellent it will be at individual tasks. That rule has surely held true for me regarding combination duck and goose calls; up until now, every one of these calls I've tried has sounded too flatulent for geese and too high and reedy for ducks.

Faulk's new combo call is a different matter, though, because it incorporates two separate calling mechanisms on one body. The goose call is bell-like and crisp, and the duck call is capable of a full range of intensities, from soft, reassuring chatter to a far-reaching highball. Of special note are two ⅜-inch holes in the center of the body that can be used to dampen the call and create special effects. They are played a little like a toy flute and produce the *chucka-chucka* mallard feeding call with amazing ease.

Faulk's Combination Duck and Goose Call comes complete with a lanyard, so you can wear it around your neck instead of fumbling for it in a pocketful of shells. Price: $18.95. Faulk's, 616 18th Street, Lake Charles, LA 70601.   —N.S.

MALLARDTONE DUCK CALL

I came by my Mallardtone in northern Canada. I had forgotten my calls, and a guest at the lodge sold me this one. Since then it's been my regular. It really blows a highball without blowing you out, and it's so responsive at lower volumes that I'd call it the easiest mouth-blown call for blowing the *chucka-chucka-chucka* feeding call. Price: $5.00. Mallardtone, 2901 16th Street, Moline, IL 61265.   —N.S.

LOHMAN NO. 300 DUCK CALL

This is a good all-around call, with a responsive low range and an assertive highball. It is essentially a mallard/black call, but it can be adapted to other species. The reed in this call is especially easy to tune. Price: $7.00. Lohman Calls, Neosho, MO 64850.

HUNTING FROM BLINDS AND PITS

The first thing to ascertain when setting up a blind or pit is whether or not there are birds using the area. Spots that look good to humans are often unattractive to waterfowl for reasons only they know.

When setting up a blind, the most important thing to remember is that it should blend into the cover in terms of color and outline. Erecting a box blind in a flat marsh is sure to shy birds, because they are not used to this new feature of the landscape. Instead, select a site that breaks up the blind's outline with a background of cattails, willows, or other such natural vegetation.

The important thing about pits is that they must be level with the ground. Be sure that the dirt you remove to bury the pit is of the same color as the surface soil. If you're digging into grass, you'll have to haul the dirt away.

I have also found that geese, especially, are very wary of field areas that could easily hide a hatch cover: for example, the chaff from an old haystack or the thick thatch of cornstalks that results from a chopper's first pass at a standing field. They might feed in these places, but often as not they'll land out in a plowed or clean-harvested part of the field and walk in, which again points up the need for being sure that birds are using the area where you plan to set up shop.   —N.S.

Oil Drum Blinds

These blinds are constructed of two oil drums welded together in a conformation that accommodates a seated hunter. They may be buried in the ground, set upon the ground, or elevated via tripod legs to a fifteen-foot-high tower blind. Their cost ranges from $109.95 to $249.00 (FOB Fort Worth), depending on the height of the tripod (five heights are available). Greens Development Company, P.O. Box 566, Fort Worth, TX 76101.

Portable Pit Blind

This molded fiberglass pit-type blind accommodates a seated hunter. It includes a cover that keeps out the weather when it's not in use and a small shelf area to hold shells and pocket stuff.

While this pit isn't exactly a palace in terms of space, in a way that's one of its advantages. Its lightness makes it perfectly portable, and it's ideal for digging into low cover and staying dry. Price: $75.00. Fiberglass Industries, Inc., 3746 Government Street, Alexandria, LA 71301.

"A peculiar virtue . . . is that the hunter ordinarily has no gallery to applaud or disapprove of his conduct. Whatever his acts, they are dictated by his own conscience."
—Aldo Leopold

263

Waterfowler Pit Blind

The Waterfowler is a roomy one-man watertight pit blind made of fiberglass. There's a wide flange around the base's exterior; in place, dirt piled on top of that flange keeps the pit from working its way toward the surface as the tide or water level raises and lowers.

As is the case with most drum-type pit blinds, the top amounts to a swing-away cover. Especially interesting about this product are the many options available: a sliding step shelf for ease of entry and exit, a sliding shelf for shells and calls, a swivel seat, and even a shallow companion blind

for your dog. Free catalog. Prices: waterfowler pit blind, $297.50; concealer cover, 65.50; dog blind (cover included), 59.50. Waterfowl Supply Company, 173 Scenic Drive, Concord, CA 94518.

Portable Two-man Blind

The Duck Inn blind receives high marks for economy, practicality, and design. It measures 43 by 60 inches on the floor, and it's 57 inches high. That's enough interior space for two men to sit comfortably, yet it's not so high that it would stand out in typical ground cover.

The blind has a full top that wards off the weather—and the prying eyes of puddle ducks as they swing overhead. Best of all, it has a peep slit in the front, along part of the sides, and across the rear; you have nearly 360-degree vision. When it comes time to shoot, the top flips up and back, affording 360-degree shooting freedom!

A few other startling facts about this blind: There's a front flap entryway, which requires no tools to set up or take down, and the fully assembled blind may be moved easily from site to site, as the whole thing only weighs 13 pounds!

Most surprising of all, perhaps, is the

price. At a time when enough plywood, studding, paint, and labor to build a permanent blind of this size would cost at least $100, the Duck Inn sells for $79.95. You can get a special carrying case for $4.95 more. Cabela's, 812 13th Avenue, Sidney, NE 69162.

Super Goose Blind

Ever hear the joke about the 500-pound canary? I have a hunch that if you use this blind you'll hear it often.

The blind is a much-larger-than-lifesize (6 feet long by 3 feet wide) replica of a Canada goose. The back swings away, and you climb inside and hide. When the birds come in, you can jump up and yell "Surprise!"

While this Trojan Horse of waterfowling is bound to elicit wisecracks and raise eyebrows, I have no doubt that it will work. Waterfowl have sharp eyes for detail and movement, but they're very poor at depth perception. Thus, the goose wouldn't look huge and out of place to incoming birds . . . just closer than it really is.

The Super Goose weighs only 50 pounds, and by turning it on its back you may use it like a sled. Put the removable head inside, and all your decoys, and it will skid over snow. Another tip: with something this big in your spread, don't use a piddling little goose call; try a diesel air horn. Price: $395.00. Neumann & Bennett's, Inc., Box 1497, Klamath Falls, OR 97601.
—N.S.

OLD GUIDE CAMOUFLAGE CLOTH

This material is a conventional camouflage pattern of an overall tan hue. Its value lies in that it is a rubberized nylon

material, impervious to wind and moisture. It would be very useful for anything you want to hide and keep dry at the same time: a blind roof, a duckboat, or a box of shells. This material can be sewn or cemented, and it is tough. Price: $3.95 per linear yard (45 inches wide). Old Guide, 105 Irving Street, Framingham, MA 01701.

THE MEANING OF CANVASBACK
by Gene Hill

The Canvasback is a now-diminishing duck that was originally created to inspire exquisite decoys and, when it was legal to take them in numbers, gluttony.

The undoing of the canvasback was a combination of many circumstances. One is the whim of nature, which brings forth more males than females and creates a lot of arguing about double-dating and poor jokes like "Who was that lady I saw you with last flight?" Another is that the artistry of the decoy proved as irresistible to the duck as it is to duck hunters. No matter how pathetic a wing shot was, and I personally know how pathetic that can be, if you had enough patience, northeast winds, and shells you could count on a duck dinner.

And canvasback was *the* duck dinner! Even the most indifferent Eastern Shore bride could toss a brace in a roasting pan and come back in a half hour and serve up a meal that grown men would fight over. But put into the hands of a sensitive chef, the canvasback took on the aura of sacredness. Take a fine establishment like the old Eager House in Baltimore: thick damask napkins a yard square tucked into the hard, starched collar of a serious trencherman; a bottle of Maryland rye whiskey close at hand; a variety of exquisite local or imported German beer that, unfortunately for us, bears not the slightest resemblance to what now passes for a similar beverage; heavy-bodied Bordeaux and Burgundies rich with the threat of gout; tureens of terrapin soup; several dozen musky-salty Chincoteague oysters, platters of cornbread and yeast biscuits; a small saddle of hare; perhaps a woodcock or two—and then, with the appetite slightly edged for its full delectation, came the canvasback! With wild rice, of course, a variety of berry sauces, pan gravy for those who chose or a thin sauce redolent of brandy, wine, orange bitters, and wild plum jelly for those who really cared. And afterward a glass of port or perhaps Madeira and, with certainty, a hand-rolled, pure Havana cigar as thick as a sash weight. This was the picture a gentleman was once delighted to envision at the mention of canvasback.

The men who provided the canvasbacks for such as the Eager House knew port only as a nautical position and believed that Madeira was the capital of Spain. Their concern with the canvasback was as exotic as the gourmet's, but the utensils were different. Their talk was of ten-gauge Levefers and Smiths. Semiautomatic Remingtons with magazine extensions that ran right up to the end of the barrel. Pungeys, deadeyes, sneak skiffs, and sinkboxes that were as cold and deadly as coffins.

They gunned by lantern light, moonlight, and in ice-shrouded fogs so thick that the only direction they knew for sure was straight down. They gunned for money, they said. But as long as the canvasback swept down to the celery-covered Susquehanna flats of the Chesapeake, they spoke of them with a tone in their voice and a wild light in their eye that had little to do with cash. They called themselves baymen, with a soft pride that is bought with the copper taste of fear and crippling frostbite—it was a way of life a lot more than a way of making a living.

And then the wild celery was gone, smothered by industrial waste, and the canvasback almost all gone with it as well . . . and a way of life . . . and the decoys and the silver tureens . . . and men who should know better—and who really do—asking, "Where did we go wrong?"

Canvasback was also the trade name of a very good, very reasonable hunting coat—also, like so many good and reasonable things, almost extinct. We seem to be still going wrong.

Gene Hill is a frequent habitué of duck blinds and goose pits from Long Island to Maryland's Eastern Shore. He has held editorial positions with *Sports Afield* and currently is associate editor of *Field & Stream.*

Smitty's Duck Blind

Smitty has put together one whale of a good pit blind. It is made of fiberglass (virtually no maintenance), and it is watertight, so it can be sunk to ground level in the middle of a boggy marsh. The seat inside swivels 360 degrees, and the hunter is surrounded by a shelf for shells, a sandwich, and calls. There is a receptacle under the seat for a can of Sterno, the heat from which is dispersed through sets of conductive fins around and under you. The blind can be used with or without a cover, and it locks up tight when not in use, keeping out rain, raccoons, muskrats, and skunks. If you have ever hunted from a blind that you had to share with a skunk, you will immediately perceive the incalculable value of this feature.

Smitty also makes a doggie blind of similar design that keeps your pal protected from some of the elements and includes a sump to catch the dripping water from a wet Lab. Both products are well worth considering if you hunt on a private, permanent site. Prices: duck blind, $450.00; doggie blind, 42.50; FOB. Henry A. Smith, 522 23rd Street, Richmond, CA 94804.

"Teal do not fly as fast as it appears. In fact, there are many ducks that fly a lot faster.
Now that you're aware of this common fallacy, try to hit one."

—Anon.

265

ED JAFFE STUDIO

Pack a Blind

Most public waterfowling areas are hunted on a first come, first served basis. Whether you have built your own blind or not, if someone gets to the spot before you, it's his for the day.

Enjoy mobility plus a blind any time, anywhere, with a portable pack blind. The blind is constructed of aluminum tubing that fits together by way of ferrules. Once the frame is put together, a brown camouflage shelter slides over the tubing like a fitted bedsheet. It is waterproof, windproof, and snug and stands 40 inches high with 22-inch interior diameter at the top and 33-inch at the bottom. The blind includes a portable vinyl seat.

There is one other pleasant feature of this pack blind: when you're done for the day, you nest the front section into the back, attach a pair of shoulder straps that come as part of the unit, and the blind becomes a backpack that's large enough to haul a dozen decoys and your shells. Price: $119.95. Orvis, 10 River Road, Manchester, VT 05254.

MARSH MAT

This product belongs to the "why didn't I think of that?" class. It is nothing more than shards of corn leaves affixed with strong stitches, spaced an inch apart, to a roll of 7½-ounce burlap backing.

The Marsh Mat comes in 40-inch high, 30-foot long rolls, enough material to cover and grass a blind for two hunters and a Lab. In addition, the mat may be sewn like any heavy canvas or cloth to make a duckboat cover or perhaps, as the manufacturer suggests, a poncho (it would have a fierce itch, I'm afraid).

The mat is an off-straw color, a shade that would surely work in a cornfield but would be a bit off around salt hay or bullrush. However, I experimented with the sample that was sent and found that it painted easily. Just take a few swipes with a brush saturated with the color that matches your marsh, and the mat takes on

a stippled camouflage appearance that looks even better than the factory sample's one-tone hue.

No, I don't think the Marsh Mat is quite as good as a careful grassing job that makes use of materials from your immediate blind area, but it is far and away the best

commercially made camouflage material on the market. Prices: corn Marsh Mat (40″x30′) $54.95; in brown or green, $59.95; Poncho, $33.95. Custom-made boat covers available on request. Rochester and Foster Co., P.O. Box 258, Fillmore, NY 14735.   —N.S.

GREENS CAMOUFLAGE NETTING

This is surely the most durable camouflage netting on the market, and it has several other noteworthy features. The backing is nylon fishnet, to which is bonded strips of PVC, a plasticlike synthetic. The PVC is crinkled, crunched, and laid on in strips so it will cast shadows and create a three-dimensional effect rather than a "wall." In addition, the PVC is colored dark and light tan and dark and light green; one overall shade predominates either side of the net. In lush green settings, use the green side. Around late-fall browns and golds, use the tan side. Another of the many advantages of this particular net is that it won't absorb water or rot or mildew.

The net measures 5 feet 7 inches by 8 feet 2½ inches and retails for $49.95. Greens will send you a small swatch of the netting free if you write and ask for it.

Another Greens product worth looking into is a portable blind frame, big enough for two, that is used in conjunction with the PVC netting: $49.95 for the frame; $98.95 for the frame and netting to cover it. Greens Development Company, P.O. Box 566, Fort Worth, TX 76101.

Camouflage Branches

There may be times when conventional camouflage doesn't quite fit in with the cover around your blind. You can buy plastic willow branches with leaves (24 inches long) for $12.95 per dozen. Waterfowl Supply Company, 173 Scenic Drive, Concord, CA 94518.

You're Not Going to Believe This One!

Need a seat for a duck blind? If so, look into the multipurpose model made by the Waterfowl Supply Company. It has a padded swivel piano-type seat and is specially designed to disperse the heat from a catalytic furnace (stove not included) around you when the furnace is placed inside.

Our vote for ingenuity of design goes not for those somewhat prosaic features but because the seat flips up and the stool (pardon the expression) converts into a commode!

Appropriately called the Growler, it costs $59.50. Waterfowl Supply Company, 173 Scenic Drive, Concord, CA 94518.

Camouflage Umbrella

Some hunting paraphernalia begins to approach the absurd, and maybe that's why I was attracted to Westwood Creations' Camouflage Umbrella. Deep down inside I had visions of a bowler, a sudden shower on Madison Avenue, and "pop" instant invisibility. But when I took one afield, darned if the thing didn't turn out to be surprisingly practical.

It is handy for shelter from pouring rain, as long as a lot of wind doesn't accompany the wet, but it is even more useful as a means to hide all the rest of the paraphernalia I drag along on a duck hunt: shells, Thermos, and especially my black Lab. Laid on its side, the opened umbrella makes a perfect hide for him, which has always been a problem when I'm using a blind constructed on the spot.

One fault in this product: the umbrella shaft is shiny chrome, and the surface doesn't hold dull, dead grass paint well; it tends to chip off when you open and close the umbrella. If this flaw were corrected, a good product would be made a lot better. Price: $17.95. Westwood Creations, P.O. Box 645, Westwood, MA 02090. —N.S.

Hunting with Duckboats

In order for duckboats to be fully effective, they must have more thorough camouflaging than a factory paint job provides. For hunting in marshes they should be a basic brown or green, depending upon the natural background, and they must then be grassed. Usually, duckboats come with grass boards. If this is an option, buy it. You can also build your own.

Grass boards are nothing more than wooden strakes attached to a duckboat's decking. They generally have a bolt-and-wing-nut arrangement that secures a second board to the top of the first. Native grasses are cut, laid down, and sandwiched in place between the top and the bottom.

Boats should be thoroughly grassed, with no patches of paint showing through, and they'll hide most effectively if you have uneven ends and sprigs of grass poking above the coaming and below the waterline.

To hide a grassed boat, find some natural feature of the shoreline like a cut or hollow into which the boat will fit. The idea is to have the side of the boat appear to fit and be part of the natural contour of the shore. You hide by lying flat on your back as the birds approach.

Open-water rigs should be painted white or gray: gray for warm-weather hunting, white when there are ice floes about. Rather than painting and repainting a grass boat, you can have a white or gray canvas cover made that conforms to the decking and secures with screw-in snaps or a drawstring around the craft's perimeter. On open water you must use two anchors, either at 45-degree angles to the bow or fore and aft to keep the boat from yawing. You will have enough trouble hitting birds from the bouncing boat without having to compensate for a side-to-side swing.

—N.S.

Camouflaged Storage Stool

Nothing is more miserable to sit on while you're waiting for ducks on some cold morning than a wet log, yet that is what I usually end up doing when I rig up a temporary blind somewhere. This stool is a whole lot better. It is made of camouflaged canvas on nonreflective olive-drab aluminum tubing, and it has storage pouches underneath for Thermos, shells, whatever. Price: $11.90. Simmons Gun Specialties, Inc., P.O. Box 533, Olathe, KS 66061. —J.B.

Simple Heater for Duck Blinds

A heat drum placed over a small portable stove makes for safe heat in a duck blind. It's also economical in that the stove may be used for cooking as well as heating. "Pure" heaters only heat. Prices: drum, $3.50; Sportster stove, $27.50. Coleman Co., Wichita, KS 67201.

DUCKBOATS

by Zack Taylor

Duckboats, gawdalmighty. Just the thought of them sets me shaking. Happens every fall. I get duckboat seizures. If I'm affluent, I buy one. If I'm broke, I build one. In between I bring the season in by fussing over the fleet. At one point I had five duckboats in the backyard—two coffin boxes, a pond box, a sneakbox, and the Zackbox. Others had astonishing things to say about the clutter of battered mud-colored veterans. Only to a duck hunter are they beautiful.

Duckboats. Okay. Let's start off on the wrong foot. It's hard to find a good duckboat. Commercial builders come and go. Few stay. Which is why I guess you see so many different kinds of boats pressed into duckboat service. Canoes. Rubber rafts. Cement-mixing boxes. All faithfully camouflaged. Some work okay; others swamp or sink or flip and kill somebody.

There are three kinds of duckboats. Access boats carry you to places where you shoot out of a blind. Any summer runabout works for this. You move it a couple of hundred yards from the decoy area and throw a camouflage net over it. A hunting boat functions as the blind itself. A canoe tucks away in grass. I dug the coffin boxes into the marsh. I've no doubt the boys with the cement-mixing-box duckboat hid it against a bank and bragged about the shooting stability of its broad, flat bottom.

Plenty of duckboats are both access boats and hunters, too. The famed sneakbox is a good example. It is seaworthy enough to cross open-water stretches yet small and light enough to conceal in a shooting spot. Hundreds of thousands of sturdy little buckets perform similar feats.

A duckboat does other good things; it keeps your gear in one spot and stores the decoys. If you trailer it, you have mobility, and it prevents theft by bringing it home at night. A decked boat keeps you warm in the coldest, windiest weather.

In many places today, a duckboat is doggone near a waterfowling must if special seasons are to be taken advantage of. You have to be able to gun different species in different areas. For this reason barge blinds are probably the hottest waterfowling vehicle going now. These are johnboats 14 to 16 feet long that are elaborately brushed or grassed and hidden in stumps or against the bank or bushes and used as a blind. Johnboats can take substantial horsepower, so the barges are fast. Yet they are low enough that, with gunners sitting crossways on the bottom and concealed by grassed-up "wings," they fool even wary blacks and mallards.

The commonest request I get is for plans for duckboats, and there really weren't any available. So when I wrote *Successful Waterfowling*, it was mostly to collect and publish as many plans as I had been able to find over the years—fourteen or so—including a plywood sneakbox. The book can be obtained from any bookstore. Crown is the publisher. Or you can send $10.00 to me at *Sports Afield*, 250 West 55th Street, New York, NY 10019, and I'll return an autographed copy.

Zack Taylor has been the boats editor of *Sports Afield* magazine for the last dozen years. He has been a waterfowler all his life.

Duckboat or Blind Paint

Duckboats and permanent blinds made of wood or canvas need a coat of flat, dull paint for protection from the elements as well as for camouflage.

For hunting in a lay-out boat in open waters free of ice, use a flat battleship gray. If you'll be laying out under cold conditions when there are ice floes about, paint the boat flat oyster white. These paints should not be hard to find, as lay-out shooting usually means big water, big water means marinas, and marinas carry a wide selection of good marine paints. Interlux was the brand I leaned to when I used to gun the East Coast, and I see no reason why the brand shouldn't be as reliable today as it was then.

Herter's catalogs a durable marine paint that is notable in that it's available in two colors: dead grass, which matches the shade of frost-killed bullrush or salt hay, and olive rush, which is close to the old army olive drab and suitable for use early in the season or in warm climates where greens predominate the landscape. A quart costs $2.97; a gallon, $7.60. It will take a gallon to do an 8-by-4-foot roofed blind, and you've got to stretch a quart to handle a one-man duckboat. Herter's, Inc., Route 2, Mitchell, SD 57301. —N.S.

THE ULTIMATE DUCKBOAT

I can go into rhapsodies over duckboats. To me they are both substance and symbol of the art, craft, and history of waterfowling, my favorite shooting sport. As this section will indicate, there are many different kinds of duckboats, none really better than another but each designed for specific hunting conditions. If there is one boat that will meet most conditions and still function admirably as a hiding place, however, it is the whale-back design from South Bay Boats.

This is the safest open-water duckboat, in terms of heavy seas, I have ever used, yet it will melt into a cut in a marsh. Low-profiled and thus easy to hide, the sharp-breaking whaleback deck will still turn back a powerful chop. At 14 feet it is large enough to carry two people or a huge spread of blocks, a Labrador, and a gunner safely. I'm not talking about an ocean trip, but I am talking about reasonable limits of wind, weather, and cargo piloted by a reasonable man.

Some of its features can only be called unique, though the phrase is timeworn. It has a recessed transom, so you can reach outboard controls without having to lean out over a big afterdeck. It has rails on the bottom, so it skids easily over ice. It rows and poles well. No, it's not as smooth as a Louisiana double-ender, but it is better than most pump-kinseed shapes. And get this: with a daggerboard as a special option, and with the addition of a sail, the hull will sail on water and even ice!

The boat is made of fiberglass. It has a 62-inch beam and a 58-by-31-inch cockpit with a 2-inch-high rolled coaming, and it weighs 180 pounds. It takes up to a 10-hp outboard, and it is available in white, marsh brown, or duckboat green. Free brochure on request. Price: basic boat, $680.00. South Bay Boats, 39 Washington Avenue, West Sayville, NY 11796.

—N.S.

LIL' DUCKER SKIFF

The most attractive thing about this duckboat is its price—$189.95, FOB. Compared to similar boats on the market, this one undercuts competition by 33 to 66 percent!

Aside from cost, it's a good, functional duckboat, modeled after the Horicon Marsh Skiff used in Wisconsin years ago. Made of fiberglass and weighing 45 pounds, the Lil' Ducker requires virtually no maintenance, and it can be car-topped by one person.

The boat measures 12 feet from bow to stern and sports a 3-foot beam. A lapstrake-type hull and double ends make it a seaworthy craft for its size, and it is easy to tow or paddle. Included in the package are full flotation, stabilizing pole holes and towing holes. Seats, an optional item, are $15.00 each, and you may order a special camouflage finish for an extra $25.00.

The Lil' Ducker has a sweet profile—low on the water, with ample coaming to turn back a chop. It is claimed to be a two-man boat, but don't bank on it. The only practical two-man boats find gunners lying side by side, and three

feet of beam is not going to afford that kind of room unless your hunting partner is a toothpick. One other feature I'd like to see on this boat are grass boards, though they should be easy enough to install yourself. White River Boat Works, 241 McHenry Street, Burlington, WI 53105.

—N.S.

"The wild gander leads his flock through the cool night, Ya-honk he says, and sounds it down to me like an invitation . . ."
—Walt Whitman, *"Song of Myself"*

269

SPORTSPAL DUCKBOAT

This specially adapted canoe has an awful lot going for it—and for the average water. It is extremely lightweight (49 pounds), so it can be hoisted to a cartop carrier by one person with ease. Not only does a canoe paddle easily, it tows easily. If you've ever walked a pumpkinseed or sneakbox full of decoys out to a blind, you'll appreciate that feature.

In place, this canoe duckboat has special stabilizers that anchor the boat rock-solid by way of bars that pass through locks and into marsh mud. There is no yawing in a current or wind drift, and the craft is so stable that you can stand on the gunwale without quivering or quaking.

The boat is marsh brown in color, and it comes with a water-repellent snap-on camouflage cover with shooting slits, camouflage paddles, two Ethafoam seats, motor mount, and towing eyes. It is advertised as a two-man duckboat, and its 14 feet of length will indeed accommodate two; but a canoe's conformation and safety dictate a back-to-back seating arrangement, which is a little impractical for shooting. Then, too, I wouldn't want to try an open-water crossing with two guys, decoys, and assorted paraphernalia in any 14-foot canoe. Call it a superb one-man duckboat that will serve two in a pinch, and don't overlook yet another feature of this attractive bucket: it makes a great cartopper for fishing as well, an advantage that duckboats designed along more traditional lines seldom afford. Price: $525.00. Sportspal, Industrial Park Road, Johnstown, PA 15904.

DOUBLE DUTY DUCKBOAT

If a pure duckboat is too specialized for the number of times you'd get to use it, American Fiber-Lite makes a nice 13-foot compromise craft that will double as a ducker and a light fishing boat. It has seats for fishing and enough room for two hunters to sit on the bottom (though not to lie down). There's enough decking so the boat would grass up well, and it has ample pitch to ward off chop, yet the cockpit is roomy enough for two anglers to cast comfortably.

The hull includes oarlocks, aluminum stern and bow handles, flotation (BIA certified), and triple-molded keels. Price: $260.70. American Fiber-Lite, P.O. Box 67, Marion, IL 62952.

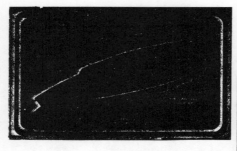

LOUISIANA DOUBLE-ENDER

The name of this duckboat is the Cajun Classic Kayak, as strange an association of regional terms as calling it an Eskimo Classic Pirogue.

In fact, it's a Louisiana double-ender, borrowing some lines from the pirogue, and it is an ideal boat for shooting in protected waters. It poles or paddles with ease in either direction, and it threads the needle eyes between hummocks, heads, and cypress knees like a curling snake. Its low profile makes it virtually disappear when you tuck it up against a bank.

The boat weighs a mere 75 pounds, is 12 feet 2 inches long, and has a 39-inch beam. A very nice one-man duckboat at a very reasonable price: $180.00. Fiberglass Industries, Inc., 3746 Government Street, Alexandria, LA 71301.

The Slipper Scull Boat

Sculling up on a flock of ducks achieved the status of an art in the days of market gunning. While the sport survived in a few select spots, like northern California and on the Great Lakes, it was generally ignored by most waterfowlers. Recently, however, sculling has undergone a revival, and several builders are making scull boats.

One of the prettiest ones I've seen is appropriately dubbed the Slipper. It's a two-man rig, 18 feet long, yet it weighs a featherlike 85 pounds. It's extremely narrow in beam (3 feet 6 inches), so it's easily propelled by a sculling oar. The coaming sweeps up to a point 11 inches above the waterline: low enough so as not to present too great a profile to a raft of birds, yet high enough so it should break and tame a

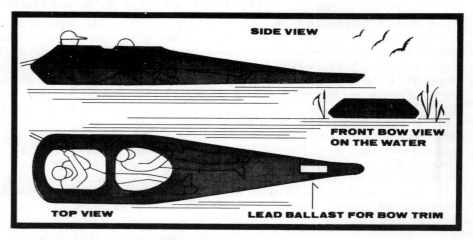

SIDE VIEW

FRONT BOW VIEW ON THE WATER

TOP VIEW

LEAD BALLAST FOR BOW TRIM

2- to 2½-foot incoming chop.

The slipper comes with a sculling oar and a detachable motor mount. It's available in gray for open-water shooting and marsh brown if you hunt around streams, swamps, or bogs. Price: $575.00 FOB. Witham Boats, Fox Point Road, Newington, NH 03801.

OUTBOARD FOR

Evinrude offers a trim package for the waterfowler. Their six-horse engine has a deserved reputation as a dependable unit. It's easy-starting, even on mornings when pane ice coats your favorite pond, and it has enough power to plane a 16-foot aluminum johnboat with two hunters aboard when you have to run down a lively cripple.

It has a gearshift, which is an absolute must if you use your boat to pick up decoys. Without neutral, you'll foul decoy lines in the prop, which isn't just a pain in the neck; on a stormy day it can be deadly dangerous. And you'll use reverse a lot when you inadvertently drift out of reach of a bobbing decoy.

For all its power and maneuverability, it's also a very compact engine, small enough to tuck under the decking of a grassboat or easy to hide ashore.

PROTECTS AGAINST THEFT

HELPS KEEP MOTOR FROM VIBRATING LOOSE

DOUBLES AS A CONVENIENT CARRYING HANDLE

OUTBOARD MOTOR LOCK

If you're accustomed to leaving your outboard on your duckboat or towing skiff, prudence dictates that you lock the motor to the transom. The Master Outboard Motor Lock is a case-hardened steel sleeve that fits over the transom clamps and locks into position. The lock can't be reached with bolt cutters or the steel broken, as is the case with a standard padlock threaded through the transom clamps.

The lock is made of marine brass and the sleeve is protected by vinyl, so it should have a long life in salt water. It's also available in keyed-alike locks if you have two or more motors.

Another pleasant feature of this locking system: when the motor is off the boat, the sleeve makes an ideal carrying handle. Price: $10.95. Master Lock Company, Milwaukee, WI 53201.

Outboard Remote Control

Here's a product worth considering when your waterfowling brings you up against a lively cripple. Best described as a manual remote control, this gadget allows both shift and throttle control with the same hand. When a duck dives, you can back up, zoom forward, or drift in neutral without taking your eyes off the bird to shift. (Another tip for that same cripple: carry a large-mouthed, long-handled fisherman's landing net. It makes snaring the bird a hundred times easier than by hand.) Price: Remote Control Adapter Kit, $27.50 from your Johnson or Evinrude dealer.

DUCK HUNTERS

Evinrude, through its subsidiary, Outboard Motor Corporation, also offers two optional pieces of equipment that fit well with the waterfowling scene: a propeller guard which, bolted up to the lower unit, creates very little drag and protects the propeller from snags, stumps, and damaging rocks when you putt around in shallow water; and a canvas carryall in a camouflage pattern which, in addition to its other qualities, described elsewhere, fits nicely over the power unit of a six-horse engine for quick, effective camouflage. (This eliminates the need to paint the engine dull, dead grass and also eliminates lost cash should you want to sell the motor someday.) Prices: 6 hp motor, $575.00; prop guard, $19.95; carryall, $14.95. Contact your local Evinrude dealer or write Evinrude Motors, 4143 27th Street, Milwaukee, WI 53216.

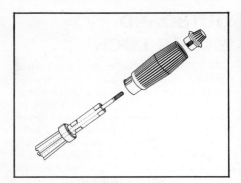

OUTBOARD EXTENSION HANDLE

This gadget is the perfect solution to a lot of problems that arise when you're waterfowling with the aid of a boat.

An easily installed male receptacle replaces the twist throttle on the motor. A 30-inch female handle snaps onto the receptacle. This handle is telescoped. By removing a bolt, the handle will extend up to 4 feet. This allows for easy steering of a duckboat with a large afterdeck, because it eliminates a long reach. It also allows you to steer any boat while standing. You can see down into the water and thus are in a better position to spot snags and crippled birds than when sitting. The handle also allows you to get farther forward in a small boat, for a better distribution of weight. With it a 5-hp motor will get a 14-foot johnboat up on plane. Price: $12.95. Gil's, 3715 Minnehaha Avenue, Minneapolis, MN 55406.

Custom Camouflage Boat Cover

This is a net-type camouflage boat cover with drawstrings, so it can be cinched in place between the gunwales and the waterline. There are snap closures down the center, so you can sit anywhere with your head and torso free to shoot.

A cover like this has many applications, but the best, I think, is as a means to hide a rowboat or johnboat used to gain access to a blind. These are also good for marshbrown duckboats that you wish to convert temporarily to open-water layout boats. Soak the netting in a diluted white or gray acrylic paint (use water until the paint is broth thin rather than pea soupy), let it dry, and it's ready to use. Price: covers for 12-, 14-, and 16-foot boats $23.97, $27.97, and $30.87 respectively. Herter's, Inc., Route 2, Mitchell, SD 57301.   —N.S.

Floatable Carryall

Hunting around water, be it in a duck blind or on a deer stand, usually finds some part of your gear getting wet. The most frequent offenders are cardboard shell boxes that break at the bottom and scatter the shells over the marsh. Then, too, soggy sandwiches aren't exactly gourmet fare; and if you bring a camera along, you'll want to keep it out of spray and splashy mud.

Outboard Motor Corporation's camouflage Carryall is a practical solution to this problem. It measures 16 by 9 by 16 inches and has a 300-pound capacity. Constructed of 6-ounce canvas duck, the carryall is sufficiently water resistant to keep gear safe from spray or a sudden downpour. Should it fall overboard, it floats.

Another notable feature: it folds flat when empty for easy storage when not in use. $14.95 from your Johnson or Evinrude dealer.

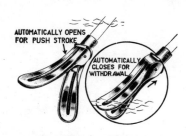

Duckbill Head for Pushpoling Duckboats

Poling a duckboat is often the only way to get across a shallow, muddy marsh. This device resembles the upper and lower halves of a duck's bill. It expands as you push, opening up to expose a large, flat surface to the soft bottom. As you retract the pole, the "bills" close, cutting down on water resistance. Without such a head, pushpoles are bound to get stuck in the mud. Staff tested. Price: $2.89. Herter's, Inc., Route 2, Mitchell, SD 57301.

FLOTATION CLOTHING

Cold weather and cold water can be a dangerous combination, and the typical waterfowler faces both in the course of a season. If you're a poor swimmer, a non-swimmer, or an aficionado of open-water sculling or layout boats, consider wearing flotation clothing.

Its greatest asset is that it will be on your back at all times. Mae West-type life jackets are difficult to don in an emergency situation, and that difficulty is compounded by the bulky clothing you'll surely be wearing. Then, too, modern flotation clothing is reasonably comfortable to wear and is good insulation against the cold.

Vest-type preservers are the least constraining. The Sterns line offers a vest in either brown or green camouflage, with four pockets and Velcro closures. The zipper is rustproof and heavy-duty, with a tab large enough to grab with gloves on. Price: $35.25.

Vests are best worn as outerwear in warm weather or under a conventional parka or camouflage suit when it's cold. Patterns available include forest green and green or brown camouflage. They incorporate patch pockets, a zippered game pocket, a waterproof hood that folds away into the collar, and a two-way zipper protected by a storm flap. Pants and jacket, windproof and waterproof, may be purchased separately. Prices: vest, $35.25; pants, $60.50; jacket, $80.50. Stearns Manufacturing Company, P.O. Box 1498, St. Cloud, MN 56301.

"Getting up too early is a vice habitual in horned owls, stars, geese, and freight trains. Some hunters acquire it from geese."
—Aldo Leopold

273

SIMMONS FLOTATION COAT

This meets all Coast Guard specifications for a personal flotation device yet is a warm camouflage coat very well adapted to waterfowling. Two-way zipper, drawstring hood, big pockets with inside shell loops. In sizes Small, Medium, Large, and Extra Large. Price: $55.00. Simmons Gun Specialties, Inc., P.O. Box 533, Olathe, KS 66061.

ROYAL FLEXNET CAMOUFLAGE SUIT

Of the several commendable features in this wet-weather hunting outfit, most notable is the batwing shoulder cut, which allows you to mount a gun and swing without binding.

The camouflage pattern is well conceived and does a better job of blending into marshy, woodsy backgrounds than the standard army pattern. It is also available in green or brown, to better match local hunting conditions.

The Flexnet material is waterproof, yet it provides for some transfer of internal moisture. This is a problem with most waterproof foul-weather gear when it gets involved in outdoor sports. Exertion makes for perspiration, and you get wet from your own sweat. With Flexnet, some of this moisture can escape.

Other features indicate that this suit was thoughtfully designed: cuffs that snap tightly around your wrists in two locations and allow for heavy undergarments, or the lack of them, and a jacket length that is sufficient to drain water over, not into, a pair of hip boots. Prices: parka, $37.20; pants, $20.40; suit, $57.60. Royal Sports Clothing, 8530 Page Avenue, St. Louis, MO 63114.

Peter Storm Overjacket

If you do a lot of waterfowling in the kind of weather that finds *you* growing webbed feet, look into the line of outdoor clothing made by Peter Storm. These products are designed for sailors, not hunters, hence there are no camouflage patterns, but the designs used and the materials employed are just the thing for wet weather.

For example, their Bulkflex overjacket is the only waterproof garment we've run into that actually breathes (it's knitted). It's guaranteed not to form condensation on the inside. Other products include things like oiled wool sweaters, sou'westers, and watch caps, most of which are available in olive drab or green shades. Overjacket price: $46.00. Peter Storm, Smith Walk, Norwalk, CT 06851. Free catalog.

Down Hunting Coat for Cold Ducks

Klamath Koat for Klammy Konditions

If you're used to waterfowling when the weather's really soggy, the Klamath Koat might be for you. It's a super storm suit designed especially for the hunter, with nice details like shell-loop pockets that are protected by a camouflage outer flap, so the glint of shells won't spook incoming birds.

It is available in brown or green traditional camouflage pattern, and the waterproof outer shell is lined with poplin to absorb any dampness from condensation. The hood is visored and can be snugged tightly against your face. The nylon zipper is protected from the strongest gale by two storm flaps, and the waist and cuffs are adjustable. Prices: jacket, $52.00; pants, $19.95. Columbia Sportswear, 6600 North Baltimore Street, Portland, OR 97203.

When the weather really gets cold, toward the end of a northern duck season, and any moisture that falls is going to be snow, down makes for a great insulator without the kind of bulk that will interfere with your shooting. This jacket is filled with duck down, and it includes among standard features handwarmer pockets, a removable hood, a corduroy nonchafe collar, and a storm-flap front with snap fasteners. Price: $84.00. Duxbak, 825 Noyes Street, Utica, NY 13502.

BERGAN & KLINEBERG

EDDIE BAUER, INC.

REVERSIBLE LIGHT VEST

A light vest does wonders to keep you warm on cool marsh mornings. Wear it under your camouflage clothing. When the day warms up, take it off and stow it, or stow your camou top and wear the vest green side out. These vests are also great around big-game camps—just about any kind of hunting situation—for supplemental warmth. Dacron fill. Price: $12.50. Duxbak, 825 Noyes Street, Utica, NY 13502.

Mosquito-Net Camouflage Parka for Hot Hunting

For duck hunting in warm climates or dove hunting down south, this mesh parka will keep you shaded, well ventilated, and hidden. It includes a zipper front, an attached hood with a face net, and two slash side openings, so you can reach your pockets. Also good camouflage in cold climates when worn over any kind of warm clothing. A super buy at $10.00. Duxbak 825 Noyes Street, Utica, NY 13502.

CAMOUFLAGE HOODED SWEATSHIRT

Ideal for duck hunting when the weather's a bit cool. Outer and inner layers are 100-percent cotton jersey knit; inner insulation, polyester thermal foam. There are two large pockets up front where you can tuck your hands, and wrist and waist are stretchknit to fit snugly. Full-length zipper.

This jacket's available in camou for duck, dove, and archery hunters and in red for gun-toting deer hunters. Price: $11.95. Eddie Bauer, 1737 Airport Way South, Seattle, WA 98134.

REED CAMOUFLAGE PATTERN

No, that isn't the creature from the black lagoon; it's someone inside a reed-pattern camouflage coat, with a face mask. Although I haven't tried one personally, this garment appears to be the best thing a duck hunter can put on his back. It should blend into the striped shadows of a fall marsh far better than splotchy conventional camouflage, and the mask covers one of the most persistent giveaways of your presence, the shine off your face.

One inherent problem with face masks and hoods, though, is that they seldom turn when you do. Turn your head, and more often than not you see the inside of your slicker. Should this problem arise with this garment, consider a pair of lensless glasses. Sew the glasses to the mask eyeholes, and your headgear will be firmly attached to your temples and will turn when you do. Price: reed pattern camouflage coat, $39.95. Hunters' Things, P.O. Box 30903, Raleigh, NC 27612.

—N.S.

"Iron" Camouflage Face Mask

This expanded-vinyl face mask comes in a five-color camouflage pattern. The inside is lined to reduce sweating. The advantages of this mask lie in an unobstructed view that doesn't change when you turn your head and because it can be worn over glasses. Also handy for costume parties if you want to go as the Man in the Iron Mask. Price: $3.19. Cabela's, 812 13th Avenue, Sidney, NE 69162.

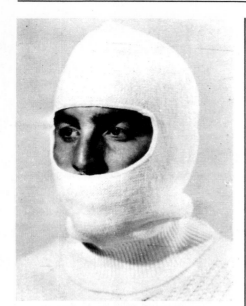

FACE MASK FOR COLD-WEATHER HUNTING

Knitted face masks perform three functions: They hide you, they keep your face (and more important your sinuses) warm, and they heat the air you breathe in. Kolpin's All Season camouflage masks are knitted from 100-percent acrylic yarns, which means they won't itch. They have an extra-long neck tube to seal off drafts, and they come in four color patterns: red camouflage for big-game hunters, brown and green camouflage for archers and duck hunters, and pure white—an ideal color for hunting any animal when there's snow on the ground. Price: $8.75. Kolpin Manufacturing, Inc., P.O. Box 231, Berlin, WI 54923.

Solid-Fuel Handwarmer

This is an interesting (but untested by us) concept in handwarmers. The fuel is a small, solid, dry stick that you light on one end. Once it gets going, you close the lid on the fuel holder and that's it. It supposedly lasts five to twelve hours. The metal case is covered with velveteen to pevent hot spots. Price: $3.95. Brookstone Company, 125 Vose Farm Road, Peterborough, NH 03458.

DUCK HUNTER'S HAND-WARMING MITT AND MUFF

This combination glove and muff was designed by a past president of Ducks Unlimited. It will keep your hands warm on the coldest day. The mitt hand holds your gun. It is fleece-lined on the inside and leather on the outside, with thumb and trigger finger separate from the mitten that's around what's left of your fingers. The muff is fleece and leather, too, and it keeps your trigger hand warm. You can either go bare-handed or, in really bitter weather, wear a light wool or knit shooting glove.

ED JAFFE STUDIO

The Duck Hunter's Mitt is available in right- or left-hand models, and one size fits all. Price: $21.50. Orvis, 10 River Road, Manchester, VT 05254.

WATERPROOF GLOVES FOR SETTING DECOYS

If the weather's cold enough for you to need gloves, you should never go into the water with them on—your regular gloves, that is. Get them just a litle damp and their ability to hold warmth will be cut in half.

Instead, when you're retrieving a bird, setting out or winding in decoys, don a pair of waterproof rubber gloves. The best kind are gauntlets that come up and over your cuffs, as water tends to drain directly

off their tops when you bend your elbow rather than onto your sleeve. If weather and water are bitterly cold, wear liners inside the rubber gloves. Prices: gauntlet with jersey liner, $3.49; special thermal liner for extreme cold, $1.39. Cabela's, 812 13th Avenue, Sidney, NE 69162.

Armpit-high Waterproof Gloves

These gloves are by far the best for picking up blocks in cold weather, as it is nearly impossible for water to drain back against your clothing. We can't track down a mail-order source for the goodies or even a manufacturer's address, as they are not sporting goods items but are tools of the lineman and the electrician. Your local power company undoubtedly uses them, so you might check there. Electrical supply wholesale houses (in the Yellow Pages) should carry them, too. Price: $18.00–$28.00, depending on the thickness of the rubber.

Over-the-Shoe Waders

Over-the-shoe waders were common fifteen years ago, but now they have fallen into disfavor, and I can't figure out why. They're great, because you wear them over your hunting boots and get a nice, snug fit for walking. They're also slightly less expensive than waders with a built-in foot.

These boots are nylon coated, with rubber on the outside and neoprene on the inside, and they are chest high. Price: $49.50. Tidewater Specialties, 430 Swann Avenue, Alexandria, VA 22301.   —N.S.

For other cold-weather items (socks, boots, heavy clothing, etc.), see section I, Big Game.
For other camouflage items, see section VI, Archery.

Royal Red Ball Cahill Waders

These are truly comfortable waders. They are tailored, so there is no low crotch to snag on barbwire fences or stop you short when you try to step up. The legs, too, are form-fitting, without dumpy folds that make you feel like a blimp.

The pair I tried out had insulated boots, and my feet stayed perfectly warm in 35-degree water and 25-degree air with only two pairs of socks. I did note, however, that the Tuff-Guard upper material, a kind of woven nylon, absorbs water. As it dries, evaporation cools the material. My feet stayed warm, but my legs got chilly, so in the future I'll wear insulated rather than cotton long johns when duck hunting in cold weather.

This same material, however, becomes a plus under most conditions in that it is highly ozone-resistant, and it's the ozone in the air that destroys wading boots. The boots are also reinforced for extra protection.

Clearly, this is a well-made wader, with a long life span. Price: $49.70. Royal Sports Clothing, 8530 Page Avenue, St. Louis, MO 63114.   —N.S.

Stocking-foot Chest Waders

The one thing a stocking-foot wader has going for it is that it's light, so if you have a long way to walk to your blind and the weather's warm, they might be for you. However, waders like this are notorious for developing leaks due to snags and cuts, so I wouldn't recommend them for cold-weather use.

This particular wader is one of the most snag-resistant on the market. It is one-piece latex rubber, with no seams, and is quite flexible. If it does puncture, it can be repaired like an inner tube. Adjustable elastic web straps and an inside pocket are included, but the shoes are not (you can wear common tennis shoes, or special wading shoes). Prices: waders, $22.69 from Cabela's, 812 13th Avenue, Sidney, NE 69162; special wading shoes, $57.50 from Leonard, 25 Cottage Street, Midland Park, NJ 07432.

The Indestructible Wader

If you've thrown up your hands at $50.00-chest waders that last just one season, look into the Super Industrial wader by Royal. As the name implies, they are of industrial quality and are extra tough. A few examples of where I've seen them used will indicate their quality. They are standard equipment for the Montana Fish and Game Department, commercial clammers and fishermen on the East Coast use them; and so do most of the duck-hunting guides on the Great South Bay. Captain Critter claims he gets three to four years' use out of a pair, and he's both a duck guide and a clammer, so he uses them year round.

They do have two characteristics that don't exactly lend themselves to duck hunting: they are heavy and they are black.

Locating them can be a problem, as they are not marketed as a sporting goods item but in commercial fishing supply stores, farm supply stores, and occasionally in electrical supply stores. They're usually priced from $70.00 to $80.00. Royal Red Ball, Naugatuck, CT 06770.

Quick-Release Wader Suspenders

These suspenders have a snap-release feature for safety and ease in getting in and out of them. They have an H-type strap, so you don't have to cross them to keep them from slipping off your shoulders. Price: $4.35. Tidewater Specialties, 430 Swann Avenue, Alexandria, VA 22301.

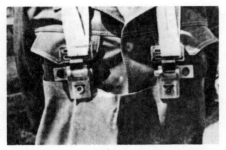

Safety Device for Wader Suspenders

If your wader suspenders don't have a quick-release feature, this product will do it. It is a three-part system; an adjustable wader strap lock is joined to the wader's button snap by way of a clevis and pin. The pins have a large ring on the end. Should you go into the drink, all it takes to free the wader straps is to pull the pins loose. Price: $3.99 per pair. Jay Gee Enterprises, P.O. Box 871, Albany, NY 12207.

Goose Hunting on Maryland's Eastern Shore

Easton, Maryland, is known as the goose capital of the East, and W. Raymond Marshall III runs a guiding operation three that includes over 1,000 acres of fields, marshes, and blinds.

Hunting techniques include pits, fence rows, and water blinds, and the birds are brought in to decoys. One of the more ex-

STOP OZONE DAMAGE TO RUBBER GOODS

The real enemy of rubber waders, slickers, and hunting boots isn't use; it's ozone, which dries the rubber and causes it to check. Armor All is a spray-on polymer that arrests ozone damage and protects rubber by sealing it off from the air. Use it on all your rubber goods twice a year, and you'll prolong their life considerably. Price: $3.98. Very Important Products, 3901 Westerly Place, Suite 101, Newport Beach, CA 92660.

citing aspects of this particular hunt is the calling. Mr. Marshall is a recognized master goose caller, and there are few sights and sounds more beautiful in the outdoors than goose music and the rush of wings as a flock of big Canadas fly down your gun barrel.

Basic rates run $55.00 each for a party of four. Along with waterfowling, Marshall also books hunts for deer, dove, and quail at amazingly reasonable rates. Contact W. Raymond Marshall III, P.O. Box 171, Trappe, MD 21673.

Goose Hunting in Northern Canada

Is goose hunting up around James Bay and Hudson Bay all they say it is? Yes, it is, and then some. Canadas come in to piles of mud and newspaper and crude mouthy honks like chickens to barnyard corn. Daily limits are the rule, not the exception.

What's the secret? No secret at all. The birds are just dumb. By the time they get to Maryland's Eastern Shore, or Punky Down's 'tater patch out on eastern Long Island, or Cairo, Illinois, or Gary De-Cock's cornfield along the Yellowstone, they've been educated by dozens of hunters packing long tom 12s and 10s with magnum loads of twos and BBs. The lessons make an impression.

If you've thrown in the towel after having these birds examine your attempts at a decent invite and then turn you down, go get 'em where they live *before* they get their Ph.D.s.

Cost: five-day goose hunt, September 1 to October 8 at Cape Jones or Roggin River goose camps, James Bay, Canada, $650.00 per person. Contact Den Austin, P.O. Box 520, Rawdon, Quebec, JOK 1SO, Canada.

SPORTSMAN'S HIP BOOTS

Before you buy hip boots consider this: will you ever be hunting over deep water? If the answer is yes, buy chest waders, because it's a sure thing that a time will come when you'll need their extra height—probably when chasing a lively cripple or when a decoy anchor line lets go and a block starts to drift away.

However, if you always hunt around shallow water, hip boots are lighter, cheaper, and, to some extent, more comfortable than chest waders. Royal makes a top-of-the-line hipper, with nylon lining and a reinforced toe. The price varies from store to store, but they're generally in the $20.00–$30.00 category. Royal Red Ball, Naugatuck, CT 06770.

W. RAYMOND MARSHAL III

ARGENTINE GOOSE HUNT

Most foreign waterfowl hunts are a European-style shoot, with birds driven or passing over stands. If you're into the beauty and excitement of waterfowl tolling to decoys, Braniff Airlines books a four-day Argentine goose and duck hunt which is conducted from blinds and pits, with birds shot over decoys.

The geese strongly resemble North American Canadas and blue geese in size, color, and habit. Huge flocks of the birds invade the fields and marshlands of western and central Argentina during the southern winter (March through July). There are no seasons or bag limits, so you can bang away all day if you wish. Downed birds are never wasted, though; the local farmers and workers love them.

Lodgings are in chalet-type hotels with bars and big fireplaces. The food is first class, and it is served with a wide selection of native and European wines. The price of the package includes airport reception, transfers, three nights' lodging, all meals, hunting permits, guides, transportation to and from your blind, retrievers, and care of downed game. Costs: tour, $420.00 per person, with group rates reduced to 40 percent; air fare, $1,088.00, Miami to Buenos Aires. Contact Safari Outfitters, Inc., 8 South Michigan Avenue, Chicago, IL 60603.

Hunt Shinnecock Bay with Captain Critter

Captain Critter (Errol Carter) hunts out of a floating blind on Shinnecock Bay, New York. The blind is a masterpiece of comfort and camouflage, with full cooking and eating facilities aboard. Critter serves ham and/or sausage and eggs (scrambled—he can't fry an egg without breaking the yolk), soups, and hot sandwiches. Chestnuts are normally roasting on the starboard heater.

He hunts black duck early in the season, broadbill late in the season, and geese whenever they're around. Aside from his guiding chores, he does superb imitations of John Wayne and Gabby Hayes and swears that Polish polkas played on his portable radio bring in ducks better than a call. A good hunter and a great guy, at bargain rates: $100.00 daily for parties up to four. Contact Errol Carter, 180 Vail, East Quogue, NY 11937.

Part IV

VARMINT AND TARGET SHOOTING

THAT'S MARKSMANSHIP

- 1879: Adam Bogardus shoots at 5,000 glass balls in six hours with a 12-gauge shotgun and misses 156.
- 1884: Annie Oakley shoots at 5,000 glass balls with a 16-gauge shotgun and misses 228.
- 1886: Doc Carver shoots at 60,000 balls over a ten-day period, using a .22, and misses 50.
- 1907: Al Topperwein shoots at 72,500 wooden blocks in ten days with a .22 and misses 9.
- 1959: Tom Frye shoots at 100,010 wooden blocks in thirteen days with a .22 and misses 6.

VARMINT RIFLES AND CARTRIDGES

Any gun that is used to hunt varmints—nongame animals—might be termed a varmint rifle, but today a varmint gun is thought of as a very accurate rifle, chambered for a smaller-bore, fast centerfire cartridge. Because of the accuracy factor they are usually bolt actions, but occasionally other actions are used, especially single shots. The calibers run from .17 to .25, with the centerfire .22s being the classic varmint rounds.

This definition is fairly broad, and there might be three additional divisions within it. One would be the "pure" varmint rifle. These guns are used entirely for varmint hunting and have heavier-than-normal barrels (which are stiffer, promoting accuracy; they also "hold" steadier). A second division would be the sporter varmint rifle, which also might be used entirely for varmint hunting, but it would have a standard-weight barrel, making it easier to use if much walking were involved. The third category would be combination guns. These would be chambered for the larger varmint rounds—the 6mms and .25s—and would have standard-weight barrels and perhaps variable scopes; they would be usable on big game as well as varmints.

For "pure" varmint shooting the centerfire .22s are the No. 1 choice, as they are more accurate, on the average, than any other class of cartridges. There are a number of reasons for this. One is that they kick very little, and another is that the report is comparatively mild. Most people shoot better when they aren't getting knocked around and their ears aren't being stunned. Still another reason might be that more care is taken in the manufacture of many of the .22 varmint cartridges simply because they *are* going to be used by varmint hunters who demand sufficient accuracy to knock off smallish critters at ranges up to ¼ mile. A fourth reason perhaps is that the .22 hole (actually .224 inch) in a barrel leaves more steel in the barrel than other, larger calibers, as most manufacturers leave outside barrel diameters the same in most calibers. This, like the heavy barrel, promotes stiffness and accuracy.

The centerfire .22s range from the .22 Hornet (believe it or not, this bullet started out in life as a black-powder round back in the late 1800s) through the .222 family. This group consists of the .222 Remington, its slightly larger .222 magnum brother, and the similar .223 (which is the 5.56mm used in the Vietnam War, up to the .22-250 and .220 Swift. Muzzle velocities in these various classes of cartridges (they all use bullets of 45 to 55 grains in factory loads) run from around 2,700 fps for the Hornet to the

3,100 to 3,300 range for the .222s, up to 3,600 to 4,000 fps for the largest rounds.

As you go up the ladder in power, flatness of trajectory (very important when you are aiming at targets smaller than a breadbox) becomes more of a characteristic, while accuracy declines slightly. Notice that I said *slightly*, as there are far too many .22-250s that will group inside ½ inch at 100 yards for anyone to ever call it an inaccurate round. But the fact remains that the .222s offer the optimum in shootable accuracy, a statement that's supported by the fact that they hold most of the benchrest records.

In practical terms, each type of hot .22 is best for a certain type of shooting. The Hornet excels in crowded country at ranges under 200 yards, simply because it doesn't bark as loud. Its size, however, limits it to these fairly close ranges. The .222s can be used at up to 300 yards and are especially suitable for targets such as prairie dogs and ground squirrels, where pinpoint accuracy is needed. For longer ranges and larger animals, such as coyotes, the .22-250 and .220 Swift are the kings, although there are those who say that they simply don't have enough power for game bigger than 20 pounds much past 300 yards.

If it weren't for the last factor and another—wind—we would be well off simply with the hot .22s for most varminting. But their light bullets of low sectional density can be blown around incredibly by even a 10-mph breeze at longer ranges. For these situations, the 6mms (.243 inch) and .25s are better, because they shoot more efficient bullets. They start off a bit slower than the fastest .22s, with most .24- to .25-caliber varmint loads having muzzle velocities in the

3,200 to 3,400 range, but because the bullets are more efficient, they shoot just as flat at longer ranges. Their accuracy is not quite as good generally, but a heavy-barreled .243 or .25-06 can be tuned to group well under an inch. Because of the wind-drift factor, they are more accurate in practical terms at long ranges. Of course, these are the rounds that are used for big game as well. If used for this purpose, you must forego the heavy barrel, but the kind of accuracy that can be squeezed from one of these light sporters is surprising. I have a .243, for instance, that weighs only 7½ pounds with scope and sling, yet with selected handloads it will stay inside 1 inch and very often under ¾ inch at 100 yards when shooting five-shot groups. This is entirely adequate for most varminting.

Other rounds can be used for varminting. Most popular big-game rounds up to .30 caliber are available in at least one varmint factory load. These loads are light, thin-jacketed bullets driven at higher velocities—the 100-grain .270, the 125-grain 7mm magnum (though this is used as a big-game load, too), the 110- and 125-grain .308 and .30-06. These high velocities ensure breakup on ground or game. The 100-grain .270 load, especially, is very suitable, but these loads kick harder than the smaller rounds, and as a result, their accuracy leaves something to be desired. But for the man who wishes to give varminting a try before he breaks the piggy bank and dashes down to the hardware store for a new .222, they are a good option. Let me warn you, though: if you try it, you might like it, and then you *will* want another rifle.

—J.B.

WEATHERBY VARMINTMASTER

This is a scaled-down version of the Mark V Weatherby. It is not a heavy-barreled varmint gun but is very accurate nonetheless. Originally, it was chambered only for the .224 Weatherby magnum, a miniature belted round with slightly less power than the .22-250, but because the ammo was hard to get, they started chambering the gun for the .22-250 as well, and sales went up. Both are good rounds, and the rifle is very nice: the standard Weatherby stock design, well finished, what might be called a slightly flashy rifle. Available with 24- or 26-inch barrel; weight, 6½ pounds. Price: $429.50. Weatherby, Inc., 2781 Firestone Boulevard, South Gate, CA 90280.   —J.B.

WINCHESTER 70 VARMINT

Again, simply a heavy-barreled version of the regular 70, with target scope block on barrel, this gun has all the virtues of the regular 70: quick lock time, good trigger, nice handling. In calibers .222, .22-250, and .243. Weight about 9¾ pounds; barrel, 24 inch. (Why did they ever drop the .220 Swift?) Price: $265.00. Winchester-Western, 275 Winchester Avenue, New Haven, CT 06504.   —J.B.

"Up the airy mountain, / Down the rushy glen,
We daren't go a-hunting / For fear of little men."
—William Allingham

281

SAVAGE 65-M: RIMFIRE VARMINTER

This little gun is chambered for the .22 magnum, which was thought up by Winchester as a round to plug the gap between the .22 long rifle and the .22 Hornet. It is an OK 125-yard varmint round, though it costs about as much to shoot as handloads in Hornets or .222s: $3.00 for a box of 50. I have a .22 magnum and can't get wildly enthusiastic about it; it doesn't really offer much of an advantage over the regular .22 rimfire and is less accurate than the Hornet and .222, with less range. For the nonhandloader who wants to dabble in varminting (close range), it might be the choice, however. Clip is five-shot, barrel 22 inches, weight 6 pounds. Price: $66.80. Savage Arms, Springdale Road, Westfield, MA 01085. —J.B.

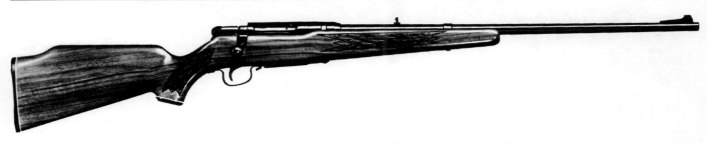

SAVAGE 340: ECONOMY VARMINTER

This is a nonconventional bolt-action gun designed for slightly lower pressures than most bolts. It comes with a side mount for scoping, since the receiver bridge is split (à la Mannlicher). It is available in .22 Hornet, .222, and .223, all of which are good, low-recoil, low-cost rounds. Accuracy in this gun is limited by the light barrel, the trigger (it isn't the best in the world, but it is better than might be expected), and the fact that the barrel is screwed to the fore-end of the stock, which could be helped with a bit of judicious gunsmithing. I've fooled around a little with one in .222 with factory ammo, and it seemed that it would do the job for most casual varminting on chuck-sized game up to 200 yards or so. Possibly with some handloads and tuning it would have been very acceptable (groups ran 1½ to 2 inches at 100 yards). Something tells me that with a more attractive stock design they'd sell a few more. The best part: price, $122.00. Savage Arms, Springdale Road, Westfield, MA 01085. —J.B.

SAVAGE 112-V: ESPECIALLY FOR VARMINTING

Unlike most "varmint" specials on today's market, this isn't just a regular centerfire gun with a heavy barrel screwed into the standard action on a standard stock. This is a single-shot, bolt-action version of the Savage 110, with the magazine left out to promote stiffness (which helps support the heavy barrel) and a stock especially designed for varminting. The receiver is drilled and tapped for regular mounts as well as having a target scope block on barrel. Barrel is 26 inches; weight, 9¼ pounds. Available in .222, .223, .22-250, .243, .25-06, and the spectacular .220 Swift. Price: $229.35. Savage Arms, Springdale Road, Westfield, MA 01085. —J.B.

SAKO 74 HEAVY BARREL AND SPORTERS

This action has an excellent reputation for accuracy. With the heavy barrel in calibers .222, .223, .22-250, and .243, it will rival any. Weight is about 8½ pounds. Adjustable trigger.

The little Sako sporter .222 is also very popular for back-country varminting because of its weight: 6½ pounds. Accuracy is excellent with this gun, too; most go under an inch at 100 yards with factory ammo, some less. This standard rifle is also available in other calibers and the .220 Swift (though these are a bit heavier). Price for any of the Sako sporters is $329. The Garcia Corporation, 329 Alfred Avenue, Teaneck, NJ 07666.   —J.B.

MOSSBERG 800 V/T

This is a heavy-barreled version of Mossberg's 800 big-game gun. It is available in .243 and .22-250, weight about 9½ pounds, with sling swivels, recoil pad, 24-inch barrel, and the price is reasonable: $187.50. O. F. Mossberg & Sons, Inc., 7 Grasso Avenue, North Haven, CT 06473.   —J.B.

COLT AR-15 SPORTER

This is a civilian version of the M-16 military rifle, which was used during the Vietnam War. This one, of course, is semiauto only; the military version can be either semiautomatic or fully automatic. It is chambered for the 5.56mm round, which in commercial terms is the .223 Remington. The most practical application for this rifle in sporting use is on running varmints, like coyotes and foxes. Its light recoil and straight-back push make it extremely fast on the repeat shot. As a big-game rifle its uses are nil, in spite of the fact that it was used for targets about as big as deer (people), because the small bullet only kills well with multiple hits (as in fully automatic fire). For long-range varminting at stationary targets, it probably wouldn't be as good either, since it shouldn't be any more accurate than the military version, which has a standard 3.5-inch accuracy maximum at 100 yards. This translates out to around 10 inches at 300 yards, out where the woodchucks are. It isn't easily scopable with standard scopes, though a 3x scope and mount especially adapted for it are available as an option. Price of the rifle is $297.50 with 5-shot magazine, and the scope and mount runs $90.00. Colt Industries, Firearms Div., 150 Huyshope Avenue, Hartford, CT 06102.   —J.B.

"Here lived and loved another race of beings. Beneath the same sun that rolls over your heads the Indian hunter pursued the panting deer."
—Charles Sprague, The American Indian

283

HARRINGTON & RICHARDSON 317

This is a cute little rifle (5¼ pounds), chambered for the .17 Remington and the .223. It has a 20-inch barrel and a six-round magazine.

The .17 especially matches its mood. This is essentially a .222/.223-sized case necked down to take .172-inch bullets of 25-grain weight (the Remington 700 BDL is also chambered for this round). It is of extremely high velocity and is the only factory-loaded cartridge besides the .220 Swift with a muzzle speed of over 4,000 fps. Because of the tiny .17 bullet, which has a very low ballistic qualities, it can never match even the .22s in range and power. In practical terms it is a 250-yard varmint round. Its virtues are much the same as the small .22s, (the .222 and the .223): light recoil, light report, economy of reloading. Perhaps its greatest virtue is the light report, for it certainly doesn't kill any better than the .222. For crowded areas it would be a very good choice, and also for those who even shy from .22-250 recoil.

The problems involved with this caliber are getting the ammo and finding a .17-caliber cleaning rod.

This round is also favored by some hunters who use it on furbearing varmints, such as foxes and coyotes, as it doesn't chew up the hide like bigger rounds do. For this use, however, you must be ultra-careful about shot placement on coyotes, owing to the fact that the little bullet can blow up on a shoulder blade and not kill.

Price of the 317 is $285.00. Harrington & Richardson, Inc., Industrial Rowe, Gardner, MA 01440.　　　　—J.B.

RUGER NO. 1 SPECIAL VARMINTER AND NO. 3 SINGLE SHOT

The No. 1 Special Varminter is a heavy-barreled version of the Ruger single shot. Its caliber selection in varmint rounds is rather limited—.22-250 and .25-06 (it would be nice if they'd put one of the 6mms in there)—but it's a very good gun. Barrel length is 24 inches, weight 9 pounds, which would go up to 10 or 10½ with a scope. It's equipped with a scope block for target-type scopes. Price: $265.00.

Ruger also makes the No. 3 single shot, a carbine model of the No. 1, in .22 Hornet. Barrel length is 22 inches; weight is 6 pounds. It's drilled and tapped for standard scope mounts and would make a very good light varminter. Price: $165.00. Sturm, Ruger & Co., Inc., Lacey Place, Southport, CT 06490.　　　　—J.B.

VARMINT AMMO

Varmint ammo is designed primarily for three things: accuracy, flat trajectory, and high disintegration (on both animal and ground). The accuracy must be worked out in your own rifle, though most factory loads in .25 and under these days are very good; above that you take your chances.

The flat trajectory is easily taken care of by using light bullets. These lose energy fast, but their flight to 300 yards is noticeably flatter than that of heavier bullets, and the energy factor is not critical, as the targets are usually small and don't take much to do them in.

The high disintegration factor is why varmint loads shouldn't be used on big game, in spite of their explosiveness. While they will kill deer and even larger animals if they get into the chest cavity, all too often they don't. A high-speed 55-grain

.22 bullet, because of its thin jacket and high rotational velocity, will usually fly apart on the shoulder blade of a deer. I have seen them fail to penetrate a coyote's shoulder. If you insist on shooting bigger game with a .22 varmint gun, by all means use the specially designed bullets put out by some handloading companies. These have heavier jackets than varmint bullets.

There is one varminting situation where high disintegration isn't wanted. When shooting furbearers, such as fox and coyote (when last seen, prime coyote hides were going in my neighborhood for $60 to $100), you don't want to tear up that precious hide. Factory loads are available in .222 and .223 Remington with full-metal-jacketed (nonexpanding) bullets for this use.　　　　—J.B.

REMINGTON "ACCELERATOR"— SUPER VARMINT ROUND FOR THE .30-06

The Remington .30-06 Accelerator is a new concept in metallic ammo; it fires a .224 55-grain bullet (like that used in most centerfire .22 varmint rounds) out of a .30-06 rifle at a muzzle velocity of 4,080 fps. The .30-06 thus becomes even more versatile than it is now; with a box of Accelerators, an adaptor for .30 carbine rounds, and some regular 180-grain loads, the hunter (even the nonreloader) would be set for varmints, small game, and big game—all with one rifle.

The Accelerator works with a sabot-type plastic sheath surrounding the .22 bullet. The plastic sabot is .30 caliber and falls away after the projectile leaves the muzzle of the rifle—Remington publicity says at about 14 inches. Accuracy is supposed to be equal to that of a regular shell; in other words, it should match the individual gun's accuracy.

Accuracy was the main thing I was wondering about when I received some sample Accelerators; I had had experience with the 55-grain bullet in .22-250s and .220 Swifts and was pretty sure about what it would do to most varmints. I tested the load for accuracy in two guns: a Remington pump with a 3x scope and an Interarms Mauser with a 3–9x mounted. The bolt gun gave the best groups, because of the action and the higher-powered scope. Three 3-shot groups at 100 yards averaged a hair under an inch—adequate accuracy indeed for varminting! The pump gun didn't do quite as well, but it did well enough for shooting at running varmints, such as coyotes and jackrabbits, out to 250 yards; most groups were under 2 inches. Recoil is moderate, running about like .22-250 or .220 comeback, certainly less than a .243, so the Accelerator would be a nice round with which to start somebody on a big-game rifle.

After all that, I just couldn't resist running out to my favorite jackrabbit flat to see what one of the Accelerators would do to one of the big hares. I was especially in-terested in using the rounds in the Remington pump, as this combination on running jacks would seem to be very good practice for running deer. My partner and I split the shooting; he took the standing shots with the bolt gun while I took the running shots with the speedy pump. We got four jacks, and the rounds proved flawless both in functioning through the actions and in bullet performance.

These Accelerators can be used in any manually operated .30-06 just as they are, but they must be single-worked through semiautos because they just don't have enough oomph to make the action go around. Just like regular ammo, it comes in twenty-round boxes, priced at $9.95. If the Accelerator is a commercial success, we'll probably see it in other calibers in the future and, I hope, as a reloading component. Remington Arms Co., Inc., 939 Barnum Avenue, Bridgeport, CT 06602.

WINCHESTER-WESTERN "SOLIDS" FOR FURBEARERS

This is a 55-grain full-metal-cased bullet, available in .222 and .223, designed not to put big holes in the hides of furbearers. Velocity at the muzzle is 3,020 in the .222 and 3,240 in the .223, which is slightly higher than might be desirable, as these bullets have a tendency to tumble at velocities of much over 2,800, which creates a bigger wound. They will, however, still tear up less hide than normal soft-points. Care must be taken as to where you shoot these, because they ricochet more easily than regular varmint loads. More care, too, must be given to bullet placement; they don't tear up as much vital tissue as regular loads and hence don't kill as well. Prices: $5.50 for a box of twenty in .222; $6.00 for a box of twenty in .223. Winchester-Western, 275 Winchester Avenue, New Haven, CT 06504. —J.B.

VARMINT SIGHTS

There ain't no irons about this type of sight. Varminting is simply a scoped business, and that's it. And forget about your big-game scopes for even 200-yard stuff; you'll need more than 4x. A 6x is the absolute minimum for serious varminting, and more is better. Don't be shy about buying power in a varmint scope, because you'll be shooting at stationary targets (usually) and will have plenty of time to pick them up even in their small field of view.

The 6x is at its best on smaller varmint rigs—.22 Hornet or .222—or on guns used primarily for running varmints—of which there aren't too many. I have a 6x on a .243 that I use mainly for jackrabbits and coyotes—a perfect fit. But if I were doing much rock chuck hunting, I'd put more power on top—like at least 10x. The better you see, the better you shoot. If I were going in for super long-range varminting, I'd seriously consider the newer receiver-mounted target scopes of 20x or so, though I don't think I'd mess around with conventional target-block types that mount on the barrel and receiver. There is no need to these days.

Two features to look for in a varmint scope: a precise reticle and an adjustable objective lens, if you go for more than 6x. There's no sense in going out after chucks with a reticle that will cover three or four of the little fellas, and there's no sense in aiming at a prairie dog if parallax is pointing you off in another direction. —J.B.

REDFIELD 6–18X: BIG VARIABLE

This scope covers just about all varminting situations, from running coyotes to prairie dogs at 400 yards. Parallax-focusing objective, weight 18 ounces. Also available with Accu-Range range-estimating reticle. Prices: With Accu-Range, $186.40; without, $171.90. Redfield, 5800 East Jewell Avenue, Denver, CO 80222. —J.B.

"Hunting was the labour of the savages of North America,
but the amusement of the gentlemen of England."
—Samuel Johnson

285

BUSHNELL BANNER 10X WITH RANGEMASTER

A scope of around 10x is what many varmint hunters feel is about right for most varminting. Equipped with the range-compensating Rangemaster system, this 10x should be deadly in the hands of a good distance estimator. Weight is 14.6 ounces, objective is 40mm. Price: $89.95. Bushnell Optical Co., 2828 East Foothill Boulevard, Pasadena, CA 91107.   —J.B.

LYMAN 6X-P

This is a rarity among 6x scopes: it features a parallax-focusing objective. For smaller varmint guns, such as the .17, the Hornet, the .222 family, and especially for light rifles, it would be a good choice. Price: $124.95. Lyman also makes good 8x and 10x scopes in the same style for the same price. Lyman Products for Shooters, Route 147, Middlefield, CT 06455.   —J.B.

ECONOMY-PRICED 3X TO 9X SCOPE

This Valor 3x to 9x variable scope includes a wide-angle effect, a duplex reticle, and a rubber ring on the eye relief. It comes with a screw-on Amber Glo filter and is priced at an affordable $65.00. Precise Imports Corp., 3 Chestnut Street, Suffern, NY 10901.   —F.S.

WOODCHUCK
by Nick Sisley

I counted, "One thousand one. One thousand two. One thousand three." Then it appeared above the low grass, as I'd hoped. The short, black tail looked like the head of a serpent as it twitched first to one side, then to the other. Finally it quivered. Then it disappeared from my scope. My shot had been perfect; now I was certain. The chuck hunt was over.

The woodchuck, or groundhog, is a burrowing animal that ranges over the eastern half of the United States, as far south as the northern tips of Mississippi, Alabama, and Georgia. It also can be found through most of Canada, including the Canadian Rockies, and is plentiful over much of this range. Riflemen find chucks challenging targets. They are beneficial to many game animals and furbearers, because they burrow holes underground that other mammals use for refuge and shelter. The farmer finds the woodchuck a pest, because if they are plentiful they can do considerable damage to crops. They can also be the cause of costly repairs to expensive farm machinery if the farmer doesn't see their excavations at hay-cutting time. As a result, chuck hunters are often welcomed, even by landowners who post their property against hunting other species.

Chuck hunting is a summer sport, so pursuit of these critters provides an excellent tune-up for fall big-game seasons. I've had several Western guides tell me that experienced Eastern woodchuck hunters who travel west in the fall to hunt antelope and mule deer are usually excellent shots, and they know how to dope the wind and estimate range.

In addition to being great practice for big game, the woodchuck, *Marmota monax,* is an excellent rifle challenge in its own right. There are two ways to hunt this animal—either from long-range vantage points or by using hunting and stalking skills to get as close as possible.

The hunter who takes pride in making long-range clean kills may possess a great deal of sophisticated equipment. He normally takes up his stand where he can overlook a wide expanse of chuck country. If he's lucky, the hay will have been cropped recently, making the chucks easier to see. Patience is required. The long-range buff may arrive at his predetermined spot at three in the afternoon, and he may stay until sunset.

His rifle is usually a high-velocity 22-caliber centerfire or one of the 6mms—maybe even a wildcat cartridge. The barrel is heavy to aid tack-driving accuracy, but since this hunter doesn't move around much, the extra weight is no problem. His scope will probably be somewhere between 8x and 24x. Some scopes are almost two feet long! These precision optical instruments have quarter-minute clicks, so that accuracy can be controlled to the finest degree. Tripods may also be utilized, so that the rifle can be shot from either a sitting or a prone position. Little if any gun movement is encountered with these precise tools. Two hunters often go out together and one checks the shots through a spotting scope, in case there is a miss. The hunter who shoots chucks at long range always wants to know if the shot was high or low, right or left. If he pulled the trigger smoothly, where the bullet struck gives him an indication of how he may have misjudged range or wind.

Chuck hunters who "walk 'em up" aren't as plentiful as they were a decade ago. Long-range whistle-pig hunting requires a lot of skill, but I personally prefer to get as close as possible before pulling the trigger. Perhaps I am from the old school, but I feel the kill is anticlimactic in hunting. To me it is what I have done to arrive at the point of pulling the trigger that gives me satisfaction. Depending on where the individual chuck is first spotted, it may take a great deal of hunting skill, work, and ingenuity to get within 10, 30, 100, or 200 yards.

Many techniques can be utilized to narrow the range between the hunter and the quarry. I always use a lightweight rifle—either a varmint caliber or big-game medicine—because I'm usually on the move. Sneaking up on chucks improves hunting skills considerably. In this day and age there are too many people finding too many ways to eliminate or reduce physical exertion. Good physical condition is always important if you expect to be a competent outdoorsman. By sneaking up on chucks and staying on the move, I am better prepared physically for the big-game seasons that follow.

However or wherever you hunt it, the woodchuck is a worthy challenge. It looks around constantly for danger and presents a small target. For the rifle buff, there's no better way to spend a lazy summer day than in pursuit of the woodchuck.

Nick Sisley is a full-time free-lance writer and photographer who specializes in small-game and varmint hunting. He lives in Pennsylvania.

HUNTING THE TIZI N' TICHKA PASS LIZARD
by Chuck Durang

Parallel to the coast of northwest Africa run the Atlas Mountains, traversing Morocco from its southwest corner to northern Tunisia. It is there that Dr. Alfred Stonewhistle and I went to seek big game. I made the passage from India by tramp steamer; Dr. Stonewhistle traveled by rail.

Our arrival in a small camel-fat-processing town on the Moroccan coast created a buzz of inattention. We were, however, welcomed by the Bedouin chieftain Hassan Ben Sober, who was to guide us in hunting the Tizi n' Tichka Pass Lizard.

"Africa is a plateau," he said, by way of greeting. "Upon a basement of Archean rocks, highly metamorphosed and much intruded by granites of various ages, rest numerous sedimentary rock sequences, mostly nonmarine in origin." It developed that this was the only English he knew; hence, we departed immediately for Tizi n' Tichka.

The pass is only some 7,438 feet above sea level, and the climb is mostly through sparse vegetation. We came upon only two instances of danger the entire way. The first was a Jaguar in the brush; we stole the hubcaps, as we had not brought a mess kit. The second was an apelike man who appeared on the trail ahead of us as we neared the pass. He was clad in a garment made entirely of butterfly wings and moved very slowly. As we drew near, he halted us with a call in Pidgin English.

"Hey, hunter, watch out for pigeons up on the ledge." He went on to exhort us to turn back, as the terrible lizard was in the midst of its mating season. And, indeed, we heard its call from up the trail ahead: "Hoo-hah! Oh, boyo-boyoboy. Whee! Whoops!"

The ape-man then explained that he, Edgar Mice Burrows, was appointed by his mountain tribe to assure that the lizard mated undisturbed, for if this was not so, the lizard was in a foul mood for the rest of the year and made a practice of eating small children, census takers, and tourists, which upset the economy of the village something fierce. The mating season would last a week. As we had not the time to wait, I contented myself with creeping up to a rock overhang and taking a photograph, the only one today extant of this breed of lizard.

It is, of course, unpublishable.

Chuck Durang once lived in the geographical center of Fargo, North Dakota. He is currently working on a book about his travels titled "Roller Skating the Great Divide with Gun and Camera."

HOW TO CALL WILDLIFE
by Byron W. Dalrymple

New York: Funk & Wagnalls, $7.50.

While the title of this book suggests that it's about calling only, there's a lot more crammed between the covers. In addition to calling techniques for game and varmints, Dalrymple discusses personal camouflage, blinds, and how to select a likely stand.

I particularly liked his assertion that old-line purists make calling seem more difficult than it is. From my experience with this craft, the calling is really pretty easy. It's the patience that's difficult.

In addition to technique, the author also does an excellent job of reviewing the equipment (mouth calls, electronic calls, cassettes, camouflage cloth and clothing, decoys, etc.) associated with bringing the game to you. The only flaw in this work, and it's a minor one, is that its flavor is decidedly Southwestern. It's a solid education in calling wildlife, and with a few variations Dalrymple's savvy should work for anyone anywhere.
       —N.S.

*"The crow looks rusty as he rises up,
bright is the malice in his eye."*
—Wallace Stevens

287

Burnham Bros. Catalog: Varminting and Hunting in the Southwest

These folks specialize in varminting equipment but also carry some general hunting stuff. They have an excellent selection of electronic and manual calls, shooting lights, amplifiers, and recordings. If you need some special equipment for varminting, you'll probably find it here.

Notable, too, is the slant of their hunting equipment. It's decidedly southwestern; the items that are listed are suited to those conditions. For example, they stock snakeproof puttees, snakebite kits, lightweight camouflage clothing, water purifiers, and lightweight shooting vests. Good stuff. Free catalog. Burnham Bros., P.O. Box 100A., Marble Falls, TX 78654.

Records, Cassettes, and Tapes for Calling Game

Burnham Bros. stocks virtually every kind of game call recording you could ever want for an electronic caller: grown jackrabbit squeals, half-grown jackrabbit screams, hand squeaking, crows in bunches fighting an owl, grown cottontail squeaks, yellowhammer distress cries, cardinal distress cries, wild turkeys on roost at daybreak, wild turkey tom trying to pick a fight, quail distress cries, quail calling, horn rattling, coyote barking and howling, baby kid goat in distress, terrified screams of baby house cat, deer distress cries, javelina distress cries, rat distress cries, meadowlark distress cries, baby red fox distress cries, bantam chicken squalls, Plymouth Rock chicken squalls, deer fawn bleats, mallard quacks, ringtail cat barks, snarling and growling bobcats, the distress cries of a hunter with his *cojones* caught in a No. 4 jump trap, and Kate Smith singing "When the Moon Comes over the Mountain." Prices: $2.50 to $5.95 each. Free catalog. Burnham Bros., P.O. Box 100A, Marble Falls, TX 78654.

OLT COYOTE AND FOX CALLS

The Olt people make all sorts of game calls: duck calls, dove calls, deer calls, crow calls, turkey calls, elk calls, pheasant calls, quail calls—well, they make calls enough to bring everything except the mice out of the woods. I tried a couple of their predator calls, one a jackrabbit and one a cottontail. These calls are designed to imitate the dying sounds of those two animals; the jackrabbit call is supposed to be more effective for luring coyotes in this part of the country (eastern Montana) and the cottontail call for foxes. I'd never called predators before but decided to try the jackrabbit call in an area where there were a lot of them (and where you find jackrabbits you'll find coyotes, believe me). My first couple of stands were unsuccessful, but on the third I called up a young coyote and mule deer doe! I had never heard a dying jackrabbit, probably since I hunt them with centerfire varmint rifles, but I had heard the sound cottontails make. The only directions I had in calling were those that were included with the call.

Since then I've called some more and talked with other varmint-callers, and the most important thing in calling seems to be not how you call but where you call. Camouflage clothing, whether green and brown for warm months or white for snowy, helps a great deal, and so do the Olt calls. Send for their catalog. P. S. Olt, Pekin, IL 61554.

—J.B.

PORTABLE CASSETTE CALLER

The C-101 is a portable cassette Superscope (made by Sony). It's calling range can be boosted with an amplifier. The unit includes record, fast-forward, play, and stop-eject mode selectors (piano-key type), an AC cord and inlet jack, and a remote-control input jack.

This is a reasonably priced unit that should be good for varminters who do a lot of moving around afoot (it weighs under 4 pounds). Price: $59.95. Burnham Bros., P.O. Box 100A, Marble Falls, TX 78654.

CLOSE-RANGE PREDATOR CALL

While fox, coyote, and bobcat may come freely to a standard predator call, they often hang just out of good gun range or skulk in the brush. This high-pitched squealer call amounts to an offer they can't refuse. Price: $3.75. P. S. Olt, Pekin, IL 61554.

ADJUSTABLE PREDATOR CALL

This call can be adjusted to imitate cottontail and jackrabbit death squeals, as well as the high-pitched close-in call that brings foxes and coyotes running. Price: $5.00. Faulk's, 616 18th Street, Lake Charles, LA 70601.

OWL HOOTER CALL FOR CROWS

This owl and turkey hooter call was designed for turkey hunting (for some unknown reason, hooting owls drive tom turkeys to frenzied gobbling), but it works on crows, too. Owls and crows are natural enemies, and the hoot often elicits scolding caws in return, giving away the crows' positions. Price: $6.95. P. S. Olt, Pekin, IL 61554.

CROW CALL

This is the call I've used for years. It has soft, responsive reeds, yet good tonal and distance range. Price: $5.25. P. S. Olt, Pekin, IL 61554.   —N.S.

DECOYS FOR CROW HUNTING

The common way that crows are decoyed is to place a few full-bodied crow decoys in a tree. Then place an owl decoy near those crows, where it can be easily seen. The best spot is atop a pole in the middle of an opening, but when the leaves are off the trees you can perch the owl on (or hang it from) a bare branch. Around the base of the pole, or beneath the owl, set out more decoys on the ground. Strips of black cloth or stuffed black socks will work, but silhouette crow decoys are better. Find a good hide, start blowing on a crow call, and get ready for the action. Prices: owl decoys, $4.97 each, and full-bodied crow decoys, $1.97 each, from Herter's, Inc., Route 2, Mitchell, SD 57301; silhouette crow decoys, $2.25, from P. S. Olt, Pekin, IL 61554.

Hoisting an owl decoy high enough to be seen by passing crows can be chancy work if you rely on trees. Instead, tote along sections of electrical conduit or hollow aluminum tubing with dowel plugs for ferrules.

The Best Crow Hunting in the World?

I know . . . you hear those kinds of claims about everything, but if Cobb Creek Lake isn't the best, it's got to be close to it. It's located near Eakly, Oklahoma, and the lake's north end harbors the largest crow roost in the Midwest. Motels and stores and bars and marinas have sprung up around this roost to house and feed the crow hunters, some of whom come from a thousand miles away to shoot there. We started seeing large numbers of crows ten miles from the roost and estimate that we saw 10,000 birds in all—which had to be but a small part of the total winter population (this was in early December).

Cobb Creek Lake also has excellent waterfowling, should your shoulder get tired from so much crow shooting, though you'd surely go nuts trying to pick out the ducks from the unending flocks of crows flying low over the water.   —N.S.

Eight-Track Electronic Game Callers

This is a brand-new game caller—the first eight-track system with fine tuning. It's audible for a mile or more yet distortion-free up close. It features a push-button cartridge ejector, program repeat circuit, and an illuminated push-button channel selector. The unit comes with a 25-watt speaker and is powered by twelve alkaline flashlight batteries. Price: $159.50. Burnham Bros., P.O. Box 100A, Marble Falls, TX 78654.

Varminting Tips from Wiley Coyote

Last fall turned up an instructive evening in the art of coyote hunting. I spent the weekend with Bruce Eakins, a rancher in western Oklahoma who is so enamored of coyote calling that his CB friends gave him the handle of "Wiley Coyote."

Bruce's rig is pretty impressive: a '59 Chevy panel wagon with wide tires, an electronic caller mounted over the cab, red-filtered airplane landing lights and spotlights up front, and a CB.

Bruce's night technique is to park the rig just below the rim of a high bluff so he can see and scan the terrain below without the wagon's being fully exposed. He serenades the varmints on his stereo while he scans the brush with the red spotlight for the telltale glint of eyes. When they appear, he turns the light off momentarily so the critter will work in closer. When he feels the time is right, the lights go on and all hell breaks loose. He works each spot for about an hour.

Two incidents Bruce recounted that night bear witness to the effectiveness of the technique. A bobcat once came in so fast that there wasn't time to shoot. All Bruce could do was watch as the cat clawed at the rear tire of his van and tried to climb up to the squealing speaker. Another time, while Bruce was hunting with a friend, a bobcat actually jumped into the open rear of his rig and proceeded to claw and gnaw away at the speaker. That cat wasn't dumb, either. In the wild rush to get some distance between them, the cat got away clean.

Bruce is also a superb mouth caller. His dying rabbit call sends chills up your spine, and it excites the ear and mind. He prefers to use a mouth call during the day, while lying down on a hilltop in full camouflage. On a windy day he calls fifteen to twenty seconds at one-minute intervals. When it is cold and still and sound carries far, he waits five minutes between calls. When he gets a coyote close in, he makes another sound, a very high-pitched squeak, by blowing on the back of his hand. This not only brings 'em up close but leaves his call hand free to shoot.

—N.S.

Coon Squaller

This call is designed to imitate the squalls and snarls of fighting raccoons. Other coons in the vicinity come running to see what the argument is all about. Price: $4.95. Faulk's, 616 18th Street, Lake Charles, LA 70601.

THE COMPLETE BOOK OF TRAPPING
by Bob Gilsvik

Radnor, Pa.: Chilton Books, $10.95.

The catalog staff considered trapping, and the consensus was that it wasn't really hunting, so we chose not to list trapping items. If you've got any questions about trapping, however, this book is the place to start. It's a brand-new book that examines products for the trapper, how to trap (where to make your sets and how to put them together most enticingly), the habits of furbearing animals, and the tools and knowledge needed to prepare pelts.

It is complete because it goes beyond trapping for fun and profit and gets into capturing pesky critters like skunks, raccoons, and field mice who are raising hell with your house. There is also a chapter on live trapping, if you've been aching to discipline the neighbor's cat but don't want to do permanent damage. All in all, an excellent reference work.

Shooting Light Mounts on Gun

The Burnham shooting light is designed to be mounted on a telescopic sight tube or on a single-barreled shotgun and is designed to withstand the shock of recoil. The light has a manual switch, and it comes with two 9-volt mercury batteries. Yet another practical feature: it accepts a snap-on red filter. Prices: light, $17.95; filter, $2.95. Burnham Bros., P.O. Box 100A, Marble Falls, TX 78654.

Animal Scents

If you have need for an animal scent for your trapping or varminting, Burnham Bros. stocks fox, coyote, cat, rabbit, and deer scents for $2.00 each. Burnham Bros., P.O. Box 100A, Marble Falls, TX 78654.

THE COON HUNTER'S HANDBOOK
by Leon F. Whitney and Acil B. Underwood

New York: Holt, Rinehart & Winston, $5.95.

The authors are experts at following the dogs they have bred and at outwitting what some hunters feel is America's smartest game animal. Coon hunts, coon-hunt field trials, coon dogs, coon skins, coon lore, and coon dinners are all discussed in the text.

Portable Spotlights

Varmint hunting at night, launching a duckboat in the predawn darkness, or checking out your recvees on a lonely, dark road are typical times when a portable spotlight comes in handy. Dick Cepek sells a 12-volt, 35,000-candlepower hand spotlight for $6.95 that plugs into a cigarette lighter and is small enough to fit into your car or truck's glove compartment.

If you really want to blast someone's corneas, he also stocks a 300,000-candlepower spotlight with a halogen bulb for $25.95. This item should also be useful for spotting enemy aircraft and attracting crowds on opening night at the theater. Dick Cepek, Inc., 9201 California Avenue, South Gate, CA 90280.

For camouflage clothing for varmint hunting, see sections on clothing for waterfowlers and archers. For warm boots, underwear, hats, etc., see sections on clothing for big-game hunters.

Trap and Skeet Gun Features

Trap guns are usually choked tight (improved modified or full) and have long barrels (30-inch) because of the range of the targets. They are also usually heavier, because stouter loads are used in them. Monte Carlo stocks (butt stocks with a high comb and low butt plate) are favored to position the eye correctly and to maintain an erect head position, which is less tiring over a long match.

Skeet guns are choked more openly (skeet choking is about like improved cylinder) and are stocked with a little more drop at heel (lower butt stock). Barrels are shorter, 26-inch probably being the most popular, and weights are less.

Competition guns are also equipped with wide ventilated ribs to provide a good sighting plane and to disperse heat from the barrels. Good recoil pads are also standard, in order to take the sting out of long matches.
—J.B.

THE EXPERT'S BOOK OF THE SHOOTING SPORTS
edited by David E. Petzal

New York: Simon & Schuster, $9.95.

This book is a collection of essays and advice from America's most noted outdoorsmen and writers on their specialties. John Amber has a chapter on custom guns, Howard Brant writes on skeet shooting, Steve Ferber contributes his knowledge of handgun target shooting, and John Gilmore covers benchrest shooting. Other chapters are devoted to various aspects of hunting, optics, target shooting, and maintenance, all written by sportsmen with equally fine credentials.

Petzal has done other "expert" books—on big-game and small-game hunting—and he has written an excellent book on the .22. While they're all fine reading and full of information, *The Expert's Book of the Shooting Sports* holds a special place on my library shelves. I keep it among the reference works in my office rather than in my collection of outdoor literature. That alone is testimony to the depth, breadth, and quality of knowledge that is contained between its covers.
—N.S.

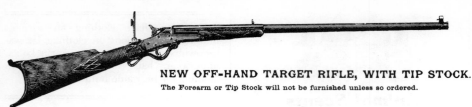

SHOTGUNS AND SHOOTING
by Edmund S. "Ted" McCawley, Jr.

New York: Van Nostrand Reinhold Company, $4.95 (paper).

The most notable thing about this book is its point of view. Rather than focusing on the game or on hunting techniques, it concentrates on the shotgun and its proper use as the real stepping-stones to enjoyment of all shooting sports associated with the arm.

It's a rather different approach, but when you think about it, it is a correct one. Such matters as barrel length, stock dimensions, and chokes are lucidly explained, along with the different systems that may be used to hit a moving target. These are followed by chapters on claybird shooting and the shotgun's role in upland, waterfowl, and big-game hunting. There's also a good chapter on the basics of shotshell reloading.

Simmons Illusion: Same Look, Different Gauge

In going from gauge to gauge in competition shotgunning, the smaller-gauge barrels are thinner. This bothers shooters who wish to maintain the same feel and look between guns as much as possible. The Illusion is simply a roof over smaller-gauge barrels, which makes them appear the same size as the 12-gauge. If you already have a set of smaller-gauge barrels for your double or a barrel for the Remington 110 auto, this conversion costs $135.00; if you wish Simmons to include it on their barrels ($600.00 in double guns), it is $75.00. Simmons Gun Specialties, Inc., P.O. Box 533, Olathe, KS 66061. —J.B.

Simmons Exact Impact Ventilated Rib and Uni-Single Trap Gun

By the simple means of a rib that is adjustable for elevation, trap guns can now be precisely adjusted to an individual shooter's preference. The version pictured is on Simmons' Uni-Single trap gun modification, which involves making a double into a single-shot for purposes of weight-saving and straight-line recoil (most single-barrel guns have a higher recoil line). These conversions aren't exactly cheap: the installation on the rib is $575.00, and Uni-Single barrels for Remington, Browning, or Perazzi guns run $600.00, or $350.00, if you're willing to let them work your gun over. For serious trap shooters only. Simmons Gun Specialties, Inc., P.O. Box 533, Olathe, KS 66061. —J.B.

Savage 333-T

This is a relatively inexpensive ($451.15) trap gun, yet of high quality. Chambering is standard 12-gauge, choking improved modified and full. Features include selective trigger, extractors, extrawide ventilated rib, Monte Carlo stock, manual safety; 7¾ pounds. Savage Arms, Springdale Road, Westfield, MA 01085. —J.B.

"That low man goes on adding one to one, / His hundred's soon hit; / This high man, aiming at a million, / Misses an unit."
—Robert Browning, "A Grammarian's Funeral"

291

Remington 3200 Skeet

Choked skeet and skeet, naturally, this gun comes with 26- or 28-inch barrels. It has the same coil-spring, shroud-locking, fast-lock-time 3200 action that is in Remington's regular field gun. The separated barrels have an added advantage in competition shooting in that heated barrels cool faster and impact change is less, since the hot barrel does not put undue pressure on the cool one. A barrel selector combined with the safety is a standard feature in the regular model. This gun weighs 7¾ pounds and is priced at $835.00. It is also available in trap version for $865.00. Remington Arms Co., Inc., 939 Barnum Avenue, Bridgeport, CT 06602.   —J.B.

WINCHESTER MODEL 12 TRAP

There is only one way you can get the famed Model 12, and that is direct from the factory. Available with either a standard trap or Monte Carlo comb, it is equipped with a recoil pad, a 30-inch barrel, and a ventilated rib. It weighs about 8¼ pounds. Price is $525.00 for a Monte Carlo-stocked gun; $10.00 less for regular stock. Winchester-Western, 275 Winchester Avenue, New Haven, CT 06504.   —J.B.

PERAZZI MT-6

Competition IV

PERAZZI

Perazzi MT-6

The latest in the Perazzi line of trap and skeet shotguns imported by Ithaca, the MT-6 is a trap gun, available with the Perazzi interchangeable choke tubes, which are similar to the Winchoke system in that they thread into the gun's muzzle. The MT-6, like other Perazzis, can be had in varying custom stock dimensions and features fully separated barrels that can be adjusted for point of impact. It comes in its own lined hard case and retails, in case you're interested in running down to the hardware store to pick one up, for $2,495.00.

Perazzi is the acknowledged best maker of competition shotguns in the world. If you don't feel you can afford an MT-6, their Competition IV trap single-barrel (with changeable choke tubes) only costs $1,995.00. Ithaca Gun Company, Inc., 123 Lake Street, Ithaca, NY 14850.

GETTING STARTED IN TRAPSHOOTING
by Ted McCawley

Midsummer in central Ohio is usually hot and muggy—sometimes to a fearsome degree. Late-afternoon thunderstorms are common, and occasionally the rain comes down so hard it turns the flat ground into a quagmire. To many people these climatic facts of life provide compelling arguments for being somewhere else at that time of year if they can possibly arrange it. But one large group of sportsmen and sportswomen respond to these conditions as readily as Pavlov's dogs. Who are they? Why, trapshooters, of course.

In the middle of August every year, thousands of them flock to Vandalia, Ohio, a small town outside of Dayton which is the home of the Amateur Trapshooting Association of America and the site of its annual Grand American tournament. This event lasts nine days and is a classic spectacle of the sporting world. Competitors representing a broad cross section of the population from every part of the country meet there, with a common bond of interest in shooting at clay targets with a shotgun.

The thousands who attend the "Grand" every year (and its companion event for skeet shooters, the National Skeet Shooting Championships) represent the best shotgunners in the country. Known as "registered shooters," many of them spend a good part of their leisure time touring the country to participate in formal tournaments. In the case of trapshooters, they often compete for cash prizes, and for the best of them the rewards can be considerable.

Although there are over 60,000 registered trapshooters in the United States, they represent only a small portion of the total number of devotees of this fast-growing sport. There are countless others who shoot only at local clubs and never compete in the big-time events. What are the attractions of this game and how does the average sportsman get started?

As practiced in the United States, trapshooting falls into three different categories—16-yard, handicap, and doubles. All three are shot over the same field, and they have many similarities. (A fourth category, international trap, is shot over an entirely different layout, and even though it is the type of trap shot at the Olympics, not too many people participate in it in this country.)

A standard trap field consists of five shooting stations, each 3 yards apart, located on a semicircle 16 yards from a low shed in which the "trap" (a mechanical device that throws the targets) is located. Each station has a path behind it which extends to a point 27 yards in back of the trap house. Additional shooting positions are located on these paths at 1-yard intervals.

For all three types of conventional trap, a squad consists of five shooters, with one stationed on each position. In 16-yard and handicap events, they shoot in turn until each has fired at five targets. Then each shooter moves to the right to the next station (the shooter in position number five moves to position number one), and the process is repeated until each competitor has shot at five targets from each station.

For doubles, the procedure is essentially the same except that ten targets (two pairs of five) are thrown at each station. Thus, a complete round of singles, whether 16-yard or handicap, involves shooting at twenty-five targets, while a round of doubles involves fifty targets.

In all three types of trapshooting, targets are thrown at the call of "pull" from each shooter. For singles events, the traps are set to throw targets at roughly seventy different random angles within an arc of 44 degrees. Vertical angles remain constant, while horizontal angles change constantly, so that shooters cannot know for sure exactly where the next target is going. Normal targets fly about 50 yards from the trap before hitting the ground and reach a maximum height of about 18 feet.

In handicap events, shooters compete from various yardages, which are based on their average scores in past events. Thus, the better shooters are positioned farther back of the trap house than those less skilled. For doubles, all shooters stand at the 16-yard positions. At each call of "pull," two targets are thrown simultaneously, flying at extreme angles to the right and left. Normal practice is to shoot first at the bird flying closer to straightaway and then go after the other. Doubles is usually rated as the hardest of the three types of trap.

Standard procedure in all three events is for the shooter to put his gun to his shoulder, in firing position, before calling for the target. Since the traps these days are generally operated by electricity, the clay birds fly almost instantaneously, making quick reactions a necessity.

To be able to hit flying targets takes a good deal of coordination of eye, mind, and body, but the basic skills can be learned by anybody with normal reflexes. The secret is to remember that a flying target is moving, and in order to hit it you have to put the charge of shot where the target is going to be rather than where it is at the moment you pull the trigger. This involves learning how much to lead targets at the various shooting positions and how to figure angles of target flight. Obviously, for a straightaway shot no horizontal lead is needed, while for an extreme right or left angle quite a bit is required. There are numerous books and several films that give details on these finer points of the game. The best way to learn them, however, is by actually shooting.

The standard gun for trapshooting is one with a full-choke 12-gauge barrel. Although beginners can start with field guns, those who get serious about the game soon graduate to specialized trap guns. While these can be of any action style, they generally have ventilated ribs and straighter stocks than field guns. The most popular barrel length is 30 inches, and guns are generally bored full choke or modified trap. Shells used are generally specialized target loads with Nos. 7½, 8, or 8½ shot.

Getting started in trap is easier than many people think it might be. Most commercial gun clubs are interested in helping new shooters and will try to get them started in special novice squads, so that they aren't embarrassed by their lack of skill at the outset. In addition, it's a simple matter to buy an inexpensive mechanical trap and some clay targets and set up your own informal field as long as you are sure of plenty of room for safety. The major gun and ammunition manufacturers are interested in promoting clay target shooting and can provide information on how to set up both formal and informal facilities. Obviously, they also manufacture the equipment involved.

Whether your interest lies in sharpening your shooting eye for hunting on a setup in the back forty or winning a title at the Grand American, trapshooting can provide hours of fun and challenge. Physical strength is not a big factor in success, and men and women can compete on relatively even terms. It's a great family sport, and it's not unusual to see kids not much bigger than their guns smoking targets alongside septuagenarians. All of them are having a good time, and this is one good reason the sport keeps growing.

Edmund S. "Ted" McCawley, Jr., is public relations manager for the Remington Arms Company, and in that capacity he gets to shoot an awful lot of clays. He's been tested and certified by one member of the staff, Sil Strung, who under his brief tutelage learned to outshoot her husband.

Trius Target Traps

No, Junior, these aren't for catching targets; they're for letting them go. Strange name, but that's what they call 'em. Trius is the best name in traps, and they make a variety of sturdy traps at reasonable prices. The Birdshooter model pictured will serve the average gunner's purposes. It's priced at $38.95 and will throw singles and doubles in every direction except down. Trius Products, Inc., P.O. Box 25, Cleves, OH 45002.

Hand Trap for Clay Pigeons

The Melco brand trap is my pick of the crop for several reasons. First, it may be used by a right- or left-hander; second, it can throw two birds at a time; and third, it is adjustable. Each clay can be set for different flight patterns. I also find that this hand trap breaks the least clays, though that judgment is a bit unfair, since all the other traps I've used were obviously designed for a right-hander. Price: $5.95. Burnham Bros., P.O. Box 100A, Marble Falls, TX 78654.
—N.S.

Trap Thrower

This is the hand trap that gets my vote. It has an adjustable spring mechanism to match the pressure that holds the pigeon in place to your swinging style. You load the pigeon and cock the head, and the combined power of the swing of your arm and the flick of the head really sends the clays out there. Price: $6.50. Precise Imports Corp., 3 Chestnut Street, Suffern, NY 10901.
—F.S.

Super Trap and Skeet Tosser

Remington's Model 4100 (trap) and Model 4100s (skeet) clay target traps enjoy a reputation as reliable performers with unusually low accidental target breakage. Features include a seven-stack, rotating target magazine, with a capacity of 154 targets, and a loading system that permits faster reloading than competitors' traps. The system boasts an overall breakage rate of less than 1 percent, and the Model 4100s can be easily adapted to international skeet. Price: $2,920.00. Remington Arms Co., Inc., 939 Barnum Avenue, 06602.

TARG-A-Launch Beer Can Throwing Device

This gadget launches beer cans up to 40 yards. To send 'em flying, you break open the launcher, insert a .22 blank, close the launcher, snap a beer can onto the top of it, pull back a spring-loaded plunger, and let it go. The plunger strikes the .22 blank, and rapidly expanding gases launch the can up, up, and away.

Sound great? It is, kinda, but don't forget that you've got to pick up all those beer cans when you're done unless you do your target practice at the town dump. Price: $24.50. Tidewater Specialties, 430 Swann Avenue, Alexandria, VA 22301.

SUPER PIGEON

The Super Pigeon isn't some breed of bird from planet Krypton but a plastic target meant to be thrown from a trap, just as clay pigeons are. It is constructed of two halves that resemble miniature Frisbees; these come apart when struck by shotgun pellets, allowing the Super Pigeon to fall to the ground. There is a small tab that keeps the two halves together so you don't have to look for both parts. Super Pigeon is colored international orange, which makes it easy to find, and since it doesn't disintegrate like a clay pigeon, it can be snapped back together and thrown again, at least until it's so full of holes that it can't fly or won't snap together. This also means that your faithful dog can bring it back to you, which saves wear and tear on your legs and gives the dog some practice. The people who make it claim that each one will take about thirty hits, so if you buy the pro pack at $21.95, that means thirty rounds of whatever you want to shoot, or the equivalent of 750 clay targets—actually more, since a missed Super Pigeon can be used again, something that isn't usually possible with a clay target. Unless you average 99 percent, that comes out to a little bit of savings. Also, since this target doesn't litter fields, farmers will be much more willing to let you practice on their land. Super Pigeon is also available in ten-packs for $8.95 or five-packs for $4.95. Include 50 cents for postage and handling if you order by mail. Super Pigeon Corporation, P.O. Box 428, Princeton, MN 55343.

CLAY PIGEONS

Clay pigeons for trap and skeet shooting are made by the following folks:

Remington Arms Co., Inc, 939 Barnum Avenue, Bridgeport, CT 06602

Trius Products, Inc., P.O. Box 25, Cleves, OH 45002

Winchester-Western, 275 Winchester Avenue, New Haven, CT 06504

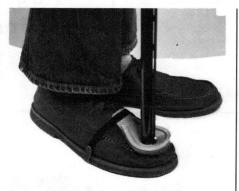

MUZZLE REST

If you get tired of holding your gun on the line, rest your arm between birds with this toe rest. The felt underside won't scar shoes, and the ridge on top prevents the muzzle from slipping off your foot. Elastic banding around the shoe sole anchors the rest in place. Price: $2.50. Kolpin Manufacturing, Inc., P.O. Box 231, Berlin, WI 54923.

KOLPIN MANUFACTURING, INC.

WATER BUFFALO SHELL BAG

This shell bag is practical, and it is also a sure conversation starter. Crafted from imported water buffalo leather, it contains two compartments: one for live shells and one for empties and comes with an adjustable belt. Each compartment holds twenty-five shells. Price: $22.00. Kolpin Manufacturers, Inc., P.O. Box 231, Berlin, WI 54923.

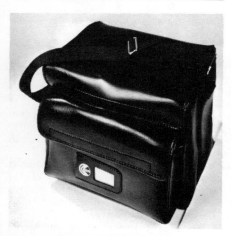

CLAYBIRD'S SHOULDER BAG

Here's an answer to several logistic problems for the trap or skeet shooter. This expanded vinyl shoulder bag contains two compartments; one holds eight boxes of shells, and the other holds eight boxes of empties. The large front pocket will hold your shooting glasses, hearing protectors, and other accessories. Price: $23.00. Kolpin Manufacturing, Inc., P.O. Box 231, Berlin, WI 54923.

ADJUSTABLE COMB FOR TRAP AND SKEET SHOOTERS

Trap and skeet shooters prefer high combs on their stocks, since this helps compensate for a rising target. Because of cheek placement and its relation to sighting, the higher the comb, the higher the point of pattern impact.

Adjustable combs are an aid, since targets rise more rapidly under certain

wind conditions, Convert-A-Stock is a system whereby pads of separate thicknesses can be added to or subtracted from the comb of a stock. The pads are held in place by a bootlike device that in turn is pinned to either side of the stock by a Velcro strip. Price: $16.50. Meadow Industries, Meadow Lands, PA 15347.

"Hunters, like poets, are born, not made. The art cannot be taught on paper."

—Nessmuk

295

Spot Shot

Indoor Practice with Your Shotgun

Here's a safe, inexpensive way to sharpen up your shooting eye without noise, kick, or damage to your living room walls. The Spot Shot is a high-intensity spotlight that fits inside the barrel of a side-by-side or over/under shotgun. When you squeeze the trigger, it projects a beam of light that's the same size as an improved cylinder shot pattern at any distance between 1 and 40 yards.

Practice up by snap shooting the lampshade or the picture of great grandfather over the mantel. For pass shooting get someone to move a second beam of light along a darkened wall and try to wipe it out with the Spot Shot's beam.

The Spot Shot is powered by three AA batteries that come with the unit, so you can use it away from electrical connections.

One word of caution; shotgun pellets move at around 1,200 feet per second. The speed of light is around 180,000 miles per second. Don't depend on this gadget to help correct any leading problems you might have. The Spot Shot is available in 12 and 20 gauge. Price: $39.95. Orvis, 10 River Road, Manchester, VT 05254.

TRAP AND/OR SKEET GUN TAKEDOWN CASE

This gun case would do the finest trap or skeet gun proud. It is made of leather-covered wood and is put together like a fine cabinet. The case is fully lined, the top half made for a receiver and fore-end and the bottom half holding up to four barrels. Price: $115.00. Gun-Ho, 110 East 10th Street, St. Paul, MN 55101.

TRAP AND SKEET SHOOTING: FOR MORE INFORMATION

Amateur Trapshooting Association
P.O. Box 246, West National Road
Vandalia, OH 45377
Ron Mosier, General Manager

National Skeet Shooting Association (amateur)
P.O. Box 28188
San Antonio, TX 78288
Carroll E. Bobo, Executive Director

Pacific International Trapshooting Association
3847 Glenwood Loop, Southeast
Salem, OR 97301
Gordon E. Hull, Secretary-Manager

SHOOTER'S CASE FOR TRAP AND SKEET

This Clubhouse Shooter's Case measures 16 by 13 by 8 inches. Inside, it has a removable upper tray that is designed to hold loose shooting items like glasses, ear protectors, and scorecards; the bottom section will hold ten boxes of shells. The case is made of molded Royalite and is rainproof. Price: $45.00. Gun-Ho, 110 East 10th Street, St. Paul, MN 55101.

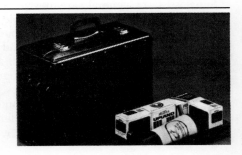

ABSORPTIVE LENSES FOR SHOOTERS
by Kurt Roeloffs, O.D.

Shooting glasses and sunglasses are like any other product in that there is a great variety in quality and performance, and no one pair is best for all situations. Either one purchases several pairs, each to accomplish a specific purpose, or one can accept a reasonable compromise.

The yellow filters, better known as shooting glasses, serve a specific purpose: to make a target stand out from its surrounding background and to sharpen the target picture. Yellow filters block out a great portion of the reds, greens, blues, and violets. The human eye is most sensitive to light-wave frequencies in the area of 5,800 angstroms units, and these glasses allow full passage of waves in that area. The effect is to sharpen visual acuity by eliminating chromatic aberration. No matter how well one sees, one is certain to see any given object more distinctly with yellow lenses. This is most apparent when looking at block targets, such as skeet and trap and fixed rifle or pistol targets. Black appears blacker, and the background, which usually consists of a parade of colors, appears washed out and more uniform in contrast, so not only does a shooter see the target more sharply, but the lenses serve to separate the target from the rest of the visual field. This great advantage in target shooting is largely lost, however, in the field. Animal coloring is generally not black and is mostly designed to allow an animal to blend in with its surroundings. Yellow filters will not help pick out game unless it is silhouetted against snow or a white overcast. (Another use for yellow lenses is driving in haze or fog. Again, dark objects are more readily discerned in these conditions.)

Yellow lenses are available in glass and in plastic. For the outdoorsman glass is far superior, since it resists scratching and will not warp and distort vision as is the case with plastic.

Bausch & Lomb's Kalichrome and American Optical Company's Hazemaster are good quality shooting glasses. I would suggest that you purchase them from a local optician or optometrist, who will be glad to professionally fit them; also, replacement lenses, frame points, and temples are readily available. The minor savings gained by purchase through a gun shop or catalog are quickly lost in achieving a comfortable fit and prompt repair. Prices range from $25.00 to $35.00, depending on frame type. Also, shooting glasses can be ground in any prescription, including bifocals.

Sunglasses, in general, are designed to reduce overall brightness and glare. They are available in three basic colors; green, gray, and brown. Any good-quality sun filter will absorb the harmful ultraviolet and infrared rays and reduce overall brightness. Use of such a lens will prevent constant squinting and the resultant fatigue of facial muscles and will prevent red, itching, burning, scratchy eyes, which all of us have experienced from a day outdoors. Color selection is largely a matter of personal preference.

Green lenses tend to enhance the greens and browns, while gray lenses give a more accurate, truer color representation. Gray lenses are generally the darkest filters, but they tend to reduce figure-ground separation, an undesirable effect for the hunter, especially in woods and other dark or shaded areas.

Brown lenses tend to improve figure-ground separation and especially reduce blue light. Browns appear browner and therefore sharper. This is a definite advantage when shooting birds against a blue sky; the birds appear in sharper definition. Specific cloud formations are more apparent, which is an advantage in analyzing the approaching weather; this is of benefit to pilots, fishermen, and yachtsmen.

Poor-quality brown lenses tend to give everything a reddish cast and are, therefore, undesirable. Anyone wanting to buy brown sunglasses should get American Optical Company's Cosmetan. Unfortunately, these do not come factory-assembled, and therefore, the cost is higher. Again, all three colors are available in prescription form, and purchase from an optometrist or optician will permit proper adjustment and prompt repairs.

Polaroid lenses are of no particular value to the hunter and target shooter. Polaroid filters selectively eliminate light that is reflected vertically. They eliminate the sheen on water surfaces and allow the wearer greatly improved visibility beneath the water surface, making fish, submerged objects, bars, and holes much more visible. No boatsman or fisherman should be without Polaroid lenses. Inexpensive Polaroid lenses are available everywhere, but they warp and scratch easily. Such glasses should be considered expendable and should be replaced once or twice a year.

Better-quality Polaroid sunglasses are laminated lenses with a polarizer sandwiched between two layers of glass. These are available only through an optometrist or optician and can be made in prescription form also.

Over-the-counter sunglasses appear very attractive from the cost point of view. There are certain hazards. Quality control is generally poor, and the consumer often ends up with unwanted small amounts of random prescriptions and distortions. This can lead to reduced visual acuity and/or headaches or other forms of eyestrain. Absorption curves are never published, so the desired effect is not guaranteed. Many types are not repairable, and over the long haul frequent replacement may be more expensive than a pair of prescription-quality lenses and frames. Acceptable quality ready-to-wear sunglasses range in price from $12.00 to $40.00. Top-quality pairs start at about $20.00.

Kurt Roeloffs, O.D., is a well-known Long Island angler and shooter. He practices optometry and lives in Patchogue, New York.

"That's a hell of a place to lose a cow."
—Supposedly said by the first man ever to view the
awesome chimneys, cliffs, and arroyos of Utah's Bryce Canyon

297

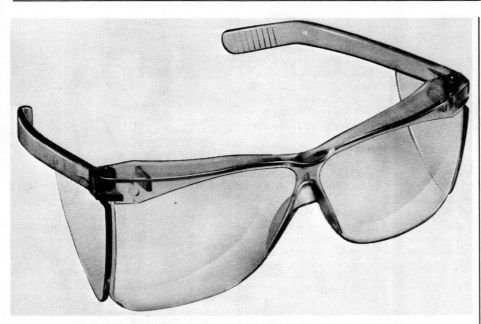

MARBLE'S SHOOTING GOGGLES

Marble's shooting goggles give you wraparound protection without a lot of distortion. The flat side-shields protect your eyes and filter without bending your vision. They're available in two colors, amber and green. Price: $2.39. Marble's, P.O. Box 111, Gladstone, MI 49837.

BUSHNELL SHOOTING GLASSES

Bushnell lenses are made of ground glass and are hardened so as to resist breakage by impact or blow-back. They are distortion- and aberration-free and are constructed in such a way as to sit high on the bridge of your nose when you assume a sighting posture.

These glasses have gold wire frames and come in a reinforced case, which ensures against accidental breakage. Available in yellow ($32.95) and green and gray ($27.95). Bushnell Optical Co., 2828 East Foothill Boulevard, Pasadena, CA 91107.

THE SPORTSMAN'S EYE
by James Gregg

New York: Macmillan, $2.95.

James Gregg is a practicing optometrist and a professor at Los Angeles College of Optometry. This book brings together his professional knowledge and his knowledge of outdoor sports. Visual perception and acuity are examined from several points of view: improving visual skills, visual defects that hamper you outdoors, how animals see, corrective lenses, and exercises that improve and test your ability to see as a sportsman. There is also excellent advice on optical aids (binoculars and spotting scopes, as well as glasses) and on vision as it relates to photography.

It's surprising that this book hasn't become something of a minor classic of outdoor literature, for it is the only work that deals specifically with the hunter's greatest asset—eyes. All the tips and tricks of the hunter's trade lead to one undeniable truism: if you see your game before it sees you, you have succeeded. The kill may be tangible proof of that success, but to a truly experienced hunter it is almost an afterthought.

In a nutshell, the eyes have it, and this book tells you how best to use and protect them.

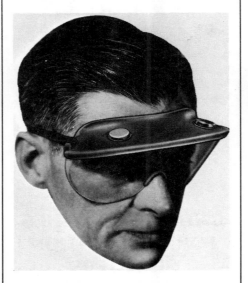

VISORGOGS

These glasses are held on your head by an elastic band. They are available in clear pale blue and light and dark green tints. Lenses are replaceable. Of special note is a top-venting system that keeps fogging to a minimum. Price: $3.70. Jones & Company, 325 Massasoit Avenue, East Providence, RI 02914.

#1119

"Adventurer"

Chrome frames and temples with plastic encased ear grips give these handsome sturdy styled sportsglasses added visual appeal. Tinted, ground glass lenses cut the sun's glare to provide comfortable clear, distortion-free viewing in the woods, on the water, or on the courts. Hard case fits belt.

TASCO SHOOTING GLASSES

These are tinted either yellow or green and are of good-quality glass. I wear prescription glasses, so my wife tried them. She says they're excellent, with no distortion that she could note. The frames are rugged, and the lenses are large enough for good protection. Price: $29.95. Tasco Sales, Inc., 1075 Northwest 71st Street, Miami, FL 33138.   —J.B.

AIR FORCE STYLE SPORT GLASSES

These good, conventional sunglasses are a neutral gray shade, the same color selected for Air Force pilots (theoretically, the best color for discerning objects against the sky). They are made of impact-resistant glass and have wire frames and plastic-tipped temples. Price: $15.95. Bushnell Optical Co., 2828 East Foothill Boulevard, Pasadena, CA 91107.

Hearing Protectors

Don't shoot your hearing. The constant concussion of rifle or shotgun fire on the range can permanently damage your ability to hear certain sounds. These hearing protectors are designed to reduce harmful high-frequency and impact noise while still allowing the wearer to hear warnings and sounds in the speech frequency range. Cold-resistant vinyl ear seals adjust to fit all head and ear contours. Price: $12.50. Marble's, P.O. Box 111, Gladstone, MI 49837.

Simmons Suede International Shooting Vest

This vest has an extended pad for international-style shooting (where the gun is held in a low position until the target appears). Suede, naturally. Price: $135.00. Simmons Gun Specialties, Inc., P.O. Box 533, Olathe, KS 66061.   —J.B.

E-A-R Plugs

These earplugs are made of a polymer foam. They are first compressed with the fingers, then inserted in the ear, where they expand to fit the individual ear canal perfectly. Because of this tight fit they're much more effective than regular earplugs and actually are just about as effective as earmuffs. They can be reused almost indefinitely, though periodic washing is advised. They are comfortable, and regular speech can be heard while wearing them (only at a short distance). They are bright yellow, which helps me a great deal since I always seem to be dropping them. When used in conjunction with muffs, they would provide the ultimate in ear protection. Prices: 45 cents a pair; 30 cents a pair for twelve pairs or more. Write to E-A-R Corporation, 376 University Avenue, Westwood, MA 02090, and include 50 cents for postage.   —J.B.

BOB ALLEN CATALOG: CLOTHES FOR COMPETITION SHOOTERS

The Bob Allen people specialize in clothing for trap and skeet shooters. Their catalog contains twenty pages of vests, coats, jackets, and pants that are sure to go well with the country club set. Classy hunting clothes are included, plus some target equipment, such as leather reloader's pouches for spent shells. Free catalog. Bob Allen Sportswear, P.O. Box 477, Des Moines, IA 50302.

MESH SHOOTER'S VEST

To keep you cool when it's scorching hot on the line, this vest is made from a polyester honeycomb mesh and has a zipper front. It includes two breast-pocket shell loops and an extended international-style quilted gun cloth pad. Price: $34.95. Bob Allen Sportswear, P.O. Box 477, Des Moines, IA 50302.

Shooting Shirt for Warm-weather Trap and Skeet

This nylon shooting shirt features a long tail and shoulder padding available for right- or left-handers. It comes in red, green, blue, gold, brown, and maroon in sizes from small through extra large. Price: $13.95. John Hall Plastics, P.O. Box 1526, Alvin, TX 77511.

"They ain't screwin' our sheep, they're eatin' 'em."
—*Comment heard during a sheepmen's meeting regarding the
possibility of sterilizing coyotes as a means of control*

299

HEAVYWEIGHT EL MONTE SHOOTING VEST

This international-style shooting vest has the added luxury of generous leather trim. Gabardine material, with zipper front; open-top bellows shell pockets; long, international-type shoulder pads; and loops for extra shells. Price: $39.95. Bob Allen Sportswear, P.O. Box 477, Des Moines, IA 50302.

Standard Shooter's Vest with Insert-A-Pad

This classic shooter's vest has a reloader's pouch in the back and open-top bellows pockets that will hold a box of shells apiece. The vest also has an Insert-A-Pad feature which allows you to slip a foam rubber insert behind the butt pad, thus giving your shoulder a break. Pads come in ⅛-, ¼-, and ⅜-inch thicknesses. Price: $17.95. Bob Allen Sportswear, P.O. Box 477, Des Moines, IA 50302.

TRAP AND SKEET GLOVES

When you're shooting in warm weather, the oils and perspiration from your hand can damage gun steel and make your gunstock slick and hard to handle. The Claybirder shooting glove absorbs perspiration, yet its skin-thin leather affords maximum trigger and handling sensitivity. The gloves have capeskin leather palms and backs, with stretch nylon between the fingers for a skintight fit. This is also a good glove for any warm-weather hunting. Available in two-tone brown or black and in sizes from small through extra large. Price: $8.95. Bob Hinman Outfitters, 1217 West Glen, Peoria, IL 61614.

REFLECTIONS ON RIMFIRES

by David E. Petzal

Most big-game hunters are rotten shots. They are rotten shots because they don't practice shooting fundamentals, such as trigger squeeze, breath control, and the rapid assumption of the prone, kneeling, and standing positions. The reason they don't practice is largely laziness, but also because shooting a centerfire rifle on a regular basis is expensive, noisy, and, in some cases, painful.

I have long been an advocate of practicing on a year-round basis with a .22 rimfire rifle. It is effective, and compared to the expense of shooting up centerfire ammo, it is dirt cheap. The basics that you rehearse with a .22 can readily be carried over into anything from a .243 to a .300 magnum, provided that the rimfire you use bears a close resemblance to your centerfire arm.

There's my beef. The rimfire rifles on the market today are designed, almost without exception, for kids or are sort of a compromise between a big-game rifle and a gun for Junior. The stocks are too short, have far too much drop along the comb, possess rotten trigger pulls and scabrous sights, and are grooved for tip-off mounts, which rank right along with crabs and pimples as a curse on mankind.

Today there are only a couple of .22s that are real, honest-to-God rifles. One of them—the Remington 541-S—costs $160.00, and the Savage/Anschutz 54 is just about twice that price. These are serious firearms. I don't care for the styling on either of them, but do they produce! The Anschutz especially, which is based on that firm's world-beating Super Match 54 target rifle, is often accurate to a degree that's spectacular.

Somebody is missing a bet here. I think there is a demand for a conservatively styled .22 bolt-action that is also a first-rate gun. The Winchester Model 52 Sporter, which has not been made for some time, sold for around $150.00 in 1955; today, in first-class condition, it brings six times that amount. Even taking into consideration the massive inflation we've had in the intervening two decades, that's a lot of money to spend on a rifle. The 52 was a veritable jewel among guns—first class all the way. It was a conservative, elegant piece of machinery, and them what has 'em today ain't lettin' go of 'em.

I understand that the Anschutz 54 sells very well, so obviously there are those who take the rimfire seriously enough to shell out serious money. Wouldn't it be nice if Winchester could bring back the 52 Sporter? Or if Sturm, Ruger cooked up a rimfire version of its classic Model 77 centerfire? They would not sell as quickly as tickets to *Jaws*, but they would sell in sufficient numbers to justify their existence.

The kids can have their pumps, autos, levers, and single-shots made from Crackerjack parts at Crackerjack prices. But there are those of us who delight in a rifle that works with precision and puts its bullets in a quarter-sized group at 50 yards, a gun without white line spacers or a glaring finish or a tin trigger guard or useless iron sights. I enjoy the hell out of the .22. It was the first gun I ever shot and owned. The magic of shooting, which has never lessened for me, is inextricably tied to those little cartridges. If only we had a few more good guns to feed 'em into.

David E. Petzal has been a shooter for more than twenty years. He is managing editor of *Field & Stream* magazine and has written a book on rimfires, *The .22 Rifle*, published by Winchester Press.

Mossberg 144 Rimfire Target Rifle

Here is an inexpensive target gun that is stocked for either prone or position shooting and is equipped with receiver sight and sling swivels. It has an adjustable hand stop. A good way to start out in target shooting. About 8 pounds. Price: $103.50.

O. F. Mossberg & Sons, Inc., 7 Grasso Avenue, North Haven, CT 06473.

—J.B.

ANSCHUTZ TARGET RIFLES
AND
ELEY MATCH .22 AMMUNITION

Savage Arms imports these rifles from West Germany, and by all accounts they're the best rimfire target arms made, although American rifles are catching up. The rifle pictured is the Model 1411, which is stocked for prone American-type matches. At the 1976 National Matches held at Camp Perry, (probably the most prestigious American target event), more shooters used these rifles in the prone event than any other make. Anschutz .22 target rifles are priced from $342.55 to $610.00, depending on style, and they're available with both right- and left-hand stocks. Anschutz also makes a fine match air rifle in two grades, the Model 64 at $162.50 or the Model 250 at $370.25.

Savage also imports Eley Match .22 ammunition from England, which before the recent advent of Winchester's Super Match Gold ammo, was virtually unchallenged in the field of accurate .22s. Savage Arms, Springdale Road, Westfield, MA 01085.

Rings and Bases for Mounting a Scope on a .22

If you're having trouble locating a scope-mounting system for your .22, look into the Redfield line. They have bases and ring mounts in ¾ inch and 1 inch for most rifles. Prices: bases, $3.50 to $6.60; rings, $10.80 to $13.20. Redfield, 5800 East Jewell Avenue, Denver, CO 80222.

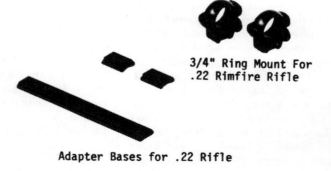

3/4" Ring Mount For .22 Rimfire Rifle

Adapter Bases for .22 Rifle

1" Ring Mount For .22 Rimfire Rifle

Regular .22LR meets a full can of pop from 100 feet.

Stinger meets a full can of pop from 100 feet.

SAME LENGTH

Regular .22LR   Stinger

.22 AMMUNITION

If you're looking for special .22 ammunition, try Omark Industries. These folks manufacture all the standard .22 loads, as well as oddballs like CB caps ($2.54 per 100), plastic-globed shotshells, sometimes known as ratshot ($1.59 per 20), and a .22 long-rifle cartridge known as the Stinger ($1.95 for 50) that is the hardest-hitting load of its kind. Omark Industries, P.O. Box 856, Lewiston, ID 83501.

Redfield

Precision Target Sights

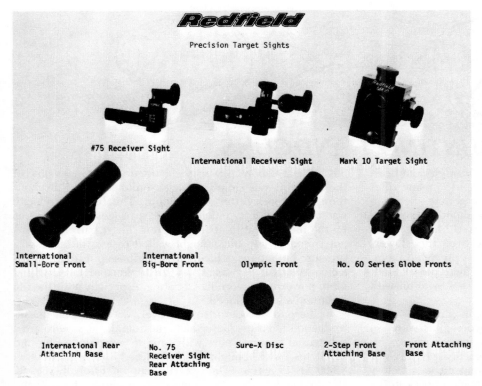

#75 Receiver Sight

International Receiver Sight

Mark 10 Target Sight

International Small-Bore Front

International Big-Bore Front

Olympic Front

No. 60 Series Globe Fronts

International Rear Attaching Base

No. 75 Receiver Sight Rear Attaching Base

Sure-X Disc

2-Step Front Attaching Base

Front Attaching Base

.22 MATCH SIGHTS

A full line of .22 match, Olympic, and big-bore competition sights are available from Redfield. The top of the line is the Mark 10 target sight, precision-machined to inaccuracies of less than 0.0003. The total adjustment for windage or elevation is 36 minutes of angle. Each click is ¼ or ⅛ moa, with accuracy of plus or minus $1/32$ moa (.031 inch at 100 yards). The Mark 10 retails for $204.70.

The 75 is a more economical target rear sight, with ¼-inch micrometer click adjustments. Graduations are marked in white, and one side of the elevation staff is left blank for range markings. Price: $23.20.

The International Match small-bore front is a good companion to either rear sight. It's extra long for sharp contrast and a clear sight picture. This front sight comes with six clear inserts and six skeleton inserts. Price: $27.00. Other competition sights from $9.20 to $46.00. Redfield, 5800 East Jewell Avenue, Denver, CO 80222.

Plinker's Delight and Birds in Flight: Two Tough Targets

If plinking with a .22 is your idea of fun, these targets will test the best. They amount to bird outlines that spin on an axle when hit. Plinker's Delight revolves on a vertical axis and Birds in Flight spins horizontally.

Aside from proving immediate and obvious confirmation of a hit or miss, they'll also sharpen your eye on moving targets. They may be used with rifles or pistols that range from pellet guns up to .38 S & Ws, and when not in use they fold flat for storage. Prices: Plinker's Delight, $19.95; Birds in Flight, $29.95. Arbruster Manufacturing Company, Inc., 124 Smathers Street, Waynesville, NC 28786.

THE TRICKIEST TARGET

If you want some inexpensive winter fun and some of the trickiest target shooting there is, plink away at inflated balloons on crusted snow when there's a breeze blowing.

Targets for Big Bores, .22 Rifles, and Air Guns

Regulation targets for small-bore and air-gun shooting competition and big-bore

sighting-in are sold by Outers'. Big-bore targets are calibrated to scope adjustments, so you will know how many clicks, right or left, up or down, it will take to get a test group of three shots right on the button. Price: $1.00 for ten targets. Outers Laboratories, Inc., Route 2, Onalaska, WI 54650.

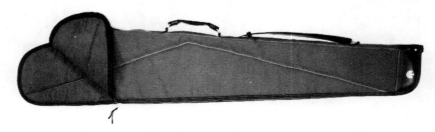

TARGET GUN CASE

This oversized canvas case will accommodate .22 target rifles with oversized scopes and/or bipods attached. Other features include humidity-deterrent padding, a full-length zipper, a steel-reinforced handle, and an adjustable sling. Price: $30.00. Kolpin Manufacturing, Inc., P.O. Box 231, Berlin, WI 54923.

HUNTING HANDGUNS

There seems to be a trend in hunting handguns and cartridges that might be analogous to the trend in game rifles of fifty to seventy-five years ago. That period—between 1900 and 1925—was when the first flat-shooting, smaller-bored rifles started to become the preferred hunting arms. These guns had numerous advantages over the slower, bigger-bulleted black-powder weapons that preceded them, including lighter recoil, increased down-range power, and, perhaps most important of all, a flatter, easier-to-hit-with trajectory.

For many years it seemed that handgun cartridges were limited in the same way that black-powder guns were, in that the only practical way to increase power was to increase bore and bullet size. Maximum practical velocity was considered to be about 1,500 fps. This speed in a factory cartridge was first reached by the .357 magnum back in the

30s. When a more powerful cartridge was brought out, in the 1950s, it was simply a bigger-bulleted round at about the same velocity: the .44 magnum. This limit on velocity was imposed not so much by the cartridges themselves as by the mechanical limits of the guns. Short barrels, actions not suited to any but straight-walled cases, the necessary pressure limitations of handguns—all these put limits on velocity. Also, there wasn't any great demand for anything more powerful or more flat-shooting, especially after the .44 magnum was introduced.

In the past decade or so, however, we have seen the introduction of faster, flatter handgun rounds, and there are a substantial number now with muzzle velocities of around 2,000 fps, which might be considered the equivalent of 3,000 fps in a rifle. The .221 Remington Fireball, the .22 Remington Jet, the .256 Winchester magnum, the .30 and

PISTOL & REVOLVER GUIDE
by George C. Nonte, Jr.

Chicago: Follett, $6.95 (soft cover).

A modern classic by a world-renowned expert on fire-arms, this third edition has been expanded and revised to reflect the latest information, specifications, and illustrations on the newest developments in handguns. Covers automatics, pistols, and revolvers, and today's high-performance ammunition, plus tips on modern target- and combat-shooting techniques. Includes chapters on the history of the handgun, how to shoot handguns, care and maintenance of handguns, even hunting with a handgun. With a directory of goods and services for the handgun buyer and owner.

CASE LINED WITH CHAMOIS SKIN, CONTAINING COMBINATION REVOLVER AND SINGLE SHOT TARGET PISTOL.

A complete outfit consisting of: 1 .38 Model 1891 Revolver, 3¼-inch barrel; 1 Pair Interchangeable Target Stocks; 1 Hollow Brass-Handled Screw Driver, with 4 blades; 1 Interchangeable Single Shot Barrel (6, 8 or 10-inch, .22, .32 or .38 calibre); 1 Brush wiper.

From an old gun catalog

.357 Herrett semiwildcats, and the .357 and .44 auto mag rounds all can reach this level in certain guns with certain loads. Also capable of this performance are the "rifle" rounds now found in the Thompson/Center Contender, such as the .22 Hornet, .218 Bee, .222, .25-35, and .30-30. Each of these represents a substantial gain in range, in terms of both retained energy and velocity, over the more conventional hunting rounds. This has been made possible by the new guns that have been introduced, which in turn were demanded by shooters. As more and more skilled handgun hunters realized that they were being limited by the available equipment, better equipment became available, both through the traditional sources and through the efforts of handgunners such as Steve Herrett and Lee Jurras. Scopes are now fairly common on handguns, which has also aided development; again, this situation occurred fifty years ago with rifles.

Advances in handgun equipment are not likely to be as universally accepted as advances in rifles, because handgunning is a less universal sport. Few people have the time, perseverance, and resources required to practice with a handgun until they can take full advantage of its capabilities. An aspiring rifleman may walk into a store, buy a rifle and ammo, and with less than 100 rounds of practice be able to consistently take big game at 100 yards. To acquire the same skill, the handgunner must shoot at least 1,000 rounds of ammunition a year and preferably more. Serious handgun hunting demands that a shooter be willing to give a great deal of his time and energy. The rewards are great, but most of us lack either the time, skill, or money to earn them, so the majority of handgunning equipment will always be geared to the average shooter, who probably can't even take advantage of the range of the .38 special.

The aspiring handgun hunter should keep the cost-of-practice factor in mind when contemplating his first purchase. In all aspects the rimfire .22 comes out on top as the first gun. It can be shot at low cost (about 2 cents a shot), and the initial cost of the arm is lower than for a centerfire. While it is just as cheap or cheaper to shoot a .357, say,

with cast-bullet handloads, the nonreloader must make an initial investment in loading equipment before taking advantage of this. The shooter who buys a .22 is making a minimal investment and is also buying an easier-to-shoot arm.

The .22 is a good gun for small game and for shorter-range shooting at small varmints. The small-capacity long-rifle round loses very little velocity in a handgun barrel as compared to a rifle barrel and is effective out to 50 yards or so on small game (though few of us can hit small game at that range). A revolver with an interchangeable .22 magnum cylinder can give you added power for varminting, while allowing you to use low-cost standard .22 ammo for practice.

Varmint handguns are becoming more specialized, just as in rifle varminting. Single-shot flat-shooting guns equipped with long eye-relief scopes are capable of astounding accuracy.

When you speak of big game and the handgun, you are generally speaking of deer-sized game, as the handgunners with the skill and time to try for larger game are few and far between, although they are growing in numbers. A good minimum for deer is the fine old .357 magnum, and indeed it is often the minimum legal caliber for deer in those states that allow handgunning for big game. The semiwildcat .30 and .357 Herretts (they are chambered in factory guns but must be reloaded) are also good, with the .41 and .44 magnums second; the auto mag rounds are good choices, too. The rifle rounds in the T/C Contender that are considered deer rounds are the .25-35 and .30-30. If you are going after elk or other large game, you might be advised to stick to the over-.40-caliber guns, as they still represent the ultimate in handgun power. They are also the most difficult to master because of the relatively severe recoil. It is unlikely that we'll see anything more powerful than the .44 magnum (both in regular and auto mag form) introduced in the near future, at least until the problem of recoil is solved.

—J.B.

HANDGUN HUNTING
by George C. Nonte, Jr., and Lee E. Jurras.

New York: Winchester Press, $8.95.

The emphasis in this book is on the hunting most readily available in the United States but also includes African animals and other exotics. Handgun hunting of one kind or another is possible in almost every state, say the authors, but until now there has not been much information and guidance on it. This book includes the history of the sport, best types of arms, where to hunt and what game to hunt for, selecting ammunition, handloading, choosing equipment and accessories, customized guns, techniques for hunting predators as well as large game, hunting pronghorns and other species that demand long-range accuracy, tuning your handgun, using muzzleloaders, and pursuing dangerous game such as bear, boar, and African animals.

AUTO MAG: MOST POWERFUL HANDGUN

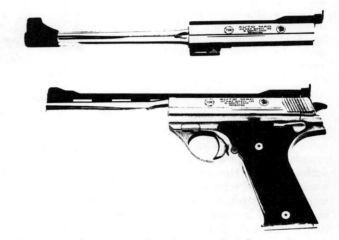

The auto mag pistol is strictly a big-game gun. The .44 auto mag round is the most powerful factory handgun cartridge, with a 180-grain bullet starting out at about 1,800 fps. The .357 auto mag round uses a 125-grain bullet at 1,900 fps. Both are extremely flat-shooting for handgun rounds.

The auto mag itself is a massive gun, weighing in at 57 ounces for the .44 and 54 ounces for the .357. Barrel lengths are 6½ and 8½ inches; a 10½-inch can be obtained on special order. A conversion unit which uses the same frame and magazine is available to interchange calibers. The basic gun costs $500.00; the Custom Hunter, with laminated wood grips, holster magazine, and Magnaporting (a recoil-reduction machining, which is advised for auto mag pistols because of the severe recoil), runs $750.00. Barrel units cost $195.00.

There is also an Alaskan model, which features a 12½-inch barrel and shoulder stock. Because of the longer barrel, a 265-grain bullet can be driven at about 2,000 fps from this gun. It is mainly a status weapon, as it will do nothing that the Ruger .44 carbine won't do, and it costs $945.00, which is about eight times as much as the carbine. The weight is about the same: 5 pounds 10 ounces. You also must pay a $200.00 federal tax on this gun, because the barrel is under the legal 16-inch limit for shoulder-held rifled arms.

The Backpacker is yet another version; it weighs in at a relatively petite 3 pounds with a 4½-inch barrel, and the regular 7-round magazine has been reduced to 5. It runs $785.00.

Jurras also does a great deal of custom and tuning work on auto mags. The gun itself is a marvelous firearm, and perhaps the best choice for those who go after really big game. The only problem seems to be in getting ammo (as it has been all along), and as of now the situation is still iffy. Due to the fact that most handgunners who want to use the auto mag are also handloaders, this hasn't really affected sales, although with good distribution of factory stuff through a well-known company, popularity would have to rise, even with the high cost of the gun. Because cases for both calibers are basically shortened .30-06 or .308 size, obtaining brass for forming is no big problem, and data for loading the auto mag rounds are easily available, notably in the *Speer Reloading Manual #9*. Write to Lee E. Jurras & Associates, Inc., P.O. Box 847, Roswell, NM 88201.

—J.B.

Smith & Wesson Model 29 .44 Magnum

This is the gun in which the .44 magnum was originally introduced. Perhaps it is still a slightly better choice than other handguns for big game, simply because the ammo is more available than for the auto mag and the stock shape lets it handle recoil a little better than single-action revolvers. It is available in a 4-, 6½-, or 8⅜-inch barrel, with weight running 43 to 51½ ounces, depending on barrel. The front sight is a ramp with a red blade, and the rear sight is the S & W click-adjustable micrometer. Available in blue or nickel. Prices: 8⅜-inch barrel, $256.00; 4- or 6½-inch barrel, $248.00. Smith & Wesson Co., 2100 Roosevelt Avenue, Springfield, MA 01101.

—J.B.

"You can always tell an old soldier by the inside of his holsters and cartridge boxes. The young ones carry pistols and cartridges: the old ones, grub."
—George Bernard Shaw, Arms and the Man

305

COLT SINGLE-ACTION ARMY

Probably the most famous handgun in American history, the single-action army has been in more Westerns than John Wayne. It was out of production for a time, but now it's back. You can obtain it in .45 Colt or .357 magnum calibers, with a 4¾-, 5½-, or 7½-inch barrel. The .45 can be handloaded to near-.44 magnum performance and makes an excellent big-game gun; the .357 is probably still the best all-around cartridge for revolvers that we have. The stock is available in either hard black rubber or walnut, and the finish can be either case-hardened or nickel (nickel is available in the 7½-inch barrel only). The New Frontier is a version of the single-action army with adjustable sights and is probably more practical for the serious hunting handgunner; it is available in the same calibers but with walnut stock and case hardening only, and the 4¾-inch barrel is not available. Prices range from $246.50 to $294.000.

For the shooter who is not sure he wants the weight, kick, power, and expense of a .45 or .357, Colt makes a scaled-down .22 single-action. I've carried one with a 4¾-inch barrel on most of my big-game hunts as a side arm for ten years now, and my father carried it for ten years before that.

It's as tight as the day it was made, although the finish is a little worn. The newer version comes with 4⅜-, 6-, or 7½-inch barrel and with two cylinders, one for .22 long-rifle and one for .22 magnum. There is also a version with adjustable sights. They are excellent for taking small game and for finishing off large game. Prices range from $96.50 to $113.50. Colt Industries, Firearms Div., 150 Huyshope Avenue, Hartford, CT 06102. —J.B.

THOMPSON/ CENTER CONTENDER

This single-shot handgun's salient feature is its barrel-switching capability. The Contender itself retails for $155.00 for the plain-barreled model, with a few dollars more for bull barrel and ventilated rib, and extra barrels are available for $57.00 to $67.00. Calibers available run from .22 long-rifle up to .44 magnum, thus covering every handgun hunting situation you could imagine. Some of the calibers are the .30 and .357 Herrett rounds (wildcats based on the .30-30 rifle case and two of the best choices for handgunning big game), the .218 Bee (obsolete in rifles, but an excellent handgun caliber), and .25-35 and .30-30 rifle calibers.

The Contender features .357 and .44 magnum barrels, with choke for shotshells in those calibers. T/C sells both shot capsules and shells in those calibers loaded with 4, 6, 7½ and 9 shot and claims performance equal to the 2½-inch .410 load, which some people might say is damning with faint praise, although it makes for an interesting weapon. Shot charges are ⅝ ounce in .44 and ½ ounce in .357. T/C also sells their Lobo 1½x handgun scope, with mounts for most popular handguns. Price is $44.50 for the scope and $7.50 for mounts.

Just in case you're interested, the .30 Herrett pushes a 125-grain bullet at 2,273 fps and the .357 Herrett a 158-grain at 2,108, which is almost a .30-30 power and should be fine on deer-sized game out to 150 yards or so. Dies are $20.00, with a trim die for $12.00. Thompson/Center Arms, Farmington Road, Rochester, NH 03867.

COLT WOODSMAN .22 AUTO

This is one of the most popular of hunting .22 handguns. The 4-inch barreled Sport model weighs in at 29 ounces and has a magazine capacity of ten long-rifle shells. Rear sight is fully adjustable, accuracy is superb. Price: $154.50. Colt Industries, Firearms Div., 150 Huyshope Avenue, Hartford, CT 06102.   —J.B.

RUGER SINGLE-SIX .22 REVOLVER

This gun comes with two cylinders—one for regular .22 shells and one for .22 magnums—adjustable sights, and all the standard Ruger quality. Barrel lengths are 4⅝ to 9½ inches, available in stainless steel in 5½- and 6½-inch barreled versions. Prices: $92.25 to $141.75. Sturm, Ruger & Co., Inc., Lacey Place, Southport, CT 06490.   —J.B.

New Model Blackhawk®

New Model Super Blackhawk®

RUGER BLACKHAWK AND SUPER BLACKHAWK

This is the gun that brought the single-action revolver back. The Blackhawk is chambered for the .30 carbine, .357 magnum, .41 magnum, and .45 Colt, with extra cylinders available for the 9mm Parabellum and .45 ACP (to be fired in the .357 and .45 Colt guns respectively). The Super Blackhawk is for the .44 magnum. Barrel lengths are 4⅝, 6½, and 7½ inches in the regular Blackhawk and 7½ inches only in the Super Blackhawk. Features include an adjustable rear sight, ramp front, and a transfer bar system that allows you to keep all six cylinders loaded instead of having your six-shooter really being a five-shooter as with most single-actions. The Blackhawk is also available in .357 magnum in stainless steel. Prices are $119.75 for all regular Blackhawks, $142.80 for dual-cylinder models, $149.75 for stainless .357, and $170.00 for the Super Blackhawk. Again, like all Ruger products, one of the very best values on the market. Sturm, Ruger & Co., Inc., Lacey Place, Southport, CT 06490.   —J.B.

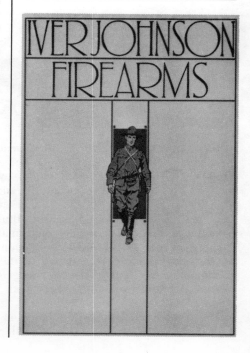

SMITH & WESSON MODEL 34 .22/32 KIT GUN

This is an excellent, lightweight (22½-ounce) .22 revolver that is well suited either to small-game hunting or simply as a sidearm for general outdoor activity. The barrel is available in 2- or 4-inch length, the 4-inch model being the only real choice for the sportsman. Rear sight is click-adjustable for windage and elevation. Prices: blued, $127.00; nickel, $138.00. Smith & Wesson Co., 2100 Roosevelt Avenue, Springfield, MA 01101.   —J.B.

IVER JOHNSON'S "S" SIDEWINDER

This is a deluxe version of IJ's little double-action .22 revolver. It costs a bit more ($73.00 versus $56.60) but is worth it in terms of what you get: better sights. The regular Sidewinder's sights are fixed; the "S" has a nice ramp front and an adjustable rear. It is a Western-styled, dual-cylinder model; weight is 30 ounces; cylinder is 6-shot. The Sidewinder is available in 4¾- and 6-inch barrels and in a nickel-finish version for about $5.00 extra; doing without the .22 magnum cylinder can knock about $5.00 off the price. Iver Johnson's Arms, Inc., 109 River Street, Fitchburg, MA 01420.   —J.B.

"There is no arguing with Johnson: for when his pistol misses fire, he knocks you down with the butt end of it."
—Oliver Goldsmith, on Boswell's Life of Samuel Johnson

307

REMINGTON XP-100

This single shot is Remington's lone entry into the handgun field. There are those who debate whether it truly qualifies as a pistol, because basically it uses the same bolt-action as is used in the Remington 600 series of carbines. It looks more like a Flash Gordon-type of device than a conventional handgun to many conservative handgunners, but they can't argue about the fact that it can be held in one hand and fired fairly well, although in normal use it is held with both hands or over a rest. The .221 Fireball round that fits it is a shortened .222, which in factory form drives a 50-grain bullet at 2,650 fps from the 10½-inch barrel of the XP-100. This is not spectacular in rifle terms, but it is the .220 Swift of handgunning and has the highest velocity ever achieved by a factory handgun cartridge. The gun itself is very accurate, because of both the excellent Remington action and trigger and the stable nylon stock, with groups of 1 to 1½ inches at 100 yards not uncommon. This would beat most factory *rifles*. The XP-100 is equipped with sights and ventilated rib, but most end up scoped. It is drilled and tapped for scope mount bases and comes with a zippered carrying case. Weight is 3¾ pounds. Price: $169.95. Remington Arms Co., Inc., 939 Barnum Avenue, Bridgeport, CT 06602. —J.B.

TARGET PISTOL FEATURES

American shooting matches usually involve revolvers and autos in both big bore and small bore, while international matches are held with single-shot pistols in "free" competition and with specially chambered (.22 short) autos in "rapid fire" competition.

Most target pistols come with click-adjustable rear sights, stop-adjustable triggers, and thumb-rest stocks. Their front sights are usually blade, and they are often undercut to reduce reflection.

—J.B.

COLT PYTHON .357

Equally suitable for target shooting, police work, or hunting, the Colt Python has a ventilated rib, adjustable sights, and a target hammer and trigger. It comes in three barrel lengths—2½, 4, and 6 inches—with the 6-inch model the most practical for target shooting and hunting. Prices: blued, $289.95; nickel, $299.95. Colt Industries, Firearms Div., 150 Huyshope Avenue, Hartford, CT 06102.—J.B.

COLT GOLD CUP NATIONAL MATCH

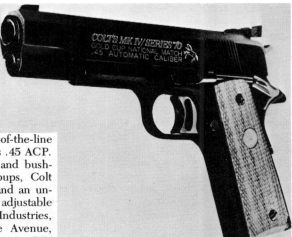

This gun represents the top-of-the-line for Colt target pistols. Caliber is .45 ACP. It features an accurizer barrel and bushings that aid in tightening groups, Colt Elliason adjustable rear sight, and an undercut front sight. The trigger is adjustable for stop. Price: $264.95. Colt Industries, Firearms Div., 150 Huyshope Avenue, Hartford, CT 06102. —J.B.

SMITH & WESSON NO. 41 TARGET PISTOL

Available with or without muzzle brake and in a special .22 short version for international shooting, this pistol features a micrometer rear sight and ⅛-inch Patridge undercut front sight. Barrel length is 7⅜ inches; the magazine holds ten rounds; and the gun weighs about 44 ounces. Trigger is adjustable for stop. Price: $184.00. Smith & Wesson Co., 2100 Roosevelt Avenue, Springfield, MA 01101. —J.B.

Harrington & Richardson Auto Target Pistols

H & H .22 rimfire pistols are made in a variety of configurations, but all on the same basic design, and are available at reasonable prices. Designs for American matches and also those conforming to international specifications range in prices from $180.00 to $219.00. All feature click sights, triggers that are adjustable for stop, and ten-shot magazines. Pictured is the Standard Citation with bull barrel ($180.00). Harrington & Richardson, Inc., Industrial Rowe, Gardner, MA 01440.

—J.B.

Single Shot Target Pistol.

WITH AUTOMATIC SHELL EXTRACTOR, REBOUNDING LOCK, ADJUSTABLE TARGET SIGHTS.

The Ammunition best adapted to this arm is the .22 Long Rifle Cartridge. Penetration, 5½ ⅞-in. pine boards.

This Pistol is also bored to take the regular S. & W. .32-10-88 and .38-15-146 Cartridges. Gallery charges in same shell, .32-4-46 and .38-4-70.

Lengths of Barrels and Weights.—.22 calibre, 6-in., 1 lb. 4¾ oz.; 8-in., 1 lb. 6½ oz.; 10-in., 1 lb. 8¾ oz. .32 and .38 calibre barrels are 2 to 4 oz. lighter.

Finish.—Biued or Nickel Plated. Black Rubber Target Stocks.

The Lock Frame of this Pistol is identical with that of the S. & W. .38 calibre Single Action Revolver, model '91, and the barrels and stocks of the two arms are interchangeable.

From an old gun catalog

International 211

HAMMERLI TARGET PISTOLS

The Hammerli line of precision target pistols, very popular among international shooters, is highly regarded everywhere in the world. There are models in both centerfire and rimfire types; the P240, for instance, comes in .38 special and a .22 long-rifle conversion kit is also available. The P240 itself runs $720.00, and the conversion kit is an extra $300.00. The 120 free pistol (single shot) is priced at $210.00, and the .22 semiauto International 211 is $572.00. All Hammerli pistols come with micrometer-adjustable sights and adjustable triggers; various types of adjustable grips are standard also, with left-hand versions priced slightly higher. All the pistols come with cleaning rods, tools (screwdrivers and Allen wrenches of the proper size), spare parts that take the most wear (firing pins, springs, etc.), and detailed instruction manuals, and the more expensive models, such as the P240, come with lined carrying cases. Imported by Gil Hebard Guns, P.O. Box 1, Knoxville, IL 61448.

HANDGUN TARGET SHOOTING: FOR MORE INFORMATION

National Shooters League
504 Lyons
Laramie, WY 82070
Robert O. and Gifford C. Burgess, Co-directors

United States Revolver Association
59 Alvin Street
Springfield, MA 01104
Stanley A. Sprague, Executive Secretary

HANDGUN AMMO

Handgun hunters who are after small game with .22s have to make the same choice as small-game rifle hunters: whether to use the more explosive hollow-point ammo or the solid-tipped type. I usually prefer the hollow-point, because shots are not always well placed when using a handgun, and the hollow-point allows a margin for error not found in solids. When using larger handguns for small game, nonexpanding bullets are preferred, usually lead bullets at medium velocity.

Varmint hunting at its extreme requires jacketed bullets, because the high velocities involved are not feasible with lead bullets. Hollow-points give better expansion in the not-quite-so-hot rounds, such as the .38 and .357, while guns with muzzle velocities of over 2,000 fps can usually use soft-points. For closer ranges these types of expanding bullets are advisable for the larger varmints, such as coyotes, because of their killing power, but for smaller varmints almost any load can be used as long as it is suitably accurate.

There are two schools of thought concerning big-game handgun bullets. One holds that you need a good expanding bullet of strong construction, and the jacketed hollow-point is the most reliable in this respect. Often soft-points only expand reliably when used in the faster, smaller-bored guns, such as the .25-35, .30-30, .30 Herrett, and .357 Herrett rounds available in the Contender, or the .357 auto mag. The big over-.40 guns need the hollow-points if expansion is desired, although the father of big-bore handgun hunting, Elmer Keith, feels that penetration is the most essential aspect with these guns, especially for game bigger than deer. He feels that the bullet is big enough around anyway, so he uses a hard-alloy lead bullet. It is difficult to argue with his results.

Speer Plastic Handgun Ammo

Speer makes plastic bullets and cases in the more popular handgun rounds —.38/.357, .44, and .45—for inexpensive, short-range practice. The bullets are powered by a primer (a magnum type is recommended) and are reusable. No tools are needed to load the shells; you simply press in a new primer and a recovered bullet (an old rug in a cardboard box stops them nicely), and they're ready to go again. Prices: $2.00 for fifty cases; the same for fifty bullets in .38/.357; $2.25 for .44. Bullets only are available in .45, to be used in .45 ACP metal cases. Speer, Inc., 1023 Snake River Avenue, Lewiston, ID 83501.   —J.B.

FORSTER WAX BULLET KIT FOR FAST DRAW AND INDOOR PISTOL PRACTICE

These are propelled only by a primer; the kit includes everything needed to shoot except primers. The compound is formulated for good accuracy and yet is soft enough so that it won't cause injury in case of an accident. Available in .38 special or .45 Colt (cases are modified for the wax). Extra cases can be had for $5.00 per fifty, and 14 ounces of wax costs $1.00. The whole kit includes cases, wax, and deprimer. Price: $6.60. As the Forster catalog says, "Quick-draw practice should only be done with wax bullets to avoid the painful results that can occur when regular ammunition is fired prematurely." Amen. Forster Products, 82 East Lanark Avenue, Lanark, IL 61046.   —J.B.

HANDGUN SIGHTS

Preferably, sights on the hunting handgun should be adjustable, as fixed sights are only really suited for close ranges and one load. If you use a variety of loads, such as a low-power cast bullet load for small game and a jacketed bullet at high velocity for larger stuff, adjustable sights are a necessity. They should also be rugged; sights that are bent or put out of adjustment easily are worthless. This is something to think about when considering a lower-priced gun.

Arguments rage back and forth over the best type of handgun sight, but nothing beats a good wide-bladed post front on a ramp and a click-adjustable rear.

Handgun scopes are just now coming into their own. They are plagued with the same problems, mostly involving mounting, that first were encountered with rifle scopes.

Most handguns simply aren't manufactured with scope mounting in mind. There are any number of ways to hang a scope on a handgun, but the best involve drilling and tapping by a skilled gunsmith. There are some mounts that replace grips; these work fairly well, but if you want a custom grip, you are up the creek. Fortunately, the handguns that are most often scoped are arms like the T/C Contender, which are chambered for longer-ranged rounds. The Contender is easily scoped because it was made to be.

Handgun scopes are now good products; in the past some have not been able to stand up to the recoil velocity of larger hunting guns. They are normally of under 2½x and have long eye relief, because a handgun is held much farther from the eye than a rifle. —J.B.

MMC HANDGUN SIGHTS

The Miniature Machine Company micrometer-adjustable handgun sights have a very good reputation among serious handgunners and are available for most popular models. Pictured is the Colt .45 auto installation, which requires a competent gunsmith for application. The advantages of the MMC sights are that they are designed so the original low factory front sight need not be replaced, that it usually requires a minimum of work to install (sometimes none), and that it is precisely machined so there is little or no slack in adjustments. Prices, complete with bases: $37.90 to $40.05. Miniature Machine Co., 210 East Poplar, Deming, NM 88030.
—J.B.

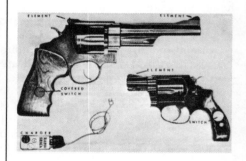

EL-TRONIC NIGHT SIGHT

These are electronically lighted open sights for shooting in dim light. Developed primarily for police work, they would also be useful to the hunter who prefers not to scope his handgun, and they would be very helpful in thick timber.

The standard setup is a red front sight and a yellow rear. The mechanics involve a battery in the grip and tiny wires leading to the sights; the setup is unobtrusive and is switched on by the pressure of the middle finger in a normal shooting grip, so that the sights aren't on all the time. Batteries keep the sight going for up to six hours continuously; a charger is available, too. At the present time it's only available in certain Smith & Wesson, Colt, and Ruger models and as a front sight on the AR-15 and M-16 rifles. Base price is $69.50; a covered switch is $5.00 extra. More models may be available. For info write Cap Cresap, 21422 Rosedell, Saugus, CA 91350.

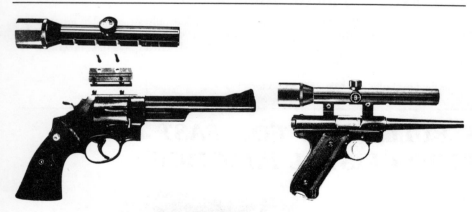

Bushnell Handgun Scopes and Mounts

There are two Bushnell Phantom handgun scopes, a 1.3x and a 2.5x. Eye relief on both is up to 21 inches; weight is 5½ ounces for the smaller scope and 6½ ounces for the larger one. Prices are $42.50 and $49.50 respectively.

There are two basic types of Bushnell handgun mounts; both of these are available to fit most popular handguns and mate with the dovetailed bottom of Phantom scopes. One is a single-piece; the other a two-piece. Price for either: $9.95. Bushnell Optical Co., 2828 East Foothill Boulevard, Pasadena, CA 91107. —J.B.

Thompson/Center Lobo Handgun Scope

This is a 1.5x that weighs 5 ounces, introduced after T/C's original Puma scope was found to have problems coping with magnum recoil. The Lobo is theoretically strong enough to mount on any handgun. It has a dovetailed bottom that mates with the T/C mounts available for the T/C Contender, Smith & Wesson, and Ruger guns. (The Contender doesn't require drilling and tapping for this mount because the rear sight screw holes are used; the others do require drilling.) Price for the Lobo is $44.50; all mounts are $7.50. Thompson/Center Arms, Farmington Road, Rochester, NH 03867.   —J.B.

Sport Specialties' .45 Auto Scope Mount

This will fit all commercial and military models of the Colt .45 ACP. It simply replaces the left grip and is built to accept Bushnell Phantom scopes. Price: $14.25. Sport Specialties, P.O. Box 774, Sunnyvale, CA 94088.   —J.B.

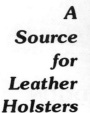

A Source for Leather Holsters

This company makes and markets leather holsters that will fit just about any handgun without a scope. Styles include Western, fast-draw, belt, speed, and shoulder holsters. They also make wide, Western-style rifle slings and leather police accessories. Typical price for a holster and belt: $30.00 to $35.00. Catalog, $1.00. American Sales & Manufacturing Company, P.O. Box 677, Laredo, TX 78040.

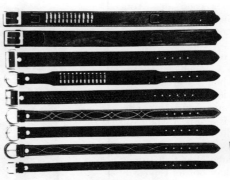

Thompson/Center Contender Holster

This holster is made in two styles, for scoped and unscoped Contenders. It can be worn either on the shoulder, which is usually preferred with handguns of the Contender's size, or on the belt. It is also available in left- or right-handed models at no extra cost. Light tan with oil finish. Prices: $27.95 for scoped; $25.95 for unscoped. Thompson/Center Arms, Farmington Road, Rochester, NH 03867.   —J.B.

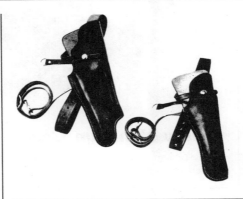

SAFARILAND HOLSTERS AND BELTS

These are all top-grade products. Safariland has a large variety of sporting holsters available for just about every gun imaginable, with prices running about $14.95 to $25.95 for plain leather (brown or black) and $21.50 to $28.95 for lined patterns (plain or basketweave). All feature big, secure snaps and lockstitching. The belt loop is 2¼ inches.

They also have belts in a variety of styles, both with and without belt loops, in widths from 1¼ to 2¼ inches, at prices from $7.50 to $28.50. A handy accessory to the belts is their sliding belt ammo carrier; this is a loop-type carrier that holds six rounds and is available in either .38/.357 or .44/.45 caliber sizes for $2.75. Safariland, 1941 Walker Avenue, Monrovia, CA 91016.   —J.B.

HOLSTERS AND BELTS

One of the charms of handgun hunting is that both hands are free, so you can roam wherever you like without having to hang onto your gun or adjust the sling or cope with any of the numerous small hassles involved in other types of hunting. All your equipment can be carried on a belt: gun, ammo, and knife.

Most guns are easily carried on a belt, but certain requirements should be observed. The holster should fit the gun well, keep it in place, and be reasonably weatherproof. Leather is the best material for this: good, stiff leather from the back of the animal. Horsehide is best, but as it is in much shorter supply than cowhide it is more expensive.

Your belt ought to get equal consideration. It should be made of good, stiff leather, wide enough to support the weight of the equipment (at least 2 inches), and with a good buckle. There is nothing more frustrating than having your gunbelt come loose in the hills, especially if you're also using it to hold up your pants.

Cartridge loops are not really the best way to carry ammo. They are slow and limit a single belt to a single weapon (it simply doesn't work to try to put .22 shells in .357 loops!) so an ammo holder of the slide-on type that can be positioned anywhere on the belt is a good idea. Your ammo and knife can be carried on one side of the belt and your gun on the other, thus balancing the load.

Larger guns are usually carried in a shoulder holster; this is much more comfortable than a belt when any great weight is involved, (and a loaded .44 magnum with holster can get up around 4 pounds. The shoulder holster is also best when you anticipate much belly-crawling, because the belt holster picks up dirt when you paw through the gumbo after that trophy pronghorn. The shoulder holster can easily be protected in such a situation by wearing a vest or coat.
—J.B.

Bianchi Holsters

This company, best known for police equipment, also makes a fine line of sporting holsters for most popular guns. They are available in various styles, both black and tan finished, and prices run $12.95 to $31.50. Fast-draw rigs (with belts) and a minimal selection of sporting belts are also available. Bianchi, 100 Calle Cortez, Temecula, CA 92390. —J.B.

Classy Handgun Case

This two-gun case is made of leather-covered wood and is fully lined. It opens up fully and lies flat for easy gun removel. It is also a good case for spotting scopes. Price: $45.00. Gun-Ho, 110 East 10th Street, St. Paul, MN 55101.

UNIVERSAL PISTOL CASE

Any sidearm under 13 inches in length can be housed in this soft expanded-vinyl pistol case. It includes a full-length zipper, a moisture-resistant lining, a locking ring, and two inside pockets for cleaning gear and accessories. Price: $9.00. Kolpin Manufacturing, Inc., P.O. Box 231, Berlin, WI 54923.

PROTECTO PLASTICS, INC.

FOUR-HANDGUN CASE

To hold up to four handguns, try this ABS plastic gun case. It is foam-lined (the foam is easily cut with a razor if you want the custom look of specific receptacles) and includes a lock and carrying handles. There are many other kinds of cases made by this company. Free catalog. Price: $28.95. Protecto Plastics, Inc., 201 Alpha Road, Wind Gap, PA 18091.

GUN CONTROL: THE REAL ISSUE

Logic is a marvelous tool; it is the basis of reason, the mold that casts the unassailable argument. Yet I would question the veracity and perhaps even the honesty of any logician or philosopher who doesn't recognize the validity of logic's alter ego, the subjective.

Subjectiveness may be defined as gut reaction, feeling rather than thinking, the smell of a wild rose. By its very nature, it can't be described well. By logic's very nature, it can be described with exactitude and with eloquent precision.

Logical arguments concerning gun control come close to canceling one another out, and consequently it is a perennial issue; one that will probably never be resolved logically.

You are right when you maintain that handguns are essentially weapons, that handguns contribute to crime, that any gun is capable of killing people.

You are just as right to maintain that handguns provide healthy, honest, legal recreation; that they are a deterrent to crime when criminals know you have one; that guns don't kill people—people kill people.

Perfect logic can be called to the court of human conscience, and it will ably defend each position. So perhaps we should examine the subjective for a definitive decision.

What is the gut reaction to guns? I'd say fear and freedom. The fear reaction occurs on the part of people who don't understand them, who view them as a symbol of evil.

The fear can be proven illogical. Guns are machines, like cars and drop hammers and electric drills, no more deserving of consideration as threatening, animate objects than rocks or sticks or knives. There is no reason to fear guns—only rocks, sticks, knives, and guns in the hands of frightened people.

And how about freedom? Sure, there's the freedom to swing your arms until you touch the tip of my nose, and that's part of guns. So is the freedom of a fall morning—cold, clear, and colored red and yellow. But there is a deeper freedom in *free* gun ownership that should touch us all. It is the freedom of a government so sure of its commitment to freedom that it can allow its citizens to keep and bear those very instruments that could lead to its destruction.

I'm aware that the citizen/patriot/soldier is not much of a threat against an army with automatic weapons, and nuclear warfare, but that's logic. Guns are a symbol, a subjective entity, and the right of ownership of them cannot be described logically. The need for gun ownership hearkens back to 1776; that's why provisions were made in that ultimate statement of freedom we call the Constitution to "keep and bear" them. I would distrust any government that removed this very positive symbol of freedom from it citizens, and you would, too. That, not madmen or criminals or Nazism, is the real issue in gun control. —N.S.

TARGET SHOOTING

The image that many hunters have of the target shooter is one of a specialized machine, someone who isn't a good shot in practical situations. Stories abound concerning target shooters and world champions who can't hit a deer at 100 yards or who miss quail right and left. These are told in much the same manner as the one about the Abercrombie & Fitch-equipped fly fisherman who was outfished by a little kid with a bent pin and a can of worms.

The truth is that a good target shot, given a little experience in the game fields, will shoot the pants off of any of us lesser mortals. And the other side of the coin is that even Dead-eye Joe down the street, who never misses a deer (or so he says), can benefit both from target shooting and the knowledge of firearms that target shooting provides.

For instance, take benchrest shooting. This sport seems silly to a great many hunters, because it consists of a bunch of grown men trying to put as many bullets into the same spot as possible. Hell, they aren't even tryin' to hit a bull's-eye! Well, the benchrest game was started by varmint hunters who wanted to prove whose rifle was the most accurate, and many of the advances in accuracy, both in ammo and in guns, are incorporated not only in today's factory-made varmint guns but in the deer rifles and ammo that Dead-eye Joe—and you—shoot. So even if you never

try to shoot a string of shots for group in your life, you owe the benchresters a debt every time you buy a box of shells at the hardware store. It's a better product because of them.

The same goes for the other shooting sports: small-bore target, military match, big-bore, handgun, skeet, trap. The advances made in every kind of target shooting are felt in sporting arms and ammunition, even if you never partake of the paper-punching or clay-busting sports. So don't go looking at the target shooters and world champions with a jaundiced eye. While their guns may sometimes seem strange and their clothing may be nothing you'd dare wear to deer camp, they can teach you a few things. In fact, if you do ever take part in one of the target sports, whether through a round of skeet at the country club or a sanctioned rifle match, you'll learn a lot about shooting that can't be taught in the deer woods. Remember, too, that they are shooters and gun enthusiasts just like you, and that they all started somewhere. Like most sports, shooting is 10 percent talent and 90 percent practice, something which natural shot Dead-eye Joe may never admit. But then, you'd never find him on a target range either. If you are one of the many who likes to shoot as much as he likes to hunt, try the target sports. You might even like it.   —J.B.

TARGET RIFLE FEATURES

The biggest difference between various types of target rifles is in the stock. There are three main kinds of target shooting: position (which involves all the standard shooting forms: standing, kneeling, sitting, and prone), prone, and benchrest. Each type of shooting requires a different stock to match the position. Position stocks must necessarily be of an all-around design. (Free rifle stocks, used primarily in international competition, are essentially position stocks that are fitted with hook, butt plates, grips, and other features not allowed in most American position matches.) Prone stocks can be more specialized, because they will be used only in the prone position. Benchrest stocks are only used when shooting over rests, with the shooter sitting at a bench, so they are also specialized.

Depending on the rifle, it may be drilled and tapped for target sights, it may have target-type scope blocks fitted, or it may include sights. Most target rifles also have adjustable triggers, the degree of adjustability depending on the rules

under which they'll be used. Many of the big-bore rifles are fitted with stainless steel barrels, since these resist heat erosion more than ordinary carbon steel.

Most stocks are made of wood, sometimes laminated (like plywood) to minimize warping. Most are of plain finish; target rifles are meant to be shot, not looked at. The latest type of stock material is fiberglass (actually, a shell of fiberglass cloth and resin), which has become popular in matches where a maximum weight is part of the requirements, as they weigh at least 1½ pounds less than the average wooden stock of the same dimensions. Also, they do not warp with changing moisture and hence are consistent in their relationship with the metal parts of the gun. This helps to maintain accuracy. They are often painted in amazing colors. There is nothing weirder for the average hunter to look at than a fiberglass-stocked benchrest rifle with its unblued stainless barrel, its stock of international orange, and its extended scope.   —J.B.

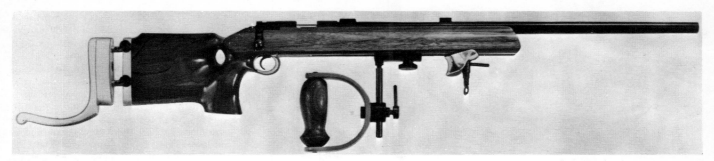

Winchester 52 International Match "Free" Rifle

International match shooting involves position shooting but with fewer restric-tions on the rifle. That's why you see all those whatchamacallits hanging all over this gun; they help to hold it steady and con-trol is better. While there are fewer restric-tions on the rifle in international matches, the targets are a hell of a lot tougher. Only iron sights are used. There are two courses: small-bore (rimfire) and big-bore (centerfire). The Winchester 52 is a rimfire and runs 13½ pounds. Cost is $585.00. Also available in a model for prone inter-national competition for $475.00. Win-chester-Western, 275 Winchester Avenue, New Haven, CT 06504. —J.B.

Remington 40-XR Position Rifle

This is basically the same gun as Rem-ington's 40-XC except that it fires the .22 rimfire. There are various types of rimfire (small-bore) position matches, with dif-ferent rules—high school, college, NRA, and international—but all require the same sort of rifle. Shooting is in ten-shot strings at ranges from 50 feet to 50 meters, in all standard shooting positions, depend-ing on whose sanction the match is under. Most rules are for iron sights only, for which the 40-XR is drilled and tapped. Redfield Olympic front and rear sights are available at an extra charge. Single shot. Price: $275.00; $55.25 for the sights. Rem-ington Arms Co., Inc., 939 Barnum Av-enue, Bridgeport, CT 06602. —J.B.

Remington 40-XC National Match Course Rifle

Though the Winchester M-70 is most prevalent at big-bore matches, the Rem-ington 40-XC is a perfectly good rifle. The National Match Course involves ten shots from a standing position at 200 yards, ten rapid-fire shots from a sitting position at 200 yards (time limit of sixty seconds with bolt gun), ten rapid-fire from prone at 300 yards, and twenty slow-fire shots at 600 yards from prone. Obviously, it's a tough competition. It's made even tougher by the fact that only iron sights are allowed.

The 40-XC is a fine National Match gun, chambered for the .308 Winchester, with a stock that is well designed for all posi-tions. It includes a hand stop behind the front swivel, which helps, with the aid of a heavy shooting glove, to protect the forearm hand in recoil, because with nor-mal sling use that hand is pushed up hard against the front swivel. It has an adjust-able butt, a clip slot on the receiver (for stripper clip loading—a must when you're firing ten shots in sixty seconds from a five-shot magazined rifle), and it's drilled and tapped for metallic sights. Stainless steel, 24-inch barrel, weight 11 pounds. Price: $450.00. Remington Arms Co., Inc., 939 Barnum Avenue, Bridgeport, CT 06602.

—J.B.

SPRINGFIELD ARMORY

Springfield Armory M-1A: Civilian Rifle for Military Matches

One version of the over-the-course match for big-bore rifles involves what is known as the service rifle match, in which shooters must use one of the recent military rifles: the M-1 Garand, the M-14, or the M-16. The M-14 is the rifle that replaced the Garand, and it fires the 7.62mm NATO round (.308 Winchester). The M-16 is the 5.56mm (.223) rifle that was used in Vietnam. The preferred match gun of the three is the M-14, because it is a more consistent performer than the Garand. The M-16 is practically worthless for the larger ranges (300 and 600 yards), especially in the wind, because of its light and inefficient bullet. Until Springfield Armory brought out the M-1A (which, in spite of its name, is an M-14), civilian rifle clubs that shot against military teams were essentially limited to the Garand, since the military M-14 is shootable as either a semi-automatic or full-automatic weapon and is outlawed for civilian use. The M-1A is strictly semiauto and hence can be used by civilian clubs, so they aren't at a disadvantage when competing against military teams. It is available in three grades: standard rifle, $342.50; target, $457.50; and super match (which has a premium barrel), $511.75. Two magazines are included. Springfield Armory, 111 East Exchange, Geneseo, IL 61254. —J.B.

Shilen Benchrest Rifles: Among the Very Best on the Rest

Long known for barrels, rifles, and benchrest gunsmithing, the Shilen company knows how to put together an accurate rifle. Available with either Claro walnut or fiberglass stock, in thumbhole or conventional style, this rifle comes with Shilen's match grade stainless barrel. Tell Shilen what scope you are going to mount, and they'll make up the rifle to make the weight class you're looking for (10½ or 13½ pounds). You can get the fiberglass stock in a choice of colors (love that robin's egg blue!). Takes six months for delivery. Price: $650.00 without scope or mounts. Shilen Rifles, Inc., 205 Metro Park Boulevard, Ennis, TX 75119.

—J.B.

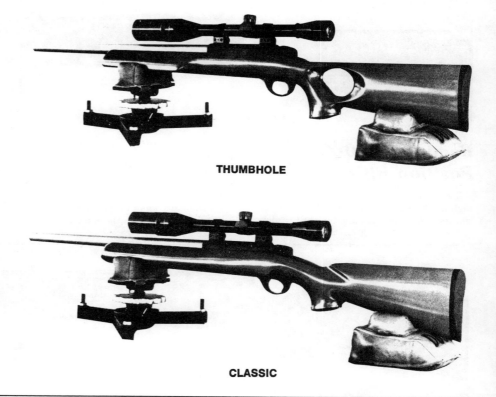

THUMBHOLE

CLASSIC

Remington 700 Varmint Special in .308: Factory Metallic Silhouette Gun

The fastest growing of the target sports is metallic silhouette shooting, where shooters fire offhand at metal outlines of chickens, javelinas, pigs, turkeys, and bighorn sheep at ranges from 200 to 500 meters. This is done with basic hunting rifles, which must not weigh more than 8 pounds 13 ounces (4 kilograms). No slings are allowed and all shots count; there are no sighters. Scoring is easy; if the silhouette falls over, it counts as a hit.

Hunters who always looked down their noses at target shooting are finding that MS shooting is a hell of a lot of fun and good practice, too. As the competition gets more serious, an increasing number of rifles specifically designed for this kind of shooting will come out, but as of now there's just one: Remington's Varmint Special in .308. The .308 is the most popular

"The cowman who cleans his range of wolves does not realize that he is taking over the wolf's job of trimming the herd to fit the range. . . . Hence we have dustbowls,"
—Aldo Leopold

317

Remington 700 Varmint and 40-X Series

The Remington 700/40-X bolt action is the basis of more fine, accurate varmint and benchrest rifles than any other, and it's the action that is the basis for any accurate firearm. In major benchrest competitions usually over half the shooters use this action in their rifles, more than all other actions put together. Aside from its excellent trigger and fast lock time, the 700/40-X's basic action design, which is a round bolt in a round sleeve, encourages the strength and concentricity that is necessary in any superaccurate rifle. It is a stiff action, which easily mates up with the barrel, due to its round design, and aids in making sure that the chamber is perfectly lined up with the bolt. So, after the bench shooter finishes weighing each case, drilling out his flash holes, trimming the necks to make sure they're all of uniform thickness, and spinning the whole cartridge in an alignment gauge to make sure everything is as close to center as possible, he's sure that his rifle is just as accurately centered. If it wasn't, all the rest of the steps would be useless, at least insofar as bench competition is concerned, where winning groups at 100 yards usually measure around 2/10ths of an inch.

For the long-range varmint hunter there's the Model 700 Varmint Special, with a heavy barrel, which is priced at $259.95. It comes in all popular varmint calibers and is now also available in .308 Winchester for silhouette shooting.

For the really insane varmint hunter, probably the Rangemaster centerfire target rifle would be better yet. It features a stainless-steel barrel for longer barrel life, a stock that is more suitable for scope sighting, and target scope blocks on the barrel. It's also available in a single-shot model, which probably would be slightly more accurate because of having no magazine cut to reduce stiffness in the action. It's available for $395.00 base price in just about all varmint calibers and also in big-bore calibers, such as 7mm Remington and .300 Winchester magnum, for long-range target shooting.

For the bench shooter there's the 40-XBR, which retails for $425.00. It also features a stainless-steel barrel and comes in the smaller .22 centerfire chamberings, which are the most popular for bench shooting, as well as .308 Winchester and the 6x47, a wildcat bench cartridge that is made by necking up the .222 magnum to 6mm. It's probably the most accurate factory rifle made.

caliber for MS shooting, because of its accuracy, combined with enough punch to knock over the sheep at 550 yards. This gun makes the weight limit (which doesn't include sights), and with the quick lock time of the 700 action (very necessary in offhand shooting), it is a natural. Price: $259.95. Remington Arms Co., Inc., 939 Barnum Avenue, Bridgeport, CT 06602.

—J.B.

MODEL 70 TARGET RIFLES

The Model 70 Rifle is favored for high-powered rifle matches, such as 1,000-yard target shooting and High Power National Match-type competition, which feature ranges from 200 to 600 yards. Needless to say, such rifles are usually chambered for higher-powered, heavier-bulleted rounds than benchrest rifles normally are, in order to buck the wind and to shoot flatter at long distances. The advantage of the Model 70 action in this type of shooting lies not only in its excellent trigger and fast lock time, which are equalled by other rifles, but in its flat-bottomed action, which resists the torque that occurs when a high-powered round, such as the .300 Winchester magnum or 7mm Remington magnum, is fired and the action tends to twist away from the spin of the bullet in the barrel. Such sudden stress can change the point of impact in a rifle enough to move the next shot out of the X at 1,000 yards if the receiver isn't solidly bedded against any such twisting action, which the flat bottom of the M-70 guards against. As in benchrest shooting, most shooters eventually get rifles built up with custom stocks and precision barrels, but the man with a factory M-70 target rifle has no need to be shy. The Model 70 Target runs $400.00; the Model 70 International Army Match, $500.00 The Army Match is available only in .308 Winchester; the Target model in .308 and .30-06. Winchester-Western, 275 Winchester Avenue, New Haven, CT 06504.

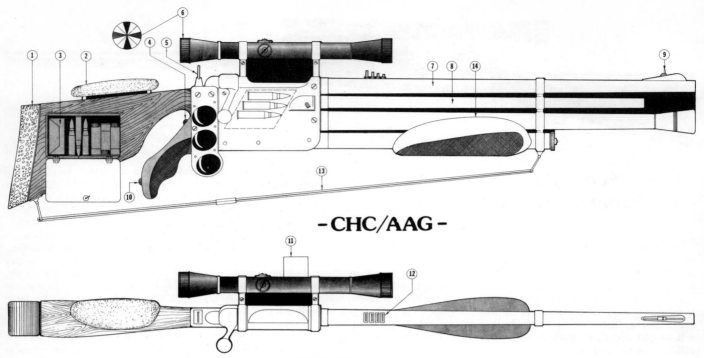

-CHC/AAG-

THE CHC-AAG

The CHC-AAG (Complete Hunter's Catalog All-Around Gun) is the answer to anything, anywhere, anytime. Features include:

1. Recoil pad, 2 inches thick, tapered, made out of East Indian vulcanized bat hide.

2. Adjustable cheek piece, for any height of sight.

3. Spare ammo carrier that holds three shotgun shells, three high-powered rifle shells, and a box of fifty .22 long-rifle shells and comes with lock and key.

4. Tang safety (of course!) for all three actions.

5. Micrometer-adjustable receiver sight.

6. A 1–20x variable scope with adjustable objective on swing-over mount. Reticle has two posts, duplex cross-hair, dot and plain cross-hair reticles. Dot is range finder. Simply look on the handy Eye-Size chart accompanying rifle and find out what the average size eye is of the game you'll be hunting. Feed this info into top turret adjustment computer and, when you see your game, adjust power until dot just covers eye; your scope automatically resets itself for the distance involved.

7. A .375 H&H barrel, the perfect all-around caliber, especially since we've heard Remington is soon to bring out their sabot loads in calibers from .17 to .35 so that all calibers will be represented. The best is the .22 varmint load with a 55-grain bullet at 7,610 fps.

8. A .22 long-rifle barrel, on semiauto action.

9. Sliding bead front sight (for use with both iron and shotgun sights).

10. Release knob for adjustable pistol grip.

11. Magazine for .22—holds 20 long-rifle shells.

12. Folding leaf rear sight, sighted for .375 H&H at ranges of 100, 200, 300, and 400 yards.

13. Sling, one-piece shooting type.

14. Three-inch 12-gauge barrel with adjustable choke on pump action.

—J.B.

POSITION RIFLE SHOOTING
by Bill Pullum
and Frank T. Hanenkrat

Chicago: Follett, $5.95 (soft cover).

A landmark in shooting literature, this is the most up-to-date book for the competitive rifleman. Specifically concerned with three-position riflery—the target-shooting style used all over the world in competitions ranging from local matches to the Olympic Games—this book contains everything a competitor needs to know to become a champion: the psychology of successful shooting, how to train your body and your mind, how to use the physics of shooting equipment, positions, coaching techniques, and much, much more.

THE ACCURATE RIFLE
by
Warren Page

New York: Winchester Press, $8.95.

This book deals mainly with benchrest shooting: the rifles, techniques, components, etc. It is written by the former gun editor of *Field & Stream,* who is also a topflight benchrest shooter. Naturally, it is most useful to the benchrest shooter, but many techniques and much equipment can be adapted by the varmint hunter, in particular, as well as the long-range big-game hunter. This is a good, concise book, written by one of the best firearms authors ever.

THE HANDY SPORTSMAN
by
Loring D. Wilson

New York: Winchester Press, $10.95.

Even the inexperienced craftsman can master the skills needed to make low-cost, high-quality hunting and fishing gear. Necessary tools and materials are introduced and then projects arranged so that new techniques are learned chapter by chapter. Some of the twenty-nine sporting accessories include a custom loading bench, spinner center, game carrier, and shotgun case. Written in an easy-to-read, humorous style.

SIGHTING IN: WHY AND HOW

There are two mistaken notions regarding sighting in a rifle that cause more grief and pain than any other bunch of misconceptions combined. The first of these is that once a rifle is "on" it will stay that way, in spite of advancing time, storms, accidents, and the fickle nature of guns themselves. The other notion is that once a rifle is sighted in with one type of ammunition it will be sighted in with all other types.

There are a number of reasons why a rifle will not stay sighted in, the biggest of which is that most guns are made of both wood and metal. The metal parts usually do not change the point of impact, unless some screws happen to get loose, but wood does. Wood is a porous substance; it shrinks, expands, twists, and turns with changing moisture in the air. To a great many shooters it does not seem logical that the "handle" of a gun would have anything to do with how it shoots. All they can think of is the rigid relationship between the sights and the barrel and action. But the relationship of stock to metal is a subtle one, one that is nearly always changing, however slightly.

Let me give you an example. About ten years ago I loaned a very accurate .308 to a friend who wanted to go antelope hunting. It hadn't been sighted in since the previous season, and since it had merely reposed in a gun rack, we both assumed it was "on." He got a shot at a standing buck at 150 yards and missed completely. When we tried the gun by shooting at a small rock on a hill, the bullet struck about *two feet to the left* at 150 yards. Examination showed that the stock had warped in the fore-end; when tension was relieved, the rifle shot to nearly the same spot it had the year before without any sight adjustment. This is an extreme example. The rifle was a 99 Savage, and the fore-end must have been putting considerable pressure on the barrel in order to change the impact that much. Most of the time impact change from wood warpage will not be much, but it can easily be enough to miss (or wound) a deer at 100 yards.

Warping wood is still the number-one reason why rifles change their point of impact from season to season, but there are many others. Oil or solvent getting on the stock and softening the wood, a bent action screw, a loose scope,

a bent scope, a slight nick in the muzzle—all of these can affect both the point of impact and accuracy. Just taking the stock off a bolt-action gun and then replacing it will very often change the point of impact a few inches; very rarely is the tension on the screws exactly the same once they are screwed down again.

OK, so you accept the fact that sighting in is not a permanent thing. You check your rifle out. All screws, both in stock and scope mount, are tight. The stock is not bearing overly hard on any portion of the barrel. The eyepiece of the scope is screwed down correctly, the set-ring is locked. You have the correct ammo and the barrel is clean. Let's sight it in.

The first step is to get the barrel and sights pointing somewhere together. If the rifle is a bolt-action or single-shot, where you can look through the barrel from the breech, everything is relatively easy. The simplest way to bore-sight (align scope and barrel visually) with these rifles is to clamp them in a padded vise and adjust the bore so that when you look through it some obvious object can be seen. Then adjust the sights until they are on the same object. If you don't have a vise, you can improvise a rest with a rolled-up jacket or a cardboard box with notches cut in two opposite sides. In any case, you can get the barrel and sights pointing in the same direction.

If your gun is a lever, pump, or semiauto, there are two options. You can get it collimated by a gunsmith (he'll use a little device that attaches to the end of the barrel) or you can set up a target at short range for the initial alignment. About 25 yards is the most popular. Even if your rifle is way off, it will still print somewhere on a two-by-two-foot target at that range. Shoot from a rest of some sort, and adjust the sights until the bullets strike where you are aiming.

None of these methods is exact; your gun still isn't necessarily sighted in. It might be, but more likely it is off a few inches at 100 yards, the traditional sight-in range. I have sighted in rifles hundreds of times, and only twice in my recollection have I had the bullets strike exactly where I wanted them to after bore-sighting, collimation, or 25-yard sight-in. So you either avail yourself of a shooting range in your neighborhood or find a safe open area to shoot in, with an adequate backstop. If you are setting up your own target, a cardboard box is handy; simply tack the target to it, weight the box with a chunk of wood (rocks can cause ricochets) to keep it upright, and pace off 100 steps (or measure 100 yards if you are of a precise turn of mind). Fire three shots at the target over some sort of rest, such as a rolled-up jacket, from prone or over the hood of a car if you don't have a bench, making sure that you place the fore-end of the rifle on the rest and not the barrel. Some shooters prefer to put their hand between the rest and the rifle. In any case, squeeze those shots off as carefully as possible; then examine the target. If the initial alignment was carefully done, you should be somewhere on a 2-by-2-foot target. The three shots should be reasonably close together; some guns put the first shot from a clean barrel to a different spot than from a fouled one. If this appears to be the case, you should go back and fire at least one more shot to make sure of the initial point of impact. I have found that accurate rifles that have had as much of the solvent rubbed out of the barrel as possible very often shoot the first shot from a clean bore to the same place as from a dirty barrel. If your rifle is reliable in this respect, it is a good thing. If necessity demands that you clean your barrel in the woods, it won't be necessary to fire a fouling shot to be accurate. This is an individual thing with guns, however, and you must test your own.

Now, if you are sure of where the gun is shooting, you measure in inches how far the center of your group is from the bull's-eye, then turn the dials of the scope the number of clicks (which vary from scope to scope—in hunting scopes, increments are from ¼ to 1 inch in value) needed to move impact that far. After you've turned the dials, you might tap them with an empty cartridge case, as sometimes the adjustments don't "take." In recent years I have found scopes to be more reliable in adjustment than those of five or more years ago, but it is still a good idea to tap the dials. Wait until the barrel is cool (rifles will often shoot to different places from a hot barrel than they will from a cool one, and in most hunting you'll be shooting through a cool barrel), and fire another three-shot group. You should now be somewhere close to where you want to be on the target. If not, only minor adjustments should be necessary.

If you are using iron sights, the procedure is the same as with the scope, except you adjust differently, at least with open sights. The easiest rule of thumb is to move the rear sight in the direction that you want the bullet's impact to go; usually the rear sight is the adjustable one. If you want the rifle to shoot higher, move the rear sight higher. If you want it to shoot more to the left, move the rear sight to the left. Receiver sights can either be adjustable by means of simple set screws or they might have click adjustments as with scopes. In either case, the same rules hold true.

One typical mistake that many hunters make is to sight "dead-on" at 100 yards. Even with the flattest-shooting calibers, your bullet will soon drop enough below point of aim to interfere with shot placement. A .270 130-grain bullet, for example, will be close to a foot low at 300 yards with this sight-in. A better idea is to sight in so that the bullets strike slightly high at 100 yards; for big-game hunting 3 inches is not too much, and it is the best sight-in system for long-range hunting. With this sighting the same .270 bullet will still be about 3 inches up at 200 yards, will strike "right on" at 275, and will not drop 3 inches below point of aim until it gets out around 340 yards. It will not be a foot low until it reaches 400 yards. Thus you have added about 100 yards to the useful range of your gun. For most shooting, which does not involve range over 250 yards, 2 inches high is enough. Most rifles in the 2,700+ muzzle velocity range will then be on at about 200 yards, a few inches low at 250. Very fast varmint guns can be sighted in 1 inch high and still be close enough to "on" for even small targets out to 250–300 yards. For small-game hunting with .22s, a 60-yard sight-in is about right; the bullet will strike about 1 inch high at 30 yards and 1 inch low at 75, with high-velocity long-rifle ammo.

So your rifle is now sighted in. It is your job to practice with it until you know its trajectory at the ranges you'll be shooting at. For this you should select one load and one load only for a given sight-in, especially if you are going to be shooting at longer ranges. Because of the barrel's vibrations, different loads, even of the same bullet weight, will often shoot to different points of impact. In spite of advertising, not all loads with the 150-grain bullet, say, in the .30-06 will have the same velocity. Bullet shape will be slightly different. This difference usually isn't enough to cause misses on big game at 100 yards, but it can cause a misplaced shot at 200. It *can* cause misses at longer ranges or with smaller game. Conversely, not all loads will shoot to different places, but you can never be sure without testing.

—J.B.

A Target You Can Set Your Sights On . . .
Literally

The Squaresighter target from Universal is square rather than round. The lateral and horizontal centers of the target are graduated, much like the cross hairs on heavy artillery sighting devices. With this system it's easy to determine sight adjustments once you establish an optimum point of impact.

Another plus with this target: its blue, gray, and orange color format better defines the point of aim and adds to the ease of sight adjustment. Price: 10 targets, $3.00. Universal Sporting Goods, Inc., 7920 Northwest 76th Avenue, Miami, FL 33166.

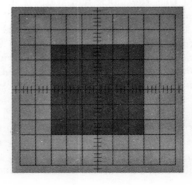

"You mean there's a Senator for all this?"
—Gary Snyder, on a mountaintop from which he
could see 100 miles in all directions

321

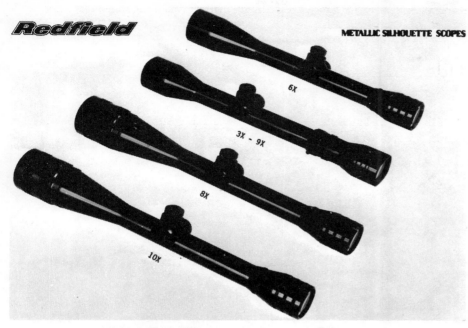

METALLIC SILHOUETTE SCOPES

6X

3X - 9X

8X

10X

Redfield Target Front Sights

There are two versions of the Redfield target international front sight: small-bore and big-bore. The small-bore is the larger of the two (the big-bore is of lightweight alloy to resist recoil loosening), and both conform to international specifications. Both cost $27.00. Redfield, 5800 East Jewell Avenue, Denver, CO 80222.   —J.B.

3200 Target Scope

For rim and centerfire rifles this scope provides exceptionally clear optics, so you can read wind and mirage and see exactly where the reticle is on the target. The ¼ minute-of-angle adjustments are accurate to plus or minus ¹/₃₂ moa with each click. This scope comes standard with sunshade, lens caps, ring mounts, and a styrene carrying case. Available in 12x, 16x, 20x, and 24x, with three types of reticles, including an optional ⅛-inch dot for a few bucks extra. Price: $244.90. Redfield, 5800 East Jewell Avenue, Denver, CO 80222.

Redfield MS for Big-Bore Competition

The Redfield MS is specifically designed for metallic silhouette competition shooting. Accuracy to .01 minute of angle is claimed over its 200- to 500-meter adjustment range. The fixed-power models provide 12 moa adjustments in one revolution of the finger knob, allowing a shooter to go from the chicken silhouette, through the javelina and turkey, to the sheep with less than 360-degree rotation. Thus, you don't have to keep track of how many times you've turned the knob when setting.

Windage and elevation adjustments are standard on all models, and you have a choice of 4-plex or dot reticles. Available in 6x, 8x, 10x, 12x, and 3x–9x variable, with Accu-Range. The 3x–9x scope sounds great for varmint shooting as well. Prices: 6x 4-plex, $109.00; 3x–9x variable, with Accu-Range and dot reticle, $202.00. Redfield, 5800 East Jewell Avenue, Denver, CO 80222.

LYMAN 20XLWBR Scope

Lyman LWBR: Receiver-mounted Target Scope

Internal adjustments, receiver mounting, light weight, and Lyman quality all make the LWBR (lightweight benchrest) scope a great bargain at $189.95 for either 20x or 25x. Weight is 15¼ ounces. Available with either ¼- or ⅛-inch click. Lyman Products for Shooters, Route 147, Middlefield, CT 06455.   —J.B.

Lyman Super-Targetspot and Three-Point Mount

For the shooter who wants a conventional target scope, this is the classic. In 10, 12, 15, 20, 25, and 30 power, it's 24 inches long and weighs 25 ounces. Comes with Lyman three-point rear mount and front mount. Price: $204.95. Mounts are available separately for $30.00 and $15.00 for the rear and front respectively. Case is available for $29.95. Lyman Products for Shooters, Route 147, Middlefield, CT 06455.   —J.B.

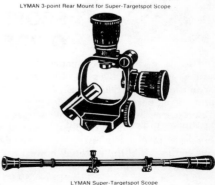

LYMAN 3-point Rear Mount for Super-Targetspot Scope

LYMAN Super-Targetspot Scope

TARGET RIFLE SIGHTS

Iron sights are all that are allowed at many matches, which means receiver sights. Target model receiver sights are more precise but necessarily more fragile and bulky than hunting sights. They cost more, too—often as much as scopes for hunting rifles. The big factor is that they often will be used at various ranges, and the adjustments must be precise, with no play or backlash. Front sights are often built to include a small spirit level to prevent canting the rifle, which is very important at longer ranges. An odd thing about iron sights for target rifles is that small-bore sights are larger and bulkier than big-bore sights, as the big-bore sight must be light in order to "ride" with the recoil of centerfire rounds. If a sight is too heavy, the repeated battering of a day's match can shear the mounting screws.

There are two types of target scopes available, the traditional receiver-and-barrel mounted type and the new receiver-only mounted scopes, which mount just like hunting scopes. There are both externally adjustable scopes, which require adjustable mounts and internally adjustable scopes of the traditional type. All the new receiver-mounted scopes are internally adjustable. The receiver-mounted scopes are lighter and easier (and cheaper) to mount and don't interfere with barrel vibrations or tension, so look for them to become more and more popular. They have practically taken over the benchrest game.
—J.B.

On the hunt... accuracy insurance

On the range saves time & ammo

Exclusive expandable arbors for .22 to .45 calibers

Check scope alignment with instant reminder "Zero-in" Graph.

BUSHNELL BORESIGHTERS

Bushnell makes two good boresighters (collimators). The smaller and lower-priced of the two is the Truscope, which can fit in your pocket. It comes with one expandable arbor (.243 to .308), and there are two other arbors available to cover .22 up to .45 caliber rifles. Price of the Truscope is $24.95; the arbors run $5.95.

Their other boresighter is the Professional model. It has the same range of arbors, though none are included. It is more exact, but larger and heavier. Prices: $32.95; arbors are $5.95 each or all three for $16.50. Bushnell Optical Co., 2828 East Foothill Boulevard, Pasadena, CA 91107.
—J.B.

TASCO SCOPE GUIDE

This is a simple collimator that fits scopes with objectives of 15, 20, and 32mm in rimfire style and 20, 32, and 40 mm in big-bore style. It is designed for Tasco scopes but works on other scopes of like size. It is made of plastic, and the problems involved in using it are mainly due to the flex of the material; however, it will get you on target at 100 yards if your target is at least 2 by 2 feet. Price: $9.95. Tasco Sales, Inc., 1075 Northwest 71st Street, Miami, FL 33138.
—J.B.

"Shooting Stick" Field Rifle Rest

This gadget ensures accuracy for scope shooters and for all still hunting—varmints, fox, deer, gophers, turkey, woodchuck, etc. A handy hunting aid where precise bullet placement is essential. Easy to carry, fully adjustable to 26 inches. Price $19.95. Hoppe's Penguin Industries, Inc., P.O. Box 97, Parkesburg, PA 19365.

Hoppe's Rest Bags and Benchrest

Hoppe's rest bags are ready to fill; the rear is grooved for the butt stock, and the front is slightly concave and built to fit Hoppe's tripod-type rest. This rest is equipped with screw-type anchors to attach it to wooden benches; these anchors are also reattachable for use on metal or concrete. The bags are available in leather or vinyl. Prices: $5.95 for the front, $9.95 and $10.95 for the rear; the rest is $34.95. Hoppe's, Penguin Industries, Inc., P.O. Box 97, Parkesburg, PA 19365. —J.B.

MATS AND PADS FOR RIFLE COMPETITION

If you're serious about .22 or big-bore competition shooting, you'll want shooting mats and kneeling pads for the comfort and stability they afford.

The Ehmke Manufacturing Company makes a 72-by-30-inch mat for prone shooting. It is padded with polyester foam and made of army duck canvas. The mat includes two extendable wings and a nonslip rubber pad for an elbow rest. Price: $21.50.

Their kneeling pad measures 10 by 6 inches. It is olive drab army duck and is treated for water and mildew resistance. Price: $3.75. Ehmke Manufacturing Company, Belfield Avenue and Wister Street, Philadelphia, PA 19144.

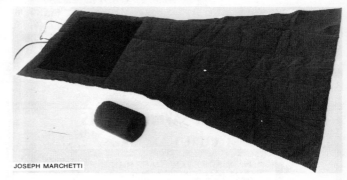

JOSEPH MARCHETTI

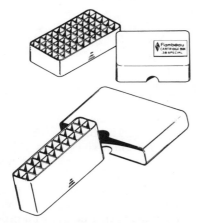

Cartridge Cases for Clean, Well-formed Shells

These are polyethylene cases with individual shell compartments and tight-fitting tops. They keep shells separated and clean and bullets perfectly formed. They also serve as a receptacle for spent casings that are due for reloading. Capacity and dimensions vary with shells, but they hold from twenty to fifty rounds each. Specify caliber and type of arm (ex/.38 cal. pistol). Price: 88 cents. Cabela's, 812 13th Avenue, Sidney, NE 69162.

The Sand Bagger Rifle Rest

This gun rest is designed to eliminate the need for a shooting bench or rifle range when sighting in your rifle. It will provide the stability required to sight in your rifle accurately from the hood or trunk of your car.

The Sand Bagger is fully adjustable both vertically and horizontally. It is also collapsible, for ease of carrying and storing. It is made of durable aluminum alloy and is strong enough to withstand the repeated concussion of even the big magnum caliber rifles. The tripod tips and front and rear rest forks are coated with a special nonslip plastic that won't scratch your car or the stock of your rifle. Price: $44.95. Progressive Products, P.O. Box 41, Holem, WI 54636. —F.S.

ADAPTER CARTRIDGE CONVERTS HIGH-POWER RIFLES TO PLINKERS

If the cost of .222 shells puts brakes on your plinking pastimes, this device will convert a .222 Remington chamber so that it will accept a .22 long-rifle. The gadget is essentially an extension of the bolt head and firing pin.

Other conversions available:

.22 LR in .220 Swift
.22 LR in .221 Fireball
.22 LR in .223
.22 LR in .22-250
.22 WMR in .222 Remington

.22 WMR in .22-250
.30 M-1 Carbine in .30-06
.30 M-1 Carbine in .30-.30
.30 M-1 Carbine in .308

Price: $11.95 each. Burnham Bros., P.O. Box 100A, Marble Falls, TX 78654.

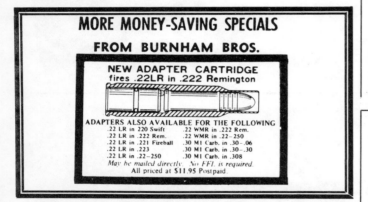

MORE MONEY-SAVING SPECIALS FROM BURNHAM BROS.

NEW ADAPTER CARTRIDGE
fires .22LR in .222 Remington

ADAPTERS ALSO AVAILABLE FOR THE FOLLOWING
.22 LR in 220 Swift   .22 WMR in .222 Rem.
.22 LR in .222 Rem.   .22 WMR in .22-250
.22 LR in .221 Fireball   .30 M1 Carb. in .30-.06
.22 LR in .223   .30 M1 Carb. in .30-.30
.22 LR in .22-250   .30 M1 Carb. in .308
May be mailed directly. No FFL is required.
All priced at $11.95 Postpaid.

KOLPIN MANUFACTURING, INC.

SANDBAG RIFLE RESTS

If you're a shotgun reloader, save your old shot bags. Filled with sand, they make a good sturdy rest on the target range. You can also buy contoured rifle rests that have a flat bottom and a special fill funnel, which makes loading and emptying sand easy. Price: One-piece rest, $5.00; two-piece rest, $8.50. Kolpin Manufacturing, Inc., P.O. Box 231, Berlin, WI 54923.

RIFLE TARGET SHOOTING: FOR MORE INFORMATION

International Benchrest Shooters
R. D. 1, Robinson Road
Mohawk, NY 13407
Mrs. James Stekl, Receiving Secretary

National Benchrest Shooters Association
607 West Line Street
Minerva, OH 44657
Bernice McMullen, Secretary—Treasurer

National Board for the Promotion of Rifle Practice
Forrestal Building, (West) Room 1E053
Washington, DC 20314
Col. Jack R. Rollinger, Executive Office

National Rifle Association of America
1600 Rhode Island Avenue, Northwest
Washington, DC 20036
Maj. Gen. Maxwell Rich, Executive Vice-president

DAISY AIR GUNS

Daisy, the most famous American name in BB guns, has something for just about everyone. The best known, however, is 1105, the bottom-line BB gun, which costs $13.95 (inflation hits everywhere—my first Daisy was under five bucks!) but is still a great value. This is a simple, spring-loaded air gun that not only can teach the rudiments of marksmanship at a reasonable price but will develop strong biceps in young shooters, since the spring takes just a little bit of effort to cock. The sights are a fixed open rear and a post front. These will also teach the youngster the value of Dad's toolbox the day he goes looking for a file and a pair of pliers to "adjust" his sights. Its 350-shot magazine is great. It's inaccurate beyond 30 feet, and even that range is doubtful with the smooth bore and irregular BB ammo, but it will take just about any kind of abuse. I know; I had two of them as a youth, and the only reason the first one died is that it got run over by a truck. We even used to stuff Kleenex down the bore for wadding, then some sand, and shoot houseflies out of the air. Simply a wonderful gun.

Daisy has an array of arms ranging from the 1105 up to the Daisy/FWB target rifle and pistol, both of which retail in the $300.00 range. Write to them at Daisy, P.O. Box 220, Rogers, AR 72756.

—J.B.

"Nocturnal coon-hunts frequently result disastrously to other animals [as] a party of hunters will return with a varied bag . . . including skunk, woodchuck, cat, etc."
—Charles Hallock, 1877

325

PLINKING ARMS: FUN GUNS

Plinking is a form of target shooting where there are no rules and very rarely bull's-eyes. Plinking is Saturday-afternoon shooting at tin cans or shooting at an indoor range with BB guns. Although competition can result, it is informal and without pressure. There are no gold medals awarded for the best plinker on the block.

Any gun can be used to plink, but something like a .460 Weatherby is not only not very much fun for kids to shoot (and kids are at least the excuse for 90 percent of the plinking in the world) but kind of expensive at over a buck a shot. Plinking guns are thought of as inexpensive guns, not necessarily accurate, that use inexpensive ammunition. Guns favored for plinking include .22s and CO_2 and air guns. There are even forms of shotgun plinking, with .22 shotshells being used. Other plinking guns might include your favorite deer rifle used with cast-bullet handloads (which cost about as much to make as .22 shells cost to buy) or handguns using wax or plastic bullets.

Once you get down to it, the bottom line is where plinking is at. The .22s are fairly inexpensive at about 2 cents a shot. CO_2 guns vary, but with an average of fifty shots from a 25-cent carbon dioxide cylinder and 250 pellets running about $1.00, you're getting by for under a penny a shot. BB guns are the cheapest of all in air-rifle formation, as power doesn't cost you anything but arm exercise, and BBs can be had for about 1/10 of a cent apiece. Extremely reasonable.

The only thing hindering plinking and its fun is the increasing difficulty of finding a place to plink. And it's increasingly difficult to get even air-gun ammo in certain areas because of restrictive gun laws. I can't tell you how I felt when I moved from Montana to Minneapolis at the age of twelve and found that I couldn't buy BBs even with a note from my father. It seems that you must be eighteen to buy even air-gun ammo in most states. This is probably a sound law in many urban areas where vandalism is a problem, but it is an infinitely sad thing to find our government looking over the shoulders of little kids with their first Daisy.

—J.B.

Armies with Air Rifles

The principle of powering a projectile by compressed air dates back hundreds of years. Today BB guns and air rifles are associated with indoor target shooting and a kid's first gun, but they were instruments of war in the eighteenth century.

The Austrians found this weapon so effective for close-in fighting that in 1790 they expanded the use of air rifles from four men to a 1,300-man corps. When they used the "silent rifle" against Napoleon's troops, so many men were killed that Napoleon ordered that any man found carrying an air rifle be shot on sight or hanged immediately.

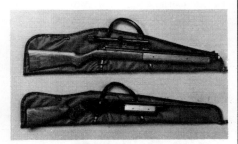

AIR RIFLE CASE

This vinyl gun case comes in 37- and 40-inch lengths, which will accommodate most air rifles. Features include lining, moisture-resistant padding, wraparound handle, and hang-up loop. Prices: unscoped rifle case, 6.95; scoped rifle case, $8.00. Kolpin Manufacturing, Inc., P.O. Box 231, Berlin, WI 54923.

Benjamin Air Rifles

At the age of twelve and in our clique, the word Benjamin was synonomous with Weatherby and Browning today. They were regarded as the hardest-hitting pellet rifles on the market—the ultimate plink—and the squirrels, rabbits, and pheasants in Alley Pond Park soon learned of their pump-up fury.

Benjamins are still guns to be reckoned with. They'll shoot under a ¾-inch group at 25 feet, with 1-inch penetration into soft pine. Approximate muzzle velocity: 750 fps.

These air rifles are available in autofeed BB or single-shot pellet styles, with peep and telescopic sights as accessories. They are chambered for BB, .177-caliber, or .22-caliber ammunition. Price: $62.45. Benjamin Air Rifle Co., 1525 South 8th Street, St. Louis, MO 63104.   —N.S.

Hy-Score Air Guns: Lots of Zip for Match or Field

Air guns have come a long way since Daisy's Red Ryder. Hy-Score's Model 809 M features a break action (which means you break it once and it's ready to fire), a standard firearm feel and weight, a match trigger and peep sight, and a muzzle velocity of 700 fps! It's advertised as a "match or field gun," because the Olympic-style peep sight can be quickly converted to a four-aperture rear sight. Given the speed of the projectile and a 7-grain oval nose pellet, this gun is capable of competition accuracy and killing power for small game at around 100 feet. Price: $109.95.

If you don't mind pumping up an air gun and want real power, the same company makes a lever-action No. 894 that delivers a smashing 775 fps. The rifle comes furnished with a special removable weight, which stabilizes the barrel for greater accuracy, a precision rear click sight and a hooded front sight, and a detachable military-type sling. The receiver will accept a scope mount. Price: $84.95. From your nearest Hy-Score dealer or S. E. Laszlo, 200 Tillary Street, Brooklyn, NY 11201.

Hy-Score makes a wide selection of .22- and .177-caliber rifles and pistols, ranging in cost and quality from a $4.95 junior pellet air pistol to a $200.00 Supermatch recoilless target gun used in international and Olympic competition. Hy-Score air guns include models that are powered by

AIR GUN CATALOG

CO_2 gas, by a pump-up lever, and by break action. Several of these guns have a muzzle velocity in excess of 700 fps, which is really zipping along for a pellet gun.

Hy-Score makes pellets in .22 and .177

caliber, and they're available in 7-grain oval penetrating designs and in 8-grain pure lead wadcutters. The entire Hy-Score air gun and implement line is featured in a catalog that you can have for $1.00 from S. E. Laszlo, 200 Tillary Street, Brooklyn, NY 11201.

STEVENS 72 CRACKSHOT .22

These guns were great favorites in the early 1900s. They only cost a few bucks and were reliable arms. The price is now just a little bit higher—$69.50—but the

reliability and the style are still there. Falling-block, octagonal barrel, case-hardened frame, and a walnut stock with oil finish. Weighing only 4½ pounds and only 37

inches long, this is a super plinking rifle. Savage Arms, Springdale Road, Westfield, MA 01085.   —J.B.

ROSSI GALLERY MODEL .22

This is styled after the Winchester pump .22 that used to grace shooting galleries and farmhouse doors. It holds twenty short, sixteen long, and thirteen

long-rifle shells and shoots 'em as fast as you can shuck the action. Available in blue or chrome, in carbine or rifle (16¼- and 23-inch barrels, respectively), for either

$110.00 or $120.00, the higher price for chrome. Weighs about 5½ pounds. The Garcia Corporation, 329 Alfred Avenue, Teaneck, NJ 07666.   —J.B.

Smith & Wesson Model 80 BB Rifle

This really isn't a rifle, as the barrel is smoothbored; it's a semiauto CO_2 gun, with a fifty-shot spring-forced magazine. Tang safety, grooved for .22 scope mounts. Weight 3¼ pounds. Price: $37.50. Smith & Wesson Co., 2100 Roosevelt Avenue, Springfield, MA 01101.   —J.B.

"Better to hunt in fields, for health unbought,
Than fee the doctor for a nauseous draught."
—John Dryden

327

M-19A ANNIHILATOR: A CHILDHOOD FANTASY COME TRUE

I am truly glad that this gun wasn't around when I was a kid. Well, maybe the neighborhood would have survived the arrival of a BB machine gun, but more likely it would have been terrorized.

Perhaps I am being overcritical of my childhood tendencies, but there is no doubt that the Annihilator is a fantasy gun, a legal machine gun at a low, low price. It has no use for anything except plinking, but it is the *supreme* plinking gun. Imagine, for one moment, standing in front of a row of tin cans; suddenly, you point the deadly black Annihilator in their general direction (there being no sights), press the trigger, and with a sinister sputtering hiss you mow the dreaded Nazi cans down (when I was a kid, gunfights, if they weren't between cops and robbers or cowboys and Indians, were Marines and Nazis), thus saving the day for America and the free world.

The sample of the Annihilator that I have is well built and handles nicely. It would gladden my heart to say that it is perfect, but, alas, it isn't so. The system by which it works—Freon gas used in air conditioners, which is available at automotive stores for about $1.50 a can—doesn't work all that well in weather below 55 degrees or so, as the release of the gas cools the can and lowers the pressure so that nothing happens. In warmer weather it quickly heats up again, aided by hand heat, but on the first day I used it, it took around fifteen minutes for pressure to build up again, the temperature being around 40 degrees. In warmer weather it works fine.

It can also be used with compressed air (not over 60 psi), but this necessitates a tank, which naturally cuts down on portability. Freon is relatively inexpensive, however; one can will last for enough shooting to satisfy most plinkers. It should be pointed out that the Annihilator is a gun to be used only under the supervision of adults, because the Freon, while not dangerous, needs care in handling and requires some strength in applying to the gun. This is not to mention the possible effect on neighborhood dogs and cats that might wander within range of a child-wielded Annihilator. Price: $29.00, and $2.00 for postage and handling. LARC International, P.O. Box 340007, Coral Gables, FL 33134. You must send a signed statement that you are over eighteen.
—J.B.

Quick Load: Clip for Tube-Magazine .22s

Sometimes it seems as though tube-magazine .22s shoot forever, especially at plinking targets when filled with .22 shorts. Thing is, they seem to take forever to load, too, and all too often shells end up on the ground instead of in the magazine. The Quick Load is a solution to this problem, at least in part. It consists of nine plastic tubes of about ¼-inch inside diameter, which hold fourteen long-rifle or twenty shorts and which all can be fitted inside a 1½-inch diameter plastic tube. Thus you can preload at home (lightning arithmetic gives me 126 long-rifle rounds if all the tubes are loaded) and fast-load in the field. Just take the spring-loaded plunger out of the magazine, hold a Quick Load over the end of the magazine, and presto—fourteen more shells into your favorite .22. The large tube, which carries all the small tubes, also has a plastic belt loop, so you can supposedly carry it afield. I say supposedly; it doesn't look to be stout enough to carry my huntin' ammo on a serious hunt, but for plinking it looks to be fine. Price: $7.45 for the set. Eastern Associates, 149 East Javelin, Carson, CA 90745.
—J.B.

Crosman Model 70 Bolt CO₂ Rifle

This is built to look and feel like a centerfire bolt-action big-game rifle, and it does a reasonably good job of it. The sample I have came one afternoon, and I handed it to a friend, saying, "Take a look at my new oh-six." He seemed suspicious, because it's pretty light (about 5 pounds), and so he looked at the muzzle, which is recessed and is apparently about .30 caliber. I had to tell him it was a CO₂ gun!

The M-70 is a single-shot, with a hardwood stock that is sized big enough to be comfortable for most teenage and adult shooters. It is also grooved for .22-type scopes. The only not-so-real spot is the trigger, which on my sample anyway is rough and creepy and heavier than the advertised 4½ pounds. The gun is very accurate, however, especially since the .177 pellets I got ahold of weren't the most uniform in the world and ran anywhere from 7 to 8 grains in weight, with unsquare skirts. After a fifty-shot period, where the barrel seemed to need breaking in, the M-70 shot very respectably, averaging groups of under ½ inch at 30 feet. Most were just one ragged hole. As a matter of fact, on a dare I shot a tack off the target. Part of the time a Weaver 4x .22 scope was used, and during the other part iron sights were used. Actually, they are plastic and much better than those found on many other CO₂ guns, being both adjustable for windage and elevation (precisely adjustable). The rear is a semibuckhorn and the front a big post.

This would be an excellent gun for either the younger shooter who is getting started or an adult who wishes to practice up before game season with a gun resembling his deer rifle. It is safe to shoot inside. Muzzle velocity is advertised at 600 fps, which is powerful enough to take some small game and pests out to 50 feet or so. Price: $49.95. Crosman Arms Co., 980 Turk Hill Road, Fairport, NY 14450.

—J.B.

MARKSMAN REPEATER AIR PISTOLS

MARKSMAN AIR PISTOL

This is a solid, inexpensive ($12.00) air pistol, patterned after the Colt 1911 .45, that will teach the rudiments of handgun handling. While it isn't very accurate (irregular BB ammunition in a smoothbore seldom is), it will still hit a tin can at 20 feet if it's held and squeezed right. With one of Marksman's steel BB trap targets, which come in various sizes and styles— some motorized in the manner of shooting galleries—you can shoot the same projectiles over and over again. I know one shooter who kept himself entertained after having a serious heart attack by setting up a Marksman target across his bedroom and plinking away at it during the three months he was laid up. Pellets and darts can be shot with it, too, but must be single-loaded. In repeat fire it can hold up to twenty BBs. A fun gun. Marksman Products, 2133 Dominguez Street, Torrance, CA 90509.

—J.B.

Semiautomatic Pellet Rifles

If you're tired of hand-loading each pellet, the Precise/Minuteman Mark II pellet rifle accepts a preloaded magazine of twenty-five pellets. Design features include a break action, modified Monte Carlo butt stock, a Bavarian target cheekpiece, a thumb rest, and a pistol grip. It also has a grooved receiver for a scope.

The velocity of this gun is rated at 650 fps with .177-caliber pellets, and incidentally, it looks like it came right out of a James Bond movie. Prices: $100.00 for gun; 60 cents per box of four pellet tubes. Precise Imports, 3 Chestnut Street, Suffern, NY 10901.

CROSMAN SUPER BBs

These are uniform BBs, a little more accurate than the average. Like other BBs, they are copper-plated steel. Prices run from 50 cents for 350 to $4.25 for 5,000. Crosman Arms Co., 980 Turk Hill Road, Fairport, NY 14450.

—J.B.

The Super Slingshot, or if Huck Finn Had Had One, Hannibal Would Have Been Leveled

WILLIAM CHENEY

The Wrist Rocket slingshot offers some revolutionary developments in the time-honored beany shooter. Strong, surgical rubber tubing has greater recovery than common rubber banding, and the prongs are springy as well. The biggest improvement, however, is the wrist cradle, which rests against your forearm as you draw. This steadies the slingshot for accurate aiming and means that less of the rubber's recovery is absorbed by your hand and arm. It hits harder. Another aiming aid lies in the contoured pistol grip. Forked oak branches never shot like these!

A 25-caliber steel ball fired from this slingshot is rated at a velocity of 230 fps, more than enough energy to kill game up to 50 yards. Prices: Wrist Rocket slingshot, $5.50; steel ball ammo, $1.25 for 170; extra rubbers, $1.50. Orvis, Manchester, VT 05254.

"Whether 'tis nobler in the mind to suffer
The slings and arrows of outrageous fortune . . . .?"
—Shakespeare, *Hamlet*

329

WHAM-O
"Since 1948"

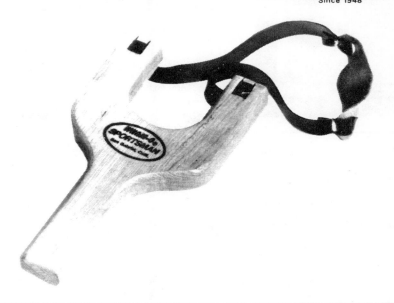

WHAM-O SLINGSHOT

The venerable Wham-O slingshot has been around a long time. For many of us, to discard a forked willow and buy one was a major step in our gradual ascent from peashooters and popguns to big-game rifles.

Wham-Os have changed little over the years, testimony perhaps to their durability. The stock is hardwood, the banding pure rubber, and the pouch leather. The banding is affixed to the stock by way of a simple notching system that makes changeover of worn rubbers quick and easy. The slingshot comes prepackaged with a bunch of steel ball bearings for ammunition and an extra rubber. Prices: $3.50 for the slingshot; $1.50 for an extra set of rubbers. Wham-O Manufacturing Company, 835 East El Monte Street, San Gabriel, CA 91776.

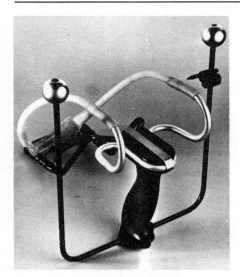

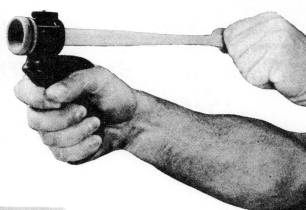

TOURNAMENT SLINGSHOT

Look what they've gone and done to the venerable art of the beany shooter! A forked willow, rubber bands, and the back patch off a pair of Levi's has grown into this Falcon 300 tournament slingshot. Features include stabilizer weights to steady hand and wrist motion, a molded handle, close-set prongs to cut down on wrist pressure, and, would you believe, an adjustable sighting device. Price: $15.00. Saunders Archery Company, P.O. Box 476, Industrial Site, Columbus, NE 68601.

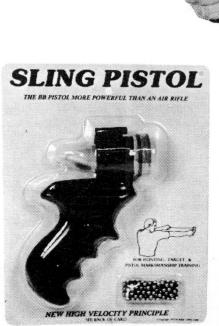

SLING PISTOL

A new twist in an old friend. The sling pistol is a kind of slingshot, but instead of horns, the missile is fired through a hole. Propulsion is provided by way of a latex rubber tube that looks like a baby nipple when it's relaxed. Drop a BB in the nipple pocket, draw it back, and let it fly.

The handle is contoured and molded of ABS plastic, the rubber is replaceable, and the "pistol" has a sight. Manufacturers claim superpower with this gadget, though we can't say because we have not tried it. For the price you can't go wrong. Even if it doesn't work it will make a great conversation piece. Price: $2.39. Cabela's, 812 13th Avenue, Sidney, NE 69162.

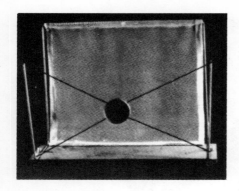

INDOOR/OUTDOOR SLINGSHOT TARGET

The backstop catches pellets, and they fall where they can be retrieved and re-used. The target center is a 3½-inch cup, which spins when it's hit. Price: $15.00. Saunders Archery Company, P.O. Box 476, Industrial Site, Columbus, NE 68601.

For Those Who Want to Be Somebody: How About World Champion Beany Shooter?

The interest in individual competitive sports has climbed to yet another fever-pitch level. There is now a U.S. Open Indoor Slingshot Tournament held each year in conjunction with the U.S. Open Indoor Archery Championships.

Norman Ekdahl, 1st U.S. Open Champion (Pro/Am)

If you'd like to enter or wish to know more about the agonies and ecstasies associated with Pro/Am beany-shooter competition, write Saunders Archery Company, P.O. Box 476, Industrial Site, Columbus, NE 68601.

RUBBER BAND RIFLE

Here's a way to enjoy safe, legal target shooting anywhere. The RBG 100 is a styrene plastic rifle that uses rubber bands for ammunition. There are no darts, BBs, pellets, stones, or other implements of destruction—just rubber bands, the kind we used to zing across the classroom when the teacher wasn't watching.

You load the gun by stretching rubber bands from the barrel end to a trip mechanism that will handle five "bullets"; and the bands are released with each pull of the trigger.

The gun is reasonably accurate up to 20 feet (you can hit a paper cup about four times out of five), and it has a range up to 60 feet. It comes packaged with a cardboard target, instructions, and thirty rubber bands. This is the perfect first gun for kids just out of the cap pistol stage and fun for adults, too. Price: $14.95. AJK Recreational Shooting Products, 7 Wellington Road, Lincoln, RI 02865.

A PRIMER IN SLINGSHOT AMMUNITION

Rocks, in some respects, are the purist and purest way to go. Finding just the right round rock is an exercise comparable to making your own archery tackle, handloading ammunition, or tying flies. They are the least accurate, since you never find a perfectly round rock; hence they are also the most sporting.

BBs are reasonably accurate, but they are so small that they never realize full energy potential. Seven or eight BBs in a slingshot pouch at one time create a shotgun effect, but they're only good at very close ranges.

Marbles are accurate, but penetration is poor. They don't kill much game, but they sure thump it. They're also a bit heavy for target work and require a lot of elevation at medium ranges.

Ball bearings around ⅜ inch in diameter are extremely accurate, and the most professional ammunition of all. They realize full energy potential, they are perfectly round so they don't drift off target, and they have good penetration. They are expensive to buy (around $1.25 for twenty-five).

Buckshot is my all-around favorite, economy, accuracy, and energy taken into consideration. The best way to buy this stuff is via shotgun reloading equipment suppliers. A 5-pound bag of shot costs around $4.00; a twenty-five-pound bag is around $15.00. Don't ask me how many pellets are in each bag, but 25 pounds should last you a lifetime. —N.S.

Backstops

You will also need a good backstop for any range. A backstop for Pellet guns, Fig. 3, using 3/8" plywood, 1/32" sheet steel, wire, sand, and clip-type clothespins. A cardboard box filled tightly with newspapers makes an ideal BB gun backstop, Fig. 4. It is always wise to take the added precaution of hanging a large piece of canvas or a blanket as a backdrop behind the backstop.

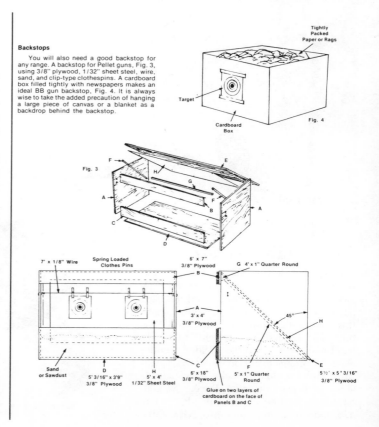

"The mountain sheep are sweeter, / But the valley sheep are fatter;
We therefore deemed it meeter / To carry off the latter."
—Thomas Love Peacock

331

THROWING KNIVES

There is nothing quite so damn foolish as a throwing knife. Even in expert hands they're not all that reliable, and the one unbreakable rule of hand-to-hand combat is "never throw your weapon away."

Still, I must confess to a certain satisfaction with the solid thunk of a thrown knife as it buries deep in wood, and you might find the same to be true, so here are a few guidelines on the knives.

It is always best when a throwing knife is one piece, blade and handle punched out from the same slab of steel. It's OK to have some rawhide or vinyl wrapped around the handle, but when you start getting into slab handles or rattail tangs, the constant rapping will eventually break them off.

Throwing knives should be made of soft steel with a Rockwell Hardness of around 54–56, so they will bend rather than break. If you throw a carbon steel hunting knife, you'll eventually break the point, and it will not be the knife's fault. Hunting knives are not throwing knives or vice versa.

Only the point on a throwing knife need be sharp. If you sharpen the edges, you're asking for a cut at some point in your throwing career.

If you're going to have more than one throwing knife, buy them all alike. Different-sized knives have a different balance, and consequently they must be thrown differently to stick.

One source of throwing knives that I can recommend is Coast Cutlery, 1109 Northwest Glisan Street, Portland, OR 97209. They make a pretty little 3-ounce throwing knife, with dipped vinyl on the handle. It comes complete with a sheath for $3.95.

—N.S.

NEVER-FAIL-TO-STICK THROWING KNIFE

If you can't master the art of throwing a conventional knife, this is the blade for you. It is an eight-sided star that looks like a large, sharp rowel from a spur. Set it to whirling in the air, and it has to stick in whatever it hits. Price: 97 cents. Herter's, Inc., Route 2, Mitchell, SD 57301.

WHY HANDLOAD?
by Jon R. Sundra

When anyone writes about getting started in handloading, the emphasis is usually on the economics involved. We're told, for example, that it takes X number of dollars for a box of factory .30-06 cartridges, but that we can reload those same twenty cases for only Y number of dollars, thus saving what amounts to a good hunk of change.

Fact is, though, that I've never met anyone who actually started handloading because he wanted to save money. Nor have I ever known anyone to actually save money once he started. The guy who starts rolling his own soon finds that although he's realizing a per shot saving of as much as 40 percent, he's shooting five times as much as he used to!

One could say, then, that the net result of handloading is that it's more—not less—expensive than shooting factory ammo.

The kicker, of course, is the fun derived. How does one place a value on the enjoyment and satisfaction derived from those hours spent at the loading and shooting bench? One can't.

To the shooter who has enough interest in firearms to even contemplate handloading in the first place, the hobby itself acts as a sort of catalyst. By that I mean that once one gets started, handloading literally forces one to learn such things as trajectories, bullet shape and mass, burning rates, relative accuracy. . . . Things once considered ethereal, if not downright boring, suddenly hold a practical interest and fascination for the reloader.

If I had to throw out a figure, I'd venture to say that the average handloader is at least three times as knowledgeable about ballistics and firearms as the nonhandloader. Though knowledge is not what starts one to load his own ammo, it's something that just naturally happens. In short, we learn in spite of ourselves.

The other and equally important half of handloading is that is provides options—thousands of them. The shooter who uses factory ammo has but a few. By options I mean the right combination of case, powder, and bullet to provide optimum accuracy in a given rifle or handgun. For every firearm—handgun, long gun, even shotguns—there are combinations that group or pattern better than others.

The man shooting factory ammo must be satisfied with whatever accuracy he gets. The only options open to him are to try various brands of ammunition to see which gives him the best accuracy. But once he becomes interested enough in his gun's performance to actually try various ammo brands, chances are he's well on his way to becoming a handloader. I say that because in experimenting with more than one make of ammunition in a given bullet weight, our shooter is going to see that there are differences in accuracy. Brand X may not only group tighter than brand Y, but chances are that point of impact (assuming the same sight setting) is also going to be different. When that happens and he starts to reason why, the whole concept of handloading (aside from the fun and satisfaction) becomes clear: each firearm is unique, and only as a handloader can one hope to extract its full potential.

Jon Sundra is a noted authority on shooting. He is hunting editor of *Shooting Times Magazine*, field editor of *Hunting* magazine, technical editor of *Rifle Magazine*, and East Coast editor of *Shooting Industry Magazine*.

LOADING MANUALS

The loading manual is to the handloader what the road map is to the traveler or the repair manual to the mechanic. The experienced reloader, mechanic, or traveler can often do without the help, but every so often he needs it. The beginner gets lost without it.

Loading manuals that concern rifle and handgun ammunition include information on specific types of powders (given in grains, an avoirdupois measure, *not* in grains of powder) matched with specific bullet weights. The muzzle velocity of each combination is listed. This is bare information; many manuals go far beyond it and give barrel length of the test weapon, case make, primer make, pressure, bullet type, depth of bullet seating, down-range velocity and energy, trajectory, temperature at the time of testing, and the color of the technician's hair. In a way, this information is useful; in some ways it is not. Shotgun manuals tread on even thinner ice. Instead of being a simple combination of bullet, case, powder, and primer, the shotshell is a complex sort of thing, with a small difference in components often drastically changing pressure and performance. Often something such as a type of wad, which a shooter wants to use simply because it is available or cheap, is not included in specific shotgun data, and the information that can be inferred is at best an approximation.

So what does a manual tell us? In absolute terms, not much. It is only a guide, as there to too many variables involved ever to give loading data the blessing of absolute conviction. In truth, most rifle-handgun manuals just tell us that a certain combination of components did a certain thing in a certain gun on a certain day. They don't tell us anything, except in a general way, about what will happen when we put X powder into Y case behind Z bullet and fire it in *our* gun. As a matter of fact, each manual will tell you different things, as each test will produce slightly different results, even if the combination of gun and load are identical. This confuses and worries the aspiring reloader to no end, as do warnings listed by manufacturers on their products that go something like this: "We have no control over how this will be used, so we can't guarantee a damn thing." The variations between individual guns and components are also why every loading manual you pick up will advise you not to start with the maximum load listed but to reduce it by 5 to 10 percent. Understandably, this also worries the novice.

This confusion and worry on the part of the beginner is a good thing. If it doesn't scare him off completely, it makes him very careful. He starts his loads out low, looks carefully for signs of rising pressure, and always consults his manual when using a new component. I have met only one dangerous reloader in my life, and nobody would shoot with him. He always took the top load in the book and worked up, and he was always trying to make a .30-06 out of a .30-30. It

was a tribute to today's sporting arms that he'd never been seriously injured.

He was the exception. The rest of us are careful, just as we are reasonably careful when we cross the street. I have fired many thousands of rounds of reloaded ammo in my guns and have yet to come close to anything resembling an accident. The reason that I and millions of other reloaders can make this statement is that we *are* careful, and we use the guides that are available to us.

I have on my shelf copies of all recently published American loading manuals and some that are not so recent. I know deep down in my heart that they are not all necessary to my sport, but each has some bit of information, something that sets it apart from the others, that makes is useful to me. They also provide a cross check of sorts. For the beginner such an array is unnecessary. One good manual will give him all the information he needs to start loading, and when he feels the need for another manual, he will get it. As a matter of fact, the loading manual should be the first thing the aspiring loader buys, before presses, scales,

From an old gun catalog

Directions for the Use of Reloading Tools.

To Remove the Exploded Cap.—Place the head of the shell in the base, and force the cap out with the punch.

To Open the Mouth of Crimped Shells.—Press the shell in the short barrel (at the large end), place it on the base with the head in the countersink, and push in the short plunger, using sufficient force to straighten the edge of the shell.

To Re-Cap the Shells.—Place the shell in the hole on one side of the mould (with the head inside), place the cap in the orifice of the head, and press it home by the handles of the mould.

To Cast the Bullets.—Use one ounce of tin to one pound of lead. Keep the moulds tightly closed when running the metal, as otherwise the bullet will be cast too large and will not enter the shell.

To Charge the Shell.—Press in the reloader (at the large end); place it on the base with the head in the countersink; put in powder with the measure, *using no more than one measure full*; place the bullet in the reloader, butt down, and drive it home with the plunger until the shoulder of the plunger strikes the reloader (using the mallet or hand).

To Crimp the Shells Loaded with Conical Bullets.—Place the head of the cartridge in the countersink in the base, and drive the crimper over it until the end of the crimper meets the base.

N.B.—The groove in conical bullets must be perfectly filled with tallow before loading.

The cartridges loaded with round balls must be greased by dropping one drop of melted beef tallow into the shell above the ball.

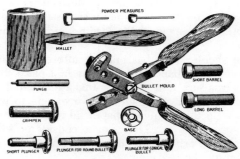

NEW MODEL RELOADING TOOLS.

For Reloading Smith & Wesson Cartridges.   For Reloading the Winchester .32, .38 and .44. Winchester Reloading Sets are recommended.

Cartridge Shells can be reloaded a number of times with perfect safety, making a great saving in the cost of ammunition.

SPEER RELOADING MANUAL NO. NINE

components, or anything else. A good one—and by that I mean one that tells you the basics of loading as well as giving data—is the best investment a reloader can make. Above all the others I'd recommend the manuals of the three major custom bullet firms: Speer, Sierra, and Hornady. They give information on techniques and have fairly complete data. Which one you select may hinge on what shell you plan to load for. The .358 Winchester round, for instance, can be found in the Sierra and Hornady books, but not the most recent Speer. The .357 auto mag may only be found in the Speer manual. For shotgun loading the most complete manual is the Lyman Shotshell Handbook. It is the very best; I cannot recommend a loading manual more highly.

After you get your first manual, read it carefully and abide by the limitations both suggested and imposed by it until you are more experienced. If you approach reloading with care and a good manual, you will be rewarded by fine ammo and an intriguing sport. You will also never be in any more danger than when you are watering your lawn.

—J.B.

Speer was the first custom bullet manufacturer to bring out a comprehensive reloading manual. The Speer Manual No. 1 was published in 1954; since then eight others have come along to keep pace with developments in powders and cartridges. Each has had loading data and commentary on a great variety of the more popular centerfire cartridges, both standard and wildcat, along with articles written by top gun authorities and basic instruction in reloading techniques. The No. 9 manual is the most up-to-date of them all. It features an article on benchrest loading techniques (some of which are useful to all reloaders interested in any degree of accuracy) and a new testing of actual factory cartridge velocities. This list has been in the Speer manuals for quite a while now and is one of the main reasons that the factories have started listing the velocities of their cartridges from hunting-length barrels, instead of the long test barrels which give high, unrealistic velocities. For instance, the 7mm Remington magnum was originally listed as driving 175- and 150-grain bullets at 3,070 and 3,260 fps; it's now listed with the same bullets at 2,860 and 3,110 for 24-inch barrels. Price: $6.95. Speer, Inc., 1023 Snake River Avenue, Lewiston, ID 83501.

LYMAN SHOTSHELL HANDBOOK, 2ND EDITION

This is the most complete shotshell handbook ever compiled. It has more loads, more information, and more helpful hints on shotshell loading than any other book. All standard gauges are included: 10, 12, 16, 20, 28, and .410. Nothing else approaches it in the field of shotshell loading. Price: $6.95. Lyman Products for Shooters, Route 147, Middlefield, CT 06455.

—J.B.

RCBS RELOADING GUIDE

This small booklet contains the basic information on reloading. It is surprisingly complete, with loading data for the most popular calibers, as well as articles by leading gun writers. It is concerned with rifle and pistol ammo only and costs $2.00. RCBS, Inc., 605 Oro Dam Boulevard, Oroville, CA 95965.

NOSLER RELOADING MANUAL

This book contains what many reloaders have been waiting for for years: data for Nosler bullets, both for loading and in terms of ballistic coefficients, trajectories, etc. It also has some interesting articles by well-knwon shooters and some basic reloading techniques. My one criticism is that the selection of cartridges is somewhat thin, with semipopular rounds like the 6.5 mm Remington and .284 Winchester having been left by the wayside. It is a good book, however, for those who use Nosler bullets. Price $5.95. Nosler Bullets, Inc., P.O. Box 671, Bend, OR 97701.

SIERRA RELOADING MANUAL

Sierra's manual is a looseleaf binder in which pages can be inserted. Instead of publishing complete updated manuals that would keep up with new components and cartridges, the Sierra people just published a few more pages and sell them as a supplement to the original manual, thereby saving both themselves and shooters time and money.

The Sierra manual has a large amount of technical ballistic data, and it was the first to include wind-drift data for its bullets (naturally, all loads given are for Sierra bullets). The only flaw that I've found is their wide use of the Universal Receiver for test barrels. Most of the barrels they use with this device are 26 inches long, which is 2 to 4 inches longer than most barrels on sporting arms today, and so velocities are not what they should be in most shooters' guns. Nonetheless, it is an excellent manual. Price: $5.95; supplement, $3.45. Sierra Bullets, 10532 South Painter Avenue, Santa Fe Springs, CA 90670.
—J.B.

HODGDON DATA MANUAL

This manual is full of data for Hodgdon powders for rifle, handgun, and shotgun loads. Starting load, maximum load, and velocity/pressure data are given for rifle and handgun loads, as well as all particulars involving gun and load. Price: $2.95. B. E. Hodgdon, Inc., 7710 West 50 Highway, Shawnee Mission, KS 66202. —J.B.

HORNADY RELOADING HANDBOOK VOL. II

This book contains data on rifle and handgun rounds and complete trajectory figures on all Hornady bullets, with standard info such as ballistic coefficients, drop, and retained energy (out to 500 yards in rifle calibers). For whatever reason, I've found that Hornady's velocity figures match actual results more closely than those of other manuals. Of course, this depends on gun and components, as well as other factors, but Hornady's seem to be most consistent with real performance, perhaps because they choose test guns that are more like standard sporting arms than the highly tuned rifles used by other loading companies. Price $6.95. Hornady Manufacturing Co., P.O. Box 1848, Grand Islands, NE 68801. —J.B.

OHAUS CASE LENGTH GAUGE

This is an inexpensive ($3.50) vernier-type gauge and comes with a chart that lists 120 popular calibers and their lengths. While not as exacting as a shop-type metal caliper, this plastic gauge will do for most reloaders' needs. Ohaus Scale Corp., 29 Hanover Road, Florham Park, NJ 07932. —J.B.

THE COMPLETE BOOK OF PRACTICAL HANDLOADING
by John Wootters

New York: Winchester Press. $12.50.

This is an up-to-the-minute guide for the rifleman and shotgunner. Many gunners, particularly those interested in target sports such as position rifle shooting, trapshooting, and skeet, turn to handloading as an obvious way to reduce expenses of their sport. Almost immediately the beginning handloader discovers that what he thought might be drudgery is instead a satisfying hobby, rewarding for its own sake; and instead of merely duplicating expensive factory-made cartridges and shells, he begins to experiment with different powders, bullet weights, primers, and other variables. Here is practical instruction in ballistics, metallurgy, chemistry, physics, and handloading technique.

RELOADER'S GUIDE
by R. A. Steindler

Chicago: Follett, $6.95 (soft cover).

Commercially produced ammunition is becoming expensive. The third edition of this practical book has been updated and revised to reflect the changes in this economical and rewarding adjunct to shooting and hunting. It contains the latest technical data, expanded loading tables, tips on solving handloading problems, bullet casting, swaging, and cartridge case conversions, and is illustrated with diagrams and photographs of the latest techniques and equipment.

ACKLEY HANDBOOK FOR SHOOTERS AND RELOADERS

This two-volume set has plenty of data in it for both standard and wildcat rounds. Some of the data for wildcats is sketchy and seems to be on the hot side, but that's the way it is with wildcats; each inventor wants his baby to be the best, and so he loads it up to the maximum. It is a good guide, however, and includes much technical information for the more serious home-grown ballistician. Also included is a fair amount of P. O. Ackley's own cartridge-design theory, which makes sense and supplies a lot of information to the shooter, too.

The volumes cost $10.00 apiece or $19.50 for both (the first contains most of the technical info; the second volume is a continuation of the first, with data on the newer wildcats included). P. O. Ackley, 2235 Arbor Lane, Salt Lake City, UT 84117. —J.B.

"Tiger, tiger, burning bright / In the forests of the night,
What immortal hand or eye / Could frame thy fearful symmetry?"
—William Blake

335

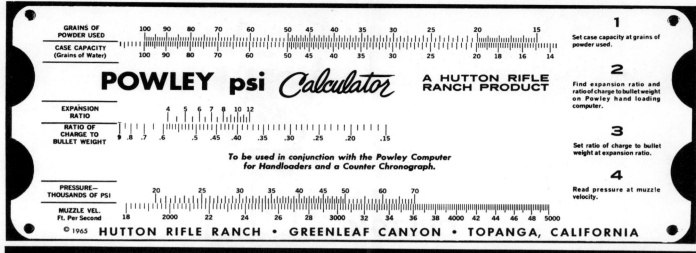

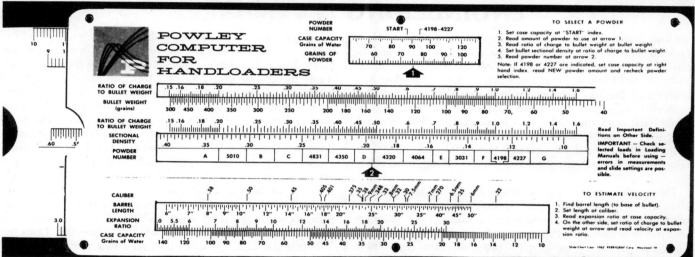

Powley Computer and Calculator for Handloaders

These are slide-rule-type figgerin' machines that are a must for any ballistics nut or handloader. The method by which they're used is too much to go into here; what they do, however, is figure out a starting load with the correct powder (it's based on the Dupont IMR series but can be correlated to other powders) for a given bullet weight for *your* gun. It also figures very closely the velocity for this load and pressure, and can help you in calculating maximum loads and their velocities, especially if you have one of those little boons to mankind, an electronic calculator. Don't get the idea that it takes the place of a chronograph, because it doesn't. The velocities figured, while usually very close, are still only estimates and for one powder only. (The powder recommended is usually one that fills the case nearly full and delivers top velocity at allowable pressures; more uniform ignition results when the case is full.) But it is fun and handy, especially for offbeat cartridges or bullet weights that manuals don't cover. Price for the computer and calculator is $8.50. Other ballistics aids are also available. Hutton Rifle Ranch, 1802 South Oak Park Drive, Rolling Hills, Tucson, AR 85710.

MEC SHOTSHELL LOADERS

Mayville sells some of the best shotshell loading equipment around. In addition to their excellent line of loaders, which range in price from $79.20 for the 600 Jr. to $445.60 for the Hydramec 650 (which features hydraulic power), they make a complete line of shotshell accessories. They have a wad dispenser for plastic wads, automatic primer feeding systems, case conditioners—just about anything you need to load shotshells. Mayville Engineering Company, Inc., Mayville, WI 53050.

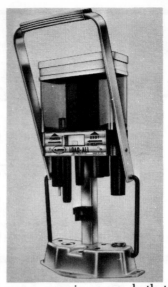

LEE CUSTOM ENGINEERING

How many reloaders have started their careers with a Lee loader? This is a little like asking, How many angels can dance on the head of a pin? Nobody knows. Millions? Trillions? All I know is that I was one of the multitudes. My loader and the old Russian military gun that was my first centerfire rifle cost the same—$10.00 each. That was a while back—but the loader now retails for just $10.98 and I still see some of those old Westinghouse-built Moisin-Nagant rifles around—for $30.00 to $40.00 each. The Lee people have been doing a terrific job in holding down inflation.

They make a whole line of inexpensive hand-type tools of all sorts—for reloading rifle, pistol, and shotshells; for trimming cases; for measuring powder; for starting crimps—just about anything you can imagine. All excellent. They even make an inexpensive pistol machine rest. Their new Target Model rifle loader contains everything (except a powder scale) anyone needs to produce ammo equal to any and costs just $28.98. It trims, primes, reams out the case necks, and straight-line seats the bullets.

The one drawback to Lee loaders is that they are basically limited, due to their non-full-length-sizing design, to bolt-action rifles and double-barrel shotguns, because of these guns' abilities to squeeze slightly oversized cases into their chambers. There are exceptions—I had an old Savage 99 .308 that took Lee loads slickly, and there's a 20-gauge pump gun in my rack that will generally chamber Lee-loaded shotshells—but for every gun that does, there are half a dozen that don't, especially if you use the same shotshells in several guns. Lee's latest product takes care of that, at least in the shotshell world. The Load-All press sizes, loads, and crimps shells that, according to Lee, are as good as factory new. I wouldn't dispute the point, I've been using a 12-gauge model for about a dozen boxes now, and it does just that. It might not be as fast as a hydraulic, automatic, electronic supertool, which loads five shells every time you pull the handle, but then it only costs $29.98. Absolutely the best shotshell loading value on the market. It's no trick to load a couple of boxes in fifteen or twenty minutes once you get used to it, and they'll run through even the finickiest autoloader. The only difference that I can see between the Lee tool and other shotshell presses is that it can't be switched to another gauge. Economically, this isn't a big problem, as die sets for most loaders run almost as much as a new Lee Load-All, but for the man who loads a lot of different gauges it might turn into a hassle. But for the average loader who uses the 12-gauge and maybe the 20 there shouldn't be any problem (the Load-All loads both 2 ¾-and 3-inch shells in eithe gauge). It's also available in 16 gauge, and hopefully there'll be a .410 in the future. Lee Custom Engineering, Inc., Hartford, WI 53027.   —J.B.

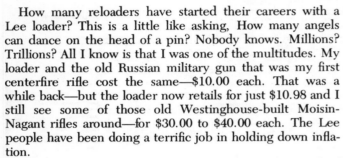

RCBS ROCKCHUCKER PRESS AND RELOADING DIES

The Rockchucker press has enough leverage to swage bullets as well as to do all the normal metallic handloading chores. It costs $67.50 and is a superlative piece of equipment. RCBS dies are equally good; they cost $15.00 in most popular calibers.

If you have an old 450x400x3¼ Nitro Express or a 7x72 Rimmed or a .276 Pedersen, don't despair; write to RCBS. They can supply you with custom dies for most calibers for between $24.00 and $30.00.

It is too bad RCBS only makes metallic-loading equipment, as I'd just about commit a felony to get my hands on a shotshell press with their name on it. They're that good. RCBS, Inc., 605 Oro Dam Boulevard, Oroville, CA 95965.   —J.B.

OEHLER CHRONOGRAPHS

For various reasons, such as loading their own ammunition or having a rifle with an odd barrel length or just plain curiosity, a great many shooters would like to know exactly what velocity they are getting. Factory ballistics tables are closer to the truth than they were in former years, but they are based usually on one barrel length, and even if the barrel length is the same as the shooter's rifle or handgun, variations in individual arms and ammunition will give different results. To say that factory ammunition for the .30-06, using the 150-grain bullet, gives 2,910 fps from the muzzle (this is the industry standard now, taken from a 24-inch barrel) is simply not realistic. Not only do most factory-made .30-06 rifles come with 22-inch barrels, one brand of ammunition is bound to give slightly different results from another, and different rifles, even if they come off the assembly line consecutively, will have minute variations in chamber and bore dimensions that will give different velocity results. The handloader is even more in the dark, as he sometimes loads for guns that are chambered for wildcat cartridges and for which no factory ammunition exists. Oehler Research makes an excellent line of chrono-

graphs—some say the very best—for reasonable prices. These run from the Model 10A Chronograph System for $99.95, which includes the chronograph, cables, screen holders, battery, and fifty screens, to the Model 81 Machine Gun Chronograph, which lists for $10,900.00. The Model 10A will do for most shooters; it is a standard breaking screen system wherein the readout is converted to feet per second by means of a velocity table. For the shooter who would be shooting and chronographing more than a couple of hundred rounds per year, the 11/61 System with Skyscreens would make sense. This system, which is becoming very popular, is photoelectric, with no breakable screens to shoot through and replace with each shot. Instead, you simply shoot over the screens, take the readout, and reset the chronograph to shoot again. The 11/61 System runs $199.95—twice as much as the 10A—but you don't ever have to buy screens (screens for the 10A run $8.95 per 100), so you'll eventually make up the difference. Very quickly, if you shoot a lot. Oehler Research, Inc., P.O. Box 9135, Austin, TX 78766.

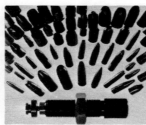

D. R. CORBIN SWAGING DIES

This company markets a very complete line of bullet swaging dies in just about all handgun and rifle calibers. The dies are made so that you can adjust them to produce a wide range of bullet weights, in half-, three quarter-, and full-jacketed styles. They also make a tool that enables you to use fired .22 long-rifle cases for bullet jackets in .22 and 6mm calibers. They

work surprisingly well; this is the way that Vernon Speer got his start in the bullet-making biz.

Their swaging dies run $39.50 to $50.50 for most kinds and can be used in compound-type reloading presses, such as the RCBS Rockchucker, or in Corbin's special press, which runs $69.50. The .22-case jacket-maker is $16.50. Corbin also

makes canneluring tools, core swages, and excellent swaging lubes. These products are fully described in their *Handbook and Catalog*, which is also an excellent swaging manual. It costs $2.00. Corbin Manufacturing and Supply, P.O. Box 44, North Bend, OR 97459. —J.B.

LYMAN BULLET MOLDS

LYMAN Double-Cavity Bullet Mould

Lyman molds are high quality and the equal of any on the market. They come in a greater variety of calibers, weights, and styles than those of any other company—in calibers from .22 on up to .69 musket miniés and in one-, two-, and four-cavity molds. Also available are round-ball molds in sizes from .235 to .735. Blocks cost $15.00 for single, $18.00 for double, and $36.00 for four-cavity, with hollow-base or hollow-point designs (available only in single-cavity) running $21.00. Handles cost $6.50 to $9.50, depending on size. I've been using single and double Lyman

molds in their popular 358156 gas-check semiwadcutter (for the .38 and .357) and have had excellent results. Bases are square and true, and weights run very consistently. Accuracy has been the equal of any cast bullet I've ever used.

I also have a variety of Lyman accessories in my casting equipment, such as ladles, pots, etc., and all of it is excellent stuff, well designed and worthy of the No. 1 company in casting. Lyman Products for Shooters, Route 147, Middlefield, CT 06455. —J.B.

PACIFIC POWDER MEASURE

Powder measures aren't necessary for reloading, but they sure make things go a lot faster. This Pacific tool is a micrometer-adjustable type and comes with two drop tubes (17–30 caliber and 30–45 caliber) and a bench stand. It easily converts to left-hand operation. Also available are extra metering assemblies which allow you to switch from rifle to pistol charges; these run $9.00. The measure costs $34.00.

Pacific also makes a good line of presses and metallic-loading dies, case trimmers, scales, etc. For more info write to Pacific Tool Company, Division of Hornady Mfg. Co., P.O. Box 2048, Grand Island, NE 68801. —J.B.

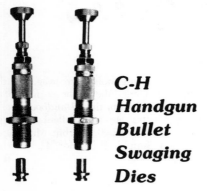

C-H Handgun Bullet Swaging Dies

These are inexpensive dies for swaging jacketed handgun bullets. They have a ⅞-14 thread, so they can be used in any well-built loading press. They will swage three quarter-jacketed bullets (that have the jacket up over the curve of the bullet so that no lead contacts the barrel) in weights from 110- to 250-grain. They come in .38/357, .41, .44, and .45 caliber and are priced at $29.95 for solid-point and $30.45 for hollow-point style.

Also available from C-H is a core cutter for making cores for swaged bullets out of lead wire. Price: $7.50. C-H Tool & Die Corp., P.O. Box L, Owen, WI 54460. —J.B.

Lyman Mould Master and Bullet Sizer-Lubricator

Unless nobody objects to the smell of lead-casting in the kitchen (and old lead pipe can have some pretty weird smells), probably the best bet is an electric furnace. Not only do these have a power source of their own (eliminating hotplates, torches, etc.), but they are precisely controllable as to temperature and draw the metal from the bottom of the pot, which helps in consistency and is nice because you can completely empty the furnace when you're done.

The Lyman Mould Master comes complete with an ingot mold, and operates on 115-volt AC current. It regulates heat between 450 and 850 degrees (which should take care of just about all casting requirements) and has an 11-pound capacity. It costs $74.95.

After you get your bullets cast, you must usually size them to precise bore diameter and lubricate them. The Lyman 450 Sizer-Lubricator does both easily. It costs $42.50, and dies for changing bullet diameter cost $7.50; the top punch, which conforms to the shape of your bullet and is necessary if you change to a different caliber, costs $2.50. Lyman Products for Shooters, Route 147, Middlefield, CT 06455. —J.B.

LYMAN Mould Master
Bullet Casting Furnace with Mould Guide

LYMAN 450 Bullet Sizer/Lubricator

C-H 333X PISTOL PRESS

This is a semiprogressive pistol press (each case must be hand-moved along to each separate station) which will load a reasonable number of rounds per hour (150 according to C-H) for the shooter interested in target shooting.

It is within the price range of the average shooter at $114.00, which includes steel dies (tungsten-carbide dies included for $9.00 extra). It is available in calibers 30 M-1, 9mm Luger, 38 special, 357 magnum, 44 magnum, 45 ACP, and 45 Colt. Conversion dies for changing to another caliber, which includes dies, powder bushings, and shell holders, cost $35.90 for steel or $47.40 for tungsten carbide. C-H Tool & Die Corp., P.O. Box L, Owen, WI 54460. —J.B.

"The earth gets tired of being exploited. A country wears out quickly unless man puts back into it all his residue and that of all his beasts."
—Ernest Hemingway

339

REDDING NO. 1 POWDER SCALE

This is a simple, low-cost scale ($17.50) that is as accurate as any on the market. Its capacity isn't quite as large as some, and it doesn't have a damping system, but it handles 99 percent of all reloading. The lack of a damping system, which slows down the swing of the beam, isn't the sin that a great many reloaders think it is; I've used a No. 1 for years, and once you get used to the manner in which it's used, it is as fast as any other system and perhaps a bit more accurate. I couldn't recommend a scale more highly.

Redding also makes a good line of presses, measures, and case trimmers. Redding-Hunter, Inc., 114 Starr Road, Cortland, NY 13045.

—J.B.

LEE BULLET CASTER

Another solid value for the economy-minded loader, the Lee caster is a nonadjustable, electric pot, which sells for $14.98. It comes with a 6-foot cord, and it is guaranteed for two years. Lee Custom Engineering, Inc., Hartford, WI 53027.

—J.B.

LEE SIZING AND LUBING TOOLS

For those bullet casters who are not willing to put up with the expense of a press-type luber-sizer or who do not have the space, the Lee company has a simple hand tool for each purpose. The Lube Cutter is a tube-type tool; it is used by melting lube and pouring it around standing bullets, then pushing the tool down over the bullets. The Lee Sizer is a cylinder and punch, available in sizes from .225 to .457. Both tools are slower and somewhat messier to use than a press tool, but in typical Lee fashion they do the job just as well and cost only a fraction as much as other types. The Lube Cutter can be had for $1.98, the Sizer for $3.98; or they can be bought together in a kit, along with some Hodgdon bullet lube and a melting pan for $6.98. Lee Custom Engineering, Inc., Hartford, WI 53027.

—J.B.

THUMLER TUMBLER

These tumbler cleaners are available in various sizes and are very handy things to have around. While there actually isn't any difference in performance in tarnished or polished brass, a tumbler is a quick and easy way to remove resizing lubricant from cases, or lubricant from swaged bullets. It will also clean out dirty primer pockets. The Thumler Tumbler is available in sizes from 3-pound capacity on up to 12-pound, which is used by commercial loaders. It may also be used for polishing rocks, if you are so inclined. Barrels are made of rubber for quiet tumbling, and various polishing medias are available, the most useful of which for the reloader would be the brass-polishing type. Prices range up to $49.95; the polishing agent is $1.95 per pound. Randal Marketing Corp., 2 Pennsylvania Plaza, Suite 1500, New York, NY 10001.

—J.B.

B-Square Micrometer

A micrometer is one of a reloader's—at least a serious reloader's—basic tools. In fact, unless you are tied to large production, I'd rate it ahead of a powder measure in terms of usefulness. You can get a serviceable mike for about the price of a powder measure, and it will do much more—measure bullet diameters, help in determining working loads (by measuring case-head expansion), measure slugs from bores—any number of things. This B-Square model is $20.00 in the most useful 0–1-inch size and is accurate to .0001 inch. It comes with a fitted case. B-Square Company, P.O. Box 11281, Fort Worth, TX 76109.

—J.B.

B-Square Dial Caliper

A dial or vernier-type caliper is not as necessary for precision loading as a good micrometer, but it is handy. This model is accurate to .001 inch and is stainless steel. All measuring faces are hardened, and its 6-inch capacity is enough for all case-length measuring. Price: $42.00. B-Square Company, P.O. Box 11281, Fort Worth, TX 76109.

—J.B.

BULLET PULLERS

The bullet puller is an exceedingly useful tool. Not only will it pull old military bullets from salvage rounds, it also takes the bullets out of cartridges loaded with an unsuitable powder charge or rounds that otherwise must be corrected.

Actually, you don't need a bullet puller to pull bullets: simply put the cartridge in your press with the die removed, run the case up through the hole where the die goes in, grab the bullet with a pair of pliers, and pull the cartridge away. Presto! Bullet out! It is likely to be deformed or at least scratched, but if you are not concerned with using the bullet again, this will do the job.

If you do want to use bullets again, the commercial bullet puller is the ideal tool. There are two types, basically: kinetic and gripping. The kinetic type is a hammer that has a shell holder built in. You put the cartridge in the holder, rap the hammer on a solid surface, and everything—bullet and powder—comes out into a hollow in the puller. The gripping type may either be pliers that have bullet-diameter holes drilled in them or a screw-down collet; both of these are used in the same manner as the pliers method

noted above. The pliers and collet types are somewhat quicker and less noisy, but you must buy a different size (most of the time) for each caliber, and if none of the cylinder part of the bullet is showing above the case, they sometimes don't grip well enough to get the bullet out. For most situations they are a good choice, however.

RCBS, Inc., 605 Oro Dam Boulevard, Oroville, CA 95965, makes both collet and kinetic type pullers. The kinetic type has a three-jaw chuck that grips the case; it costs $12.95. The collet type is ⅞-14 threaded to fit presses; it costs $3.75 without collet. Collets are available in calibers from .17-.45 and cost $3.25 each.

A good pliers-type puller is made by Corbin Manufacturing & Supply, Inc., P.O. Box 44, North Bend, OR 97459. It offers an advantage over other pliers types in that it has four holes in various diameters, all precise caliber-sized; some pliers pullers have only one hole. The sizes include .22 and .30 in all models, with .243, .25, 6.5mm, .270, and 7mm available in various combinations with those two. Price: $9.50. —J.B.

RCBS Powder Trickler

When using maximum loads in any gun, the powder should generally be weighed, unless your powder measure is of such absolute accuracy and reliability that you would stake your life on it. A reasonably fast way to weigh such charges is to set your measure to throw a charge slightly underweight, and then dump it in the scale pan and bring it up to weight with a powder trickler. The RCBS trickler, like most, is a screw-feed device that lets powder out a kernel or two at a time. It is of the proper height so that it can be set next to the scale, ready to trickle. Price: $4.50. RCBS, Inc., 605 Oro Dam Boulevard, Oroville, CA 95965. —J.B.

RCBS Stuck Case Remover

It happens to everyone at least once: you don't lube the case well, and it goes into the die and then won't come out. Usually, you end up pulling the head off the case. You can get the case out by drilling and chiseling, but you're likely to scratch the die and cuss a whole lot. The easiest solution is a case remover. The RCBS puller is a tap and drill (¼-20), with which you tap the bottom of the case and then pull the case out by means of a hex-head screw which braces against a steel cylinder. It works on the same basic principle as a screw-type gear puller. Price: $4.50. RCBS, Inc., 605 Oro Dam Boulevard, Oroville, CA 95965. —J.B.

"Three jovial huntsmen, and a-hunting they did go;
And they hunted, and they hollo'd, and they blew their horns also."
—Anon.

341

Pacific Chamfer Tool

Of the same basic design as most chamfering tools, the Pacific model has a steel stud projecting from the outside-deburring end, which keeps the case from slipping off and poking you in the hand. Chamfering tools without this feature are always attacking me in various nefarious ways. Lord knows why, as I am basically a kindly sort. Pacific Tool Company, P.O. Box 2048, Grand Island, NE 68801.

—J.B.

Pacific Powder Funnel

Powder funnels are not necessary (obviously any fool can make a little paper funnel to get the powder into the case) but are a joy to possess, as they make life easier and keep the powder off the rug. The Pacific funnel is made of aluminum, which eliminates the static electricity problems that plastic funnels sometimes have. Like most funnels, the Pacific is usable with various calibers. It comes in three sizes: 17, 22-270, and 28-45. Price: $2.00. Pacific Tool Company, P.O. Box 2048, Grand Island, NE 68801.

—J.B.

C-H GI Decapper and Primer Pocket Swager

To take advantage of cheap surplus GI brass, you must have a means of removing the crimped-in primer and then a means of eliminating the remaining crimp, which keeps ordinary primers from being seated. This C-H tool does both; the deprimer is rugged and will put up with heavy crimps, and the swaging system is precise. Primer pocket swagers usually work better than reamers and are more exact. Price: $5.95. C-H Tool & Die Corp., P.O. Box L, Owen, WI 54460.

—J.B.

C-H Tungsten Carbide Expander Balls

Tungsten carbide expander balls eliminate the need to lube inside of case necks and will never wear down. C-H models are available in .22-.32 calibers in popular sizes except 6.5mm and fit C-H dies, along with others. Price: $5.50. C-H Tool & Die Corp., P.O. Box L, Owen, WI 54460.

—J.B.

RCBS PRIMER TRAY

A primer flipper (which is what this RCBS product is) is not necessary, but like many handy little gadgets it speeds things up, makes life a more tolerable thing, and helps to satisfy the American gadgetry urge. Actually, for loading in any large amount it is almost a necessity. All it does is flip the primers over so they are all right side up. For the price of $1.00 you can't beat that. RCBS, Inc., 605 Oro Dam Boulevard, Oroville, CA 95965.

—J.B.

LYMAN EASY SHOTSHELL LOADER

This is a relatively low-cost shotshell press that can be switched between 12, 16, and 20 gauges. It can be used with the Lyman adjustable powder bar, which costs $13.00, and it may be converted with the $19.50 conversion kit. It will not roll crimp. Price: $59.95. Lyman Products for Shooters, Route 147, Middlefield, CT 06455.

—J.B.

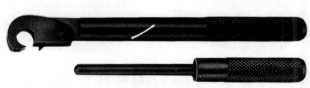

RCBS BERDAN DECAPPER

Berdan-primer cases are getting to be more and more scarce, which is a nice thing, as they were always a pain in the . . . well, anyway, they were a hassle. But if you own a European rifle for some metric-designated caliber and all you can get are Berdan cases, this is the tool. It is much handier and less messy than the old fun water method, where you fill the case with H_2O and then shove a caliber-sized punch down into it until the primer is forced out by the water pressure. The only practical place I ever found to do that trick was the kitchen sink, and my wife never enjoyed it. Price: $10.00. RCBS, Inc., 605 Oro Dam Boulevard, Oroville, CA 95965.

—J.B.

OHAUS SCALES

Ohaus scales have the best reputation in the business, and while they are perhaps not any more accurate—at least in practical terms—than other makes of scales, they usually incorporate mechanical advantages that make them easier to use. They range in price from $27.50 for the 5-0-5 (with magnetic dampening and agate bearings) on up to the lab-type 304 at $95.00, which includes Ohaus's powder trickler and stand. The most practical for the precision-minded loader, however, might be the 10-10. At $39.50 it offers a bigger weight capacity than any scale in its class (1,010 grains), a setting system that is micrometer-controlled, and Ohaus's Approach to Weight system, which tells the shooter when the weight is approaching the desired level before the beam moves. Ohaus Scale Corp., 29 Hanover Road, Florham Park, NJ 07932.　—J.B.

C-H CORE CUTTER

A core cutter is a tool that cuts lead wire for use in swaging bullets. You can do the same thing with a hacksaw and vise, but it won't be nearly as precise: any excess and you'll be wasting lead and putting a strain on your press and dies; cut too small a core and you'll wind up with an underweight, inaccurate bullet. The core cutter is the way to go. This C-H tool will cut lead wire up to ⅜ inch in diameter, which is good for bullets up to .45 caliber or so, and at the price you can't beat it, especially since it is consistent and much easier than any jerry-rigged method. Price: $7.50. C-H Tool & Die Corp., P.O. Box L, Owen, WI 54460.　—J.B.

Shell Catcher for Remington's 1100

If you're both a reloader and 1100 owner, you've got problems retrieving your hulls unless you own one of these. It's a snap-on gadget that decreases the size of the breech opening just enough so the base of the ejected shell hangs up. The hull can then be removed by hand. Good for only one shot at a time. Price: $4.95. Cabela's, 812 13th Avenue, Sidney, NE 69162.

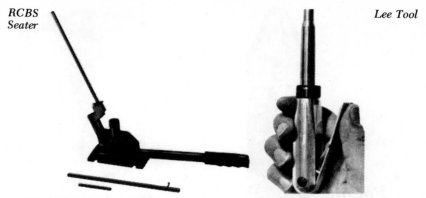

RCBS Seater

Lee Tool

PRIMING TOOLS BY RCBS AND LEE

A priming tool isn't essential, as most reloading presses and even the little Lee Loader come with some sort of arrangement for seating primers, but some shooters, especially those concerned with precision, prefer separate priming tools because they are more sensitive and hence can detect when the primer is fully seated. The RCBS seater is essentially a miniature bench-mounted press which uses standard RCBS shell holders and can be fitted with an automatic primer feed. It also can be adapted for Berdan priming. Price is $25.50 without shell holder; this includes primer feed tubes for both large and small American primers. (RCBS, Inc., 605 Oro Dam Boulevard, Oroville, CA 95965.

The Lee tool is, as usual with this company's products, a simple hand tool that is just as effective as any other tool on the market. A great many reloaders feel that this is the most sensitive of all the priming tools. It costs $2.98; shell holders are $1.80. Lee Custom Engineering, Inc., Hartford, WI 53027.　—J.B.

SHOTGUN RELOADER'S POUCH

This receptacle for empty hulls slips onto any belt and hangs low on your side, so there's no hassle finding the hole. When you've picked 'em all up, the bottom of the case opens by way of a zipper. Holds over 100 empties. Prices: canvas pouch, $8.00; vinyl, $7.00. Kolpin Manufacturing, Inc., P.O. Box 231, Berlin, WI 54923.

For bullets for reloading, see additional information and specs on bullets in the Big Game section.

RELOADING COMPONENTS

Components are all the things necessary to make ammunition: bullets, powders, primers, wads, shot, and cases. Sometimes these can be made by the individual loader, such as in cast bullets, but most often they must be purchased. The reloading market is so huge now it would be almost impossible to list all components of all types, and prices fluctuate constantly, particularly with lead products such as bullets and shot. Here, however, are some samples that will give you an idea of what to expect.

Rifle bullets (conventional type)	$5–$8 per 100, depending on caliber
Handgun bullets (jacketed)	$5–$7 per 100
Shot	$15–$18 per 25 pounds
Brass cartridge cases (rifle)	$2.50–$4 per twenty
Brass cartridge cases (handgun)	$6–$10 per 100
Shotgun shells (empty)	$5–$8 per 100
Primers (rifle and pistol)	$8–$10 per 1,000
Primers (shotshell)	$15–$18 per 1,000
Powder	$5–$8 per pound
Wads (plastic cup type)	$2–$4 per 250
Wads (paper/felt)	$2–$3 per 1,000
Gas checks	$5–$8 per 1,000
Jackets (for swaging)	$8–$20 per 1,000

As stated before, prices will fluctuate. Powder, in particular, has gone up in the past few years, as it is primarily a petroleum product. Certain types of components that are more expensive to manufacture than conventional types, such as Nosler bullets, will cost more.

The main thing to remember when purchasing components is that in spite of the fact that most manufacturers can't put guarantees on their products simply because of the use they might be put to or the guns they'll be fired in, there are no inferior products on the market. When poor performance or, God forbid, an accident occurs, it can almost always be traced to the incompetence of the shooter or some other factor. When used correctly, with care and forethought, each component on the market works very well.

It is this vast array of components that gives the reloader an edge over the shooter limited to factory-loaded ammunition.

—J.B.

Federal Brass

Federal's latest entry into the components field is their brass for most popular calibers. I've been using their cases for .270 loading for years (from factory loads) and have found them to be the equal of any. Their shotshells, wads, and primers are all of excellent quality, too. Federal Cartridge Corp., 2700 Foshay Tower, Minneapolis, MN 55402.

—J.B.

Winchester-Western Components

Winchester markets all sorts of components, including its own brand of ball powders, bullets, shot, wads, cases, and primers. All of them are very good and are competitively priced. Their ball powders for rifle reloading are especially nice, as they meter better than log-type IMR powders and are available in burning speeds to suit just about all cartridges. I've been using their 785 (the slowest burning) lately in 6mm and .270 loads, and it gives excellent accuracy and top velocity. It is also supposed to burn somewhat cooler than other powders, thereby cutting down on barrel erosion. You can find data for loading with WW components in their free handbook, "Ball Powder Loading Data," by writing to Winchester-Western, 275 Winchester Avenue, New Haven, CT 06504.

—J.B.

Remington 10-Gauge Wads

Remington now has available as a component its Power-Piston plastic wads in 10 gauge, which should bring the big 10 into the reloading twentieth century and finally put patterns on a par with the smaller gauges. Heretofore only conventional paper and felt wads were available to 10 enthusiasts, thus effectively reducing the percentage of undeformed shot in any load. No price is yet available on these, but they should run around $3.00 to $4.00 for 250. Remington Arms Co., Inc., 939 Barnum Avenue, Bridgeport, CT 06602.

—J.B.

Alcan 10-Gauge Wads

For a long time 10-gauge enthusiasts had to rely on Alcan 10-gauge wads (conventional type) in order to keep their boomers booming. Now, with the resurgence of the big bore, several companies have brought out plastic wads, which produce better patterns, and Alcan probably will, too. For those who wish to get the conventional type, however, Alcan still makes 'em. Alcan (Smith & Wesson Ammunition Co.), 2399 Foreman Road, Rock Creek, OH 44084.

—J.B.

Sources of Components

	Rifle Bullets	Handgun Bullets	Shot	Brass	Shotgun Shells	Primers	Powder	Wads	Gas Checks	Jackets
Alcan—Smith & Wesson Ammunition Co. 2399 Foreman Road Rock Creek, OH 44084					X	X	X	X		
Bitterroot Bullet Co. P.O. Box 412 Lewiston, ID 83501	X									
Colorado Custom Bullets P.O. Box 215 American Fork, UT 84003	X									
E. I. Dupont de Nemours & Co., Inc. Explosives Department 1007 Market Street Wilmington, DE 19898							X			
Federal Cartridge Corp. 2700 Foshay Tower Minneapolis, MN 55402				X	X	X		X		
Hercules Powder Co. 910 Market Street Wilmington, DE 19899							X			
Herter's, Inc. Waseca, MN 56093	X	X		X	X	X	X	X	X	X
B. E. Hodgdon, Inc. 7710 West 50 Highway Shawnee Mission, KS 66202						X	X	X		
Hornady Mfg. Co. Box 1848, Grand Island, NE 68801	X	X							X	
Lyman Products for Shooters Route 147 Middlefield, CT 06455									X	
Norma-Precision P.O. Box E Lansing, NY 14882	X	X		X			X			
Nosler Bullets, Inc. 600 Northwest Meadow Drive Beaverton, OR 97005	X									
Remington Arms Co., Inc. 939 Barnum Avenue Bridgeport, CT 06602	X	X		X	X	X		X		
Sierra Bullets 10532 South Painter Avenue Santa Fe Springs, CA 90670	X	X								
Speer, Inc. 1023 Snake River Avenue Lewiston, ID 83501	X	X		X		X				X
Winchester-Western 275 Winchester Avenue New Haven, CT 06504	X	X	X	X	X	X	X	X		

HODGDON POWDER

Hodgdon is one of the big names in powder, the company having made its start after World War II by selling surplus military powder (two types that became popular as 4895 and 4831). The supply of 4831, one of the most widely used rifle powders, dried up a couple of years ago, and now it is being produced in Scotland. It is still very popular, but at about $6.00 a can it is much more expensive than the old military stuff, which went for about $2.00 just before it disappeared. The Hodgdon company of late has become involved in the mounting numbers war and is producing powders with identical designations to other companies' lines, such as 205, (fortunately for reloading confusion, this has been discontinued by the Norma company), 3031, 4064, etc., which means that we'll just have to be more careful about which powder we use. The situation that occurred a couple of years ago, when Dupont brought out *their* 4831 (which is faster-burning and produces higher pressures than the Hodgdon with equal charges), is likely to be duplicated with other powders unless you keep one step ahead of this numbers game. B. E. Hodgdon, Inc., 7710 West 50 Highway, Shawnee Mission, KS 66202.　　　—J.B.

Remington UMC

Page 153

Paper Shot Shells

"Nitro Club"

(Reg. U. S. Pat. Off.)

(U. S. Patent, March 12, 1912)

From an old Remington catalog

Shooters Accessory Supplies Bullet Jackets

A good source for rifle jackets for swaging is Shooters' Accessory Supplies, 3091 North Bay Drive, North Bend, OR 97459. They have jackets in many styles and sizes; prices are available on request.　　—J.B.

Lyman Gas Checks

Lyman offers a complete selection of gas checks in just about all popular calibers from .22 through .45. Price: $9.50 per 1,000. Lyman Products for Shooters, Route 147, Middlefield, CT 06455.

　　　—J.B.

Speer Bullet Jackets

In addition to their excellent line of bullets for both rifle and handgun, Speer also markets one half and three quarter jackets for handgun bullet swaging in calibers .30, .38/.357, .41, .44, and .45. Prices run from $15.00 to $18.40 per 1,000. Speer, Inc., 1023 Snake River Avenue, Lewiston, ID 83501.　　　—J.B.

BENCHREST LOADING

The benchrest loader does the same things as any other metallic-cartridge reloader, except he does them more painstakingly. Where the average shooter makes sure that his brass is all of the same make, that his power charges are consistent, and that his bullets are all seated to the same depth, the benchrest loader takes each minute aspect of the cartridge and makes sure it is as consistent as possible.

Not only does he use tools that aid in putting the shell together in a very precise way, but he uses gauges to check the components and the loaded round. Micrometers, calipers, depth gauges—all have their place in the bench loader's scheme of things. Case necks are turned—a tiny shaving of the brass—either with a special tool or on a lathe-type trimmer until they are of equal thickness. Flash holes are gauged, and sometimes a drill bit is used on the inside of the case, on the end of the flash hole, so that holes are of the same length. Primer pockets are gauged and primers delicately seated. Bullets are seated in dies that align the case precisely with the projectile. The correct powder charge is arrived at by painstaking testing, but interestingly enough it does not have to be weighed to exacting tolerances, as most people who are unfamiliar with bench techniques suppose. There are other factors that probably cancel this factor out, so most powder charges are simply measured (although with *good* measures). All this exactitude is combined with weighed and matched cases that have been previously fired in a perfect chamber.

This may seem to have no bearing on normal loading, but we all can make some use of bench techniques, varmint hunters in particular. Probably the most important ingredient in accurate loading, aside from good tools and components, is the neck-turning technique. Often neck-turning alone can shrink groups by 50 percent. But even if you never shoot a group over sandbags in your life or try for a woodchuck 300 yards distant, the knowledge of loads and guns that bench shooters have amassed is now affecting the quality of the equipment that you buy.

　　　—J.B.

BENCHREST BULLETS

It used to be that most serious benchrest shooters made their own bullets in precision swaging dies, but most shooters are now going over to the commercially produced match bullets. The demand for these bullets is such that almost every major custom-bullet firm is making them, at least in .22 caliber, with 6mm and .308 diameters also available. These precision bullets are not only highly concentric (the center of gravity as close as possible to the dimensional axis), but the bases are squared to the axis and weight is held to minimal tolerances (under .01 grain and most often less). It is the base that has the most to do with accuracy, and bullet spinners actually test the quality of the base rather than the roundness of the bullet (even in hunting loads, bullets are rarely out of round). The following companies make benchrest bullets: —J.B.

Hornady Mfg. Co.
P.O. Box 1848
Grand Island, NE 68801

Shilen Rifles, Inc.
205 Metro Park Boulevard
Ennis, TX 75119

Nosler Bullets, Inc.
600 Northwest Meadow Drive
Beaverton, OR 97005

Speer, Inc.
1023 Snake River Avenue
Lewiston, ID 83501

Remington Arms Co., Inc.
939 Barnum Avenue
Bridgeport, CT 06602

Winchester-Western
275 Winchester Avenue
New Haven, CT 06504

Sierra Bullets
10532 South Painter Avenue
Santa Fe Springs, CA 90670

Lee Target Model Loader

Except for a good powder scale, this hand-type loader includes every tool that you need to produce ammunition second to none. It neck-sizes, reams the neck out so that the neck is of even thickness, trims the case to length, primes the case with the sensitive little Lee priming tool, and straight-line seats the bullet. While it might not have the same exactness of a custom-made die, it has closer tolerances than most production tools, and its careful use will produce highly accurate ammo. Price $28.98. Lee Custom Engineering, Inc., Hartford, WI 53027. —J.B.

Shilen Loading Dies

Shilen can supply their own neck-sizing/decapping tool and the popular Wilson straight-line bullet seater at prices of $20.00 and $19.50 respectively, in calibers .222, .22-250, 6x47, and 308. These calibers are the most popular for bench rifles (excepting the .22-250, although there are still a few rifles made for it); the dies are of the standard hand-type, where you use a soft mallet or an arbor-type press to do the work. Shilen Rifles, Inc., 205 Metro Park Boulevard, Ennis, TX 75119. —J.B.

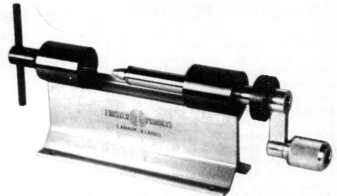

FORSTER CASE TRIMMER

One of the basic tools of the metallic-cartridge reloader is the case trimmer, and it is one that is often overlooked by the beginner. A case trimmer is a tool that trims cartridges for length by taking brass from the mouth of the case. This is necessary with many rifle rounds because, with firing, the brass tends to "flow" forward. This extra length, when it butts up against the front of the chamber, does bad things for accuracy and at its worst can cause severe pressure problems, since the case is actually being crimped in against the bullet. Another situation where case trimming is sometimes necessary is when pistol rounds headspace on the front edge of the case (i.e., forward progress of the shell into the chamber is stopped by the edge of the case butting up against the front of the chamber). It isn't likely that accidents will occur if length isn't exactly correct in such a situation, but this ammo is more accurate if it all headspaces in the same way.

The Forster case trimmer is known as a lathe type. It actually is a miniature metal lathe and is the original of its kind. It has an advantage over the other commonly used trimming device, something called a "trim die." This is a die that fits into a loading press; the case is run into it, and all the case that comes up through a hole in the top of the die is filed away. The lathe trimmer is quicker and more precise, because it automatically squares the neck with the axis of the shell. The trim die is more expensive than the lathe type, as you must buy a separate die for each caliber. An RCBS trim die, for instance, costs $8.10. A Forster trimmer, complete for one caliber, costs $17.50, but all you need for other calibers, in most instances, is the pilot, which costs 60 cents.

There are other jobs that the Forster tool can do. Neck-reaming, which must be done when necks become too thick (this is caused by the same forces that lengthen cases but isn't as common), is easily done with the proper attachment. Neck reamers cost $6.50. You can hollow-point solid-tipped or soft-point bullets with the appropriate tool ($5.50), outside-turn necks to uniform thickness ($13.50), ream primer pockets of GI brass ($5.50), or clean primer pockets ($1.15). There is even a power-operated Forster tool that attaches to a drill press; the price is $15.50. It uses all the same attachments as the hand-operated type. Forster Products, 82 East Lanark Avenue, Lanark, IL 61046.

"There is a pleasure in the pathless woods,/ There is a rapture on the lonely shore . . . I love not man the less, but Nature more."

—Byron

347

B-SQUARE BENCHREST GAUGES

This company markets gauges for most benchrest-type precision measuring. All except one of their gauges work with their dial indicator, which is accurate to within ±.0001 inch. By itself, the indicator costs $31.50, but if you buy it with any other B-square tools, the additional cost is only $15.00. The gauges that are available include a cartridge gauge (which reads run-out on loaded rounds), a bullet spinner (for checking bases), and a case neck gauge (which measures neck thickness after turning). Prices are $34.95 for the cartridge gauge, $34.95 for the bullet spinner, and $29.95 for the case neck gauge.

Their one other gauge is a primer pocket gauge, which—naturally—measures primer pockets. If the depth of each pocket isn't consistent with that of the other cases, firing pin force varies from shot to shot and affects ignition.

This tool has a built-in dial indicator that is accurate to ±.001 inch and costs $39.95. B-Square Company, P.O. Box 11281, Fort Worth, TX 76109. —J.B.

CCI BENCHREST PRIMERS

The primer is the only cartridge component that bench loaders have no real control over. They can work brass over extensively, swage their own bullets, fiddle around with different powders and charges until their fingers feel numb, but a primer can only be weighed and measured, and then there is still no assurance that it will act just like its brother. CCI has now brought out benchrest primers made especially for precision shooting that are more painstakingly put together than their regular primers. Dimensions, charge weights, everything is to closer tolerances. They are available in both large and small rifle sizes and are priced slightly higher than regular CCI primers: about $1.50 per 100 in my neck of the woods. Omark Industries, P.O. Box 856, Lewiston, ID 83501.

—J.B.

B-SQUARE ARBOR PRESS

While some loaders use old bottle cappers, a rugged arbor press that is especially made for bench loading is a better bet. The B-Square model is easily changed from right- to left-handed operation, has a removable base, and is powerful and precise enough for any sizing or seating job. Price: $49.95. B-Square Company, P.O. Box 11281, Fort Worth, TX 76109. —J.B.

CUSTOM ARMS: PACHMAYR AND GRIFFIN & HOWE

While there are many fine gunsmiths and firms both in the United States and abroad that will gladly take your money in return for a fine, handcrafted, custom-made-to-your-specifications rifle, shotgun, or other arm, the two most prestigious firms in the nation are New York-based Griffin & Howe and Los Angeles-based Pachmayr. Both have long, hard-earned reputations as the best gun-crafting shops around, and so they're not cheap. Just how much they'll charge to take your Mauser action and make it into a finely tuned .270 sporter, or how long it will be before they can deliver a custom 20-gauge side-by-side with two sets of barrels, is impossible to determine, as each custom gun is indeed a creation unto itself. It would be a fair guess to say that even if you provide the basis for the gun in terms of action and possibly barrel(s) and wood, you are talking about a minimum charge of around $500.00 and several months' time. In the case of a finely engraved sporter with the best wood and 32-line checkering, you are most likely talking about thousands of dollars. The only way to really find out is by writing to them.

—J.B.

Griffin & Howe, Inc.
589 Broadway, 4th Floor
New York, NY 10012

Pachmayr Gun Works, Inc.
1220 South Grand Avenue
Los Angeles, CA 90015

MCGOWEN GUNSMITHING AND BARRELS

The McGowen company does numerous gunsmithing chores and installs its own barrels on most actions. Bolt handle alteration, scope base mounting, trigger installation, etc., are also part of their services. They also do bluing and install Fajen stocks on their rifles. Their barrels are of Douglas contour and come in more calibers than the Douglas brand. The price for a chambered, threaded, crowned, and ground barrel is $43.95, with installation $8.00 for '98 Mausers and $12.00 for other bolt actions. They also sell Mauser '98 bolt actions with McGowen barrels installed for $83.95. To bring these up to top grade you'd have to have the bolt altered ($10.00), the safety altered ($8.00), scope bases fitted ($16.00 for Redfield), a Timney trigger installed ($18.00), a push-button release put in the floorplate ($4.00), and the trigger guard streamlined ($4.00), bringing the cost to $143.95, not including bluing, which is $25.00 extra. With shipping it would run around $170.00 total, which isn't a bad price if you desire a Mauser-actioned sporter these days. This doesn't include stocking.

They also do rechambering and reboring work for $35.00 a gun, so that a shot-out .270 can be cheaply converted to .280 or .30-06 or your '06 converted to .300 Winchester magnum. There are any number of other combinations.

A quarter will get you their list of services and prices. Write to McGowen Rifle Barrels, Route 3, St. Anne, IL 60954.

—J.B.

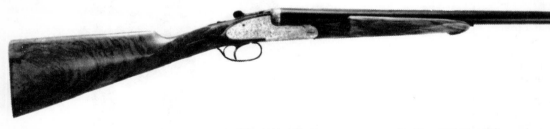

ORVIS CUSTOM SHOTGUNS

The Orvis company makes custom side-by-sides (box-lock) in either straight-grip or pistol-grip style. These are nice-handling, conservatively designed guns and are available in 20 or 12 gauge. They weigh 6 and 6½ pounds respectively and are Spanish-made. There are a great many options available. Prices start at $1250.00.

For more information contact Ben Upson, Orvis Shooting School Director, Manchester, VT 05254.

—J.B.

Simmons Gun Specialties Services

The Simmons company specializes in shotgun work, although they do some rifle work, such as bluing. They do just about any kind of rebluing, and they refinish, rechecker, or stock shotguns, especially for trap and skeet shooting. Prices on bluing run from $27.50 for bolt rifles up to $150.00 for double guns (this is difficult and expensive because of the solder between the barrels, which doesn't take kindly to the heat of bluing processes). They also do repair work, such as removing dents, opening up chokes, and installing sights. Their prices are reasonable in most cases, and their stocking also seems to be priced competitively; fancy wood styles cost $70.00 to $100.00. Simmons Gun Specialties, P.O. Box 533, Olathe, KS 66061.

—J.B.

"Hunting doesn't degrade an animal. It's not as bad as what we do to our domestic animals; they become more debased as they become suited to our purpose."
—Patrick Hemingway

349

DB-2. FIELD STYLE STOCK and BEAVERTAIL FOREND on Winchester Model 21 double. Hand carving available at additional cost.

PA-3. COMPLETELY FINISHED and CHECKERED Texan style buttstock and standard forend on Remington Model 58.

A-5. FINISHED AND CHECKERED ALASKAN STOCK for Springfield 1903 A3, fluted at point of comb, with standard checkering pattern.

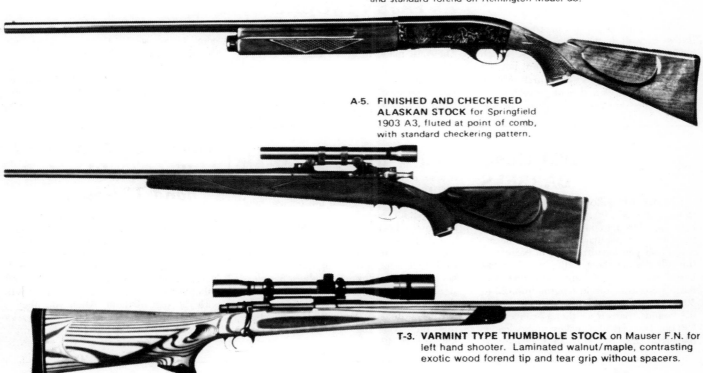

T-3. VARMINT TYPE THUMBHOLE STOCK on Mauser F.N. for left hand shooter. Laminated walnut/maple, contrasting exotic wood forend tip and tear grip without spacers.

BISHOP STOCKS

The Bishop company makes stocks of just about every sort and supplies such accessories as butt plates and pads, stocking tools, and checkering kits. In addition, they do custom stock work, with prices starting at about $90.00, and they supply blanks. The Alaskan stock shown costs (in lowest grade) $19.95 in ready-to-finish form. If it is fitted to your rifle and finished by the Bishop shop, it costs $67.95; the same service with checkering costs $102.95. The "low" grades of wood are not bad wood; they are simply plain, straight-grained American walnut without any fancy figure and are actually better for hunting rifles than fancier-figured types, which tend to shift and change the gun's point of impact. The shop also does carving; the standard job will cost about $200.00. They also sell stocks in other woods, such as screw-bean mesquite, claro walnut, French walnut, hard maple, and myrtle wood. Prices for the fancy grades in fitted, finished stocks will go up to $400.00. Bishop also has various types of laminates available in both walnut/walnut and walnut/maple styles, such as the varmint thumbhole stock shown.

If you want to do the stock work yourself, they also sell an excellent kit, which includes wood rasps, chisels, and a bottoming tool, along with three checkering tools, for $36.50. The checkering set can also be had alone for $7.25. I've been using one for a while now, and although it isn't of professional quality, it is a good low-cost set for the aspiring checkerer. E. C. Bishop & Son, Inc., P.O. Box 7, Warsaw, MO 65355.
—J.B.

HARRY PHILPOTT

FAJEN STOCKS

Fajen supplies stocks of conventional design as well as their interesting Aristocrat (pictured) and Regent styles, which are swept-line designs. These are not the California-style stocks with high Monte Carlo cheekpieces and hook grips but are modified classic stocks that actually handle recoil in heavy rifles much better than some of the "classic" designs I've seen. They are made in styles that are acceptable to most conservative shooters as well as in flashier types. Prices run from $13.95 for unfinished low-grade Aristocrats to close to $200.00 for finished and checkered Regents. Fajen also sells a line of very good target stocks in prone, free, and thumbhole types. They also supply grip caps, butt plates, pads, sling swivels, etc. of name brand types as well as stockmaking kits. Reinhart Fajen, Inc., P.O. Box 338, Warsaw, MO 65355.　　—J.B.

DOUGLAS BARRELS

Douglas Ultrarifled barrels are second to none. For $75.00 (plus postage) you can have one fitted to most popular bolt actions in most popular calibers and be assured that you have the best in barrels. If the rifle doesn't shoot well with a Douglas barrel, there is something else wrong. The barrels are available in lengths from 22 to 30 inches and in finished weights from 2 to 9¾ pounds. Barrels for the .17 caliber run $90.00. Douglas also makes muzzleloader barrels in .32, .36, .40, .45, .50, and .54 calibers in 44-inch length (which, of course, can be cut to any lesser length) for $45.00 or $47.50, depending on the diameter of the barrel. These are octagon and threaded for breech plugs. Pistol barrels for muzzleloaders run $17.50. All the above prices are for unblued barrels; Douglas doesn't do any bluing or action work except for opening up the bolt face if necessary for magnum cartridges. Stainless steel barrels are also available for those shooters who want an erosion-resistant barrel; these run $100.00. Douglas Barrels, Inc., 5504 Big Tyler Road, Charleston, WV 25312.

When You Can't Find a Widget with a Left-hand Thread . . .

Try the Brookstone Company, 207 Vose Farm Road, Peterborough, NH 03458. They specialize in hard-to-find items. Tools, cookware, knives, blacksmith supplies, and general arcana. They have an illustrated catalog that they'll send you, and although their prices are right up there with the rest of them, when you need a puukko knife or a pair of left-handed scissors, they'll probably have a few around.　　—N.S.

(Actual Size)

Personalized Stock Shield

This police-type stock shield, engraved with your initials, requires no inletting or special stock preparation. The soft gold or silver molds to the contours of your stock, and it's held in place by a metal nail on the shield's back. It can also be glued with epoxy for a more secure attachment. Prices: silver, $4.00; gold, $5.00. Indicate initials you wish engraved (up to three). Bob Hinman Outfitters, 1217 West Glen, Peoria, IL 61614.

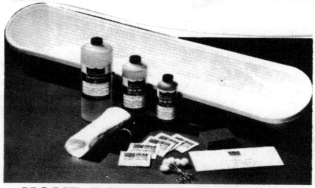

HOME BARREL BLUING KIT

No matter the claims, a tank bluing is bound to produce a more even, professional bluing job on a bare barrel than any swab-on, touch-up bluing solution. Here's a complete kit, including a bluing tank, that contains enough materials to blue around ten barrels.

Aside from the 36-inch tank, the kit includes a quart of bluing concentrate, a quart of steel cleaner and degreaser, 8 ounces of blue and rust remover, swabs, wipes, steel wool, sponge applicator, and service cloths—everything you'll need to get the job done right. Price: $24.95. (Bluing materials are also available separately and in large quantities.) Birchwood Casey, 7900 Fuller Road, Eden Prairie, MN 55343.

"In works of labor or of skill / I would be busy too,
For Satan finds some mischief still / For idle hands to do."
—*Isaac Watts, "Divine Songs"*

351

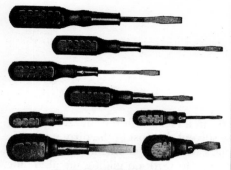

GUNSMITH'S SCREWDRIVER SET

The fine screws used on most arms require a special screwdriver with an extremely sharp, perfectly flat head. Workshop-type screwdrivers tend to burr fine screws.

This set of eight screwdrivers ranges in tip size from 5/16 to 3/32 inch and in overall length from 3 7/8 to 8 inches. The blades are carbon steel, and the shanks are square, so you can turn them with a wrench. Square hardwood handles for a good grip. Price: $19.95. Brookstone Company, 125 Vose Farm Road, Peterborough, NH 03458.   —N.S.

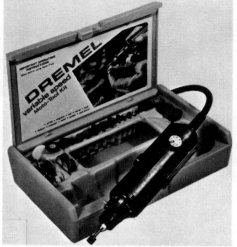

DREMEL MOTO-TOOL

I've used one of these tools for fifteen years, and it's been one of the most relied-upon in my workshop for sporting goods cleanup and repair. Basically, it's like an oversized dentist's drill that you hold in your hand. There are all kinds of grinders, polishers, drills, and abrasives that are attached like drill bits, which may be used to sharpen knives, saw blades, and axes, to remove rust, and to do reasonably delicate grinding in gunsmith work. They're also ideal for cleaning and polishing guns and for carving and shaping operations in gunstock inletting work. A pocket-sized machine shop. Price: Moto-Tool kit with thirty accessories, $44.95. Dremel Manufacturing Co., 4915 21st Street, Racine, WI 53406.   —F.S.

Slip-on Recoil Pads

Slip-on recoil pads serve two functions: they cushion recoil and they also increase stock length, should the trigger pull on a gun be too short for you. What's more, they do it without altering the appearance of the original stock.

Burnham Bros. stocks two kinds of these "butt boots," one with a honeycombed cushion for maximum stock absorption and one with a solid cushion. Prices: $3.10 and $1.95 respectively. Mention make of gun when ordering. Burnham Bos., P.O. Box 100A, Marble Falls, TX 78654.

—N.S.

Do-It-Yourself Recoil Pad

This recoil pad kit includes a white spacer and honeycombed rubber butt plate. Easy to install, it effectively dampens kick. Price: $5.95. P. S. Olt, Pekin, IL 61554.

Wonder Glue Sets in Sixty Seconds

If you have to do a repair job on a gun or other hunting equipment that resists being held in a clamp, this glue sticks in a minute. Just hold the part in place with your fingers. The resulting bond is rated at 5,000 psi tensile strength, and it is water-, temperature-, and chemical-resistant. This glue is *not* recommended for polyethylene, Teflon, paper, or leather. Price: 2 grams, $2.50. Brookstone Company, 125 Vose Farm Road, Peterborough, NH 03458.   —N.S.

GUN CARE
AND
MAINTENANCE

The most obvious thing that the owner of a rifle, shotgun, or handgun should do is "clean" it. To many people this only involves cleaning the bore, and often they aren't aware of why or how to do that.

Cleaning the bore is indeed the most important aspect of maintaining a gun but not the only aspect. Keeping the action operating (also usually a job of "cleaning") and the stock in good shape is also important. Simply cleaning the barrel is akin to only changing the oil in your car and leaving the other maintenance aspects alone.

The barrel is a good place to start, however. The reason we clean the bore in modern guns is not to prevent corrosion, as was primarily the case in the days of corrosive powders and primers, but to strip away any buildup of projectile material that is in the bore. This can range from the gilding metal of high-powered rifle bullets to the lead of handgun and .22 bullets to the plastic of modern shot cups. Each of these, in its own way, interferes with the efficiency of the weapon.

The tools you'll need are a cleaning rod of appropriate size, a bore brush (either soft metal or tough plastic) that attaches to the rod—it should be of slightly over bore size—some patches and a cleaning rod tip to take them, and a solvent. There are other tools that can be useful for each type of weapon, but the ones I've mentioned are basic to all.

The hardest stuff to get rid of is gilding metal (copper alloyed with zinc) fouling, which is what most rifle bullets are jacketed with. It builds up in barrels and interferes with accuracy. As an experiment one time I shot sixty rounds through a very accurate .270 without cleaning it. The groups at the start of the shooting were under 1¼ inches in size, with most under 1 inch. After fifty shots they had opened up to 2½ to 3 inches, and the coppery metal had built up to a point where it was very apparent when I examined the muzzle of the gun. This is an extreme case, as most rifles should be cleaned every fifteen to thirty shots for the best accuracy. I put the rifle in a vise (another handy tool for cleaning, although not necessary) and took out the bolt. I then fitted a rod guide into the space left by the bolt. This is a tube of bolt size that has a hole in it large enough to admit the cleaning rod; it prevents the rod from rubbing the throat of the barrel and impairing accuracy. I then fitted the bore brush to the cleaning rod (in some guns the brush must be fitted after the cleaning rod is inserted into the rod guide, and then the rod guide inserted into the action), dipped the brush in my favorite solvent, and ran the brush through the bore ten times. If this had been an ordinarily fouled barrel, I would have then run clean patches through the bore until they came out clean. This barrel was so heavily fouled that I ran one clean patch through and then another liberally doused with solvent, instead. I then stood the rifle on its muzzle in a rack, with the muzzle on a rag.

This was to let the solvent do most of the dirty work. The solvent I used, Hoppe's No. 9, has ammonia in it, as should all solvents that are used to work on gilding metal fouling. Ammonia dissolves the copper in the fouling and leaves a greenish compound; in heavily fouled bores this is one way of getting most of the fouling out. Note that I said most, as some will still be apparent in the grooves of the barrel; but this small amount will not harm accuracy, and indeed some target shooters feel a little fouling fills up the pores in the metal and smooths the barrel, aiding accuracy.

Another way to get heavy fouling out is to use one of the mildly abrasive bore cleaners on the market; these can quickly remove all gilding metal from the bore. Their disadvantage is that unless they are carefully used they can harm some soft steels. They are also messier than most solvents and very hard to get out of the other parts of the rifle, should you slip up.

I left the .270 overnight and the next morning ran clean patches through the bore until they came out clean, which usually takes about a dozen patches. These patches should be tight in the bore but not so tight that they'll get stuck; otherwise they won't get into the rifling grooves and do the job. I then stuck a rag over a 20-gauge bore brush, put it on a shotgun cleaning rod, and wiped out the chamber of the .270. This step is especially important for lever, pump, and auto rifles, because they don't have the primary extraction power of the bolt, and a dirty chamber can cause them to malfunction. With any gun, however, it is advisable to wipe out the chamber after cleaning, to get solvents and pieces of dirt out. The solvent can cause severe bolt thrust by lubricating the walls of the chamber and not allowing the cartridge to stick to it during firing, and if there are pieces of dirt in the chamber, the chamber itself can become scratched when an entering round scrapes the dirt against it.

The next step was to wipe out the action of the rifle, to remove dirt and any solvent that might have accidentally gotten into the magazine or other parts of the action. A rod guide helps to prevent this in bolt rifles, and a rag in the magazine of other types helps to soak up solvent, too.

This same cleaning procedure is advisable for all rifles, at least the minimum bore treatment of solvent and brush. Guns that must be cleaned from the muzzle must be protected from the passage of the cleaning rod. The easiest way to do this is to go to your nearest hamburger emporium and grab a few plastic drinking straws. Cut off a piece about 3 inches long and slit one end with a scissors about 1 inch down the straw in four places. Insert the straw into the muzzle of the gun with the slit end facing out; you can bend the tabs created by the slits back over the face of the muz-

"For heathen heart that puts her thrust / In reeking tube and iron shard,
All valiant dust that builds on dust / And guarding calls not thee to guard."
—Rudyard Kipling

353

zle and either hold or tape them there while you run the cleaning rod down the barrel. This will effectively protect the muzzle.

This same basic cleaning procedure holds for shotguns and handguns as well, although unless you're using jacketed bullets in a handgun, you won't be encountering gilding metal fouling. Leading, the same sort of fouling but caused by lead bullets or shot, is much easier to remove than gilding metal. Cast bullets sometimes will lead barrels, depending on the hardness of the lead alloy and the velocity of the load. Leading is much easier to see than gilding metal fouling; it looks like dark streaks in the bore.

Chambers must be cleaned in shotguns and handguns, too. A brush just oversized enough is handy. This is sometimes hard to find for the larger shotgun gauges (a 20-gauge chamber can be cleaned with a 12-gauge bore brush), but a brush wound with cloth and then with a few pieces of steel wool will work, as long as you use it with care.

The .22s are sometimes a problem. Much of the newer .22 ammo will cause severe leading, and so the notion that you don't have to clean .22s (which came into being when noncorrosive fouling was developed) isn't as valid as it once was. Their barrels are often of very soft steel, so extra care must be taken not to harm the chamber or muzzle. Paste abrasives aren't advised for most .22 steel, and as the fouling is usually soft lead, they aren't really necessary. Most leading is removed with a brush and solvent.

With the new shot cups another type of fouling has cropped up: plastic. This usually builds up in the forcing cone just ahead of the chamber and in the choke. It can cause high pressures as well as bad patterns. A brush with solvent cures it, but it isn't as readily apparent as gilding metal or lead fouling, so make sure to clean the barrels often if you suspect your gun may have this problem. If plastic fouling is occurring, the plastic will drop out of the muzzle during cleaning in the form of plastic dust or flakes; it is readily apparent on a dark background.

Cleaning rods for rifles and handguns should preferably be made of steel and be one piece. Aluminum, brass, and plastic-coated rods tend to pick up bits of abrasive dirt, which scratches the bore when the rod is run through. The connections in multiple-piece rods do the same thing. If you are forced to use a soft rod in a rifle or pistol, wipe it off after every pass and use a rod guide if cleaning through the breech. Definitely use some protection when cleaning through the muzzle. If it is a takedown rod, sand the connections so they won't rub. Shotgun rods can easily be of softer metal, as they are normally stiff enough not to rub the bore.

The "problem" guns in cleaning are those with rough bores that pick up fouling easily. This may result from a manufacturing defect or through neglect, as with rust pits. A shotgun barrel can be polished to eliminate this, but if the pitting is acute in a handgun or rifle, the only solution may be a new barrel or perhaps a reboring job.

As was noted, if you lube some part of the gun (and all moving parts will last longer if you do), be sure to wipe the parts off. The thin film that remains will be sufficient for all purposes of lubricating. Excess lube can damage stocks by soaking in and softening the wood, and it also has a tendency to pick up grit. There are many solvent and lubing products on the market which come in spray cans with small plastic tubes that can direct whatever you're spraying into the tiniest crevices in a gun. To a certain extent this is helpful, but if you spray where you can't wipe it off, you may end up with a bad grime problem, especially if you hunt in a dusty area. Cotton-tipped swabs and pipe cleaners are cheap and help to get lube and dirt out of almost all spots.

If you are going to be storing a gun for a while in a damp climate, it's best to protect it with some sort of rust preventive, especially in the bore. The wax that you use on furniture will protect the stock and also enhance its appearance.

All screws should be degreased (with alcohol, acetone, etc.) and set up tightly with screwdrivers that fit. Either buy a set of gunsmith's screwdrivers or file the tips of your present screwdrivers until they are square and fit the screws well; many gun screws are made of fairly soft metal and tear easily.

Do not take guns down beyond what is advised in the owner's manuals. If something seems wrong or if it is an old gun, take it to a gunsmith; unless you are familiar with how guns go together you might not be able to reassemble what you have put asunder. Normal cleaning is sufficient in most cases to keep arms operating safely and well.

—J.B.

Uni-Kit Cleans Rifles, Shotguns, Pistols

Marble's Uni-Kit is designed to clean all firearms. The secret is in the cleaning rod, which is small enough for rifle bores but will accept large shotgun cleaning brushes. Pistols are cleaned with just one section of the three-section breakdown rod. Kit includes patches and nonfreeze gun oil. Price: $5.95. Marble's, P.O. Box 111, Gladstone, MI 49837.

Corbin Benchrest Bore Cleaner

When I have a barrel really fouled by gilding metal, lead, or whatever, I just about always reach for Corbin's bore cleaner. It is a fine abrasive in light oil, and ten strokes with a bore-cleaner-soaked patch will remove more fouling than all-day scrubbing with most solvents. It can also be used as a very gentle lapping compound, but normal use only removes fouling. It's also very effective on rust if you should ever be that unlucky. Price: $1.98 for a 2-ounce jar. Corbin Manufacturing and Supply, P.O. Box 44, North Bend, OR 97459. —J.B.

HOPPE'S STEEL CLEANING RODS

The best type of cleaning rod for rifle cleaning is a one-piece steel rod. Such a rod has no ferrule connections, which tend to catch dirt and scratch the bore, and the steel won't pick up dirt like aluminum or brass. Hoppe's makes two one-piece rods, in .22 and .30 sizes. Actually, the smaller one can be used on everything between .22 and .28, and the .30 can be used on bigger bores, with the use of appropriate patches, brushes, etc. Price is $3.25 each. They also have a .17 caliber one-piece rod and kit, complete with No. 9, oil, patches, and .17 brush, priced at $6.99. Penguin Industries, Inc., P.O. Box 97, Parkesburg, PA 19365. —J.B.

The Tico Tool: Bore-length Brush for Shotguns

The Tico tool is a 34-inch-long brush of nylon. Actually, it feels like fur and is a nice pink, which will be absolutely stunning next to your other cleaning rods. It is supposed to revolutionize shotgun cleaning, but it doesn't—quite. Supposedly, you run the tool into a shotgun barrel, twirl it a few times, and presto! the bore is clean. If you wish to oil the bore, you just put a dab of oil on the end attachment and draw the tool back through the bore. Unfortunately, the nylon really doesn't take out anything tougher than loose powder fouling; leading, plastic fouling, and the tough kind of powder buildup that occurs at the front of the chamber and the forcing cone seem to ignore the Tico tool. It has some really nice applications, though, in that it will take moisture right out of the barrel if you happen to get your gun wet (as happens in waterfowl hunting) and because the oiler, which is nothing more than a short section of the nylon rod, can stay oiled and ready in the capped hollow handle. This feature would be handy on a hunting trip, when the gun would probably be fired again the next day anyway. One handicap is that it's one-piece, and the 3-foot length is kind of awkward in a vehicle. It comes with a plastic carrying tube and costs $6.95. Tico International, 460 Bryant Street, San Francisco, CA 94107. —J.B.

HOPPE'S CHAMBER-CLEANING KIT

One of the problem spots in gun cleaning is the chamber. It is not so hard to handle in handguns, because it's usually of bore diameter, and standard brushes and patches can be used. For rifles a .410 or 28-gauge brush is adequate if really needed, but with the larger shotgun sizes bore brushes often just rattle around in all that empty air. Hoppe's makes a chamber-cleaning kit that will work for 12- to 10-gauge guns, priced at $3.65. It includes a short rod and a special short brush. Penguin Industries, Inc., P.O. Box 97, Parkesburg, PA 19365. —J.B.

THE GUN OWNER'S BOOK OF CARE, REPAIR AND IMPROVEMENT
by Roy Dunlap

New York: Harper & Row, $9.95.

Roy Dunlap is one of the very best gunsmiths alive, and he is also a good, straightforward writer. This book, although *not* a gunsmithing book, explains to the average gun owner how to make a great many repairs and modifications on his arms that would otherwise have to be done by a gunsmith, such as trigger adjustments, stock repair and finishing, cleaning, and just about everything else that can be accomplished by the average handyman who doesn't have the skill or access to major gunsmithing tools, such as metal lathes, drill presses, milling machines, and welding equipment. Mr. Dunlap is also the author of *Gunsmithing* (Stackpole Co.), probably the best work on that subject ever done, which is a good book for the more advanced gun tinkerer, but the average shooter would be well off with *The Gun Owner's Book;* it will save him money and increase his knowledge of arms and how they work—something that will make us all better—and safer—shooters. —J.B.

CLEANING ROD COILS UP

Kleingunther's offers the Schukra steel collapsible cleaning rod. This rod is made of a series of small steel cylinders which, when tension is applied by means of a lever attached to a cable that runs through the cylinders, stiffen up and serve their function very well. The end is threaded for standard brushes (rifle sized), and when collapsed the rod fits into a pocket-sized plastic case. Rigid, it's 26 inches long, so it will handle most rifle barrels, and its steel construction prohibits the tendency of dirt and fouling to adhere to the rod and harm the bore (as happens with many soft-metal and plastic-coated rods). Price: $10.95. Kleingunther's, P.O. Box 1261, Seguin, TX 78155.

Safe-Site Bore Inspector and Cleaning Aid

The Safe-Site is a combination mirror and periscope that allows you to inspect the bore of a rifle for obstructions and dirt. To use it, you insert one leg of the device in the chamber and hold it under a strong light. You can check for barrel obstructions at the breech and evaluate the condition of the bore by looking down the muzzle.

Safe-Site fits calibers .270, .30-30, .32, .300, .30-06, .308, .44, and larger (including shotguns). Price: $1.49. Marble's, P.O. Box 111, Gladstone, MI 49837.

BORE INSPECTION

When sighting down the bore after cleaning a rifle or shotgun, use a piece of aluminum foil as a reflector on the other end. It shows up fouling and corrosion better than a mirror or white paper.

HOPPE'S NO. 9

One of the most wonderful smells in the world is that of good old No. 9. I can't understand why my wife doesn't like it. A solvent for both powder and metal fouling and a preservative rolled into one, it has yet to be improved upon. Price: $1.10 for 2 oz.. Hoppe's also makes other fine shooting products, from cleaning rods to deer scents, which you can find out about in their catalog. Frank A. Hoppe Div., Penguin Industries, Inc., Parkesburg, PA 19365.   —N.S.

Gun Scrubber for Cold-weather Hunting

Automatics are the most sensitive sporting arm when it comes to malfunctions due to cold weather, but virtually any kind of action may go on the fritz when built-up lubricants and powder residues harden in cold temperatures.

As the season progresses and temperatures drop, make it a practice to clean actions, especially automatics, to avoid misfires and sticky bolts. Gun Scrubber is a powdered aerosol degreaser that softens dirt, grease, and powder fouling and blasts it away from hard-to-get-to parts. In all but the most extreme cases, it works without having to disassemble the gun. Price: Gun Scrubber, $3.25. Birchwood Casey Products, 7900 Fuller Road, Eden Prairie, MN 55343.

GUN ACTION CLEANING TIP

To clean a dirty rifle or shotgun action without taking it apart, remove the stock and, if possible, the barrel. Drench the action with a commercial solvent like Gun Scrubber, if it is available. Lighter fluid, carbon tet, or alcohol may be used as a substitute in a pinch.

While the solvent is still wet, immerse the action in boiling water and detergent. Mr. Clean is typical of the kind of household cleaners that will work. If they're not around, dish soap is second best. You need very little of either; 1 teaspoon per gallon is ample.

Dunk and swish the action around until you're reasonably sure the hot water has reached all moving parts. Dunk the action once again in pure boiling water to remove any detergent residues.

The trick is to use very hot water and to keep the metal in it until it, too, gets hot. The hot water and detergent dissolves the gunk, and the hot metal evaporates any clinging water drops when the action is taken from the pot.

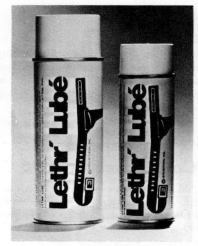

ZIP AEROSOL PRODUCTS

We have tried samples of Zip products: Degunge (a degreaser), Engarde (a nonoily lubricant), and Lethr Lube, which is supposed to "penetrate, lubricate, soften and protect all leather goods"; it seems that it does do all those things.

Degunge is handy for degreasing scope-mounting holes and other hard-to-reach places; it comes with a plastic-tube attachment that reaches most anywhere. It evaporates quickly and degreases well (it smells as if it contains acetone, so make sure you don't breathe too deeply).

Engarde is a light, moisture-displacing, nonoily lubricant which can also be used as a cleaning solvent for lighter gun-cleaning chores, such as leading and plastic build-up in shotguns. It doesn't seem to attract dirt the way the popular WD-40 does, probably because it's lighter and so cuts down on gumming, too. Price for each: $2.00 for an 8-ounce can. Zip Aerosol Products, 21322 Deering Court, Canoga Park, CA 91304.

G96 PRODUCTS

The G96 brand is on a bunch of stuff from Jet-Aer. Among other things they sell gun blue in cream and liquid form, black-powder solvent, antigrease compound, cleaning solvent, silicone antirust treatment, wood finishes, leather waterproofing, bug spray, etc., etc., ad infinitum—all of it very good stuff.

One of the more effective rust-preventing substances on the market is silicone. Used properly, it actually enters the pores of metal and gives it very effective protection. For wet climates G96 Silicone Spray is doused on warmed metal and rubbed in; for drier climes the Silicone Gun Mitt protects metal from fingerprints and gives guns a nice shine. Prices: 15-ounce can of spray, $2.25; gun mitt $1.75. Jet-Aer Corporation, 100 6th Avenue, Paterson, NJ 07524.

Cold Blues by G96

Cold bluing compounds aren't meant for complete arms, although they are sometimes used on double shotguns where heat would harm the solder holding the barrels together, but for touch-up work they are fine. There are two G96 cold blues, a paste and a liquid. The paste is somewhat more effective in producing an even finish, while the liquid gets into hard-to-reach spots. Like any liquid blues they work better if the metal is heated and thoroughly degreased before application. The paste is available in a 2-ounce jar for $2.50 or a 4-ounce tube for $3.98. The liquid comes in a 2-ounce bottle for $1.50. Jet-Aer Corporation, 100 6th Avenue, Paterson, NJ 07524.

—J.B.

Hoppe's Pure Linseed Oil

One of the big advantages of the traditional oil finish on a gunstock is that minor scratches can be easily fixed up by the application of a little more boiled linseed oil. Hoppe's markets it in a handy touch-up size bottle (2 ounce) for $1.45. Penguin Industries, Inc., P.O. Box 97, Parkesburg, PA 19365.

—J.B.

Numrich Parts for All Sorts of Guns

If you are in need of parts, the people to contact are at Numrich. They carry parts for many sporting and military guns, not to mention gunsmithing supplies. You need a new barrel for your No. 3 Quackenbush air gun? Ask Numrich. You need a clip for your old .35 Remington Model 8 auto rifle? Only a buck from Numrich. Their parts catalog also has exploded drawings of many guns (especially handguns) and is well worth the asking price of $2.00. Numrich Arms Corporation, West Hurley, NY 12491.

—J.B.

Safariland Leather Products

In addition to their fine line of leather products for both sporting and police uses, these people also market a leather maintenance kit that includes a leather conditioner that softens and restores old, cracked leather and some leather dressing which, when applied, results in a protective, glossy film that doesn't discolor the leather and is guaranteed not to crack or peel. Also included in the kit are a couple of wool applicators that are reusable, as both the conditioner and the dressing rinse out in warm water. The kit costs $2.50. For information on their other products, send $1.00 to Safariland, 1941 South Walker Avenue, Monrovia, CA 91016.

Mittermeier Shotgun-barrel Dent Remover

It happens to most of us at least once in a lifetime: either you stand a shotgun up in a corner or you unexpectedly bump the barrel on a rock or somehow, somewhere you simply notice a dent in the barrel. It may be a small dent, but it isn't a good idea to just leave it there no matter how tiny. Even if it isn't big enough to be dangerous in itself, it can pick up fouling and cause problems. In any case, you either go to the local gun wizard or try to get it out yourself, which really isn't all that difficult if you have one of the Mittermeier dent removers. These are bore-sized plugs that are expandable (by means of a tapered thread and screw) to fit most bores, as some shotgun barrels are slightly under- or oversized. Small dents in soft barrels can often be removed just by driving the lubricated plug through the bore, but often a rawhide hammer is needed to really get the dent out. In any case, it comes with instructions (although very basic) and costs $6.75, or $19.75 for a set of three: 12, 16, and 20 gauges. Frank Mittermeier, Inc., 3577 East Tremont Avenue, New York, NY 10465.

—J.B.

Armoloy Plating: Effective Rust Prevention

If you shoot in an area where rust is a real problem, such as most coastal areas, you might consider the Armoloy process for your guns. It is a very hard (70 Rockwell) electro-deposited chromium plating that effectively stops corrosion and reduces friction between moving parts. Under most circumstances buildup of the process is not over .0002 inch, so even the interiors of bores can be processed and protected. The process doesn't affect tensile or other properties of the base material and can be used on all ferrous and nonferrous metals except aluminum, magnesium, and titanium, which really don't need the process anyway. It can be applied not only to firearms but to bullet molds, loading dies, etc., as well. Prices for handguns are $40.00 for revolvers and $45.00 for autos; rifles and single-barreled shotguns are $50.00, side-by-sides are $60.00, and over-unders are $65.00. Specific portions of arms can be plated, too, with interiors of barrels running in price from $8.25 for autos to $25.00 for double shotguns. For additional specifics and sending instructions, write to Armoloy Company, 204 East Daggett Street, Fort Worth, TX 76104.

—J.B.

"Get out the hounds; I'm well to-night, and young again and sound;
I'll have a run once more before they put me underground."
—George Walter Thornbury, "The Death of th'Owd Squire"

357

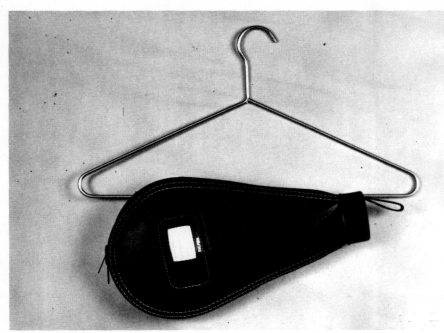

Clothes Closet Cases for Rifles, Shotguns, and Pistols

Store your shoulder arms and pistols out of the way and in an unlikely spot by hanging them in a clothes closet. The Hang In There gun glove accepts unscoped rifles and shotguns up to 52 inches in length. The inside is padded and lined, and the full-length zipper operates in such a way that your gun won't fall out when you open it up.

The Hanger Holster contains two Velcro snaps that fasten to the bottom of a clothes hanger. The full zipper has two tab pulls that can be padlocked together for complete security. In addition, the pistol case can be worn on your belt and can be used just like a holster. Sizes from 7 to 15 inches. Prices: Hang In There case, $16.00; Hanger Holster, $12.50. Kolpin Manufacture, Inc., P.O. Box 231, Berlin, WI 54923.

Gun Insurance

Your sporting arms are a valuable investment, and as such they should be protected by some sort of insurance. Homeowner's policies might not cover loss of your guns away from home from theft, fire, accident, or explosion, and if you have many guns, there's a chance they're not even covered inside your house.

Check on the status of your firearms with your insurance agent. If they are not insured under your present policy, he can write a floater that will cover whatever kind of potential loss you wish to insure.

Another possibility is insurance through the National Rifle Association of America, 1600 Rhode Island Avenue, Northwest, Washington, DC 20036.

Members of that organization may insure their guns through a special group policy at a rate of 3.24 percent of the declared value of their firearms for three years' protection.

Part V

BLACK-POWDER GUNS AND OTHER COLLECTIBLES

Collector's Item

A seventeenth-century American flint-lock was recently purchased by a London collector for a reported $300,000.

THE "SINGLE-SHOT" THAT REALLY IS

by Ed Park

Most of my big-game hunting has been done with a scope-sighted, bolt-action, repeating .30/06, into which I feed accurate handloads. With such a combination, given a solid rest for same and a deer-sized animal standing still, it is pretty much an assassination out to maybe a quarter mile. I need no holdover to around 300 yards and not a lot on out to 400. I can work that bolt pretty rapidly now for follow-up shots, and in twenty-five years of shooting with the same gun I've yet to have a misfire from reloads or factory ammo. But this is no big deal, for the same can be said of any of the modern high-powered rifles.

In recent years I've been spending more time stomping the hills and canyons with a heavy, long-barreled, iron-sighted beast. It has a logical range of maybe a third that of my '06, plus the annoying problem of sometimes not going off! And when it does, which I'll admit is most of the time, I shoot with the sure knowledge that I have just one shot, for I'm now doing a lot of my big-game hunting with a black-powder muzzle-loader.

To begin with, the muzzle-loader is the closest thing we have to a true single-shot. We read of so-called single-shots, such as the fine Rugers or Brownings—and they are fine rifles, to be sure—but with a mere flick of the fingers, the action is opened, the empty brass ejected, and a live round inserted. Elapsed time? Maybe four seconds, six on a cold day. Even an archer can get off his second shot in less than ten seconds.

But with a front-stuffer it takes a bit of time to pour the powder charge down the barrel, ram a new ball home, and fumble a new cap onto the nipple—all necessary steps for that second shot. It may take thirty seconds—sufficient time for a healthy deer to lope a quarter mile or so.

The end result is that the muzzle-loader hunter does not figure on shot number two or three. He thinks "one," knowing fully that if that first shot is not good, his chances for a follow-up are nil.

He therefore approaches a hunt with an attitude different from that of the usual big-game hunter. First, he experiments with the variables, and practices on paper, until he knows the exact limitations of both his rifle and himself. *Then* he goes hunting.

And "hunting" it is, with the "hunt" once more put back into the word, for he knows his primitive weapon will take game for him only if he gets well within range and is certain of that one shot. He realizes he must become more familiar with his game, its habits and its habitat. He must hone his spotting and stalking skills, and learn the art of patience while sitting on a stand or waiting for his target to move so a closer approach is possible. He must, in essence, once again become a hunter rather than merely a shooter.

And while learning all this and doing all this, it is difficult not to learn a lot of other truths, such as what this sport of hunting is all about. When he is forced to work at his sport and to get closer to all outdoors, he can't help but learn that just to be out there in the blaze of autumn, whether game is taken or not, is well worthwhile.

He is now really hunting, and while a kill is the stated objective of the hunt, there is much more to it than that. Sure, the same feelings can be learned when using more modern equipment, but somehow the learning comes easier when limitations are self-imposed—such as when a hunter chooses to hunt with a primitive weapon.

This, then, is why I welcome the disadvantages of my heavy, inefficient black-powder rifle; this is the appeal I have recently found in hunting with a muzzle-loader.

Ed Park is a full-time free-lance writer and photographer from Oregon. He is president of the Northwest Outdoor Writers Association and sits on the board of directors of the Outdoor Writers Association of America.

BLACK POWDER GUN DIGEST
edited by Toby Bridges

Chicago: Follett Publishing Company, $6.95 (paper).

This book starts with the history of black powder and contains many articles on techniques for building, shooting, and loading for black-powder arms. It also contains a list of black-powder arms available today (although the list has grown since publication in 1972) and articles by such notables as Dean Grennell, Turner Kirkland, Bob Zwirz, and Skeeter Skelton.
—J.B.

MUZZLELOADERS' HANDBOOK AND BLACK POWDER HANDBOOK
edited by C. Kenneth Ramage

Middlefield, Conn.: Lyman Products for Shooters, $6.95 each.

These are large-format, softbound books, and they contain a wealth of info for the black-powder enthusiast. The *Muzzleloaders' Handbook* contains articles on many aspects of front-stuffer shooting and a catalog section of related products, both Lyman's and other companies'. The *Black Powder Handbook* is a fine source of information on techniques for shooting, casting, and cleaning and has the most extensive ballistics information I've yet seen for black-powder arms. Naturally, the charts are made up of primarily Lyman bullets, although they can be interpolated for other makes (and is there really all that much difference between round balls of the same diameter no matter which mold they came out of?). I would rate the *Black Powder* book especially high on the list of must-gets for the black-powder shooter, as it not only includes facts about loads and muzzle velocities but trajectory info and much other technical data as well.
—J.B.

BLACK POWDER GUIDE
by George Nonte

Chicago: Follett Publishing Company, $6.95 (paper).

The author of this second edition is one of the most competent technical firearms writers in the country, and so the book contains an amazing amount of information on the care and feeding of black-powder weapons, including a good article on cannon. There are also several basic load tables with some ballistic information, a glossary, and a list of books and periodicals that might be of interest to those who are involved with black-powder weapons, although many (if not most) of these are not specifically black-powder publications. This book is highly recommended to anyone interested in the more technical aspects of black-powder shooting.
—J. B.

MUZZLE-LOADING ASSOCIATIONS AND CLUBS

National Muzzle-Loading Rifle Association
P.O. Box 67
Friendship, IN 47021
Mrs. Maxine Moss, Office Editor

Brigade of the American Revolution
P.O. Box 207
Vails Gate, NY 12584

The American Mountainmen
P.O. Box 259
Lakeside, CA 92040

Black-Powder Booklet

"Shooting Black Powder Guns" is a 34-page booklet published by Thompson/Center Arms Co. It details the component parts of black-powder shooting, the nature of the propellant, loading tools, bullets, patches, and rods and explains how to load black-powder arms. It concludes with instruction on proper gun maintenance.

The illustrations are clear, the writing interesting and concise, and the text thorough. A good introduction to black-powder shooting that should answer most beginners' questions and get you safely primed, loaded, and ready to shoot in a matter of minutes. Price: $1.00. Thompson/Center Arms Co., Farmington Road, Rochester, NH 03867.

Single Barrel Muzzle-Loading Shot Guns.

No. 5 SINGLE SHOT GUN.

No. 1, Boys' Gun. Very plain, iron barrel, common lock and mountings, without rib, varnished stock, weight 4½ pounds, 30 inch barrel, 25 to 30 bore, range 20 yards............ $2 50

No. 2, Boys' Gun. Same style as No. 1, but is a stronger and better made gun, weight 5 to 5½ pounds, 12 to 16 bore, 24 to 36 inch barrel, range 30 to 40 yards............ 3 00

No, 3, Youths' size. Browned iron barrel, ribbed, varnished stock, side lock, 5 to 7 pounds weight, 12 to 16 bore, 34 to 38 inch barrel, range 30 to 40 yards............ 3 50

No. 4 G. Boys' American single barrel shot gun, made of *Springfield rifle barrels*, bored perfectly smooth, from 16 to 25 bore, 30 to 34 inch barrel, 5 to 6 pounds weight, oiled walnut stock, good lock, blue mounting, a perfectly safe and reliable gun, yet so cheap as to be within the reach of all, range 45 yards... 4 00

No. 5 G, Men's size. Made of *Springfield barrels*, same as No. 4 boys', but larger, heavier, and 12 to 25 bore, 6 to 7 pounds weight, 30 to 40 inch barrel, range 50 to 60 yards............ 5 00

No. 6. Same as No. 5, with ribbed barrel, solid breech............ 8 00

No. 7. Extra heavy, large bore, *Springfield barrel*, heavy breech, good lock, ribbed barrel, 10 bore, 30 to 36 inch; 12 bore, 34 to 38 inch; 14 bore, 34 to 40 inch; 18 bore, 37 inch; all 8 to 8¾ pounds.. 9 00

From an old gun catalog

"They earned a name that lives in song, those woodsmen stout and plucky
Whose hair and rifles both were long—the Hunters of Kentucky."
—Arthur Guiterman, "The Tall Men"

361

THE MODERN MOUNTAIN MAN

by Don Davis

Let us first define the modern mountain man, also known as a primitive; one is the same as the other. There is no variation; you're either a primitive/mountain man or not.

The true modern mountain man is probably the most individualistic of all muzzle-loading shooters. He deviates not from the trails of the old-timers of early frontier days. This includes affecting their mannerisms, customs, mode of life, and their various primitive or rendezvous-type skill matches.

The rules for a rendezvous are very strict inasmuch as you must come in appropriate costume and carry nothing into the camping area but the bare necessities. A lot of the boys bring in wild game they have gotten during the hunting season, and the stews you will find cooking in iron pots over a campfire are numerous and sometimes unusual.

There are a great many primitive-style shoots all over the United States, and there are some in Canada. They are widely advertised in muzzle-loading magazines, and you shouldn't have any trouble locating one close to you.

As you come down Friendship Road during the National Matches, for example, you will notice, on one side of Laughery Creek, a huge settlement of tents and the like, all surmounted by sixty or more tepees. It is a stirring sight, early in the morning, to see the smoke coming out of the teepees and campfires, all surrounded by a mist. It truly looks much the same as the old-time rendezvous, the "place appointed for a meeting." There are no cars allowed in this area.

Walking over the bridge and into the primitive area, you will see what, in effect, approximates the old frontiersman or mountain man. He will be dressed somewhat as follows.

Almost always the knee-high moccasins of deerskin. Buckskin pants with a fringe and, in cold weather, a buckskin coat and probably a fur hat; in warmer weather, a buckskin shirt or old-style colonial-type cotton shirt with wide sleeves. Also, in the summertime, most of them wear hats with wide brims, but of the early type.

Around the waist is a wide belt, from 2 inches on up. This belt is very important; on it you will see a large knife in a sheath and a "possibles" bag, which holds a variety of items, such as glasses, pipe, and perhaps flint and steel, with a box of tinder. This bag is important, too, for there are no pockets in proper buckskins. At the back of the belt you will see a tomahawk, with or without a sheath. The belt buckle is commonly made of hand-forged iron.

A leather hunting bag will be seen hanging on the right-hand side, and on this you will find a powder horn for the rifle powder and a smaller one for priming powder, in the case of a flintlock, which is the most common. On the strap of this bag is a smaller knife called the patch knife, which is used to cut patches for the round ball at the muzzle. These are of infinite variety.

The rifle itself is most commonly a flintlock, but you do see some caplocks around. It will have up to around a 42-inch barrel, full stocked, probably with curly maple.

In the Western sections especially you will find the type of rifles we refer to as the Plains or Hawkens style. These usually have a 34- to 38-inch barrel, are well adapted for the longer shots you must take, especially when hunting, and are usually half stocks.

The calibers range on the Pennsylvania/Kentucky style from .32 to .50, while the Hawkens types are up around .50 and .54 calibers.

Also notice that you will see no "production" guns in this group. Almost all the rifles are custom or home made. A great many of the shooters make their own rifles or buy ones that are made for them. Maybe they'll run onto one at a shoot.

Now this is a picture of a more or less typical mountain man/primitive. They go to great lengths to keep things as they were in the old days and seek to emulate, as closely as possible, the very feel of the old days. I've shot with them a lot, and I envy them their attitudes.

They are very skillful with both the knife and the tomahawk as throwing instruments. There are many contests with them.

Fire-building with flint and steel is another popular contest. Some of these fellows can start a fire about as fast as you can get your lighter out of your pocket and light it.

Most of them are dead shots with the rifle. They shoot at a mark or X center on a charred board, shoot the candle match, split the ball on an ax, and hold many other challenging matches.

They tend to run together, although you'll find them in their costumes at almost any muzzle-loading shoot. They are superior target shooters, but their true love is primitive style.

The primitives are a fun-loving bunch, and you'll find yourself cordially received in their midst—if you keep the rules. At night you'll hear the fiddles and banjos going as they visit around their campfires. It's all very cheerful and informal.

Incidentally, they allow no cars in the rendezvous areas, so you'll have to walk in. Try it, and I think you'll run into the most typical Americana that you'll find any place.

So, the next time you see a shooter dressed and equipped in the manner described above, pay close attention to him and maybe you'll get caught up in the primitive game. It's a lot of fun, and I think that you'll thoroughly enjoy yourself.

Don Davis lives, shoots, and writes out of Friendship, Indiana, the home of the National Muzzle-Loading Rifle Association. Don shoots all styles and has won a great many muzzle-loading matches.

DIXIE GUN WORKS CATALOG

If you need anything, anything at all, in the realm of black powder and antique guns, these are the people you should contact. I don't think there is anything you could want that you wouldn't find in their catalog. As a matter of fact, after looking through it it's hard *not* to want a lot of things, some of which you've never even heard of before.

Let me back up a minute. Take it from the top, as they say. On the cover of the catalog, in the upper right-hand corner, is the price—$2.00—and a request for you to send $3.00 if you like the book. Farther down the cover is a suggestion to read Matthew 7:12, which is the golden rule. Inside the cover is a short essay on the use of the word weapon and its relationship to gun control. The next several pages are taken up with a history of Dixie Gun Works written by Turner Kirkland, the mildly, wonderfully crazy founder and owner of the company. There are photographs of guns, of employees, and of Turner in his younger years. Farther on there's an article on restoring a 1912 Cadillac (Turner's also an old car nut). The Dixie Gun Works catalog really doesn't start to become what you'd expect a catalog to be until page 62, where postage rate tables are printed. After that you will find muzzle-loading guns, parts for 1873 Springfields, kits for muzzle-loading guns, parts for *all sorts* of old guns, army surplus from the Civil War, brass buttons, wad punches, powder measures, a history of flints, home gunsmithing tools (such as band sanders and taps and dies), pure mutton tallow (for lubricating patches), hot air balloons (stuck for no apparent reason between plastic name plates and cast-iron pistol-shaped bootjacks), leg irons, bear traps, gold coins, flags, fifes, pewter spoons, swords, swagger sticks, knives and everything you need to make them, crossbows, suits of armor, tomahawks and everything you need to make *them,* Eddie (one of the employees who is posing as a rough drill sergeant in a Smokey Bear hat—you can buy the hat but not Eddie), coon bones, scalplocks (they don't actually say they're of real human hair but the implication is there), beads, duplicates of medals (such as the one given to John Paul Jones for the capture of the *Serapis*), ten pages of cannon and supplies (including cannonball molds—the Phoenix Iron Works cannon, Civil War Manufacture, with minimal restoration as they've "been maintained in excellent condition," complete with carriage and trailer, runs $5,995), and books on anything having to do with guns, cartridges, paraphernalia, and gun collecting. All these things are displayed by members of the Dixie Gun Works staff, who all look happy. The last part of the book deals with shooting black-powder guns and is as complete a rendition of that subject as you're likely to find (and you can find out how to make old-time hardtack). There are also listings of serial numbers on old guns. All the above isn't a hundredth of what you'll find in the catalog. Worth the price just to read it. One of the great books of the twentieth century. Dixie Gun Works, Inc., Highway 51, South, Union City, TN 38261.
—J. B.

DIXIE YORK COUNTY, PENNSYLVANIA, RIFLE

I tested a sample of a percussion model of this rifle and also a kit of the rifle in flintlock version. Both are excellent, rugged firearms, .45 caliber and weighing just 7½ pounds. They are perhaps not as fancy as some other muzzle-loading rifles, but they are great guns for the price ($150.00 for the ready-made gun in percussion; $95.00 for the kit in flintlock). Accuracy is all you can expect from general muzzle-loading arms.

About 70 per cent of the muzzle-loading guns in use today are made either from kits or parts by the owners, showing that it's something of a do-it-yourself sport. I encountered little difficulty in putting together the flintlock kit that Dixie sent me. However, there are a few things that can help anyone in attempting something like this, especially if they've had little gunsmithing experience. The Dixie catalog itself has a great deal of information on building guns, as do other publications, but, for what it's worth, here are a few suggestions. First, don't attempt a complete stock-making job on your first gun unless you've had an awful lot of experience in conventional stock-making processes. The kit I put together is just about totally inletted and shaped; all that you need to do is some final fitting and sanding, then the finish. The most difficult part of putting together a muzzle-loading kit is in finishing the brass fittings. Brass scratches much more easily than harder metals, so you have to be careful. Use nothing rougher than a very fine file on it, and don't try to hurry the job. You can get the brass as smooth as a mirror by using fine, wet sandpaper and then steel wool and finally polishing with jeweler's rouge. I finished mine as a hunting rifle and didn't buff it up, as I think too much shine in a hunting gun is bad news. On a display or target gun it wouldn't matter.

There are many bluing and browning supplies on the market, but probably the majority of home-grown guns will either be blued by the local gunsmith or cold-blued or browned. The most important thing to remember in using any of these commercial chemical solutions is that the metal must be polished, degreased (with carbon tetrachloride, alcohol, acetone, etc.), and then *heated* for the best results. There are a few different ways of heating, such as over a gas burner or with a propane torch. I usually hold the barrel under hot tap water and then quickly degrease with acetone.

Make sure the barrel is mounted solidly. Since I prefer to take the barrels out of black-powder guns to clean them (to avoid getting solvents and dirt on the stock), I didn't use the pins that come in the Dixie kit that are supposed to go through the forestock and hold the barrel by two brass tabs. Taking them out would loosen them eventually and probably damage the stock (by being punched out), so I drilled and tapped a 8-32 hole on the underside of the barrel and fitted a screw though the ramrod slot of the stock to hold

Thompson/Center Arms for Black-Powder Hunting

This company specializes in black-powder guns for the hunter. Their products include two pistols and three rifles that are ready to shoot right from the factory, and a Hawken rifle kit that you put together yourself.

Available are .36, .45, .50, and .54 caliber rifles in percussion or flint ignition, and each firearm boasts accuracy and lightness. Thompson/Center also markets black-powder accessories (their Maxi-Ball is reputed to be unusually accurate at long ranges) and individual gun parts. Free catalog. Thompson/Center Arms, Farmington Road, Rochester, NH 03867.

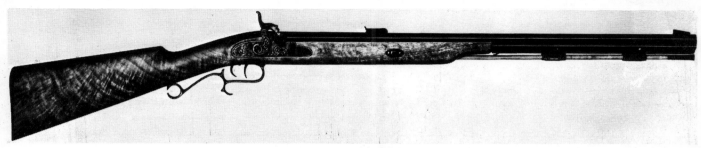

Renegade
Black-Powder Big-Game Rifle

This caplock rifle is chambered for .54 caliber, a load of sufficient beef to stop most North American big game dead in its tracks. With a 400-grain bullet the Renegade develops a muzzle energy of 2,016 foot pounds, which is right up there in the smokeless-powder class.

The Renegade comes with a blued, octagon-rifled barrel that may be removed for cleaning, double set triggers, adjustable sights, and an American walnut stock. It is not a particularly fancy rifle, so if you're looking for a display piece, shop around elsewhere. But as a hunting arm, its performance is indeed impressive. Prices: caplock rifle, $165.00; with accessory kit (all you'll need to shoot except for the powder), $177.35. Thompson/Center Arms, Farmington Road, Rochester, NH 03867.

the middle of the barrel firmly in place (the tang screw and fore-end tip screw are easily accessible). Just a suggestion; most modern black-powder solvents are excellent products, but they can damage stock finishes.

Most black-powder gunstocks are maple and are usually stained, because maple is a very light-colored wood. Turner Kirkland gives a couple of good old-time recipes for stain in the catalog; there are many modern commercial products that work well, too. A commercial linseed oil finish might be more authentic than a varnish over the stain; it depends on what you prefer.

Building a muzzle-loader is a rewarding experience, something easily done by the home hobbyist. All you need are a few files, some sandpaper, screwdrivers, and a lot of elbow grease and patience. And after the first is together you'll want another. Dixie sells kits for all sorts of rifles, pistols, revolvers, and shotguns, but I'm willing to bet you'll want to make up a gun out of loose parts, one that will be totally unlike any other in the world. Like the short-barreled .31 with the tang sight that I'm dreaming about. Or how about a .54 or a 20-gauge or . . . ? The possibilities are endless, and the Dixie catalog sells a selection of barrels, locks, stocks, and triggers that will keep you daydreaming for, well, days. Dixie Gun Works, Highway 51, South, Union City, TN 38261.

—J.B.

Seneca Light Hunting Rifle

At 6 pounds the Seneca caplock rates as one of the lightest black-powder hunting arms on the market. It is available in .36 and .45 caliber; the lighter bullet is for small game up to turkey and coyotes, and the .45 caliber is suitable for deer.

The rifle comes with double set triggers, adjustable open sights, an octagon-rifled barrel, and a walnut stock. While this isn't a fancy gun, it is attractive enough to be as at home on your den wall as it is comfortable to carry afield. Prices: Seneca caplock, $205.00; with accessory kit, $232.50. Thompson/Center Arms, Farmington Road, Rochester, NH 03867.

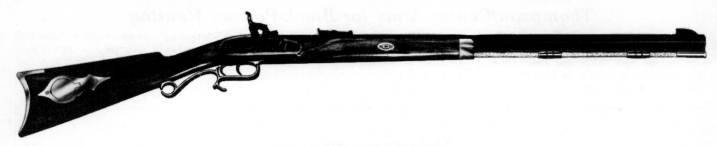

Hawken Rifle Kit

If you're modestly versed in gunsmithing and wood finishing, here's a way to own a quality black-powder gun at a two thirds to half the price of a finished gun.

The kit includes a walnut stock, rifled barrel, lock, double set triggers, hunting sights, a hooked breech system, and brass trim. The gun can be assembled using standard home workshop equipment. Complete instructions included. Prices: Hawken percussion (.45 or .50 caliber), $130.00; Hawken flintlock (.45 or .50 caliber), $140.00. Thompson/Center Arms, Farmington Road, Rochester, NH 03867.

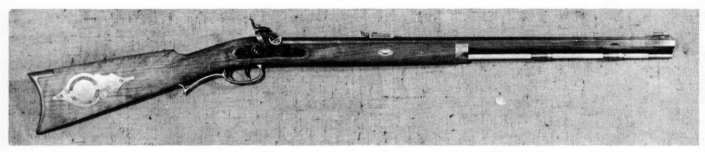

Dixie Hawken Percussion Rifle and Kit

Pictured is the kit just as it comes, fully assembled but unfinished. All that's needed is finishing the stock, bluing or browning the barrel, and polishing the brass. Costs $139.95 or $190.00 finished, in percussion only. This is probably the best bet for somebody wanting a hunting rifle. The barrel is a good hunting length, 28 inch, and it comes in .45 or .50 caliber. The .50 is better for deer hunting, since a .50 ball will weigh about 180 grains as opposed to about 130 for the .45 (round balls give better accuracy in most muzzleloaders, owing to the common rifling twists used and to the fact that minié balls, which are supposed to expand and "take" the rifling without a patch, generally don't fit the bore as well as a patched ball). The rear sight is fully adjustable. For really big game, such as elk and moose, a .54 or even .58 might be better, but for the average hunter this gun will do fine. Dixie Gun Works, Highway 51, South, Union City, TN 38261.

ERNEST PAPPAS

SHILOH SHARPS REPLICAS

The Sharps rifle was one of the big three rifles of the West, along with the Winchester and the Hawken. There is hardly a story involving buffalo that doesn't involve a Sharps in one way or another. The Shiloh people are now offering a replica, in both rifle and carbine form, of the original Sharps gun (noncartridge), which was one of the first successful breech-loading designs. Both guns are .54 caliber in standard form, although you can have .50 and .45 on special order. The rifle is 47 inches long and weighs 8¾ pounds; the carbine 39 inches and 7¾ pounds. They cost $375.00 and $345.00 respectively. Shiloh Products, Inc., 37 Potter Street, Farmingdale, NY 11735.

—J.B.

"The dusky night rides down the sky, / And ushers in the morn;
The hounds all join in glorious cry, / The huntsman winds his horn."
—Henry Fielding

365

Browning Enters Black-Powder Field

The Jonathan Browning Mountain Rifle leads off Browning's entry into the black-powder market. Aside from the kind of good looks that have long been a part of Browning quality, this gun boasts a single set trigger that can be adjusted to between 2 ounces and 2 pounds of pull. Unset, the trigger pull rates between 4 and 5 pounds.

Other features worthy of note include a breech plug system that reduces rear thread stress and ensures a more perfect gas seal, simplified barrel removal for easy cleaning, and fully adjustable buckhorn sights.

The octagonal barrel is 1 inch "on the flats" and 30 inches long. It rests in a half stock with a semicheek piece. Browned finish, caplock, available in .45, .50, and .54 caliber. Price: $274.95. Browning, Route 1, Morgan, UT 84050.

Hopkins & Allen Double Gun: Low-cost Repeater

The big problem with muzzle-loading rifles used in hunting is the slow second shot. An easy solution to the problem is to build a double rifle, but the usual construction of a double gun—two barrels using one set of sights—involves expense, not just in having two barrels and two locks but in regulating the barrels to shoot to the same point of impact. The Hopkins & Allen double gun gets around that by using one lock for two revolving barrels. Each barrel has its own set of sights and is sighted in individually. It is a percussion lock of .45 caliber and weighs only 8½ pounds, very good for a double gun. Price complete is $159.95; in kit form, $109.95. It's claimed that a shooter practiced with the gun can get two shots off in two seconds or thereabouts. Numrich Arms Corp., West Hurley, NY 12491.

—J.B.

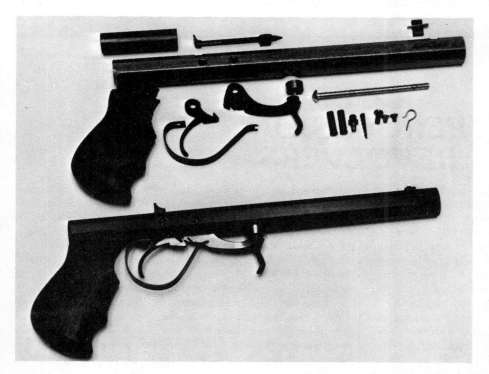

Simple, Fast Ignition: Hopkins & Allen Underhammer Arms

The underhammer black-powder design is an extremely simple one (the trigger and hammer contact directly and there is no lock plate), and it also provides a more direct, reliable means of ignition, because the flash hole can be straight, instead of 90 degrees curved as in the usual side-hammer-lock design. This promotes both reliability and accuracy. This lock design is included both in H & A pistols and rifles, and they're available both as kits and fully finished. The Boot pistol kit costs $29.95; the Heritage Model rifle kit, $99.95. Both are in either .36 or .45 caliber. The pistol and five models of underhammer rifles are available complete; the pistol runs $39.95; the rifles, $134.95 to $149.95, all except one—again, both in .36 or .45. The exception is the Deer Stalker, which is in .58.

Hopkins & Allen also have kits and rifles of more conventional types, mostly Kentucky. The kits run $109.95 to $129.95, and the complete guns cost $244.95 in percussion and $249.95 in flint. Numrich Arms Corp., West Hurley, NY 12491.

—J.B.

Second Model Brown Bess Musket

This is the less expensive version of the Brown Bess that Dixie sells. It retails for $250.00 (the No. 1 runs $450.00). It's .74 caliber, and the big, heavy lock will probably give the best ignition of any flintlock around. This is a replica of the gun that figured prominently in the American Revolution, and the barrel, lock, and ramrod are left bright as on the original. The smoothbore barrel is 42 inches long, so it's no brush gun, though it can be used with either ball or shot for the man who wants one gun (smoothbore barrels are serviceably accurate for hunting out to 50 yards or so, depending on the gun and how it's loaded). Dixie Gun Works, Inc., Highway 51, South, Union City, TN 38261.

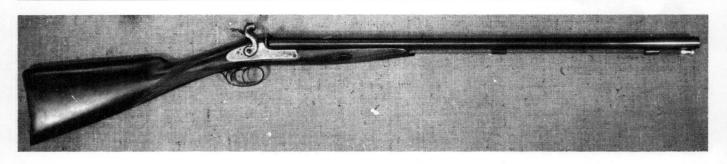

DIXIE DOUBLE-BARREL SHOTGUN

This is Dixie's best-selling shotgun. It's a 12-gauge, with browned, 30-inch barrels choked modified and full. You can load this gun with plastic shot cups. Lock, tang, and trigger are case-hardened light gray and engraved. It uses standard No. 11 caps. This is the shotgun Turner used in Africa. Price: $175.00. Dixie Gun Works, Inc., Highway 51, South, Union City, TN 38261.

COLT PERCUSSION REVOLVERS

In 1974 Colt resumed production of the Third Model Dragoon percussion revolver. No, they didn't reintroduce it or market a replica, they resumed production, right where they left off in 1860, with serial number 20,901. There are certain differences, of course, the main one being the materials used. There are some minor markings, I understand, by which you'll be able to tell a new Dragoon from the old, in order not to get collectors confused (and conned), but the dimensions and mechanics are the same. It is the same .44 as the old model, which means, in the great American tradition of confusing caliber designations, that it shoots a .457 round ball), but costs just a little bit more, inflation being what it has been over the past hundred years or so. Still, it is considerably cheaper than the few grand you'd have to lay out for an original. Retail price is $284.95; you can also buy accessories from Colt, such as a brass bullet mold and powder flask, in order to keep everything semiauthentic.

The Colt 1851 Navy is also back in production. This is .36 caliber, which usually comes out to .375, and is a little less of a shock to the pocketbook, running an even $200.00. It is also less of a shock to the arm, as it weighs in at 2½ pounds, compared to the Dragoon's 4. It has the squareback trigger guard that was relatively rare on the original.

These are high-quality arms, in the Colt tradition, and their price partially reflects the cost of the Colt name. There are lower-priced guns that shoot as well, but if you must have a genuine Colt, there isn't any choice. Colt Industries, Firearms Div., 150 Huyshope Avenue, Hartford, CT 06102.

—J.B.

Forster Tap-O-Cap: Make Your Own Percussion Caps

The black-powder shooter is one of the biggest do-it-yourselfers in the world. He makes his own rifles, casts his own bullets, cuts his own patches, and now he can even make his own percussion caps. The method used isn't as romantic, perhaps, as browning your own barrel in a 200-year-old recipe or casting bullets over a fire, but it works. The Tap-O-Cap is a punch that makes the cap body out of metal (aluminum beverage cans) into which are fitted the charge disks from a roll of toy pistol caps. What? Yes, it's true, and now you can have an excuse for emptying a six-pack on a Saturday afternoon. You have to be careful in punching out the caps with the paper puncher included, or you'll be surprised. They don't hurt; hell, I can remember having black fingernails from all the caps I popped with my hands when I was a kid.

The Tap-O-Cap is fairly expensive— $12.95—and unless you shoot an awful lot you won't save money as the last time I looked, Dixie caps were going for $7.00 per 1,000 and Alcan for about $15.00, plus you have to figure in the cost of toy caps and all that beverage drinking. But it does work, and it is an easy-to-use, well-designed tool. If percussion caps are hard to come by in your neck of the woods, you might try it. Forster Products, 82 East Lanark Avenue, Lanark, IL 61046.

—J.B.

DIXIE 1860 ARMY REVOLVER

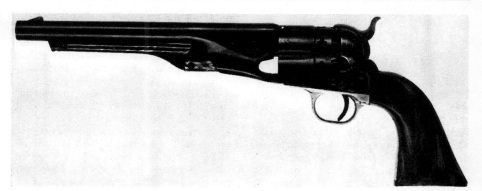

The catalog says, "We know when you buy one (or more) of these revolvers you will agree with us that they are the finest on the market." Now, these folks at Dixie are honest, so believe them. Here's what Turner has to say about their Philadelphia Derringer: "Some of the other fellows sell this same gun, but they will not tell all the facts about it. I do not think it is high quality, although it is a good serviceable shooting gun. There is definitely some room for improvement in its quality." Now, you have to believe just about anything he says after that, don't you? I do. I haven't fired one of these, but I'm taking Turner's word. It's a good gun. Retails for $89.95. Caliber is .45, and it is cut for shoulder stock (also available from Dixie). They also sell many other revolvers, which are more suitable for sporting purposes than pistols and are often surprisingly accurate. Dixie Gun Works, Highway 51, South, Union City, TN 38261.

—J.B.

RUGER OLD ARMY REVOLVER

This percussion revolver is the standard .44 caliber, which uses a .457 round ball. It's not a replica, as are a great many of the black-powder revolvers on the market today, but a modern black-powder gun. If you go for tradition and nostalgia, this might not be your arm, but if you want a shooting black-powder revolver, look into it. The gun has a fully adjustable target rear sight and a ramp front, a departure from the cocking-piece fixed rear and blade front on traditional revolvers. It's also available in stainless steel, as well as the blued style, and all the springs are coil instead of the traditional flat type. A very good gun, and it has one of Ruger's typical virtues: an incredibly low price for the quality. The nonstainless version costs $125.00, the stainless, $167.50. Sturm, Ruger & Co., Inc., Lacey Place, Southport, CT 06490.

DIXIE PISTOLS

For the shooter who would like to fool around with black powder at little expense, these are the items. Also good for hanging on the wall. The Spanish percussion pistol pictured is made in Spain and is .40 caliber; it costs only $45.00. Their most popular model is the Kentucky pistol, which retails for $89.95 or in kit form for $58.40. Caliber is .45. They also have various derringers, including a replica of the gun John Wilkes Booth used to kill Lincoln. You can get an overcoat pistol kit for $23.50. You won't be able to hit anything smaller than the proverbial broad side of a barn with most black-powder pistols, but they all do go bang and make a big cloud of smoke, which is where the fun is anyway. Dixie Gun Works, Inc., Highway 51, South, Union City, TN 38261.

PATRIOT .45 TARGET PERCUSSION PISTOL

The manufacturer claims this to be the world's most accurate black-powder handgun. Features include a walnut stock with ebony ramrod, a coil-spring lock, a hooked breech system, double set triggers, brass trim, adjustable target sights, and a rifled steel barrel.

The Patriot is available with or without an accessory pack (contains all the molds, tools, and measures needed to shoot). Prices: $125.00 without accessory pack, $152.50 with. Thompson/Center Arms, Farmington Road, Rochester, NH 03867.

Do-It-Yourself Pistols from Classic Arms

Classic Arms has three pistols in their kit line: the New Orleans Ace (a single shot), the Snake Eyes (a double-barrel side-by), and the Duck Foot (a four-barreled weapon that's a real oddball, with each barrel pointing in a slightly different direction on the same horizontal plane). The last is not much for target work, but it would sure throw shot around the room.

These guns are sold in kit form. I put together the New Orleans Ace. It isn't so complex that you need special tools or a lot of knowledge to do it, but then it isn't exactly child's play either. There was no inletting, drilling, or tapping required (the pieces are 90 percent completed), but when I finished, I felt I'd accomplished something.

All three kits are shooting models (although it costs an extra $2.00 for a rifled barrel), and the finished product looks good enough to hang on a wall. Great gifts for yourself or for friends who are antique buffs, and at a price that is right. Free color brochure. Price: Snake Eyes kit, $29.95. The other kits are in the same price range. Classic Arms, 547 Merrick Road, Lynbrook, NY 11563.

—N.S.

This company makes a good line of black-powder products, including both completed firearms and kits of the more popular types, all at competitive prices. They also sell parts, such as locks, furniture, and barrels, and all accessories, but the selection is somewhat limited compared to some of the larger companies.

ULTRA-HI PRODUCTS

They only sell three molds—.44, .50, and .69 caliber—although they do deal in a good selection of round balls. They also publish an excellent "Muzzleloader's Manual,"

which is one of the better books on this subject for the beginner, because it covers all the basics and doesn't get into some of the complexities that very often only confuse the neophyte. It's written by Hank Goodman and costs $2.95. Ultra-Hi Products Company, Inc., 150 Florence Avenue, Hawthorne, NJ 07506.

DIXIE BULLET MOLD

This is an old-time bullet mold that doesn't have a sprue cutter, so you have to cut the sprue off by hand after the bullets are molded. It isn't really much of a problem; I just drilled a ⅜-inch hole in a piece of 2 by 4, put the bullet in the hole with the sprue lying on the block, and tapped a knife through the sprue next to the bullet. It isn't quite as clean and sharp as a mold-mounted sprue cutter, but it does all right. The mold is one piece; you can't just buy mold blocks and put them on the handles to change calibers as you can with Lyman-type molds, but if you only use one or two calibers, there's no problem. It's available in any round ball size (they have a listing of .078 to 1.377 inches, which should take

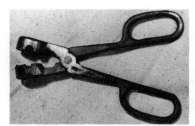

care of most guns) in .001 increments, in round or conical (nonhollow base). They also sell molds for special old guns, such as the Burnside .54 carbine, and uncherried (blank) molds for do-it-yourselfers. The style I tried was for a .444 round ball; the first dozen balls all measured just that in a micrometer. Price: $9.95. Dixie Gun Works, Inc., Highway, 51, South, Union City, TN 38261.   —J.B.

BLOWN BARRELS

The use of an old rag or a worn bedsheet for patching material can cause a blown barrel in your muzzle-loader. If there is sufficient powder residue in the barrel, the worn patch can hang up partway down the barrel when you ram the ball home. The patch in the bore then becomes a likely candidate for a barrel obstruction. Play it safe; use new patching material and keep your bore clean.

"But as some muskets so contrive it / As oft to miss the mark they drive at,
And though well aimed at duck or plover, / Bear wide, and kick their owners over."
—John Trumbull, McFingal

369

PYRODEX, THE BLACK-POWDER SUBSTITUTE

With the tremendous upsurge in black-powder shooting, there has been an attendant increase in the demand for something to use instead of black powder. This demand is not necessarily due to the flash, smoke, and fouling of black powder, because those three things are part of what differentiates the stuff from smokeless and are part of its charm (well, at least the smoke and flash are; I don't know many people who are crazy about the fouling). The biggest problem with black powder is that it's more dangerous than other powders; it is an explosive instead of a progressive-burning substance like smokeless, and it ignites at a lower temperature than smokeless (about 350 degrees Fahrenheit).

We now have a smokeless substitute. Actually, from the smell, feel, and results it might best be called semi-smokeless, as it appears at least partly to be a modification of black powder and not a completely new substance. The best part of Pyrodex is that it ignites at about 600 degrees, which means it is even safer than smokeless, and it passes the Department of Transportation tests for a "smokeless propellant." These tests are amazingly simple: you pile a bunch of boxes of known size and weight on top of a specified bunch of whatever it is you're testing and then ignite the test material. If the resultant ignition leaves a hole in the ground, then it is an explosive; if not, it's a safe-to-transport propellant. Black powder leaves a hole, and this is the reason why it can't be shipped in the same manner as smokeless.

How well does Pyrodex work? It does nicely for most shooting. I've been testing it (there are three types: rifle-shotgun, pistol, and cartridge), and I must say that in some ways it is easier to use than conventional black powder and in some ways it isn't. Because of the high ignition tempera-ture, it really isn't suitable for use in flintlocks, for instance, although it can be ignited by using a priming charge of black powder (about 10 grains or so) behind the Pyrodex charge. This involves a complex loading procedure and is, in general, a pain. Even in percussion guns it's not quite the same as black powder, because the higher ignition requirements here necessitate the use of a hot cap (the Dixie cap was used in my tests and worked well) and somewhat more compression than is used in normal loading. By this I don't mean that I have to jump up and down on the ramrod; I just lean a little more. There were no misfires, but hangfires were a problem until I got used to the loading procedure.

Pyrodex going off is just about the same as black powder: a good healthy flash and enough smoke to satisfy anyone. The nicest thing about the stuff, at least to me, was the minimal fouling. It does occur, but it doesn't build up as with black powder, and I found I was able to shoot as long as I wanted to without stopping to clean out the bore. In fact, a Pyrodex-fouled barrel seems to be slightly lubricated and makes for easier ramming. Very nice!

I've also tested the cartridge-type Pyrodex in an original Springfield trapdoor (just the type of gun it was intended for), and it answers a long-standing need. I used magnum primers (CCI) just to make sure of ignition and never had a problem.

You don't sub Pyrodex grain for grain for black powder: in most cases there is about a 20-percent reduction. Because it's competitively priced with black stuff ($4.50 per 1-pound can) you'll actually save a little by shooting it. For loading info write to B. E. Hodgdon, Inc., 7710 West 50 Highway, Shawnee Mission, KS 66202.   —J.B.

Finishing Kit for Do-It-Yourself Muzzle-Loaders

Putting together a muzzle-loading kit is half the fun of black-powder shooting. When it comes to finishing touches, look into the Birchwood Casey line of gun blues and stock finishes. Barrel browning, bluing, and stock finishes are sold separately or in kit form. The Muzzle Loaders Barrel and Stock Finishing Kit contains plum brown barrel finish, cleaner-degreaser, stock finish and stain, sandpapers, steel wool, swabs, wipes, and everything else you'll need to do a first-class job. Price: $7.95. Free catalog. Birchwood Casey Products, 7900 Fuller Road, Eden Prairie, MN 55343.

PRELOADS FOR MUZZLE-LOADERS

You can make premeasured "cartridges" for your muzzle-loaders with dime-store balloons. Drop a ball into a balloon and tie it off with light thread. Next, pour in the powder charge and tie it off. Carried thusly, the powder and ball are at the ready and are waterproof at well. Use different-colored balloons for different loads.

DIXIE HORNS AND FLASKS

Probably the most romantic piece of equipment to the black-powder shooter, aside from his Kentucky rifle, is the powder horn. Powder horns invoke memories of Dan'l Boone tossing a charge down the barrel and then knocking somebody or something off with the ramrod; the horn also recalls the buffalo, as a great many horns were made of bison headgear before the herds were slaughtered.

Dixie doesn't offer any buffalo horns, and they don't advise pouring powder directly from their horns, but they do offer a good selection of complete horns, kits, and cowhorns. I've been using a priming horn (fully finished) and a large horn made from one of their kits; both are well worth the price. The priming horn is a small horn, about 5 inches long, and is very well finished with brass fittings and a thong groove; price is $8.95. The horn kit supplies you with a large cowhorn about 10 to 12 inches long, an end plug of maple, a wood peg for the pouring end, and brass nails for finishing all for $3.95. This makes up into a horn large enough for most shooters' needs. I've been using the priming horn for most percussion shooting lately, since it holds enough powder for a day's hunting, and I use the large horn only when working up loads.

For those who prefer them, Dixie also sells a complete selection of flasks, including some shaped like shotgun butts, priced from $7.95 to $37.50. They also supply such items as spouts, horn tips for powder measures, leather for thongs, etc., etc., ad infinitum. Dixie Gun Works, Inc., Highway 51, South, Union City, TN 38261.

—J.B.

HOPPE'S BLACK-POWDER CLEANING KIT

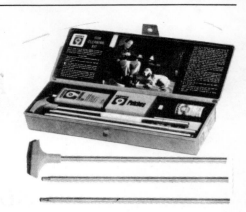

This kit is made especially for large-caliber long barrels and contains a bottle of Hoppe's No. 9 Plus (a special formula for black-powder fouling), an extra-long cleaning rod with slotted end, Hoppe's lubricating oil, and six cloth patches soaked in moisture-displacing lubricant. It comes in a black plastic box. The price for the whole thing is $8.80. Penguin Industries, Inc., P.O. Box 97, Parkesburg, PA 19365.

—J.B.

Uncle Mike's Leather Products for Black-Powder Shooting

Michaels of Oregon has three suede items for black-powder enthusiasts: a "possibles" bag (to hold all the paraphernalia that black-powder people need), a bullet bag, and a patch knife sheath. The possibles bag has an adjustable shoulder strap and a beavertail flap; it sells for $12.95. The bullet bag is drawstring type and costs $6.95; the sheath is $2.95. Michaels of Oregon, P.O. Box 13010, Portland, OR 97213.

—J.B.

UNCLE MIKE'S FIBERGLASS RAMROD

This is available in .45, .50, .54, and .58 calibers, and it is made of three pieces of brown fiberglass, so it won't break so easily. The ramrod is fitted with brass joints. Included are a cleaning jag and a "worm." Price: $10.95. Michaels of Oregon, P.O. Box 13010, Portland, OR 97213.   —J.B.

"By the rude bridge that arched the flood, / Their flag to April's breeze unfurled,
Here once the embattled farmers stood, / And fired the shot heard round the world."
—Ralph Waldo Emerson

371

UNCLE MIKE'S MUZZLE GUARD

This is a brass fitting that acts as a protective sleeve for the interior of black-powder rifle muzzles. It fits any muzzle-loader from .45 to .50 caliber and also comes with any of the Michaels' cleaning rods. Price: $1.00. Michaels of Oregon, P.O. Box 13010, Portland, OR 97213.

—J.B.

GREEN RIVER PATCH KNIFE FROM NAVY ARMS

This is a high-quality patch knife that comes complete with black leather sheath for $15.00. The handle is riveted in four places, and the blade is serrated on one side (Lord knows why). Navy Arms Company, 689 Bergen Boulevard, Ridgefield, NJ 07657.

—J.B.

KOLPIN MANUFACTURING, INC.

Frontier Gun Case for Muzzle-Loaders

This brown suede leather case has fringing for that woodsy look and a wraparound handle for carrying strength and long life. There's a lint-free red lining inside and a nylon zipper that runs one third the length of the case. When ordering, specify size. Cases come in 48-, 52-, and 60-inch lengths.

The case also has a matching ball bag and shooter's shoulder pouch made of the same fringed brown suede. The pouch has two compartments for shot and cleaning accessories, and it's modeled on an authentic original. The ball bag closes by a drawstring, and it, too, is patterned after the original thing. Prices: frontier gun case, $34.00; shooter's pouch, $16.00; ball bag, $6.00. Kolpin Manufacturing, Inc., P.O. Box 231, Berlin WI 54923.

Hard-shell Case for Kentucky Long Rifles

Kentucky long rifles and other black-powder weapons seldom fit in conventional gun cases. This hard-shell case of ABS plastic measures 65 inches by 11 inches by 3½ inches. It's lined with polyurethane foam and will encase two rifles. Price: $65.00. Protecto Plastics, Inc., 201 Alpha Road, Wind Gap, PA 18091.

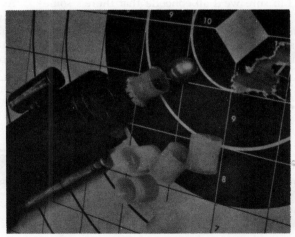

PLASTIC PATCHING MATERIAL

The Poly Patch is a one-piece polyvinyl plug with a hemisphere dug into each end. It eliminates cloth patches and lubing and is reputed to be 50 percent faster than conventional loading techniques. The Poly Patch is available in .36, .45, .50, .54, and .58 caliber at $1.95 per bag of 100. Butler Creek Corp., P.O. Box GG, Jackson Hole, WY 83001.

TASCO No. 1860 EARLY AMERICAN STYLED RIFLESCOPE 4X15mm

TASCO No. 1903 EARLY AMERICAN STYLED RIFLESCOPE 4X15mm

TASCO EARLY AMERICAN SCOPES

There's always been an argument among black-powder shooters about how authentic their sport should be. Some shooters do everything the old way, at least as much as possible: wearing homemade buckskins, shooting original and not replica rifles, and casting their bullets over an open fire. At the other extreme are shooters who only care that their guns shoot black powder; they use automatically regulated-temperature melting pots, and it isn't rare to see modern variable scopes on their arms. Most of us fall somewhere in between, but I'm sure we'd all concede that there's something slightly incongruous about a gleaming, big-objective variable on an old (or old-looking) Kentucky coal-burner. Tasco now has old-timey looking scopes for the black-powder enthusiast. Their No. 1860 4x15 is a full-barrel-length, brass-tubed type equipped with a cross-hair reticle; the No. 1903, a shorter style for turn-of-the-century breech-loaders, features an adjustable mount and is also 4x15. The small objective would give poor contrast in dim light, but these scopes probably wouldn't be used on purely big-game rifles, where poor light conditions are most likely to be encountered. Latest info gives list price at $99.95; bases are included and are available for a wide variety of arms. And yes, there *were* scopes for hunting rifles before this century. As a matter of fact, they were in use by some snipers in the Civil War, and a few buffalo hunters used them on their big Sharps rifles. These Tasco products are faithful representations of the early scopes. Tasco Sales, Inc., 1075 Northwest 71st Street, Miami, FL 33138.   —J.B.

RON KUSSE

A fine example of a collectible gun, a .410-gauge Winchester Super Model 42 Skeet. In like-new condition and enhanced by a beautiful walnut stock and forearm, all nicely checkered. This gun has not been made in a number of years and is hard to find in this grade and condition.

THE COLLECTIBLE GUN

by Ron Kusse

Gun collectors collect guns for various reasons. The hunter collects shotguns or rifles that are suited to the kinds of game he hunts. In a sense, this is a collection.

Most of the time, though, when a collection is talked about, it is not working firearms that are spoken of but the "collectible gun," meaning guns that are difficult to obtain.

The value of a collection need not be in the rarity of the guns therein but in the rarity of the guns in fine condition. Most gun collectors tend to collect a specific type of weapon, such as military, early American, early European, dueling pistols, black-powder guns, high-grade rifles or shotguns, and drillings, and there is one collector I know of who specializes in miniature handguns (not over 1½ inches long) that all fire live ammunition.

High-quality guns are, of course, the optimum choice for the collector; for example, good quality American-made doubles, the older hand-fitted pump shotguns, and discontinued lever and bolt-action rifles. There are hundreds of fine collectible guns that are waiting to be found by the canny collector.

Probably the first thing to look at when a gun is presented to you for inspection is the overall appearance, such as no excessive wear on the bluing, no large obvious gouges in the wood, and in general a well-cared-for look. First of all, the gun should be unaltered; a shotgun that seems in excellent condition but has 2 inches cut off the stock is severely limited in its value as a collector's item. A replacement stock, if it can be detected (and in most cases it can be), will lower the value of the gun. Another gun of the same model may not be in as good overall condition but will be worth more and is more desirable if it is completely unaltered. Some obvious faults to avoid are cracks and checking in the stock and/or forearm, barrels on shotguns that have been altered (such as sawed-off or bored out), not true to choke, bulging or pitting in shotgun barrels, and screws that have been butchered with the wrong size screwdriver.

Something that might not be obvious in rifles are holes that are drilled and tapped in the receiver for various types of sights or scopes after leaving the factory. All these things will lower the value of the gun as a collectible. Some extras that are often overlooked by even experienced collectors are cleaning rods, original boxes, sales slips, or instruction manuals that are specifically intended for the gun you are contemplating buying. Sometimes these accessory items, combined with the gun, can make the whole package worth a great deal more.

The collectible gun may be found in other than obvious places, such as stores and gun shows. Rural-area gun stores are very good sources, because their general clientele is more interested in hunting guns than in Dad's or Grandpa's old side-by-side or lever action. So never pass up a gas station in the country that has a sign reading "Guns for Sale."

An interesting example lies in the Catskill region of New York State, sixty miles from New York City. This area holds one of the finest stockpiles of quality unused collectors' guns in the world. Many sportsmen in New York City purchase fine-quality guns for their gun rooms and collections, generally with the idea of using them. But the pressures of business and the lack of opportunity minimizes the number of times these guns can be used to the point that some of these arms are never fired. In a slow but steady stream, these quality guns filter out into the rural areas surrounding New York City, making it fertile ground for the collector. And I suspect all large cities in the United States experience this same phenomenon.

Ron Kusse is currently a vice-president of the H. L. Leonard Rod Company and in his spare time writes and lectures throughout the eastern United States.

THE AMERICAN SPORTING COLLECTOR'S HANDBOOK
edited by Allan J. Liu

New York: Winchester Press, $10.00.

In America the days of making handcrafted, one-of-a-kind rods, guns, and reels are virtually gone. The old craftsmen have carved their last waterfowl decoys. Limited-edition books and prints have sold out, and many have become classics. Yet thousands of these treasures are still around—undiscovered or at least unappreciated—and ownership is widespread. In fact, there is hardly an attic in America that doesn't harbor some "tool" from field or stream. Recently, several astute collectors have begun to realize the value of these long-neglected items, and prices of sporting art and accessories have doubled and redoubled in the span of a few years. In this book eighteen experts, each writing on a subject on which he is an authority, tell all they know about the complete range of sporting collectibles. Specific price lists help the collector to evaluate both his holdings and the market. The standard reference for sportsmen, collectors, and dealers in art and antiques.

GUN COLLECTOR'S DIGEST
edited by Joseph J. Shroeder, Jr.

Northfield, Ill.: Digest Books, $6.95 (soft cover).

Arms collecting can mean many things. It can involve rifles, handguns, swords, ammunition—in fact, almost anything having to do with sporting or military arms. And you don't have to be rich to collect, either. Many enthusiasts make up collections of versions of Mauser rifles that were made before World War II, or variations of U.S. military ammo (though these pastimes can get expensive, too). Collecting should be, and is, a hobby for just about anyone. *Gun Collector's Digest* features articles by collectors on subjects as diverse and as specialized as antique air guns, firearms photography, and the 10mm Dutch East Indies revolver. Also included in the book are a list of gun collectors' groups and shows, a list of periodicals that might interest the collector, and another list of books on the subject. A highly recommended and worthwhile book for any aspiring collector.
—J.B.

Collector's Record Books

Gun and knife collectors will find these record books useful. They are 6-by-9-inch loose-leaf notebooks that come with removable record sheets for twenty-five knives or twenty-five guns (ten shotguns, ten rifles, and five pistols). Extra record sheets are available for $1.50 per twenty-five. Aside from a means to catalog your collection, these notebooks also provide excellent documentary evidence in case of fire or theft. When ordering, specify straight or folding knives or guns. Price: $7.50 each. A. G. Russell Co., 1705 Highway 71 North, Springdale, AR 72764.

Stoeger's Gun Trader's Guide

The *Gun Trader's Guide* is a rundown of twentieth-century firearms you're likely to find either on dealers' shelves or in other shooters' hands. It gives descriptions, approximate values, and manufacturing dates. The latest edition is the seventh. Price: $6.95. Stoeger Publishing Co., 55 Ruta Court, South Hackensack, NJ 07606.

COLLECTING ASSOCIATIONS AND CLUBS

American Society of Arms Collectors, Inc.
6550 Baywood Lane
Cincinnati, OH 45224
Robert F. Rubendunst, Secretary-treasurer

International Cartridge Collectors Association, Inc.
4065 Montecito Avenue
Tucson, AZ 85711

In addition, there are many state and local organizations. A complete list of these can be found in the *Gun Collector's Digest*.

REPRODUCTIONS OF OLD GUN CATALOGS

Collectors are usually nostalgia nuts, and even those who aren't will feel a twinge of longing for the past when they look over these old gun catalogs, faithfully reproduced on high-quality paper.

Nearly 100 years of classic catalogs are available, from the 1862 Rifleman's Handbook ($2.00), written by John Pease for the Union troops at the start of the Civil War, to a 1950 Walther P-38 operating manual ($2.50) in English, with exploded views of components.

While the prose is interesting, the art in many of these old catalogs is classic, from fine line drawings to funky photos, illustrating testimonials from famous shooters of the day. Many illustrations contained in *The Complete Hunter's Catalog* originated from these old gun catalogs.

But the real clincher is when you take a look at the prices charged for fine, engraved weapons at the turn of the cen-

tury. Nostalgia nut or no, I promise you'll weep for the loss. Free illustrated catalog available on request. The Personal Firearms Record Book Company, P.O. Box 2800, Santa Fe, NM 87501.

"Oh, bright as a berry, / They're red and they're rare, / The setters from Kerry, / And Cork and Kildare!"
—Patrick Reginald Chalmers, "The Red Dogs"

375

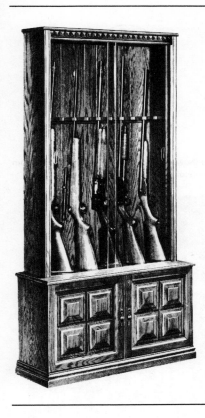

Standing Gun Cabinet

A gun is as much a work of art as it is a functional tool. It's also a kind of memory bank. Look upon the 12-gauge side-by-side that was your dad's or the .30-06 you carried up the slopes of the Rocky Mountains, and memories swirl like smoke from a barrel.

One way to display that art and enjoy those memories is by way of a gun cabinet. This standing cabinet is made of solid oak and oak veneers. It holds up to ten guns behind glass-encased doors that are secured with a ratchet lock. Barrel racks and stock pits are lined with green felt, and the cabinet at the base holds ammo, cleaning kits, and soft cases under a separate lock.

The cabinet is of Mediterranean styling and measures 74 high by 37 inches wide and 13½ inches deep. It will accept guns up to 52 inches long. Price: $210. Bob Hinman Outfitters, 1217 West Glen, Peoria, IL 61614.

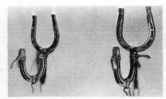

Display Racks for Antique and Collectible Firearms

The display racks in this line are all individual hangers. The motif is decidedly Western; hangers are fashioned after spurs, horseshoes, and saddle cinches (in case you're unfamiliar with saddles, these hangers are suspended from polished aluminum D rings, and the gun is racked inside a cowhide leather belt that is decorated with floral patterns). If you don't like things Western, there's also a set of gun cradles made of polished aluminum that will pass for early Yankee. All display racks are lined to protect the finish on your guns. Price: $2.95 to $5.95. San Angelo Co., P.O. Box 984, San Angelo, TX 76901.

Morton Booth Gun Cabinets for Long Guns and Handguns

This company is the largest maker and supplier of gun cabinets in the United States, with thirty-eight different types of cabinets and finishes to choose from. Most of their cabinets feature stand-up display, glass doors, and locks on gun doors and sliding drawers located at floor level.

Their cabinets are made to house six to twelve guns, and they are available in a wide variety of woods and finishes. A sampler of styles and prices would include:

• No. 620, a picture-frame-type pistol cabinet in walnut finish that houses up to eight guns on a pegboard back with a felt green finish, $60.00.

• No. 248, an eight-gun rifle/shotgun cabinet in walnut or maple finish with dustproof doors, decorator hinges, felt padding for barrels and butt plates, two keyed-alike locks, $146.00.

• No. 408, an elegant solid walnut gun cabinet for eight guns, $280.00.

• No. 770, an economy-class walnut-finish six-gun cabinet without a glass door, but with an underdrawer, $92.00.

• No. 612, stylish storage for twelve guns in a hand-rubbed solid walnut or solid maple cabinet with two drawers and like-keyed locks, $400.00. Morton Booth, P.O. Box 123, Joplin, MO 64801.

RUSTIC,
DO-IT-YOURSELF
GUN RACK

MICHAELS OF OREGON DISPLAY AIDS

This firm has quite a few low-priced gun racks and other display items available. The simplest are their hook-type racks for wall mounting; these come in oakleaf or contemporary (whatever that means) styles in two-, three-, and four-gun sizes and are priced at $10.95, $15.95, and $19.95 respectively. Also available is a rustic rack made for one long gun, which is a wall-hanging style and includes a storage shelf for ammo, cleaning equipment, etc. It comes as a do-it-yourself kit (only needs finishing) and costs $10.95. A handy accessory to this might be their locking chest, which comes with a skeleton key. It is roomy enough to store ammo, bolts, and other sundry items. Price: $25.95. Michaels of Oregon, P.O. Box 13010, Portland, OR 97213.

—J.B.

Photo shows how lock securely rachets locking pin into bore of any rifle including all shot guns.

Bargain Gun Cabinet: Finish It Yourself

This is an unfinished pine gun cabinet with a lot of expensive features: glass, dustproof doors, floor-level drawer, both with locks and finished hinges. It holds up to six guns, and at $74.97 it is the cheapest cabinet that we've been able to find with these features. Herter's, Inc., Route 2, Mitchell, SD 57301.

SECURITY GUN SAFES

Public relations hyperbole being what it is, it's refreshing to run into a product that is correctly and even honestly named. This one is. It is secure, it is for guns, and it is comparable to a safe.

Twelve guns, along with shelves for ammo, cameras, handguns, etc., are housed in a 63-by-24-by-17-inch steel cabinet. Two locks, protected by a hood, are out of reach of hammers, saws, or bolt cutters. A large padlock secures the locking system; it, too, is out of reach of anything but the right key.

The safes may be bolted to the wall or floor for added protection, and they are guaranteed against forced entry for three years. Price: $412.00. Security Gun Chests, P.O. Box 5497, Roanoke, VA 24012.

NEW Master ARMORLOCK No. 37-D

For EXTRA PROTECTION in Today's Jungle

FOR TRAILER HITCH   FOR HASPS   FOR CHAIN & CABLE

ARMORLOCK PADLOCK

When you have to padlock anything, from hunting camp to a trailer hitch or a hard-shell gun case, consider the Armorlock.

It is a conventional padlock in its basic design, but the shackles are protected on one side by a revolving guard that defies a hacksaw and on the other side by a ¾-inch armored bolt-cutter barrier. In place on a hasp, or chain and cable, you just can't get at the shackles, and the internal mechanism is engineered to defy shimming or rapping. This looks like a lock that would test Willie Sutton. Just don't lose your key. Price: $5.95. Master Lock Co., Milwaukee, WI 53201.

Security Gun Locking System

This looks like a good idea that combines a foolproof locking system with a display technique. A padded butt keeper of steel and aluminum, which can be bolted or screwed in place, accepts the rifle or shotgun butt. A male locking device, which also can be bolted or screwed into a wall, goes into the barrel and locks in place. The gun is out in the open, but it cannot be removed from the wall or cabinet without being unlocked. With this system guns can be mounted anywhere, in any attitude. If you have several guns, units can be keyed alike. Price: $25.00. Trico Security Products, 2309 Wyandotte Road, Willow Grove, PA 19090.

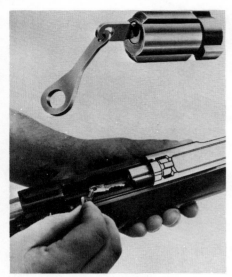

Cease-Fire Bolt-Action Lock

This is a short, locking safety device that renders a bolt gun inoperable. It can't be forced out without destroying the action, so that any gun so equipped is useless to a thief, and it also keeps firearms safe from children. The bolt need only be drawn back to install. Price: $9.95. Michaels of Oregon, P.O. Box 13010, Portland, OR 97213.   —J.B.

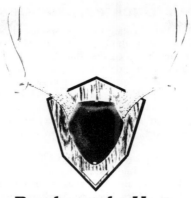

Ready-made Horn Mount

If you want a token of your trophy and can't afford the cost of a taxidermist, San Angelo makes a quality do-it-yourself horn mount.

Everything is supplied but your rack. Their kit contains a highly polished hardwood plaque, a brass plate (should you wish some kind of permanent inscription), and a green or red velvet skull cover.

To mount a set of antlers, cut off the top of the deer's skull with horns attached, lay them on the plaque, and bolt the skull cover in place. There's no more to it than that. A real bargain at $8.95. San Angelo Co., P.O. Box 984, San Angelo, TX 76901.

Hoppe's Sportsmen's Knobs

These are simple wooden knobs, with nails running lengthwise through them. You drive the nail into a wall and hang things on it: guns, hats, a bag of onions, anything your heart desires. You can buy six for $2.25. Penguin Industries, Inc., P.O. Box 97, Parkesburg, PA 19365.
                              —J.B.

Knife Collector's Club

If you're interested in collecting knives, this organization should be a good one to join. Member services include bulletins, catalogs, and news about knives; advance notice on new knives before prices go up; discounts on knives; first crack at low serial numbers and premier grades; and a free consultation and information service.

The club is the brainchild of A. G. Russell, who's carved out a reputation as a number-one authority on custom and collectible knives. Membership seems reasonable enough: $5.00 per year. Contact A. G. Russell Co., 1705 Highway 71 North, Springdale, AR 72764.

METAL ENGRAVER HELPS TRACE THEFTS

The Dremel electric engraver will carve permanent marks on virtually all materials, including hardened steel and glass. Use it to put identifying marks on guns, outboard motors, and household valuables. If it's common knowledge that you've done this, chances are these items won't be ripped off. Even if they are, should the police catch up with the crooks, they're easy to identify as yours. Price: $14.95. Dremel Manufacturing, 4915 21st Street, Racine, WI 53406.   —F.S.

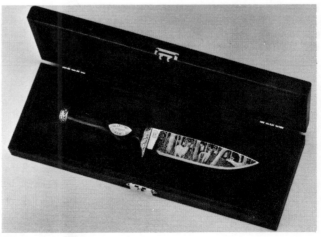

Smith & Wesson's Knife Collector's Series

Smith & Wesson's line of quality hunting knives provide the basis for their collector's series. A limited edition (1,000) of each of their knife types, which have been styled and engraved by Blackie Collins, a noted custom knifemaker. Artwork includes an acid-etched game scene on the blade, a sculptured sterling silver guard and pommel, and engraved escutcheons on the handle. Each knife is numbered and is issued in a richly lined mahogany presentation case. A fine specimen is the Outdoorsman. Price: $300.00. Smith & Wesson Co., 2100 Roosevelt Avenue, Springfield, MA 01101.

Belt Buckles, Buckles, Buckles

If you're looking for a personalized belt buckle, this is the place to start. Morgano & Feuer has a catalog that lists over 500 different belt buckles, and at incredibly reasonable prices. There are brass buckles, pewter buckles, rawhide buckles, and hand-enameled buckles; square, round, large, and small, that depict just about every sport, pastime, or interest imaginable.

There are the predictable Colt and Winchester arms buckles; more esoteric Buick, Mack Truck, and Volkswagen buckles for car buffs; Africa buckles; Marlboro buckles; hunting dog buckles; camera buckles; a Polish Armed Guard buckle, which features a pistol that fires backwards; and the doubtful subtlety of a buckle that simply reads, "Bullshit."

If their vast selection doesn't satisfy you, they'll engrave or cast your own design. Prices on production buckles run $7.50 for enameled models to $4.50 for pewter, and they'll sell you a leather belt for your buckle for around $3.50. Morgano & Feuer Enterprises, Inc., 28 Rockne Street, Staten Island, NY 10314.

If the Place You Hunt Sounds Like a War on Opening Day . . .

Dress right for the occasion. Unique Imports, 610 Franklin Street, Alexandria, VA 22314, offers a free catalog that includes roomfuls of military collectibles, from the Civil War through Korea. There are hats and helmets, knives and bayonets, gas masks, insignia, uniforms, and replica (nonfiring) guns from about any period that strikes your fancy.

They also accent the unusual, like a specifically designed bayonet that cuts wire, the Gurkha Kukri knife ("never unsheathed unless it draws blood"), and a recording of the songs of Fascist Italy (1922–43), among others.

This well-illustrated catalog lists about every war memento or associated book (would you believe three volumes on bayonets of the world?) you'd ever have need for, and believe it or not, there are even a few items listed there that would be useful afield.

Magazine for Decoy Carvers and Collectors

Hillcrest Publications puts together a quarterly magazine called *North American Decoys* that features things like new developments in carving and collecting, coverage of decoy shows across the nation, old decoys and decoy makers, and classified and display ads. It costs $12.00 annually.

These same folks publish a whole slug of books that deal with carving, collecting, and art associated with waterfowl and waterfowling. Hillcrest Publications, P.O. Box 246, Spanish Fork, UT 84660.

North American DECOYS

MAINE OLDSQUAW (14")
Carved by unknown bayman in the Monehegan Island area of Maine, circa 1910. This colorful and somewhat rare bird was heavily hunted in the Great Lakes and New England area at the turn of the century.

THE WOODEN DECOYS OF

If you're a tradition-bound waterfowler who glories in the lines of a Barnegat Bay sneakbox and the tales of the days when you could shoot seventy-five canvasback, look into what the Wooden Bird Factory can do for you.

They make wooden decoys—the solid, gracefully carved blocks of yesteryear—and at a price that means you can afford to use these marvelous bits of antiquity as working blocks.

Essentially, these folks offer you a basic block shape—mallard, pintail, wood duck, bluebill, and others—and give you the option of choosing the material from which it is made and whether the block is painted or unpainted. In other words, if you're interested in a working rig, you can buy a baker's dozen of rough-finished, unpainted decoys, made from cedar or pine, for $99.50. You weight, finish, paint, and rig them yourself and, along the way, really get close to what waterfowling is all about.

"Nature I loved; and next to Nature, Art.
I warm'd both hands against the fire of life."
—Walter Savage Landor

379

WILDLIFE ART *by Maynard Reece*

Depictions of birds, mammals, and fish have been created by man for ages. The prehistoric cave paintings of early man and the tombs of ancient civilizations are reminders that man has always had an intense interest in animals.

From about 1300, artists started putting their drawings on wood, then later on paper and canvas. Wildlife art was popular among art collectors and museums until the early 1900s. Artists such as Winslow Homer, Thomas Eakins, John Audubon, Frederic Remington, and Charles Marion Russell were painting hunting and fishing scenes of early America; most of their works eventually found their way into the largest art museums in the country.

With the new wave of modernism, impressionism, cubism, regionalism, and other facets of modern art flourishing in the early 1900s, museums started collecting more of this type of work, and the realism of wildlife art fell into disfavor.

The public wasn't as prone to switch their allegiance to other forms of art. Some bird-lovers, hunters, fishermen, and outdoor people in general still collected wildlife art, but little of it ever found its way back to art museums, since the interest there had turned to other art forms.

Most wildlife artists turned to magazines, books, and advertising to make their living in this specialized field. As nature photography, especially color photography, became more prevalent with better equipment, a simple matter of economics began to phase out a large share of wildlife art in the commercial field.

The sale of wildlife art to art collectors as well as to birders, hunters, and fishermen began to gain momentum. This has increased in recent years, until now there is a sizable market for this type of art.

Two major things have occurred to increase the interest in this field. Man suddenly began to run out of natural resources and started to accelerate the pollution of his own environment. This awakened a new awareness that he was just another animal on this earth and could actually eliminate himself from an existence that he took for granted. A great many people began to take interest in the natural world around them and began to join in the effort to slow down man's disastrous insistence on destroying himself and his environment. This interest has stimulated collectors, people publishing material to educate the public on this danger, and organizations trying to save this environment, and has increased the sales of wildlife art.

The second thing that occurred because of this new interest was the emphasis on prints, particularly limited edition prints. Every type of collector began buying prints of wildlife at a fraction of the cost of acquiring an original painting. Now every home can afford a favorite bird or mammal on the wall, a nostalgic scene of his duck marsh, or a painting of a natural river, bog, lake, forest, or brook. These things are being destroyed by industry, agriculture, highways, subdevelopments, and the relentless crunch of misguided civilization. By buying and viewing these prints the public is learning about and appreciating the natural world around us.

Museums are now becoming aware of this interest in wildlife art. Man's interpretation of animals in their natural habitat has once again found its way back to the walls of the art museums, to be viewed by millions of people who are interested in the natural world in which we live.

Maynard Reece is one of America's premier wildlife artists. His waterfowl paintings and sketches hang in museums and private collections in the United States and Europe. His artistry has also graced a number of migratory bird stamps.

BIRD FACTORY: DISTINCTION

If you're interested in a decorative decoy, the same block patterns are available in cherry, butternut, or walnut and in three finishes: rough, feather smooth, or carved. You can also buy a fully painted block, if you want a decorative decoy that you can slap on the mantel right now. Prices on these more exquisite stool run from $9.95 to $49.95 each, depending on the wood and work involved in their production.

Along with standard postures, species, and shapes, the Wooden Bird Factory offers classics like the Laing sleeping black duck, the Mason bluebill, half ducks for wall framing, and shorebirds. These are a marvelous release for the repressed artist in you, and a source of treasured Christmas and birthday presents for your blind partners. The Wooden Bird Factory, 8600 Highway 7, St. Bonifacius, MN 55375.

—N.S.

BEN SCHMIDT CANVASBACK (16")

Ben Schmidt (1884-1968) was a well-known regional carver living in Detroit, Michigan. His rugged birds were noted for their big water stability, and their effective decoying characteristics. Some hunters still use Ben's classic designs.

GRAY FOX FAMILY
33 X 25

EASTERN CHIPMUNK
12 X 9

OAKGROVE PINTAILS
28 X 40
16 X 20

BOBWHITE QUAIL
24 X 21

FLYING SNOWY OWL
33 X 25

ART
BY
JEANIE MCCOY

If you have a yen for an original painting or a drawing of wildlife native to the Rocky Mountains, look into the art of Jeanie McCoy. She lives and works near Ennis, Montana. Her paintings are noted for accuracy of color and proportion and for a three-dimensional quality that makes you want to reach out and touch her subjects.

Ms. McCoy works in all mediums—oil, pastel, and watercolor—and handles each with equal skill. For further information contact Bill McCrea, P.O. Box 415, Fairfield, MT 59436.

WATERFOWL ART

There's a subtle statement about the beauty and the poetry of waterfowling made through the existence of and interest in waterfowl art. There are more prints, paintings, etchings, and sketches of waterfowl created and sold annually than art depicting any form of the shooting sports. And when you think about it, it isn't too surprising. The decoy hunter, with stool that he paints himself and then sets down on some calm pond to imitate nature, is a kind of artist himself.

If you have an interest in waterfowl art, one outlet we know of is The Depot, Rural Route 3, Sullivan, IL 61951. Along with a gallery of over 100 framed hunting prints, they furnish investment information, news about new print releases, and secondary market data regarding the purchase of art.

They also provide a by-mail total information service. For an annual fee of $3.00, you're sent a monthly newsletter that illustrates and gives prices on available wildlife art. Small, full-color reproductions of featured prints often accompany this newsletter, and they alone are worth the price of a subscription.

SKETCHES BY JOI

Joi Wedekind, 89-74 221st Street, Queens Village, NY 11427, is a talented portrait and scenic artist, who is at home in just about any medium from pencil to oil. She has had extensive experience working from photographs (for an example of her work, see the sketches of the staff at the end of this book) as well as life, and her work appears in galleries in New York, Florida, and Puerto Rico. Send her your favorite hunting photo, and ask for a price.

ECONOMY WILDLIFE PRINTS

Anticipation is part of hunting. To help you pass away those winter days with nostalgic memories of last year's hunt, we recommend your looking into the variety of hunting scenes and prints that have been reproduced on heavy artist stock.

These prints come in full color and are available in a variety of sizes. Labrador print, 20 by 24 inches, is priced at $9.95, postpaid. Canadian Game Bird Products, Ltd., 1237 56th Street, Delta, British Columbia, Canada.   —P.S.

DECOY NEEDLEPOINT KITS

Rosey Greer can dig it; you might, too. These kits contain a pressed design on canvas, necessary yarn, needles, and complete instructions. The finished needlepoint measures 12 by 17 inches. Available in wood duck decoy and pintail decoy. Price: $20.00 each. Tidewater Specialties, 430 Swann Avenue, Alexandria, VA 22301.

GAME POSTERS FOR DEN OR WORKSHOP

If the musty smell of an old decoy from the attic calls up dreams of a bygone era, if finding the remains of an old shotgun shell among the autumn leaves makes you wonder about the bird, the gun, and the man who once used it, you'll probably love Remington's game posters.

The style of art, the quality of reproduction, and the funky didacticism of these reproductions are out of those times when birds were abundant two miles outside town and when "hunter" was synonymous with "gentleman."

Four posters are currently available in the Know Your

Game series: Upland Birds, Waterfowl, Big Game, and Hunting Dogs. The subjects are portrayed in color, and a brief description of their identification and behavior accompanies the artwork. While they were originally intended to be an educational device, that's not their real worth. Like a weathered old decoy or Great-Grandpa's Damascus side-by, they just feel good to have around. Price: $3.00 each. Remington Arms Co., Inc., 939 Barnum Avenue, Bridgeport, CT 06602.

SPORTING LIFE CATALOG—

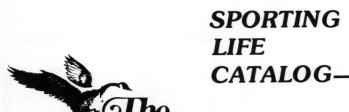

The Sporting Life is a Georgetown (D.C.)-based gallery with branches in Memphis and Milwaukee. A few of the artists they represent constitute a Who's Who of wildlife art: Guy Coheleach, Peter Corbin, Leroy Neiman, Maynard Reece, Chet Reneson, and Larry Toschik.

The first thing that impressed (or rather surprised) me about this catalog is that while it pretends to champagne tastes, a lot of the art advertised is within the limits of a beer pocketbook. $600.00 for a Corbin original is not outrageous; nor is $85.00 for a signed and numbered Maynard Reece print. Rest assured that there are ample paintings in the $1,000 to $2,000 class, but the majority of them are affordable.

*"The old hound wags his shaggy tail, / And I know what he would say:
It's over the hills we'll bound, old hound, / Over the hills and away."*
—George Meredith

383

Carving Kit for Beginners

If you're a duck hunter with a creative urge but have never tried wood carving before, this kit contains rough-shaped bodies, heads, and wings for two miniature decoys, including an extra wing and head should your knife slip. Finished, one decoy is in a flying posture, the other in a sitting position.

Along with the basic bodies, you get the tools you'll need to finish the job: a knife, sandpaper, nails, patterns, and instructions for carving and painting (the paint is not included). You have your choice of a mallard/black duck, a bluebill, or a Canada goose. If you know a little bit about carving and duck proportions, these can be easily altered to conform to just about any species of waterfowl you'd like to depict. Price: Duck carving kit, $12.50. Bob Hinman Outfitters, 1217 West Glen, Peoria, IL 61614.

DO-IT-YOURSELF BUMPER STICKERS

If you've had a yen to respond to anti-hunting inanities, like "I Brake for Animals" (who in their right mind doesn't?) and "Support Your Right to Arm Bears," we know of two people who will custom print your own slogan on a bumper sticker: Headline Printers, P.O. Box 1114, Billings, MT 59103, and Oleet & Co., Inc., 60 Claremont Plaza, Mount Vernon, NY 10553. Cost is based on the number of characters. Price range is $5.00 to $10.00 per dozen.

The possibilities are limited only by your imagination. You could do something like "Hunters Pay for Conservation," but to my way of thinking that's a little stodgy. Some of my favorites have been "The Sonoran Desert, Love It or Leave It," "Save Furbish Lousewort," and "Save a Tree, Eat a Beaver."   —N.S.

The Sporting Life also catalogs the kind of trinkets you might associate with a gallery—brass canvasback bookends ($50.00), a shotshell ashtray ($15.00), and Richard Bishop glasses with game birds fired on (six for $28.80). Like their art, these wares are quality and seem to be offered at a fair price.

Art and artifacts aside, the catalog itself is graphically attractive. The prints offered for sale are faithfully reproduced, many of them in color, and the goods are seductively displayed. A good source of presents for the sportsman who has everything, including good taste. Free catalog. The Sporting Life, 3029 M Street Northwest, Georgetown, Washington, DC 20007.

PRINTS AND PRETTY THINGS

Part VI

ARCHERY

RECURVE VS. COMPOUND: THE LOWDOWN

So you're thinking of buying another bow, and you want to know which one is better, the recurve or the compound? Judging by most standards, the compound is, by far.

There are three big advantages to the compound bow. The most important is that it is harder-hitting and of a flatter trajectory than a recurve of comparable weight. This is because the compound bow accelerates the arrow more smoothly than a recurve. Because of the compound's breakaway feature, where peak draw weight is achieved halfway through the draw and then is relaxed as you continue to draw, when you release the bowstring the arrow is "pushed" at ever-increasing pressure. In a recurve, the maximum thrust is at the maximum draw length. Rather than being pushed, the arrow is walloped by the string in a recurve, which results in sympathetic reactions in the arrow shaft that, in lay terms, could best be described as "whips, snaps, and jingles." The net result is a slower-moving, lower-energy, less-accurate arrow in flight.

That breakaway point is of monumental significance in another respect. Depending upon the amount of reduction in a particular compound, a bow that peaks out at 50 pounds will deliver between 38 and 25 pounds of pull on your fingertips at full draw. This means you can probably pull and hold a much heavier, more powerful bow than you're used to, a feature that again translates to an increased effective range and greater accuracy.

Finally, compounds are adjustable. Some models have adjustable peak draws, where you can vary the draw weight up to 20 pounds by turning a cam. In other words, when you're developing form, you can crank a 60-pound compound down to 45 pounds so as not to get arm-weary. As hunting season approaches, you can "train up" to 60 pounds. Then, some compounds have adjustable draw lengths. If everyone in your family likes to shoot, you can change draw lengths to suit them all. And there are compounds available with *both* peak draw weight and draw length adjustments.

At this point perhaps I should digress, because the implication is clear: that buying a compound "loaded"—that is, with all these features—is always the best deal. 'Tain't so. There is a valid comparison to be made between that assumption and one holding that a Cadillac Seville is the best car on the market because it offers the most features. Try taking one up a jeep road. Or match it against a Triumph at a rallye. In fact, of those people I've spoken to whom I consider experts, all but one felt (given brand preferences) that the less adjustment there was, the better the bow would perform. But realize that these folks were expert bowmen who knew just what they wanted. All of them were just as quick to agree that adjustable bows could very well suit other tastes.

With this ringing praise of the compound, do I then relegate the recurve to museums and junk heaps? Not at all. The recurve is plainly a less-efficient weapon, but that's really no measure of a hunting implement or its popularity. A 7mm magnum automatic combines firepower and accuracy that makes a .45 caliber caplock black-powder rifle turn pale, yet there are an awful lot of folks who are hunting and shooting black-powder guns today.

The recurve has two things the compound will never achieve: the first is grace, and grace is one of the prime attractions of archery; the second is that it's primitive, several steps removed from the machinelike efficiency of the compound and perhaps several steps closer to the essence of hunting. The compound will never replace the recurve. Rather, it will assume a separate niche in the minds of archers. Both have their place, and both are here to stay.
—N.S.

RECURVE AND COMPOUND: A TEST

In order to get some idea of the differences in performance and handling between the two styles of bows, rather than differences in manufacturing excellence, I tested two Brownings: a 60-pound Compound Stalker I and a 55-pound Wasp recurve. The arrows were Browning glass shafts with field points.

The first test was conducted at 25 yards, and the target was a pie plate in the middle of stacked hay bales. Shooting the recurve, I buried the arrow just beyond the crest, about two thirds of the shaft's length.

When I released the compound, the arrow simply disappeared. The flight was so fast that I couldn't track it by eye, as I could with an arrow cast from a recurve. It went completely through the bale and plunked into the dirt about 25 feet behind it. I noted, too, that I had nicked the top of the pieplate with the arrow from the compound. The arrow from the recurve rested about an inch below the pie plate. I had held on the same spot for each shot.

Next I stationed a friend out in the field in front of my house and stuck a piece of lath in the ground. With him double-checking the point of impact, I held on the top of the lath and released, once with the compound and once with the recurve.

I feel obligated at this point to mention that I am not a tournament archer. I don't always hit pie plates at 25 yards, so there was some margin for elevational error. At any rate, the compound's point of impact was 52 feet beyond the recurve's.

Finally, our distance test. I shot an arrow into the air with the recurve. It was easy to track, and the point at which it reached ultimate elevation and turned around was plain to the naked eye. When I shot the compound, we lost the arrow. It went too fast to track, and we never saw it turn around, which made for mutual apprehension for a while.

Since we didn't see it come down, we theorized that perhaps the shaft stuck up there. Our assumption was proven false a few days later when I found the arrow in my upper pasture, about 150 yards away from where it had been shot.

One problem with the compound was revealed by subsequent shooting. Along with my inability to consistently hit pie plates, I also have been known to misnock an arrow now and then. Whenever the bow was inadvertently thus "dry fired," the string jumped its idler pulleys and wedged between the clevis and the pulley. It takes two to wrench the cable free and get it back on the trolley, and it doesn't do the string any good either.

Admittedly, a bow should never be "dry fired," but it can happen accidentally, and unless you have a hunting buddy nearby, a misnocked arrow would draw your day's hunting up short.

Another thing I noticed while hunting with a compound is that they are not really any easier to get through brush than a recurve. True, the limbs are shorter, but the extensive stringing tends to ensnare brush and, I feel, cancels out the short-limbed advantages.

Still, I feel right in saying that the compound is superior in its performance and is a system to be reckoned with in the woods.

—N.S.

THE ARCHER'S TOUGHEST TROPHY

by Fred Bear

There are various definitions of what constitutes a tough-to-obtain bowhunting trophy. My own is that of an animal so well attuned to its environment and with senses so finely honed that it takes all the skill a woodsman can muster to consistently be successful in pursuit of that species' more mature males.

Some animals are potentially dangerous to pursue, and this in itself adds spice to the hunt. It does not necessarily make them difficult to stalk; just difficult to collect once the hunter encounters them. In this category I would list such animals as the polar, Kodiak, and grizzly bears on our continent and, farther afield, the elephant, cape buffalo, lion, and leopard. In my experience, the polar bear has to be the riskiest of our North American game to go up against with the bow. He is big, aggressive, and often shows no fear of man. I was saved from a possible mauling or worse twice by my guide's rifle on hunts for these kings of the Arctic ice before I finally succeeded in taking one unaided with the bow.

In another category of hunting toughness are those animals whose habitat is so barren, restrictive, or hard to get into that successful stalks are difficult. Among these would be classed the various species of mountain sheep and the Rocky Mountain goat, as well as the Asiatic buffalo and, again, the polar bear.

A subcategory might include those animals whose habits—for instance, being largely nocturnal—make them difficult to encounter. Good examples would be our mountain lion, when dogs are not used to run or tree it, and the Asiatic tiger, if native beaters are not employed.

However, after some forty-five years of pursuing the various species of big game, I firmly believe that anyone who can successfully and consistently outwit white-tailed deer is the peer of any hunter anywhere. The craft and cunning of this animal is legendary. Both the Western mule deer and the elk are plenty smart, but they live in more open country, for the most part, and are thus easier to locate, to call, and to stalk.

Archery Museum

The Fred Bear Archery Museum is located 1½ miles west of Grayling, Michigan, and if you're into the historical aspects of the bow and arrow, it's well worth a look. The Bear people claim it's the most extensive private collection of archery-oriented artifacts in existence, with tools, weapons, and art displayed from North American Indians, Japan, the Battle of Marathon in 490 B.C., Malaysia, the South Pacific, Africa, Tibet, Mongolia, China, Persia, Arabia, and more.

There's also an extensive display of taxidermy, mostly trophies collected by Fred Bear himself: elephants and lions, polar bear and virtually all other North American big game. Upstairs there's a museum theater which seats seventy people, where half-hour movies of Bear's hunting adventures are shown during the peak season.

The museum is open seven days a week year round. For further information write Fred Bear Archery Museum, Grayling, MI 49738. —F.S.

The Let-off Letdown

A compound bow with a 50-pound peak draw weight and with 50-percent let-off would mean that at full draw you would only be holding back 25 pounds. There are some obvious advantages to this: less muscle fatigue, the ability to hold the draw for longer times, and the fact that archers who aren't built like Tarzan can still handle a heavy bow. But like all things that seem too good to be true, there is a catch.

The more let-off in a bow, the less energy is stored in the string. Although two compounds may be rated at equivalent peak draws, the compound with less let-off will drive the arrow flatter and faster (hence with more energy) than a bow with a lot of let-off. In general, it may be said that bows in the 25-to-35-percent let-off range will perform better as hunting bows than those in the 35-to-50-percent range. —N.S.

ALLEN'S COMPOUND SPEEDSTER

This bow is made by the people who brought you the compound in the first place. Every compound, no matter what its name or appearance, is licensed under the Allen patent.

We selected the Speedster at the suggestion of a well-known archery authority who claimed it was, dollar for dollar, the best buy on the market.

No. 7507 is non-adjustable, with a draw weight of 50 pounds at either 27-to-29-inch or 29-to-31-inch draw. It has a 40-percent let-off, is 48 inches overall, and has laminated glass limbs. The Speedster is available in right- or left-hand grips and in two colors, black or brown.

While I didn't shoot the bow personally (we couldn't find a left-hander), the fellow I was with, by no means an accomplished archer, was able to place arrows within the second ring consistently at 20 yards. He was obviously impressed with the bow's handling and smooth let-off, because he subsequently bought one. Price: $79.50. Other Allen compounds from $89.50 to $275.00. Allen Archery, Inc., Billings, MO 65601. —N.S.

While deer are often referred to as creatures of habit, they can and do change their ways and are often found where you least expect them. The larger bucks are often highly individualistic in their routines. They are familiar with every feature of their home range and are highly adept at skulking, hiding, and evading the hunter. Their senses are whetted keen by hundreds of years of being pursued. Their hearing is acute, their sense of smell keen, and their ability to spot movement phenomenal.

Whitetails are often overlooked by inexperienced hunters in discussing tough trophies, simply because they are North America's most common and most heavily hunted big-game animal. Most of the really large bucks obtained by bowmen have been ambushed from elevated blinds. Purely chance encounters, of course, account for some. The ultimate test of an archer's skill as a woodsman, however, comes in the still hunt, wherein he travels quietly through known deer cover, moving slowly and either across or into the wind. Once having sighted the quarry, his job has just begun, as he must stalk to within adequate range of his weapon, which is generally some 30 to 40 yards. Anyone who can do this successfully with a large whitetail buck has certainly accomplished a great deal and deserves respect.

The whitetail's adaptability and stealth have brought it through years of changing environment and, in many areas, within the fringes of civilization. In our distant future, I would guess that the whitetail may be America's last surviving species of large game to be found in huntable numbers.

Fred Bear needs little more introduction than his name. If modern archery has a father, it is he. If one man personifies the term sportsman, it is he. Fred Bear has taken virtually every spieces of big game in the world, and he has done it with a bow and arrow.

JENNINGS TWO-WHEEL COMPOUND TWINSTAR HUNTER

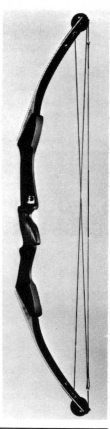

In a very broad sense, four-wheel compounds are preferred to two-wheel compounds by target archers because they can be more finely tuned. Two-wheel compounds are more attractive to hunters because they are simpler—cleaner, if you will.

The Jennings folks claim that their new bow, the Twinstar Hunter, offers the best of both worlds: the clean lines of a two-wheeler, with a 10-pound weight adjustment, a 1-inch draw length adjustment, and a 40-to-50-percent let-off. Other features of this bow include an adjustable arrow rest, interchangeable grips (including an insulated grip for cold-weather hunting), and machined Delrin step-wheel eccentrics with bushings. Also, the bow is tapped and drilled for a sight, stabilizer, cushion plunger, and a bow quiver. Price: $265.82. Jennings Compound Bow Company, 28756 North Castaic Canyon Road, Valencia, CA 91355.

Jennings Arrowstar Hunter: A Top-Drawer Four-Wheeler

This bow was the pick of the crop by a friend and well-known archer who wishes to remain anonymous. He was highly impressed with its ability to be precisely tuned and its cable clearance. Said he, "If you want one bow for match archery and hunting, and you're serious about both, this is the one I'd suggest."

Features include 10-pound weight adjustments, 1-inch draw adjustments, 25 or 40 percent let-off, depending on eccentrics, interchangeable grips, an adjustable arrow rest carriage with a cushion plunger and an arrow rest, magnesium eccentrics, and aluminum idler wheels and pylons, and the bow is drilled and tapped for sights, quiver, stabilizer, and cushion plunger.

The bow may be ordered in draw lengths from 23 to 33 inches and in peak weights from 45 to 70 pounds. Price: $315.82. Jennings Compound Bow Company, 28756. North Castaic Canyon Road, Valencia, CA 91355.

Jennings Sidekick II: An Economy-class Compound

The Sidekick is a two-wheeler with a 20-pound weight adjustment (40-to-60-pound draw weight). It has a 40-to-50-percent let-off, and it is available in nonadjustable draw lengths from 29 to 31 inches. The bow is drilled and tapped for a sight, a stabilizer, a cushion plunger, and a bow quiver, and it comes with a center shot adjustment with an arrow rest.

This is the toughest bow Jennings makes, and it is an eminently affordable hunter at $99.80. Jennings Compound Bow Company, 28756 North Castaic Canyon Road, Valencia, CA 91355.

I do set my bow in the cloud . . .
Even as Nimrod the mighty hunter.
—Genesis

389

BROWNING COMPOUND STALKERS I AND II

The 4-wheel Compound Stalker I has an adjustable draw length but no adjustment on the peak draw. It comes in 50- and 60-pound peak draw weights. The Stalker II is nonadjustable in the same weights. The Stalker I has a 30 or 40 percent let-off; the Stalker II has a 35 or 50 percent let-off. The Stalker I is only 40½ inches axle to axle, which is something of an advantage in brush to the II at 47 inches.

The Stalker is one of the fastest bows made. Chronograph tests have recorded a 241-feet-per-second flight using a 450-grain hunting arrow. To my knowledge that's a speed second to none in a production bow (remember this is with a hunting, not target, arrow). Also interesting: Browning walked away with the distance championships of the National Archery Association. Like I say, their bows have zip.

Of note, too, are the good looks of this bow. It's about as graceful as a compound can get, with lots of wood and solid, rather than levered, limbs. Price: Stalker I and II, $157.95. Browning, Route 1, Morgan, UT 84050.

BROWNING®

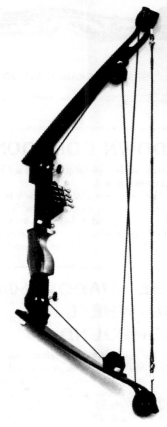

THE RIGID HUNTER COMPOUND BOW

Several features set this bow apart from the competition: it is all aluminum, and at 34 inches it is a very short bow and thus may be snaked through brush a little easier than most other compounds; it is also adjustable from 35 to 70 pounds pull, with only a common crescent wrench needed for the changeover.

The limb construction is such that the bow will stand free on a flat surface (arrow rest and grip facing down), and it has a draw length of 26 to 32 inches.

It is isn't exactly a graceful-looking device when compared to other products, but then the same criticism was leveled at the first compounds by all of us who were then enamored of the recurve. It's a little noisy, too, but you can dampen vibration with rubber banding. Price: $174.95. Rigid Archery Products, Inc., 445 Central Avenue, Jersey City, NJ 07307. —F.S.

JENNINGS ARCHERY CATALOG

If you're unfamiliar with the machinations of a compound bow, this catalog should be required reading. There are excellent soft-sell sections on "What Makes a Good Compound Bow," "The Two- and Four-Wheel Concept," and "How to Choose a Compound Bow." To some extent these are self-advertisements, but to a much larger extent they are solid, well-written explanations of the workings and qualities of compounds. Other sections of nonproduct interest are the essays on competitive archery and the future of bow hunting. And there is, of course, a complete listing of Jennings's excellent bows and accessories.

It is also an attractive catalog visually, with lots of original color art, as well as the standard photographs. Highly recommended, at a price that's hard to beat: free. Jennings Compound Bow Company, 28756 North Castaic Canyon Road, Valencia, CA 91355.

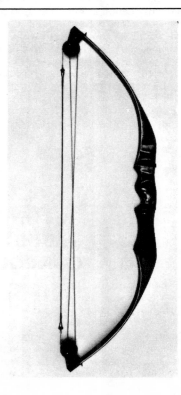

STAG COMPOUND BOW

This is a one-piece two-wheel compound with a continuous glass backing. In addition to its unusually graceful appearance, the manufacturer claims the Stag will not jump its cable terminals. The Stag comes tapped for a stabilizer and/or bow-fishing reel, and the riser has a flat surface for easy sight mounting. Nonadjustable, 45-to-55-pound draw weights, 40-to-50-percent let-off. Price: $112.00. Stemmler Archery Company, Southford Road, Middlebury, CT 06762.

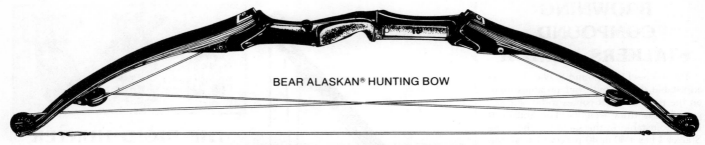

BEAR ALASKAN® HUNTING BOW

TAKEDOWN COMPOUND BOW

Bear's Alaskan is a top-of-the-line compound bow with a takedown feature for ease of storage and transport. Standard equipment includes needle-bearing eccentric wheels, a bristle arrow rest, an adjustable nylon arrow plate, a cover plate for installation of a bowsight, a magnesium handle with a pistol grip, and a Converta-Accessory insert.

The bow is available in black or camouflage colors, in draw lengths from 25 to 34½ inches, and it has a 33-to-36-percent let-off, depending on the eccentric wheel size. This four-pulley compound is available in draw weights from 35 to 70 pounds, in right- or left-hand models. It's Bear's best compound hunter. Price: $152.00. Bear Archery Company, Rural Route 1, Grayling, MI 49738.

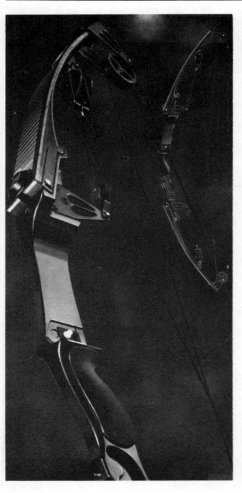

THE SHADOW 600 SIX-WHEEL COMPOUND

The manufacturer claims this is archery's most uncomplex compound, with no fine tuning required. The bow's self-compensating design keeps the bow in balance and unaffected by your method of release.

The Shadow 600 measures 44 inches axle to axle, and it has an adjustable draw weight of 45 to 55 pounds or 55 to 65 pounds. Let-off at full draw is 30 percent, plus or minus 3 percent, and it is tapped for stabilizers, quivers, and such. It comes in nonadjustable draw lengths of 28, 29, 30, and 31 inches. Free catalog. Price: $193.70. Ben Pearson, P. O. Box 270, Tulsa, OK 74101.

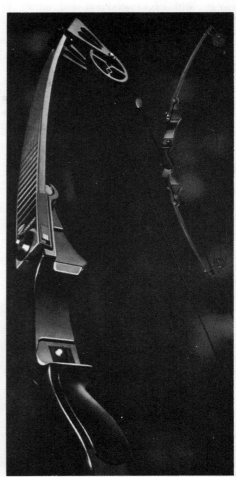

ECONOMY TAKEDOWN COMPOUND

Ben Pearson's Shadow 100 is a takedown two-wheel compound, with an adjustable peak draw weight of 50 to 60 pounds. It boasts a 45-percent let-off and a short (41¾ inch axle to axle) frame. It sounds like something to look into if you're looking for a bargain. Price: $94.95. Ben Pearson, P. O. Box 270, Tulsa, OK 74104.

Bear *Whitetail Hunter Compound Bow*

This is an economically priced, six-wheel compound that is reputed to have the best cable clearance and arrow alignment on the market. The weight control system allows your choice of 50-, 55-, and 60-pound peak weights on the same bow.

It is 44 inches axle to axle, with a 50-percent let-off and a draw length of 28 to 30½ inches. This compound comes with a Bear Weatherest, and it's predrilled and tapped for bowfishing rigs, stabilizers, and a quiver. It also has a predetermined locater for a Berger Button and a bowsight. Price: $94.00. Bear Archery Company, Rural Route 1, Grayling, MI 49738.

JAGUAR RECURVE BOW

A well-made recurve at a reasonable price, the Jaguar is laminated wood and glass, 60 inches long, with a draw length of 29 inches. It is available in draw weights of 45, 50, and 55 pounds and in left-hand models. Price: $40.26. Stemmler Archery Company, Southford Road, Middlebury, CT 06762.

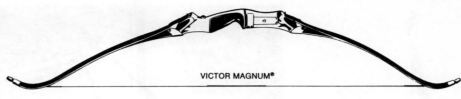

VICTOR MAGNUM®

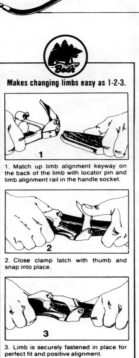

Makes changing limbs easy as 1-2-3.

1. Match up limb alignment keyway on the back of the limb with locator pin and limb alignment rail in the handle socket.

2. Close clamp latch with thumb and snap into place.

3. Limb is securely fastened in place for perfect fit and positive alignment.

BEAR TAKEDOWN RECURVE

Fred Bear is the granddaddy of the takedown bow. This Victor Magnum comes in draw weights from 25 to 70 pounds and includes a vinyl arrow rest, arrow plate, accessory insert, and special grip as standard equipment. Price: $140.00. Bear Archery Company, Rural Route 1, Grayling, MI 49738.

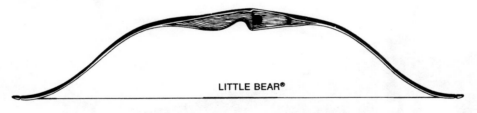

LITTLE BEAR®

Little Bear Recurve: Not Just Kid Stuff

If you want a good bow for a youngster, look into the Little Bear by Bear Archery. While it is designed for use by the younger set (20-pound draw weight, 24-inch draw), it's not a toy but a scaled-down recurve with Bear quality construction. This bow is also sold as a kit, which includes three cedar arrows, an arm guard, a four-color target, a glove, and a quiver. Prices: bow, $25.85; kit, $31.90. Bear Archery Company, Rural Route 1, Grayling, MI 49738.

Crossbows: *Maligned and Misunderstood*

If you've heard that crossbows are rifle-accurate long-range devices, if you have heard that they are illegal for hunting, and if you have heard that they're unsporting, you're like a lot of other people—wrong.

Crossbows are slightly more accurate than longbows; they will regularly deliver a bolt into a 6-inch circle at 60 yards, while a conventional archer with modern sighting equipment is hard pressed to best a 12-inch group. There is still no comparison between crossbows and rifles, which are capable of a 1-inch grouping.

In terms of distance, crossbows and longbows are comparable. A compound bow easily bests a crossbow in terms of range.

Crossbows are indeed legal to hunt with in most states, although they are limited to rifle seasons rather than special archery seasons. Arkansas, Kentucky, Alaska, Wyoming, and Indiana allow crossbow hunting during the special archery season, however.

Crossbows are no more unsporting than any other hunting arm, and they're just plain fun to shoot. If you're interested in promoting crossbow seasons or want to know more about them, contact the National Crossbow Hunters' Association, 201 Citizen's Bank Building, Wadsworth, OH 44281.

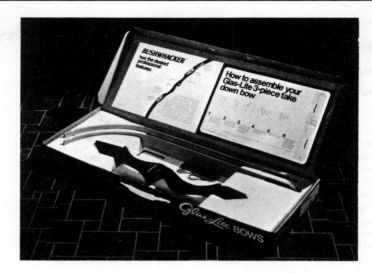

ECONOMY TAKEDOWN RECURVES

The Stinger and the Bushwacker are the lowest-priced takedown bows around.

The Bushwacker's features include a 30-inch draw, draw weights in 5-pound increments from 30 to 60 pounds, interchangeable laminated glass limbs, and an aluminum handle. It is available in right-hand model only. Price: $19.95.

The Stinger is available in draw weights from 15 to 40 pounds and is a compact 50 inches high. Limbs are interchangeable, the handle is nonreflecting black aluminum, and it is available in left-hand grip. Price: $29.95.

Both bows come packed in a stout cardboard carrying case with a plastic handle, so you save some money there, too. Plas/Steel Products, Inc., Walkerton, IN 46574.
—F.S.

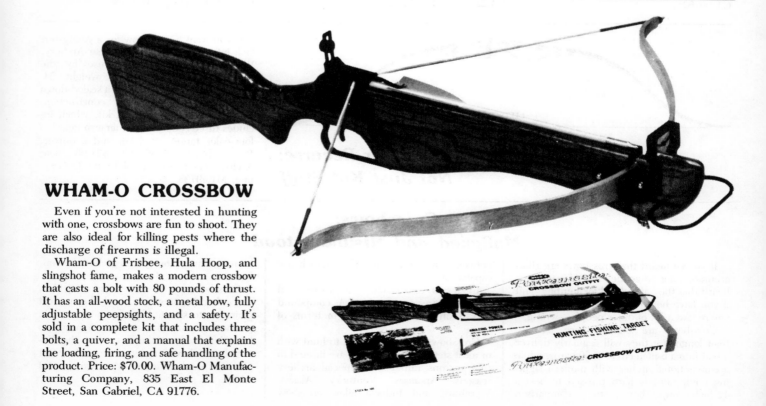

WHAM-O CROSSBOW

Even if you're not interested in hunting with one, crossbows are fun to shoot. They are also ideal for killing pests where the discharge of firearms is illegal.

Wham-O of Frisbee, Hula Hoop, and slingshot fame, makes a modern crossbow that casts a bolt with 80 pounds of thrust. It has an all-wood stock, a metal bow, fully adjustable peepsights, and a safety. It's sold in a complete kit that includes three bolts, a quiver, and a manual that explains the loading, firing, and safe handling of the product. Price: $70.00. Wham-O Manufacturing Company, 835 East El Monte Street, San Gabriel, CA 91776.

"Days, when . . . the grasp on the bow was decision,
And arrow and hand and eye were one."
—George Meredith

393

A TALE OF A TROPHY ELK

by Bill Smith

The Montana Fish and Game Department had a special elk season in December of 1973. It was held on the Upper Gallatin River, in the area that borders Yellowstone National Park.

I decided to take a crack at an elk with a rifle and zeroed out. When I applied for a second permit at the district fish and game headquarters, I was told all the permits had already been issued.

Almost as an afterthought, and as a joke, the fellow I'd been speaking to added, "But anyone can shoot an elk with a bow and arrow. You don't need a special permit for that."

It was a long shot in more ways than one, but I figured I had nothing to lose. I went down to a sporting goods store that was having a sale on archery equipment and picked up a recurve bow and half a dozen arrows.

I practiced in an empty lot near my house. It was an old sawmill, so I used a mound of sawdust as a backstop and shot at a cardboard box from about 30 yards. When I got so I could hit the box pretty consistently, I figured I was ready, and on New Year's Day, 1974, I took a drive up the Gallatin.

I had planned to scout, not hunt, but when I got into the special hunting area, I caught a glimpse of an elk high on a hillside on the other side of the river. It was in a little stand of quaking asp. I couldn't tell how big it was, but it looked as if it was in a good spot to make a play. I drove back down the canyon and got my bow and waders, and when I got back, the elk was still there.

I crossed the river and used the terrain to hide my approach. The elk was quite high and I felt that my only chance was to come down on it, so it took me a good hour and a half to get into position.

When I stepped out from behind the little ridge I'd been using as a hide, the elk lay about 30 yards away, and I could see he had one whale of a big rack. I was suddenly overcome with buck fever, but I figured, "What the hell, it's bigger than a cardboard box," and that quieted me down.

I drew and released and the shot went true. I couldn't tell where I'd hit, but I knew I connected. The elk jumped up and ran off before I could draw again, and I thought I'd lost him, but he stumbled, fell, and died about 150 yards downhill. My arrow had drilled him right through the heart.

It was a tough drag out: straight down a steep hill to the river, and then it took two men with snow machines two days to get the carcass to the nearest road.

I knew he was big and that I'd have him mounted, but I didn't realize just how big. The Fish and Game check station at the end of the canyon measured his horns, and they were pretty impressed. So was I a few months later, when I received word that my elk placed No. 6 in the Pope and Young record books.

Bill Smith lives in Gallatin Gateway, Montana. He has an unusual vocation, as well as unusual luck. He is a licensed Packard mechanic and is a collector of these classic cars.

"Your Compound Bow" Instruction Manual

This pocket-sized booklet contains all the technical information you'll need to tune, use, and care for Bear, Allen, Jennings, Carroll, Precision, or Wing compound bows. As a piece of technical writing, it is unusually clear. As a source of information, it is unusually complete.

A sampling of the subjects dealt with in this manual: how to adjust draw length and draw weight, how to adjust eccentric wheel balance and change a string, fine tuning, changing cables, matching arrows to pull weight, and proper lubrication of a compound.

At 112 pages, $4.95 seems a lot for this book, but the thoroughness of the text cannot be overlooked or underplayed. It is a compound bow owner's bible and that makes it worth the price and then some. Bear Archery Company, Rural Route 1, Grayling, MI 49738.

HOW TO TRACK AND FIND GAME
by Clyde Ormond

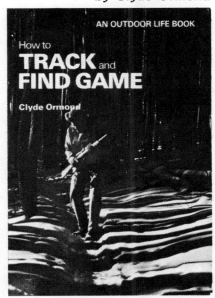

AN OUTDOOR LIFE BOOK

How to TRACK and FIND GAME

Clyde Ormond

New York: Funk & Wagnalls, $7.50 (hard cover), $4.50 (soft cover).

Correctly interpreting the signs left by animals is a major factor in hunting success. A very simple illustration of why this is so lies in a deer track. If you don't know that the hoof points point in the direction the animal is headed, you may choose the wrong way to go.

This book is an excellent primer in the art of finding your game by reading tracks, rubs, scratches, and scat, and it tells you what they suggest the animal will do in the terrain that lies ahead. The text is accompanied by clear, accurate sketches of footprint configurations and droppings, with their measurements. All North American big game is depicted, as well as many species of small game, furbearers, and varmints. Of special note is that the author goes so far as to suggest, by word and drawing, the paths that animals will take and the approach you should take on these theoretical stalks.

If you're unfamiliar with this aspect of hunting academics, this book is sure to help.

FRED BEAR'S FIELD NOTES
by Fred Bear

New York: Doubleday & Co., $8.95.

This is a book that deserved doing, if for no other reason than it records the monumental accomplishments of the grand old man of archery, Fred Bear.

While he wasn't the first to tackle the big game of the world with bow and arrow, he's surely the most famous, and the record kills he's made of such formidable quarry as the African lion, the Alaskan brown bear, and the elephant will stand forever as a tribute to someone who loved both his sport and his game. This is a man with an uncommon amount of gravel in his guts.

The writing isn't particularly inspired, yet it's exciting because it's true. Interesting, too, is the personal side of the book, its insight into the ways and days of a pioneer who blazed some tough trails to follow, with a stick of springy wood and a slender shaft.

Warning: if you read this, downing even a trophy buck deer with a compound bow and an aluminum arrow will never seem the same again.   —N.S.

MAN KIND? MAN'S INCREDIBLE WAR ON WILDLIFE
by Cleveland Amory

New York: Harper and Row, $9.95; Dell, $1.75 (paper).

This is a bitter attack on hunters and hunting, written by the founder of the Fund for Animals. Typical of Amory's attitudes is "hunt the hunter," his oft-stated proposal that hunters should stalk and shoot one another instead of animals.

The book is also illogical in Amory's ignorance of the effects of game management and in its specious arguments; for example, that you can generalize about the majority from a minority. Because one hunter, or even thousands, jacklights deer, doesn't mean that all 14 million licensed hunters do.

So why review the book?

Let's call one reason a sense of honesty. If this is a "complete" hunter's catalog, we should at least recognize this dark spectrum in the hunters' rainbow. This isn't the only book of its kind; hunting critics have been around for a long time.

Second, Amory does make some valid points. Many of the cited hunting atrocities are true. Just because the percentage of lawbreakers, thieves, and subhumans who call themselves sportsmen is small, it doesn't mean we can afford to ignore them. Thus, the book is an encouragement to clean up our act.

There is also food for thought inherent in his title. Technologically, we are in a position to engage in warfare rather than sport when we hunt. How would you classify a twenty-man deer drive? Or a heat sensor used to detect the presence of game? Or aerial hunting?

Still, this is a disappointing book. Like so many works of this nature, bile has replaced reason, and the animals the book purports to "save" lose in the process. There's no recognition of the real threat to wildlife—the bulldozers ripping at the guts of America's marshes and woodlands—nor is there any attempt to address hunting realistically, thereby enlisting the help of hunters in Amory's cause: more humane treatment of animals. So much more could have been accomplished if he had written the book for hunters instead of against them.   —N.S.

BOW HUNTING FOR BIG GAME
by Keith C. Schuyler

Harrisburg, Pa.: Stackpole Books, $8.95.

This is a valuable book in many respects. First of all, it is the sum total knowledge of a man who has spent most of his life hunting with a bow. He cares for and understands his equipment and its limitations, and he delights in all those skills that help him move in close to his game. Sound information on both these aspects of bow hunting is presented in clear, readable English. As a purely pragmatic hunting aid, the book is well worth the price.

Yet this book has a second dimension—a sense of style and a sense of soul. It is an eloquent celebration of the one-on-one challenge that begins when you take up the bow, an appreciation of the hunter and hunted alike. Good guy, good reading.

ARCHERY WORLD'S COMPLETE GUIDE TO BOW HUNTING
edited by Glenn Helgeland

Englewood Cliffs, N.J.: Prentice-Hall, $8.95.

If you're looking for good hunting advice from a broad range of opinions, look into this book. It is an anthology, with contributions by most of the recognized bowhunters in the United States. Their experiences and techniques are explained in detail and practice programs for the hunting of big-game species are outlined, as well as the equipment you'll need and the strategies you should employ when hunting anything from deer to carp.

"Bring me my bow of burning gold!
Bring me my arrows of desire!"
—William Blake

395

BROWNING CATALOG

These are the folks who used to be called Browning Arms. They changed their name to just Browning because, as this catalog reveals, they're making and/or marketing a lot more than just guns—clothing, archery stuff, knives. . . .

Of course, their guns alone would justify the time spent to drop them a card and ask for this catalog (it's free). Every gun is an example of the gunmaker's art, and their deluxe grades will make you drool. This is not only because of the quality of the products illustrated but because of the quality of the catalog itself. Of all those we've seen (and we've looked at a passel), the Browning catalog is tops artistically, with brilliant color reproduction, heavy paper, and an eye-catching layout.

It's good from the writer's point of view, too. Not only are products described in lively but clear terms, but there are many practical tips contained therein as well. For example, you are told what the markings on a box of shells means, how to shoot a pistol, where to aim to stop big game dead, and lots, lots more. Highly recommended. Browning Consumer Sales Department, Route 1, Morgan, UT 84050.

SURVIVAL KIT FOR BOWHUNTERS
by Freddie Troncoso

Listing the equipment an archer should have prior to hunting is a toughie—it usually boils down to common sense and some prior experience in woodlore. If a hunter has never taken to the woods, he should do some extensive reading starting about one year before going hunting! However, I suggest the following:

1. Spare bowstring with nocking point attached
2. Bow stringer
3. Set of precut and crimped cables (if using a compound)
4. Extra broadheads, Ferrultite, and good broadhead sharpener or file

How long the hunter plans to stay in the woods usually dictates what he should be carrying on his person or in his backpack. Here is a list of survival and first-aid goods:

1. First aid kit
2. Wire-type hand saw
3. Good compass (learn how to use it!)
4. Signaling mirror and police whistle
5. Hip flask or canteen of water
6. Matches in waterproof container
7. Candles for easy fire-starting
8. Emergency thermo blanket and sleeping bag if staying overnight
9. Dry foods and candy bars
10. Topographical map of area

I also advise all hunters to let their friends or their families know exactly where they will be hunting. In the event of an injury or mishap, a close starting geographical point would most certainly be of help to both parties in locating a missing hunter. Another rule of thumb I practice is always to hunt in pairs. There should be no need to elaborate on this advice. Many a life has been saved by a hunting companion for one reason or another.

Freddy Troncoso is contributing editor of *Archery* magazine. His column, "What's Your Problem?," is a monthly feature of the magazine.

Jennings Quivers: Six Shooter and Ace-in-the-Hole

These two quivers were designed specifically for Jennings compound bows. The Six Shooter is an economical quiver that holds up to six arrows and attaches firmly to both right- and left-hand bows. The Ace-in-the-Hole holds up to eight arrows and has a quick release feature for fast mounting or dismounting. This quiver also fits either left- or right-hand bows, and it includes adjustable arrow locks, which allow the quiver to hold large and small diameter arrows firmly in place. Prices: Six Shooter, $14.95; Ace-in-the-Hole, $24.95. Jennings Compound Bow Company, 28756 North Castaic Canyon Road, Valencia, CA 91355.

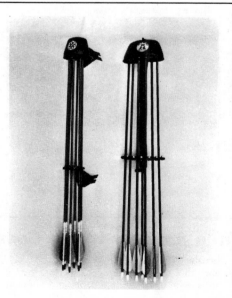

L. C. WHIFFEN COMPANY, INC.

QUIFFER BOW QUIVER

The Quiffer bow quiver is a good bet for recurve shooters. One model fits left- and right-hand bows, and it attaches instantly without any damage to the bow finish. Broadheads are protected in a cup, and it accepts any size hunting arrow. Price: $12.50. L. C. Whiffen Company, 923 South 16th Street, Milwaukee, WI 53204.

BEAR ARCHERY CATALOG

The Bear Archery catalog is pretty to look at and as complete a source for archery gear as you'll ever need.

Virtually all illustrations are in color, and there are some very nice mood shots to offset the commercial pitch: things like an archer applying camouflage makeup to his face in soft green light, a young couple sharpening broadheads in front of a fire on a rainy day, and a guy eating a typical archer's lunch—sardines right out of a can. These shots are exceptional, because they have a pervasive sense of reality as opposed to the saccharine clap-trap of "happy" families and freckle-faced, gee-whiz kids you so often see in catalogs.

The equipment listed is varied and of high quality, although the writing isn't the best (there's an awful lot of coined hyperbole like "Converta-Accessory Insert" and "Arrowdynamic Flight System" that mean little to the reader). Another thing that bothers me is that none of the equipment is priced; nor is a supplementary suggested retail price available, as in the Browning catalog.

But prices or no, this is a worthwhile catalog to have in your rack. Classy graphics, classy equipment, and a name that's synonymous with archery. Free. Bear Archery Company, Rural Route 1, Grayling, MI 49738.

—N.S.

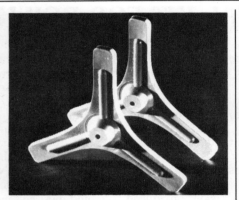

BOW SILENCERS

Bow silencers are needed to quiet the twang created by the rapid vibrations of a bowstring after the release of an arrow. The noise is often enough of a warning to cause a deer to duck the shaft.

For maximum silencing effect, move the soft rubber dampeners up and down the string until all sound is gone. (Not needed for most compounds.) Price: $1.25 a pair. Kwikee Kwiver Company, 7292 Peaceful Valley Road, Acme, MI 49610.

SNAP-ON BOW SILENCERS

The Whiffen bow silencer boasts a snap-on feature. It may be installed on the string while the bow is strung. The silencers are made of top-grade rubber and are guaranteed not to "shoot off." Price: 55 cents a pair. L. C. Whiffen Company, 923 South 16th Street, Milwaukee, WI 53204.

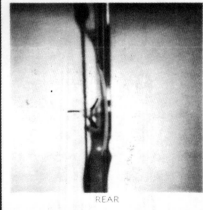

5" FLETCH – LEFT SIDE

REAR

RIGHT SIDE

Wire Witch for Four-Wheel Compounds

Some of the four-wheel compounds create vane clearance problems; when you release the arrow, the arrow fletching brushes the cables as it leaves the bow, and the arrow is deflected. This device slips over the offending cable and keeps it bent out of the way so that the fletching clears. Price: $3.95. Trueflight, Manitowish Waters, WI 54545.

"You don't go hunting to kill, you go hunting to hunt . . . there are hunters and there are killers. To the true sportsman, the kill is an anticlimax."
—Fred Bear

397

BOWSTRINGS

Bow manufacturers and marketers usually have the correct string for their models on hand, so sometimes it's best to go to the place where you bought the bow, or consult a catalog, when you need a new one (you should keep an extra around).

However, Saunders seems to stock a bowstring for everybody, such as 10-, 12-, 14-, and 16-strand bowstrings in lengths from 45 to 67 inches. These strings are available with a monofilament nylon serving ($3.00 each) or a twisted nylon serving ($2.00 each).

The length of your bow should be printed or etched into the limbs or riser (e.g., AMO 60"). If the corresponding string doesn't fit (the rule of thumb is literally just that—with your thumb extended in the thumbs-up gesture, your hand should just fit between the riser and the serving on a recurve), you can twist the string and thus shorten it by ½ inch. This twisting will also quiet your string.

If perchance you have an odd-sized bow, Saunders also sells single-loop Dacron strings. You serve and whip the second limb loop to fit your bow ($1.25 each). Compound strings are a different breed altogether. Order them by make, model, and weight. Saunders Archery Company, P.O. Box 476, Industrial Site, Columbus, NE 68601.

TEL-TALE ARROW NOCKING POINT

This is a nocking point device that performs two functions: it beds the nock of your arrow in exactly the same spot each time, and it orients the bowstring the same way each time. This latter feature is most important to the peepsight shooter. With a Tel-Tale nock, the sight will never twist out of alignment with your eye. Price: $2.20 for a package of three. J C Manufacturing Company, 6250 West 55th Avenue, Arvada, CO 80002.

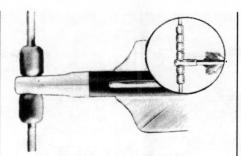

ARROW NOCK LOCKS: GREAT IDEA

As we go to press, I've just tried these once on a friend's bow, so I can't say they've been thoroughly put to the test, but I'm sure going to buy some to try out on my own.

They are semihard rubber beads, about ½ inch long and ⅜ inch in diameter, that slip over the bowstring. They do several jobs at once: provide for a nocking point, eliminate the need for an archer's glove, hold the arrow nock firmly to the bowstring, and promote a smooth release, because they roll off your fingertips. Price: 60 cents a pair. Wilson-Allen Corp., Windsor, MO 65361.   —N.S.

HEAT NOCKING POINTS

To affix these nocking points to a serving, you thread them on the string, locate your point, and heat these bands of plasticlike material with a match or candle. They shrink down in size and bond themselves to the serving. I've found this type of nocking point to be foolproof, though they won't fit over the big end loops of some compound bow strings. Price: 99 cents for a box of four. Bear Archery Company, Rural Route 1, Grayling, MI 49738.   —N.S.

UNIVERSAL COMPOUND BOW STRINGER

This gadget simplifies the job of changing a compound bowstring, which can be a formidable chore, given a compound's short, powerful limbs. Measured by recurve standards, they usually fall between 100 and 200 pounds.

Browning makes a stringer that allows you to change strings on all makes of bows without changing the tiller or draw weight or relaxing the limbs. Price: $4.50. Browning, Route 1, Morgan, UT 84050.

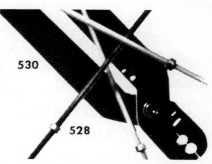

NOK-SET NOCKING POINT

This nocking point is a round, metal band that is lined with a tough, rubberlike synthetic. It clips onto the serving, and then you pinch it in place with a special pliers-like tool. While it's claimed that these won't slip, I've yet to have them stand up long using an Apache draw.

If you've got any kind of a home workshop, you might be able to save the cost of the Nok-Set pinching tool. Check your wirecutters for a wirestripping hole. The pair that I have are exactly the same diameter as the Nok-Set tool. Price: Nok-Sets (six per package), $1.68; Nok-Set tool, $1.75. Stemmler Archery Company, Southford Road, Middlebury, CT 06762.   —N.S.

Compound Bow Case for Field Use

This camouflage cotton case will accept any compound bow with quivers and arrows attached. It has a full zipper, so the case may be opened and used as a blind or

seat while you're hunting. If you prefer to hide it, it balls up into a fist-sized bundle. Price: $10.50. Kolpin Manufacturing, Inc., P.O. Box 231, Berlin, WI 54923.

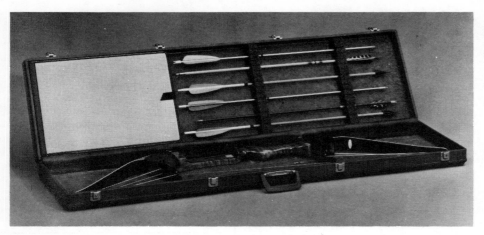

HARD-SHELL COMPOUND BOW CASE

Here's a case of class; it measures 53 by 13 by 4 inches and is made of molded plastic, fully lined. The top of the case has foam rubber slots that will accept eighteen arrows, and the lower half of the case locks a compound bow firmly in place. The case also incorporates an 18-by-12½-inch gear pocket. Price: $60.00. Gun-Ho, 110 East 10th Street, St. Paul, MN 55101.

COMPOUND BOW CASE

Carry your compound bow in padded protection with this expanded vinyl case. Green corduroy lining, full-length zipper, and wraparound handle. Bow fits inside with quiver and arrows attached. Price: $23.00. Kolpin Manufacturing, Inc., P.O. Box 231, Berlin, WI 54923.

Hard-shell Case for Longbows

If your bow is 65 inches or shorter, it will fit into this ABS plastic case. Polyurethane lined. It comes in two models: BA102 is an open case that will accommodate two bows or a bow and a dozen arrows; BA102A encases one bow and arrows and includes adjustable compartments for archery accessories. Price $65.00 each. Protecto Plastics, Inc., 201 Alpha Road, Wind Gap, PA 18091.

BRUSH BUTTONS

Recurve bows have a nasty habit of wedging grass and twigs at the point where the string first touches the limb. Brush buttons amount to a neoprene rubber half-ball that threads onto the bowstring. Snug them up against the limbs, and you'll cure this hang-up. Price: 44 cents. Herter's, Inc., Route 2, Mitchell, SD 57301.

Hard Case for Compound or Takedown Bows

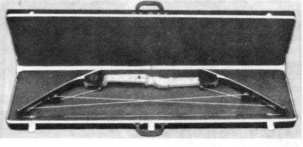

This case measures 53 by 15 by 4½ inches, large enough for most compounds (and for most rifles, too). It is foam lined, with an ABS plastic exterior. Case includes a lock and carrying handle. Price: $65.00. Protecto Plastics, Inc., 201 Alpha Road, Wind Gap, PA 18091.

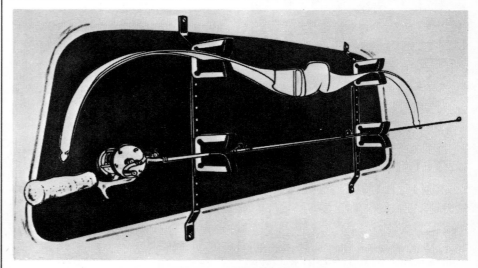

BOW RACK FOR VEHICLES

If you like to carry your bow strung and at the ready while you're driving, this rack holds the limbs firmly between jaws of soft rubber. It bolts over the rear window of most jeeps and pickup trucks and some station wagons. Price: $6.95. San Angelo Co., P.O. Box 984, San Angelo, TX 76901.

RIGHT ON THE KISSER

A kisser helps assure you a consistent draw. You slide the center-holed disk-shaped plastic kisser onto your bowstring and adjust it so it touches your lips (or cheek or brow, if you're not the kissing kind) at full draw. Clamp the bands down tightly, and they will lock it in place permanently. Price: $1.00. Saunders Archery Company, P.O. Box 476, Industrial Site, Columbus, NE 68601.

Camouflage Sleeve for Bow Limbs

If you prefer a cloth sleeve to camouflage your bow, here's a slip-on sleeve with elastic bolsters to snug it to the limbs. One size fits all bows (twist the sleeve to shorten it). Price: $3.75. Browning, Route 1, Morgan, UT 84050.

Cloth Bow Sleeves for Compounds

Conventional sock-type bow sleeves require that you remove the idlers and pulleys to slip them on the limbs of a compound bow. These camouflage sleeves wrap around the limbs and are held in place by a Velcro closure. They fit most makes of compound bows. Price: $5.50. Bear Archery Company, Rural Route 1, Grayling, MI 49738.

Adhesive Camouflage Bow Covering

A nice alternative to sleeves and socks, which get soggy and slip on the limbs when they dry, this stuff is nothing more than adhesive tape in a camouflage pattern. The adhesive never hardens, and it won't damage your bow finish when it's removed. Price: enough for one bow, $1.50. Saunders Archery Company, P.O. Box 476, Industrial Site, Columbus, NE 68601.

BOWSTRING WAX

A wet bowstring weighs a lot more than a dry one, which in turn will influence the energy transferred to the arrow and, ultimately, its path of flight. Keep bowstrings dry by applying beeswax or commercial bowstring wax. Price: $1.50 per push-out tube. Saunders Archery Company, P.O. Box 476, Industrial Site, Columbus, NE 68601.

BOW SADDLE WARMS COLD GRIPS

If you find that the grip on your bow gets cold on your hands when the weather takes a turn toward winter, Browning catalogs a bow saddle, a soft leather covering that conforms to any bow. An adhesive back holds it in place. Price: $2.25. Browning, Route 1, Morgan, UT 84050.

TOP-OF-THE-LINE ARROWS

Arrows for serious hunting really boil down to two choices: glass or aluminum. Glass is advantageous in that it won't bend out of shape like aluminum, but glass shafts are heavy. This is a positive feature in recurve bows, but it does rob you of speed and flat trajectory in a compound bow. In general, aluminum shafts are best in compound bows.

Both these shafts may be fletched with feather or plastic vanes. Again, both materials have their advantages, but it is accepted that plastic, overall, is the better performer under typical hunting conditions.

The vanes may have a straight spiral or a helical spiral. A straight spiral dampens the arrow's tendency to spin in the air, and thus a stationary broadhead drives straight and deep without expending energy to stop the spin as it enters flesh. A helical spiral spins the arrow in flight, like a football or a bullet, and it is therefore slightly more accurate than a straight fletch.

Better arrows have an adapter insert in lieu of a fixed, permanent head. This is nothing more than a threaded female receptacle that accepts the male shafts of any number of specialized heads. With this point system it is possible to do all your shooting with the same arrows, converting to field, blunt, target, and broadhead of identical weighting. These head systems are usually sold separately from the arrow.

In terms of aluminum shafts, Easton is *the* name and *the* supplier of virtually every arrowsmith in the business (Bear, Browning, Herter's, Stemmler, and the others). Glas-Lite makes one of the finest fiberglass shafts (unusually light and strong without any seams or overlap), although this field seems considerably more crowded than aluminum shafts.

—F.S.

ALUMINUM HUNTING SHAFTS: MATCHING UP WITH THE BEST

Experts agree that aluminum shafts are best. No other shaft material is comparable in terms of uniformity of weight, spine, straightness, and durability. When they are fletched with plastic vanes, they are impervious to the effects of weather and climate. Their only disadvantage is that they will bend. However, they can be straightened, which is not the case with wooden or glass shafts.

To get outfitted with the proper arrow for you, you've first got to determine length. This is most easily done with a special test arrow (see your local archery shop) that has inch increments. Use your bow (or the one you plan to buy) and loosen up by drawing it several times. Find the point where you consistently anchor the nock.

When determining this point, be sure your shoulder and arm are fully extended. In order to be consistently accurate, you must always shoot with this full extension and the same release point. It is the same with any sport, from golf to tennis to archery; consistency is the only way to perfect technique. And technique translates into skill and proficiency.

When you're at full draw, the measuring arrow will indicate proper length where it passes the window. To this figure add 1 inch to allow for the arrowhead.

The next step is to determine your true bow weight. On recurves, the bow weight is usually printed on the limbs or riser; for example, "50 lbs. @ 28″ draw." To determine actual bow weight, the rule of thumb is to add or subtract 2 pounds for every inch of draw under or over the listed draw length. If your draw length is 30 inches, actual bow weight would be 54 pounds.

"Actual bow weight" on a compound is a lot trickier to determine than on a recurve, because peak weight (the ultimate amount of pressure driving the arrow) is reached halfway through the draw. After this breakaway point, the draw weight drops off 20 to 50 percent, depending on the design and the adjustment of the bow. Because of these variables, about the only way to determine actual bow weight on a compound is by first determining your draw

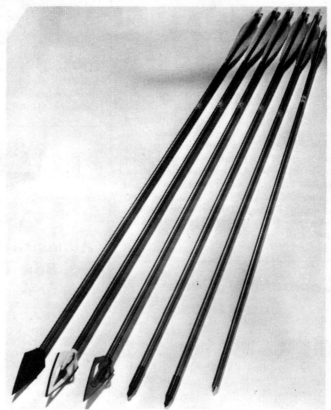

length and then measuring the pull by way of a special scale (again, at a bow shop).

Once you determine this weight, the rule is this: add draw weight to peak weight and divide by two. If peak weight is 60 pounds and draw weight is 30 pounds, you would add these two figures (90 pounds) and halve the sum (45 pounds). You would then match these weights (54 for the recurve, 45 for the compound) with a corresponding shaft.

—F.S.

COMPLETE BOOK OF THE BOW & ARROW
BY G. Howard Gillelan

The value of this book lies in that key word, complete. G. Howard Gillelan, for many years archery editor for *Outdoor Life*, discusses the bow and arrow from every conceivable perspective: historically, as a hunting weapon, as a target shooting device (including complete tournament archery rules), and even as an income-producing pursuit should you become good enough to participate in tours and tournaments.

Especially good is the emphasis it puts on target/competition form and practice. You might be the best stalker in the world, but it won't help you if you can't shoot straight. This book should help you get on target. Harrisburg, Pa.: Stackpole Books, $9.95 (second edition).

"A string may jar in the best master's hand,
And the most skilful archer miss his aim."
—Wentworth Dillon, translating Horace

401

STAINLESS STEEL ARROW SHAFTS

Stainless steel is a relatively new shaft material, but it shows some real promise. The shafts are slimmer than other, more conventional materials, yet they are the same weight. You get less drag, greater speed and range (steel shafts hold three National Archery Association flight records), and deeper penetration. In addition, these arrows are guaranteed against breaking, kinking, or cracking.

Stainless steel shafts are available unfletched with an adjustable aluminum nock at $33.45 for six or as a fletched arrow at $35.21 for six. Heads are not included. Specify draw length and peak draw weight. Hunter's International, 26422 Groesbeck Highway, Warren, MI 48089.

A WORD IN DEFENSE OF FEATHERS

It seems everybody's climbing on the plastic-vane bandwagon, and indeed, all their positive qualities taken into account, they might be best. In deference to turkeys and out of a sense of fairness, we should point out a few qualities of feathers that plastic doesn't seem to match.

Most important, feathers have more "give." If your arrow happens to scrape by a sprig of brush, the tougher plastic vanes are likely to deflect the flight of the arrow, while feathers just "lie down." Feathers also probably set up more air drag, which is both good and bad. It slows down the arrow somewhat, but it also dampens wobble in the air and sets the arrow on a straight course more quickly than plastic.

Aesthetics count, too. Plastic might be more practical, but feathers are undeniably prettier. —N.S.

PLASTIC: THE FLETCHING OF THE FUTURE

The day of the turkey feather is about to come to an end for the archer. Along with compound bows and aluminum arrows, plastic fletching promises to remove even more elements of chance and equipment failure from the hunting scene.

The advantages of plastic fletching are many. They are not affected by heat or cold, and they remain flexible under all conditions. They are not affected by water, so gone, too, are plastic bags and rubber bands to protect your arrows when it rains. The soft plastic vanes clear the bow with a minimum of deflection, and they are anchored by an epoxylike substance of thirty letters or more, which translates to NPV. This superglue adheres to wood, glass, or aluminum and eliminates lifting on the forward vane edge.

Plastic fletching is available in fluorescents and standard black and white shades. My personal choice is fluorescent red, since my groups at 30 yards don't exactly pull coffee-can tight, and without that bright color I'd spend half my waking hours searching for strays. As a matter of fact, I'm down to my last four arrows out of a set of twelve, but those four are as good as new, after a period of use that would have ruined conventional shafts. —F.S.

BEAR'S METRIC MAGNUMS

These aluminum arrows are Bear's best. They are plastic-fletched, with a helical spiral, and are reputed to be superstrong. Designed specifically for use with compound bows, these arrows are available with adapter inserts only or with the Bear Converta-head system. Price: $34.95 for a set of eight (insert only). Bear Archery Company, Rural Route 1, Grayling, MI 49738.

HERTER'S GLASS ARROWS

Herter's Farbenglas (yes, Virginia, the spelling is right; for some reason or another he calls it Farbenglas) arrows are available in either feather or plastic helical fletching. They may be ordered with either field or hunting heads or just an adapter insert. Price: $18.98 per dozen, insert only. Herter's, Inc., Route 2, Mitchell, SD 57301.

Stemmler Fiberglass Hunting Arrows

These shafts are available in plastic and in feather helical fletching, with adapter inserts. Price: $23.95 per dozen. Stemmler Archery Company, Southford Road, Middlebury, CT 06762.

HERTER'S ALUMINUM ARROWS

These are aluminum shafts with plastic helical vanes. The screw-type head adapters come separate from the shafts; you may install Herter's system or another of your choosing. Price: $24.95 per dozen. Herter's, Inc., Route 2, Mitchell, SD 57301.

CEDAR ARROWS

If you prefer wood, Herter's has the best prices we've been able to find on Port Orford cedar arrows. They come with a helical feather fletching and a point adapter that accepts a permanent head (unthreaded). Price: $9.45 per dozen. Herter's, Inc., Route 2, Mitchell, SD 57301.

Stemmler Aluminum Arrows

For those who prefer feather vanes, these arrows are available in both plastic and feather helical fletching. They are fitted with a female adapter to Stemmler's Swap-point system. These shafts are Easton's finest (XX75 Orange). Price: $42.00 per dozen. Stemmler Archery Company, Southford Road, Middlebury, CT 06762.

THE COMPLETE ARCHER
by Keith C. Schuyler

The complete archer is a composite of bursitis, arthritis, calcium deposits, and dedication. He will stand in front of a hot target throughout the summer day, punching holes in and near a bull's eye. Or he will just as eagerly climb the Rocky Mountains for a one-in-a-million chance at a goat or a sheep with a hunting arm that is still shared by some of the aborigines over the world.

From the Olympics to a rabbit thicket on the south forty, the modern archer puts his dependence upon a string and a stick to get his projectile to the target. But whether the target is a paper with colored concentric circles or a magnificent mule deer, the man, woman, or youngster who follows the sport is looking for something special.

Purely target archers are easy to understand, since competition is so typically American. But because sportsmanship is so important to the dedicated bow hunter, he will frequently also be found on the target line. This is where he develops the skill that gives him courage to seek game as common as a rabbit or as exotic as an eland, and any score in the field with the bow provides a trophy of sorts.

The truly dedicated bow hunter can best be equated with those who only angle with fur and feathered lures and use a fly rod on trout. He is quite aware that there are easier and more certain methods available to him. However, in his search for more sport, he is aware that he, too, improves his own ability and outlook through practice.

It is a fair and natural question to ask why.

This would be a difficult question for the average archer to answer when he is fighting black flies and mosquitoes near a bear bait in Maine or Quebec. Or you might catch him short with such a question when he is precariously perched on the front of a boat off Pensacola, attempting to ram a fish arrow into a shark that is capable of wrecking both him and the boat. You might even have trouble finding him on a dark night when he is trying to keep up with the dogs on a raccoon hunt.

No one person can answer for each of these followers of Roger Ascham, Sitting Bull, and Pope and Young. But deep within is a desire to meet his quarry on a more equitable basis in the knowledge that, on rare occasion, the bow hunter becomes the hunted. It adds spice to the sport and magnifies many times the successful experience. Many have expressed the opinion that they get as large a thrill from missing with the bow as with killing with the gun.

For even a comparison to be made, this hunter must have at one time used a gun. It is a matter of fact that most who hunt with the bow also utilize the gun. So there is perfect understanding, compatibility, and companionship within the two sports.

It is true that today the modern archer carries tackle far superior to that of his ancestors and predecessors. Undoubtedly, the takeover of America would have proceeded at a much slower pace, if at all, had the Indian possessed the equipment and the knowledge available to today's bowman.

But it is not improved tackle that entices the individual onto the hunting scene with his primitive arm. Rather, it is the romance associated with a bent bow and the soft swish of a deadly arrow in flight. He calls upon all his cunning to approach within a shooting distance that the good bow hunter imposes upon himself within his practical limitations. Even when everything else is perfect for the shot, the comparative slowness of a well-delivered arrow still gives a white-tailed deer time to evade it.

With apologies for self-plagiarizing, a couple of lines from the introduction to my book *From Golds to Big Game* (A.S. Barnes & Company) attempts to bring all feelings into focus:

My aim is to send the beauty to gold,
   or a kill most certain and soon;
Oh, shaft with my prayer, both humble and bold,
   be true as the sun and the moon.

Keith Schuyler regularly writes a newspaper column and two magazine outdoor columns and is the author of four books covering archery, bow hunting, fishing, and World War II experiences as a bomber pilot. He has hunted and fished much of North America, and his by-line on fact and fiction has appeared in many of the major and minor magazines, chiefly on his favorite subject, the out-of-doors.

Browning Aluminum Hunting Arrows

The Browning hunting arrow is aluminum, with plastic helical-spiral vanes. It comes with an adapter fitting that mates up to their Select-A-Point head system. Price: $39.50 per dozen. Browning, Route 1, Morgan, UT 84050.

BEAR FIBERGLASS ARROWS

The Kodiak is a fiberglass arrow with plastic, helical vanes that are available in four different sizes. The arrow tip is fitted with the Bear Converta-Head point adapter. Price: $21.95 for a set of eight (no points). Bear Archery Company, Rural Route 1, Grayling, MI 49738.

FLU-FLU ARROWS

Flu-flu arrows have a continuous, concentric, brushlike fletching which puts up a lot of wind resistance and results in a very short flight. Because of this, the arrow is ideal for backyard target practice and squirrel and bird hunting. Price: Wooden flu-flu arrows, $16.50 for six. Browning, Route 1, Morgan, UT 84050.

*"I shot an arrow into the air,
It fell to earth, I knew not where."*
—Henry Wadsworth Longfellow

403

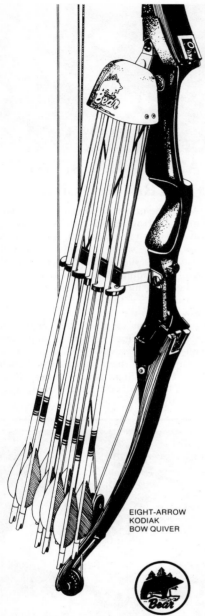

EIGHT-ARROW
KODIAK
BOW QUIVER

Converta-Quiver Holds Eight Arrows

Quivers that hold eight arrows have the largest arrow capacity we've run across. This one attaches to the bow via a snap-on clamp and a bolt or screw in the side of the riser. The Converta-Quiver fits all Bear bows and most others from 48 to 70 inches long. Bear's Kodiak quiver is affixed to the side of the bow via two screws. It fits all Bear compounds and looks as if it can be adapted to most other makes, although we haven't tried. Price: $18.69 each. Bear Archery Company, Rural Route 1, Grayling, MI 49738.

Tournament-Style Arrow Quiver

If match archery is your game, this Western-style leather quiver cases your arrows in class. It includes three separate arrow compartments and zippered pockets for pencils, scorecards, and accessories. Three brass rings hold powder pouches, arrow cleaners, yarn, and gloves, and a fourth may be used to hang the quiver when you don't want to wear it on your belt. Price: $32.00. Kolpin Manufacturing, Inc., P.O. Box 231, Berlin, WI 54923.

Kwikee Kompound Bow Quiver

KWIKEE KWIVER SYSTEM

These bow quivers are two identical arrow holders (each holds four arrows) that snap to the limbs of a bow. When arrows are plugged in place, they create extra rigidity. There is an optional Kwikee Kover that protects broadheads, and you, by snapping onto the shaft of one of the arrows in the quiver.

The advantages of this system lie in its simplicity; it goes on and comes off a bow quickly, and it is inexpensive. However, when you get down to two arrows, the quiver starts to get a little wobbly, especially when the locks are clamped over a camouflage limb cover. If you use the Kwikee Kover, the last arrow will be the one that wears it, and it will take time to remove it from the arrow shaft before you can shoot. Prices: Kwiver, $4.95; Kover, $1.95. Kwikee Kwiver Company, 7292 Peaceful Valley Road, Acme, MI 49610.

This compound quiver is affixed to the bow by means of a mounting bracket with a snap-lock feature that doesn't require screwing or bolting to remove the quiver from the bow. It holds up to six arrows in a frame made of football helmet plastic. The broadhead cup is double thickness and is lined with a soft material to prevent chatter. By way of innovation, the cup also has a foam pad for animal scents built into the liner.

The quiver fits both right- and left-handed compounds, and it's billed as fitting nearly all makes. Price: $18.95. Kwikee Kwiver Company, 7292 Peaceful Valley Road, Acme, MI 49610.

Universal Quiver for All Compounds and Recurves

This bow-mounted quiver holds six arrows, with broadheads safely protected and quieted in a foam rubber bed, surrounded by a nonbreakable plastic cup. It measures 12½ inches in length and is prefinished in nonreflective forest green. The quiver mounts on the side of the bow and may be used by right- or left-handers. In addition, it does not interfere with any bow sighting system.

There are two especially notable features of this quiver: First, it fits any bow made, compound or recurve. Second, it mounts flat and straight without creating Berger Button problems, which usually must be solved by remounting the quiver on an angle, causing balance difficulties and unwieldiness in the bow. Price: "800" quiver, $15.00. Kolpin Manufacturing, Inc., P.O. Box 231, Berlin, WI 54923.

SWEETLAND PRODUCTS

FUR TRACERS

If you tend to lose your arrows during twilight hunting trips or target practice, try these fur tracers. They are small, self-adhering strips of colored fur that go on the shaft between the nock and the vanes. Their effect on the flight of the arrow is negligible, and with these bits of fluff attached it's a lot easier to see your arrow in flight and after it's hit (or missed) its mark.

These 8-inch strips may also be wound on a bare shaft in a continuous spiral to make a flu-flu vane. Available in white, orange, or hot pink. Price: $2.00 for two 8-inch strips. Sweetland Products, 1010 Arrowsmith Street, Eugene, OR 97402.

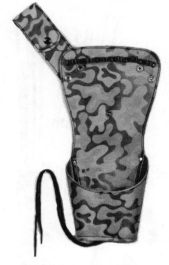

HIP QUIVER

If you don't like the heft or confusion of a quiver on your bow, the next best bet is a hip quiver. This quiver locks six arrows firmly in place. It snaps on and off your belt and ties down on your leg. Broadheads are cushioned on foam rubber and are protected by a vinyl cup. Price: $13.50. Kolpin Manufacturing, Inc., P.O. Box 231, Berlin, WI 54923.

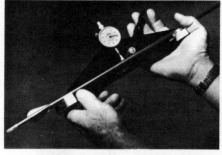

ALUMINUM ARROW STRAIGHTENER

About the only complaint we have about aluminum arrows is that they'll bend if you inadvertently mistreat them, and crooked arrows don't shoot straight. They can, however, be quickly straightened with this gadget. It amounts to a bed for the arrow, a gauge that indicates straightness, and a pressure device that gradually forces the arrow back to the straight and narrow.

At 12 inches long, 4 inches high, and 1½ inches deep, it's small and light enough to carry with you, and it won't take up a lot of room on your workbench. Price: $69.95. Stanislawski Archery Products, 7135 Southeast Cora Street, Portland, OR 97206.

Free Technical Brochure for Selecting Arrows

Easton, of aluminum shaft fame, has a clearly written brochure that fully explains, in layman's terms, the technology of choosing the correct arrow. The brochure contains an easy-to-read chart, with which you can quickly identify the best shaft for your particular bow.

Also included is information on picking the right bow, tuning bows and arrows to shooting style, and arrow care. This booklet clears up a lot of confusion and is highly recommended. Free. Jas. D. Easton Company, 7800 Haskell Avenue, Van Nuys, CA 91406.

HEADHUNTING: IN SEARCH OF THE PERFECT BIG-GAME ARROWPOINT

The key to finding an effective arrowhead lies in the way an arrow kills. Bullets kill as much by shock and tissue damage as by promoting bleeding, but an arrow kills almost exclusively by hemorrhage. There have been many ingenious ways devised to do this; for example, multibladed heads and heads with corkscrews, which are designed to take out a core of meat. I can remember spending long hours with a ⅛-inch drill bit, carefully punching holes in a fiberglass shaft, the theory being that blood from the wound would exit more easily through the hollow shaft (it didn't seem to have much of an effect), but for all the invention and experimentation, the best head is still judged to be that which does the most cutting. A three-bladed head is better than a two-bladed head, a four-bladed head is better than a three-bladed head, and so forth.

There are factors beyond the number of cutting edges to consider, however, and one of them is sharpness. The sharper the edges on an arrowhead, the more effectively it will cut. Razor sharpness is the goal. Since very few people can sharpen even a knife to razor sharpness, and arrowheads are somewhat more difficult to sharpen than a knife, I lean toward some sort of razor insert arrangement, where dull blades can be replaced with factory-sharpened ones.

One place you do not want sharpness, however, is on the arrow point. A needle-sharp point is likely to stick in bone rather than slide by it. Again, you won't bring a deer down with an arrow's shocking power; there isn't enough of it. An arrow's energy should be consumed as it cuts meat, and a relatively dull point will still be sharp enough to force entry into flesh.

Windplaning is a characteristic of some heads with unequal blade surface areas. Essentially, the largest part of the head becomes an airfoil in flight, imparting its direction to the arrow instead of the one you intended. Windplaning can sometimes be corrected by aligning the arrowhead with the fletching. Those heads least likely to windplane will have three or more blades of equal size.

There is much to be said for the convertible point system as well, not in terms of the hunting head alone but because the screw-in head feature allows you to convert your hunting shafts to target shafts with identical head weighting. As has been pointed out elsewhere, uniformity promotes consistency in archery, and it is consistency, not your eye or some inborn talent, that is the foundation of regular hits.

—N.S.

Black Copperhead Hunting and Target Heads

These folks have some new ideas in hunting head designs. We don't know how well they work, as we haven't used them, and we can't find anyone who has, but they look awfully good, so we're passing the word along.

The Archer head is best described as a target broadhead. It is a four-bladed conventional broadhead design, with an inverted v-cut tip and unsharpened edges. Both features discourage penetration, so it's a good head for shooting at bales. Weight is 125 grains. Price: $7.95 per dozen.

Target is like the Archer, except the tip is rounded. A good 125-grain head for roving target practice afield. Price: $7.95 per dozen.

Shocker is an untraditional small-game head that has broken with the blunt. It weighs 115 grains and has a heavy steel skirt midway between the rounded point and adapter ferrule. Price: $5.95 per dozen.

Talon can best be described as a four-bladed broadhead with cutaway edges near the adapter ferrule. The effect is to produce a second set of four "points" along

ARCHER
The same quality steel ferrule and tempered blades with un-sharpened edges. The V-Cut tip makes it possible to use the point for all practice shooting, even target bales, without penetration. 125 grain weight.

TARGET
Identical design as the SLICER except for unsharpened blades and the ¼" ball-round tip to retard penetration. Excellent for roving practice in wooded areas. 125 grain weight.

TALON
The newest of the Copperhead line. Extreme cutting action. 120 grain weight.

RIPPER
Saw-tooth BLACK COPPERHEAD with each of four blades form-ground after heat treating to give a total of thirteen needle-sharp penetration points. 120 grain weight.

SHOCKER
The most effective small game point produced today. Precision-steel ferrule with welded steel slug. Less than ½" penetration but maximum impact for sure small game kills. 115 grain weight.

MAGNUM
The ultimate in cutting edges for maximum penetration . . . the finest precision broadhead ever made. 115 & 130 grain weight

the cutting edge. Weight is 120 grains. Price: $19.95 per dozen.

Magnum carries the Talon idea one step farther, with two cutaways along each leading edge, creating eight extra "points." It weighs 115 and 130 grains. Price: $24.95 per dozen.

Ripper is the ultimate in cutaways, with a total of thirteen cutting points. This head can best be described as serrated. Weight is 120 grains. Price: $24.95 per dozen.

Hunter's International, 26422 Groesbeck Highway, Warren, MI 48089.

SATELLITE BROADHEAD

The Satellite broadhead is a razor-insert head, available in three- and four-bladed styles at 120-grain and 125-grain weights respectively. The inserts lock positively, front and back, and they can be replaced without removing the head from the shaft. The sharp, bullet-shaped, tempered steel head is swaged into place after assembly, and it can't come out. The head is threaded to fit most adapter systems. Price: $10.86 for six; twenty-four replacement blades, $4.66. Ben Pearson, P.O. Box 270, Tulsa, OK 74101.

SMALL-GAME ARROWS

You can make your own small-game arrows from target or big-game shafts with .32 or .38 cartridge casings. Remove the stock arrowhead and affix the pistol casing firmly on the end of the shaft with heat glue. You will probably have to do a little sanding to get a .32 casing to fit.

The blunt head kills by shock rather than penetration and thereby saves meat. It also saves arrows; pointed heads can lodge in trees, up high and out of reach.

Should you wish to convert your shafts back to field, target, or broadhead, the blunts can be quickly removed by reheating.

CLOVERLEAF ARROWHEADS

These are blunt arrowheads, with a wire four-leaf-clover design that fans out and forward from the head. If you do a lot of small-game hunting around rocky ground, they cushion the impact of the shaft and reduce arrow breakage. They are emphatically not the thing for shooting through grass, brush, or leaves, as they'll snag or hang up. Prices: 6-inch cloverleaf, $2.65; 3-inch cloverleaf, $2.40. Herter's, Inc., Route 2, Mitchell, SD 57301.

NEW ARCHERY PRODUCTS

Razorbak Broadhead: A Fine Design

Of all the heads I've looked at, this one is the finest. It has five replaceable razor edges, with a total cutting area of 7.75 inches. The point is bulletlike and is made from high-carbon steel, so it won't mushroom. Most intriguing, the head spins on an axle, the theory being that no energy of penetration will be lost upon impact. The arrow continues to spin, but the head drives on with full power.

Are they tough? The manufacturer states that "the Razorbak was ready for market when it could withstand a straight-on shot into a patio brick, from a 65# compound bow at 15 yards." That's a pretty impressive test.

The Razorbak is interchangeable with most point conversion systems (it weighs 135 grains) and comes with individual conelike safety shields, which protect its blades and your fingers. Prices: $11.25 for a four-pack of heads; $6.65 for a four-pack of replacement cartridges. New Archery Products Corp., 370 North Delaplaine Road, Riverside, IL 60546.   —F.S.

"We are not hunting targets. We are seeking to take a living creature that certainly deserves the best we can deliver."

—Keith Schuyler

407

THE RAZORHEAD WILL GET YOUR GOAT

by Marvin Tye

Bagging a Rocky Mountain goat with bow and arrow is a feat that requires a lot of dedicated effort plus the use of first-class equipment. This unique animal is a close relative of the Asian serow and the European chamois. It is found in the most rugged mountains of North America, usually on higher, more inaccessible peaks than those preferred by mountain sheep.

The goat uses its keen eyesight to spot any hunter approaching his domain from below. Once alerted to danger, the goat simply climbs higher over sheer rock walls, where it would be difficult or impossible for a man to follow.

For this reason most hunters are content to use a scope-sighted rifle to bag their goat from a range of 100 yards or more. In most cases the hunter really earns his trophy—even with a rifle.

I knew how difficult it would be to get within bow range of the elusive mountain goat, but the challenge of such a hunt appealed to me. The decision to try it was made after I talked to Salmon, Idaho, guide Ray Torrey at a Pope and Young Club meeting in Denver.

Ray is an experienced bowhunter, as well as being a first-class guide. He had bagged a record-class goat and a variety of other big-game animals with bow and arrow. Ray assured me that it would be possible to stalk to within 20 yards of goats under the right conditions. I booked a ten-day hunt with Ray in Idaho's Salmon National Forest to give me plenty of time to encounter favorable conditions for a good stalk.

The next steps were getting in shape for a rugged hunt at high altitude and selecting proper equipment. I took long walks at night wearing hunting boots near my Stone Mountain, Georgia, home and used stairs instead of elevators whenever possible.

My bow on this hunt was a 50-pound-pull Ben Pearson Stalker. It had enough power to shoot a heavy arrow for deep penetration and yet was light enough in draw to be handled easily after the exertion of a long climb. A clip-on bow quiver held six aluminum arrows.

I've always considered arrows to be the most important part of the bowhunter's tackle. They must be straight and matched to the bow for proper flight. Just as important, the broadhead point must be sharp enough to shave dry hair from the hunter's arms. A sharp broadhead produces massive hemorrhage and kills quickly and humanely.

The Bear Razorhead, manufactured by Bear Archery Company of Grayling, Michigan, is a head that I had used successfully on mule deer, whitetail deer, black bear, and a variety of other animals. It is a favorite of many American bowhunters and has probably been used to kill more big game than any other broadhead.

It features a sturdy main blade of high-carbon steel, which sharpens easily and holds an edge. A razor-steel insert can be added to make it a four-edged head that will produce maximum hemorrhage. The head can be used with or without the insert blade. I had considered leaving the insert blade out in order to get deeper penetration through the goat's thick hair and tough hide with the single double-edged blade. Ray assured me that the four-edged arrangement was best. After the hunt was finished, I was glad that I had listened to his advice.

I spotted a goat from above and stalked to within 20 yards of it. I took careful aim at a spot just behind the foreleg, low on the chest. The goat was standing slightly quartering away as the arrow hit. The shaft seemed to hit exactly in the proper location. The goat raced wildly down the mountainside and went down beside a large boulder. I worked in to close range and shot the goat once more in the chest.

Close examination showed that the first arrow had not struck the chest as I believed. It had hit the goat's leg at the point where it joined the body, just below the rib cage. The Razorhead had done its job well by severing major blood vessels. It had turned an otherwise poor hit into a sure kill and enabled me to bag a large billy that had horns large enough to be listed in the Pope and Young Club record book.

Marvin Tye is the bow-hunting editor for *Southern Outdoors* magazine and is a frequent contributor to other sports periodicals. He is a regular member of the Pope and Young Club and has taken three different species of North American big game with a bow and arrow, one of which (a black bear killed in Utah) qualified for a Pope and Young listing. He lives in Stone Mountain, Georgia.

WASP BROADHEAD

This is a 120-grain, three-bladed, replaceable razor-insert head. The bullet-shaped steel nose cone is replaceable, too, as are the rings that bind the blades to the aluminum body.

This head also has a double convertible feature. The shank of the head is threaded so that it is interchangeable with standard point conversion systems, and by removing the razor inserts, the head converts to a field/target point in its own right. Prices: $6.30 for six heads: $2.10 for eighteen blade replacements. Stemmler Archery, Southford Road, Middlebury, CT 06762.

PRACTICE HEADS

These are 125-grain rounded heads made of polyurethane. They will eventually self-destruct if shot against something hard, but they last forever when shot against a cloth backdrop and won't damage the drop. They have a 5-percent-taper core, which will fit any shaft that uses broadheads. Also available are slip-on heads that fit over target points. Price: $4.00 per dozen. Saunders Archery Company, P.O. Box 476, Industrial Site, Columbus, NE 68601.

BLUDGEON HEADS

These bludgeon heads are designed to kill small game, like rabbits and squirrels, by shock. The head looks like a flattened, inverse cone, ⅞ inch in diameter, and has six small points on the flat. It is made of tough plastic, designed so that it has some give. You thereby run less risk of damaging the shaft during an accidental collision with a rock, tree trunk, or stone wall. Available both with inside cone and threaded shank. Price: $1.50 for five. Saunders Archery Company, P.O. Box 476, Industrial Site, Columbus, NE 68601.

BEAR RAZORHEAD

Among archers this has been *the* head for a number of years, the first, to my knowledge, to use the idea of a razor insert. A small, diamond-shaped insert, with two sides razor sharp, slips into a conventional triangular broadhead at right angles. Price: $8.30 per dozen. Bear Archery Company, Rural Route 1, Grayling, MI 49738.   —N.S.

RAZORHEAD, WACA, FIELD POINT, BLUNT, TUFF-TIP

JUDO POINT

This is a bluntish small-game head, with four short, strong, springy wires jutting out from behind the head. It is useful for shooting in tall grass, as the wire catches blades and stems, preventing the arrow from digging in and often standing the arrow up so you can see the bright fletching. Price: $3.70 for six. Bear Archery Company, Rural Route 1, Grayling, MI 49738.

Browning Serpentine Arrowhead

This is a most unusual head, with two leading, flat edges from which spiral off a thin band of steel. The band twists once, like a corkscrew, and joins the butt end of the arrowhead.

It's a great idea that doesn't pan out fully in practice. Theoretically, the helical spiral fletching sends the corkscrew into flesh so it twists out a core of meat, doing ultimate damage. But the head might hang up on bone as it enters a carcass, it is very difficult to sharpen, and it is easily deflected or stopped by brush. Range tests do indicate, however, that this head has the most shocking power of any broadhead I've used. I have a hunch it would be very good for antelope out on the plains, where brush isn't a problem. But I haven't found an antelope that would let me get close enough to try out my theory. Price: $5.95 for six. Browning, Route 1, Morgan, UT 84050.   —N.S.

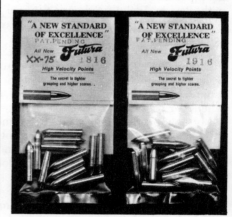

Futura: Perfection in Target and Field Points

Futura arrow points are aerodynamically designed to allow more air to flow onto the shaft and through the vanes, thereby affording better steerage. They are machined from high-carbon steel with an RC of 60, which is *hard*, and they are precision machined so that each point is alike. For aluminum shafts only. Price: $11.10 per dozen. Futura Enterprises, 1851 South Orange Avenue, Monterey Park, CA 91725.

Three-bladed Hunting Heads

These were the favorite hunting heads for many years. Three permanently fixed blades extend from a hollow shank in a triangular pattern. The hollow shank fits over an adapter or is cemented permanently to the end of the shaft. Price: $2.80 for four. Stemmler Archery Company, Southford Road, Middlebury, CT 06762.

SUPER HILBRE HEAD

This is an extremely slender triangle of sharp steel, with a diamond-shaped razor insert. While it is a very popular head, the needlelike point has been known to dig into bone and stay there, rather than slipping off to continue its flesh-cutting path. Price: $3.40 for four. Stemmler Archery Company, Southford Road, Middlebury, CT 06762.

"What! May it be that even in heavenly place
That busy archer his sharp arrows tries?"
—Sir Philip Sidney, Astrophel and Stella

409

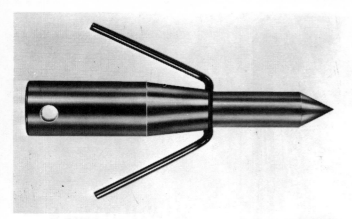

SWEETLAND ADAPTERS FOR TUBULAR SHAFTS

As far as we can determine, these folks are one of the major suppliers of head adapter systems, and target points, in the United States. Others might catalog them; Sweetland makes them.

Their target points include both the ferrule type for wooden shafts and threaded heads for tubular shaft adapter systems. Styles include blunt, field, target, parallel points, and double-barbed fish points.

They do not make hunting heads, but they make everything else you'll need to match up with the broadhead of your choice: female-threaded shaft inserts, short-nosed broadhead adapters, long-nosed broadhead adapters, single piece broadhead adapters (these remain glued in place; the head is noninterchangeable), and nock adapters for glass shafts.

Of special note in this product is a tiny vent hole that is drilled in the shaft inserts. This eliminates the occasional problem, when you're fitting your own tackle, of the insert's "walking" back out of the shaft due to built-up air pressure while the glue is still soft.

	Per 12	Per 100
Field points, tapered hole	$1.50	$10.00
Target points, tapered hole	1.50	10.00
Blunt points, tapered hole	1.25	9.00
Field points, parallel hole	1.50	10.00
Target points, parallel hole	1.25	9.00
Headshrinkers	1.25	9.00
Flight points	1.50	10.00
Fish points ($1.00 each)	9.60	—
Stab. bushings ($1.00 each)	9.60	—
Shaft inserts, female thread	$2.25	16.00
Field points, threaded 125 Gr.	2.25	16.00
Field points, threaded 150 Gr.	2.50	17.50
Broadhead adapters, short	2.25	16.00
Broadhead adapters, long	2.50	17.50
Blunts, threaded	2.25	16.00
Single piece broadhead adapters	2.50	17.50
Nock adapters	2.00	14.60

Sweetland Products, 1010 Arrowsmith Street, Eugene, OR 97402.

SWEETLAND PRODUCTS

SWAP POINT SYSTEM

Stemmler's Swap Point system is typical of most convertible head systems. Their aluminum/glass shaft adapter goes inside the hollow shaft ($1.68 per dozen). They also have a wood arrow adapter that ferrules onto the tip of a wooden shaft ($2.10 per dozen). The adapter accepts a field head ($1.68 per dozen), a target head ($1.68 per dozen), or the broadhead of your choice.

When putting together one of these systems, the only thing to be aware of is the head weights of your practice points. In order to achieve consistency and accuracy, your practice points should weigh the same as your hunting broadheads.

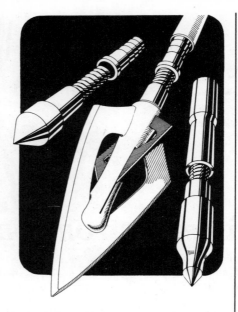

Stemmler Archery Company, Southford Road, Middlebury, CT 06762.

BOWHUNTER'S SHEATH KIT

All the basic necessities for your equipment are housed in the belt sheath—a hunting knife, a file, and a stone for sharpening both knife and broadheads—and there's an extra pocket for small stuff like bowstrings. Price: $19.50. Bear Archery Company, Rural Route 1, Grayling, MI 49738.

BROWNING SELECT-A-POINT HEAD SYSTEM

(Specify shaft size when ordering)

Item	Per 12
Wood adapter	$2.50
Glass or aluminum adapter	$2.00
Broadhead adapter*	$2.00
Points: target, field, blunt	$2.00

Browning, Route 1, Morgan, UT 84050.

*This is a screw-in adapter with a conical point onto which may be cemented the ferrule-type broadhead or field point of your choice.

POPE AND YOUNG RECORD BOOK

This book is the official listing and scoring of all trophy North American big game taken by bow and arrow. It's the Boone and Crockett book of the archery world.

In addition to trophies and their respective ratings, the book also contains articles about bow hunting and profiles of big game, such as deer, elk, caribou, pronghorn, moose, bear, sheep, and mountain goats.

The full name of this work is *Bow Hunting Big Game Records of North America*, and you'll probably find it in your local library's reference stack. If it's not there or you want a copy of your own, you can order it from The Pope and Young Club, 600 East High Street, Milton, WI 53563, for $17.50.

—F.S.

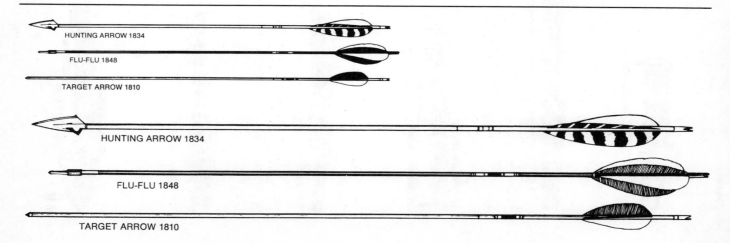

HUNTING ARROW 1834

FLU-FLU 1848

TARGET ARROW 1810

HUNTING ARROW 1834

FLU-FLU 1848

TARGET ARROW 1810

"The archer is a special kind of hunter because it is his personal strength as well as his skill that ultimately kills the game."

—*Dave Petzal, in conversation*

411

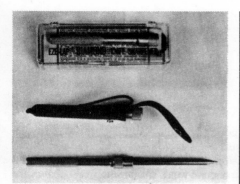

EZE-LAP DIAMOND SHARPENERS

These are hand-held honers, with a surface of powdered diamond. They are reputed to be extremely fast-cutting (although I haven't tried one) and capable of imparting fine keenness to the edge.

The Knife Sharpener is a sharpening rod that is carried in its own aluminum or brass handle (specify which you prefer). The handle/rod is carried in a belt-looped sheath. Price: $19.95.

The Hone and Stone is a flat, hand-sized metal file, with diamond dust on the tip section. It's small enough to carry comfortably in a back pocket or in a spare knife sheath. Price: $4.95.

Both sharpeners look especially well suited to sharpening broadheads in the field. Eze-Lap Diamond Products, P.O. Box 2229, Westminster, CA 92683.

—N.S.

DIXIE STUDIO

Arrow Puller for Buried Broadheads

Next to loss, sinking a broadhead deep into a tree is the greatest gobbler of expensive hunting arrows.

The VORCO Arro-puller is a plierslike device that clamps down hard on the edge of a broadhead and then rockers back, working the arrow free without danger of breakage.

The end opposite the pliers head is a chisel, so you can dig down to the vanes of a completely buried head. The tool comes with a small file to sharpen arrows. Both items are housed in a durable leather carrying case you can wear on your belt. Price: $15.95. Van's Archery Supplies, P.O. Box 929, St. George, UT 84770.

POINT RETRIEVER FOR ARROWS

This is a simple arrow puller for use with threaded conversion-head systems. If your broadhead sticks in a stump or a tree, unscrew the arrow and screw this handle to it. Wiggle it back and forth and the head will work its way out.

This retriever is also useful when sharpening arrows, and it even converts your broadhead to a makeshift knife in the field. Price: $3.30. Jen-Lin Manufacturing Company, Archery Division, P.O. Box 211, Hummelstown, PA 17036.

MATCH ARCHERY
by Glenn Helgeland

I like to watch a good archer shoot. I watch *only* him or her (if it's a her, there's even more incentive to watch); I don't even look at the target.

Because good archers make it look so easy. They've got themselves and their bows under such control that a shot sequence has the same watchable, enjoyable grace you see in a slow-motion film of a bounding impala.

Why do I get such a kick out of watching that muscular poetry? For two reasons: (1) I know the sport well enough to know what it took in time and effort and sheer determination for each good archer to reach that level; and related to this, (2) when I shoot the bow, a bystander would quite possibly get the impression that I'm locked in a strenuous wrestling match with that bow and quite likely to lose two of three falls.

As with any sport, no outsider can fully appreciate the talent and skill that an expert employs to make the act look easy. My dad played a lot of sandlot baseball so long ago that sandlots were rare and hayfields were more common. Because of this he has more than the usual interest in baseball and much more than the usual understanding of the game. He also used to get madder than hell at ball games he took us to when my brothers and I were kids, because about three times a game a batter would clout one on a line between a couple of infielders or blast one a hundred miles up and forty miles back, and one of the infielders would make a wild leap for the liner and just snag it or the outfielder would just barely catch up with the fly ball. The crowd would go absolutely bananas and beat their palms together until they blistered. And my old man would sit there and seethe for a couple of seconds, then he'd growl—just loud enough so us kids could hear—"If that guy had been in better position [referring to an infielder, usually], or gotten a better jump on the ball and turned the right way when he took off [the outfielder here], he wouldn't have had so much trouble getting the job done."

Believe me, folks, that sank in. To this day I do not like it when a person makes an easy play look tough; nor do I like to listen to a crowd go crazy over a fly ball that is destined to be nothing more than a big out and quite obviously so, even if the outfielder does need to drift back quite a bit. Nor do I cotton to the rah-rah types who can't back up their rah-rah as well as they'd like you to believe they can; I played high school football with a couple of them and that was enough. More people ought to realize the yawning chasm between someone who makes a tough play look easy and someone who makes an easy play look tough.

I'm no smarter than you are and probably no dumber. We most likely have similar interests; if not, I never would have written for this book and you never would be reading it. So it probably won't come as any shock to you when I say that you might get a kick out of archery. It's a sport that will give you back as much as you put into it or as little as you put into it. It's so diverse that no one can tell you this is the way to enjoy archery. You can shoot in the backyard with the kids, you can shoot field archery over outdoor ranges that simulate hunting conditions, you can shoot under extremely strict rules, such as those who aim for the Olympics do, or you can take your bow and arrows (and a jug of wine, a loaf of bread, and Omar Khayyam, too, if you wish) into the wilderness or forest, usually a woods near home, and just wander around and shoot at stumps and clumps of grass and things like that. If you do this, you'll need to use a special point called a judo point, which has four short wires pointing in four directions, because it will stop immediately upon impact. Shoot a regular field point under such conditions and there's a good chance I'll be a grandfather before you find your arrow (unless my kid does something ghastly or you're shooting into a good backstop).

Some archers are technical nuts who aren't satisfied until they can find *the absolute* bow and arrow combination that will give them another couple of feet per second speed on the arrow, and they're not satisfied when they do, because they figure if they could get that speed, maybe they ought to hunt around for a faster combination. But there are also a good many of us who just like to get out there and draw that bow and let it go and watch an arrow fly. Lord, it's pretty; especially on a long shot. A good arrow leaps out of the bow and then bores through the air, just daring anything to push it off course, until it lands with a whap somewhere in the target. If it hits the middle, fine. If not, it still was fun seeing that arrow arc out there the last half of the distance. That's something *I* did. I set up that bow. I tuned it. I drew and shot it. That arrow could have fish-tailed all over the place; but it didn't, because I did everything right.

Top archers say the sport is 95 percent mental. I believe that, because there aren't five people on earth who can each claim 1 percent of the frustration and stupidity I feel when I make a lousy shot; and there aren't 95, 9,500, or 9,500,000 who could feel what I feel when I bring that bow up, draw the arrow, aim well and properly, and maintain such mental control over my muscles that I shoot when I'm ready to shoot . . . and the arrow goes right where it should. Right where I intended it to go. Right where I *knew* it would go.

The only way you could feel that way would be to do it yourself. Then you'll know.

Glenn Helgeland is editor and associate publisher of *Archery World* and *Archery Retailer* magazines and has edited *Archery World's Complete Guide to Bowhunting*.

BOWHUNTING FOR WHITETAILS

by G. Howard Gillelan

Without a doubt, hunting whitetails is the greatest challenge for archers. It's true that a bow-shot Alaska moose makes a spectacular trophy and that downing a brown bear or a caribou with an arrow is a memorable experience. But the whitetail, according to bowhunters who have bagged numerous big-game species, requires the greatest hunting expertise, as well as the ability to put the broadhead-tipped hunting arrow in the right spot.

Odocoileus virginianus virginianus is one of the smartest critters in the wild, which is one reason the species is thriving in unprecedented numbers. To get a smart whitetail with a bow, the emphasis must be on the bowman's hunting skills.

Of course, the archer must have the right equipment and know how to use it with accuracy, but the best archery tackle and marksmanship are meaningless unless the bowhunter can get really close to his target, preferably less than 30 yards. That's not because a hunting arrow won't do the job at longer ranges. It's capable of taking game at 200 yards or more, but no archer can place his arrow in an animal's vitals at such a range.

So the challenge of bowhunting for white-tailed deer is in getting within a few paces of a wary animal. Nationwide, the average successful bow-shot at whitetails is in the neighborhood of 25 yards.

For a bowman, of the three methods of hunting whitetails with the bow—stalking or still-hunting, driving, and hunting from a stand—the last-named method is by far the best. As a consequence, the choice of a stand is of the utmost importance. Whether it's in the fork of a tree or a platform up the tree's trunk or a blind on the ground, the bowhunter's stakeout must be in a place the deer are using.

To ensure setting up on the best possible stand, the smart bowhunter spends considerable time in checking out his hunting areas for the most likely locations for his ambush. He ascertains the prevailing winds, then looks for tracks, droppings, game trails, rubbing trees, and buck scrapes. Of all the forms of deer sign the most meaningful are the buck scrapes, which outline the perimeters of a buck's claimed territory during the rut.

It's possible for a bowhunter to nail a doe, or even a good buck, at the edge of a field, where the animals use well-defined trails to enter their feeding grounds. If you want to see deer and get a good shot at a whitetail, the borders between grain fields and woods are a good bet. But if a bowhunter can hunt during the rutting season, his best chance is to go deeper into the woods and locate the scrapes. That's where the action is for big bucks.

As for the shooting part, a hunting archer should practice enough so that he can consistently hit a 12-inch bull's-eye from a variety of distances between 10 and 30 yards. If he can do that, and if his broadheads are razor-sharp, he'll get a deer, providing he's a good hunter.

Camouflage clothing and a camouflaged bow are musts. Scents are recommended, not necessarily to lure deer but because they tend to mask human scent. Generally, deer calls do more harm than good. The exception is horn-rattling, which can properly be considered a deer call. It's effective, and the technique is not too difficult to master, but it works only when bucks are rutting.

The bowhunter's equivalent of the rifleman's Boone and Crockett Club is the Pope and Young Club, named after two pioneers in modern bowhunting. Using Boone-Crockett scoring standards for measuring archers' North American big-game trophies, the Pope and Young Club maintains listings of record animals shot with a bow. It's reassuring to sportsmen to know that new records for trophy animals are regularly established. That proves three things: (1) the quality of North American big game is not declining, (2) bowhunters are increasing in numbers, and (3) bowhunters are steadily improving in skill.

G. Howard Gillelan, the archery editor of *Outdoor Life* since 1959, is the author of six books on archery and bowhunting and has bagged whitetails, moose, and mule deer with his bow. According to one of his publishers, he has written more words on archery than anyone else in the history of the sport.

Robin Hood Archery Catalog

In terms of completeness and organization, this free archery catalog is the best we've seen. The Robin Hood folks list every conceivable piece of archery tackle you'd ever need, each class of equipment is tab-indexed so you can find it quickly, and individual products are described and pictured in plain (if unimaginative) progression. The net effect is a display of products that you can scan and locate fast. One criticism: retail prices are not listed in the catalog, but the accompanying price list is easy to match up to the products. Robin Hood Archery, Inc., 215 Glenridge Avenue, Montclair, NJ 07042.

No-screw Sight Attachment Bracket

If you don't like the idea of drilling into your bow to attach a sight, look into the sight attachment bracket made by Saunders. It's a stickum-type backing on a copper plate, to which is affixed a mounting bracket for the sight. Saunders claims it will conform to any bow and leaves no marks when it's removed. Price: $2.50 per pair. Saunders Archery Company, P.O. Box 476, Industrial Site, Columbus, NE 68601.

FLEETWOOD ARCHERY RACK: ECONOMICAL

A do-it-yourself, economy archery rack that holds three bows horizontally, and twenty-four arrows vertically. Made of redwood, with metal wall hangers and accessory hooks. Price: $11.84. Fleetwood Archery, P.O. Box 37, Onalaska, WI 54650.

BLUNT-HEAD PRACTICE TARGET

The target consists of a frame that stretches a spring-loaded synthetic net with the shape of a deer on it. The boiler room is a suspended plate. When you hit it, it spins. The backstop is guaranteed to catch arrows from the heaviest compound, as long as they have a blunt head. This target breaks down for easy transport, and it may be towed to simulate a moving animal. May be used indoors or out. Price: $35.00. Saunders Archery Company, P.O. Box 476, Industrial Site, Columbus, NE 68601.

Reversible Camouflage Jacket and Pants

Here's a hunting outfit that will see you through an entire season. One side of this jacket/pants combo is green camouflage to match the verdant greens of early archery seasons. The other side is fall brown, for bow and arrow hunting after the frosts or duck hunting on a fall marsh.

Jacket includes two slash pockets and a breast pocket with a hidden zipper. The pants have two roomy cargo pockets. The camouflage pattern is broad to match big leaves, and both pants and jacket are 100-percent cotton and are machine washable. Prices: jacket, $11.49; pants, $12.95. Cabela's, 812 13th Avenue, Sidney, NE 69162.

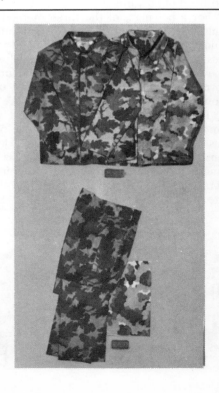

Mail Order Archery Accessories

If you have trouble locating a specific archery accessory in your local sporting goods store, write the Whiffen Archery Company, 923 South 16th Street, Milwaukee, WI 53204, and ask for their catalog and a price list. They have a very thorough selection of just about every piece of equipment an archer would need, except bows. They catalog shafts, finished arrows, sights, clothing, heads, arm guards, tackle, and more, with prices at or slightly below manufacturers' suggested retail.

Powder Pouch for Match Shooters

Smooth out your release by smoothing your fingertips with talc powder. This powder pouch is made of leather and has a clear vinyl flap that protects the powder from rain and dampness. It includes a cloth dispenser, a scorecard clip, a pencil holder, and a clip that fits over your belt or a quiver pocket. Price: $2.75. Kolpin Manufacturing, Inc., P.O. Box 231, Berlin, WI 54923.

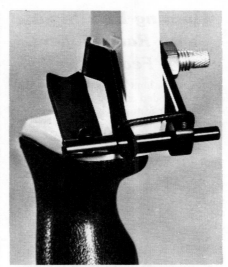

Pacesetter II Arrow Rest

The Pacesetter II arrow rest is secured to the sight window by a clamp and bolt that passes through the bow. The rest is adjustable by way of an allen screw, which allows the shaft it bears upon to slide left or right. The arrow rest is a semifirm plasticlike material selected for toughness and quietness, and when adjusted properly, the rest allows for complete clearance of vanes as the arrow leaves the bow.

The manufacturer claims this rest to be impervious to weather and slick under all conditions. Launcher arms are replaceable (although they're supposed to last a lifetime), and the rest will fit right- or left-handed bows. Price: $11.10. Golden Key Archery Products, 1851 South Orange Avenue, Monterey Park, CA 91754.

SPRING-TYPE ARROW REST

For those who prefer a spring-type arrow rest, this product is adjustable in three directions: across, back and forth, and up and down. There is also a tension adjustment on the spring. Available in right- or left-hand rests, target or hunting styles. Specify when ordering. Prices: rest, $19.95; extra springs, $4.00 each. Stanislawski Archery Products, 7135 Southeast Cora Street, Portland, OR 97206.

Comanchero Hunting Release

This is a simple release that fits the palm of your hand. The serving is accepted in a slot in the face of the release, and a tongue laps in front of the slot and holds the serving as you draw. The tongue is part of a levering device, with a trip that extends from the rear of the release. Depress the trip with your thumb and the serving is released. A simple, effective gadget. Price: $14.95. Browning, Route 1, Morgan, UT 84050.

BARNER BOW RELEASE

A bow release is comparable to a trigger on a gun. It promotes smooth, consistent releases of the arrow and string and thus enhances accuracy. The moving parts of these releases are made of heat-treated tooled steel. The outer steel housing is finished in black oxide. Flex handle. Prices: hammer and slot release, $65.00; string release, $45.00. Barner Release, P.O. Box 382, Bozeman, MT 59715.

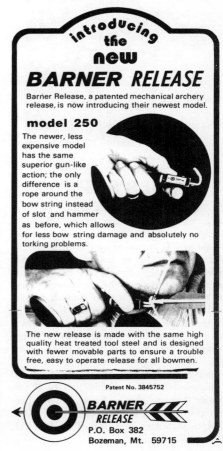

ALUMINUM PEEPSIGHT

Peepsights that rest in the string are simple and reliable sighting devices. This one packs an added guarantee; if it breaks, return it with a self-addressed stamped envelope and you'll get another one free. $3/64$- and $1/16$-inch holes. Price: $3.25. Stanislawski Archery Products, 7135 Southeast Cora Street, Portland, OR 97206.

Hunting Bow Sight with Rangefinder Feature

Browning's hunting bow sight is a standard color-coded adjustable pin sight with a rangefinder feature. The rangefinder is a square viewing port, across which is stretched fluorescent monofilament at graduated intervals. Its range is 20 to 60 yards. You identify range by fitting the borders of your target to the proper box. For example, if a deer, belly-to-back, fits into the second slot, the animal is 30 yards away. The 30-yard mark is color coordinated with the 30-yard sight pin. Put the 30-yard sight pin on the critter's boiler room, and you've got venison in the pot. Price: $9.95. Browning, Route 1, Morgan, UT 84050.

Handwarmers for Cold-Weather Archers

Keep your string hand warm, flexible, sensitive, and ready to fire by carrying it inside this belt-mounted hand warmer with its heavy pile lining. You can make this gadget downright toasty by dropping a catalytic handwarmer in first.

Or take the chill off your bow hand with a bow muff, a mitten that slips over the bow handle. Only the outside of the muff insulates: or, put a different way, there is no material between the bow and your hand. The bare-hand grip permits maximum feel for control and sensitivity when you shoot, yet your hand stays warm. Prices: handwarmer, $6.00: bow muff, $5.00. Kolpin Manufacturing, Inc., P.O. Box 231, Berlin, WI 54923.

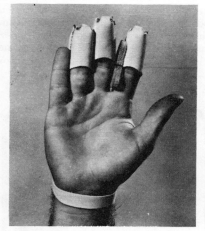

FINGER-SPACING ARCHER'S GLOVE

Finger pinching was a minor problem with recurves, but the short limbs of a compound compound the problem, you might say. It is caused by the angles of the string becoming so acute at maximum draw that they force your fingers up against either side of the arrow nock. This, in turn, interferes with a smooth release and causes erratic flight in the arrow.

An easy way to eliminate this problem is to use an archery glove with a finger spacer—a tab attached to the inside index glove finger. It prevents your fingers from coming together on the shortest-limbed compounds. Also available in tabs if you prefer them to gloves. Prices: finger-spacing glove, $4.75; finger-spacing tab, $3.00. Kolpin Manufacturing, Inc., P.O. Box 231, Berlin, WI 54923.

EDDIE BAUER, INC.

COTTON CHAMOIS CAMOU SHIRT

The most comfortable material ever loomed is cotton chamois, and it's just the right weight for the first part of the archery season, when the weather is still summerlike but the morning's cool. This shirt has extra-long shirttails and, praise be, a whisker-proof nylon collar lining that won't chafe your neck when you do a lot of looking. Price: $18.50. Eddie Bauer, 1737 Airport Way South, Seattle, WA 98134.

CAMOUFLAGE SWEATERS

A sweater is just the right garb for many early fall mornings, when it's not cold enough for heavy clothing yet too frosty for light coveralls. These 100-percent-acrylic sweaters won't itch, and they're available in brown, green, and blaze orange camouflage patterns, with matching knit watch caps, in sizes small through extra large. Prices: sweaters, $31.00; watch caps, $8.75. Kolpin Manufacturing, Inc., P.O. Box 231, Berlin, WI 54923.

"I indignantly deny the allegation of efficiency. I admit only this: that making archery tackle is an effective alibi for being late at the office."

—Aldo Leopold

417

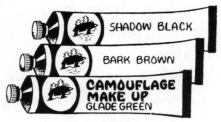

CAMOUFLAGE MAKEUP

In a duck blind or with a bow, it's central to success to mask your presence. It's easy to break up your outline with camouflage clothing, but your face still shines like a beacon, and the human face is recognized by wildlife immediately.

Just dulling the shine and changing the telltale color helps. You can accomplish this with burnt cork or, in a pinch, mud. Either is better than nothing.

If you really want to do a good job, use camouflage makeup. It comes in three shades—brown, green, and black—and has a cold cream base, so it's easy to remove. As a pleasant little extra, the makeup also contains insect repellent.

Apply it in a pattern, just like camou clothing. Pay particular attention to your eyes. Close them, then raise your eyebrows and get some color into the sockets. If you don't, your eyeballs will gleam like a headlamp on a fast freight. Price: makeup kit, $3.69. Cabela's, 812 13th Avenue, Sidney, NE 69162.

HUNTMATE BRUSH REST

One inherent problem with plastic vanes is that they don't give as much as feathers. If they brush against something solid, they deflect. The Huntmate Brush Rest is a nylon-bristled rest that holds the shaft ½ inch above the rest base. The bristles act to provide the give that feathers normally have, and the arrow clears the bow without deflection. Price: $2.50. Saunders Archery Company, P.O. Box 476, Industrial Site, Columbus, NE 68601.

ARCHERY RACK

Store your archery gear in style. This rack accepts five bows and twenty-four arrows in prominent display. It includes a pull-out accessory drawer, a place to hang shooting gloves, and built-in bow quiver holders. The rack is made of wood-grained plastic. Price: $26.95. Cabela's, 812 13th Avenue, Sidney, NE 69162.

KWIK LOK ARROW HOLDER

This device locks your arrow to your bow and on the string, so that you don't have to use your hands to keep it in place. It releases automatically as you draw. Installation requires no drilling; just press the plate in place and the adhesive backing does the rest. Price: $3.50. Saunders Archery Company, P.O. Box 476, Industrial Site, Columbus, NE 68601.

Adjustable String Peepsight

The beauty of this type of peepsight is that you can slide it up and down the string, testing it and you for the perfect position. Once in the right place, the sight may be fixed in permanent position without the need for any serving. Scored surface keeps reflected light to a minimum. Price: $2.00. Saunders Archery Company, P.O. Box 476, Industrial Site, Columbus, NE 68601.

ARCHERY TARGET FACES

If you need something to shoot at, Saunders Archery Company will oblige. They have paper target faces that include bull's-eyed pictures of pheasant, bobcat, fox, turkey, blue jay, deer, lion, and Richard Nixon. If you prefer more conventional targets, they have both paper- and cloth-skirted targets in color and black and white, including PAA regulation indoor and outdoor tournament targets. Price range: 6 cents to $6.60. Saunders Archery Company, P.O. Box 476, Industrial Site, Columbus, NE 68601.

SCORE-MORE SIGHT

This is a single pin-type sight, with lateral and vertical adjustments. There's no need to drill, tap, or screw into the bow to mount it. Guaranteed against breakage, except sight pin, which is replaceable. Price: $6.00. Saunders Archery Company, P.O. Box 476, Industrial Site, Columbus, NE 68601.

Jennings Hunting Sight: Clean and Simple

The Buckshot hunting sight by Jennings is trim and tough, with three adjustments: master, vertical, and horizontal. Positive contact between all parts stops rattles and ensures against the pins or bracket being knocked out of alignment. It can be mounted on any bow on the market, although untapped bows must be drilled. Price: $9.95. Jennings Compound Bow, Inc., 28756. North Castaic Canyon Road, Valencia, CA 91355.

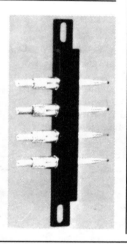

COBRA BOWSIGHT

Four sighting pins are color-coded and placed at 1-inch intervals on this bow sight. It has a flat-black aluminum-alloy frame, brass pins, and knurled thumb nuts. Mounts on the back of the bow. Price: $10.00. Stemmler Archery Company Southford Road, Middlebury, CT 06762.

NEW ARCHERY PRODUCTS

Flipper II Arrow Rest

This is a sweet rest, because it's simple. There's no drilling or bolting required to mount it on your bow, just a clean surface and some strong stickum tape that comes with the rest.

The housing is made of nylon, from which protrudes a spring-loaded steel arm. The arm is covered by a Teflon sleeve. You lay the arrow on top of the arm, draw, and release. As the arrow leaves the bow, the arm folds out of the way. Price: $4.25. New Archery Products Corp., 370 North Delaplaine Road, Riverside, IL 60546.

—F.S.

Mohair Arrow Rest and Plate

If you appreciate the beauty inherent in simplicity, this is about the simplest rest in the business. It is a self-adhesive patch of mohair that you paste to the bottom of the sight window. A leather plate pastes on the side of the window to quiet the sound of the shaft as it leaves the bow. Price: $1.12. Stemmler Archery Company Southford Road, Middlebury, CT 06762.

FULL-SIZE TARGET FACES

These targets measure 35 by 45 inches and portray five different full views of a white-tailed deer. They are in sepia tone, and the target area is outlined on each pose. Price: $5.49 per set. Cabela's, 812 13th Avenue, Sidney, NE 69162.

WEATHEREST ARROW REST

This arrow rest was specifically designed to accommodate plastic-fletched arrows. Adhesive-backed, so there's no installation hassle, it comes in right- and left-handed models. Price: $1.72. Bear Archery Company, Rural Route 1, Grayling, MI 49738.

HUNTING STABILIZER

Target shooters have long used stabilizers to improve their score. A stabilizer can best be described as a counterweight that extends from the bow back and is used to dampen vibrations, torque, and to get a more balanced feel in the bow. Problem is, target stabilizers are up to a yard long, which gets a little cumbersome in the brush.

Bear Archery markets a short hunting stabilizer that won't get in your way. It fits all Bear bows and can be adapted to most other makes with a special adapter. Comes with camouflage cover. Price: $14.00. Bear Archery Company, Rural Route 1, Grayling, MI 49738.

*"The antique Persians taught three useful things—
To draw the bow, to ride, and speak the truth."*
—Byron, Don Juan

419

BOW-FISHING RIG

Bow fishing, shooting trash fish like carp and gar with an arrow, is an exciting way to keep your archer's eye on target during the off-season.

Bear Archery markets two bow-fishing rigs. The Converta Bow-Fishing Rig includes a reel that mounts on the back of the bow, 50 feet of 90-pound test line, and a fiberglass arrow with plastic fletching and a harpoon head. This rig fits all Bear bows except for the White Bear and the Little Bear.

They also market a tape-on bow-fishing rig that will fit other makes. Note: if your compound or recurve is tapped for a stabilizer bar, the Converta rig might work. Prices: Converta Bow-Fishing Rig, with easy-off point, $11.50; tape-on rig, $9.75. Bear Archery Company, Rural Route 1, Grayling, MI 49738.

BERGER BUTTON

Vic Berger was the first archer ever to shoot a perfect 300 back to back. This is his favorite arrow plate—a spring tension Teflon pressure point that works like a shock absorber to minimize the effects of a bad release. Can be adjusted by a turn of a set screw. Price: $11.90. Bear Archery Company, Rural Route 1, Grayling, MI 49738.

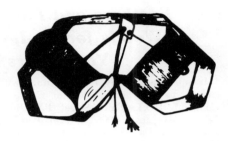

TWIN-SPIN SERVING TOOL

Spin single- or double-layer servings on your bowstring at the same time with this device. Thread spools snap into the frame, you thread the serving material through a guide and a hole, and the serving laps into place as you rotate the bobbin around the bowstring. Tension is adjusted by bending the frame. Will also make two-color servings. Price: $5.49. GT Enterprises, P.O. Box 9312, Colorado Springs, CO 80932.

—F.S.

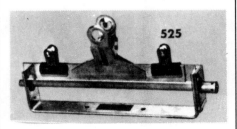

Arrow Fletcher (Straight Fletching)

This is a nice simple straight-fletcher that locks the fletching in place with spring-loaded paper clips. Easy to use and cheap. Price: $10.38. Stemmler Archery Company, Southford Road, Middlebury, CT 06762.

ARROW NOCKS

Saunders merchandises Bjorn nocks and Mycro nocks. The Bjorn nock is a pinch-type nock that locks onto the serving—a handy feature while you're hunting. Mycro nocks are conventional nocks. Prices: Bjorn nocks, $1.20 for twelve; Mycro nocks, 70 cents for twelve. State shaft size and color desired. Saunders Archery Company, P.O. Box 476, Industrial Site, Columbus, NE 68601.

PRO FLETCH PLASTIC VANES

If you wish to fletch your own shafts with plastic vanes, Saunders is one source. They have 1¾- to 5-inch long vanes in white, red, yellow, fluorescent green, fluorescent orange, and black. Price range: $2.20 to $2.50 per dozen. Saunders Archery Company, P.O. Box 476, Industrial Site, Columbus, NE 68601.

Material for Making Your Own Bowstrings

Herter's catalogs both Dacron bowstring (prewaxed) and nylon serving thread. The string material costs $2.97 for 440 yards, and the serving thread costs 95 cents for 125 yards. Herter's, Inc., Route 2, Mitchell, SD 59301.

ARROW-MAKING KIT

Herter's catalogs three kits for making aluminum, glass, and cedar arrows. Nocks, feather fletchings, and glues are provided. Prices: Aluminum, $20.50 per dozen; glass, $14.64 per dozen; and cedar, $7.55 per dozen. Herter's also sells Easton shafts alone for $15.95 per dozen. Herter's, Inc., Route 2, Mitchell, SD 57301.

BOW SQUARE

Your nocking point on the serving should be approximately ⅜ inch above a 90-degree angle formed by the intersection of the bowstring with a line drawn from the arrow rest. The easiest way to find this point is with a device called a bow square. Price: Patawatomi bow square, $3.50. Stemmler Archery Company, Southford Road, Middlebury, CT 06762.

WOOD SHAFT TAPERING TOOL

The best way to describe these gadgets is as glorified pencil sharpeners. You stick the shaft head or butt end in the hole, twist, and the ends are shaved into a cone, ready for application of heads and nocks. The tool comes with six interchangeable bushings for various shaft sizes. Price: $4.50. Herter's, Inc., Route 2, Mitchell, SD 57301.

HELICAL FLETCHER

If you prefer a helical spiral fletching, this tool will fletch one arrow every fifteen minutes. It includes a fast-changing lock that adjusts to various shaft sizes and a degree-of-spiral adjustment on each end of the fletcher that moves all three vane stations at one time. Also available as a straight fletcher. Price: $19.97. Herter's, Inc., Route 2, Mitchell, SD 57301.

MATCHED CEDAR ARROW SHAFTS

If you're into making your own cedar arrows, Cabela's lists matched Port Orford cedar shafts 31 inches long. Specify spine weight desired. Price: $2.99 per dozen. Cabela's, 812 13th Avenue, Sidney, NE 69162.

ARCHERY GLUE AND CEMENT

Archery cement for fletching and nocking wood, glass, and aluminum arrows and heat-type ferrule cement for affixing heads are both available from Cabela's. Prices: glue (¾ ounce), $2.19; cement, 99 cents. Cabela's, 812 13th Avenue, Sidney, NE 69162.

Feathers and Fine Woods for Do-It-Yourselfers

If you'd like to try making your own archery tackle, the Old Master Crafters Company, 130 Le Baron Street, P.O. Box 241, Waukegan, IL 60085, is a retail outlet for raw materials for making bows. They have, among other items, hard maple laminations, colorful woods, fiberglass, glue, etc.

Texas Feathers, Inc., P.O. Box 1118, Brownwood, TX 76801, is a good source for feathers for fletching. They have full-length, die-shaped, and bright way cut ground base feathers in select and commercial quality and in a wide range of colors, including fluorescents.

Both companies will send you a price list upon request.

EPILOGUE

A CONSUMER'S GUIDE TO ANIMAL CHARITIES AND WILDLIFE ORGANIZATIONS

In the past decade there has been a proliferation of organizations that are supposedly dedicated to the preservation and/or protection of animals, especially wildlife. Their names are impressive enough, each of them suggesting some sort of noble intent having to do with our outdoor heritage and its future. In fact, some of these organizations sound so similar that it's confusing, a situation that just might have been intentional.

What are their avowed goals? What is their approach to conservation? Most important, what is their attitude toward sport hunting?

If you ever have considered contributing time or money to such an organization, or ever will, read on to find out just what you will be supporting.

American Humane Association (1877). "A national federation of individuals and agencies for the prevention of cruelty, especially to children and animals. The American Humane Association is not opposed to regulated hunting when population factors indicate reductions are in the best interests of that species. This organization's only mandate is that such hunting be performed in the most humane manner practically available."

Ducks Unlimited (1937). "A private, nonprofit membership organization dedicated to the conservation and propagation of North America's waterfowl as a valuable natural resource." Ducks Unlimited has always recognized the role of the hunter in waterfowl conservation.

Friends of Animals (1957). "A humane conservation organization, dedicated to regaining ecological balance through preservation of wildlife's territory and elimination of human brutality to animals. 'Sports-hunting' is neither sport nor hunting. The kill-for-the-kicks boys seek to ennoble their deeds by claiming to save the animals from starvation. Wildlife belongs to all people. The destroyers of that life must, in turn, be destroyed—preferably by due legal process."

Fund for Animals. "Hunting is not a true sport, for the simple reason that there is nothing sporting about shooting the defenseless wild animals with a high-powered rifle. Hunting is not consistent with the proper conservation of the 'resource.' Hunting also adversely affects the evolutionary development of an animal species because the hunter seeks out and kills the largest and strongest animal of the herd. Moreover, hunters each year cause untold pain and suffering. It is difficult to understand why hunters cannot enjoy the wilderness and get 'close to nature' without taking the life of a fellow creature."

Humane Society of the United States. "Our ultimate goal is to develop, through education, a generation of adults who do not wish to kill any living creature for pleasure or recreation. We are aware of the tragic need to remove or eliminate excess of unwanted animals, including domestic pets. Where 'hunting' embraces this measure of responsible conduct, we are unable to object, but we are unalterably opposed to the killing of any living creature for fun or for sport."

Izaak Walton League of America (1922). "Promotes and educates the public in means to conserve, maintain, protect, and restore the natural resources of the United States. Hunting seasons should be based upon data available, and structured to assure healthy populations of games and non-game species alike. Hunting and fishing revenues (from taxes and licenses) should be used to enhance wildlife and habitat. Hunting should be characterized by the highest order of humaneness, sportsmanship, and respect for the species hunted."

National Audubon Society (1905). "To promote the conservation of wildlife and the natural environment, and educate man regarding his place within the natural ecological system. The Society has never opposed the hunting of a game species, so long as it does not deplete the wildlife resource. We do not, however, advocate hunting; our objective is wildlife and environmental conservation, not the promotion of hunting."

National Wildlife Federation (1936). "To encourage an awareness of the need for wise use and proper management of our natural resources upon which the lives and welfare of our population depends: the soils, plant life and wild life. We support the hunter-sportsman who, by legal means, crops surplus wildlife. We also understand the position of those who feel that hunting is wrong. To try to attempt to change either attitude would be like trying to stem the ocean's tide. Rather, we would hope to unite each philosophy in a common purpose and goal; to preserve wildlife habitat, the key to wildlife variety and abundance."

North American Wildlife Foundation (1911). "Sponsors wildlife research through cooperating organizations and investigations into resource conservation, restoration, and management. We recognize the sportsmen as having financed practically all of the management work since the start of the wildlife protection movement in this country. Present-day wildlife populations can be attributed almost entirely to hunters and fishermen."

Sierra Club (1892). "To protect and conserve the natural resources of this nation and the world, to study and investigate all aspects of man's environment, and to educate people in the need to preserve and to restore the quality of that environment and the integrity of natural ecosystems. We do not oppose legal sports hunting; however, we wonder if the debate over hunting doesn't dominate too much wildlife policy? Wild animals should not be valued principally in terms of whether they can serve as targets, but as a vital feature of the natural world. More and more people are finding ways to value wildlife in terms other than hunting."

Wetlands for Wildlife (1960). "Promotes the acquisition of wetlands and wildlife habitat in the United States, for ultimate transferral to the public trust, and preservation. We believe that any effort toward the conservation of wetlands would be seriously impaired without the sport hunter. He is among our most dedicated conservationists."

Wilderness Society (1935). "The national conservation organization dedicated to the preservation of wilderness, and to resist its invasion. The Wilderness Society subscribes to hunting as a legitimate use of wilderness in our national forests and certain wildlife areas."

World Wildlife Fund (1961). "Dedicated to advancing programs to save the world's threatened and endangered species of wildlife and wild areas. Makes grants to existing agencies for study, habitat improvement, and protection. World Wildlife is opposed to the hunting of any threatened or endangered species of wildlife. It neither promotes nor opposes the hunting of game that is maintained in abundance under sustained-yield programs, and recognizes that under the proper conditions hunting can be both desirable and beneficial."

TA DAH!

THE COMPLETE HUNTER'S CATALOG *FIRST-EVER* AWESOME *AWARDS FOR OTHER HUNTERS' CATALOGS*
(Ruffles and Flourishes)

In the course of writing and compiling *The Complete Hunter's Catalog*, we have had a chance to review more catalogs than most people come across in a lifetime. The following is a selected list of categories and our choices for the top three publications in each. (We have purposely kept it short to avoid the tedium that accompanies other award ceremonies—Academy, Grammy, Emmy, Harry, ad infinitum.) The envelopes, please.

The Most Complete Catalog for Hunters
Herter's, Inc., Route 2, Mitchell, SD 57301
Cabela's, 812 13th Avenue, Sidney, NE 69162
Browning, Route 1, Morgan, UT 84050

The Best-Quality Merchandise at Reasonable Cost
Cabela's, 812 13th Avenue, Sidney, NE 69162
Herter's, Inc., Route 2, Mitchell, SD 57301
L. L. Bean, Freeport, ME 04033

The Most Artistic and Informative Catalog *
Browning, Route 1, Morgan, UT 84050
Tidewater Specialties, 430 Swann Avenue, Alexandria, VA 22301
Recreational Equipment, Inc., 1525 11th Avenue, Seattle, WA 98122
Early Winters, Ltd., 110 Prefontaine Place South, Seattle, WA 98104

The Most Entertaining Catalog
Dixie Gun Works, Inc., Highway 51, South, Union City TN 38261
Timberland Footwear, P.O. Box 230, Newmarket, NH 03857
Herter's, Inc., Route 2, Mitchell, SD 57301

The Catalog with the Most Expensive Merchandise Should You Want to Impress Your Friends with Gifts
Bob Lee's Hunting World, 16 East 53rd Street, New York, NY 10022
Orvis, Manchester, VT 05257
Eddie Bauer, 1737 Airport Way South, Seattle, WA 98134

*Tied for third place in this category. Both catalogs are primarily backpacking/mountaineering oriented.

A FINAL WORD ABOUT LISTED PRICES

Manufacturers usually charge slightly more west of the Mississippi if they're based in the East and slightly more east of the Mississippi if they're based in the West. The annual rate of inflation is running from 5 to 12 percent. Many of the prices cited are 1976 figures, the lead time required for publication being what it is. In other words, chances are that the price we cite won't exactly match what you find in a sales catalog or at your local sporting goods stores.

So why bother listing them? you might ask.

Because we all concurred that a catalog should answer three questions: What does it do? Where can I get it? and How much does it cost? The cost part might be off 5 or 10 percent, but at least it gives you a ballpark figure to bounce around between your budget and the price you see quoted on a sales tag.

There are a few interesting stories connected with pricing, too. About 10 percent of the manufacturers we contacted refused to supply us with a suggested retail price. Incredible as it may seem, they were unwilling to state what a "fair" price would be. When that situation arose, we arrived at a price by locating the item in question on store shelves in four areas: New York, New York; Bozeman, Montana; Phoenix, Arizona; and San Francisco, California (we've got friends in the latter two cities). We added up the total prices of each item and divided by four. Thus, the quoted price should amount to a fair average of what's being charged for the item coast to coast.

The Complete Hunter's Catalog has been devoted to one purpose: to illustrate, evaluate, illuminate, and otherwise indicate the newest and the best in hunting equipment. Given a bottomless bank account and this book, you can outfit yourself with all the marvels of modern invention for your day afield. You can drive right up to where the game waits in an unstoppable off-road vehicle or even fly there in a helicopter outfitted with all the comforts of home. You can spot your quarry with exquisite optics or hire a guide to do it for you. During the stalk or the wait, you don't have to worry about being cold; insulated clothing and footwear will keep you living-room warm in below-zero temperatures. With practice, high-power scopes, and long-range rifles, you can down your game without ever having to get close to it. In many respects the equipment featured in this book makes getting your game nearly a sure thing.

It is the one dimension of the catalog that all of us disavow. It is not so much because of what might be the initial assumption: that highly specialized equipment will wipe out the game. Wildlife harvests are so closely monitored and regulated by management agencies that overkills are no more than a remote possibility.

Rather, it is the equation that money makes the hunter that we find troubling. Sure, you have to have some money

to buy basic equipment, and perhaps our efforts will help you do that wisely. But the breech between a sporting goods owner and a sportsman, between your holdings and your hunting, is as broad as the Grand Canyon and twice as deep.

Like all things of real value, becoming a good hunter is earned, not paid for. You earn it by expending energy in walking up a mountain, by experiencing discomfort in going over your wader tops to chase a cripple, by learning to outwit your quarry with mind and senses rather than crushing it in the gears of technology. We hope this catalog is an advertisement for these qualities, as well as for sporting goods, and this concluding thought seems to bring us full circle.

The hundred-year-old words of Mr. Hallock say it all as well today: We hope we have been a service to lovers of legitimate sport.

Norman Strung
John Barsness
Fred Scholl
Sil Strung
Wally Hansen
April 1977

THE COMPLETE FISHERMAN'S CATALOG
by Harmon Henkin

Philadelphia: J. B. Lippincott Company, $14.95 (hard cover), $7.95 (soft cover).

One Last Book Review. Are you a fisherman? If you are, and if you enjoyed this book, beg, borrow, steal, or, better yet, buy a copy of *The Complete Fisherman's Catalog*. It is an extensive examination of all those products germane to the gentle art of fishing in all its forms. There are sections on fly fishing, spinning, bait-casting, boats, books, clothing, boots—a sampling

of products every bit as incisive and exhaustive as those you've seen here.

And like our book, this one also contains original material from major outdoor sportswriters, tips on tackle and technique, and good humor. All in all, it's a fine companion to a fireside on those cold winter nights when hunting season is over and thoughts turn lightly to streams, lakes, and spring.

AND A FINAL WORD OF THANKS

To Ray Nedrud, of Nedrud's Hardware and Furniture Store in Wolf Point, Montana, and Bob Bradford and George Dieruf, of the Powder Horn Sporting Goods Store in Bozeman, Montana. These folks were of immense help to John and me by way of patience, advice, and their federal firearms permits, without which we could not have received guns and ammo through the mail for testing.

And talking about the mail, if this book has one unsung hero, it is Tom O'Rourke, the Merry Mailman of Route 3, who went far beyond the call of duty to aid us in our efforts to get segments of this manuscript out by deadline. —N.S.

ABOUT THE

Norman Strung, Editor. A transplanted Easterner who settled in Montana fifteen years ago, Norm Strung began his long association with sporting goods and the outdoors as a part-time clerk in a Long Island sport shop. He soon learned that it's more fun to use hunting equipment than to sell it, and after a brief career as a university-level teacher, he became a full-time free-lance writer, specializing in the outdoors and supplementing an initially meager income with work as a hunting and fishing guide.

Norm now works full time at hunting, fishing, and writing—in that order. His publications include over 250 feature articles in *Field and Stream, Outdoor Life, Sports Afield,* and other outdoor periodicals. He continues to keep abreast of new developments in the equipment field by way of occasional work as a products consultant. *The Complete Hunter's Catalog* is the eleventh book in which he has had a major hand.

John Barsness, Managing Editor. John Barsness has divided most of his time between two pursuits: hunting in the West and tinkering with guns, bullets, powder, and hunting paraphernalia in his extensive workshop. He is a published poet, having contributed material to *Wind* magazine and to *Four Indian Poets,* a major collection of poetry. His prose has been published in *Sports Illustrated* and *Gray's Sporting Journal.*

In addition, John is in an enviable position for the average American sportsman: he lives in Poplar, Montana, on the Fort Peck Indian Reservation. His collective hunting experience easily equals the sum total of that of the rest of the catalog staff.

Fred Scholl, Roving Editor. Fred Scholl met Norman Strung at the age of twelve, on the shores of a small carp pond on the outskirts of New York City. Since that meeting they have been friends and hunting partners, with Fred often joining Norm on hunting trips in Montana and elsewhere.

Fred's special expertise lies in hunting the Eastern Seaboard with gun and bow. His assignment was to investigate, test, and report on products for hunters that were popular around his favorite hunting haunts in Maine, New Hampshire, Vermont, and Florida.

When he's not hunting, Fred is a firefighter for the City of New York, where he makes his permanent residence.

*"Home is the sailor, home from the sea,
And the hunter, home from the hill."*
—Robert Louis Stevenson

425

SON OF THE COMPLETE HUNTER'S CATALOG

In future years we hope to bring out *The Complete Hunter's Catalog No. 2,* an update of prices, products, and reviews that will include new articles by your favorite outdoor writers and other items of interest to the sportsman and shooter.

If you're a reader with ideas on things you'd like to have included, we'd be glad to hear from you. And the same goes for manufacturers, inventors, or purveyors of brand-new sporting products, or those we inadvertently missed.

Listings are free, although we do need to know three things: (1) What does it do? (a picture usually helps), (2) Where can we buy it or write to obtain more information? and (3) How much does it cost?

Send your comments, criticisms, and/or submissions to:

The Complete Hunter's Catalog
High Country
P.O. Box 189, Route 3
Bozeman, MT 59715

STAFF

Sil Strung, Kitchen Editor. You probably assume that Sil's title refers to her duties regarding game cookery and preparation, and you're right in a way. But mainly it refers to the fact that she spent most of her time editing, reviewing, compiling, and retyping copy at a kitchen table, since she has no office.

Aside from her work as editor, critic, and secretary on the catalog staff, Sil is also an excellent hunter and has filled out her deer and antelope tags for five consecutive years. Her writing credits include contributions to *Sports Afield, The Complete Outdoor Cookbook,* and the *Winchester Hunter's Handbook,* and her photography regularly accompanies the articles and books written by her husband, Norm.

C. W. "Wally" Hansen, Art Director. Wally Hansen is a friend of the Strungs and a frequent visitor to their big-game camp. Although he holds a degree in architecture, his first love is art; his second love is the outdoors. Both persuasions have been combined in the five books Wally has illustrated for Norm Strung.

Aside from his assemblage of line art and photos, Wally also did some products testing and research for the catalog.

Wally lives in Bozeman, Montana, where he operates an architectural rendering service.